YEAR **12**

MATHEMATICS STANDARD 2

CambridgeMATHS
STAGE 6

GK POWERS

INCLUDES INTERACTIVE TEXTBOOK POWERED BY CAMBRIDGE HOTMATHS

CAMBRIDGE
UNIVERSITY PRESS

CAMBRIDGE
UNIVERSITY PRESS

University Printing House, Cambridge CB2 8BS, United Kingdom

One Liberty Plaza, 20th Floor, New York, NY 10006, USA

477 Williamstown Road, Port Melbourne, VIC 3207, Australia

314–321, 3rd Floor, Plot 3, Splendor Forum, Jasola District Centre, New Delhi – 110025, India

79 Anson Road, #06–04/06, Singapore 079906

Cambridge University Press is part of the University of Cambridge.

It furthers the University's mission by disseminating knowledge in the pursuit
of education, learning and research at the highest international levels of excellence.

www.cambridge.org
Information on this title: www.cambridge.org/9781108448079

First published 2018
20 19 18 17 16 15 14 13 12 11 10 9 8 7 6 5 4 3 2

Cover and text designed by Sardine Design
Typeset by diacriTech
Printed in China by C & C Offset Printing Co. Ltd.

*A catalogue record for this book is available from the National Library
of Australia at* www.nla.gov.au

ISBN 978-1-108-44807-9 Paperback

Additional resources for this publication at www.cambridge.edu.au/hotmaths

Contents

About the author

Greg Powers is currently the Head of Mathematics at Cabramatta High School and the coordinator of the Mathematics Head Teacher Western Network. He is an experienced classroom teacher, having taught for over 30 years in a range of different schools. Greg has been a senior marker for the HSC, educational consultant for the Metropolitan South West Region and presented at numerous MANSW inservices. He has also enjoyed several curriculum roles with the Department of Education and Training. Greg is an experienced author who has written numerous texts on mathematics and technology.

Introduction

CambridgeMATHS Mathematics Standard 2 Year 12 provides complete and close coverage of the NSW Stage 6 Mathematics Standard 2 Year 12 syllabus to be implemented in 2019 including the November 2017 syllabus update.

Now part of the *CambridgeMATHS* series, this resource is part of a continuum from Year 7 through to 12. The series includes advice on pathways from Stage 5 to Stage 6. The Year 12 resource gives access to selected previous years' lessons for revision of prior knowledge.

The four components of *Mathematics Standard 2 Year 12* — the print book, downloadable PDF textbook, online Interactive Textbook and Online Teaching Resource — contain a huge range of resources available to schools in a single package at a convenient low price. There are no extra subscriptions or per-student charges to pay.

Interactive Textbook powered by the HOTmaths platform – included with the print book or available separately *(shown on the page opposite)*

The Interactive Textbook is an online HTML version of the print textbook powered by the HOTmaths platform, completely designed and reformatted for on-screen use, with easy navigation. Its features include:

1 Most examples have video versions to encourage independent learning.
2 All exercises including chapter reviews have the option of being done interactively on line, using **workspaces** and **self-assessment tools**. Students rate their level of confidence in answering the question and can flag the ones that gave them difficulty. Working and answers, whether typed or handwritten, and drawings, can be saved and submitted to the teacher electronically. Answers displayed on screen if selected and worked solutions (if enabled by the teacher) open in pop-up windows.
3 Teachers can give feedback to students on their self-assessment and flagged answers.
4 The full suite of the HOTmaths learning management system and communication tools are included in the platform, with similar interfaces and controls.
5 Worked solutions are included and can be enabled or disabled in the student accounts by the teacher.
6 Interactive widgets and activities based on embedded Desmos windows demonstrate key concepts and enable students to visualise the mathematics.
7 Desmos scientific and graphics calculator windows are also included.
8 'Knowledge check' revision of prior knowledge using selected HOTmaths Year 10 lessons is included.
9 Every section in a chapter has a Quick Quiz of automatically marked multiple-choice questions for students to test their progress.
10 Definitions pop up for key terms in the text, and are also provided in a dictionary.
11 Each chapter has a Study Guide – a concise summary in PowerPoint slides that can be used for revision and preparation for assessment.
12 Literacy worksheets can be accessed via the Interactive Textbook, with answers in the Online Teaching Suite, providing activities to help with mathematical terminology.
13 Spreadsheet questions with accompanying spreadsheet files.

Downloadable PDF textbook *(shown on the page opposite)*

14 The convenience of a downloadable PDF textbook has been retained for times when users cannot go online.

INTERACTIVE TEXTBOOK POWERED BY THE *HOTmaths* PLATFORM

Numbers refer to the descriptions on the opposite page. HOTmaths platform features are updated regularly.

10 Pop-up definitions

9 Quick quizzes

5 Worked solutions
(if enabled by teacher)

7 Desmos calculator windows

1 Video worked examples

6 Interactive Desmos widgets

2 Answers displayed on screen

12 Printable Literacy worksheet

2 Interactive exercises with typing/hand-writing/drawing entry showing working

11 Study Guides

13 Spreadsheet question and files

4 Tasks sent by teacher

10 Dictionary

8 Revision of prior knowledge

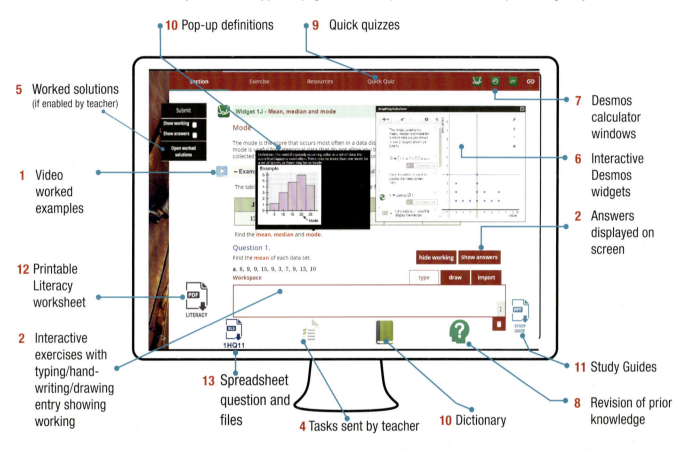

PDF TEXTBOOK

DOWNLOADABLE

14 Included with Interactive Textbook

Search functions

Note-taking

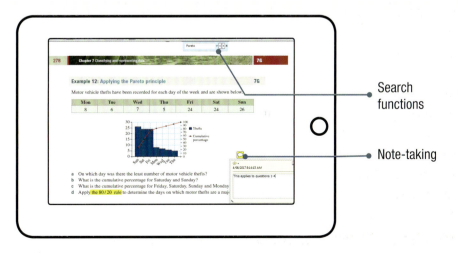

Online Teaching Suite powered by the HOTmaths platform *(shown on the page opposite)*

The Online Teaching Suite is automatically enabled with a teacher account and appears in the teacher's copy of the Interactive Textbook. All the assets and ersources are in one place for easy access. Many of them are opened by clicking on icons in the pages of the Interactive Textbook. The features include:

15 Editable teaching programs with registers, a scope and sequence document and curriculum grid.

16 Topic test worksheets A and B – based on the knowledge, skills and understanding gained in each chapter, and Revision Quiz worksheets provide HSC-standard questions for further revision for each topic, with worked solutions. NESA requirements for problem-solving investigative tasks will also be addressed.

17 A HOTmaths-style test generator provides additional multiple-choice questions, as well as digital versions of the multiple-choice questions in the test worksheets

18 The HOTmaths learning management system with class and student reports and communication tools is included.

19 Teacher's lesson notes – pop-up text boxes containing lesson notes and additional examples that can be used in class, also available as editable PowerPoint slides which can be given to students as tutorials.

Content features of the textbook

Working mathematically is integrated into each exercise using three levels.

- Level 1 – questions to develop understanding, fluency and communication. These questions are basic and straightforward in style to ensure early success. Level 1 caters for a student working at bands 1 to 3. Students going on to do HSC Standard 1 should do Level 1 questions, and Level 2 at the teacher's discretion.
- Level 2 – questions to develop problem solving, reasoning and justification. These questions extend and broaden students understanding of the concepts of the section. Level 2 caters for a student working at bands 4 to 5.
- Level 3 – questions to challenge the knowledge and understanding of the top students. Level 3 caters for a student working at band 6.

Other features:

20 The Year 11 Chapter 1 Preliminary preparation covering basic skills is accessible in the Interactive Textbook to Year 12 students. It could also be used for review during the course.

21 The textbook is divided into smaller manageable topics to assist teaching.

22 Syllabus topic focus and outcomes are listed at the beginning of each chapter.

23 Each section and exercise begins at the top of the page to make them easy to find and access.

24 Exercises are differentiated into three levels to allow teachers to assess students abilities.

25 Each exercise develops student's skills to work mathematically at their level.

26 Step-by-step worked examples with precise explanations (and video versions for most of them) encourage independent learning, and are linked to exercises.

27 Important concepts are formatted in boxes for easy reference.

28 Spreadsheet activities are integrated throughout the text, with accompanying Excel files in the Interactive Textbook.

29 Chapter reviews contain a chapter summary and multiple-choice, short-answer and extended-response questions.

30 A comprehensive glossary and HSC Reference sheet are included.

31 There are three complete HSC practice papers.

Numbers refer to the descriptions on the previous page. HOTmaths platfrom features are updated regularly.

19 Teacher's lesson notes
(Indicated by T icon in teacher's interactive textbook)

17 Test generator

Teacher's copy of interactive textbook

16 Printable test and quiz sheets

15 Teaching programs

18 Class reports

18 Student results

18 Tasks sent to students

PRINT TEXTBOOK

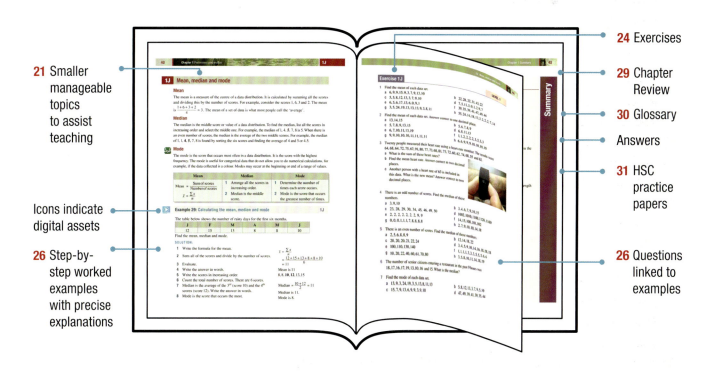

21 Smaller manageable topics to assist teaching

Icons indicate digital assets

26 Step-by-step worked examples with precise explanations

24 Exercises

29 Chapter Review

30 Glossary

Answers

31 HSC practice papers

26 Questions linked to examples

Acknowledgements

The author and publisher wish to thank the following sources for permission to reproduce material:

Cover: © Getty Images / Henrik Sorensen, Cover

Images: © Getty Images / Dallas Stribley, Chapter 1 opener / ChubarovY, 1A (1) / James F. Dean, 1A (2) / Jeffrey Davis, 1A (3) / Andrew Holt, 1A (4) / crotography, 1A (5) / Guido Mieth, 1B (1) / Bloomberg, 1C (1), 2I (1) / Westend61, p181, 1I(9), 8D (2), 9D (1), 10A (4) / designer491, p402 / Paul Bradbury, 1C (3) / Thomas Trutschel, 1C (4) / artisteer, 1D (1) / Andrew Watson, 1D (2), 3D (1), 8G (1) / antorti, 1E (1) / Dan Dalton, 1E (2) / Svetlana Zhukova, 1F (1) / Auscape/UIG, 1G (3) / Tony Nguyen, 1G (5) / Yuri_Arcurs, 1I (10) / David Sacks, 1I (11) / rvimages, 1I (12) / Darren Robb, Chapter 2 Opener / Busakorn Pongparnit, 2A (1) / NicoElNino, 2C (1) / Caiaimage/Robert Daly, 2C (2) / Gavin Hellier / robertharding, 2E (10) / Anastasiia_New, 2H (1) / Gary S Chapman, Chapter 3 Opener / Glowimages, 3A (1) / Tom Merton, 3A (1) / Richard I'Anson, 3C (1) / Manfred Gottschalk, 3C (3) / Glow Images, Inc, 3C (4) / Mario Forcherio / EyeEm, 3C (5) / Adam Gault, 3D (2), Chapter 7 Opener / PhotoAlto/Eric Audras, 3E (1) / Pete Seaward Photography, 3E (2) / Silverstock, 3E (3) / artpartner-images, 3F (1) / Thomas Barwick, 3F (2), 6D (1), 8F (1) / Hero Images, 3F (3), 5E (2) / Sam Edwards, 3F (3), 4I (1) / Johnnie Davis, 3G (1) / Burak Karademir, 3G (2) / Peter Dazeley, 3G (3), 3I (1) / Tetra Images, 3G (4) / GSO Images, 3I (2) / Universal History Archive, Chapter 4 Opener / Steven Puetzer, 4A (1) / Chris Caldicott, 4A (2) / Tim Grist Photography, 4C (1) / Tempura, 4F (1) / Sally Anscombe, 4F (2) / Alistair Berg, 4F (3) / KevinCarr, 4G (1) / Travel Ink, 4H (1) / Luis Martinez, 4H (2) / pbombaert, Chapter 5 Opener / Caiaimage/Sam Edwards, 5B (1), 9E (2) / Maximilian Stock Ltd., 5B (2) / ATU Images, 5D (1) / Michael Blann, 5E (1) / Peter Cade, 5E (3) / Roy Scott, Chapter 6 Opener / Roy James Shakespeare, 6A (1) / John P Kelly, 6C (1) / Caiaimage/Tom Merton, 6E (1) / Compassionate Eye Foundation/Gary Burchell, 6F (1) / JGI, 6F (2) / Jutta Klee, 7A (1) / Caiaimage/Gianni Diliberto, 7B (2) / p_saranya, 7B (1) / Martin Barraud, 7E (1) / Johanna Parkin, Chapter 8 Opener / Jeff Rotman, 8B (1) / Lanski, 8D (1) / franckreporter, 8F (2) / Dougal Waters, 8F (3) / Frank Herholdt, 8G (2) / Mongkol Nitirojsakul / EyeEm, 8H (1) / ollo, 8H (1) / OK-Photography, Chapter 9 Opener / Digital Vision, 9A (1) / Werner Blessing, 9B (1) / Asmita Gaikwad / EyeEm, 9B (2) / Image Source, 9E (1), 9F (4) / Steve Lee, 9E (3) / Image by Graeme Worsfold, 9F (1) / Tamara Staples, 9F (3) / Cn0ra, 9F (3) / Michael H, Chapter 10 Opener / John Keeble, 10A (1) / Howard Kingsnorth, 10A (2) / Emilija Manevska, 10A (3) / Jonathan Knowles, 10A (5) / Rafael Ben-Ari, 10A (6) / Richard Drury, 10A (7) / Photography by Andrew Katsaitis, 10G (1).

© Australian Government, Department of the Environment and Energy, 1C (2); © NSW Government, Transport.nsw.gov.au, 2C (1).

Every effort has been made to trace and acknowledge copyright. The publisher apologises for any accidental infringement and welcomes information that would redress this situation.

1

Rates and ratios

Syllabus topic — M7 Rates and ratios

This topic focuses on the use of rates and ratios to solve problems in practical contexts, including the interpretation of scale drawings.

Outcomes

- Use rates to solve and describe practical problems.
- Use rates to make comparisons.
- Interpret the energy rating of household appliances and compare running costs.
- Solve practical problems involving ratios.
- Use ratio to describe map scales.
- Obtain measurements from scale drawings.
- Interpret symbols and abbreviations on building plans and elevation views.
- Calculate perimeter, area and volume using a scale from a variety of sources.

Digital Resources for this chapter

In the Interactive Textbook:

- Videos
- Literacy worksheet
- Quick Quiz
- Solutions (enabled by teacher)
- Desmos widgets
- Spreadsheets
- Study guide

In the Online Teaching Suite:

- Teaching Program
- Tests
- Review Quiz
- Teaching Notes

Knowledge check

The Interactive Textbook provides a test of prior knowledge for this chapter, and may direct you to revision from the previous years' work.

1A Rates and concentrations

Rates

A rate is a comparison of amounts with different units. For example, we may compare the distance travelled with the time taken. In a rate the units are different and must be specified.

The order of a rate is important. A rate is written as the first amount per one of the second amount. For example, $2.99/kg represents $2.99 per one kilogram or 80 km/h represents 80 kilometres per one hour.

We are constantly interested in rates of change and how things change over a period of time. There are many examples of rates such as:

- Growth rate: The average growth rate of a child from 0 to 15 years of age.
- Running rate: Your running pace in metres per second.
- Typing rate: Your typing speed in words per minute.
- Wage rate: The amount of money you are paid per hour.

CONVERTING A RATE

1. Write the rate as a fraction. First quantity is the numerator and 1 is the denominator.
2. Convert the first amount to the required unit.
3. Convert the second amount to the required unit.
4. Simplify the fraction.

Example 1: Converting a rate   1A

Convert each rate to the units shown.

a 55 200 m/h to m/min   **b** $6.50/kg to c/g

SOLUTION:

1 Write the rate as a fraction.

2 The numerator is 55 200 m and the denominator is 1 h.

3 No conversion required for the numerator.

4 Convert the 1 hour to minutes by multiplying by 60.

5 Simplify the fraction.

a $55\,200 = \dfrac{55\,200 \text{ m}}{1 \text{ h}}$

$= \dfrac{55\,200 \text{ m}}{1 \times 60 \text{ min}}$

$= 920 \text{ m/min}$

6 Write the rate as a fraction.

7 The numerator is $6.50 and the denominator is 1 kg.

8 Convert the $6.50 to cents by multiplying by 100.

9 Convert the 1 kg to g by multiplying by 1000.

10 Simplify the fraction.

b $6.50 = \dfrac{\$6.50}{1 \text{ kg}}$

$= \dfrac{6.50 \times 100 \text{ c}}{1 \times 1000 \text{ g}}$

$= 0.65 \text{ c/g}$

The unitary method

The unitary method involves finding one unit of a quantity by division. This result is then multiplied to solve the problem.

USING THE UNITARY METHOD

1 Find one unit of a quantity by dividing by the amount.
2 Multiply the result in step 1 by a number to solve the problem.

Example 2: Using the unitary method   1A

A car travels 360 km on 30 L of petrol. How far does it travel on 7 L?

SOLUTION:

1 Write a statement using information from the question.	$30\,L = 360\text{ km}$
2 Find 1 L of petrol by dividing 360 km by the amount or 30.	$1\,L = \dfrac{360}{30}\text{ km}$
3 Multiply both sides by 7.	$7\,L = \dfrac{360}{30} \times 7\text{ km}$
4 Evaluate.	
5 Write the answer to an appropriate degree of accuracy.	$= 84\text{ km}$
6 Write the answer in words.	The car travels 84 km.

Example 3: Using the unitary method   1A

a Bella can touch type at 70 words per minute. How many words can she type in 20 minutes?
b A supermarket sells the same brand of 400 mL soft drink cans singly for $2.40, in a six-pack for $11.95, or in a carton of 24 for $39.95. Compare the cost of one can in each option, to the nearest cent.

SOLUTION:

1 Typing rate is 70 words in one minute.	a Number of words $= 70 \times 20$
2 Multiply 70 by 20 to determine the number of words typed in 20 minutes.	$= 1400$
3 Write your answer in words.	Bella types 1400 words in 20 minutes.
4 Write down the price of a single can.	b $2.40
5 Find the cost of one can in a six-pack by dividing its price by 6, and one can in a carton by dividing its price by 24, and rounding to the nearest cent.	$11.95 \div 6 \approx \$1.99$
	$39.95 \div 24 \approx \$1.66$
6 Write the answer in words.	A can bought costs $2.40 singly, in a six-pack $1.99 and in a carton $1.66.

Speed

Speed is a rate that compares the distance travelled to the time taken. The speed of a car is measured in kilometres per hour (km/h). The speedometer in a car measures the instantaneous speed of a car. They are not totally accurate but have a tolerance of 5%. GPS devices are capable of showing speed readings based on the distance travelled per time interval. Most cars also have an odometer to indicate the distance travelled by a vehicle.

SPEED

$S = \dfrac{D}{T}$ or $T = \dfrac{D}{S}$ or $D = S \times T$

D – Distance
S – Speed
T – Time

'Road sign' on the right is used to remember the formulas. Hide the required quantity to determine the formula.

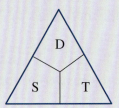

Example 4: Solving problems involving speed   1A

  a Find the average speed of a car that travels 341 km in 5 hours.
  b How long will it take a vehicle to travel 294 km at a speed of 56 km/h?

SOLUTION:

1	Write the formula.	**a** $S = \dfrac{D}{T}$
2	Substitute 341 for D and 5 for T into the formula.	$= \dfrac{341}{5}$
3	Evaluate.	$= 68.2$ km/h
4	Write the formula.	**b** $T = \dfrac{D}{S}$
5	Substitute 294 for D and 56 for S into the formula.	$= \dfrac{294}{56}$
6	Evaluate and express the answer correct to the nearest hour.	$= 5.25$ h or 5 h 15 min

Exercise 1A

Example 1 **1** Convert to the rate shown.

   a $100 in 4 h is a rate of $☐/h   **b** 240 m in 20 s is a rate of ☐ m/s

   c 700 L in 10 h is a rate of L ☐/h   **d** $39 in 12 h is a rate of $☐/h

   e $1.20 for 2 kg is a rate of ☐ c/kg   **f** 630 km in 60 L is a rate of ☐ km/L

   g 1200 rev in 4 min is a rate of ☐ rev/min   **h** A rise of 20° in 4 h is a rate of ☐ °/h

2 Express each rate in simplest form using the rates shown.

   a 300 km on 60 L [km per L]   **b** 15 m in 10 s [m per s]

   c $640 for 5 m [$ per m]   **d** 56L in 0.5 min [L per min]

   e 78 mg for 13 g [mg per g]   **f** 196 g for 14 L [g per L]

   g 20 g for 8 m^2 [g per m^2]   **h** 75 mL for 5 min [mL per min]

Example 2, 3 **3** Use the rate provided to answer the following questions.

   a Cost of apples is $2.50/kg. What is the cost of 5 kg?

   b Tax charge is $28/$m^2$. What is the tax for 7 m^2?

   c Cost savings are $35/day. How much is saved in 5 days?

   d Cost of a chemical is $65/100 mL. What is the cost of 300 mL?

   e Cost of mushrooms is $5.80/kg. What is the cost of $\frac{1}{2}$ kg?

   f Distance travelled is 1.2 km/min. What is the distance travelled in 30 minutes?

   g Concentration of a chemical is 3 mL/L. How many mL of the chemical is needed for 4L?

   h Concentration of a drug is 2 mL/g. How many mL is needed for 10 g?

Example 4 **4** Use the information provided on speed to answer the following questions.

   a Walking at 5 km/h. How far can I walk in 4 hours?

   b Car travelling at 80 km/h. How far will it travel in 2.5 hours?

   c Plane is travelling at 600 km/h. How far will it travel in 30 minutes?

   d A train took 7 hours to travel 665 km. What was its average speed?

   e Ryder runs a 42.4 km marathon in 2 hours 30 minutes. Calculate his average speed.

   f A spacecraft travels at 1700 km/h for a distance of 238 000 km. How many hours did it take?

5 Convert each rate to the units shown.

   a 39 240 m/min [m/s]   **b** 2 m/s [cm/s]

   c 88 cm/h [mm/h]   **d** 55 200 m/h [m/min]

   e 0.4 km/s [m/s]   **f** 57.5 m/s [km/s]

   g 6.09 g/mL [mg/mL]   **h** 4800 L/kL [mL/kL]

6 Mia earns $37.50 per hour working in a cafe.

   a How much does Mia earn for working a 9-hour day?

   b How many hours does Mia work to earn $1200?

   c What is Mia's annual income if she works 40 hours a week? Assume she works 52 weeks in the year.

7 A delivery driver delivers 1 parcel on average every 20 minutes. How many hours does it take to deliver 18 parcels?

8 Water is dripping from a tap at a rate of 5 L/h. How much water will leak in one day?

9 A cricket team scores runs at a rate of 5 runs/over in a match. How many overs did it take to score 90 runs?

10 A bulldozer is moving soil at a rate of 22 t/h. How long will it take at this rate to move 55 t?

11 If Leo can march at 7 km/h, how far can he march in 2.5 hours?

12 Edward saves $40/week, how long should it take to save $1000?

13 Nails cost $4.80/kg. How many kilograms can be bought for $30?

14 Alexandra jogs 100 metres in 20 seconds. How many seconds would it take her to jog one kilometre?

15 A car travels at a rate of 50 metres each second. How many kilometres does it travel in:
   a one minute?
   b one hour?

16 Convert the following speeds to metres per second. Answer to the nearest whole number.
   a 60 km/h
   b 260 km/h

17 An athlete runs 100 metres in 10 seconds. If he could continue at this rate, what is his speed in kilometres per hour?

18 Natural gas is charged at a rate of 1.4570 cents per MJ.

   a Find the charge for 12560 MJ of natural gas. Answer to the nearest dollar.

   b The charge for natural gas was $160.27. How many megajoules were used?

19 Olivia's council rate is $2915 p.a. for land valued at $265 000. Lucy has a council rate of $3186 on land worth $295 000 from another council.

   a What is Olivia's council charge as a rate of $/$1000 valuation?

   b What is Lucy's council charge as a rate of $/$1000 valuation?

20 Mira's car uses 9 litres of petrol to travel 100 kilometres. Petrol costs $1.50 per litre.

   a What is the cost of travelling 100 kilometres?

   b How far can she drive using $50 worth of petrol? Answer to the nearest kilometre.

21 Earth's radius is approximately 6400 km. (In this question, the rotation of the Earth is considered relative to the Sun, ignoring all other motion).

   a What distance does a point on the equator travel each day? Answer to nearest kilometre.

   b What is the speed of a point on the equator? Answer to the nearest kilometre per hour.

   c How long will it take a point on the equator to travel 60 km? Answer to the nearest second.

22 A motor bike is moving at a steady speed. When the speed is 90 km/h the bike consumes 5 litres of petrol for every 100 kilometres travelled.

   a The petrol tank holds 30 litres. How many kilometres can the bike travel on a full tank of petrol when its speed is 90 km/h?

   b When the speed is 110 km/h the bike consumes 30% more petrol per kilometre travelled. Calculate the number of litres per 100 kilometres consumed when the bike travels at 110 km/h.

23 A plane travelled non-stop from Los Angeles to Sydney, a distance of 12 057 kilometres in 13 hours and 30 minutes. The plane started with 180 kilolitres of fuel, and on landing had enough fuel to fly another 45 minutes.

   a What was the plane's average speed in kilometres per hour? Answer to the nearest whole number.

   b How much fuel was used? Answer to the nearest kilolitre.

1B   Heart rate

Heart rate is the number of heartbeats per minute (bpm). It is measured by finding the pulse of the body. This pulse rate is measured where the pulsation of an artery can be felt on the skin by pressing with the index and middle fingers, such as on the wrist and neck. A heart rate monitor consists of a chest strap with electrodes that transmit to a wrist receiver for display. It is used during exercise when manual measurements are difficult. An electrocardiograph is used by medical professionals to obtain a more accurate measurement of heart rate to assist in the diagnosis and tracking of medical conditions. The resting heart rate is measured while a person is at rest but awake and is typically between 60 and 80 beats per minute.

There are many different formulas used to estimate maximum heart rate (MHR). The most widely used formula is MHR = 220 − Age where age is in years.

Target heart rate

The target heart rate (THR) is the desired range of heart rate during exercise that enables the heart and lungs to receive the most benefit from a workout. This range depends on the person's age, physical condition, gender and previous training. The THR is calculated as a range between 65% and 85% of the MHR. For example, for an 18-year-old with a MHR of 202 the THR is between 131.3 (0.65 × 202) and 171.7 (0.85 × 202).

HEART RATE

Heart rate is the number of heartbeats per minute (bpm).
MHR = 220 − Age (years)

Example 5: Estimating maximum heart rate   1B

Estimate the maximum heart rate for an 18-year-old.

SOLUTION:

1	Write the formula.	MHR = 220 − Age
2	Substitute 18 for age.	= 220 − 18
3	Evaluate.	= 202
4	Write the answer in words.	Maximum heart rate for an 18-year-old is estimated to be 202 bpm.

Example 6: Interpreting trends in heart rate   1B

The table below shows the average resting heart rate for men in six age ranges and seven health categories.

Health	18–25 years	26–35 years	36–45 years	46–55 years	56–65 years	65+ years
Athlete	49–55	49–54	50–56	50–57	51–56	50–55
Excellent	56–61	55–61	57–62	58–63	57–61	56–61
Good	62–65	62–65	63–66	64–67	62–67	62–65
Above average	66–69	66–70	67–70	68–71	68–71	66–69
Average	70–73	71–74	71–75	72–76	72–75	70–73
Below average	74–81	75–81	76–82	77–83	76–81	74–79
Poor	82+	82+	83+	84+	82+	80+

a   What is the average resting heart rate for a man aged 47 years in good health?
b   What is the average resting heart rate for a man aged 25 years in below-average health?
c   What is the health of a man aged 57 years with a resting heart rate of 60?
d   What is the health of a man aged 30 years with a resting heart rate of 84?

SOLUTION:

1   Find age 47 in the age ranges.

2   Read resting heart rate for good health in the same column.

a   Age of 47 is in the range 46–55 years. Average resting heart rate is 64–67.

3   Find age 25 in the age ranges.

4   Read resting heart rate for below average health in the same column.

b   Age of 25 is in the range 18–25 years. Average resting heart rate is 74–81.

5   Find age 60 in the age ranges.

6   Find the range for resting heart rate 60 in the same column and read the health category in that row.

c   Heart rate of 60 is in the range 57–61. Health is excellent.

7   Find age 30 in the age ranges.

8   Find the range for resting heart rate 84 in the same column, and read the health category in the same row.

d   Heart rate of 84 is in the range 82+. Health is poor.

Exercise 1B

Example 5   **1**   Estimate the maximum heart rate using the formula MHR = 220 − Age for a person who is:
   a 20 years old   **b** 30 years old
   c 40 years old   **d** 50 years old
   e 60 years old   **f** 70 years old
   g 80 years old   **h** 90 years old
   i 100 years old.

2   Identify the trends in the maximum heart rate (MHR) with age.
   a Draw a number plane with 'Age' as the horizontal axis and 'MHR' as the vertical axis.
   b Plot the answers from question **1** on the number plane.
   c Join the points to make a straight line.
   d Use the graph to estimate the MHR for a person who is 25 years old.
   e Use the graph to estimate the MHR for a person who is 38 years old.
   f Use the graph to estimate the age of a person with a MHR of 155 bpm.
   g Use the graph to estimate the age of a person with a MHR of 175 bpm.

3   Calculate the target heart rate (65% to 85% of the MHR) for questions **1a** to **i**.

Example 6   **4**   The table below shows the average resting heart rate for women in six age ranges and seven
        health categories.

Health	18–25 years	26–35 years	36–45 years	46–55 years	56–65 years	65+ years
Athlete	54–60	54–59	54–59	54–60	54–59	54–59
Excellent	61–65	60–64	60–64	61–65	60–64	60–64
Good	66–69	65–68	65–69	66–69	65–68	65–68
Above average	70–73	69–72	70–73	70–73	69–73	69–72
Average	74–78	73–76	74–78	74–77	74–77	73–76
Below average	79–84	77–82	79–84	78–83	78–83	77–84
Poor	85+	83+	85+	84+	84+	85+

   a What is the average resting heart rate for a woman aged 35 years in below-average health?
   b What is the average resting heart rate for a woman aged 56 years in excellent health?
   c What is the health of a woman aged 68 years with a resting heart rate of 78?
   d What is the health of a woman aged 37 years with a resting heart rate of 59?

LEVEL 2

5 Perform an experiment to measure your heart rate.

Activity	Heart rate
Rest before walk	
End of a 15-minute walk	
3 minutes after the walk	
5 minutes after the walk	

a Copy the table. Measure your resting heart rate and write the result in the table.

b Walk quickly for 15 minutes. Measure your heart rate and write the result in the table.

c Measure your heart rate for 3 and 5 minutes after the walk. Write the results in the table.

d Draw a number plane with 'Time' as the horizontal axis and 'Heart rate' as the vertical axis.

e Plot the results from the table on the number plane.

f Do you think the first 15 minutes of the graph is a straight line?

g Did your heart rate return to the resting heart rate after 5 minutes?

h Calculate your maximum heart rate using the formula MHR = 220 − Age.

i Calculate your target heart rate. How does it compare to the results in the table?

j Complete the same experiment by jogging for 15 minutes instead of walking.

k What was the change in your heart rate at the end of the activity?

6 Use your resting heart rate measured in question **5**.

a How many times does your heart beat in 1 hour?

b How many times does your heart beat in 1 day?

c How many times does your heart beat in 1 year?

d How many times has your heart been beating since you were born?

e How many times would your heart beat if you lived to 100 years?

LEVEL 3

7 Twenty people measured their heart rate using a heart rate monitor. The results were:
64, 68, 64, 72, 75, 67, 91, 80, 77, 73, 68, 81, 73, 72, 60, 62, 74, 68, 55 and 62.

a What is the maximum heart rate?

b What is the minimum heart rate?

c What is the sum of these heart rates?

d Find the mean heart rate. Answer correct to 1 decimal place.

Parts **e** and **f** require knowledge of interquartile range and standard deviation.

e Find the interquartile range of these heart rates. Answer correct to 1 decimal place.

f Find the population standard deviation of these heart rates. Answer correct to 1 decimal place.

1C   Energy rate

The first part of this section reviews the Year 11 coverage of energy and power.

Energy is the capacity to do work. Energy exists in numerous forms, such as heat. The joule (symbol J) is the unit of energy used by the International System of Units (SI). Heat energy such as that produced by burning natural gas in the home is usually measured in megajoules (one million joules, symbol MJ).

Power

Power is the rate at which energy is generated or consumed. The watt is the International System of Units (SI) unit of power and is equal to one joule per second. The symbol for the watt is W. As for the joule, the standard SI prefixes such as milli, kilo and mega are then added and commonly used to measure power.

Electrical energy

The joule is not a practical unit for measuring electrical energy in most settings. It is more helpful to think of electrical energy in terms of the power drawn by an electrical device and the length of time the device is in use. For example, when a device with a power rating of 100 W is turned on for one hour, the amount of energy used is 100 watt-hours (Wh or W-h). This is the same amount of energy a 50 W device would use in 2 hours.

The kilowatt-hour (kWh or kW-h) is commonly used to measure electrical energy in household electricity meters. It represents the amount of electrical energy when a 1000 W power load is drawn for one hour. It is the result of multiplying power in kilowatts and time in hours. Note the conversion 1 kWh = 3.6 MJ.

Consumption is a rate expressed as an amount over time. Electrical energy consumption can be expressed in kilowatt-hours or megawatt-hours per unit of time, or megajoules per unit of time. The average annual energy use per household in Australia is 11 MWh/y or 3 MJ/y, which also equates to about eight tonnes of CO_2 emissions.

Energy rating of appliances

In Australia an energy rating label is provided for appliances such as fridges, TVs, washers, dryers and air conditioners. It allows consumers to compare the energy efficiency of similar products. Energy rating labels all have a simple star rating. The more stars on the label, the more energy efficient the appliance. The energy consumption figure is the number in the red box. It indicates the amount of electricity (kWh) the appliance typically uses to run in a year. The lower the number the less the appliance will cost to run. The running cost of the appliance is calculated by multiplying the energy consumption figure by the electricity price rate. Electricity suppliers usually give prices per kilowatt-hour. The screenshot below is from the government energy rating website (www.energyrating.gov.au/calculator).

More stars, more savings

When comparing similar sized products look for more stars to save money.

Energy Rating Labels are an Australian Government requirement on new appliances, making it easy to compare running costs.

Low score saves more

The lower the energy consumption score, the less electricity the appliance uses, and the cheaper it will be to run.

To see how much that new appliance is really going to cost you select an appliance above and calculate the running costs.

Example 7: Calculating the cost of running appliances   1C

Find the cost of running these appliances if the average peak rate for electricity is $0.21/kWh.
a   A 3.5 kW air conditioner for eight hours
b   A 200 W television for 20 hours.

SOLUTION:

1   Determine the energy (kWh) by multiplying the power rating (kW) by the hours used.

2   Determine the cost by multiplying the energy by the electricity charge.

3   Determine the energy (kWh) by multiplying the power rating (kW) by the hours used.

4   Determine the cost by multiplying the energy by the electricity charge.

a   Electricity $= 3.5 \times 8$
   $= 28$ kWh

   Cost $= 28 \times 0.21$
   $= \$5.88$

b   Electricity $= 0.2 \times 20$
   $= 4$ kWh

   Cost $= 4 \times 0.21$
   $= \$0.84$

Energy-efficient housing

BASIX or Building Sustainability Index is a scheme to regulate the energy efficiency of residential buildings. It is an online (www.basix.nsw.gov.au) program to assess and compare a house or unit design with energy and water targets.

BASIX uses information such as site location, house size, building materials, water, thermal comfort and energy. Sustainable houses feature rainwater tanks, efficient showerheads, solar hot water, performance glazing and energy-efficient lighting.

Example 8: Calculating electricity costs   1C

Christian is installing a solar PV (photovoltaic) system. His average daily consumption is 21.5 kWh. It is predicted the solar PV system will meet this need and export 6.3 kWh of energy daily to the grid. Christian's energy retailer charges $0.2167 per kWh and pays $0.08 per kWh for energy. What is the expected saving from the solar PV system each day?

SOLUTION:

1 Multiply the energy by electricity charge for daily consumption.

$$\text{Daily consumption} = 21.5 \times 0.2167$$
$$= \$4.65905$$

2 Multiply the energy by electricity charge that is exported to the grid.

$$\text{Exported} = 6.3 \times 0.08$$
$$= \$0.504$$

3 Add the two amounts to determine the saving.

$$\text{Saving} = \$4.65905 + \$0.504$$
$$= \$5.16.$$

ENERGY COSTS

1 Find the energy (kWh) by multiplying the power rating (kW) by the hours used.
2 Find the cost by multiplying the energy by the electricity charge.

Exercise 1C

Example 7

1 The Nguyen family has a clothes dryer with a 3.3 kW rating.
  a How many kilowatts of electricity does it use in a week if it is switched on for an average of 2 hours per day?
  b What is the cost of running the dryer for a week if electricity is $0.2819 per kWh?

2 A dishwasher has an energy consumption figure of 250 kWh per year. Calculate the cost of running the dishwasher for a year using the following electricity tariffs.
  a $0.1985/kWh
  b $0.2019/kWh
  c $0.2754/kWh

3 Marcus uses a 25 W ceiling fan every hour of the day.
  a How much energy does the ceiling fan use during the week?
  b What is the cost of using the ceiling fan for a week if electricity is $0.2999 per kWh?

4 Alice uses an oven with a rating of 1200 W for an average of 7 hours per week. Find the cost of the electricity for the oven at a rate of 24.11 cents per kilowatt-hour.

5 Luke received his natural gas account.

Amount used	Charges	Cost
First 6 200 MJ	2.581 cents per MJ	
Next 12 400 MJ	1.379 cents per MJ	

  a Find the cost of the first 6 200 MJ. Answer to the nearest cent.
  b Find the cost of the next 12 400 MJ. Answer to the nearest cent.
  c What is the total charge? Answer to the nearest cent.

6 Hamish uses a 12 W laptop for a total of 10 hours each day. He is charged at a rate of 25.07 cents per kilowatt-hour.
  a How many kilowatt-hours are used by the laptop during the year?
  b What is the cost of using the laptop for a year? Answer to the nearest cent.

Example 8   **7**   Eve's daily consumption of electricity is 19.5 kWh. She has a solar PV system to meet this need and export 7.5 kWh of energy to the grid. Eve's energy retailer charges $0.2425 per kWh and pays $0.10 per kWh for energy. How much is the solar PV system saving Eve each day?

8   The pie chart shows the sources of benefit to NSW of BASIX. The total benefit of BASIX for NSW to 2050 is estimated to be $294 000 000.

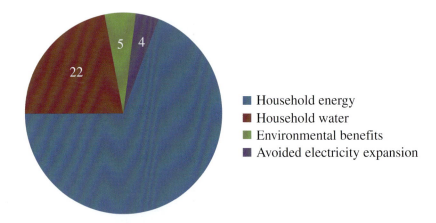

- Household energy
- Household water
- Environmental benefits
- Avoided electricity expansion

  a   What percentage of the benefits of BASIX was environmental?
  b   What percentage of the benefits of BASIX was household energy?
  c   What is the household energy saving of BASIX for NSW to 2050?
  d   What is the household water saving of BASIX for NSW to 2050?
  e   What is the environmental saving of BASIX for NSW to 2050?

9   The table shows the types of heating systems installed in new houses in one year.

Type	Number	Percentage
No active heating system	6332	
Gas fixed flued heater	2333	
Gas hydronic system	327	
1-phase air-conditioning	3357	
3-phase air-conditioning	6867	
Air-conditioning ducted	872	
Wood heating	1635	

  a   What is the total number of new houses?
  b   Copy and complete the table by calculating the percentage of each heating system.
  c   Which is the most popular heating system?
  d   How many houses installed air-conditioning?
  e   Construct a pie chart showing the proportions of each heating system.

LEVEL 2

10 The power rating of some electrical appliances is shown below.

Electrical appliance	Power rating
Air conditioner	3500 W
Clothes dryer	1800 W
Dishwasher	1600 W
Clothes washer	1300 W
TV/Computer	400 W
Refrigerator	150 W

a How much energy is used by a clothes dryer for 6 hours? Answer in kilowatt-hours.

b How much energy is used by an air conditioner for half an hour? Answer in watt-hours.

c How many hours was the dishwasher used if the cost of operating the dishwasher was $13.44? The cost of electricity is $0.2625 per kilowatt-hour.

d How many hours was the refrigerator used if the cost of operating the refrigerator was $1.38? The cost of electricity is 23 cents per kilowatt-hour.

LEVEL 3

11 An energy company charges for gas over a 3-month period are shown below.

Usage charge	First 5000 MJ	$0.02790 per MJ
	Additional MJ over 5000	$0.01675 per MJ

a Alexis used 4400 MJ of gas in this period. What is the cost of this gas?

b Matthew used 5450 MJ of gas in this period. What is the cost of this gas? Answer to the nearest cent.

c What percentage of Matthew's gas usage was charged at the lower rate? Answer correct to one decimal place.

d Stella received a gas bill for $117.18. How much gas did she use in this period?

e Claire has decided to reduce her energy bills. She has a target of $70 for gas. What is the maximum number of MJ she is allowed in this period?

f Jake used 6220 MJ of gas in this period. The gas charges are increasing by 5% in the next quarter. However, Aaron has purchased a new gas heater with a 5-star rating that will reduce his consumption by 1000 MJ. What is Jake's expected bill next quarter?

12 Access BASIX information from the website (www.basix.nsw.gov.au).

a Propose a new dwelling for a BASIX checklist.

b Determine house orientation.

c Make calculations including area and volume.

1D   Fuel consumption rate

A motor vehicle's fuel consumption is the number of litres of fuel it uses to travel 100 kilometres. The fuel consumption is calculated by filling the motor vehicle with fuel and recording the kilometres travelled from the odometer. When the motor vehicle is again filled with fuel then record the reading from the odometer and how many litres of fuel it takes to refill the tank. The distance travelled is the difference between the odometer readings.

FUEL CONSUMPTION

$$\text{Fuel consumption} = \frac{\text{Amount of fuel (L)} \times 100}{\text{Distance travelled (km)}}$$

 Example 9: Calculating a fuel consumption rate   **1D**

A medium-sized car travelled 850 km using 78.2 L of petrol.
What was the fuel consumption?

SOLUTION:

1 Write the fuel consumption formula.
2 Substitute 78.2 for the amount of fuel and 850 for the distance travelled.

$$\text{Fuel consumption} = \frac{\text{Amount of fuel} \times 100}{\text{Distance travelled}}$$

$$= \frac{78.2 \times 100}{850}$$

3 Evaluate.

$$= 9.2 \text{ L/100 km}$$

4 Write the answer in words.

Fuel consumption is 9.2 L per 100 km.

Exercise 1D

Example 9

1 Find the fuel consumption (litres per 100 km) for each of the following:

  a Lincoln's car uses 45.5 litres of petrol to travel 520 km.

  b A small car uses 36.9 litres of petrol to travel 600 km.

  c Gemma's sedan uses 55.1 litres of LPG to travel 950 km.

  d A sports car travelled 250 km using 28.5 litres of petrol.

  e Anthony's motor bike uses 167.5 litres of LPG to travel 2500 km.

  f Tahlia's car uses 121.6 litres of petrol to travel 3200 km.

2 Stephanie has bought a used car whose fuel consumption is 7.8 litres petrol per 100 kilometres. She is planning to travel around Australia. Calculate the number of litres of petrol Stephanie's car will use on the following distances. Answer correct to the nearest whole number.

  a A trip of 4049 km from Darwin to Perth.

  b A trip of 982 km from Sydney to Brisbane.

  c A trip of 2716 km from Perth to Adelaide.

  d A trip of 658 km from Melbourne to Canberra.

  e A trip of 732 km from Adelaide to Melbourne.

  f A trip of 309 km from Canberra to Sydney.

  g A trip of 3429 km from Brisbane to Darwin.

3 Charlie travels 45 km to work and 45 km from work each day.

  a How many kilometres does she travel to and from work in a 5-day working week?

  b Charlie drives a four-wheel drive with a fuel consumption of 8 L/100 km to and from work. How many litres of petrol does Charlie use travelling to and from work? Answer correct to one decimal place.

  c What is Charlie's petrol bill for work if petrol costs $1.20 per litre?

4 A family car uses LPG at a rate of 15 L/100 km and the gas tank holds 72 litres. How far can it travel on a tank of LPG?

5 Kai drives a truck whose petrol consumption is 16 L/100 km and the petrol tank is 90 litres. He is planning a trip from Moorebank to Melbourne. The distance from Moorebank to Melbourne is 840 km. Kai filled up the petrol tank at Moorebank. How many times will he need to fill his tank before arriving at Melbourne? Give reasons for your answer.

6 Natalie is planning a trip from Parramatta to Canberra using a car with a fuel consumption of 9.6 L/100 km. The distance from Parramatta to Canberra via the highway is 278 km and avoiding the highway is 363 km. The cost of LPG is 68.5 cents per litre.

  a How much will the trip cost via the highway?
  b How much will the trip cost avoiding the highway?
  c How much money is saved by travelling via the highway?

7 Austin owns an SUV with a fuel consumption of 10.9 L/100 km in the city and 8.4 L/100 km in the country. Austin travels 12 000 km per year in the city and 20 000 km per year in the country. The average cost of petrol is $1.48 per litre in the city and 12 cents higher in the country.

  a Find the cost of petrol to drive in the city for the year.
  b Find the cost of petrol to drive in the country for the year.
  c What is the total cost of petrol for Austin in one year?
  d What is the total cost of petrol for Austin in one year if the average cost of petrol increased to $2.00 in the city?

8 Eden buys a family car with a fuel consumption of 9.9 litres/100 km. Toby buys the LPG version of the family car with a fuel consumption 14.8 litres/100 km. Both Eden and Toby average 450 km in a week in the same conditions. The average price of ULP is $1.50 cents/litre and LPG is $0.85 cents per litre.

  a How many litres of fuel are used by Eden in a week?
  b How many litres of fuel are used by Toby in a week?
  c Calculate each car's yearly consumption of fuel.
  d What is Eden's yearly fuel bill?
  e What is Toby's yearly fuel bill?
  f Toby paid an additional $2400 for the LPG version of the family car. How many years will it take for the fuel savings to reach $2400 or the break-even point? Answer correct to the nearest whole number.
  g Research the current fuel prices using ULP and LPG. How long will it take for the fuel saving to exceed the initial costs?

9 Investigate the costs for two common cars on a family trip in your local area. Calculate the cost for the return trip in each case. You will need to determine the distance of the trip, fuel consumption for each car and the average price of fuel in the local area.

1E Calculations with ratios

A ratio is used to compare amounts of the same units in a definite order. For example, the ratio 3:4 represents 3 parts to 4 parts or $\frac{3}{4}$ or 0.75 or 75%.

A ratio is a fraction and can be simplified in the same way as a fraction. For example, the ratio 15:20 can be simplified to 3:4 by dividing each number by 5, which is the highest common factor of 15 and 20. Equivalent ratios are obtained by multiplying or dividing each amount in the ratio by the same number. Here the ratio 15:12 is simplified by dividing each amount in the ratio by 3, which is the highest common factor of 15 and 12.

$$\overset{\div 3 \quad \div 3}{15 : 12 = 5 : 4} \qquad \overset{\times 3 \quad \times 3}{5 : 4 = 15 : 12}$$

15:12 and 5:4 are equivalent ratios.

When simplifying a ratio with fractions, multiply each of the amounts by the lowest common denominator. For example, to simplify $\frac{1}{8}:\frac{3}{4}$ multiply both sides by 8. This results in the equivalent ratio of 1:6.

RATIO

A ratio is used to compare amounts of the same units in a definite order.
Equivalent ratios are obtained by multiplying or dividing by the same number.

 Example 10: Simplifying a ratio   1E

Write these ratios in simplest form.

a $3:\dfrac{1}{2}$

b 1.5:3.5

c $\dfrac{2}{7}:\dfrac{5}{21}$

SOLUTION:

1 Multiply both sides of the ratio by 2.
2 Evaluate.
3 Multiply both sides of the ratio by 10.
4 Divide both sides of the ratio by 5 (highest common factor).
5 Evaluate.
6 Express both sides of the ratio to a common denominator.
7 Evaluate and use the numerator as the ratio.

a $3:\dfrac{1}{2} = 3 \times 2 : \dfrac{1}{2} \times 2 = 6:1$

b $1.5:3.5 = 1.5 \times 10 : 3.5 \times 10$
$= 15:35 = \dfrac{15}{5}:\dfrac{35}{5} = 3:7$

c $\dfrac{2}{7}:\dfrac{5}{21} = \dfrac{6}{21}:\dfrac{5}{21} = 6:5$

Exercise 1E

1 Express each ratio in simplest form.

    a 15:3   **b** 10:40   **c** 24:16

    d 14:30   **e** 8:12   **f** 49:14

    g 81:27   **h** 48:32   **i** 17:51

    j 9:18:9   **k** 5:10:20   **l** 27:9:3

2 Express each ratio in simplest form. In parts e to l, the ratio has different units

    a $24:$18   **b** 3 kg to 12 kg   **c** 56 t:16 t

3 The following ratios have different units on each side. Express each ratio in simplest form after first changing to the same units on each side. So for **a**, first change the ratio to '40c to 100c' or '0.4:1'.

    a 40 c to $1   **b** 3 h to 1 day   **c** 2 mm to 1 cm

    d 1 km:250 m   **e** 3 m:50 cm   **f** 6 km:300 m

    g 7 cm:21 mm   **h** 8 months:4 years   **i** 2 L:450 mL

4 There are 14 boys and 10 girls in a class. What is the ratio of:

    a boys to girls?   **b** girls to boys?   **c** boys to the total number?

5 A clothing store has a discount sale. A dress marked at $250 is sold for $200. What is the ratio of the discount to the marked price?

6 Madeleine and Nathan invest $4500 and $2500 into a managed fund. What is the ratio of Madeleine's share to Nathan's share?

7 There were 80 blocks of land available for sale in a new land release. After one month 32 blocks have been sold. What is the ratio of sold blocks to the total number of blocks?

8 A 5 kg bag of potatoes costs $12.80. Find the cost of:

    a 1 kg   **b** 10 kg   **c** 14 kg   **d** 6 kg

9 The cost of 3 pens is $42.60. Find the cost of:

    a 1 pen   **b** 4 pens   **c** 6 pens   **d** 10 pens

10 A square has a side length of 6 cm. If the side length is doubled, what is the ratio of the area of the original square to that of the larger square?

LEVEL 2

Example 10 **11** Express each ratio in simplest form.

a $\dfrac{1}{2}:\dfrac{1}{5}$ b $\dfrac{2}{3}:\dfrac{3}{7}$ c $\dfrac{3}{4}:1$

d $\dfrac{1}{2}:\dfrac{1}{10}$ e $\dfrac{1}{10}:\dfrac{1}{5}$ f $\dfrac{2}{3}:\dfrac{3}{5}$

g $1:\dfrac{3}{4}$ h $\dfrac{2}{3}:1$ i $\dfrac{9}{10}:1$

12 Express each ratio in simplest form.

a $2x:x$ b $3y:9y$ c $4a:2$

d $4a:8a$ e $3xy:12x$ f $7m^2:m$

g $5d^2:25d^2$ h $22x:33xy$ i $16a^2b:2ab^2$

13 In an election, Aiden scored 250 votes, Billie 175 votes and Chelsea 125 votes. Find the ratio in simplest form of Aiden's votes:Billie's votes:Chelsea's votes.

14 Samantha and Mathilde own a restaurant. Samantha gets $\frac{3}{5}$ of the profits and Mathilde receives the remainder.
a What is the ratio of profits?
b Last week the profit was \$2250. How much does Mathilde receive?
c This week the profit is \$2900. How much does Samantha receive?

LEVEL 3

15 Express each of the following ratios in the form $x:1$.
a $12:8$ b $16:5$ c $1.6:1.2$ d $0.2:0.8$

16 Express each of the following ratios in the form $1:y$.
a $16:8$ b $8:15$ c $1.5:6$ d $2.4:8.4$

17 Nathan makes a blend of mixed lollies using 5 kg jelly babies, 4 kg liquorice and 1 kg skittles. Their prices are given in the table. What is the cost of the blend per kilogram?

Lolly prices	
Jelly babies	\$5.95 per kg
Liquorice	\$6.95 per kg
Skittles	\$11.90 per kg

1F   Dividing a quantity in a given ratio

Ratio problems may be solved by dividing a quantity in a given ratio. This method divides each amount in the ratio by the total number of parts.

DIVIDING A QUANTITY IN A GIVEN RATIO

1   Calculate the total number of parts by adding each amount in the ratio.
2   Divide the quantity by the total number of parts to determine the value of one part.
3   Multiply each amount of the ratio by the result in step 2.
4   Check by adding the answers for each part. The result should be the original quantity.

Example 11: Dividing a quantity in a given ratio   1F

Mikhail and Ilya were given $450 to share in the ratio 4:5. How much did each get?

SOLUTION:

1 Calculate the total number of parts by adding each amount in the ratio (4 parts to 5 parts).	Total parts = 4 + 5 = 9 9 parts = $450
2 Divide the quantity ($450) by the total number of parts (9 parts) to determine the value of one part.	$1 \text{ part} = \dfrac{\$450}{9} = \$50$
3 Multiply each amount of the ratio by the result in step 2 or $50.	4 parts = 4 × $50 = $200 5 parts = 5 × $50 = $250
4 Check by adding the answers for each part. The result should be the original quantity or $450.	($200 + $250 = $450)
5 Write the answer in words.	Mikhail got $200, Ilya got $250.

Example 12: Dividing a quantity in a given ratio   1F

A man left $6000 to be divided among his three children, Xia, Yui and Zi, in the ratio 5:8:7, in that order. How much did each get?

SOLUTION:

1 Calculate the total number of parts in the ratio by adding 5 parts to 8 parts to 7 parts.	Total parts = 5 + 8 + 7 = 20 20 parts = $6000
2 Divide the quantity ($6000) by the total number of parts (20 parts) to determine the value of one part.	$1 \text{ part} = \dfrac{\$6000}{20} = \$300$
3 Multiply each amount of the ratio by the result in step 2 or $300.	5 parts = 5 × $300 = $1500 8 parts = 8 × $300 = $2400 7 parts = 7 × $300 = $2100
4 Write the answer in words.	Xia got $1500, Yui got $2400, Zi got $2100.

Exercise 1F

Example 11 **1** Calculate how much each person receives if $100 is shared in the following ratios.

   a 7:3   **b** 2:3   **c** 11:9   **d** 7:8:10

2 Divide 240 into the following ratios.

   a 2:1   **b** 3:2   **c** 1:5   **d** 7:5

3 Share each amount in the ratio given.

   a $20 in the ratio 4:1   **b** $20 in the ratio 7:3

   c $15 in the ratio 1:2   **d** 77 drinks in the ratio 3:4

   e 100 lollies in the ratio 7:13   **f** 45 kg in the ratio 4:5

   g 160 books in the ratio 5:3   **h** 360 pencils in the ratio 2:7

   i 50 g in the ratio 1:3   **j** 60 km in the ratio 8:7

4 A bag of 500 grams of chocolates is divided into the ratio 7:3. What is the mass of the smaller amount?

5 At a concert there were 7 girls for every 5 boys. How many girls were in the audience of 8616?

Example 12 **6** Molly, Patrick and Andrew invest in a business in the ratio 6:5:1. The total amount invested is $240 000. How much was invested by the following people?

   a Molly   **b** Patrick   **c** Andrew

7 The ratio of residential area to parks in a local community is 17:3. The total area of the local community is 40 km². What is the area of parks?

8 Hayley is 15 years old and her brother is 5 years younger. If $200 is shared between them in the ratio of their ages, how much will Hayley receive?

9 In country town a census showed that there were 5 adults to every 7 children. If the population of the town was 7200, how many children lived there?

10 A punch is made from pineapple juice, lemonade and orange juice in the ratio 5:3:2.
    a How much lemonade is needed if one litre of pineapple juice is used?
    b How much pineapple juice is required to make 15 litres of punch?

11 Angus, Ruby and Lily share an inheritance of $500 000 in the ratio of 7:5:4. How much will be received by the following people?
    a Angus   b Ruby   c Lily

12 In a boiled fruit cake recipe the ratio of mixed fruit to flour to sugar is 5:3:2. A 250 g packet of mixed fruit is used to make the cake. How much sugar and flour are required?

13 A delivery load of 8.5 tonnes is to be divided between two stores in the ratio 11:6. How much will each store receive?

14 The load on a bridge is applied in three positions, A, B and C, in the ratio 5:7:5. If the total load on the bridge is 782 tonnes, what is the load taken at each point?

15 A jam is made by adding 5 parts fruit to 4 parts of sugar. How much fruit should be added to $2\frac{1}{2}$ kilograms of sugar in making the jam?

16 The perimeter of a rectangle is 42 cm. The ratio of length to breadth is 5:2.
    a What is the length?
    b What is the breadth?

17 The ratio of $5 to $10 notes in Stephanie's purse is 3:5. There are 24 notes altogether. What is the total value of Stephanie's $5 notes?

18 The three sides of a triangle are in the ratio of 1:3:5. The longest side of the triangle is 16.2 mm. What is the perimeter of the triangle?

19 A chemical solution is made by mixing acid with water in the ratio 1:24. The solution is then taken and mixed with water in the ratio 1:3. How much acid would there be in 400 mL of this final solution?

20 The ratio of the populations of town A to town B is 3:8, and the ratio of town B to town C is 5:2. If the total population of the three towns is 92 655, find the population of each town.

1G Scale drawings

A scale drawing is a drawing that represents the actual object. The scale factor of a scale drawing is the ratio of the size of the drawing to the actual size of the object. For example, a map is a scale drawing. It is not the same size as the area it represents. The measurements have been reduced to make the map a convenient size. The scale of a drawing may be expressed with or without units. For example, a scale of 1 cm to 1 m means 1 cm on the scale drawing represents 1 m on the actual object. Alternatively, a scale of 1:100 means the actual distance is 100 times the length of 1 unit on the scale drawing.

SCALE DRAWING

Scale of a drawing = Drawing length:Actual length
Scale is expressed in two ways:
- Using units such as 1 cm to 1 m (or 1 cm = 1 m).
- No units using a ratio such as 1:100.

Example 13: Using a scale   1G

A scale drawing has a scale of 1:50.
a Find the actual length if the drawing length is 30 mm. Answer to the nearest centimetre.
b Find the drawing length if the actual length is 4.5 m. Answer to the nearest millimetre.

SOLUTION:

1 Multiply the drawing length by 50 to determine the actual length.	**a** Actual length = 30 × 50 mm
	= 1500 mm
2 Divide by 10 to change millimetres to centimetres.	= 150 cm
3 Divide the actual length by 50 to determine the drawing length.	**b** Drawing length = 4.5 ÷ 50 m
	= 0.09 m
4 Multiply by 1000 to change metres to millimetres.	= 90 mm

Exercise 1G

Example13 **1** A scale drawing has a scale of 1:100. What is the actual length of these drawing lengths? Express your answer in metres.

    a 2 cm   **b** 10 mm   **c** 3.4 cm

    d 28 mm   **e** 8.5 cm   **f** 49 mm

2 A scale drawing has a scale of 1:25 000. What is the drawing length of these actual lengths? Express your answer in millimetres.

    a 2 km   **b** 750 m   **c** 4000 cm

    d 3.5 km   **e** 50 000 mm   **f** 1375 m

3 Express each of the following scales as a ratio in the form 1:x.

    a 1 cm to 2 cm   **b** 1 mm to 5 cm   **c** 1 cm to 3 km

4 The scale on a map is 1:1000. Calculate the actual distances if these are the distances on the map. Express your answer in metres.

    a Road 20 cm   **b** Shops 10 cm   **c** Pathway 5 cm

    d Parking area 10 mm   **e** Bridge 34 mm   **f** Park 80 mm

5 The scale on a map is given as 1 cm = 15 km. What is the actual distance if the distance on the map is:

    a 2.5 cm?

    b 45 cm?

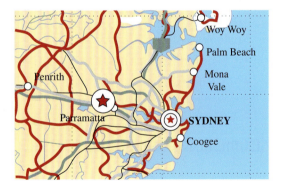

6 The scale on a map is 1:5000. Calculate the map distances if these are actual distances. Express your answer in millimetres.

    a 50 m   **b** 80 m   **c** 100 m

    d 120 m   **e** 150 m   **f** 240 m

7 The scale on a map is given as 1 mm = 50 m. If the distance between two points is 350 m, what is the map distance between these points?

8 A scale drawing has a scale of 1:75. Find the:

    a actual length if the drawing length is 15 mm

    b drawing length if the actual length is 3 m.

9 The Parkes radio telescope dish has a diameter of 64 metres. The image opposite uses a photograph of the dish.

  a Determine a scale for the image.

  b Estimate the height of the top of the antenna above the ground.

10 The scale of a model is 2:150. Calculate the model lengths if these are actual lengths. Express your answer in millimetres.

  a 75 cm
  b 180 cm
  c 300 cm
  d 45 m
  e 6 m
  f 36 m

11 A scale drawing of the space shuttle is shown opposite. The actual length of the space shuttle is 43 metres.

  a What is the scale factor?

  b Calculate the length of the wing span.

  c Calculate the width (w) of the shuttle.

  d What is the length of the nose of the shuttle?

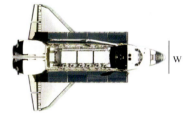

12 The total length of the Sydney Harbour Bridge is 1150 metres. A scale model is built for a coffee table of length 1.2 metres using the picture below.

  a What scale would be suitable?

  b What is the maximum height of the bridge if the scale model has a height of 20 cm?

  c Estimate the height of the bridge pillars.

  d Estimate the length of the Sydney Opera House.

1H

1H　Plans and elevations

A plan is a view of an object from the top.
It is looking down on the object. A house
plan is a horizontal section cut through
the building showing the walls, windows,
door openings, fittings and appliances. An
elevation is a view of an object from one side,
such as a front elevation or side elevation.
House elevations are rarely a simple rectangular
shape but show all the parts of the building
that are seen from a particular direction. House
elevations are a vertical section parallel to one side
of the building.

PLANS AND ELEVATIONS

A plan is a view of an object from the top.
An elevation is a view of an object from one side, such as a front elevation or side elevation.

Example 14: Drawing a plan and elevation　　　　　　　　　　**1H**

Draw the plan view, front elevation and side elevation of
this object.

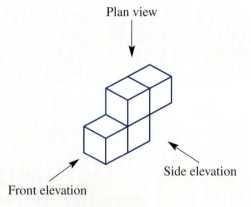

Plan view

Side elevation

Front elevation

SOLUTION:

1　Look down on the object for the plan.
2　Look from the front for the front
　　elevation and from the side for the
　　side elevation.

Plan　　　　Front elevation　　　Side elevation

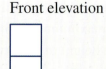
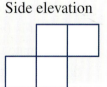

Building plans

A floor plan for a Metricon home is shown below. Building plans are a very common application of similar figures. They are drawn using a scale factor such as 1:150. This allows the dimensions of a house to be determined by measurement and calculation.

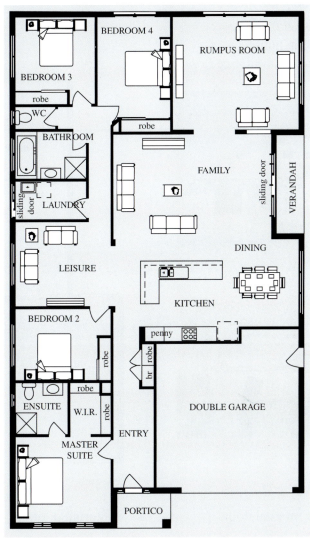

Scale 1:150

Common floor plan symbols

	Door swing – indicates direction the door opens
	Window – glass window in a solid wall
	Kitchen sink – two-compartment kitchen sink
	Shower – shower without a bathtub
	Toilet – toilet located on wall
	Bathtub – bathtub showing location of drain

Example 15: Finding measurements from a house plan   **1H**

A building plan is shown for the ground floor of
a Metricon home.

a How many internal doors are there?

b What is the meaning of PWDR?

c What is the length of the house?

d What are the dimensions of the double garage?

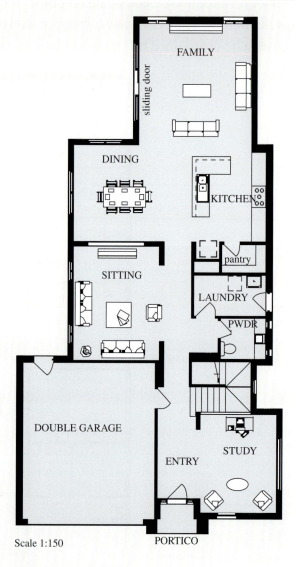

Scale 1:150

SOLUTION:

1 Count the number of internal doors
(find the door symbol).

a 4 internal doors

2 PWDR is an abbreviation for the powder
room.

b Powder room

3 Use a ruler to measure the length of the
house on the floor plan.

c Drawing length is 12.6 cm

4 Multiply the measurement by 150
(scale 1:150).

Actual length = 12.6 × 150 cm
= 1890 cm or 18.9 m

5 Use a ruler to measure the dimensions of
the double garage on the floor plan.

d Drawing length is 4.1 × 3.5 cm

6 Multiply the measurements by 150
(scale 1:150).

Actual length = 4.1 × 150 cm
= 615 cm or 6.2 m

Actual breath = 3.5 × 150 cm
= 525 cm or 5.3 m

Dimensions are 6.2 × 5.3 m.

Exercise 1H

Example 14

1 Draw the plan, front elevation and side elevation for these objects.

a Plan view

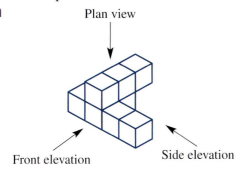

Front elevation   Side elevation

b Plan view

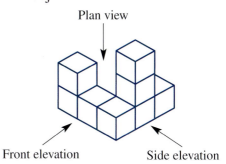

Front elevation   Side elevation

2 What are these shapes?

	Plan	Front elevation	Side elevation
a	rectangle	right triangle	rectangle
b	square with diagonals	triangle	triangle
c	circle	square	square
d	square	square	square
e	circle with centre dot	triangle	triangle

3 Draw the plan, front elevation and side elevation for these objects.

a

b

c

d

e

f

4 A section of a floor plan is shown opposite.
  a What room is shown in the diagram?
  b What symbol is used for a shower?
  c What symbol is used for a door?
  d What does 'WIR' represent on the plan?

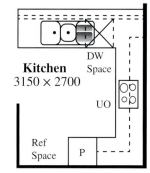

5 A section of a floor plan is shown opposite.
  a What are the dimensions of the kitchen?
  b What symbol is used for the sink?
  c What symbol is used for the cooktop?
  d What does 'Ref' represent on the plan?
  e What does 'P' represent on the plan?

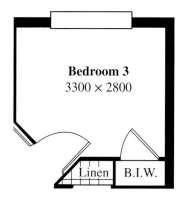

6 A section of a floor plan is shown opposite.
  a What are the dimensions of the bedroom?
  b What symbol is used for a window?
  c What does 'BIW' represent on the plan?
  d What is the length of the bedroom on the plan?
  e Calculate a scale for the floor plan.

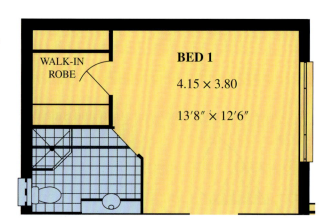

7 A section of a floor plan is shown opposite.
  a What are the dimensions of the bedroom?
  b What symbol is used for the toilet?
  c What is the length of the bedroom on the plan?
  d Calculate a scale for the floor plan.
  e What are the dimensions of the walk-in robe?
  f What is the area of the bedroom? Answer in square metres, correct to two decimal places.

Example 15 **8** A second-storey building plan is shown for a
Masterton home.

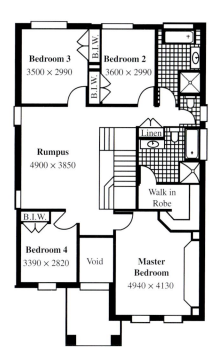

  a What are the dimensions of the third bedroom? Answer
  in metres.

  b What are the dimensions of the master bedroom? Answer
  in metres.

  c By measurement, estimate a scale for this plan.

  d By measurement, find the width of the house. Answer in
  metres.

  e Calculate the area of the void. Answer to the nearest
  square metre.

  f Calculate the area of the ensuite. Answer to the nearest
  square metre.

9 A rumpus room is built measuring 5.5 m by 4.7 m. The floor plan uses a scale of 1:100.
A concrete slab with a depth of 100 mm is used to build the rumpus room.

  a What is the area of the rumpus room on the plan? Answer in square millimetres.

  b What is the volume of concrete for the rumpus room? Answer in cubic millimetres.

  c What is the volume of concrete for the rumpus room if the slab depth is 200 mm? Answer in
  cubic millimetres.

10 The front elevation of a house is shown opposite
(scale 1:200).

FRONT ELEVATION

  a What is the width of the house? Answer
  in metres.

  b What is the height of the chimney? Answer
  in metres.

  c What are the dimensions of the front door?
  Answer in metres.

  d What are the dimensions of the window on
  the right-hand side? Answer to the nearest
  centimetre.

  e What is the area of the window? Answer to the nearest square centimetre.

  f What is the area of the large triangular gable? Answer to the nearest square centimetre.

  g What is the area of the small triangular gable? Answer to the nearest square centimetre.

11 The front elevation of a house is shown below.

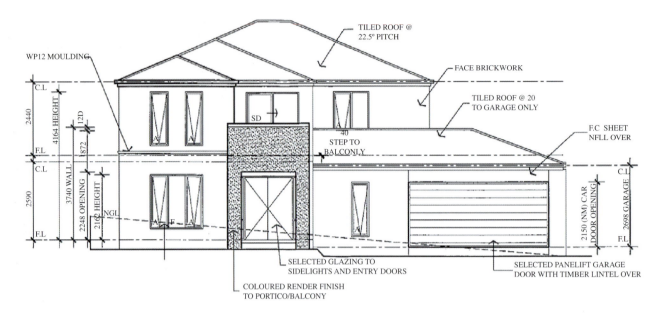

a What is the height of the first storey? Answer in metres.

b What is the height of the garage? Answer in metres.

c What is the angle of the pitch of the roof?

d How many windows are at the front of the house?

12 A building plan is shown below. The house length is 20 m and the width is 18 m.

a What are the dimensions of the living room? Answer in metres.

b What is the area of the living room? Answer to the nearest square metre.

c How much concrete was used in the concrete slab whose thickness is 200 mm? Answer to the nearest cubic metre.

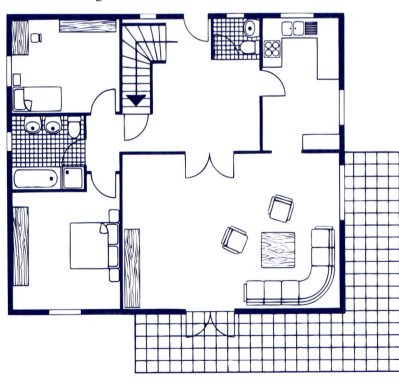

13 A building plan is shown for a Metricon home. The house length is 24 m (includes portico) and the width is 15 m (includes garage).

   a What is a suitable scale for this plan?

   b What are the dimensions of the verandah? Answer correct to the nearest tenth of a metre.

   c What are the dimensions of the double garage? Answer correct to the nearest tenth of a metre.

   d What are the dimensions of bedroom 3? Answer correct to the nearest tenth of a metre.

   e Calculate the area of the sitting room. Answer correct to the nearest square metre.

   f What is the cost of carpeting the sitting room if the cost of the carpet is $140 per square metre? Answer to the nearest dollar.

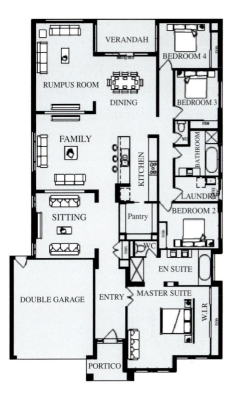

14 A section of a building plan is shown opposite. The dimensions of the family room are 5.5 metres by 6.0 metres.

   a Estimate a suitable scale for this building plan.

   b What is the combined length of the family, kitchen and sitting rooms? Answer correct to the nearest tenth of a metre.

   c The family, dining, kitchen and sitting rooms are to be tiled. Calculate the combined area of these rooms. Answer to nearest square metre.

   d Ceramic tiles measuring 300×300 mm are to be laid in these rooms. How many tiles are required?

   e What assumption has been made to the answer in part **d**?

   f The family, dining, kitchen and sitting rooms are built on a concrete slab with a thickness of 0.15 m. What is the volume of concrete used for the slab?

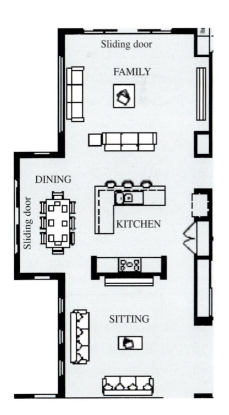

1I   Perimeter, area and volume

Perimeter

The perimeter of a piece of land can be found using aerial photographs such as those obtained from Google Earth. It is much quicker than actually measuring the land.

Steps: **1**   Determine the borders of the piece of land.

2   Access a land measurement website and view the aerial photograph of the land.

3   Using the online tools, click along the perimeter of the land.

PERIMETER

To calculate the perimeter of land, multiply the length on the aerial photograph by the scale.

 Example 16: Calculating distance using a scale   1I

This aerial view on Google Earth shows a 50 m Olympic swimming pool outlined with the 'path' tool.

a   What is the scale used on the image?

b   Use the scale to determine the length of the boat in metres.

SOLUTION:

1   Measure the length of the swimming pool.

2   Express the image length to actual length as a ratio in the same units (cm).

3   Divide both sides of the ratio by the image length (3.1).

4   Measure the length of the boat in the photo.

5   Multiply the length of the boat by the scale.

6   Evaluate using correct units.

7   Write the answer in words.

a   Length of swimming pool is 3.1 cm.
Scale 3.1 cm to 50 m (or 5000 cm).
Scale is 1:1613.

b   Boat length is 2.0 cm.
Boat length = 2.0 × 1613
$$= 3226 \text{ cm}$$
$$= 32 \text{ m}$$
Length of the boat is 32 metres.

Area

The area of a land surface can be estimated and calculated directly from scale diagrams and aerial photographs. To estimate the area of the land, divide the diagram into square grids and count the number of squares. To calculate the exact area of land, use the appropriate formula. Composite shapes are divided into plane shapes. The dimensions of the shapes are determined using the scale.

AREA

To estimate the area of land, divide it into square grids and count the number of squares.
To calculate the exact area of land, use the appropriate formula.

Example 17: Calculating the area of land   1I

A warehouse is shown on Google Earth. The red scale bar represents 42 m at the ground.

a Calculate the dimensions of the land occupied by the warehouse building using the scale. Answer correct to the nearest metre.

b Calculate the area of land occupied by the warehouse building. Answer correct to the nearest square metre.

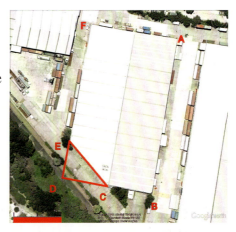

SOLUTION:

1 Measure the scale bar on the image.	**a** Scale bar is 1.2 cm, 42 m on ground.
2 Express the scale in the form 1:x by dividing 42 by 1.2.	Scale is 1 cm to 35 m.
3 Measure the length of each side.	$AB = 4.2 \times 35 = 147$ m
4 Multiply these lengths by the scale.	$BC = 1.2 \times 35 = 42$ m
	$CD = 1.3 \times 35 = 45.5$
	$ED = 1.0 \times 35 = 35$ m
	$EF = 3.2 \times 35 = 112$ m
	$AF = 2.5 \times 35 = 87.5$
5 Evaluate using correct units.	$EC = 1.6 \times 35 = 56$ m
6 Divide the area into two plane shapes.	**b** $A = lb = 147 \times 87.5 = 12\,863$ m^2
7 Write the formulas for the area of a rectangle and triangle. Calculate these areas to the nearest square metre.	$A = \dfrac{1}{2}bh = \dfrac{1}{2} \times 45.5 \times 35 = 796.3$ m^2
8 Subtract the area of the triangle from the area of the rectangle. and evaluate	$A = 12\,862.5 - 796.3 = 12\,066.2$ m^2
9 Evaluate.	
10 Write the answer in words.	Area of the warehouse is $12\,066$ m^2.

Volume of water

If water covers an area (such as the bottom of a pool, tank or reservoir), to a constant depth, its volume can be calculated using

$$V = Ah$$

where V = volume, A is the area that the water covers, and h is the depth of the water (i.e. the same as height of the water surface above the bottom). We use h because the water forms a right prism, and in Year 11 you learned that the volume of a right prism is $V = Ah$.

The trapezoidal rule for area $A \approx \frac{w}{2}(d_f + d_l)$ is used to estimate the area of a piece of land or a body of water with an irregular boundary such as a reservoir or dam. You learned it in Year 11. A is the area, w is the width between the parallel sides, d_f is the distance along the first parallel side, d_l is the distance along the last parallel side. Note that in Year 11, h was used for the width between the parallel sides, but here we will use w since h will be used for height or thickness of the shape.

So if a body of water such as a pool has a surface area of 100 square metres and the area of its bottom is also 100 square metres (because it has a constant depth), and that depth is 2 m, then its volume is 200 cubic metres.

If the area of a reservoir is A square metres, and h metres of rain falls on it (with no water running in or out), then its volume will increase by Ah cubic metres.

VOLUME USING $V = Ah$ AND THE TRAPEZOIDAL RULE FOR AREA

The trapezoidal rule:

$$A \approx \frac{w}{2}(d_f + d_l)$$

A – Area of shape
w – Width between the parallel sides
d_f – Distance along first parallel side
d_l – Distance along last parallel side

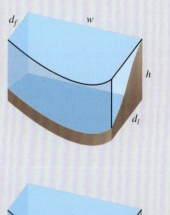

$$V = Ah$$

A – Area of the body of water or the cross-section of the prism object
h – Height or thickness

This rule only applies to bodies or prisms of uniform thickness.

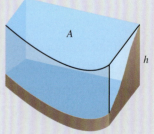

Example 18: Calculate volume with the trapezoidal rule for area **1I**

The shape of the water in a pool of constant depth with an irregularly-shaped bottom and top surface is shown. Dimensions are in metres.

a Apply the trapezoidal rule for area to approximate the volume of water in this pool.

b 100 mm of rain falls on the pool. Assume it has vertical walls that extend vertically above the water surface so that no water runs out of or into the pool, and the depth in all parts of the pool does not vary. By how much does the volume of water in the pool increase?

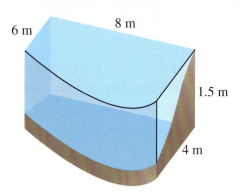

SOLUTION:

1 Write the trapezoidal rule for area.

a $A \approx \dfrac{w}{2}(d_f + d_l)$

2 Substitute $w = 8$, $d_f = 6$, $d_l = 4$, $h = 1.5$ into the formula.

$A \approx \dfrac{8}{2}(6 + 4)$

3 Evaluate to find the area of the pool in square metres.

$A \approx 40 \text{ m}^2$

4 Write the formula for volume of a right prism.

$V = Ah$

5 Substitute $A \approx 40$ and $h = 1.5$ into the formula.

$V \approx 40 \times 1.5$

6 Evaluate to find the volume of water in the pool in cubic metres.

$V \approx 60 \text{ m}^3$

7 Write the answer in words.

The volume of water in the pool is approximately 60 cubic metres.

8 Since the area of the water added is the same as the area of the pool, we can repeat steps 5 and 6 with the formula for the volume of a right prism, and just change h. It has been given in millimetres and needs to be changed to metres. There are 1000 mm in a metre. Divide 100 mm by 1000.

b $100 \text{ mm} = \dfrac{100}{1000} \text{ m} = 0.1 \text{ m}.$

9 Substitute $A \approx 40$ and $h = 0.1$ into the formula.

$V \approx 40 \times 0.1 = 4 \text{ m}^3$

10 Write the answer in words.

The volume of water in the pool increases by approximately 4 cubic metres.

Note: since the area calculated by the trapezoidal rule is an approximation, the calculations of volume using its results with $V = Ah$ in steps 5 and 9 are approximations too.

Exercise 1I

Example 16

1 The length of the Olympic swimming pool shown opposite is 50 metres.

    a Calculate a scale for the aerial photograph.
    b What are the dimensions of the aerial photograph? (Answer to the nearest metre.)
    c What is the length from A to B?
    d What is the length from B to C?
    e What is the length from C to A?
    f What is the perimeter of ABC?
    g Calculate the area of the land marked ABC. Assume a right-angle at C.

Example 17

2 A football field is shown opposite. The scale is marked by the red bar, which represents 50 m on the ground. Answer the following questions, correct to the nearest metre or square metre.

    a What is the length of the grandstand highlighted by the yellow bar?
    b Calculate the length of the field.
    c Calculate the width of the field.
    d What is the perimeter of the field?
    e What is the area of the field?
    f What is the length of the diagonal of the field?

3 Two circular buildings, A and B, at Sydney airport are shown. The red scale represents 25 m on the ground. Answer the following questions, correct to the nearest metre or square metre.

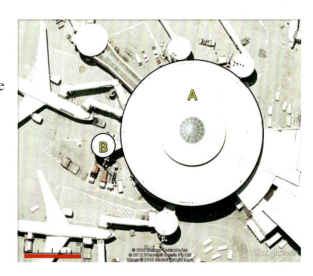

    a What is the radius of building A?
    b What is the diameter of building B?
    c What is the circumference of building A?
    d What is the area of building A?
    e What is the radius of the building B?
    f What is the circumference of building B?

4 Calculate the distance between these places, to the
nearest metre, using online tools.

a Government House to the Sydney
Conservatorium of Music

b Wynyard and Town Hall stations

c Tumbalong Park to the Archibald fountain

d University of Sydney to Moore Park

e Centennial Park to Bondi beach

f Kings Cross to Woolloomooloo

5 The map below has a scale of 1:10 000.

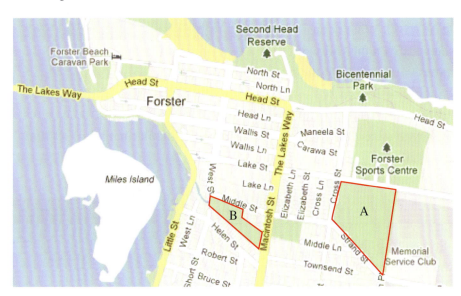

Estimate the area of the following sections of land.

a *A* **b** *B* **c** Miles Island

Example 18 **6** Find the volume using the trapezoidal rule for area and the formula for volume of a right prism
and the following sets of data.

a $w = 14$ m, $d_f = 28$ m, $d_l = 36$ m and $h = 8$ m

b $w = 9$ m, $d_f = 45$ m, $d_l = 25$ m and $h = 6$

7 The diagram shows the base of a pool. Estimate the volume of
the pool if its depth is everywhere 1.8 m. Answer correct to the
nearest cubic metre.

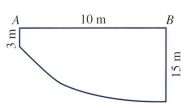

8 A farm is shown opposite. Answer the following questions correct to the nearest metre or square metre.

   a What is the perimeter of paddock A?
   b What is the perimeter of paddock B?
   c What is the perimeter of paddock C?
   d What is the perimeter of the L-shaped paddock?
   e What is the area of paddock *A*?
   f What is the area of paddock *B*?
   g What is the area of paddock *C*?
   h What is the area of the L-shaped paddock?

9 A diagram has a scale of 1:100. What is the actual area of these shapes, given the following drawing lengths? Express your answer to the nearest square metre.

   a Square with a side length of 10 mm
   b Rectangle with a length of 2 cm and a breadth of 3 cm
   c Right-angled triangle with a base length of 25 mm and perpendicular height of 40 mm
   d Circle with a radius of 20 mm
   e Semicircle with a diameter of 50 mm

10 Asha took two measurements at 120 m intervals across the irregular-shaped reservoir in the diagram. The measurements were 100 m and 80 m.

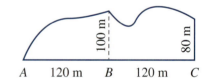

   a Estimate the surface area of the reservoir. Answer correct to the nearest square metre.
   b Asha measured the depth of water and found it to be 5 m everywhere. Estimate the volume of the reservoir. Answer correct to the nearest cubic metre.

11 150 mm of rain fell on the reservoir in question 10, which has vertical banks so no water flows in or out and the depth does not vary.

   a What is the volume of water in the reservoir after the rain?
   b After the rain, the farm that depends on the reservoir needs an extra 15000 cubic metres of water for the next month. How much rain needs to fall in that time so that when the extra water has been pumped out, the water level in the reservoir remains the same? Answer correct to the nearest millimetre.

Key ideas and chapter summary

Rate	1 Write the rate as a fraction. First quantity is the numerator and 1 is the denominator.
	2 Convert the first amount (numerator) to the required unit.
	3 Convert the second amount (denominator) to the required unit.
	4 Simplify the fraction.
Unitary method	1 Find one unit of an amount by dividing by the amount.
	2 Multiply the result in step 1 by the number.
Heart rate	Heart rate is the number of heartbeats per minute (bpm).
	MHR = 220 − Age (years)
Energy rate	Energy is the rate of power per unit of time (kilowatt hour - kWh)
	Running cost of the appliance is calculated by multiplying the energy consumption by the electricity charge.
Fuel consumption rate	$$\text{Fuel consumption} = \frac{\text{Amount of fuel (L)} \times 100}{\text{Distance travelled (km)}}$$
Ratio	A ratio is used to compare amounts of the same units in a definite order. Equivalent ratios are obtained by multiplying or dividing by the same number.
Dividing a quantity in a given ratio	1 Find the total number of parts by adding each amount in the ratio.
	2 Divide the quantity by the total number of parts to find one part.
	3 Multiply each amount of the ratio by the result in step 2.
Scale drawing	Scale of a drawing = Drawing length : Actual length
	Scale is expressed in two ways:
	• Using units such as 1 cm to 1 m (or 1 cm = 1 m)
	• No units using a ratio such as 1:100.
Plans and elevations	A plan is a view of an object from the top. An elevation is a view of an object from one side such as a front elevation or side elevation.
Perimeter	To calculate the perimeter of the land, multiply the length on an aerial photograph by the scale.
Area	To estimate the area of land, divide it into square grids and count the number of squares. To calculate the area of land, use the appropriate formula.
	The trapezoidal rule for area of land with one irregular boundary gives an approximation.
Volume of water and the trapezoidal rule	Volume of a body of water of constant depth and a trapezoidal area, or volume of rainfall falling on a trapezoidal area can be calculated using the trapezoidal rule for area $A \approx \frac{w}{2}(d_f + d_l)$ and formula for the area of a right prism $V = Ah$.

Multiple-choice

1 Christian is a courier who delivers 1 parcel on average every 25 minutes. How many hours does it take to deliver 24 parcels?

   A 10   **B** 11   **C** 12   **D** 13

2 A hose fills a 10 L bucket in 20 seconds. What is the rate of flow in litres per hour?

   A 0.0001   **B** 30   **C** 1800   **D** 7200

3 Which of the following is the slowest speed?

   A 60 km/h   **B** 100 m/s   **C** 10 000 m/min   **D** 6000 m/h

4 Eden's maximum heart rate (MHR) is 175. Which of the following heart rates is within her target heart rate (65% − 85%)?

   A 75   **B** 100   **C** 125   **D** 150

5 How much energy does a 600-watt hair dryer use in 5 hours?

   A 1.2 kWh   **B** 3 kWh   **C** 120 kWh   **D** 3000 kWh

6 What is the fuel consumption for a vehicle that travelled 340 km using 51 litres of petrol?

   A 7 L/100 km   **B** 9 L/100 km   **C** 15 L/100 km   **D** 17 L/100 km

7 The ratio of adults to children in a park is 5:9. How many adults are in the park if there are 630 children?

   A 70   **B** 126   **C** 280   **D** 350

8 A 360-gram lolly bag is divided in the ratio 7:5. What is the mass of the smaller amount?

   A 150 g   **B** 168 g   **C** 192 g   **D** 210 g

9 A scale drawing has a scale of 1:20. What is the actual length if the drawing length of an object is 20 mm?

   A 1 mm   **B** 20 mm   **C** 40 mm   **D** 400 mm

10 The scale on a map is given as 1 mm = 150 m. If the distance between two points is 600 m, what is the map distance between these points?

   A 4 mm   **B** 0.25 mm   **C** 2.5 cm   **D** 40 cm

Short-answer

1 Convert each rate to the units shown.

 a $15/kg to $/g
 b 14400 m/h to m/min
 c 120 cm/s to mm/min
 d 4800 kg/g to kg/mg
 e 14 L/g to mL/kg
 f $3600/g to c/mg

2 If 20 metres of curtain material costs $580, what would be the cost of 35 metres of the same material?

3 A motor bike travels at a speed of 100 km/h. How far does it travel in 3.5 hours?

4 A 5 kg bag of rice costs $9.20. What is the cost of the following amounts?

 a 10 kg
 b 40 kg
 c 3 kg
 d 7 kg
 e 500 kg
 f 250 kg

5 Estimate the maximum heart rate for a 22-year-old. (MHR = 220 − Age)

6 A car travels 960 km on 75 litres of petrol. How far does it travel on 50 litres?

7 Simplify the following ratios.

 a 500:100
 b 20:30
 c 28:7
 d 10:15:30
 e 12:9
 f 56:88
 g 4.8:1.6
 h $\frac{3}{4}:\frac{1}{2}$

8 Daniel and Eddie own a business and share the profits in the ratio 3:4.

 a The profit last week was $3437. How much does Daniel receive?
 b The profit this week is $2464. How much does Eddie receive?

9 Patrick mixes sand and cement in the ratio 5:2 by volume. If he uses 5 buckets of cement, how much sand should he use?

10 The ratio of Victoria's height to Willow's is 8:7. If Victoria is 176 cm tall, how tall is Willow?

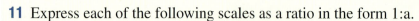

Review

11 Express each of the following scales as a ratio in the form 1:a.

   a 1 cm to 3 m   **b** 1 mm to 6 cm   **c** 1 m to 2.5 km

12 The scale on a map is given as 1 cm = 5 km. If the distance between two points on the map is 46 mm, what is the actual distance between these points? Answer in kilometres.

13 A scale drawing has a scale of 1:50000. What is the drawing length of these actual lengths? Express your answer in millimetres.

   a 4 km   **b** 1250 m   **c** 5000 cm

   d 6.5 km   **e** 20000 mm   **f** 2125 m

14 The scale on a map is 1:400. Calculate the actual distances if these are the distances on the map. Express your answer in metres.

   a bike path 180 cm   **b** town centre 20 cm   **c** street 5 cm

   d beach 210 mm   **e** river 62 cm   **f** park 60 mm

15 A section of a floor plan is shown opposite.

The longer dimension of the laundry is 3 metres.

   a Estimate a suitable scale for the floor plan.

   b What symbol is used for the bath?

   c What does 'W.C.' represent on the plan?

   d What are the dimensions of the laundry?

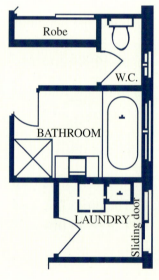

16 Use the trapezoidal rule for area and the formula for the volume of a right prism on the following set of data: $w = 6$ m, $d_f = 20$ m and $d_l = 40$ m, $h = 2.5$ m

   a to find the approximate volume.

   b to find the approximate volume of water that falls on the same area when there is 9 mm of rain.

Extended-response

17 There are 384 passengers and 144 crew in a cruise ship. If there are 22 lifeboats, enough for everyone, how many are allotted to the passengers and how many to the crew?

18 Pump A can fill a tank in 5 minutes; pump B can fill the tank in 10 minutes. How long will it take to fill the tank if both pumps are working together?

PDF
LITERACY

2 Network concepts

Syllabus topic — N2.1 Networks, N2.2 Shortest paths

This topic will develop your skills to be able to identify and use network terminology and to solve problems involving networks.

Outcomes

- Identify and use network terminology.
- Recognise the circumstances when networks can be used to solve a problem.
- Draw a network to represent a map.
- Draw a network to represent information given in a table.
- Investigate and solve practical problems involving network diagrams.
- Define a tree and a minimum spanning tree for a given network.
- Determine and use minimum spanning trees to solve problems.
- Identify the shortest path on a network diagram.
- Recognise when the shortest path is not necessarily the best path.

Digital Resources for this chapter

In the Interactive Textbook:

- Videos
- Desmos widgets
- Literacy worksheet
- Spreadsheets
- Quick Quiz
- Study guide
- Solutions (enabled by teacher)

In the Online Teaching Suite:

- Teaching Program
- Tests
- Review Quiz
- Teaching Notes

Knowledge check

The Interactive Textbook provides a test of prior knowledge for this chapter, and may direct you to revision from the previous years' work.

2A Networks

A network is a term to describe a group or
system of interconnected objects. There are
many situations in everyday life that involve
connections between objects. Cities are
connected by roads, computers are connected
to the internet and people connect to each
other through being friends on social media.
The diagram below shows the distances in
kilometres between some NSW cities. This is referred to as a network or a network diagram. Note
that the lengths of the lines in a network diagram are not generally drawn to scale.

 Networks: Basic concepts Watch the video in the Interactive Textbook for an illustration of the
terms and concepts in action.

The common terms used in a network are described below.

- A **network diagram** is a representation
  of a group of objects called vertices
  that are connected together by lines.
  Network diagrams are also called
  graphs.

- A **vertex (plural: vertices)** is a point (or dot) in a
  network diagram at which lines of pathways intersect
  or branch. In the diagram opposite, the names of the
  cities are the vertices. Vertices are also called nodes.

- An **edge** is the line that connects the vertices. In the
  diagram opposite, the line marked with 560 is an edge.
  Edges can cross each other without intersecting at a node.

- The **degree** of a vertex is the number of edges that are
  connected to it. The degree of the Broken Hill vertex is 3
  because there are three edges attached to the vertex. This
  is written as deg(Broken Hill) = 3.
  The degree of a vertex is either even or odd.
  - The degree of a vertex is even if it has an even number of edges
    attached to the vertex. For example, in the above network
    diagram the vertices of even degree are Port Macquarie,
    Bathurst and Albury.
  - The degree of a vertex is odd if it has an odd number of edges attached to the vertex. For
    example, in the above network diagram the vertices of odd degree are Sydney and Broken Hill.
  - There can be multiple edges between vertices, as shown.
- A **loop** starts and ends at the same vertex as shown in the diagram. It counts as one
  edge, but it contributes two to the degree of the vertex.

- A **directed** edge, also called an arc, has an arrow and travel is only possible in the direction of the arrow. An **undirected** edge has no arrow and travel is possible in both directions. A network or graph may have both directed and undirected edges.
- In a **directed network** or graph all the edges are directed, as in the diagram opposite, which has five vertices and six edges (arcs). It shows a path can be taken from *A* to *B* to *C*, however there is no path from *C* to *B* to *A*.

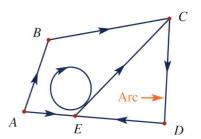

- In an **undirected network** or graph all the edges are undirected and travel on an edge is possible in both directions. The diagram opposite is an undirected graph with five vertices and six edges. It shows that there is a path from *A* to *B* and from *B* to *A*.
- In a **simple network** like the one opposite there are no multiple edges or loops.

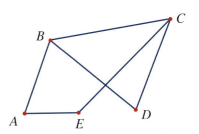

- **Labelling of vertices:** in addition to labelling vertices on a diagram, 'labelling of vertices' in a network means listing them all in curly brackets like this, using the network above as an example: *V* = {*A, B, C, D, E*}.
- **Labelling of edges:** An edge between vertex *A* and *B* would be labelled (*A, B*). A loop at *B* would be (*B, B*). A complete list of edges for the diagram above would be *E* = (*A, B*), (*B, C*), (*B, D*), (*C, D*), (*C, E*), (*A, E*).
- A **weighted edge** is an edge of a network diagram that has a number assigned to it that implies some numerical value such as cost, distance or time. The diagram opposite shows a weighted edge that indicates a distance of 200 km between Sydney and Bathurst. See also the first network on the previous page.

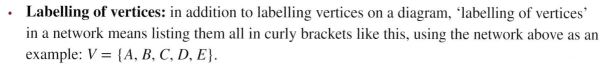

NETWORK

A network is a term to describe a group or system of interconnected objects. It consists of vertices and edges. The edges indicate a path or route between two vertices.

Example 1: Identifying and using network terminology   2A

For the network shown opposite, find the:
a number of vertices   **b** number of edges
c degree of vertex *C*   **d** number of vertices of odd degree.

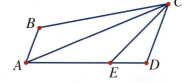

SOLUTION:

1 Count the dots in the network diagram.   **a** Five vertices
2 Count the lines in the network diagram.   **b** Seven edges
3 Count the number of edges connected to *C*.   **c** deg(*C*) = 4
4 Count the number of edges for each vertex.   **d** *A* 3, *B* 2, *C* 4, *D* 2, *E* 3
5 List the vertices of odd degree.   Two vertices of odd degree (*A, E*)

Exercise 2A

1 Copy and complete the following sentences:

    a A network is a term to describe a group or system of _____ objects.

    b In a network diagram the vertices are connected together by lines called _____.

    c A _____ is a point in a network diagram at which lines of pathways intersect.

    d The _____ of a vertex is the number of edges that are connected to it.

    e A directed graph is when the edges of a network have _____.

2 True or false?

    a Vertices are represented as a point or dot in a network diagram.

    b Directed networks are a connected sequence of the edges showing a route between vertices.

    c A loop starts and ends at the same vertex.

    d The degree of a vertex is either even or odd.

    e Degree of a vertex is odd if it has an odd number of vertices attached to the edges.

    f If an edge has a number assigned to it is called a directed edge.

    g The edges in a directed network are usually called arcs.

| Example 1 |

3 Using the network diagram shown find the:

    a number of vertices

    b number of edges

    c degree of vertex *A*

    d degree of vertex *B*

    e degree of vertex *C*

    f degree of vertex *D*

    g degree of vertex *E*.

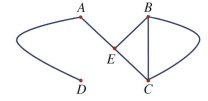

4 Using the network diagram shown find the:

    a number of vertices

    b number of edges

    c degree of vertex *A*

    d degree of vertex *B*

    e degree of vertex *C*

    f degree of vertex *D*.

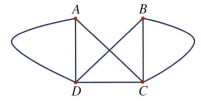

5 Using the network diagram shown find:

    a deg(*A*)

    b deg(*B*)

    c deg(*C*)

    d deg(*D*)

    e the sum of the degrees of all the vertices

    f the number of edges.

6 Using the network diagram shown find:

  a deg(*A*)

  b deg(*B*)

  c deg(*C*)

  d deg(*D*)

  e the sum of the degrees of all the vertices

  f the number of edges.

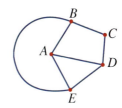

7 Using the network diagram shown find:

  a deg(*A*)

  b deg(*B*)

  c deg(*C*)

  d deg(*D*)

  e the sum of the degrees of all the vertices

  f the number of edges.

8 Find the degree of the following towns in the network diagram.

  a *A*

  b *B*

  c *C*

  d *D*

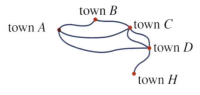

9 Using the network diagram shown find the:

  a vertex with the largest degree

  b vertex with the smallest degree

  c vertices with an even degree

  d vertices with an odd degree.

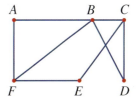

10 Using the network diagram shown find the:

  a vertex with the largest degree

  b vertex with the smallest degree

  c vertices with an even degree

  d vertices with an odd degree.

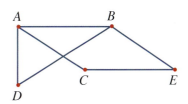

11 Using the network diagram shown find the:

  a vertex with the largest degree

  b vertex with the smallest degree

  c vertices with an even degree

  d vertices with an odd degree.

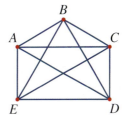

12 Using the network diagram shown find the:

   a number of vertices
   b number of edges
   c degree of vertex *A*
   d degree of vertex *C*.

13 Using the network diagram shown find the:

   a number of vertices
   b number of edges
   c degree of vertex *B*
   d degree of vertex *D*
   e number of vertices of odd degree
   f number of vertices of even degree.

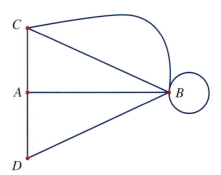

14 Using the network diagram shown find the:

   a number of vertices
   b number of edges
   c degree of vertex *A*
   d degree of vertex *C*
   e degree of vertex *F*
   f number of loops
   g number of vertices of odd degree
   h number of vertices of even degree.

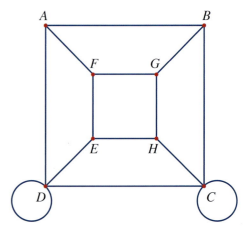

15 Consider the network diagram shown.

   a How many edges in the diagram?
   b What is the sum of the degrees of all the vertices?

   A loop is now added at vertex *A*.

   c How will this change the sum of the degrees of all the vertices?
   d How many edges are added to the graph?

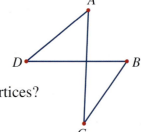

16 Draw a graph that has three vertices, two of which are of odd degree.

17 Why do you think that the sum of the vertex degrees of a graph
will always equal twice the number of edges?

2B Travelling a network

Many practical problems, such as travel routes, that can be modelled by a network involve moving around a graph. To solve such problems you will need to know about a number of concepts to describe the different ways to travel a network.

- A **walk** is a connected sequence of the edges showing a route between vertices where the edges and vertices may be visited multiple times. When there is no ambiguity, a walk in a network diagram can be specified by listing the vertices visited on the walk.

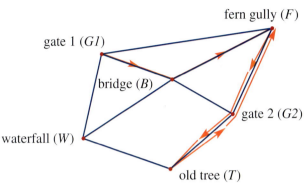

  For example, the network diagram opposite shows a walk in a forest. The forest tracks are the edges (shown in blue) and the places in the forest are the vertices. The red arrows trace out a walk in the forest and is stated as:

  $G1 - B - F - G2 - T - G2 - F$

  Note: A walk does not require all of its edges or vertices to be different.

- A **trail** is a walk with no repeated edges. For example, the network diagram opposite shows a trail in a forest. The red arrows trace out a trail in the forest and is stated as:

  $G1 - B - F - G2 - T - W - B - G2$

  Note: A trail has no repeated edges, however there are two repeated vertices (B and $G2$).

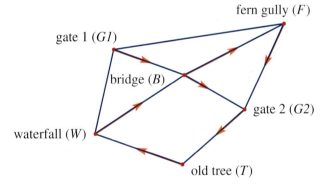

- A **path** is a walk with no repeated vertices. Open paths start and finish at different vertices while closed paths start and finish at the same vertex. Closed paths are also called circuits.

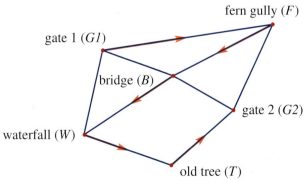

  For example, the network diagram opposite shows a path in a forest. The red arrows trace out a path in the forest and is stated as:

  $G1 - F - B - W - T - G2$

  Note: A path has no repeated edges or vertices.

- A **circuit** is a walk with no repeated edges that starts and ends at the same vertex. Circuits are also called closed trails. Alternatively, open trails start and finish at different vertices.

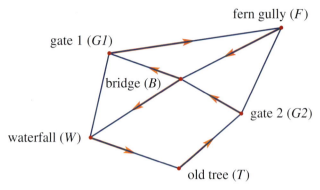

For example, the network diagram opposite shows a circuit in a forest. The red arrows trace out a circuit in the forest and is stated as:

$$G1 - F - B - W - T - G2 - B - G1$$

Note: This circuit starts and ends at the same vertex ($G1$). There are no repeated edges however the circuit passes through the vertex B twice.

- A **cycle** is a walk with no repeated vertices that starts and ends at the same vertex. There are no repeated edges in a cycle as there are no repeated vertices. Cycles are closed paths.

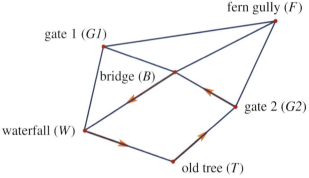

For example, the network diagram opposite shows a cycle in a forest. The red arrows trace out a cycle in the forest and is stated as:

$$G2 - B - W - T - G2$$

Note: This cycle starts and ends at the same vertex ($G2$). There are no repeated vertices or edges.

 Travelling through a network Watch the video in the Interactive Textbook to see the five types of routes that can be travelled through networks.

TRAVELLING A NETWORK

Walk is a connected sequence of the edges showing a route between vertices and edges.
Trail is a walk with no repeated edges.
Path is a walk with no repeated vertices.
Circuit is a walk with no repeated edges that starts and ends at the same vertex.
Cycle is a walk with no repeated vertices that starts and ends at the same vertex.

Type of route	Are repeated edges permitted?	Are repeated vertices permitted?
Walk	Yes	Yes
Trail	No	Yes
Path	No	No
Circuit	No	Yes
Cycle	No	No (except first and last)

Example 2: Identifying walks, trails, paths, circuits and cycles   2B

Identify the walk in each of the graphs below as a trail, path, circuit, cycle or walk only.

a

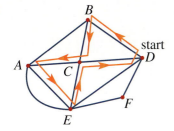

b

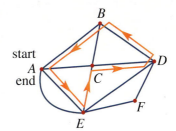

c

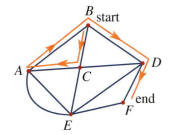

d

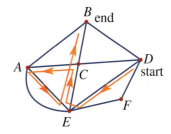

SOLUTION:

1 This walk starts and ends at the same vertex without repeated edges so it is either a circuit or a cycle. The walk passes through vertex *C* twice without repeated edges, so it must be a circuit.

a Circuit

2 This walk starts and ends at the same vertex with no repeated edges so it is either a circuit or a cycle. The walk has no repeated vertex so it is a cycle.

b Cycle

3 This walk starts at one vertex and ends at a different vertex, so it is not a circuit or a cycle. It has one repeated vertex (*B*) and no repeated edge, so it must be a trail.

c Trail

4 This walk starts at one vertex and ends at a different vertex so it is not a circuit or a cycle. It has repeated vertices (*C* and *E*) and repeated edges (the edge between *C* and *E*), so it must be a walk only.

d Walk only

Traversable graphs

Many practical problems involve finding a trail in a graph that includes every edge. You can trace out a trail on the graph without repeating an edge or taking the pen off the paper. Graphs that have this property are called traversable graphs. They will be met again in section 2D.

Traversable graph		**Non-traversable graph**	
A traversable graph has a trail that includes every edge. The trail *A–B–C–A–C* is one example.	Start *A* *B* *C* Finish	Not all graphs are traversable. It is impossible to find a trail in a non-traversable graph that includes every edge.	*A* *B* *D* *C*

Exercise 2B

Example 2   **1**   Identify the walk in each of the graphs below as a trail, path, circuit or walk only.

a

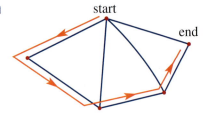

b

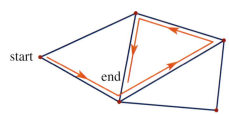

c

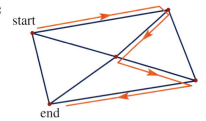

d

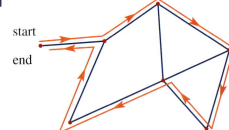

e

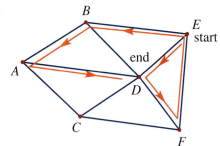

f

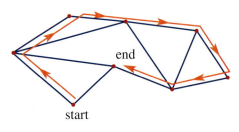

2   Using the graph below, identify the walks below as a trail, path, circuit, cycle or walk only.

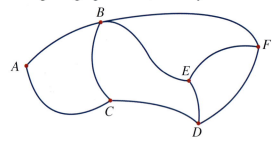

a   A–B–E–B–F

b   B–C–D–E–B

c   C–D–E–F–B–A

d   A–B–E–F–B–E–D

e   E–F–D–C–B

f   C–B–E–F–D–E–B–C–A

3 The network diagram below shows the pathway linking five animal enclosures in a zoo to each other and to the kiosk.

a Which of the following represents a trail?

i *S-L-K-M-K*

ii *G-K-L-S-E-K-M*

iii *E-K-L-K*

b Which of the following represents a path?

i *K-E-G-M-L*

ii *E-K-L-M*

iii *K-S-E-K-G-M*

c Which of the following represents a circuit?

i *K-E-G-M-K-L-K*

ii *E-S-K-L-M-K-E*

iii *K-S-E-K-G-K*

d Which of the following represents a cycle?

i *K-E-G-K*

ii *G-K-M-L-K-G*

iii *L-S-E-K-L*

4 Identify the following sequence of vertices as either a trail or cycle.

a *C–B–E–A–F–E–G–D*   **b** *D–E–A–F–C–B–D*

5 For each graph:

i Identify whether it is traversable

ii If it is traversable,

Identify a circuit including every edge.

a    **b**    **c**

6 For each graph:

i Identify whether it is traversable

ii If it is traversable,

Identify a trail including every edge.

a    **b**    **c**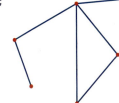

2C Drawing a network diagram

There are many situations in everyday life that involve connections between people or objects. Towns are connected by roads, computers are connected to the internet and families are connected to each other. The network diagram opposite demonstrates some of the connections on social media. When constructing a network, the graphs are either connected or not connected.

Connected graphs

A connected graph has every vertex connected to every other vertex, either directly or indirectly via other vertices. That is, every vertex in the graph can be reached from every other vertex in the graph. The three graphs shown below are all connected.

 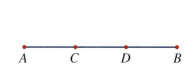 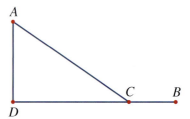

The graphs are connected because, starting at any vertex, say A, you can always find a path along the edges of the graph to take you to every other vertex. However, the three graphs below are not connected, because there is not a path along the edges that connects vertex A (for example) to every other vertex in the graph.

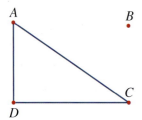 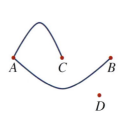 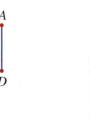

CONNECTED GRAPH

A graph is connected if every vertex in the graph is accessible from every other vertex in the graph along a path formed by the edges of the graph.

Isomorphic graphs

Different looking graphs can contain the same information. When this happens, we say that these graphs are equivalent or isomorphic. For example, the following three graphs look quite different but, in graphical terms, they are equivalent.

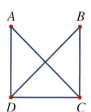

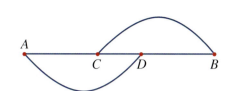

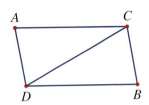

Each of the above graphs has the same number of edges (5), vertices (4), the corresponding vertices have the same degree and the edges join the vertices in the same way (*A* to *C*, *A* to *D*, *B* to *C*, *B* to *D*, and *D* to *C*). However, the three graphs below, although having the same numbers of edges and vertices, are not isomorphic. This is because corresponding vertices do not have the same degree and the edges do not connect the same vertices.

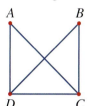

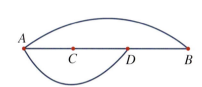

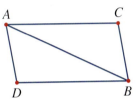

ISOMORPHIC GRAPHS

Two graphs are isomorphic (equivalent) if:
* they have the same numbers of edges and vertices
* corresponding vertices have the same degree and the edges connect to the same vertices.

Example 3: Identifying an isomorphic graph　　　　　　　　　　　　　2C

Which of the following graphs is not isomorphic to the other three graphs?

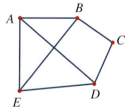

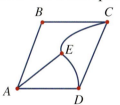

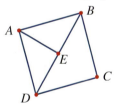

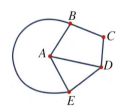

SOLUTION:

1　Check that each graph has the same number of vertices and edges.

Every graph has five vertices and seven edges.

2　Check that corresponding vertices have the same degree.

In Graph 2, vertex *B* has degree 2 and *C* has degree 3; in all others, *B* has degree 3 and *C* has degree 2.

3　Check that edges connect to the same vertices.

In graphs 1, 3 and 4, the edges are *A*–*B*, *A*–*D*, *A*–*E*, *B*–*C*, *B*–*E*, *C*–*D* and *D*–*E*, so these graphs are isomorphic.
Graph 2 does not have edge *B*–*E* and does have edge *C*–*E*, which does not appear in the other graphs, showing again that it is not isomorphic to the others.
Hence, graph 2 cannot be isomorphic to any of the other graphs shown.

Example 4: Drawing a network diagram to represent a map 2C

The map shows the main highways between the capital cities of the states and territories of Australia. Construct a network diagram of the main highway connections between the cities. Let each capital city be a vertex and the highway route between the cities an edge.

SOLUTION:

1   Vertices are the dots of the network diagram. In this situation the capital city will be a vertex.

2   Edges are the connections or pathways between the vertices of the network diagram.

3   Start by drawing a dot for each vertex (capital city).

4   Label each vertex with the name of the capital city.

5   Draw a line to represent an edge if the capital cities have a highway route between them

6   The network diagram is not connected, as Hobart does not have a highway linking it to any other city.

7   The proportions of the network diagram do not have to match the real-life situation.

The vertices will be Brisbane, Sydney, Canberra, Melbourne, Hobart, Adelaide, Perth and Darwin.

Highway routes connect the cities with the exception of Hobart.

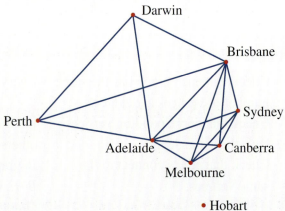

Example 5: Drawing a network diagram to represent a table   2C

A group of four students worked in pairs on four different problems. The table below shows the problem number and the two students who found the correct solution to that problem. A network diagram is to be constructed to represent the table.

Problem	Students who solved it	
1	Darcy	Beau
2	Alyssa	Beau
3	Alyssa	Claire
4	Darcy	Claire

a What will be the vertices of the network diagram?
b What will be an edge in the network diagram?
c Draw a network diagram to represent the information in the table.
d Draw an isomorphic graph of the network diagram.
e Which students have not been able to solve a problem together?

SOLUTION:

1 Vertices are the dots of the network diagram. In this situation the student will be a vertex.

2 Edges are the connections or pathways between the vertices of the network diagram.

3 Start by drawing a dot for each vertex (student).

4 Label each vertex with the student's name.

5 Draw a line to represent an edge if the students have worked together to solve the problem.

6 The network diagram is connected since the path along the edges can take you to every other vertex.

7 Isomorphic graphs have the same number of vertices and edges. They must also have to show the same connections.

8 Vertices not connected with an edge represent the students who have not been able to solve a problem.

a Alyssa, Beau, Claire and Darcy.

b Edges are drawn if the students have worked together to solve the problem.

c Network diagram

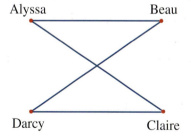

d Isomorphic graph.

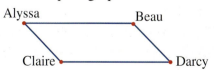

e Alyssa and Darcy, Beau and Claire

Weighted graphs

The edges of graphs represent connections between the vertices. Sometimes there is more information known about that connection. If the edge of a graph represents a road between two towns, we might also know the length of this road, or the time it takes to travel this road. Extra numerical information about the edge that connects vertices can be added to a graph by writing the number next to the edge. This is called a weighted edge. Graphs that have a number associated with each edge are called weighted graphs.

WEIGHTED GRAPH

A weighted graph is a network diagram that has weighted edges; i.e. edges with numbers assigned that imply some numerical value such as cost, distance or time.

The weighted graph in the diagram on the right shows towns, represented by vertices, and the roads between those towns, represented by edges. The numbers, or weights, on the edges are the distances along the roads. A problem often presented by this road network is, 'What is the shortest distance between certain towns?'

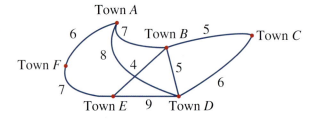

While this question is easily answered if all the towns are directly connected such as Town A to Town B, the answer is not so obvious if we have to travel through towns to get there such as Town F to Town C.

Example 6: Identifying Weighted graphs 2C

Constructing a table from a weighted graph. Construct a table from the weight graph shown opposite.

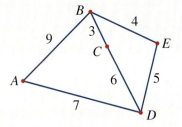

SOLUTION:

1. The vertices are the headings for the rows and columns. Headings are A, B, C, D and E.
2. A weighted edge is a value in the table. Insert 9 in the cell for AB and BA.
3. Repeat the above step for each weighted edge until all the weighted edges have been entered into the table.

	A	B	C	D	E
A	–	9		7	
B	9	–	3	–	4
C	–	3	–	6	–
D	7	–	6	–	5
E	–	4	–	5	–

Example 7: Drawing a weighted graph from a table 2C

A network diagram is to be constructed to represent the table shown below

	A	B	C	D	E	F	G
A	–	32	15	20	–	–	–
B	32	–	30	–	–	18	–
C	15	30	–	10	53	–	24
D	20	–	10	–	42	–	–
E	–	–	53	42	–	–	45
F	–	18	–	–	–	–	47
G	–	–	24	–	45	47	–

a What will be vertices of the network diagram?
b What will be the values of the weighted edges in the network diagram?
c Draw a weighted graph to represent the information in the table.
d What is the total of the weighted path from A to E via B, C and G?

SOLUTION:

1 Vertices are the headings of the rows and columns in the table.

2 Edges are the values in each cell of the table. Note: the above table is symmetrical with 22 values. The number of weighted edges is 11. That is *AB* is the same *BA*.

a Vertices are *A*, *B*, *C*, *D*, *E*, *F* and *G*.

Weighted edges: $AB = 32$, $AC = 15$, $AD = 20$, $BC = 30$, $BF = 18$, $CD = 10$, $CE = 53$, $CG = 24$, $DE = 42$, $EG = 45$, and $FG = 47$

3 Start by drawing a dot for each vertex (letter).
4 Label each vertex.
5 Draw a line between two vertices if there is a weighted edge.
6 Label the weighted edge with the correct value. Note: There can be slightly different weighted graphs drawn from the table. For example, a rotation or reflection of the above diagram.

c

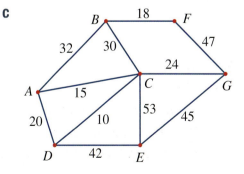

7 Add up the weights for (*A*, *B*), (*B*, *C*), (*C*, *G*), (*G*, *E*)

$32 + 30 + 24 + 45 = 131$.

Exercise 2C

1 Which of the following graphs are connected in each question?

a Graph 1 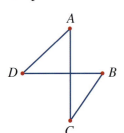 Graph 2 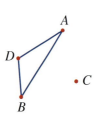 Graph 3 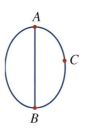 Graph 4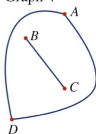

b Graph 1 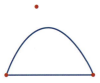 Graph 2 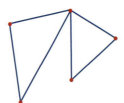 Graph 3 Graph 4

2 Draw a connected graph with:

  a three vertices and three edges   **b** three vertices and five edges

  c four vertices and six edges   **d** five vertices and five edges.

3 Draw a graph that is not connected with:

  a three vertices and two edges   **b** four vertices and three edges

  c four vertices and four edges   **d** five vertices and three edges.

Example 3   **4** Which of the following graphs is not isomorphic to the other three graphs in each question?

a Graph 1 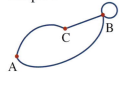 Graph 2 Graph 3 Graph 4

b Graph 1 Graph 2 Graph 3  Graph 4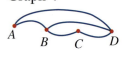

Example 4 | **5** This is a network diagram for Sydney trains.

a What are the vertices of the network diagram?

b What are the edges in the network diagram?

c Is this network diagram connected?

d How many vertices are there in the city circle (shaded circle)?

e Draw a network diagram to represent the city circle.

6 A map from a NSW region is shown.

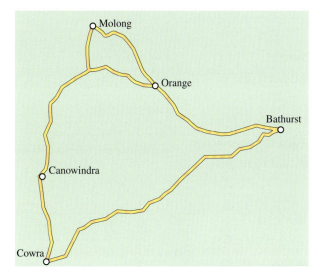

a What are the vertices of the network diagram?

b What are the edges in the network diagram?

c Is this network diagram connected?

d Draw an isomorphic graph to this network diagram.

7 A social network exists between ten students.
  - Lara is friends with Millie, Bonnie, Chris, Gabriel and Toby.
  - Millie is friends with Lara, Eden and Zac.
  - Toby is friends with Lara, Isabel, Rose and Chris.
  a Complete the network diagram below by inserting the edges.

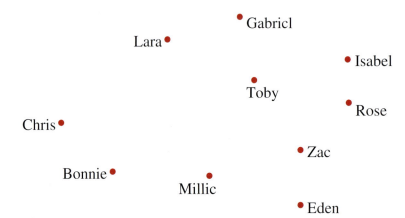

  b What do the edges of the network diagram represent?
  c Is this network diagram connected?
  d How is Bonnie connected to Rose?

Example 7 **8** Four friends live close to each other. The table opposite shows the friends and the number of minutes to walk between their homes.

  a Draw a network diagram to represent the information in the table.
  b What are the vertices of the network diagram?
  c What does a weighted edge represent in the network diagram?
  d Which friends do not have a direct path between their homes?
  e What is the shortest total walking time for Alex to leave home and visit Zac, Max and Harvey in that order, and to return home. Ignore any time spent in each house.

Friends		Minutes to walk between homes
Alex	Zac	1
Harvey	Zac	3
Max	Zac	2
Harvey	Max	4
Alex	Harvey	2

9 There are six motorways between six cities labelled A, B, C, D, E and F. The table opposite shows which cities are linked by the motorways and the length of each one in kilometres.

  a Draw a network diagram to represent the information in the table.
  b What are the vertices of the network diagram?
  c What does a weighted edge represent in the network diagram?
  d Which cities are not directly linked to city A?
  e How would you travel from city F to city D?
  f What is the shortest journey between city F and city D?

	A	B	C	D	E	F
A	–	–	–	27	51	35
B	–	–	48	24	–	–
C	–	48	–	12	–	–
D	27	24	12	–	–	–
E	51	–	–	–	–	–
F	35	–	–	–	–	–

10 Label the matching vertices in the following network diagrams.

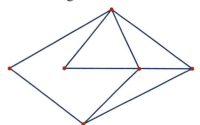

11 The first floor plan of a house is shown. Draw a network diagram by letting the rooms be the vertices and the doorways the edges. Make the hall be a vertex.

12 The table opposite describes the friendships between six people. For example, Natalie is friends with Amy, Harvey and Gabriel. Construct a network diagram to represent this table.

Person	Friendships		
Natalie	Amy	Harvey	Gabriel
Amy	Natalie	Bonnie	Louis
Bonnie	Harvey	Louis	Amy

13 Draw a network diagram of a local area network (LAN) of four computers connected through a server to a printer and scanner.

2D Eulerian and Hamiltonian walks

Eulerian trails and circuits

An Eulerian trail is a trail that uses every edge of a graph exactly once. Eulerian trails start and end at different vertices. Similarly, an Eulerian circuit is a circuit that uses every edge of a graph exactly once. Eulerian circuits start and end at the same vertex. Eulerian trails and circuits are important for some real-life applications. For example, if a graph shows towns as vertices and roads as edges, then being able to identify a route through the graph that follows every road is important for mail delivery. A graph with an Eulerian trail is an example of a traversable graph.

An Eulerian trail will exist if the graph is connected and has exactly two vertices with an odd degree. These two vertices of odd degree will form the start and end of the Eulerian trail. Eulerian circuits will exist if every vertex of the graph has an even degree. These results were discovered by the Swiss mathematician called Leonhard Euler.

EULERIAN TRAIL	EULERIAN CIRCUIT
A trail that uses every edge of a graph exactly once and starts and ends at different vertices. Eulerian trails exist if the graph has exactly two vertices with an odd degree.	A circuit that uses every edge of a network graph exactly once, and starts and ends at the same vertex. Eulerian circuits exist if every vertex of the graph has an even degree.

 Eulerian trails and circuits Watch the video in the Interactive Textbook to see them in action.

 Example 8: Identifying Eulerian trails and circuits **2D**

For each of the following graphs, determine whether the graph has an Eulerian trail, an Eulerian circuit or neither. Show one example if the graph has an Eulerian trail or Eulerian circuit.

a   **b**   **c**

SOLUTION:

1 All the vertices in the graph have an even degree (degree 2).
2 Even degree indicates there is an Eulerian circuit.
3 Start and finish from the vertex on the bottom left-hand side and travel through each edge once.

a Eulerian circuit

Start/Finish

4 Two of the vertices in the graph have an odd degree (degree 3) and the remaining vertices have an even degree (degree 2)
5 Two odd degrees indicates there is an Eulerian trail.
6 Start and finish from the vertices with the odd degrees.

b Eulerian trail

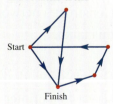

Start

Finish

7 Four vertices are odd and one is even. No Eulerian trail or circuit.

c Neither

ENRICHMENT: Hamiltonian paths and cycles

Eulerian trails and circuits are focused on the edges (though the degree of the vertices will tell you if walk is Eulerian). Hamiltonian paths and cycles are focused on the vertices. A Hamiltonian path passes through every vertex of a graph once and only once. It may or may not involve all the edges of the graph. A Hamiltonian cycle is a Hamiltonian path that starts and finishes at the same vertex. Hamiltonian paths and cycles have real-life applications where every vertex of a graph needs to be visited, but the route taken is not important. For example, if the vertices of a graph represent people and the edges of the graph represent email connections between those people, a Hamiltonian path would ensure that every person in the graph received the email message. Unlike Eulerian trails and circuits, Hamiltonian paths and cycles do not have a convenient rule or feature that identifies them. Inspection is the only way to identify them. Hamiltonian paths and cycles are named after an Irish mathematician called Sir William Hamilton.

HAMILTONIAN PATH	**HAMILTONIAN CYCLE**
A path passes through every vertex of a graph once and only once.	A Hamiltonian path that starts and finishes at the same vertex.

Example 9: Identifying a Hamiltonian path and cycle

2D

a List a Hamiltonian path for the network graph below that starts at A and finishes at D.

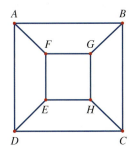

b Identify a Hamiltonian cycle for the network graph below starting at A.

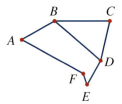

SOLUTION:

1 A Hamiltonian path involves all the vertices but not necessarily all the edges.

2 The solution $A–F–G–B–C–H–E–D$ is not unique. There are other solutions such as $A–F–E–H–G–B–C–D$.

3 A Hamiltonian circuit is a Hamiltonian path that starts and finishes at the same vertex.

4 The solution $A–B–C–D–E–F–A$ is not unique. There are other solutions such as $A–F–E–D–C–B–A$.

a $A–F–G–B–C–H–E–D$

b $A–B–C–D–E–F–A$

Exercise 2D

1 A network graph is shown opposite.
  a What is the degree of each vertex?
  b Why does this graph have an Eulerian trail?
  c List the Eulerian trail.

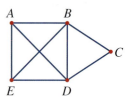

2 A network graph is shown opposite.
  a What is the degree of each vertex?
  b Why does this graph have an Eulerian circuit?
  c List an Eulerian circuit.

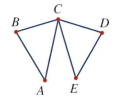

Example 8   **3** For each of the following graphs, determine whether the graph has an Eulerian trail, an Eulerian circuit or neither. Show one example if the graph has an Eulerian trail or circuit.

a

b

c

d

e

f

g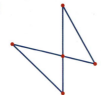

h

i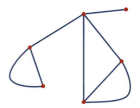

4 A road inspector lives in Town A and is required to inspect all roads connecting the neighbouring towns B, C, D and E.
  a Is it possible for the inspector to travel over every road linking the five towns only once and return to Town A? Explain
  b Show one possible route he can follow.

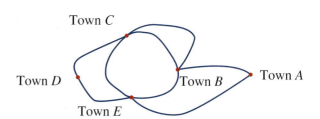

5 A network graph is shown opposite.
   a List the path shown in the graph.
   b Does the path pass through every vertex?
   c Does the path pass through every edge?
   d ENRICHMENT: Why is this path a Hamiltonian path?
   e ENRICHMENT: List another Hamiltonian path starting at *A*.

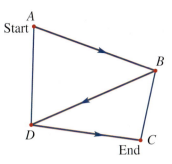

6 A network graph is shown opposite.
   a List the path shown in the graph.
   b Does the path pass through every vertex?
   c Does the path pass through every edge?
   d ENRICHMENT: Why is this path a Hamiltonian cycle?
   e ENRICHMENT: List another Hamiltonian cycle starting at *A*.

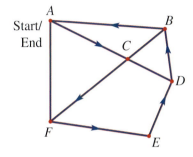

xample 9   7 ENRICHMENT: List a Hamiltonian cycle for each of the following.

   a 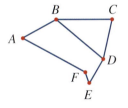   b 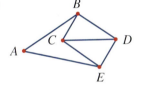   c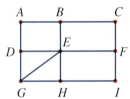

   d 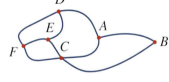   e 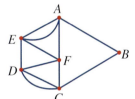   f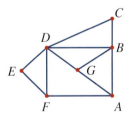

8 ENRICHMENT: A tourist wants to visit each
   of five towns shown in the graph opposite
   only once. Identify one possible route for the
   tourist to start the tour at:
   a *C* and finish at *A*. What is the
      mathematical name for this route?
   b *E* and finish at *E*. What is the
      mathematical name for this route?

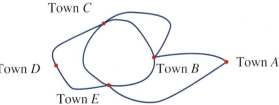

9 The graph opposite models the pathways
linking five animal enclosures in a zoo to the
kiosk and to each other.

a Explain why it is possible for the zoo's
street sweeper to follow a route that enables
its operator to start and finish at the kiosk
without travelling down any pathway more
than once.

b List one route for the zoo's street sweeper.

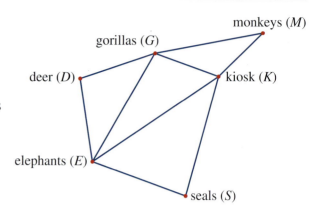

10 The graph opposite models the pathways
linking seven animal enclosures in a zoo
to the kiosk and to each other.

a List a possible route for a visitor to start
and finish their visit at the kiosk and
see all of the animals without visiting
any animal enclosure more than once.

b List a possible route for a visitor to
start their visit at the deer enclosure
and finish at the kiosk without visiting
the kiosk or any animal enclosure more
than once.

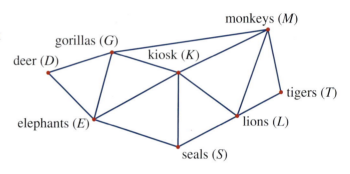

11 A postman has to deliver letters to the farms located
on the network of roads shown opposite.

a Is it possible for the postman to start and finish his
deliveries at the same point in the network without
retracing his steps at some stage? If not, why not?

b It is possible for the postman to start and finish his
deliveries at different points in the network without
retracing his steps at some stage. Identify one such
route.

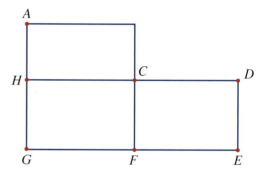

12 The network diagram shows the location of a
warehouse, W. This warehouse supplies equipment
to six factories A, B, C, D, E and F. Write the order
a manager can visit each factory, starting from W.

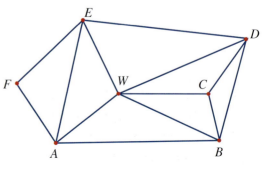

2E Network problems

Königsberg bridge problem

The town of Königsberg, or Kaliningrad as it is now known, is situated on the river Pregel in what used to be called Prussia. The old town had seven bridges linking two islands and the north and south banks of the river. A view of Königsberg is shown opposite. The Königsberg bridge problem asked whether the seven bridges could all be crossed only once during a single trip that starts and finishes at the same place.

Put in another way, can a continuous walk be planned so that all the bridges are crossed only once? Whenever someone tried to walk the route, they either ended up missing a bridge or

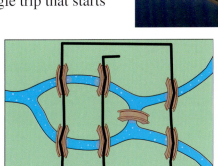
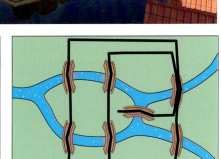

crossing one of the bridges more than once. Two such walks are marked on the diagrams. See if you can trace out a walk on the diagram above that crosses every bridge, but only once.

The Königsberg bridge problem was well known in 18th century Europe and attracted the attention of the Swiss mathematician Leonhard Euler. He started analysing the problem by drawing a simplified diagram to represent the situation, as shown below. We now call this type of simplified diagram a network diagram or graph.

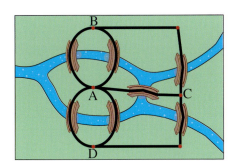
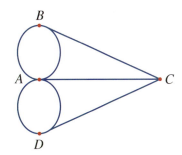

Note: All four vertices in the Königsberg bridge graph have an odd degree.

Euler was able to prove that a graph with all vertices of odd degree cannot be traced or drawn without lifting the pencil or going over the same edge more than once. Today we call this problem an Eulerian trail. The problem was solved by Euler. The seven bridges of Königsberg could not be crossed in a single walk without either missing a bridge or crossing one bridge more than once.

Example 10: Solving a practical network problem   **2E**

The network diagram opposite is used to model the tracks in a forest connecting a suspension bridge (*B*), a waterfall (*W*), a very old tree (*T*) and a fern gully (*F*). Walkers can enter or leave the forest through either gate 1 (*G1*) or gate 2 (*G2*). The numbers on the edges represent the times (in minutes) taken to walk directly between these places.

a   Construct a table to represent the weighted graph.

b   How long does it take to walk from the bridge directly to the fern gully?

c   How long does it take to walk from the old tree to the fern gully via the waterfall and the bridge?

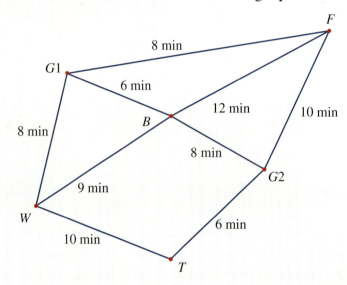

SOLUTION:

1   The vertices are the headings for the rows and columns

2   A weighted edge is a value in the table.

3   Repeat the above step for each weighted edge until all the weighted edges have been entered into the table.

a   Headings are W, G1, F, B, T and G2.
Insert 8 in the cell for WG1 and G1W.

	W	G1	F	B	T	G2
W	–	8	–	9	10	–
G1	8	–	8	6	–	–
F	–	8	–	12	–	10
B	9	6	12	–	–	8
T	10	–	–	–	–	6
G2	–	–	10	8	6	–

4   Identify the edge that directly links the bridge with the fern gully and read off the time.

5   Identify the path that links the old tree to the fern gully, visiting the waterfall and the bridge on the way. Add up the times.

b   The edge is (*B*, *F*).
The time taken is 12 minutes.

c   The path is *T–W–B–F*.
Time = 10 + 9 + 12 = 31.
The time taken is 31 minutes.

Exercise 2E

1 Investigate the Königsberg bridge problem when an eighth bridge is added as shown below.
   a Construct a network diagram to represent this situation with eight bridges. Use the labelled dots shown opposite.
   b How many vertices of odd degree are there in your network diagram?
   c Does an Eulerian trail exist in your network diagram?
   d List a continuous walk that crosses each bridge once or an Eulerian trail.

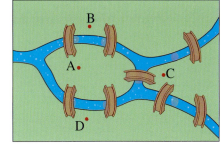

2 Investigate the Königsberg bridge problem if two bridges are added, making nine bridges as shown below.
   a Construct a network diagram to represent this situation with nine bridges.
   b How many vertices of odd degree in your network diagram?
   c Does an Eulerian circuit exist in your network diagram?
   d List a circuit that starts and ends at the same vertex, and crosses each bridge once or Eulerian circuit.

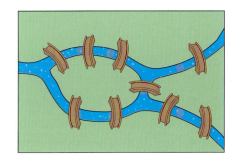

3 The roads for a garbage bin collection are shown in the network diagram. The garbage bin collection must start/end at A and travel every road only once.
   a How many vertices of odd degree in this network diagram?
   b Does an Eulerian circuit exist in this network diagram?
   c Show one possible route for the garbage bin collection.
   d List another route for the garbage bin collection.

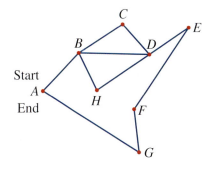

Example 10
4 Evelyn has drawn a network diagram to represent several streets for travelling from her home to school. The numbers indicate the times in minutes.
   a How long does it take to walk from home to school using the following paths?
      i $A–F–E–D$
      ii $A–F–E–C–D$
      iii $A–C–D$
      iv $A–B–C–D$
      v $A–C–E–D$
   b Which of the above walks is the longest journey?
   c Which of the above walks is the shortest journey?

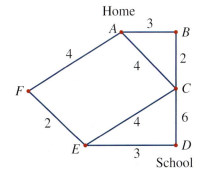

5 The network graph below shows details about air travel between Australian cities. The first graph shows the number of flights in each direction between cities, and the second graph shows capacity in each direction.

Number of flights per day

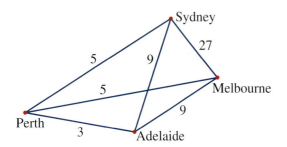

Maximum number of passengers per day

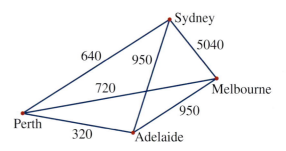

a How many flights are available per day from Sydney to Adelaide?

b How many flights are available per day between these Australian cities?

c What is the maximum number of passengers per day from Melbourne to Adelaide?

d What is the maximum number of passengers per day that can fly out of Sydney?

e Seth is wishing to fly from Perth to Melbourne but is told that the direct flights are fully booked. List any other ways of completing this journey.

f What is the greatest number of people per day that can be flown from Perth to Melbourne?

g Amy is wishing to fly from Sydney to Melbourne but is told that the direct flights are fully booked. List any other ways of completing this journey.

h What is the greatest number of people per day that can be flown from Sydney to Melbourne?

6 In this bridge problem there are six bridges as shown below.

a Construct a network diagram to represent this situation with six bridges. Label the vertices *A*, *B*, *C* and *D* to represent the river banks and the two islands. Use the edges of the graph to represent the bridges.

b It is not possible to plan a walking route that passes over each bridge once only. Why not?

c Show where another bridge could be added to make such a walk possible. Draw a graph (a network diagram) to represent this situation.

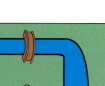

d Explain why it is now possible to find a walking route that passes over each bridge once only. Mark one such route on your graph.

2F   Minimal spanning trees

In some network problems it is important to minimise the number and weights of the edges to keep all vertices connected to the graph. For example, a number of towns might need to be connected to a water supply. The cost of connecting the towns can be minimised by connecting each town into a network or water pipes only once, rather than connecting each town to every other town. To solve these problems we need an understanding of trees.

Tree

A tree is a connected graph that contains no cycles, multiple edges or loops. The diagram below shows two network graphs that are trees and one network graph that is not a tree.

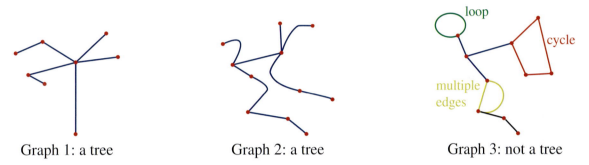

Graph 1: a tree   Graph 2: a tree   Graph 3: not a tree

Graphs 1 and 2 are trees: they are connected and have no cycles, multiple edges or loops. Graph 3 is not a tree: it has several cycles (loops and multiple edges count as cycles). For trees, there is a relationship between the number of vertices and the number of edges.
- Graph 1, a tree, has 8 vertices and 7 edges.
- Graph 2, a tree, has 11 vertices and 10 edges.

In general, the number of edges is always one less than the number of vertices. In other words, a tree with n vertices has $n - 1$ edges.

Spanning trees

Every connected graph will have at least one subgraph that is a tree. If a subgraph is a tree, and if that tree connects all of the vertices in the graph, then it is called a spanning tree. An example of a spanning tree is shown opposite. There are several other possibilities. Note: the spanning tree opposite, like the network diagram, has 8 vertices. However it has only 7 edges ($8 - 1 = 7$).

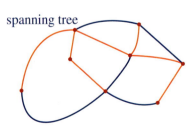

spanning tree

TREE

A tree is a connected graph that contains no cycles, multiple edges or loops.
A tree with n vertices has $n - 1$ edges.
A spanning tree is a tree that connects all of the vertices of a graph.

Example 11: Finding a spanning tree in a network   **2F**

Find two spanning trees for the graph shown opposite.

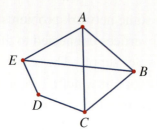

SOLUTION:

1   The graph has five vertices and seven edges. A spanning tree
        will have five (n) vertices and four ($n - 1$) edges.

2   To form a spanning tree, remove any three edges, provided
        that all the vertices remain connected, and there are no
        multiple edges or loops.

3   Spanning tree 1 is formed by removing edges *EB*, *ED* and
        CA.

4   Spanning tree 2 is formed by removing edges *EA*, *AC* and
        CD.

5   There are several other possible spanning trees.

Spanning tree 1

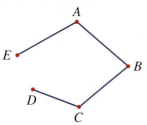

Spanning tree 2

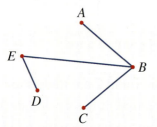

Minimum spanning trees

For a weighted graph, it is possible to determine the 'length' of each spanning tree by adding up
the weights of the edges in the tree. For the spanning tree
opposite:

Length = 5 + 4 + 2 + 1 + 5 + 4 + 1
       = 22 units

A minimum spanning tree is a spanning tree of minimum
length. It connects all the vertices together with the minimum
total weighting for the edges.

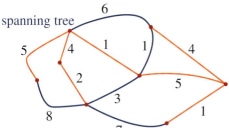

spanning tree

MINIMUM SPANNING TREE

A minimum spanning tree is a spanning tree of minimum length. It connects all the vertices
together with the minimum total weighting for the edges.

A guide to trees Watch the video in the Interactive Textbook to see trees, spanning trees and
minimum spanning trees in action.

Prim's algorithm

Prim's algorithm is a set of rules to determine a minimum spanning tree for a graph.

1. Choose a starting vertex (any will do).
2. Inspect the edges starting from the starting vertex and choose the one with the lowest weight. (If there are two edges that have the same weight, it does not matter which one you choose). You now have two vertices and one edge.
3. Inspect all of the edges starting from both of the vertices you have in the tree so far. Choose the edge with the lowest weight, ignoring edges that would connect the tree back to itself. You now have three vertices and two edges.
4. Keep repeating step 3 until all of the vertices are connected.

Example 12: Finding the minimum spanning tree   2F

Apply Prim's algorithm to find the minimum spanning tree for the network graph shown on the right. Calculate the length of the minimum spanning tree.

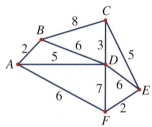

SOLUTION:

1 Start with vertex A. List the weighted edges from vertex A and find the smallest.

$(A, B) = 2$
$(A, F) = 6$
$(A, B) = 2$ is lowest.

2 Look at vertices A and B. List the weighted edges from vertex A and vertex B (apart from (A, B) which you have already found).

$(A, D) = 5$
$(A, F) = 6$
$(B, C) = 8$
$(B, D) = 6$
$(A, D) = 5$ is lowest.

3 Repeat to find the smallest weighted edge from vertex A, B or D.

$(C, D) = 3$ is lowest.

4 Repeat to find the smallest weighted edge from vertex A, B, D or C.

$(C, E) = 5$ is lowest.

5 Repeat to find the smallest weighted edge from vertex A, B, D, C or E.

$(E, F) = 2$ is lowest.

6 All vertices have been included in the graph. Draw the minimum spanning tree.

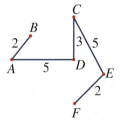

7 Find the length of the minimum spanning tree by adding the weights of the edges.

Length $= 2 + 5 + 3 + 5 + 2$
$= 17$ units

Kruskal's algorithm

Kruskal's algorithm This alternative method is covered in the Interactive Textbook.

Exercise 2F

1 Copy and complete the following sentences.

    a A tree is a connected graph that contains no cycles, multiple _____ or loops.

    b A minimum spanning tree is a spanning tree of minimum_____.

    c Prim's algorithm is a set of rules to determine a minimum _____ tree for a graph.

    d A connected graph has eight vertices. Its spanning tree has _____ vertices.

    e A connected graph has ten vertices. Its spanning tree has _____ edges.

2   **a** How many edges are there in a tree with 15 vertices?

    b How many vertices are there in a tree with 5 edges?

    c Draw two different trees with four vertices.

    d Draw three different trees with five vertices.

3 Which of the following graphs are trees?

    a    **b**

    c 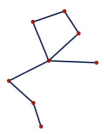   **d**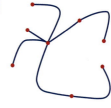

    e    **f**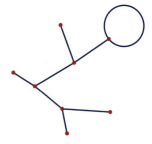

Example 11 **4** For each of the following graphs, draw three different spanning trees.

    a 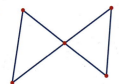   **b**    **c**

Example 12 **5** Find the minimum spanning tree and its length, for each of the following graphs.

a
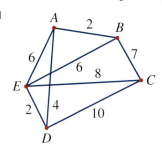

b
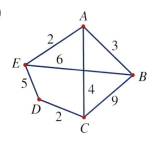

c
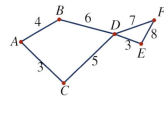

d
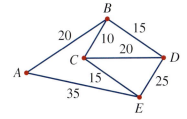

e
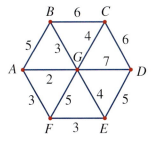

f
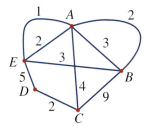

g
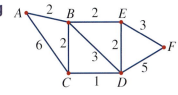

h
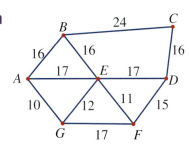

i
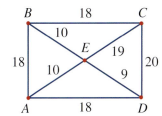

6 Water is to be piped from a water tank to seven outlets on a property. The distances (in metres) of the outlets from the tank and from each other are shown in the network opposite. Starting at the tank, determine the minimum length of pipe needed.

7 Power is to be connected by cable from a power station to eight substations (A to H). The distances (in kilometres) of the substations from the power station and from each other are shown in the network opposite. Determine the minimum length of cable needed.

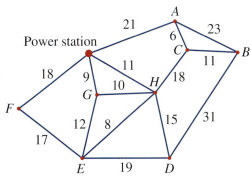

2G   Connector problems

Minimum spanning trees represent the least weight required to keep all of the vertices connected in the graph. If the edges of a graph represent the cost of connecting towns to a gas pipeline, then the total weight of the minimum spanning tree would represent the minimum cost of connecting the towns to the gas. This is an example of a connector problem, where it is important to make the cost of connecting towns or other objects together as low as possible.

CONNECTOR PROBLEMS

A connector problem uses a minimum spanning tree to find the least cost to link locations or objects.

 Example 13: Solving a minimal connector problem   **2G**

There are 11 locations that require access to power. These locations are represented by vertices on the network diagram shown. The dashed lines on the network diagram represent possible cable connections between adjacent locations. The numbers on the dashed lines show the minimum length of cable, in metres, required to connect these locations. Find the minimum length of cable needed to provide power to each location.

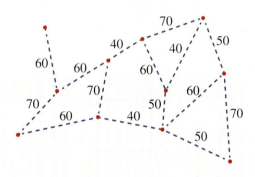

SOLUTION:

1   The cables will be a minimum length if they are placed on the edges of the minimum spanning tree for the network. A good starting point for Prim's algorithm is the vertex that is connected by just one edge. This vertex must be connected to the minimum spanning tree by this edge.

2   Follow Prim's algorithm to find the minimum spanning tree.

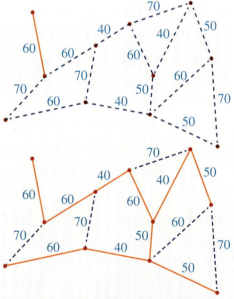

3   Find the length of the minimum spanning tree by adding the weights of the edges.

$$\begin{aligned}\text{Length} &= 60 + 60 + 40 + 60 + 50 \\ &\quad + 40 + 50 + 60 + 40 + 50 \\ &= 510 \text{ m}\end{aligned}$$

4   Write answer in words.

$\therefore$ Minimum length is 510 metres.

Exercise 2G

1 The network diagram opposite shows possible water pipes connecting six towns. The numbers on each edge represent the distance (in km) between the towns

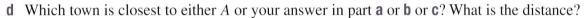

   a Which town is closest to A? What is the distance?
   b Which town is closest to either A or your answer in part **a**? What is the distance?
   c Which town is closest to either A or your answer in part **a** or **b**? What is the distance?
   d Which town is closest to either A or your answer in part **a** or **b** or **c**? What is the distance?
   e Which town is closest to either A or your answer in part **a** or **b** or **c** or **d**? What is the distance?
   f What is the shortest distance connecting water pipes to the six towns?

Example 13

2 The network diagram opposite shows possible railway lines connecting seven cities. The numbers on each edge represent the cost (in millions of dollars) in setting up a rail link.

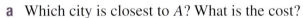

   a Which city is closest to A? What is the cost?
   b Which city is closest to either A or your answer in part **a**? What is the cost?
   c Which city is closest to either A or your answer in part **a** or **b**? What is the cost?
   d Which city is closest to either A or your answer in part **a** or **b** or **c**? What is the cost?
   e Which city is closest to either A or your answer in part **a** or **b** or **c** or **d**? What is the cost?
   f Which city is closest to either A or your answer in part **a** or **b** or **c** or **d** or **e**? What is the cost?
   g What is the minimum cost of connecting the seven cities with a railway line?

3 The network diagram opposite shows the major roads connecting eight towns. The numbers on each edge represent the distance in kilometres between the towns.

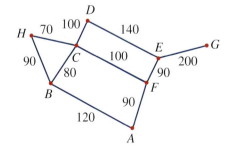

   a Which town is closest to A? What is the distance?
   b Which town is closest to either A or your answer in part **a**? What is the distance?
   c Which town is closest to either A or your answer in part **a** or **b**? What is the distance?
   d Which town is closest to either A or your answer in the parts above? What is the distance?
   e Which town is closest to either A or your answer in the parts above? What is the distance?
   f Which town is closest to either A or your answer in the parts above? What is the distance?
   g Which town is closest to either A or your answer in the parts above? What is the distance?
   h What is the minimum distance connecting the eight towns?

4 Seven towns on an island have been surveyed for
transport and communications needs. The towns
(labelled *A*, *B*, *C*, *D*, *E*, *F*, *G*) form the network
shown here. The road distances between the towns
are marked in kilometres. To establish a cable
network for communications on the island, it is
proposed to put the cable underground beside the
existing roads.

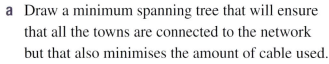

  a Draw a minimum spanning tree that will ensure
that all the towns are connected to the network
but that also minimises the amount of cable used.

  b What is the minimal length of cable required here if back-up links are not considered
necessary; that is, there are no loops in the cable network?

5 A number of towns need to be linked by pipelines
to a natural gas supply. In the network shown, the
existing road links between towns *L*, *M*, *N*, *O*, *P*, *Q*
and *R* and to the supply point S, are shown as edges.
The towns and the gas supply are shown as vertices.
The distances along roads are given in kilometres.

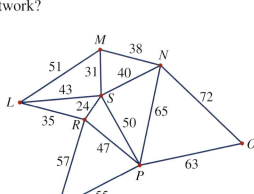

  a Draw minimum spanning tree that will ensure that
all the towns are connected to the network but that
also minimises the amount of pipelines required.

  b What is the minimum length of gas pipeline the
company can use to supply all the towns?

6 The company has constructed nine new
faculty buildings for a university in a layout
as shown. The minimum distances in metres
between adjacent buildings in the university
are shown on the edges. A computer network
is to be built to serve the whole university.

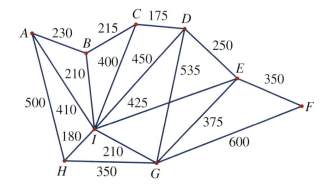

  a Draw a minimum spanning tree that will
ensure that all the buildings are connected
to the network but that also minimises the
amount of cable used.

  b What is the minimum length of cable
required to connect all the buildings?

2H Shortest path

The shortest path in a network is the path between two vertices where the sum of the weights of its edges is minimised. Finding the shortest path is often very useful. For example, if the weights of a network represent time, you can choose a path that will allow you to travel in the shortest time. If the weights represent distance, you can determine a path that will allow you to travel the shortest distance. However, be aware that travelling the shortest distance between two places is not necessarily the best path. For example, if shortest path has a speed limit of 60 km/h but another path has a speed limit of 110 km/h then the shortest path may take longer to reach the destination. In such a case, redraw the network diagram with time taken to travel each edge, rather than distance.

While there are sophisticated techniques for solving shortest path problems the method of inspection involves identifying and comparing the lengths of likely candidates for the shortest path. All of the possible paths should be listed and the length of the path calculated. When finding the shortest path it is important to be aware there can be more than one shortest path between two vertices and the shortest path may not pass through all of the vertices.

SHORTEST PATH

The shortest path between two vertices in a network is the path where the sum of the weights of its edges is minimised.

Example 14: Finding the shortest path by inspection 2H

Find the shortest path between Town C and Town F.

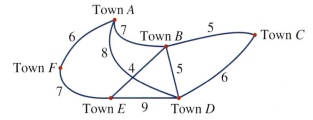

SOLUTION:

1 Identify all the likely shortest routes between Town C and Town F and calculate their lengths.
Note: Time can be saved by eliminating any route that 'takes the long way around' rather than the direct route. For example, when travelling from Town B to Town D, ignore the route that goes via Town A because it is longer.

$$C-D-E-F = 6 + 9 + 7$$
$$= 22 \text{ km}$$
$$C-B-E-F = 5 + 4 + 7$$
$$= 16 \text{ km}$$
$$C-B-A-F = 5 + 7 + 6$$
$$= 18 \text{ km}$$

2 Compare the different path lengths and identify the shortest path. Write your answer in words.

The shortest path is $C-B-E-F$.

Example 15: Finding the length of the shortest path   2H

Find the length of the shortest path between
the following vertices.

a   *A* and *E*

b   *A* and *F*

c   *A* and *G*

d   *A* and *H*

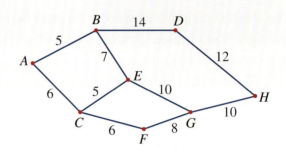

SOLUTION

1 Identify the shortest paths between vertex *A* and
     vertex *E*.

2 Add the weighted edges to find the length of the path.

3 Identify the shortest paths between vertex *A* and
     vertex *F*.

4 Add the weighted edges to find the length of the path.

5 Identify the shortest paths between vertex *A* and
     vertex *G*.

6 Add the weighted edges to find the length of the path.

7 Identify the shortest paths between vertex *A* and
     vertex *H*.

8 Add the weighted edges to find the length of the path.

a $A–C–E = 6 + 5$
$$= 11$$

b $A–C–F = 6 + 6$
$$= 12$$

c $A–C–F–G = 6 + 6 + 8$
$$= 20$$

d $A–C–F–G–H$
$$= 6 + 6 + 8 + 10 = 30$$

Example 16: Solving a shortest path problem   2H

Darcy has drawn a network diagram to represent
several streets for travelling from his home to
the shops. The numbers indicate the times in
minutes. Describe the shortest path and minimum
travelling time.

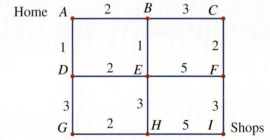

SOLUTION

1 Identify all the likely shortest routes between
     home and the shops and calculate their lengths.

2 Compare the different path lengths and identify
     the shortest path.

3 Write your answer in words.

$A–D–E–H–I = 1 + 2 + 3 + 5$
$$= 11 \text{ min}$$

$A–D–G–H–I = 1 + 3 + 2 + 5$
$$= 11 \text{ min}$$

$A–B–E–H–I = 2 + 1 + 3 + 5$
$$= 11 \text{ min}$$

$A–B–C–F–I = 2 + 3 + 2 + 3$
$$= 10 \text{ min}$$

The shortest path is $A–B–C–F–I$ and the
time taken is 10 minutes.

Exercise 2H

Example 14 **1** The numbers in this weighted graph represent time in hours. Find the length of the shortest path between the following vertices.

a *A* and *D*

b *A* and *E*

c *A* and *F*

d *C* and *F*

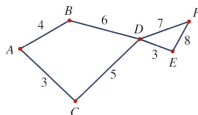

Example 15 **2** The numbers in this weighted graph represent length in metres. Find the length of the shortest path between the following vertices.

a *C* and *D*   **c** *A* and *D*

b *A* and *C*   **d** *B* and *E*

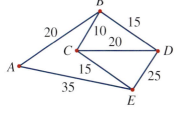

3 The numbers in this weighted graph represent cost in dollars. Find the length of the shortest path between the following vertices.

a *E* and *C*   **b** *B* and *E*

c *C* and *D*   **d** *A* and *E*

e *A* and *C*   **f** *A* and *D*

g *B* and *D*   **h** *A* to *D* to *E*

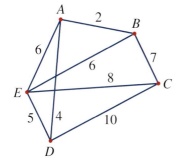

4 The numbers in this weighted graph represent time in minutes. Find the length of the shortest path between the following vertices.

a *A* and *C*

b *A* and *E*

c *B* and *D*

d *B* and *F*

e *C* and *F*

f *C* and *E*

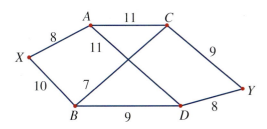

5 The numbers in this weighted graph represent distance in metres. Find the length of the shortest path between the following vertices.

a *X* and *C*   **b** *X* and *D*

c *A* and *Y*   **d** *B* and *Y*

e *A* and *B*   **f** *X* and *Y*

Example 16 **6** The network below shows the distance, in kilometres, along walkways that connect landmarks
A, *B*, *C*, *D*, *E*, *F*, *G*, *H* and *I* in a national park.

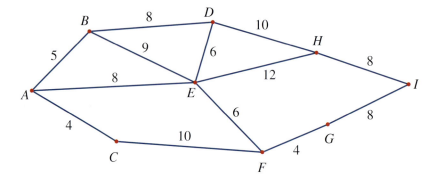

a What distance is travelled on the path *A–B–E–H–I*?

b What distance is travelled on the path *I–G–F–E–D–B–A*?

c What distance is travelled on the circuit *F–E–D–H–E–A–C–F*?

d What distance is travelled on the circuit *D–E–A–B–E–F–G–I–H–D*?

e What is the distance travelled on the shortest cycle starting and finishing at *E*?

f What is the distance travelled on the shortest cycle starting and finishing at *F*?

g Find the shortest path and distance travelled from *A* to *I*.

h Find the shortest path and distance travelled from *C* to *D*.

7 The graph below shows a mountain bike rally course. Competitors must pass through each of
the checkpoints, *A*, *B*, *C*, *D*, *E* and *F*. The average times (in minutes) taken to ride between
the checkpoints are shown on the edges of the graph. Competitors must start and finish at
checkpoint *A* but can pass through the other checkpoints in any order they wish.

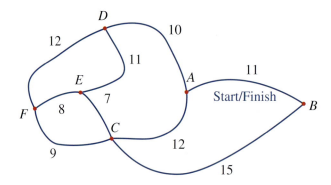

a What is the average time travelled on the circuit *A–D–E–F–C–B–A*?

b What is the average time travelled on the circuit *A–B–C–F–E–D–A*?

c What is the average time travelled on the circuit *A–C–E–D–F–C–B–A*?

d Which path would have the shortest average time?

e Will the path with the shortest average time always be the best path? Explain your answer.

8 The network below shows the time (in minutes) of train journeys between seven stations.

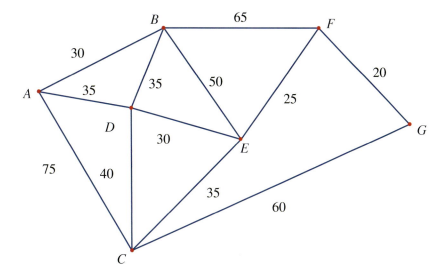

a What is the time taken to travel *A–B–E–D–A*?

b What is the time taken to travel *F–G–C–D–B–F*?

c Find the shortest time it would take to travel from *A* to *G*.

d Will the path with the shortest time always be the best path? Explain your answer.

e Find the shortest time it would take to travel from *A* to *G* if in reality each time the train passes through a station, excluding *A* and *G*, an extra 10 minutes is added to the journey.

Summary

Key ideas and chapter summary

Network	A network is a term to describe a group or system of interconnected objects. It consists of vertices and edges that indicate a path or route between two objects.
Network terminology	Network diagram, vertex, edge, degree, loop, directed network, undirected network, weighted edge, walk, trail, path, circuit, cycle, Eulerian trail, Eulerian circuit.

Drawing a network diagram	Connected graph	A graph is connected if every vertex in the graph is accessible from every other vertex in the graph along a path formed by the edges of the graph.
	Isomorphic graph	Two graphs are isomorphic (equivalent) if: • they have the same numbers of edges and vertices • corresponding vertices have the same degree and the edges connect to the same vertices.
Network problems	Weighted graph	A weighted graph is a network diagram that has weighted edges or an edge with a number assigned to it that implies some numerical value such as cost, distance or time.

Minimum spanning tree	A tree is a connected graph that contains no cycles, multiple edges or loops. A tree with n vertices has $n - 1$ edges. A spanning tree is a tree that connects all of the vertices of a graph. A minimum spanning tree is a spanning tree of minimum length. It connects all the vertices together with the minimum total weighting for the edges. Prim's and Kruskal's algorithms is a set of rules to determine a minimum spanning tree for a graph.
Connector problems	Problems using the minimal spanning tree to the find least cost to link locations or objects.
Shortest path	The shortest path between two vertices in a network is the path where the sum of the weights of its edges is minimised.

Multiple-choice

Questions **1** to **4** relate to this network diagram.

1 Which of the following vertices has the highest degree?

A Vertex B

B Vertex C

C Vertex D

D Vertex E

2 How many edges are in the network diagram?

A 4　　　　　**B** 5　　　　　**C** 6　　　　　**D** 7

3 Which of the following is a valid path?

A $A–E–B–C$　　　**B** $C–D–A–E–B–A$　　　**C** $C–D–A–E–B–C$　　　**D** $A–E–B$

4 The sequence $C–D–A–E–B$ represents:

A a walk only

B a path

C a trail

D a cycle

Questions **5** to **6** relate to this network diagram.

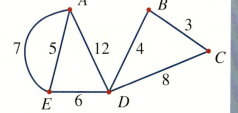

5 Which one of the following paths is a Eulerian trail?

A $A–E–D–B–C$

B $E–D–A–B–C–E$

C $A–E–D–C–B–D–A–E$

D $E–D–C–B–D–C–A$

6 What is the length of the shortest path from A to C in the network?

A 17　　　　　**B** 18　　　　　**C** 19　　　　　**D** 20

Questions **7** to **8** relate to this network diagram below.

7 What is the length of the minimum spanning tree?

A 30

B 31

C 33

D 34

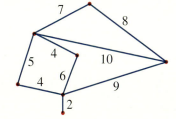

8 What is the length of the shortest path from the bottom vertex to the top vertex?

A 18　　　　　**B** 19　　　　　**C** 20　　　　　**D** 21

Short-answer

1   Find the degree of the following vertices in this network diagram.

   a *P*   **b** *Q*   **c** *R*

   d *S*   **e** *T*   **f** *U*

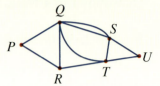

2   This network graph has six vertices.

   a What is the degree of each vertex?

   b Why does this graph have an Eulerian trail?

   c List an Eulerian trail.

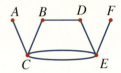

3   This network graph has six vertices.

   a What is the degree of each vertex?

   b Why does this graph have an Eulerian circuit?

   c List an Eulerian circuit.

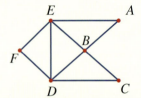

4   A chess tournament is completed between 5 players. Each game has 2 players competing against each other. This table shows the games and the players.

Match	Players	
1	Toby	Jett
2	Amy	Beau
3	Amy	Toby
4	Jett	Ellie
5	Beau	Toby
6	Toby	Ellie

   a Draw a network diagram to represent the information in the table.

   b What are the vertices of the network diagram?

   c Which players have not played a game against each other?

5 For the weighted graph shown, determine the length of the minimum spanning tree.

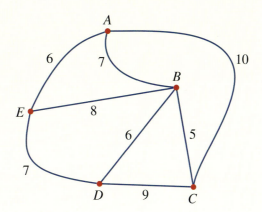

6 What is the length of the minimum spanning tree in this network?

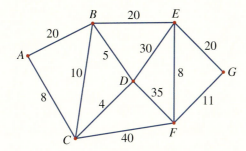

7 In this network, the numbers on the edges represent distances in kilometres.

Determine the length of:

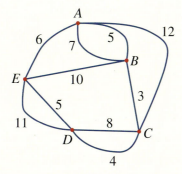

   a the shortest path between vertex *A* and vertex *D*

   b the length of the minimum spanning tree.

8 What is the length of the shortest path between *O* and *D* in this network?

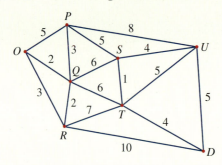

Extended-response

9 This diagram shows the network of walking tracks in a small national park. These tracks connect the campsites to each other and to the park office. The lengths of the tracks (in metres) are also shown.

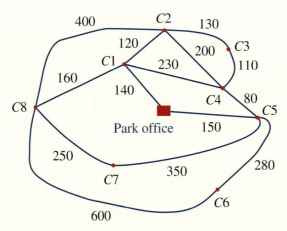

a A ranger at campsite C8 plans to visit campsites C1, C2, C3, C4 and C5 on her way back to the park office. What is the shortest distance she will have to travel?

b Each day, the ranger on duty has to inspect each of the tracks to make sure that they are all passable. Is it possible for her to do this starting and finishing at the park office without retracing her steps? Explain why or why not.

c Following a track inspection after wet weather, the head ranger decides that it is necessary to put gravel on some walking tracks to make them weatherproof. What is the minimum length of track that will need to be gravelled to ensure that all campsites and the park office are accessible along a gravelled track?

3 Investments and loans

Syllabus topic — F4 Investments and loans

This topic will develop your skills to calculate and compare the value of different types of investments, including shares, over a period of time. In addition, you will gain an understanding of reducing-balance loans and that an asset may depreciate over time rather than appreciate.

Outcomes

- Use the future value formula to calculate the compound interest.
- Compare the growth of simple interest and compound interest.
- Calculate compound interest and compare graphs for different rates and periods.
- Compare and contrast different investment strategies.
- Solve practical problems involving compound interest.
- Calculate the dividend paid on a portfolio of shares and the dividend yield.
- Calculate the depreciation of an asset using declining-balance method.
- Solve practical problems involving reducing-balance loans.
- Interpret credit card statements and solve problems involving credit cards.
- Identify the various fees and charges associated with credit card usage.

Digital Resources for this chapter

In the Interactive Textbook:

- Videos
- Desmos widgets
- Literacy worksheet
- Spreadsheets
- Quick Quiz
- Study guide
- Solutions (enabled by teacher)

In the Online Teaching Suite:

- Teaching Program
- Tests
- Review Quiz
- Teaching Notes

Knowledge check

The Interactive Textbook provides a test of prior knowledge for this chapter, and may direct you to revision from the previous years' work.

3A   Future value

Compound interest

Compound interest is calculated on the initial amount borrowed or invested plus any interest that has been charged or earned. It calculates interest on the interest. The future value formula $FV = PV(1 + r)^n$ and the compound interest formula $A = P(1 + r)^n$ are commonly used to calculate the compound interest. They are the same formula. The future value (FV) is the same as the amount (A) and the present value (PV) is the same as the principal (P).

FUTURE VALUE AND PRESENT VALUE FORMULA

$$FV = PV(1 + r)^n \quad \text{or} \quad PV = \frac{FV}{(1 + r)^n} \quad \text{or} \quad A = P(1 + r)^n$$

FV – Future value of the loan or amount (final balance)
PV – Present value of the loan or principal (initial quantity of money)
r – Rate of interest per compounding time period expressed as a decimal (or a fraction)
n – Number of compounding time periods
A – Amount

Example 1: Calculating future value and present value   **3A**

a   Blake invests $7000 over 5 years at a compound interest rate of 4.5% p.a. Calculate the future value after 5 years. Answer correct to the nearest cent.

b   Calculate the present value of an investment that has a future value of $500 000 over 8 years with an interest rate of 8.5% per annum compounded monthly.

SOLUTION:

1 Write the future value formula.	**a** $FV = PV(1 + r)^n$
2 Substitute $PV = 7000$, $r = 0.045$ (4.5% as a decimal) and $n = 5$ into the formula.	$= 7000(1 + 0.045)^5$
3 Evaluate to the nearest cent.	$= \$8723.27$
4 Write the answer in words.	Future value is $8723.27.
5 Write the future value formula.	**b** $PV = \dfrac{FV}{(1 + r)^n}$
6 The investment is compounding per month so the annual rate r, expressed as a decimal, is divided by 12 (months in a year), and time period n is in months.	
7 Substitute $FV = 500000$, $r = \dfrac{0.085}{12}$ and $n = 8 \times 12 = 96$.	$= \dfrac{500000}{\left(1 + \dfrac{0.085}{12}\right)^{96}}$
8 Evaluate to the nearest cent.	$= \$253\,916.41$
9 Write the answer in words.	Present value is $253 916.41.

Calculating compound interest

Compound interest is calculated by subtracting the principal from the amount borrowed or invested. Alternatively, finance companies provide an investment calculator as an estimate of the value of an investment.

COMPOUND INTEREST EARNED OR OWED

$I = FV - PV$ or $I = A - P$
FV – Future value of the loan or amount (final balance)
PV – Present value of the loan or principal (initial quantity of money)
I – Interest (compounded) earned

 Example 2: Finding the compound interest **3A**

Tyson invests $10 000 over 10 years at a compound interest rate of $7\frac{1}{2}\%$ p.a. Calculate:
a the amount of the investment after 10 years, correct to the nearest cent;
b the interest earned after 10 years, correct to the nearest cent.

SOLUTION:

1 Write the future value formula.

2 Substitute $PV = 10\,000$, $r = 0.075$ $\left(\text{decimal equivalent of } 7\frac{1}{2}\right)$ and $n = 10$ into the formula.

3 Evaluate.

4 Write answer in words.

5 Write the formula.

6 Substitute $FV = 20\,610.32$ and $PV = 10\,000$ into the formula.

7 Evaluate.

8 Write in words.

a $FV = PV(1 + r)^n$
$\qquad = 10\,000(1 + 0.075)^{10}$

$\qquad = 20\,610.3156...$
$\qquad \approx \$20\,610.32$
Amount is $20610.32

b $I = FV - PV$
$\qquad = 20610.32 - 10000$

$\qquad = \$10610.23$
Interest earned is $10\,610.21$

Exercise 3A

Example 1   **1**   Calculate the future value, to the nearest cent, for each of the following.

a   Present value = $400, Compound interest rate = 3% p.a., Time period = 2 years

b   Present value = $26000, Compound interest rate = 8% p.a., Time period = 4 years

c   Present value = $48000, Compound interest rate = 3.95% p.a., Time period = 10 years

d   Present value = $3000, Compound interest rate = $5\frac{1}{2}$% p.a., Time period = 5 years

e   Present value = $18000, Compound interest rate = 10% p.a., Time period = $2\frac{1}{2}$ years

f   Present value = $65000, Compound interest rate = 5.9% p.a., Time period = $3\frac{1}{4}$ years

g   Present value = $240000, Compound interest rate = 11.3% p.a., Time period = 4.5 years

h   Present value = $14000, Compound interest rate = $2\frac{1}{4}$% p.a., Time period = $7\frac{3}{4}$ years

2   Use the formula $FV = PV(1 + r)^n$ to calculate the value of an investment of $16000, over a period of 2 years with an interest rate of 5% compounding annually.

Example 2   **3**   Sophia and Isaac invested $27000 for 6 years at 9% p.a. interest compounding annually. What is the amount of interest earned?

4   What is the interest earned if $15 720 is invested for 5 years, compounding yearly at 8% p.a.? Answer to the nearest dollar.

5   Find the amount $7800 will grow to if it is compounded at 6% p.a. for:

a   3 years   b   10 years   c   30 years.

6   Jett sold his car for $35 600. He invested this amount at 7.2% p.a. with interest compounded annually. What is the value of his investment in 15 years?

7   Bonnie wishes to invest $5000 for a period of 8 years. The following investment strategies are suggested to her. How much interest is earned on each investment strategy? Answer to the nearest dollar.
    a   Simple interest at 7% p.a.
    b   Compound interest at 7% p.a. compounded annually
    c   Simple interest at 14% p.a.
    d   Compound interest at 14% p.a. compounded annually

8   Which of the following is the best investment over 10 years? Justify your answer.
        Investment A: Simple interest at 5% p.a. with $70 000
        Investment B: Compound interest at 5% p.a. compounded annually with $70 000.

9   Calculate the present value, to the nearest cent, for each of the following:
    a   Future value = $34 000, Interest rate = 4% p.a., Time period = 4 years
    b   Future value = $87 000, Interest rate = 5% p.a., Time period = 12 years
    c   Future value = $190 000, Interest rate = 3% p.a., Time period = 15 years
    d   Future value = $200 000, Interest rate = $12\frac{1}{4}$% p.a., Time period = 5 years
    e   Future value = $4600, Interest rate = 15% p.a., Time period = $2\frac{1}{2}$ years
    f   Future value = $60 000, Interest rate = 6.25% p.a., Time period = $1\frac{1}{4}$ years
    g   Future value = $320 000, Interest rate = 5.5% p.a., Time period = $9\frac{3}{4}$ years
    h   Future value = $450 000, Interest rate = $9\frac{1}{2}$% p.a., Time period = 25 years

10 Find the present value of money in a bank account if the future value after 4 years earning 9% p.a. compound interest, paid annually, is $5000. Answer to the nearest dollar.

11 Calculate the future value, to the nearest cent, for each of the following.
    a   Present value of $680 invested for 4 years at 5% p.a. compounded biannually
    b   Present value of $5000 invested for 6 years at 6% p.a. compounded quarterly
    c   Present value of $1400 invested for 3 years at 4.2% p.a. compounded monthly
    d   Present value of $780 invested for 5 years at 9.8% p.a. compounded weekly
    e   Present value of $290 invested for 7 years at 10% p.a. compounded fortnightly

12 Which of the following is the best investment over 25 years? Justify your answer.

Investment A: Simple interest at 4% p.a. with $100 000

Investment B: Compound interest at 4% p.a. compounded annually with $100 000

Investment C: Compound interest at 4% p.a. compounded biannually with $100 000

Investment D: Compound interest at 4% p.a. compounded quarterly with $100 000

Investment E: Compound interest at 4% p.a. compounded monthly with $100 000

13 Calculate the present value, to the nearest dollar, for each of the following:

a Future value of $1243, interest rate at 6% p.a. compounded biannually for 5 years

b Future value of $8200, interest rate at 4% p.a. compounded quarterly for 8 years

c Future value of $1580, interest rate at 4.8% p.a. compounded monthly for 4 years

d Future value of $19 600, interest rate at 8% p.a. compounded weekly for 3 years

e Future value of $3800, interest rate at 5% p.a. compounded fortnightly for 7 years

14 Find the future value of a bank account after 3 years if the present value of $4000 earns 4.6% p.a. interest compounding quarterly.

15 Alexander invested $16 400 over 6 years at 7.4% p.a. interest compounding monthly.

a Calculate the value of the investment after 4 years.

b Calculate the compound interest earned.

16 What sum of money would Max need to invest to accumulate a total of $100 000 at the end of 7 years at 8% p.a. interest compounding biannually? Answer to the nearest cent.

17 What sum of money needs to be invested to accumulate a total of $40 000 after 10 years at 9.25% p.a. interest compounding monthly? Answer to the nearest cent.

18 How much more interest is earned on $60 000 if interest of 8% p.a. is compounded quarterly over 6 years than if simple interest of 8% is earned over the same time? Answer to the nearest cent.

19 Mikayla invests $200 000 for 10 years at 6% p.a. interest compounded quarterly. Abby also invests $200 000 for 10 years, but her interest rate is 6% p.a. compounded monthly.

a Calculate the value of Mikayla's investment at maturity.

b Show that the compounded value of Abby's investment is greater than the value of Mikayla's investment.

c Explain why Abby's investment is worth more than Mikayla's investment.

3B Investment graphs

Simple interest graphs

When graphing simple interest make the horizontal axis the time period (n) and the vertical axis the interest earned (I). Simple interest will increase by a constant amount each time period. This will result in a straight-line graph.

SIMPLE INTEREST GRAPHS

1 Construct a table of values for I and n using the simple interest formula.
2 Draw a number plane with n the horizontal axis and I the vertical axis. Plot the points.
3 Join the points to make a straight line.

Example 3: Constructing a simple interest graph   3B

Draw a graph showing the amount of simple interest earned over a period of 10 years if $1000 is invested at 8% p.a. Use the graph to estimate the interest earned after 7.5 years.

SOLUTION:

1 Write the simple interest formula.
2 Substitute $P = 1000$, $r = 0.08$ and n into the formula.
3 Draw a table of values for I and n.
4 Let $n = 0, 2, 4, ...$ Find the interest (I) using $I = 80n$.
5 Draw a number plane with n as the horizontal axis and I as the vertical axis.
6 Plot the points $(0, 0)$, $(2, 160)$, $(4, 320)$, $(6, 480)$, $(8, 640)$ and $(10, 800)$.
7 Draw a straight line between the points. Simple interest graphs are linear.
8 Read the graph to estimate I ($I = 600$ when $n = 7.5$).

$I = Prn$
$= 1000 \times 0.08 \times n$
$= 80n$

n	0	2	4	6	8	10
I	0	160	320	480	640	800

Simple interest on $1000 at 8% p.a.

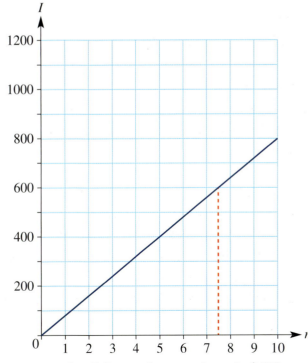

9 Write the answer in words.

Interest after 7.5 years is approximately $600.

Compound interest graphs

When graphing compound interest make the horizontal axis the compounding time periods (*n*) and the vertical axis the interest earned (*I*). Compound interest will increase by a different amount each time period. This will result in an exponential curve.

COMPOUND INTEREST GRAPHS

1 Construct a table of values for *I* and *n* using the compound interest formula.
2 Draw a number plane with *n* the horizontal axis and *I* the vertical axis. Plot the points.
3 Join the points to make an exponential curve.

Example 4: Constructing a compound interest graph   **3B**

Draw a graph showing the interest earned over a period of 10 years if $1000 is invested at a compound interest rate of 8% p.a. Use the graph to estimate the interest earned after 7.5 years.

SOLUTION:

1 Write the future value and interest earned formulas.

2 Substitute $PV = 1000$, $r = 0.08$ and n into the formula.

$$FV = PV(1 + r)^n \qquad I = FV - PV$$
$$= 1000 \times (1.08)^n \qquad = PV(1 + r)^n - PV$$
$$= 1000(1.08)^n - 1000$$

3 Draw a table of values for *n*, *FV* and *I*

4 Let $n = 0, 2, 4, \dots$ Find the future value and interest earned.

n	0	2	4	6	8	10
FV	1000	1166	1360	1587	1851	2159
I	0	166	360	587	851	1159

5 Draw a number plane with *n* as the horizontal axis and *I* as the vertical axis.

6 Plot the points (0, 0), (2, 166), (4, 360), (6, 587), (8, 851) and (10, 1159).

7 Draw an exponential curve (not a straight line) between the points.

8 Read the graph to estimate *I* when $n = 7.5$ years ($I = \$780$ when $n = 7.5$).

Compound interest earned on $1000 at 8% p.a.

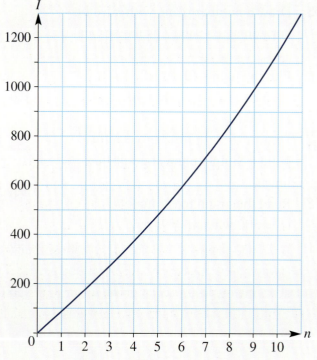

9 Write the answer in words.

Interest on the loan after 7.5 years is about $780.

Exercise 3B

Example 3

1 Harvey invested $2000 at 6% per annum simple interest for 5 years.

   a Simplify the simple interest formula ($I = Prn$) by substituting values for the principal and the interest rate.

   b Use this formula to complete the following table of values.

n	0	1	2	3	4	5
I						

   c Draw a number plane with n as the horizontal axis and I as the vertical axis.

   d Plot the points from the table of values. Join the points to make a straight line.

   e Use the graph to find the interest after $2\frac{1}{2}$ years.

   f Extend the graph to find the interest after 6 years.

   g Estimate the interest earned after 6 years using the graph.

2 Olive invested $800 at 7% per annum simple interest for 6 years.

   a Simplify the simple interest formula ($I = Prn$) by substituting values for the principal and the interest rate.

   b Use this formula to complete the following table of values.

n	0	1	2	3	4	5	6
I							

   c Draw a number plane with n as the horizontal axis and I as the vertical axis.

   d Plot the points from the table of values. Join the points to make a straight line.

   e Use the graph to find the interest after $2\frac{1}{2}$ years.

   f Extend the graph to find the interest after 7 years.

   g Estimate the interest earned after 7 years using the graph.

3 Ellie is comparing three different interest rates for a possible investment.

   a Draw on the same number plane the graph to represent the interest earned over 5 years on:

     i $1000 invested at 4% per annum simple interest

     ii $1000 invested at 6% per annum simple interest

     iii $1000 invested at 8% per annum simple interest.

   b How much does each investment earn after 5 years?

   c Use the graph to estimate the interest earned after $3\frac{1}{2}$ years.

   d Find the time for each investment to earn $200 in interest.

Example 4   **4**   Ava invested $2000 at 6% per annum interest compounding annually for 5 years.

    a   Substitute the present value and the interest rate into the formula $FV = PV(1 + r)^n$ to obtain an expression for the future value.

    b   Substitute the future value expression and the present value into the formula $I = FV - PV$.

    c   Use these formulas to complete the following table of values. Answer to nearest dollar.

n	0	1	2	3	4	5
FV						
I						

    d   Draw a number plane with n as the horizontal axis and I as the vertical axis.

    e   Plot the points from the table of values. Join the points to make a curve.

    f   Extend the graph to find the interest after 6 years.

    g   Compare the interest earned after 5 years by Harvey in question **1** with Ava in question **4**.

5   Dylan invested $800 at 7% p.a. compound interest, paid annually, for 6 years.

    a   Substitute the present value and the interest rate into the formula $FV = PV(1 + r)^n$ to obtain an expression for the future value.

    b   Substitute the future value expression and the present value into the formula $I = FV - PV$.

    c   Use these formulas to complete the following table of values. Answer to nearest dollar.

n	0	1	2	3	4	5	6
FV							
I							

    d   Draw a number plane with n as the horizontal axis and I as the vertical axis.

    e   Plot the points from the table of values. Join the points to make a curve.

    f   Use the graph to find the interest earned after $2\frac{1}{2}$ years.

    g   Compare the interest earned after 6 years by Olive in question **2** with Dylan in question **5**.

6   Bailey is comparing three different interest rates for a possible investment.

    a   Draw on the same number plane the graph to represent the interest earned over 5 years on:

      i $1000 invested at 4% per annum interest compounding annually

      ii $1000 invested at 6% per annum interest compounding annually

      iii $1000 invested at 8% per annum interest compounding annually.

    b   What is the approximate value of the interest on each investment after 5 years?

    c   What is the approximate value of the interest on each investment after $3\frac{1}{2}$ years?

    d   Find the approximate time for each investment to earn $200 in interest.

    e   Compare the interest earned after 5 years by Ellie in question **3** with Bailey in question **6** using the 8% interest rate for each.

LEVEL 2

7 Draw a graph showing the amount of interest paid over a period of 6 years if $1000 is invested at a compound interest rate of 10% p.a. Use the graph to estimate the interest after $5\frac{1}{2}$ years.

8 Mick is comparing three different interest rates for a possible investment.
   a Draw a graph to represent the interest earned for 6 months on:
     i $100000 invested at 6% p.a. simple interest
     ii $100000 invested at 9% p.a. simple interest
     iii $100000 invested at 12% p.a. simple interest.
   b How much does each investment earn after 2 months?
   c How much does each investment earn after 6 months?
   d Find the time for each investment to earn $3000 in interest.

9 Laura is comparing three different interest rates for a possible investment.
   a Draw a graph to represent the amount earned over 6 months on:
     i $100000 invested at 6% p.a. interest compounding monthly
     ii $100000 invested at 9% p.a. interest compounding monthly
     iii $100000 invested at 12% p.a. interest compounding monthly.
   b What is the approximate value of each investment after 2 months?
   c How much does each investment earn after 6 months?
   d Find the time for each investment to earn $3000 in interest.

LEVEL 3

10 The table below gives details for an investment product. The compound interest earned is paid quarterly.

Investment	Rate of compound interest
A	4% p.a.
B	6% p.a.
C	8% p.a.
D	10% p.a.

Ethan is prepared to invest $50000 in the above product.
   a Draw a graph to represent the interest earned of these investments after 3 years.
   b What is the approximate value of investment B after 2 years?
   c What is the approximate value of investment C after 18 months?
   d Find the approximate time for investment D to earn $10000 in interest.

3C Appreciation and inflation

Appreciation

Appreciation is the increase in value of
items such as art, gold or land. This increase
in value is often expressed as the rate of
appreciation. Calculating the appreciation is
similar to calculating the compound interest.
For example, a painting worth $100 000 that
has an annual rate of appreciation of 10%
will be worth $110 000 after one year (an
increase of $10 000). In the second year its
value will increase by $11 000. The amount of
appreciation has increased.

APPRECIATION

$FV = PV(1 + r)^n$ or $A = P(1 + r)^n$
FV – Future value of the item
PV – Present value of the item
r – Rate of appreciation per compounding time period expressed as a decimal
n – Number of compounding time periods

Example 5: Finding the appreciated value   3C

Joel bought a unit for $690 000. If the unit appreciates at 9% p.a.,
what is its value after 7 years? Answer to the nearest dollar.

SOLUTION:

1 Write the formula for appreciation $FV = PV(1 + r)^n$. $FV = PV(1 + r)^n$
2 Substitute $PV = \$690\,000$, $r = 0.09$ (9% expressed as a $= 690\,000(1 + 0.09)^7$
  decimal) and $n = 7$ into the formula.
3 Evaluate. $= 1\,261\,346.993$
4 Write the answer to the correct degree of accuracy. $\approx \$1\,261\,347$
5 Answer the question in words.   Unit is valued at $1 261 347.

Inflation

Inflation is a rise in the price of goods and services or Consumer Price Index (CPI). It is measured by comparing the prices of a fixed basket of goods and services. If inflation rises then a person's spending power decreases. The inflation rate is the annual percentage change in the CPI. In Australia, the Reserve Bank aims to keep the inflation rate in a 2% to 3% band.

Calculating inflation is similar to calculating appreciation or compound interest.

INFLATION

Inflation rate is the annual percentage change in the CPI.
Use the formula $FV = PV(1 + r)^n$ to calculate the future value of an item following inflation.

Example 6: Finding the price of goods following inflation   3C

a   What is the price of a $650 clothes dryer after one year following inflation? (Inflation rate is 2.6% p.a.)

b   What is the price of a $400 clothes dryer after three years following inflation? (Inflation rate is 3.2% p.a.)

SOLUTION:

1	Write the formula for inflation.	**a** $FV = PV(1 + r)^n$
2	Substitute $PV = 650$, $r = 0.026$ and $n = 1$ into the formula.	$= 650(1 + 0.026)^1$
3	Evaluate correct to two decimal places.	$= \$666.90$
4	Write the answer in words.	Clothes dryer will cost $666.90.
1	Write the formula for inflation.	**b** $FV = PV(1 + r)^n$
2	Substitute $PV = 400$, $r = 0.032$ and $n = 3$ into the formula.	$= 400(1 + 0.032)^3$
3	Evaluate correct to two decimal places.	$= \$439.64$
4	Write the answer in words.	Clothes dryer will cost $439.64.

Exercise 3C

Example 5   **1**   A vintage car was bought for $70 000 and appreciated at the rate of 6% p.a. What will be the value of the car after 4 years? Answer correct to the nearest cent.

2   The price of a house has increased by 4.5% for each of the last two years. It was bought for $490 000 two years ago. What is the new current value?

3   William bought the following antiques.
  a   Tall boy valued at $4450. Each year its value appreciated by 5%. Calculate the value of the tall boy after 3 years. Answer correct to the nearest cent.
  b   Table valued at $6200. Each year its value appreciated by 4%. Calculate the value of the table after 5 years. Answer correct to the nearest cent.
  c   Chair valued at $1250. Each year its value appreciated by 9%. Calculate the value of the chair after 4 years. Answer correct to the nearest cent.

4   A collection of dolls was valued at $1500 four years ago. If it appreciated at 12% p.a., find its current value. Answer correct to the nearest cent.

5   The price of a diamond ring has increased from $3400 to $5300 during the past five years due to inflation. What is the rise in the price of the ring?

Example 6   **6**   The average inflation for the next five years is predicted to be 3%. Calculate the price of the following goods in five years time. Answer correct to the nearest cent.
  a   3 L of milk for $3.57
  b   Loaf of bread for $3.30
  c   250 g honey for $4.50
  d   800 g of eggs for $5.20

7   If the inflation rate is 5% p.a., what would you expect to pay to the nearest dollar in four years time for a house that costs:
  a $280 000?
  b $760 000?
  c $324 000?
  d $580 000?
  e $1 260 000?
  f $956 000?

8 The graph on the right shows the value of cricket memorabilia for the past 6 years.

    a What was the value of the memorabilia after 4 years?

    b What was the initial value?

    c How much did the memorabilia appreciate each year?

    d Find the equation of the straight-line graph in terms of V and n.

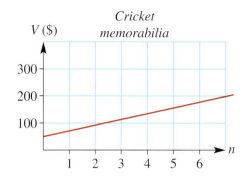

9 The following blocks of land have increased in value this year. What is the rate of appreciation? Answer correct to two decimal places.

    a $328\,000 to $352\,000
                    b $256\,000 to $278\,000

10 Hayley invested $700 on rugby memorabilia. It appreciated over 7 years at 8.2% p.a. interest compounding annually.

    a What is the value of the investment after 7 years? Answer correct to the nearest cent.

    b Calculate the amount of appreciation.

11 An investment is appreciating at a rate of 8% of its value each year. Kumar decides to invest $20\,000.

    a What will be the investment's value after 5 years? Answer correct to the nearest cent.

    b How much does the investment increase during the first 5 years?

    c When will the investment at least double in value? Answer to the nearest year.

12 The cost of a certain car has increased during the past two years from $45\,200 to $49\,833 following inflation. What was the annual inflation rate?

3D Shares and dividends

Shares

A share or stock is a part ownership in a company. Shares are bought and sold on the stock market or stock exchange, such as the ASX (Australian Securities Exchange). The ASX provides current information about share prices, market data, tools and resources for investment. When a company is first listed on the ASX the initial price is called the face value. The price of a share will change according to the performance of the company. The current price of a share is called the market price. The amount paid when a share is bought is called the cost price or issued price. The amount paid when a share is sold is called the selling price.

The share price can change each day, or even minute-by-minute. The changes are shown on screens and also on the ASX website. As well as tables of share prices over time, the website provides charts (graphs) of prices and the volume of shares traded.

Shares are bought and sold using a broker. A broker receives a brokerage fee when shares are traded or a percentage value of the transaction. There are many different types of brokers, such as CommSec. Goods and Services Tax (GST) of 10% is charged for buying and selling shares.

Example 7: Calculating the cost of shares   3D

Lucy bought 500 shares at a market value of $6.80 each. Brokerage fees incurred were $33 including GST. What is the total cost of purchasing the shares?

SOLUTION:

1 Write a word equation for the total cost to be calculated.

    Cost = (No. of shares × price) + brokerage fee

2 Substitute 500 for no. of shares, $6.80 for price and $33 for brokerage fee.

    Cost = (500 × 6.80) + $33

3 Evaluate.

    = $3433

4 Write answer using correct units and in words.

    Cost of the shares is $3433.

Dividends

The owners of a share are entitled to share in the company's profits. Profits are given to shareholders as a dividend. A dividend is a payment given as an amount per share or as a percentage of the issued price. A dividend are issued twice per year: interim and final dividend. The dividend yield is the annual rate of return. It is calculated by dividing the annual dividend by the share's market price.

		Dividend History		
Type	Cents per share	Frank %	Ex Dividend Date	Dividend Pay Date
Interim	62.00	100	8/5/2018	1/7/2018
Final	74.00	100	8/11/2017	21/12/2017
Interim	62.00	100	14/5/2017	2/7/2017
Final	69.00	100	9/11/2016	15/12/2016
Interim	56.00	100	15/5/2016	3/7/2016

DIVIDENDS

A dividend is a payment given as an amount per share or a percentage of the issued price.

$$\text{Dividend yield} = \frac{\text{Annual dividend}}{\text{Market price}} \times 100\%$$

$$\text{Dividend} = \text{Dividend yield} \times \text{Market price}$$

Example 8: Calculating the dividend and dividend yield   3D

The share price of a company is $28.42.
 a   The predicted dividend yield is 3.5%. What would be the dividend?
 b   The company decides to pay a dividend of $1.12. What is the dividend yield?

SOLUTION:

1	Write the quantity to be found.	**a**	Dividend = 3.5% of $28.42
2	Express the dividend yield as a decimal and multiply it by the share price.		$= 0.035 \times \$28.42$
3	Evaluate correct to two decimal places.		$= \$0.99$

Dividend is $0.99

4 Write the formula to calculate the dividend yield.

b $\text{Dividend yield} = \dfrac{\text{Annual dividend}}{\text{Market price}} \times 100\%$

5 Substitute the annual dividend of 1.12 and the market price of 28.42 into the formula.

$= \dfrac{1.12}{28.42} \times 100\%$

6 Evaluate correct to two decimal places.

$= 3.94\%$

Dividend yield is 3.94%

Exercise 3D

Example 7 **1** A broker charges a fee of $33 to trade shares. What is the total cost for these shares?
   a 150 shares, market price of $19.70
   b 340 shares, market price of $2.41
   c 60 shares, market price of $92.35
   d 2000 shares, market price of $1.68
   e 208 shares, market price of $49.61
   f 3900 shares, market price of $56.23

Example 8 **2** Molly buys 3000 shares with a market price of $6.20. She pays a brokerage fee of $22.50. How much does she pay altogether?

3 Calculate the dividend yield (to two decimal places) on the following shares.
   a Market price of $33.70 and a dividend of $0.84 per share
   b Market price of $22.08 and a dividend of $1.63 per share
   c Market price of $20.58 and a dividend of $1.00 per share
   d Market price of $37.72 and a dividend of $2.11 per share
   e Market price of $45.43 and a dividend of $2.86 per share
   f Market price of $4.00 and a dividend of 10 cents per share

4 A company with a share price of $8.40 declares a dividend of 56 cents. What is the dividend yield correct to two decimal places?

5 Calculate the total dividend received on the following shares. (Answer correct to two decimal places.)
   a 500 shares with a market price of $4.80 and a dividend yield of 5.2%
   b 80 shares with a market price of $88.10 and a dividend yield of 4.4%
   c 2200 shares with a market price of $9.56 and a dividend yield of 6.1%
   d 890 shares with a market price of $22.30 and a dividend yield of 1.9%
   e 3400 shares with a market price of $56.30 and a dividend yield of 4.6%
   f 780 shares with a market price of $12.58 and a dividend yield of 8.1%

6 A share with a market price of $1.30 has a dividend yield of 9.2%. What is the dividend per share correct to two decimal places?

7 Tipeni bought 100 shares in a bank for $35.60 each. He sold them two years later for $48.90 each and paid a brokerage fee of $32.95.

   a What is the profit made on these shares?

   b What is the profit as a percentage of the cost of the shares?

8 Cooper bought 2500 shares for $5.60 each.

   a Cooper is charged a brokerage fee of 6.2 cents per share. What is the total cost of purchasing the shares?

   b Two months later a dividend of 36 cents per share was paid. What was the total dividend Cooper received?

   c Cooper sold the shares after receiving the dividend for $5.75 each. He was charged a brokerage fee of 6.2 cents per share. What was the profit on these shares?

9 The dividend yield on a company was 5%. How much is the dividend if you owned 500 shares with a market value of $4.80?

10 A company started trading on the ASX with a face value of $8.40. This graph shows the share price over time.

   a What was the share price at the beginning of June?

   b How much has the share price decreased during the 3 months?

   c What is the percentage decrease in the market value over the three months? Answer correct to two decimal places.

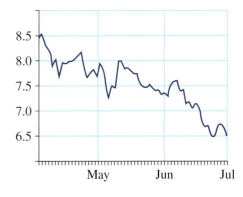

11 A spreadsheet can be used to record and graph the price of a share over time. The Excel file in the Interactive Textbook shows you how. Choose a company listed on the ASX and record its share price over a week and create a graph of the price. You will need to choose a company that is actively traded, with frequent changes of price.

3DQ11

12 A company has an after tax profit of $128 million. There are 200 million shares in the company. What dividend per share will the company declare if all the profits are distributed to shareholders?

13 Lauren owns 400 $3 ordinary shares and 300 $2 preference shares. The current prices of the ordinary shares and preference shares are $4.20 and $3.60 respectively. The dividend on the ordinary shares is 55c and on the preference shares is 3%. Calculate Lauren's total dividend.

3E Declining-balance depreciation

Declining-balance depreciation occurs when the value of the item decreases by a fixed percentage each time period. For example, if you buy a car for $20000 and it depreciates by 10% each year then the value of the car after one year is $20000 − $2000 or $18000. After the second year the value of the car is $20000 − $2000 − $1800 or $16200. Notice that the amount of depreciation has decreased in the second year. Depreciation calculations have similarities with compound interest, except that the depreciation is subtracted from the value not added to it.

DECLINING-BALANCE DEPRECIATION

$S = V_0(1 - r)^n$

S – Salvage value or current value of an item. Also referred to as the book value.
V_0 – Purchase price of the item. Value of the item when $n = 0$.
r – Rate of depreciation per time period expressed as a decimal.
n – Number of time periods.

Example 9: Calculating the declining-balance depreciation   3E

Eva purchased a new car two years ago for $32000. During the first year it had depreciated by 25% and during the second it had depreciated 20% of its value after the first year. What is the current value of the car?

SOLUTION:

1   Write the declining-balance depreciation formula. $S = V_0(1 + r)^n$
2   For the first year, substitute $V_0 = 32000$, $r = 0.25$ and $= 32000 \times (1 - 0.25)^1$
    $n = 1$ into the formula.
3   Evaluate the value of the car after the first year. $= \$24000$
4   Write the declining-balance depreciation formula. $S = V_0(1 - r)^n$
5   For the second year substitute $V_0 = 24000$, $r = 0.20$ $= 24000 \times (1 - 0.20)^1$
    and $n = 1$ into the formula.
6   Evaluate the value of the car after the second year. $= \$19200$
7   Write the answer in words.   Current value is $19200.

Example 10: Calculating the purchase price **3E**

Angus buys a car that depreciates at the rate of 26% per annum. After five years the car has a salvage value of $17 420. How much did Angus pay for the car, to the nearest dollar?

SOLUTION:

1 Write the declining-balance depreciation formula. $\qquad\qquad S = V_0(1 - r)^n$

2 Substitute $S = 17420$, $r = 0.26$ and $n = 5$ into the $\qquad 17420 = V_0 \times (1 - 0.26)^5$
formula.

3 Make V_0 the subject of the equation. $\qquad\qquad V_0 = \dfrac{17420}{(1 - 0.26)^5}$

4 Evaluate. $\qquad\qquad\qquad\qquad\qquad\qquad\qquad\qquad = \$78503.59621$

5 Express the answer correct to the nearest $\qquad\qquad\qquad = \$78504$
whole dollar.

6 Write the answer in words. $\qquad\qquad\qquad$ Angus paid $78 504 for the car.

Example 11: Calculating the percentage rate of depreciation **3E**

Madison bought a delivery van four years ago for $27 500. Using the declining-balance method for depreciation, she estimates its present value to be $8107. What annual percentage rate of depreciation did she use? Answer to the nearest whole number.

SOLUTION:

1 Write the declining-balance depreciation formula. $\qquad\qquad S = V_0(1 - r)^n$

2 Substitute $S = 8107$, $V_0 = 27500$ and $n = 4$ into $\qquad 8107 = 27500 \times (1 - r)^4$
the formula.

3 Make $(1 - r)^4$ the subject of the equation. $\qquad (1 - r)^4 = \dfrac{8107}{27500}$

4 Take the fourth root of both sides. $\qquad\qquad\qquad 1 - r = \sqrt[4]{\dfrac{8107}{27500}}$

5 Rearrange to make r the subject. $\qquad\qquad\qquad\qquad r = 1 - \sqrt[4]{\dfrac{8107}{27500}}$

6 Evaluate. $\qquad\qquad\qquad\qquad\qquad\qquad\qquad\qquad = 0.26314528$

7 Express the answer correct to the nearest whole number. $\qquad = 26\%$

8 Write the answer in words. $\qquad\qquad\qquad$ Rate of depreciation is 26%.

Exercise 3E

Example 9 **1** A motor vehicle is bought for $22 000. It depreciates at 16% per annum and is expected to be used for 5 years. What is the salvage value of the motor vehicle after the following time periods? Answer to the nearest cent.

  a One year

  b Two years

  c Three years

2 Emma purchased a used car for $6560 two years ago. Use the declining-balance method to determine the salvage value of the used car if the depreciation rate is 15% per annum. Answer to the nearest dollar.

3 Bailey purchased a motor cycle for $17 500. It depreciates at 28% per year. Answer to the nearest dollar.

  a What is the book value of the motor cycle after 3 years?

  b How much has the motor cycle depreciated over the 3 years?

4 A new car is bought for $52 000. It depreciates at 22% per annum and is expected to be used for 4 years. How much has the car depreciated over the 4 years? Answer to the nearest dollar.

5 Chloe purchased a car for $19 900. It depreciates at 24% per year. Answer to the nearest dollar.

  a What is the salvage value of the car after 5 years?

  b How much has the car depreciated over the 5 years?

6 The depreciation of a used car over four years is shown in the graph below.

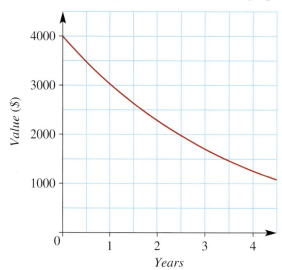

  a What is the initial value of the used car?

  b How much did the used car depreciate during the first year?

  c When is the value of the used car $2000?

  d When is the value of the used car $1500?

  e What is the value of the used car after 4 years?

  f What is the value of the used car after $1\frac{1}{2}$ years?

Example 10 | **7** Sarah buys a car that depreciates at the rate of 20% per annum. After six years the car has a salvage value of $6400. How much did Sarah pay for the car, to the nearest dollar?

Example 11 | **8** A hatchback vehicle was purchased for $16 980 three years ago. By using the declining-balance method of depreciation, the current value of the vehicle is $9614. What is the annual percentage rate of depreciation, correct to two decimal places?

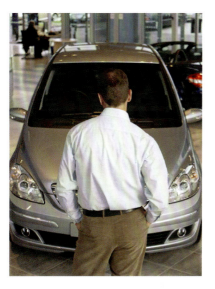

9 A new car is valued at $35 000. After one year using the declining-balance method, it is valued at $25 500.
   a Determine the annual percentage rate of depreciation. Answer correct to three decimal places.
   b What is the value of the new car after three years? Answer correct to the nearest dollar.

10 Philip and Amy spent $200 000 on a luxury car 7 years ago. Its current value is $104 350. Using the declining-balance method, find the percentage depreciation rate over this period. Answer correct to one decimal place.

11 Jessica invested $18 820 to buy a new car for her business. How many years would it take for this car to depreciate to $4520? Assume declining-balance method of depreciation with a rate of depreciation of 30%. (Answer to the nearest year.)

12 A motor vehicle is bought for $32 000. It depreciates at 16% per annum and is expected to be used for 5 years.
   a How much does the motor vehicle depreciate in the first year?
   b Copy and complete the following depreciation table for the first five years. Answer to the nearest dollar.

Year	Current value	Depreciation	Depreciated value
1			
2			
3			
4			
5			

   c Graph the value in dollars against the age in years.

3F Reducing-balance loans

Reducing-balance loans are calculated on the balance owing and not on the initial amount of money borrowed as with a flat-rate loan ('flat' meaning the interest rate does not change during the life of the loan). As payments are made, the balance owing is reduced and therefore the interest charged is reduced. This can save thousands of dollars on the cost of a loan. The calculations for reducing-balance loans are complicated and financial institutions publish tables related to loans.

LOAN REPAYMENTS

Total to be paid = Loan payment × Number of repayments
Total to be paid = Principal + Interest

Example 12: Using a table for a reducing-balance loan 3F

The table below shows the monthly repayments for a reducing-balance loan. Calculate the amount of interest to be paid on a loan of $200 000 over 13 years.

Term	Amount of the loan			
	$100 000	$150 000	$200 000	$250 000
12 years	$1664	$2096	$2794	$3493
13 years	$1700	$2150	$2856	$3569
14 years	$1726	$2218	$2898	$3622

SOLUTION:

1 Loan is $200 000 and time period is 13 years.

2 Find the intersection value from the table ($2856).

3 Multiply the intersection value by the number of years and 12 (months in a year) to determine the total to be paid.

4 Substitute the total to be paid ($445 536) and principal ($200 000) into the formula.

5 Evaluate.

6 Write the answer in words.

Total to be paid
= Loan payment × Number of repayments

= 2856 × 13 × 12
= $445 536

Total to be paid for the loan is $445 536.

Total to be paid = Principal + Interest
445 536 = 200 000 + I
= $245 536

Interest paid is $245 536.

Example 13: Using a table for a reducing-balance loan　　　3F

The table shows the monthly payments for each $1000 borrowed. Molly is planning to borrow $280 000 to buy a house at 8% per annum over a period of 20 years.

Interest rate	Period of loan		
	10 years	**15 years**	**20 years**
6% p.a.	$11.10	$8.44	$7.10
7% p.a.	$11.61	$9.00	$7.75
8% p.a.	$12.13	$9.56	$8.36

a What is Molly's monthly payment on this loan?
b How much would Molly pay in total to repay this loan?
c How much would Molly save if she repaid the loan over 15 years?

SOLUTION:

1 Find the intersection value from the table for interest rate 8% p.a. and time period 20 years.

a $8.36

2 Multiply the intersection value by the number of thousands borrowed (280).

Monthly repayment = $8.36 × 280
　　　　　　　　= $2340.80

3 Multiply the monthly repayment by the number of years and 12 (months in a year) to determine the total to be paid.

b Total to be paid
= Loan repayment × Number of repayments
= 2340.80 × 20 × 12

4 Evaluate.

= $561 792

5 Write the answer in words.

Total to be paid for the loan is $561 792.

6 Repeat the above calculations using 15 years instead of 20 years.

c 15 years
Monthly repayment = $9.56 × 280
　　　　　　　　= $2676.80

Total to be paid
= Loan repayment × Number of repayments
= 2676.80 × 15 × 12
= $481 824

7 Subtract the total to be paid for 15 years from the total to be paid for 20 years.

Amount saved = $561 792 − $481 824

8 Evaluate.

= $79 968

9 Write the answer in words.

The amount saved is $79 968.

Fees and charges for a loan

Banks and financial institutions charge their customers for borrowing money. A loan account is created and an account service fee is charged per month. In addition to this fee there are a number of other loan fees and charges, depending on the financial institution. Many of these fees are negotiable and customers are advised to compare the fees and charges with the interest rate charged. Fees and charges for a loan may include:

- loan application fee – costs in setting up the loan.
- loan establishment fee – initial costs in processing the loan application.
- account service fee – ongoing account-keeping fee.
- valuation fee – assessment of the market value of a property.
- legal fee – legal processing of a property.

Graph of a reducing-balance loan

The graph below shows the amount owed after each month on a reducing-balance loan. The amount borrowed is $50 000 at an interest rate of 10% p.a. It illustrates the difference between making repayments of $500 per month and making repayments of $1000 per month. When paying $500 a month, it takes 215 months to pay off the loan, and the interest charged is $57 500. However, when paying $1000 a month, it only takes 65 months to pay off the loan, and the interest charged is $15 000. Each graph is a gradual curve as each payment reduces the amount owed and slowly decreases the interest charged.

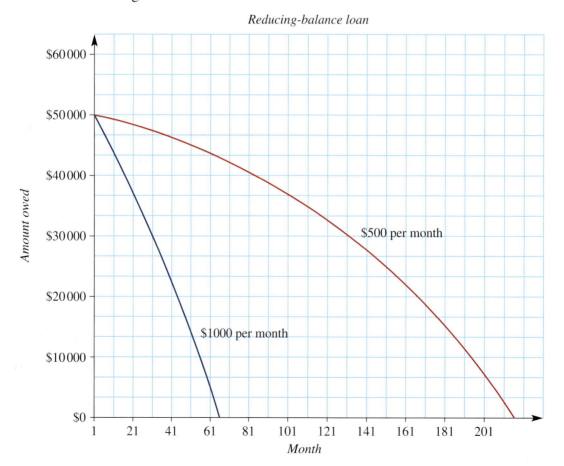

Reducing-balance loan

Exercise 3F

Example 12 **1** Tyler is considering an investment loan from the bank at an interest rate of 9.9% p.a. reducible (i.e a reducing balance loan). The table below shows the monthly repayment for an investment loan.

Term	Investment loan				
	$50 000	**$75 000**	**$100 000**	**$125 000**	**$150 000**
5 years	$1060	$1590	$2120	$2650	$3180
10 years	$658	$987	$1316	$1645	$1974
15 years	$534	$801	$1068	$1336	$1603

   a What is the monthly repayment for a loan of $75 000 over 15 years?
   b What is the monthly repayment for a loan of $150 000 over 10 years?
   c What is the monthly repayment for a loan of $100 000 over 5 years?
   d What is the monthly repayment for a loan of $50 000 over 15 years?
   e What is the monthly repayment for a loan of $125 000 over 5 years?

2 Kevin is applying for an investment loan from a bank of $75 000 over 5 years using the table in question **1**.
   a What is the monthly repayment?
   b What is the total amount paid for this loan?
   c What is the interest paid on this loan?

3 The table below shows the monthly repayments per $1000 on a bank loan.

Term	7.00%	7.25%	7.50%	7.75%
10 years	$16.39	$16.78	$17.18	$17.58
15 years	$15.33	$15.87	$16.44	$17.02

Calculate the monthly repayment on the following loans.
   a $310 000 at 7.50% p.a. for 15 years   **b** $120 000 at 7.00% p.a. for 10 years
   c $450 000 at 7.75% p.a. for 10 years   **d** $180 000 at 7.25% p.a. for 15 years

4 Blake is borrowing $35 000 at 7% p.a. for 10 years. Use the table in question **3** to answer these questions.
   a What is the monthly repayment?   **b** How much interest will he pay?

Example 13 **5** This table shows the monthly payments for a loan of $1000 for varying interest rates. Jack is planning to borrow $340 000 to buy a house at 10% p.a. over a period of 15 years.

Interest rate	Period of loan		
	10 years	**15 years**	**20 years**
7% p.a.	$11.61	$9.00	$7.75
8% p.a.	$12.13	$9.56	$8.36
9% p.a.	$12.67	$10.14	$9.00
10% p.a.	$13.22	$10.75	$9.65

a Calculate Jack's monthly payment on this loan.

b How much does Jack pay in total to repay this loan?

c How much interest does Jack pay on this loan?

d How much would Jack save if he repaid the loan over 10 years?

6 Hannah and Mitchell borrow $180 000 over 20 years at a reducible interest rate of 8.5% p.a. They pay $1754 per month.

a Calculate the total amount to be paid on this loan.

b How much interest do they pay on the loan?

7 The graph opposite shows the amount owed each month on a reducing-balance loan. Use the graph to estimate the answer to these questions.

a How much was borrowed?

b How much is owed after 20 months?

c How much is owed after 40 months?

d How much is owed after 60 months?

e When is the amount owing $20 000?

f When is the amount owing $60 000?

g When is the loan paid?

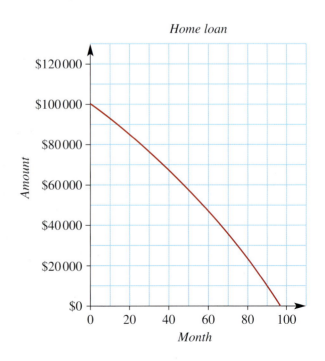

Home loan

LEVEL 2

8 Mr and Mrs Smith intend to borrow $400 000 at 8% p.a. reducible interest for a term of 20 years. Use the table in question **5** for the following calculations.

  a What is their monthly repayment?
  b Find the total amount to be repaid.
  c What is the interest paid for this loan?
  d How much would they save if they repaid the loan over 15 years?
  e How much would they save if they repaid the loan over 10 years?
  f What is the equivalent flat interest rate charged per annum on this loan? Answer correct to two decimal places.

LEVEL 3

9 Abbey borrows $160 000 over 8 years at an interest rate of 21.2% p.a. reducible. She pays $1600 per fortnight.

  a How much will Abbey pay back altogether?
  b What is the interest paid for this loan?
  c What is the equivalent flat interest rate charged per annum on this loan? Answer correct to one decimal place.

10 The formula below converts a flat rate of interest to the approximate equivalent reducible interest rate.

$$E = \frac{2NR}{N + 1}$$

  E – Reducible rate of interest per annum as a decimal
  R – Flat rate of interest per annum expressed as a decimal
  N – Number of repayments in the loan

Use the formula to calculate the approximate reducible interest rate for these loans. Answer correct to two decimal places.

  a Loan of $20 000 over 3 years at 12% p.a. flat interest with monthly repayments
  b Loan of $50 000 over 5 years at 8.5% p.a. flat interest with monthly repayments
  c Loan of $58 000 over 4 years at 9% p.a. flat interest with quarterly repayments
  d Loan of $7000 over 12 months at 15% p.a. flat interest with biannual repayments
  e Loan of $62 000 over 6 years at 11% p.a. flat interest with quarterly repayments
  f Loan of $25 000 over 2 years at 19% p.a. flat interest with biannual repayments
  g Loan of $70 000 over 24 months at 15% p.a. flat interest with monthly repayments

3G   Credit cards

Credit cards are used to buy goods and services and pay for them later. The time when interest is not charged on your purchases is called the interest-free period. If payment is not received when the statement is due then interest is charged from the date of purchase. Interest on credit cards is usually calculated daily on the outstanding balance using compound interest.

The interest rate is usually much higher than for other kinds of loans and credit facilities.

CREDIT CARDS

$$\text{Daily interest rate} = \frac{\text{Annual interest rate}}{365}$$

$FV = PV(1 + r)^n \quad I = FV - PV$

FV – Amount owing on the credit card

PV – Principal is the purchases made on the credit card plus the outstanding balance

r – Rate of interest per compounding time period expressed as a decimal

n – Number of compounding time periods

I – Interest (compound) charged on the outstanding balance

Example 14: Calculating the cost of using a credit card   3G

Samantha has a credit card with a compound interest rate of 18% p.a. and no interest-free period. Samantha used her credit card to pay for clothing costing $280. She paid the credit card account 14 days later. What is the total amount she paid for the clothing, including the interest charged?

SOLUTION:

1   Write the formula for compound interest.

2   Substitute $P = 280$, $r = (0.18 \div 365)$ and $n = 14$ into the formula.

3   Evaluate.

4   Express the answer correct to two decimal places.

5   Answer the question in words.

$FV = PV(1 + r)^n$

$= 280\left(1 + \dfrac{0.18}{365}\right)^{14}$

$= 281.9393596$

$= \$281.94$

Clothing costs $281.94

Desmos widget 3G Credit card interest rate compared to a bank loan

Exercise 3G

1 A credit card has a daily interest rate of 0.05% per day. Find the interest charged on these outstanding balances. Answer correct to the nearest cent.

  a $840 for 12 days

  b $742.40 for 20 days

  c $5680 for 30 days

  d $128 for 18 days

  e $240 for 6 days

  f $1450 for 15 days

2 Joel has a credit card with an interest rate of 0.04% compounding per day and no interest-free period. He uses his credit card to pay for a mobile phone costing $980. Calculate the total amount paid for the mobile phone if Joel paid the credit card account in the following time period. Answer correct to the nearest cent.

  a 10 days later

  b 20 days later

  c 30 days later

  d 40 days later

  e 50 days later

  f 60 days later

3 Calculate the compound interest charged on these outstanding balances. Answer correct to the nearest cent.

  a Balance = $6820, Daily interest rate of 0.08%, Time period 70 days

  b Balance = $23 648, Daily interest rate of 0.06%, Time period 35 days

  c Balance = $1550, Daily interest rate of 0.05%, Time period 20 days

  d Balance = $35 800, Daily interest rate of 0.09%, Time period 100 days

  e Balance = $4500, Daily interest rate of 0.05%, Time period 27 days

  f Balance = $7680, Daily interest rate of 0.04%, Time period 180 days

4 Andrew's credit card charges 0.045% compound interest per day on any outstanding balances. Calculate how much interest Andrew is charged on an amount of $450, which is outstanding on his credit card for 35 days. Answer correct to the nearest cent.

5 Olivia received a new credit card with no interest-free period and a daily compound interest rate of 0.05%. She used her credit card to purchase food for $320 and petrol for $50 on 18 July. This amount stayed on the credit card for 24 days. What is the total interest charged? Answer correct to the nearest cent.

6 Jhye used his credit card to buy a holiday to New Zealand. The cost of the package was $6500. The charge on the credit card is 1% interest per month on the unpaid balance. How much does Jhye owe for his holiday after six months? Answer correct to the nearest cent.

7 Calculate the amount owed, to the nearest cent, for each of the following credit card transactions. The credit card has no interest-free period.
  a Transactions = $540, Compound interest rate = 14% p.a., Time period = 15 days
  b Transactions = $270, Compound interest rate = 11% p.a., Time period = 9 days
  c Transactions = $1400, Compound interest rate = 18% p.a., Time period = 22 days
  d Transactions = $480, Compound interest rate = 16% p.a., Time period = 18 days
  e Transactions = $680, Compound interest rate = 10% p.a., Time period = 9 days

8 Calculate the interest charged for each of the following credit card transactions. The credit card has no interest-free period. Answer correct to the nearest cent.
  a Transactions = $680, Compound interest rate = 15% p.a., Time period = 20 days
  b Transactions = $740, Compound interest rate = 12% p.a., Time period = 13 days
  c Transactions = $1960, Compound interest rate = 17% p.a., Time period = 30 days
  d Transactions = $820, Compound interest rate = 21% p.a., Time period = 35 days
  e Transactions = $1700, Compound interest rate = 19% p.a., Time period = 32 days

9 Luke has a credit card with a compound interest rate of 18.25% per annum.
  a What is the daily percentage interest rate, correct to two decimal places?
  b Luke has an outstanding balance of $4890 for a period of 30 days. How much interest, to the nearest cent, will he be charged?

10 Alyssa uses a credit card with a no interest-free period and a compound interest rate of 15.5% p.a. from the purchase date. During April she makes the following transactions.

Transaction details		
04 April	IGA Supermarket	$85.00
09 April	KMart	$115.00
12 April	David Jones	$340.00
27 April	General Pants	$80.00
28 April	JB-HIFI	$30.00

  a What is the daily compound interest rate, correct to three decimal places?
  b Alyssa's account is due on 30 April. What is the total amount due if you disregard the amount of interest to be paid?
  c How much interest has Alyssa paid on the IGA transaction during the month? Answer correct to the nearest cent.
  d How much interest has Alyssa paid on the KMart transaction during the month? Answer correct to the nearest cent.

11 Charlie's credit card has up to 55 days interest free and is due on the 22nd of each month. The interest rate is 15.4% p.a. compounding daily. Charlie buys furniture costing $5160 on 25 October. How much interest is he charged if he pays the balance on 22 December? Interest is charged from the date of purchase if the total amount owing has not been paid by the due date.

12 Harry buys two Blu-ray DVDs for $29.90 each and a shirt for $84.95 on his credit card. This amount stays on his credit card for 75 days. There is a 45-day interest-free period and a daily interest of 0.05% compound on his credit card.

  a How much did Harry spend on his credit card?
  b Calculate the amount Harry owes on the credit card.
  c What was the interest charged on these purchases?
  d What would be the interest charged if Harry's credit card did not have a 45-day interest-free period?

13 Sarah and Joshua each use their credit cards to buy holiday packages to Adelaide. The cost of the package is $1700 for each person.
  a The charge on Sarah's credit card is 0.9% compound interest per month on the unpaid balance. It has no interest-free period. Sarah pays $800 after one month and another $500 the next month. How much does she still owe on her credit card?
  b The charge on Joshua's credit card is interest-free in the first month, and 1.4% compound interest per month on any unpaid balance. Joshua pays $800 after one month and another $500 the next month. How much does he still owe on his credit card?

14 Emily's August credit card statement shows an opening balance of $1850, a purchase of $2450 on 5 August, and another purchase of $55 on 14 August. The minimum payment is 3% of the closing balance. The initial credit charge is 1.6% compounding per month of any amount outstanding.
  a What is the closing balance on this credit card for August?
  b Calculate the amount of interest charged for the month of August.
  c What is the minimum payment, to the nearest cent, required for August?
  d What is the opening balance for October if Emily paid the minimum payment in September for interest charged in August and made no purchases in September?

3H   Credit card statements

Credit card statements are issued each month and contain information such as account number, opening balance, new charges, payments, refunds, reward points, payment due data, minimum payment and closing balance. The credit card statement includes the date and cost of each purchase and could be regarded as a ledger. A ledger documents your spending.

If the minimum payment is not made by the due date, the consequences can be expensive. You may be charged a late payment fee and, of course, you will be charged interest on it.

Example 15: Reading a credit card statement   3H

Your Bank
Your Bank of Australia
ABN 12 345 678 901

Page number	1 of 2
Statement begins	5 Oct
Statement ends	5 Nov

MR JOHN CITIZEN
123 SAMPLE STREET
SUBURBIA NSW 2000

Enquiries
Credit Card   **13 2221**
(24 hours a day, 7 days a week)

Your Bank Awards   **13 1661**
(8am to 8pm Mon-Fri)

MasterCard 5353 1801 0001 0001

Opening balance	$207.72
New charges	$460.14
Payments/refund	-$207.72

Payment due date

> 30th November

Minimum payment

> $25.00

Closing balance

> $460.14

Your Bank Awards 1000123456

Opening points balance	50,500
Total points earned	460
points redeemed	-15,600

Total Points Balance

> 34,910

Answer the following questions using the above credit card statement.

a What is the credit card account number?   **b** What is the opening balance?

c What is the payment due date?   **d** What is the minimum payment?

e What is the closing balance?

SOLUTION:

1	Read the number after 'MasterCard'.	**a**	5353 1801 0001 0001
2	Read 'Opening balance'.	**b**	Opening balance is $207.72.
3	Read the box 'Payment due date'.	**c**	Payment due date is 30 Nov.
4	Read the box 'Minimum payment'.	**d**	Minimum payment is $25.00.
5	Read the box 'Closing balance'.	**e**	Closing balance is $460.14.

Exercise 3H

Example 15

1 Use the credit card statement opposite to answer these questions.
  a What is the due date?
  b What is the cost of the purchases?
  c What is the closing account balance?
  d What is the minimum amount due?
  e What payment was made last month?
  f How much interest was charged?
  g What was the opening balance?
  h What is the cardholder's credit balance?

2 The transactions on a credit card are shown below.
  a What is the credit limit?
  b What is the account balance?
  c How many transactions are shown?
  d What is the available credit?

Account summary	
Opening balance	**$743.42**
Payments and other credits	$743.42
Purchases	$172.91
Cash advances	$0.00
Interest and other charges	$0.00
Closing account balance	**$172.91**
Cardholder credit balances	4511.88
Payment summary	
Card balances renewal	$4684.79
Monthly payment	$10.00
Due date	**21/04/2020**
Minimum amount due	**$10.00**

Account summary			
Available credit	**Account balance**		**Credit limit**
$15 549.18	$3950.82		$19 500.00
	Payment due date	**Minimum payment due**	
	7 Dec		$57.00
Last 5 transactions View more			
Date	**Transaction description**	**Debit**	**Credit**
30 Nov	WW Petrol	$24.38	
29 Nov	Coles	$55.03	
29 Nov	Woolworths	$34.63	
28 Nov	Myer	$49.13	
28 Nov	David Jones	$23.40	

  e How much was spent on 29 November?
  f How much was spent on 28 November?
  g Where was $49.13 spent on 28 November?
  h Where was $24.38 spent on 30 November?
  i What is the payment due date?
  j What is the minimum amount due?

3 Create the spreadsheet below.

3HQ3

	C10	▾	f_x =SUM(C5:C9)	
	A	B		C
1				
2	Worksheet to create a ledger			
3				
4	Date	Details		Amount
5	20-Nov	Manly Vale Pharmacy Manly Vale		-$20.00
6	25-Nov	Manly Vale Pharmacy Manly Vale		-$18.95
7	01-Dec	Virgin Mobile North Sydney		-$25.00
8	05-Dec	Target 78 Brookvale		-$12.99
9	05-Dec	Pulse Warringah Brookvale		-$30.98
10				-$107.92

a How many transactions are shown on the ledger?

b How much has been spent at Manly Vale Pharmacy?

c If the account begins on 15 November and ends on 14 December, how many days does it account for?

d If the card has a $5000 credit limit, what is the available credit on 14 December?

e If the minimum payment is $10 and is paid on the due date, what is the balance owing?

f This credit card charges 0.06% per day compound interest on the unpaid balance. What is the interest charged per day on the closing balance? Answer to the nearest cent.

4 Consider the credit card statement shown opposite.

a What is the opening balance?

b What is the credit limit?

c What is the available credit?

d What is the closing balance?

e How much has been spent on purchases, cash advances and special promo debits this month?

f How much interest and other charges were paid last month?

Visa Account number	4557 0756 0833 1234
Credit limit	$12 000
Available credit	**$6 361**
Account summary	
− Opening balance	$5 821.31 DR
+ Payment & other credits received	$781.25 CR
− Purchases, cash advances & special promo debits	$511.93 DR
− Interest & other charges	$86.26 DR
= Closing balance	$5 638.25 DR

g This credit card charges 0.05% per day compound interest on the unpaid balances.

    i What is the interest charged per day on the closing balance? Answer to the nearest cent.

    ii How much interest would be paid on the closing balance for a year? Answer to the nearest cent.

5 The transactions on a credit card with an opening balance of $5246.84 are shown below.

Date	Card	Transaction details	Debit	Credit
21 Nov		Opening balance	$5246.84	
22 Nov	6378	AAMI	$627.13	
23 Nov	6378	Priceline	$155.14	
23 Nov	6360	Primus	$89.15	
23 Nov	6378	Utopia Hair Design	$32.50	
23 Nov	6378	Cue	$199.00	
23 Nov	6378	Coles	$14.00	
24 Nov	6378	Hungry Jack's	$19.25	
25 Nov	6378	Optus	$74.94	
26 Nov	6378	General Pants		$45.00
26 Nov	6360	Eway Electronic Toll	$100.50	
29 Nov	6378	Big W	$31.99	
29 Nov	6378	Price Attack	$72.90	

a What is the opening balance?
b What is the total of new charges and credits made on this account?
c If the card has a $30 000 credit limit, what is the available credit on 1 December?
d How many transactions were completed using card 6360?
e How many transactions were completed using card 6378?
f Which transaction was a credit?
g What was the transaction date for Coles?
h What is the closing balance?
i This credit card charges 21.9% p.a. compound interest on the unpaid balances. What is the interest charge for 120 days on the closing balance? Answer to the nearest cent.

6 Payment details for a credit card are shown opposite.
a What is the closing balance if the minimum payment was paid on the 30 September?
b This credit card charges 18.75% p.a. compound interest on the unpaid balance. What is the interest charged for the next 60 days? Answer to the nearest cent.

Payment details

Closing balance	$5638.25	DR
Available credit	$6361.00	

DUE NOW

Past due/overlimit amount	$5.00
Due date 30 September	
Monthly payment	$140.96
Total minimum payment	$145.96

3I   Fees and charges for credit card usage

Banks and financial institutions charge their customers an annual card fee for maintaining a credit card account. In addition to this fee, customers may be charged fees for late payment, cash advances and balance transfers. The late payment fee applies if the minimum payment has not been received by the due date. Interest is charged for retail purchases and the amount still owing from the previous month.

FEES AND CHARGES FOR CREDIT CARD USAGE

- Annual card fee – maintaining credit card account
- Interest charge – interest charged for retail purchases
- Late payment fee – when minimum payment has not been received by the due date
- Cash advances – withdrawing cash from the credit card account
- Balance transfers – moving balance to another account, often held at another institution

Example 16: Calculating fees and charges   3I

Hilary has a debit of $6000 on a credit card with an interest rate of 14.75% p.a. that compounds daily. She decided to transfer the balance to a new card with a 0% balance transfer for 6 months. However, after 6 months the new card reverted to an interest rate of 19.75% p.a that compounds daily. Is Hilary better off after 12 months?

SOLUTION:

1   Write the formula.

2   Substitute $PV = 6000$, $r = 0.1475$ and $n = 365$ into the formula.

3   Evaluate correct to two decimal places.

Old card $FV = PV(1 + r)^n$

$$= \$6000\left(1 + \frac{0.1475}{365}\right)^{365}$$

$$\approx \$6953.39$$

4   Write the formula.

5   Substitute $PV = 6000$, $r = 0.1975$ and $n = 182.5$ (6 months only) into the formula.

6   Evaluate correct to two decimal places.

New card $FV = PV(1 + r)^n$

$$= \$6000\left(1 + \frac{0.1975}{365}\right)^{182.5}$$

$$\approx \$6622.57$$

7   Calculate the saving by subtracting the future value of the new card from the old card.

Saving $= \$6953.39 - \$6622.57$

$= \$330.82$

8   Write the answer in words.

Hilary is better off with the new card by $330.82.

Exercise 3I

1 Alicia's bank charged an annual credit card fee of $350, a cash advance fee of $2.50 and a late payment fee of $20. Calculate Alicia's banking costs for the year if she made:

  a 11 cash advances and 4 late payments.

  b 20 cash advances and 12 late payments.

  c 50 cash advances and 6 late payments.

  d 0 cash advances and 12 late payments.

  e 100 cash advances and 0 late payments.

  f 0 cash advances and 0 late payments.

2 The table below shows the credit card usage charges for four banks.

Bank	Annual fee	Cash advance	Late payment
A	$225	$2.00	$15
B	$200	$2.20	$20
C	$250	$1.80	$12
D	$240	$1.90	$16

  a What is the cost of the cash advance fee at bank B?

  b What is the cost of the late payment fee at bank D?

  c Which bank has the lowest annual fee?

  d Which bank has the highest cash advance fee?

  e Calculate the difference between the late payment fees at bank C and bank D.

  f Calculate the difference between the cash advance fees at bank B and bank C.

  g What is the average annual fee for these banks?

  h What is the average late payment fee for these banks?

  i What are the annual banking costs for 30 cash advances and 1 late payment at:

    i Bank A?   **ii** Bank B?

    iii Bank C?   **iv** Bank D?

  j What are the annual banking costs for 100 cash advances and 6 late payments at:

    i Bank A?   **ii** Bank B?

    iii Bank C?   **iv** Bank D?

3 Elijah's bank charged an annual credit card fee of $320, cash advance fee of $2.30 and late payment fee of $18. What are Elijah's banking costs for the year if he made 80 cash advances and had 1 late payment fee?

4   The table below shows the banking charges for credit card usage.

Fee	Charge
Cash advance	5%
Late payment	$20
Balance transfer	1%

Find the cost of the following activities. Answer to the nearest cent.
a   1 cash advance of $400.
b   10 cash advances of $50.
c   100 cash advances of $100.
d   1 balance transfer of $3580.
e   1 balance transfer of $8620.
f   1 balance transfer of $10000.
g   2 late payments and 3 cash advances of $300.
h   10 late payments and 20 cash advances of $200.
i   5 late payments and 50 cash advances of $80.

Example 16   **5**   George purchased a laptop on his credit card for $2500. Interest is charged at 0.04% per day. He decided to transfer the balance to a new card with a 0% balance transfer for 90 days. How much does he save in the first 180 days on the following new cards? Answer to the nearest cent.
a   Interest rate of 0.03% per day   **b**   Interest rate 0.04% per day
c   Interest rate of 0.05% per day   **d**   Interest rate 0.06% per day
e   Interest rate of 0.07% per day   **f**   Interest rate 0.08% per day

6   Annabelle has a debit of $8000 on a credit card with an interest rate of 12% p.a. She decided to transfer the balance to a new card with a 0% balance transfer for 6 months. How much does she save in the first 12 months on the following new cards whose interest rate compounds daily? Answer to the nearest cent.
a   Interest rate of 12% p.a.   **c**   Interest rate of 16% p.a.   **e**   Interest rate of 20% p.a.
b   Interest rate 14% p.a.   **d**   Interest rate 18% p.a.   **f**   Interest rate 22% p.a.

7   Emily's August credit card statement shows an opening balance of $1850, a purchase of $2450 on 5 August, and another purchase of $1055 on 14 August. The minimum payment is 3% on the closing balance. The credit charge is 0.05% per day compound interest on the outstanding balance. Answer the following questions to the nearest cent.
a   What was the total cost of the purchases in August on the credit card?
b   What is closing balance on this credit card for August?
c   What is the minimum payment to the nearest cent required for August?
d   Calculate the amount of interest charged for the month of September if Emily paid the minimum payment in August.

Key ideas and chapter summary

Future value formula	$FV = PV(1 + r)^n$ or $PV = \dfrac{FV}{(1 + r)^n}$ or $I = FV - PV$ FV – Future value of the loan or amount (final balance) PV – Present value of the loan or principal (initial quantity of money) r – Rate of interest per compounding time period as a decimal (i.e. convert percentage rates to decimal) n – Number of compounding time periods I – Interest (compounded) earned.
Investment graphs	**1** Construct a table of values for A and n using the simple interest formula or the future value formula. **2** Draw a number plane: n horizontal axis, A the vertical axis. Plot and join the points.
Appreciation and inflation	Use the formula $FV = PV(1 + r)^n$ for appreciation and inflation. Inflation rate is the annual percentage change in the CPI.
Shares and dividends	Dividend is a payment given as an amount per share or a percentage of the issued price. $\text{Dividend yield} = \dfrac{\text{Annual dividend}}{\text{Market price}} \times 100\%$

Declining-balance depreciation	$S = V_0(1 - r)^n$ S – Salvage value or current value
	                           V_0 – Purchase price of the item
	                           r – Rate of interest per time period (decimal)
	                           n – Number of time periods.

Reducing-balance loans	Total to be paid = Loan repayment × Number of repayments Total to be paid = Principal + Interest
Credit cards	$\text{Daily interest rate} = \dfrac{\text{Annual interest rate}}{365}$ $FV = PV(1 + r)^n$ FV – Future value or the amount owing on the credit card PV – Present value or the purchases made on the credit card r – Rate of interest per compounding time period as a decimal n – Number of compounding time periods.
Fees and charges for credit card usage	Annual card fee, interest charge, late payment fee, cash advances, balance transfers.

Review

Multiple-choice

1   Holly invests $8000 at 10% p.a. interest compounding annually. What is the future value after 3 years? (Answer to the nearest dollar.)

   A $242   B $2648   C $8242   D $10648

2   Nathan borrows $3000 at 10% p.a. interest compounding annually. What is the interest earned after 2 years? (Answer to the nearest dollar.)

   A $30   B $60   C $600   D $630

3   A painting was bought for $460000 and appreciated at the rate of 7% p.a. What will be the value of the painting after 4 years? (Answer to the nearest dollar.)

   A $473016   B $492200   C $588800   D $602966

4   Chloe brought 800 shares at a market value of $10.20 each. Brokerage costs incurred were $38 including GST. What is the total cost of purchasing the shares?

   A $48.20   B $8160   C $8198   D $30400

5   A car depreciates in value from $39000 to $12250 in 4 years using the declining-balance method for depreciation. What is the annual rate of depreciation to the nearest whole number?

   A 17%   B 18%   C 25%   D 26%

6   The table shows the monthly repayment of $1000 on a reducing-balance loan. What is the monthly repayment on $290000 at 8.75% for 20 years?

Term	8.00%	8.25%	8.50%	8.75%
20 years	$6.38	$6.77	$7.17	$7.57

   A $1850.20   B $1963.30   C $2079.30   D $2195.30

7   Lachlan borrows $245000 over 20 years at a reducible interest rate of 6.5% p.a. He pays $1856 per month. What is the total paid on this loan?

   A $200440   B $318500   C $445440   D $563500

8   A credit card has a daily interest rate of 0.05% per day (no interest free period). Find the interest charged on $1530 for 14 days. Answer correct to the nearest cent.

   A $0.77   B $10.74   C $76.50   D $1540.74

Short-answer

1 Calculate the future value, to the nearest cent, for each of the following.
  a Present value = $920, Compound interest rate = 5% p.a., Time period = 4 years
  b Present value of $2100 invested for 3 years at 6.1% p.a. compounded monthly

2 Calculate the present value, to the nearest cent, for each of the following.
  a Future value = $26 000, Interest rate = 4.9% p.a., Time period = 3 years
  b Future value of $10 400, Interest rate at 9% p.a. compounded quarterly for 5 years

3 What sum of money would Emma need to invest to accumulate a total of $200 000 at the end of 10 years at 12% p.a. interest compounding biannually? Answer to the nearest cent.

4 An investment is appreciating at a rate of 4% of its value each year. Ruby decides to invest $480 000.
  a What will be the value of the investment after 10 years? Answer to the nearest dollar.
  b How much does the investment increase during the first ten years?

5 The average inflation for the next three years is predicted to be 2.5%. Calculate the price of the following goods in three years' time. Answer to the nearest cent.
  a 2 L of soft drink for $2.80
  b Apple pie for $4.60
  c Hamburger for $6.00
  d Bottle of water for $1.60
  e Punnet of strawberries for $4.50
  f 500 g of chicken breast for $8.90

6 Mia bought 50 shares in a bank for $82.64 each. She sold them two years later for $68.90. The brokerage fee paid for buying and selling the shares was $35.95. What was the loss on these shares?

7 A company with a share price of $2.42 declares a dividend of 12 cents. What is the dividend yield correct to two decimal places?

8 Ebony purchases 1000 shares at $16.90 per share. Her broker charges $20 plus 1.5% of the purchase price. Calculate the brokerage for this purchase.

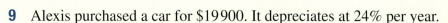

Review

9 Alexis purchased a car for $19 900. It depreciates at 24% per year.

   a What is the salvage value of the car after 5 years? Answer to the nearest dollar.

   b How much has the car depreciated over the 5 years?

10 Paige takes out a loan of $21 000 over 36 months. The repayment rate is $753.42 per month.

   a How much will Paige pay back altogether? Answer to the nearest dollar.

   b What is the equivalent simple interest rate per annum for the loan, correct to one decimal place?

11 James borrows $280 000 and repays the loan in equal fortnightly repayments of $1250 over 20 years. What is the flat rate of interest per annum on James's loan, correct to two decimal places?

12 Madison has a credit card with an interest rate of 17% p.a. compounding daily and no interest-free period. Madison used her credit card to pay for shoes costing $170. She paid the credit card account 26 days later. What is the total amount she paid for the shoes including the interest charged? Answer to the nearest cent.

13 Hayley's bank charged an annual credit card fee of $300, a cash advance fee of $4.00 and a later payment fee of $20. Calculate Hayley's banking costs for the year if she made:

   a 9 cash advances and 5 late payments
       b 15 cash advances and 7 late payments.

Extended-response

14 Benjamin uses a credit card with a no interest-free period and an interest rate of 18.5% p.a. compounding daily from and including the purchase date and due date. Benjamin's account is due on February 28. During February he makes the following transactions.

Transaction Details		
06 February	Coles	$278.00
07 February	Myer	$87.00
18 February	Big W	$259.00
18 February	Jag	$120.00
20 February	Bunnings	$460.00
21 February	Woolworths	$300.00

How much interest will Benjamin pay during the month on the following transactions? Answer correct to the nearest cent.

   a Coles transaction
                 b Myer transaction

   c Big W transaction
                 d Jag transaction

   e Bunnings transaction
            f Woolworths transaction

Practice Paper 1

Section I

Attempt Questions 1–15 (15 marks).
Allow about 20 minutes for this section.

---

1 A 4 L tin of paint is made using a mixture of blue, white and green paint in the ratio $3:5:2$. How much blue paint is needed per tin?

A 300 mL

B 1200 mL

C 1800 mL

D 2000 mL

2 A car is travelling at a constant speed. It travels 60 km in 3 hours. This situation is described by the linear equation $d = mt$.

What is the value of m?

A 0.05

B 3

C 10

D 20

3 A bank charges 0.05753% simple interest per day on the amount owing on a credit card. What is the interest charged in four weeks on a balance of $1200?

A $19.33

B $27.61

C $69.04

D $276.14

4 The ratio of 1.5 m to 10 cm is:

A $1.5:10$

B $1:15$

C $15:10$

D $15:1$

5 What is the amount of interest paid on a $150 000 loan over 25 years if the interest rate is 7.2% p.a. compounding annually? No payments are made before the end of 25 years. Answer to the nearest dollar.

A $10 800

B $27 000

C $703 023

D $853 023

6 A car uses on average 7 L per 100 km in fuel. How much fuel would be used on a trip of 382 km?

   A 26.74 L

   B 34.72 L

   C 38.20 L

   D 54.57 L

Use the following network graph to answer questions **7** to **10**.

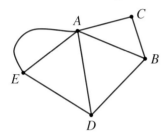

7 What is the degree of vertex *B*?

   A 1

   B 2

   C 3

   D 4

8 How many edges are there in the graph?

   A 5

   B 6

   C 7

   D 8

9 How many even vertices are there in the network diagram?

   A 1

   B 2

   C 3

   D 4

10 The graph has:

   A an Eulerian trail but not an Eulerian circuit.

   B several Eulerian trails but no Eulerian circuits.

   C an Eulerian circuit.

   D neither an Eulerian trail nor an Eulerian circuit.

11 Lucy has planted red and white rose bushes in the ratio 2:3. How many white rose bushes are there if she planted a total of 30 rose bushes?

A 6

B 12

C 18

D 20

12 Which symbol represents a toilet in a floor plan?

A

B

C

D

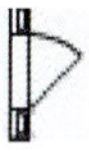

13 The daily interest rate for the outstanding balance on a credit card was 0.037%. The interest charged for 29 days was $9.12. The simple interest charged for 29 days was $9.12. How much was the outstanding balance? Answer to the nearest dollar.

A $246

B $850

C $971

D $24 649

14 Nicholas uses a 1.6-kilowatt dishwasher for a total of 2.5 hours. He is charged at a rate of 27.4 cents per kilowatt-hour. What is the cost of using the dishwasher?

A $1.10

B $1.12

C $4.00

D $109.60

15 Aiden breathes about 15 times each minute. How many times would he breathe in 9 hours?

A 90

B 216

C 8100

D 486 000

Section II

Attempt Questions 16 – 18 (45 marks).

Allow about 70 minutes for this section.

All necessary working should be shown in every question.

Question 16 (15 marks)   **Marks**

a A group of 3 people share a sum of $1200 in the ratio $5:3:8$. How much does   **2**
each person receive?

b The diagram shows a site plan.

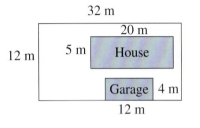

Not to scale

   i   What is the total area of land of the house and garage?   **1**

  ii   What percentage of the site is taken up by the house and garage? Answer correct to   **2**
the nearest whole number.

 iii   There is a brick wall, 800 mm high, along the northern boundary of the site.   **1**
What is the area of the brick wall in square metres?

  iv   600 bricks are needed to build 10 square metres of wall. How many bricks   **1**
were used to build the wall in part **iii**?

   v   The guttering around the perimeter of the house is to be replaced. Guttering   **2**
costs $60 per metre. How much will the new guttering cost?

c Oscar bought 1000 shares for $6.40 each. He received a dividend of 5.5% on his   **3**
purchase price. Oscar sold these shares for $7.20 each after 3 months. Calculate
Oscar's profit from the dividend and the sale of these shares.

d The table below shows the banking charges for credit card usage.

Fee	Charge
Cash advance	5%
Late payment	$30
Balance transfer	1.25%

   i   Find the cost of 40 cash advances for $100.   **1**

  ii   Find the cost of a balance transfer of $7000   **1**

 iii   Find the cost of 6 late payments and 5 cash advances of $200.   **1**

Question 17 (15 marks)   **Marks**

a A network graph is shown below.

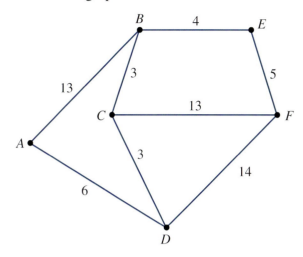

   i Does this graph have an Eulerian circuit? Give a reason.   **1**

  ii Find the minimum spanning tree and its length for the network.   **2**

 iii What is the length of the shortest path from *A* to *E* in the network?   **1**

  iv What is the length of the shortest path from *A* to *F* in the network?   **1**

   v What is the length of the shortest Hamiltonian cycle for the network?   **2**

b A rectangular poster is to be made to advertise energy-efficient housing. It is to be 1.6 m long and 1 m wide.

   i Draw a scale drawing of the rectangle using the scale 1:20.   **1**

  ii Outline two features of an energy-efficient house that could be part of the poster.   **2**

c A painting was bought for $695 at the beginning of 2017. It is expected that the painting will appreciate in value by 8% each year. What will be the value of the painting at the end of 2027? Answer to the nearest dollar.   **2**

d The two figures below are similar.

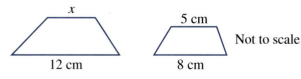

   i What is the scale factor, in simplest form?   **1**

  ii What is the length of the unknown side in the above trapezium?   **2**

Question 18 (15 marks)   **Marks**

a A network diagram is shown below.

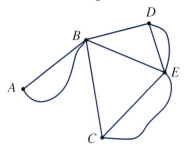

   i What is the degree of vertex E?   1

   ii Give an example of a Hamiltonian path in this graph.   1

b i Mia has a debit of $15 890 on a credit card with an interest rate of 17% p.a.   2
     compounded annually. How much interest is charged if she makes no payments
     for 2 years?

   ii Mia transferred the debit to a new card with a compound interest rate of 20% p.a. The   2
     new card has a 0% balance transfer for 6 months. How much is saved after 2 years?

c Layla uses a hot water unit with a rating of 12 kW for 10 minutes per day.

   i How much electricity is used each day?   1

   ii Electricity is charged at 15.25 cents per kWh. What is the electricity cost of using   1
     the hot water unit for one week?

d Nathan bought a new car for $45 000. When will the depreciated value of the car   2
fall below $10 000 using the declining-balance method of depreciation if the rate of
depreciation is 15% p.a.?

e The diagram below shows the network of pipes providing water from a reservoir to
six small settlements. These pipes connect the settlements to each other and to the
reservoir. The lengths of the pipes (in km) are shown.

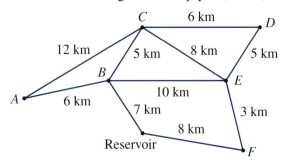

The pipe inspector plans to start her inspection at the reservoir, travel along each of
the pipes and return to the reservoir without having to travel along any pipe section
more than once.

   i What is the technical name for the route she wants to follow?   1

   ii Explain why such a route is possible for this network of pipes.   1

   iii Name one such route she could follow.   1

   iv The system of pipes is due for replacement. What is the minimum length of pipe   2
     that can be used to service all of the settlements?

4

Non-right-angled trigonometry

Syllabus topic — M6 Non-right-angled trigonometry

This topic is focused on solving problems involving right- and non-right-angled triangles in a variety of contexts.

Outcomes

- Solve problems using trigonometric ratios in one or more right-angled triangles.
- Solve problems involving angles of elevation and depression.
- Solve problems involving compass and true bearings.
- Determine the sign of trigonometry ratios involving obtuse angles.
- Calculate the area of a triangle given two sides and an included angle.
- Use the sine rule to find lengths and angles.
- Use the cosine rule to find lengths and angles.
- Use trigonometry to solve a variety of practical problems.
- Construct and interpret compass radial surveys and solve related problems.
- Investigate navigational methods used by other cultures.

Digital Resources for this chapter

In the Interactive Textbook:

- Videos
- Desmos widgets
- Literacy worksheet
- Spreadsheets
- Quick Quiz
- Study guide
- Solutions (enabled by teacher)

In the Online Teaching Suite:

- Teaching Program
- Tests
- Review Quiz
- Teaching Notes

Knowledge check

The Interactive Textbook provides a test of prior knowledge for this chapter, and may direct you to revision from the previous years' work.

4A   Right-angled trigonometry

Trigonometric ratios are defined using the sides of a right-angled triangle. The hypotenuse is opposite the right angle, the opposite side is opposite the angle θ and the adjacent side is the shorter side next to θ.

The trigonometric ratios $\sin \theta$, $\cos \theta$ and $\tan \theta$ are defined using the sides of a right-angled triangle.

$$\sin \theta = \frac{\text{opposite}}{\text{hypotenuse}} \qquad \cos \theta = \frac{\text{adjacent}}{\text{hypotenuse}} \qquad \tan \theta = \frac{\text{opposite}}{\text{adjacent}}$$

$$\sin \theta = \frac{o}{h} \text{ (SOH)} \qquad \cos \theta = \frac{a}{h} \text{ (CAH)} \qquad \tan \theta = \frac{o}{a} \text{ (TOA)}$$

In trigonometry an angle is usually measured in degrees, minutes and seconds such as $31°05'51''$ (31 degrees 5 minutes 51 seconds). It is important to remember that one degree is equal to 60 minutes ($1° = 60'$) and one minute is equal to 60 seconds ($1' = 60''$). Calculators may also measure angles in decimal degrees such as 31.0975, and a button like this $\boxed{\circ \, ' \, ''}$ or this $\boxed{\text{DMS}}$ is provided to convert between decimal degrees and degrees/minutes/seconds. Make sure also that the degree mode (not radian mode) is selected on your calculator.

RIGHT-ANGLED TRIGONOMETRY

The mnemonic 'SOH CAH TOA' is pronounced as a single word.

     SOH: **S**ine-**O**pposite-**H**ypotenuse

     CAH: **C**osine-**A**djacent-**H**ypotenuse

     TOA: **T**angent-**O**pposite-**A**djacent

The order of the letters matches the ratio of the sides.

Example 1: Finding an unknown side in a right-angled triangle   4A

Find the length of the unknown side x in the triangle shown. Answer correct to three decimal places.

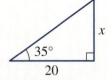

SOLUTION:

1   Identify the sides of the right-angled triangle that are relevant to the question.

     The opposite side is the unknown, the adjacent side is 20.

2   Determine the ratio that uses these sides (TOA).

$$\tan \theta = \frac{o}{a}$$

3   Substitute the known values and x for o.

$$\tan 35° = \frac{x}{20}$$

4   To make x the subject, multiply both sides of the equation by 20.

$$20 \times \tan 35° = x$$
$$x = 20 \times \tan 35°$$

5   Press 20 $\boxed{\tan}$ 35 $\boxed{\text{exe}}$ or $=$.

$$= 14.00415076$$

6   Write the answer correct to three decimal places.

$$= 14.004$$

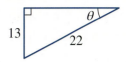

Example 2: Finding an unknown angle in a right-angled triangle   **4A**

Find the angle θ in the triangle shown. Answer correct to the
nearest minute.

SOLUTION:

1	Identify the relevant sides of the right-angled triangle.	Opposite = 13, hypotenuse = 22
2	Determine the ratio that uses these sides (SOH).	$\sin \theta = \dfrac{o}{h}$
3	Substitute the known values.	$\sin \theta = \dfrac{13}{22}$
4	Make θ the subject of the equation.	$\theta = \sin^{-1}\left(\dfrac{13}{22}\right)$
5	Press SHIFT $\boxed{\sin^{-1}}$ (13 ÷ 22) $\boxed{\text{exe}}$ or =. or Press SHIFT $\boxed{\sin^{-1}}$ 13 $\boxed{a^{b/c}}$ 22 $\boxed{\text{exe}}$ or =.	= 36.22154662
6	Convert decimal degrees to degrees and minutes using $\boxed{\circ\,\prime\,\prime\prime}$ or $\boxed{\text{DMS}}$ on your calculator.	= 36°13′
7	Write the answer correct to the nearest minute.	

Example 3: Application requiring the length of a side   **4A**

A vertical tent pole is supported by a rope tied to the top of the pole and to a
peg on the level ground. The peg is 2.5 m from the base of the pole and the rope
makes an angle of 63° to the horizontal. What is the length of the rope between
the peg and the top of the tent pole? Answer correct to two decimal places.

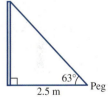

SOLUTION:

1	Identify the unknown side and call it x, and identify the relevant sides of the right-angled triangle.	Adjacent is 2.5 m, hypotenuse is the unknown x.
2	Determine the ratio that uses these sides (CAH).	$\cos \theta = \dfrac{a}{h}$
3	Substitute the known values, and x for h.	$\cos 63° = \dfrac{2.5}{x}$
4	Multiply both sides of the equation by x.	$x \cos 63° = 2.5$
5	Divide both sides of the equation by cos 63°, so x is now the subject of the equation.	$x = \dfrac{2.5}{\cos 63°}$
6	Press 2.5 ÷ $\boxed{\cos}$ 63 $\boxed{\text{exe}}$ or =.	= 5.506723161
7	Write the answer correct to two decimal places.	= 5.51
8	Write the answer in words.	Length of the rope is 5.51 m.

Exercise 4A

1 Find the value of the following trigonometric ratios, correct to two decimal places. Your calculator must be in degree mode and needs to have a degrees/minutes/seconds button which you press after entering the degrees, so you can then enter the minutes.

a $\sin 33°$

b $\cos 70°$

c $2 \tan 51°$

d $7 \sin 24°$

e $\cos 42°15'$

f $\tan 55°28'$

g $2 \cos 62°59'$

h $8 \sin 15°42'$

2 Given the following trigonometric ratios, find the value of θ to the nearest degree. Remember the $\sin^{-1}$, $\cos^{-1}$ and $\tan^{-1}$ buttons give angles from the trigonometric ratio.

a $\sin \theta = 0.4712$

b $\cos \theta = 0.3412$

c $\tan \theta = 0.3682$

d $\tan \theta = \dfrac{5}{8}$

e $\sin \theta = \dfrac{1}{2}$

f $\cos \theta = \dfrac{1}{4}$

Example 1 **3** Find the length of the unknown side x in each triangle, correct to two decimal places.

a
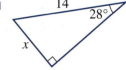

b

c
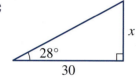

d
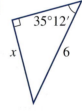

e
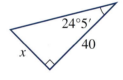

f
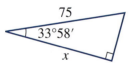

Example 2 **4** Find the unknown angle θ in each triangle. Answer correct to the nearest minute.

a
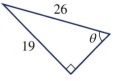

b

c
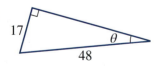

d
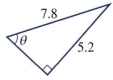

e
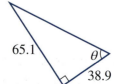

f
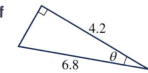

LEVEL 2

5 Find the length of the unknown side x in each triangle, correct to two decimal places.

a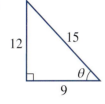

b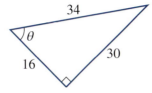

c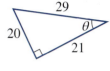

6 Find the unknown angle θ in each triangle. Answer correct to the nearest degree.

a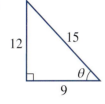

b

c

7 A balloon is tied to a string 25 m long. The other end of the string is secured by a peg to the surface of a level sports field. The wind blows so that the string forms a straight line making an angle of 37° with the ground. Find the height of the balloon above the ground. Answer correct to one decimal place.

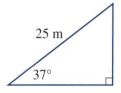

8 A pole is supported by a wire that runs from the top of the pole to a point on the level ground 5 m from the base of the pole. The wire makes angle of 42° with the ground. Find the height of the pole, correct to two decimal places.

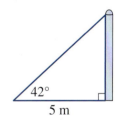

9 Ann noticed a tree was directly opposite her on the far bank of the river. After she walked 50 m along the side of the river, she found her line of sight to the tree made an angle of 39° with the river bank. Find the width of the river, to the nearest metre.

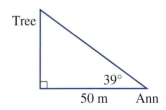

10 A ship at anchor requires 70 m of anchor chain. If the chain is inclined at 35° to the horizontal, find the depth of the water, correct to one decimal place.

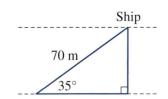

11   A pole casts a shadow of 5.4 m long. The sun's rays make an angle of 36° with the level ground. Find the height of the pole to the nearest metre.

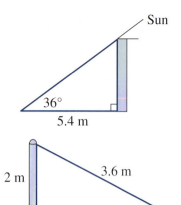

12   A vertical tent pole is supported by a rope of length 3.6 m tied to the top of the pole and to a peg on the ground. The pole is 2 m in height. Find the angle the rope makes to the horizontal. Answer correct to the nearest degree.

Example 3   13   A 3 m ladder has its foot 1.5 m out from the base of a wall. What angle does the ladder make with the ground? Answer correct to the nearest degree.

14   A shooter, 80 m from a target and level with it, aims 2 m above the bullseye and hits it. What is the angle, to the nearest minute, that his rifle is inclined to the line of sight from his eye to the target?

LEVEL 3

15   A rope needs to be fixed with one end attached to the top of a 6 m vertical pole and the other end pegged at an angle of 65° with the level ground. Find the required length of rope. Answer correct to one decimal place.

16   A wheelchair ramp is being provided to allow access to first floor shops. The first floor is 3 m above the ground floor. The ramp requires an angle of 20° with the horizontal. How long will the ramp be? Answer correct to two decimal places.

17   A plane maintains a flight path of 19° with the horizontal after it takes off. It travels for 4 km along the flight path. Find, correct to one decimal place:
   a   the horizontal distance of the plane from its take-off point.
   b   the height of the plane above ground level.

18   Two ladders are the same distance up the wall. The shorter ladder is 5 m long and makes an angle of 50° with the ground. The longer ladder is 7 m long. Find:
   a   the distance, correct to two decimal places, the ladders are up the wall
   b   the angle, to the nearest degree, the longer ladder makes with the ground.

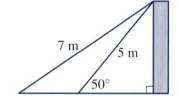

19   A pole is supported by a wire that runs from the top of the pole to a point on the level ground 7.2 m from the base of the pole. The height of the pole is 5.6 m. Find the angle, to the nearest degree, that the wire makes with the ground.

4B Angles of elevation and depression

The angle of elevation is the angle measured upwards from the horizontal. The angle of depression is the angle measured downwards from the horizontal.

ANGLE OF ELEVATION	**ANGLE OF DEPRESSION**

The angle of elevation is equal to the angle of depression as they form alternate angles between two parallel lines. This information is useful to solve some problems.

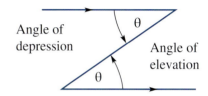

 ## Example 4: Angle of elevation 4B

A park ranger measured the top of a plume of volcanic ash to be at an angle of elevation of 41°. From her map she noted that the volcano was 7 km away. Calculate the height of the plume of volcanic ash. Answer correct to two decimal places.

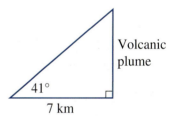

SOLUTION:

1 Draw a diagram and label the required height as x.

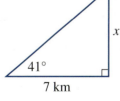

2 Determine the ratio (TOA). $\tan \theta = \dfrac{o}{a}$

3 Substitute the known values. $\tan 41° = \dfrac{x}{7}$

4 Multiply both sides of the equation by 7. $7 \times \tan 41° = x$

              $x = 7 \times \tan 41°$

5 Write the answer correct to two decimal places. $x = 6.085\,007\,165$

              $= 6.09$

6 Write the answer in words.   The height of the volcanic plume was 6.09 km.

Example 5: Finding a distance using angle of depression 4B

The top of a cliff is 85 m above sea level. Minh saw a tall ship. He estimated the angle of depression to be 17°.

a How far was the ship from the base of the cliff? Answer to the nearest metre.

b How far is the ship in a straight line from the top of the cliff? Answer to the nearest metre.

SOLUTION:

1 Draw a diagram and label the distance to the base of the cliff as x and the distance to the top of the cliff as y.

a

85 m, 17°, y, 17°, x

2 Determine the ratio (TOA).

$$\tan\theta = \frac{o}{a}$$

3 Substitute the known values.

$$\tan 17° = \frac{85}{x}$$

4 Multiply both sides of the equation by x.

$$x \times \tan 17° = 85$$

5 Divide both sides by $\tan 17°$.

$$x = \frac{85}{\tan 17°}$$
$$= 278.022...$$
$$\approx 278\,\text{m}$$

6 Write the answer correct to nearest metre.

7 Write the answer in words.

$\therefore$ The ship is 278 metres from the base of the cliff.

8 Determine the ratio (SOH).

b $$\sin\theta = \frac{o}{h}$$

9 Substitute the known values.

$$\sin 17° = \frac{85}{y}$$

10 Multiply both sides of the equation by y.

$$y \times \sin 17° = 85$$

11 Divide both sides by $\sin 17°$.

$$y = \frac{85}{\sin 17°}$$
$$= 290.7258...$$
$$\approx 291\,\text{m}$$

12 Write the answer correct to nearest metre.

13 Write the answer in words.

$\therefore$ The ship is 291 metres from the top of the cliff.

Exercise 4B

Example 4

1 Luke walked 400 m away from the base of a tall building, on level ground. He measured the angle of elevation to the top of the building to be 62°. Find the height of the building. Answer correct to the nearest metre.

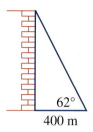

2 The angle of depression from the top of a TV tower to a satellite dish near its base is 59°. The dish is 70 m from the centre of the tower's base on flat land. Find the height of the tower. Answer correct to one decimal place.

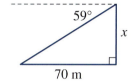

Example 5

3 When Sarah looked from the top of a cliff 50 m high, she noticed a boat at an angle of depression of 25°. How far was the boat from the base of the cliff? Answer correct to two decimal places.

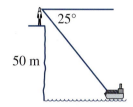

4 The pilot of an aeroplane saw an airport at sea level at an angle of depression of 13°. His altimeter showed that the aeroplane was at a height of 4000 m. Find the horizontal distance of the aeroplane from the airport. Answer correct to the nearest metre.

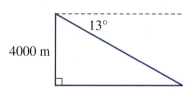

5 The angle of elevation to the top of a tree is 51° at a distance of 45 m from the point on level ground directly below the top of the tree. What is the height of the tree? Answer correct to one decimal place.

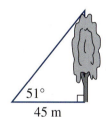

6 A iron ore seam 120 m slopes down at an angle of depression from the horizontal of 38°. The mine engineer wishes to sink a vertical shaft, x, as shown. What is the depth of the required vertical shaft? Answer correct to the nearest metre.

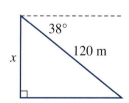

7 Jack measures the angle of elevation to the top of a tree from a point on level ground as 35°. What is the height of the tree if Jack is 50 m from the base of the tree? Answer to the nearest metre.

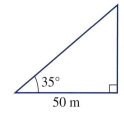

8 A tourist viewing Sydney Harbour from a building 130 m above sea level observes a ferry 800 m from the base of the building. Find the angle of depression. Answer correct to the nearest degree.

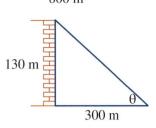

9 What would be the angle of elevation to the top of a radio transmitting tower 130 m tall and 300 m from the observer? Answer correct to the nearest degree.

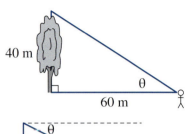

10 Lachlan observes the top of a tree at a distance of 60 m from the base of the tree. The tree is 40 m high. What is the angle of elevation to the top of the tree? Answer correct to the nearest degree.

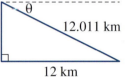

11 A town is 12 km from the base of a mountain. The town is also a distance of 12.011 km in a straight line to the top of the mountain. What is the angle of depression from the top of a mountain to the town? Answer correct to the nearest tenth of a degree.

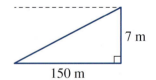

12 Find, to the nearest degree, the angle of elevation of a railway line that rises 7 m for every 150 m along the track.

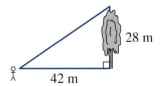

13 The distance from the base of the tree is 42 m. The tree is 28 m in height. What is the angle of elevation measured from ground level to the top of a tree? Answer correct to the nearest degree.

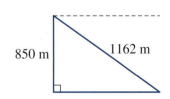

14 A helicopter is flying 850 m above sea level. It is also 1162 m in a straight line to a ship. What is the angle of depression from the helicopter to the ship? Answer correct to the nearest degree.

15 The angle of elevation to the top of a tree from a point A on the ground is 25°. The point A is 22 m from the base of the tree. Find the height of the tree. Answer correct to nearest metre.

16 A plane is 460 m directly above one end of a 1200 m runway. Find the angle of depression to the far end of the runway. Answer correct to the nearest minute.

17 A rocket launching pad casts a shadow 35 m long when the angle of elevation of the sun is 52°. How high is the top of the launching pad? Answer correct to nearest metre.

18 A communication tower is located on the top of a hill. The angle of elevation to the top of the hill from an observer 2 km away from the base of the hill is 6°. The angle of elevation to the top of the tower from the observer is 8°. Find, to the nearest metre, the height of the:

a hill

b hill and the tower

c tower.

19 Jack is on the top of a 65 m high cliff. He observes a man swimming out to sea at an angle of depression of 51°. Jack also sees a boat out to sea at an angle of depression of 30°. Find, to the nearest metre, the distance:

a *x* of the man from the base of the cliff

b *y* of the boat from the base of the cliff

c from the man to the boat.

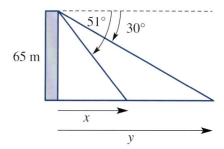

20 A lighthouse stands on the top of a cliff. A sailing boat is located 75 m from the base of the cliff. The angle of elevation to the top of the cliff and the top of the lighthouse is 42° and 50° respectively. Find the height of the lighthouse, correct to the nearest metre.

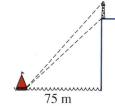

21 A plane is flying at an altitude of 880 m. Kayla is standing on the ground, she observes the angle of elevation to the plane as 67°40′ and 25 seconds later the angle of elevation had changed to 24°30′.

a How far had the plane flown in that time? Answer to the nearest metre.

b What is the speed (to the nearest km/h) of the plane?

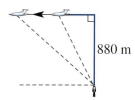

22 The angle of elevation from a boat out to sea to the top of a 350 m cliff is 13°. After the boat travels directly towards the cliff, the angle of elevation from the boat is 19°. How far did the boat travel towards the cliff? Answer correct to the nearest metre.

4C Compass and true bearings

A bearing is the direction one object is from another object or an observer or a fixed point. There are two types of bearings: compass bearings and true bearings.

Compass bearings

Compass bearings use the four directions of the compass: north, east, south and west (N, E, S and W). The NS line is vertical and the EW line is horizontal. In-between these directions are another four directions: north-east, south-east, south-west and north-west (NE, SE, SW and NW). Each of these directions makes an angle of 45° with the NS and EW lines.

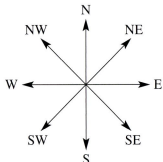

A direction is given using a compass bearing by stating the angle either side of north or south. For example, a compass bearing of S50°W is found by measuring an angle of 50° from the south direction towards the west side.

Example 6: Understanding a compass bearing 4C

Find the compass bearing of:
a A from O
b B from O.

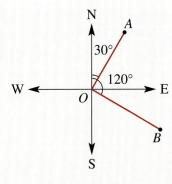

SOLUTION:

1	Determine the quadrant of the compass bearing.	**a** The line OA is in the north/east quadrant.
2	Find the angle the direction makes with the vertical (north/south) line.	30°
3	Write the compass bearing with N or S first, then the angle with the vertical line and finally either E or W.	Compass bearing of A from O is N30°E.
4	Determine the quadrant of the compass bearing.	**b** The line OB is in the south/east quadrant.
5	Find the angle the direction makes with the vertical (north/south) line.	$180° - 120° = 60°$
6	Write the compass bearing with N or S first, then the angle with vertical line and finally either E or W.	Compass bearing of B from O is S60°E.

True bearings

A true bearing is the angle measured clockwise from north around to the required
direction, and it is written with the letter T after the degree or minutes or seconds
symbol. True bearings are sometimes called three-figure bearings because they
are written using three numbers or figures. For example, 120°T is the direction
measured 120° clockwise from north. It is the same bearing as S60°E.

The smallest true bearing is 000°T and the largest true bearing is 360°T. The eight directions of the
compass have the following true bearings: north is 000°T, east is 090°T, south is 180°T, west is
270°T, north-east is 045°T, south-east is 135°T, south-west is 225°T and north-west is 315°T.

The bearings in the following diagrams are given using both methods.

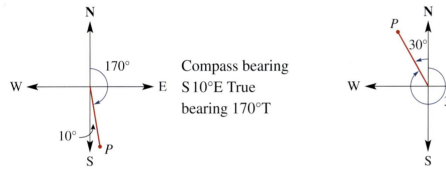

Compass bearing
S 10°E True
bearing 170°T

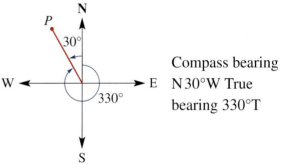

Compass bearing
N 30°W True
bearing 330°T

COMPASS BEARING	TRUE BEARING
A direction given by stating the angle either side of north or south, such as S60°E.	A direction given by measuring the angle clockwise from north to the required direction, such as 120°T.

Example 7: Understanding a true bearing   4C

Find the true bearing of:
a   C from O
b   D from O.

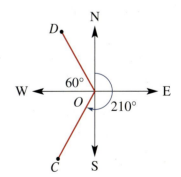

SOLUTION:

1	Find the angle the bearing makes in the clockwise direction with the north direction.	**a** 210°
2	Write the true bearing using this angle. Add the letter 'T'.	C from O is 210°T.
3	Write the true bearing of west.	**b** 270°T
4	Add angle between west and D to true bearing for west.	270° + 60° = 330°
5	Write the true bearing using this sum. Add the letter 'T'.	D from O is 330°T.

Exercise 4C

1 State the compass bearing and the true bearing of each of the following directions.
   a NE   **b** NW   **c** SE   **d** SW

Example 6, 7 **2** State the compass bearing and the true bearing of each of the following directions.

a
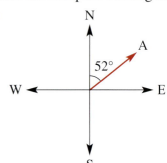

b
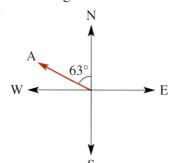

c
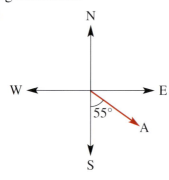

d
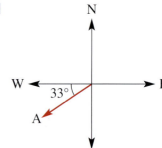

e
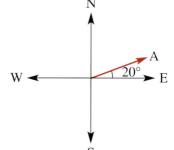

f
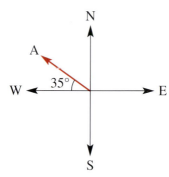

g

h

i
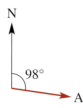

j
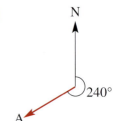

k
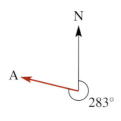

l
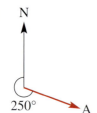

3 Sketch each of these bearings on a separate diagram.
   a N10°E   **b** S25°W   **c** N60°W   **d** S42°E
   e 300°T   **f** 105°T   **g** 219°T   **h** 050°T

4 Aaron runs a distance of 7.2 km in the SE direction. How far east
has Aaron run? Answer correct to one decimal place.

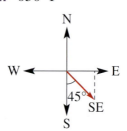

5 A plane is travelling on a true bearing of 030° from *A* to *B*.

   a What is the compass bearing of *A* to *B*?

   b What is the true bearing of *B* to *A*?

   c What is the compass bearing of *B* to *A*?

6 The diagram shows the position of *P*, *Q* and *R* relative to *S*. In the diagram, *R* is NE of *S*, *Q* is NW of *S* and ∠*PSR* is 155°.

   a What is the true bearing of *R* from *S*?

   b What is the true bearing of *Q* from *S*?

   c What is the true bearing of *P* from *S*?

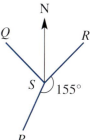

7 The bearing of *E* from *D* is N38°E, *F* is east of *D* and ∠*DEF* is 87°

   a Find the values of *x* and *y*.

   b What is the compass bearing of *E* from *F*?

   c What is the true bearing of *E* from *F*?

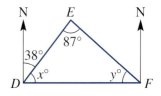

8 Riley travels from *X* to *Y* for 125 km on a bearing of N32°W.

   a How far did Riley travel due north, to the nearest kilometre?

   b How far did Riley travel due west, to the nearest kilometre?

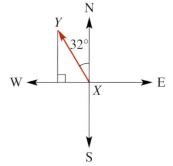

9 Mia cycled for 15 km west and then 24 km south.

   a What is the value of θ to the nearest degree?

   b What is Mia's true bearing from her starting point?

   c What is Mia's compass bearing from her starting point?

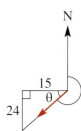

10 A boat sails 137 km from Port Stephens on a bearing of 065°T.

   a How far east has the boat sailed? Answer correct to one decimal place.

   b How far north has the boat sailed? Answer correct to one decimal place.

11 A ship sails 5 kilometres west, then 5 kilometres south.

   a What is the compass bearing of the ship from its original position?

   b What is the true bearing of the ship from its original position?

12 Harry travelled for 8.5 km on a bearing of S 30°W from his home.

   a How far west is Harry from home? Answer correct to two decimal places.

   b How far south is Harry from home? Answer correct to two decimal places.

   c What is the compass bearing of his home from his current position?

13 A cyclist rides 15 km on a bearing of 290°.

   a How far north is the cyclist? Answer correct to one decimal place.

   b How far west is the cyclist? Answer correct to one decimal place.

   c What is the true bearing of the cyclist's starting position from the cyclist's current position?

14 Amelia walked from point A for 1 hour in the direction N 51°E to reach point B. She then walked 2 hours heading south past C until she was at point D. Amelia was walking at constant speed of 5 km/h for the entire journey. Answer the following questions, correct to two decimal places where necessary.

   a What was the distance walked from A to B?

   b What was the distance walked from B to C?

   c What was the distance walked from C to D?

   d Calculate the distance between A and C.

   e Calculate the distance between A and D.

   f What is the compass bearing needed for Amelia to return to her starting point?

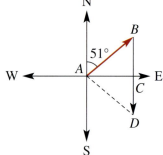

15 A plane left from O and travelled 350 km in the direction 225°T to reach P. It then changed direction and travelled due north for 500 km to reach point N.

   a What was the distance from P to M? (Answer correct to two decimal places.)

   b What was the distance from M to O? (Answer correct to two decimal places.)

   c What was the distance from M to N? (Answer correct to two decimal places.)

   d What is the angle θ, correct to the nearest degree?

   e What is the true bearing of N from O?

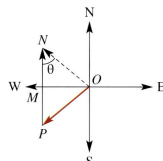

16 Oscar drives at a speed of 80 km/h on a bearing of 125°T for 2.5 hours. How far is Oscar east of his starting position? Answer to the nearest kilometre.

4D | Trigonometry with obtuse angles

When the angle θ is acute (0 to 90°) all the trigonometric ratios are positive. However, when the angle θ is obtuse (90° to 180°) the sine ratio is positive, the cosine ratio is negative and the tangent ratio is negative. These results are stored in the calculator's memory. For example, pressing cos 120° will result in −0.5, as 120° is an obtuse angle and the cosine ratio is negative. However, by pressing sin 120° the result is 0.866, as the sine ratio for an obtuse angle is positive.

ACUTE ANGLE (0 TO 90°)	OBTUSE ANGLE (90° TO 180°)
$\sin \theta$ – positive	$\sin \theta$ – positive
$\cos \theta$ – positive	$\cos \theta$ – negative
$\tan \theta$ – positive	$\tan \theta$ – negative

Example 8: Finding a trigonometric ratio of an obtuse angle 4D

Find the value of the following obtuse angles, correct to two decimal places.
a sin 164.25° **b** tan 124°30′

SOLUTION:

1 Press $\boxed{\sin}$ 164.25 $\boxed{\text{exe}}$ or =.

2 Press $\boxed{\tan}$ 124 $\boxed{\circ\prime\prime}$ $\boxed{\text{exe}}$ (or $\boxed{\text{DMS}}$) 30 $\boxed{\circ\prime\prime}$ $\boxed{\text{exe}}$ or =.

a sin 164.25° = 0.2714404499
= 0.27

b tan 124°30′ = 1.455009029
= −1.46

Example 9: Finding an obtuse angle from a trigonometric ratio 4D

a Given cos θ = −0.5178, find the value of θ to the nearest degree.
b Given tan θ = −1.32, find the value of θ to the nearest minute.

SOLUTION:

1 Press SHIFT $\boxed{\cos^{-1}}$ −0.5178 $\boxed{\text{exe}}$ or = .

2 Press SHIFT $\boxed{\tan^{-1}}$ −1.32 $\boxed{\text{exe}}$ or = .

3 To find the obtuse angle, add 180° to the negative angle (−52.85).

4 Convert the answer to minutes by using the $\boxed{\circ\prime\prime}$ or $\boxed{\text{DMS}}$.

a cos θ = −0.5178
θ = 121°

b tan θ = −1.32
θ = −52.8533133
= 180 − 52.8533133
= 127.1466867
= 127°09′

Exercise 4D

1 Without using a calculator, state whether these ratios are positive or negative.

    a $\tan 134°$ **b** $\sin 92°$ **c** $\cos 153°$

    d $\tan 178°$ **e** $\cos 142°30'$ **f** $\sin 100°10'$

    g $\cos 92°46'$ **h** $\tan 125°54'$

2 Find the value of the following trigonometric ratios, correct to two decimal places.

    a $\sin 140°$ **b** $\cos 91°$ **c** $\tan 115°$

    d $\cos 129°$ **e** $\tan 99°$ **f** $\sin 174°$

    g $\cos 156°$ **h** $\tan 168°$

Example 8   **3** Find the value of the following trigonometric ratios, correct to one decimal place.

    a $\sin 90°09'$ **b** $\cos 147°20'$ **c** $\tan 173°53'$

    d $\cos 102°35'$ **e** $\sin 92°51'$ **f** $\tan 123°54'$

    g $\tan 148°7'$ **h** $\cos 107°17'$

4 Find the value of the following trigonometric ratios, correct to two decimal places.

    a $5\tan 149°$ **b** $3\sin 105°$ **c** $10\cos 101°$

    d $12\tan 122°$ **e** $-3\sin 132°$ **f** $-8\cos 153°$

    g $-7\tan 163°$ **h** $-9\cos 108°$

Example 9   **5** Find the value of the obtuse angle θ to the nearest degree.

    a $\cos \theta = -0.4625$ **b** $\tan \theta = -0.6582$

    c $\sin \theta = 0.6291$ **d** $\tan \theta = -\dfrac{3}{4}$

    e $\cos \theta = -\dfrac{3}{8}$ **f** $\sin \theta = \dfrac{1}{2}$

6 Find the value of the obtuse angle θ to the nearest minute.

    a $\tan \theta = -1.7356$ **b** $\cos \theta = -0.5196$

    c $\sin \theta = 0.6456$ **d** $\cos \theta = -\dfrac{1}{5}$

    e $\tan \theta = -1\dfrac{1}{3}$ **f** $\sin \theta = \dfrac{4}{7}$

7 Find the value of the obtuse angle θ to the nearest degree.

    a $\cos \theta = -0.45$ **b** $\tan \theta = -1.85$

    c $\sin \theta = 0.83$ **d** $\tan \theta = -\dfrac{1}{6}$

    e $\cos \theta = -\dfrac{5}{7}$ **f** $\sin \theta = \dfrac{1}{4}$

8 The cosine ratio of an obtuse angle θ is -0.7. What is the value of θ, correct to the nearest minute?

9 Find the value of the following trigonometric ratios, correct to two decimal places.

a $\dfrac{5\sin 36°}{\sin 98°}$

b $\dfrac{7\sin 25°}{\sin 138°}$

c $\dfrac{4\sin 156°}{\sin 34°}$

d $\dfrac{11\sin 139°}{\sin 28°}$

e $\dfrac{6\sin 128°5'}{\sin 8°9'}$

f $\dfrac{2\sin 109°28'}{\sin 23°1'}$

g $\dfrac{8\sin 17°25'}{\sin 120°5'}$

h $\dfrac{3\sin 77°4'}{\sin 90°19'}$

10 Find the value of the obtuse angle θ to the nearest degree.

a $\tan\theta = -\dfrac{1}{\sqrt{3}}$

b $\cos\theta = -\dfrac{\sqrt{2}}{5}$

c $\sin\theta = \dfrac{\sqrt{3}}{2}$

d $\cos\theta = -\dfrac{\sqrt{3}}{2}$

e $\tan\theta = -\dfrac{7}{\sqrt{3}}$

f $\sin\theta = \dfrac{1}{\sqrt{2}}$

11 Find the value of the obtuse angle θ to the nearest minute.

a $\cos\theta = -\dfrac{2}{\sqrt{10}}$

b $\tan\theta = -\dfrac{\sqrt{11}}{2}$

c $\sin\theta = \dfrac{\sqrt{5}}{4}$

d $\tan\theta = -\dfrac{\sqrt{3}}{3}$

e $\cos\theta = -\dfrac{3}{\sqrt{11}}$

f $\sin\theta = \dfrac{\sqrt{10}}{8}$

12 Find the value of the obtuse angle θ to the nearest degree.

a $\tan\theta = -2:3$

b $\cos\theta = -1:5$

c $\tan\theta = -9:8$

d $\theta = \cos^{-1}(-2:9)$

e $\theta = \tan^{-1}(-1:2)$

f $\theta = \cos^{-1}(-5:6)$

13 Given that $\cos\theta = -0.8$ and angle θ is between $90°$ and $180°$, find the value of:

a θ to the nearest degree

b $\tan\theta$, correct to two decimal places

c $\sin\theta$, correct to one decimal place.

14 Given that $\tan\theta = -2.3$ and angle θ is between $90°$ and $180°$, find the value of:

a θ to the nearest minute

b $\cos\theta$, correct to three decimal places

c $\sin\theta$, correct to four decimal places.

4E Area of a triangle

The area of a triangle can be calculated in a triangle without a right angle. It requires that two sides and the included angle are known. The area of a triangle is half the product of two sides multiplied by the sine of the angle between the two sides (included angle).

This result is derived by constructing a perpendicular line of length h from B to D.

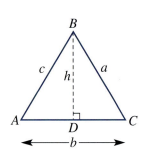

Area of a triangle is calculated using the formula:

$$A = \tfrac{1}{2}bh$$

In $\triangle BCD$, $\sin C = \dfrac{h}{a}$

$$h = a \sin C$$

Substituting $a \sin C$ for h into $A = \tfrac{1}{2}bh$

$$A = \tfrac{1}{2}ba \sin C$$
$$= \tfrac{1}{2}ab \sin C$$

Similarly, by constructing perpendiculars from C and A, we can obtain the other two results below.

AREA OF A TRIANGLE

$$A = \tfrac{1}{2}bc \sin A$$

$$A = \tfrac{1}{2}ac \sin B$$

$$A = \tfrac{1}{2}ab \sin C$$

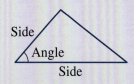

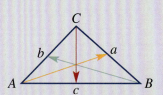

Area of a triangle is half the product of two sides multiplied by the sine of the angle between the two sides (included angle).

Example 10: Finding the area of a triangle

Find the area of the triangle to the nearest square centimetre.

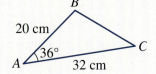

SOLUTION:

1 Write the formula.

2 We are given two sides b, c and the angle A between these sides (included angle).

3 Substitute values for b, c and A.

4 Evaluate.

5 Write, correct to the nearest square centimetre.

$$A = \tfrac{1}{2}bc \sin A$$

$$= \tfrac{1}{2} \times 32 \times 20 \times \sin 36°$$
$$= 188.0912807$$
$$= 188 \text{ cm}^2$$

Exercise 4E

Example 10

1 Find the area of each triangle, correct to one decimal place.

a
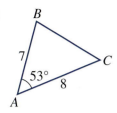

b
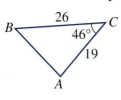

c
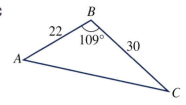

d
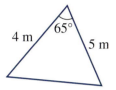

e
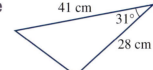

f
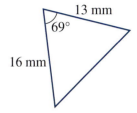

2 In triangle *ABC*, side *a* is 36 cm, side *b* is 48 cm and angle *C* is 68°. Find the area of the triangle. Answer correct to two decimal places.

3 In triangle *XYZ*, side *x* is 4 m, side *y* is 7 m and angle *Z* is 34°. Find the area of the triangle. Answer correct to two decimal places.

4 Find the area of triangle *DEF* if *DF* = 5 cm, *EF* = 6 cm and ∠*DFE* = 40°. Answer correct to the nearest square centimetre.

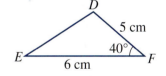

5 Find the area of each triangle, correct to one decimal place.

a
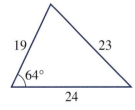

b
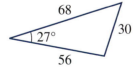

c
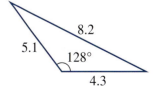

d
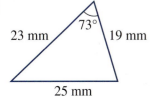

e
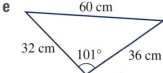

f
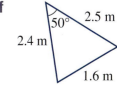

6   In triangle *DEF*, the length of *DF* is 21 cm, *EF* is 28 cm, ∠*FDE* is 64° and ∠*DEF* is 43°. Find the area of triangle *DEF* to the nearest square centimetre.

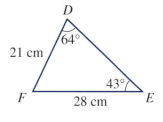

7   A parallelogram *PQRS* has *PS* = 4 cm, *SR* = 5 cm and ∠*PSR* = 40°.

   a   What is the area of triangle *PRS*? Answer correct to one decimal place.

   b   What is the area of parallelogram *PQRS*? Answer correct to one decimal place.

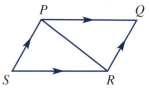

8   A drawing of a farmer's property is shown below.

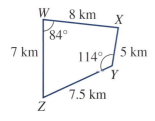

   a   What is the area of triangle *WXZ*? Answer correct to one decimal place.

   b   What is the area of triangle *XYZ*? Answer correct to one decimal place.

   c   Find the total area of the property in square kilometres. Answer correct to one decimal place.

9   The triangle *ABC* has an area of 243 m^2, *BC* = 30.1 m and ∠*BCA* = 54°21′. What is the length of *AC* in metres, correct to one decimal place?

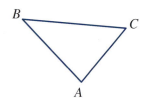

10   A rhombus *ABCD* has a side length of 13 cm and *ADC* = 64°35′. What is the area of the rhombus? Give the answer correct to the nearest square centimetre.

11   A triangle has an angle of 129°56′ with one arm of this angle 15 cm long. What is the length of the other arm of this angle if the area of the triangle is 69.94 cm^2? Answer correct to the nearest centimetre.

4F The sine rule

Trigonometry is also applied to non-right-angled triangles. The sides of the triangle are named according to the opposite angle.

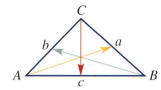

- Side a is opposite angle A.
- Side b is opposite angle B.
- Side c is opposite angle C.

The sine rule relates the sides and angles in a triangle. It states that 'Side a divided by the sine of angle A is equal to side b divided by the sine of angle B and is equal to side c divided by the sine of angle C'.

This result is derived by constructing a perpendicular line of length h from C to D.

$$\text{In } \triangle BCD, \sin B = \frac{h}{a} \qquad \text{In } \triangle ACD, \sin A = \frac{h}{b}$$

$$h = a \sin B \qquad\qquad h = b \sin A$$

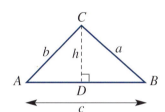

The values of h must be equal to each other.

$$a \sin B = b \sin A$$

$$\frac{a}{\sin A} = \frac{b}{\sin B}$$

Similarly, by constructing a perpendicular line from B it can be shown that

$$\frac{a}{\sin A} = \frac{c}{\sin C}$$

We can combine these two rules to obtain the result below.

THE SINE RULE

Sine rule relates the sides and angles in a triangle.

- To find a side, use $\dfrac{a}{\sin A} = \dfrac{b}{\sin B} = \dfrac{c}{\sin C}$

- To find an angle, use $\dfrac{\sin A}{a} = \dfrac{\sin B}{b} = \dfrac{\sin C}{c}$

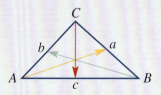

Sine rule is used in a non-right-angled triangle given:
- two sides and an angle opposite one of the given sides, or
- two angles and one side.

Example 11: Using the sine rule to find an unknown side 4F

Find the value of x, correct to one decimal place.

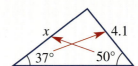

SOLUTION:

1 Check that the sides and angles are opposite each other.

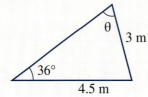

2 Write the sine rule to find a side.

$$\frac{a}{\sin A} = \frac{b}{\sin B}$$

3 Substitute the known values
($a = x$, $A = 50$, $b = 4.1$ and $B = 37$).

$$\frac{x}{\sin 50°} = \frac{4.1}{\sin 37°}$$

4 Multiply both sides of the equation by $\sin 50°$.

$$x = \frac{4.1 \times \sin 50°}{\sin 37°}$$

5 Evaluate.

$$= 5.218849806$$

6 Write the answer correct to one decimal place.

$$= 5.2$$

Example 12: Using the sine rule to find an unknown angle 4F

Hannah is standing 4.5 m from the base of a 3 m sloping wall. The angle of elevation to the top of the wall is 36°. Find the angle θ at the top of the wall, to the nearest minute.

SOLUTION:

1 Check that the sides and angles are opposite each other.

2 Write the sine rule to find an angle.

$$\frac{\sin A}{a} = \frac{\sin B}{b}$$

3 Substitute the known values
($a = 4.5$, $A = \theta$, $b = 3$ and $B = 36$).

$$\frac{\sin \theta}{4.5} = \frac{\sin 36°}{3}$$

4 Multiply both sides of the equation by 4.5.

$$\sin \theta = \frac{4.5 \times \sin 36°}{3}$$

5 Evaluate.

$$= 0.8816778784$$

6 Write the answer correct to the nearest minute.

$$\theta = 61°51'$$

7 Write the answer in words.

The angle at the top of the wall is 61°51'.

Exercise 4F   LEVEL 1

1 For each triangle, state the lengths of sides *a*, *b* and *c*.

a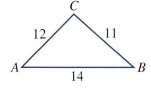

b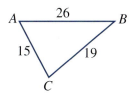

c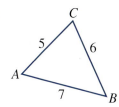

2 Find the value of *x*, correct to two decimal places.

a $x = \dfrac{5 \times \sin 65°}{\sin 46°}$

b $x = \dfrac{10 \times \sin 76°}{\sin 25°}$

c $x = \dfrac{3 \times \sin 100°}{\sin 18°}$

d $\dfrac{x}{\sin 40°} = \dfrac{8}{\sin 62°}$

e $\dfrac{x}{\sin 58°} = \dfrac{4}{\sin 78°}$

f $\dfrac{x}{\sin 21°} = \dfrac{29}{\sin 120°}$

Example 11 **3** For each triangle, find the length of the unknown side *x*, correct to two decimal places.

a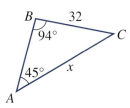

b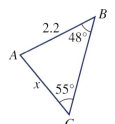

c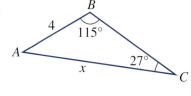

d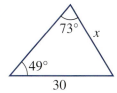

e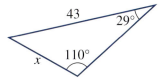

f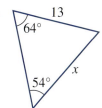

4 Find the length of the unknown side *x* in each triangle, correct to two decimal places.

a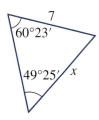

b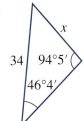

c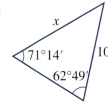

5 Given the following trigonometric ratios, find the value of A to the nearest minute.

a $\sin A = \dfrac{12 \times \sin 71°}{18}$

b $\sin A = \dfrac{25 \times \sin 65°}{32}$

c $\sin A = \dfrac{24 \times \sin 103°}{40}$

d $\dfrac{\sin A}{50} = \dfrac{\sin 53°20'}{65}$

e $\dfrac{\sin A}{187} = \dfrac{\sin 73°30'}{236}$

f $\dfrac{\sin A}{6} = \dfrac{\sin 61°46'}{7}$

Example 12 **6** Find the unknown angle θ. Answer to the nearest degree.

a

b
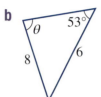

c
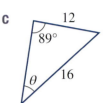

d
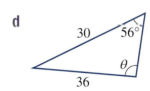

e
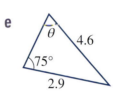

f
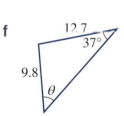

7 Find the unknown angle θ. Answer to the nearest minute

a
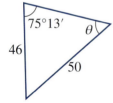

b
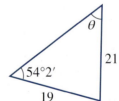

c
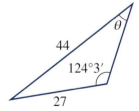

8 Find the value of the pronumeral in following questions, correct to two decimal places.

a In triangle ABC, $A = 56°$, $B = 75°$ and $a = 15$. Find b.

b In triangle XYZ, $X = 107°$, $Y = 45°$ and $x = 30$. Find y.

c In triangle PQR, $P = 118°$, $Q = 34°$ and $p = 59.5$. Find q.

9 Find the value of the pronumeral in following questions, correct to the nearest degree.

a In triangle DEF, $D = 46°$, $d = 10$ and $f = 5$. Find angle F.

b In triangle ABC, $B = 102°$, $b = 18$ and $c = 13$. Find angle C.

c In triangle RST, $R = 68°$, $r = 15$ and $t = 8$. Find angle T.

10 Find the length of the unknown side, x, in each triangle, correct to two decimal places.

a
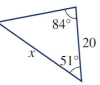

b
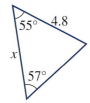

c
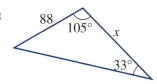

d
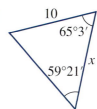

e
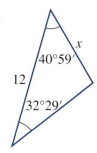

f
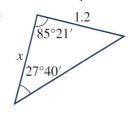

11 Benjamin is planning to build a triangular garden for his daughter. The vertices of the triangle are named PQR. He measured PQ as 2.7 m, QR as 3.1 m and $\angle PRQ$ as 57°. Use the sine rule to find the size of $\angle RPQ$, correct to the nearest degree.

12 Triangle ABC has $\angle ABC = 71°$, $\angle BCA = 69°$ and $\angle CAB = 40°$. The length of AB is 10.
  a What is the value of a, correct to one decimal place?
  b What is the value of b, correct to one decimal place?

13 Triangle XYZ has sides $YZ = 30$ cm, $XY = 24$ cm and $\angle YXZ = 54°$.
Use the sine rule to:
  a Find the size of angle XYZ. Give your answer to the nearest degree.
  b Find the size of y. Give your answer to the nearest centimetre.

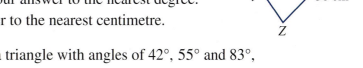

14 Find the length of the longest side of a triangle with angles of 42°, 55° and 83°, given that the length of the shortest side is 8.6 cm. Answer correct to one decimal place.

15 Sienna was located at *X* and saw a fire in the direction N15°E. Seven kilometres to the east of *X* at *Z*, Dylan saw the fire in the direction N50°W.

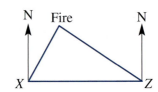

a How far is *X* from the fire? Answer in kilometres, correct to one decimal place.

b How far is *Z* from the fire? Answer in kilometres, correct to one decimal place.

16 A man at *R* measures the angle of elevation to a plane at *P* as 45°15′. The plane travels 15 km from *P* to *Q*. The man then measures the angle of elevation to the plane at *Q* as 35°42′.

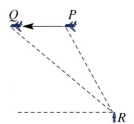

a What are the sizes of ∠*PRQ*, ∠*PQR* and ∠*QPR*?

b What is the distance from *R* to *P*? Answer in kilometres, correct to one decimal place.

c What is the distance from *R* to *Q*? Answer in kilometres, correct to one decimal place.

17 Chelsea is travelling due east from *A* to *B*. Unfortunately, the road is blocked and she makes a detour by travelling from *A* to *C* a distance of 30 km, on a bearing of 040°. Chelsea then turns and travels southeast until she reaches *B*.

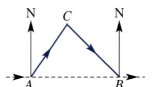

a What are the sizes of ∠*CAB* and ∠*CBA*?

b How far did Chelsea travel from *C* to *B*? Answer correct to the nearest kilometre.

c What was the extra distance travelled on the detour? Answer correct to the nearest kilometre.

LEVEL 3

18 Harrison measured the angle of elevation to the top of the mountain as 28°. He moved 140 m closer to the mountain and measured the angle of elevation to the top of the mountain as 43°. How far in a straight line is Harrison from the top of the mountain at his new position? Answer correct to the nearest metre.

19 The captain of a ship, *A*, sighted the smoke of a volcanic island in the direction N53°E. A captain on another ship, *B*, 30 km due east of the first ship saw the smoke in the direction N42°W.

a How far is ship *A* from the volcano? Answer correct to one decimal place.

b How far is ship *B* from the volcano? Answer correct to one decimal place.

c The ship closer to the volcano is travelling at 20 km/h. How long will it take for this ship to reach the volcano? Answer to the nearest minute.

4G The cosine rule

The cosine rule is another formula that relates the sides and angles in a triangle. It is applied to problems where three sides and one angle are involved. The cosine rule is derived by constructing a perpendicular line of length h from B to D. Let the distance from A to D be x and hence the distance from C to D is $(b - x)$.

In $\triangle ABD$ using Pythagoras' theorem:

$$c^2 = h^2 + x^2 \ldots \text{①} \Rightarrow h^2 = c^2 - x^2$$

In $\triangle ABD$, $\cos A = \dfrac{x}{c}$

$$x = c \cos A \ldots \text{②}$$

In $\triangle BCD$ using Pythagoras' theorem

$$\begin{aligned} a^2 &= h^2 + (b - x)^2 \\ &= h^2 + b^2 - 2bx + x^2 \\ &= h^2 + x^2 + b^2 - 2bx \\ &= c^2 + b^2 - 2bx & \text{From ①} \\ a^2 &= b^2 + c^2 - 2bc \cos A & \text{From ②} \end{aligned}$$

Similarly, by constructing perpendiculars from C and A, we can obtain the other two results below.

THE COSINE RULE

To find the third side given two sides and the included angle in $\triangle ABC$,

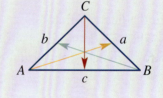

$$a^2 = b^2 + c^2 - 2bc \cos A \qquad (a \text{ is opposite } \angle A)$$
$$b^2 = a^2 + c^2 - 2ac \cos B \qquad (b \text{ is opposite } \angle B)$$
$$c^2 = a^2 + b^2 - 2ab \cos C \qquad (c \text{ is opposite } \angle C)$$

To find an angle given three sides (rearrangements of the above formulas):

$$\cos A = \frac{b^2 + c^2 - a^2}{2bc} \qquad \cos B = \frac{a^2 + c^2 - b^2}{2ac} \qquad \cos C = \frac{a^2 + b^2 - c^2}{2ab}$$

Example 13: Using the cosine rule to find an unknown side   4G

Find the value of x, correct to two decimal places.

SOLUTION:

1   Write the cosine formula to find a side. $c^2 = a^2 + b^2 - 2ab \cos C$

2   Substitute the values for a, b, c and C. $x^2 = 12^2 + 6^2 - 2 \times 12 \times 6 \times \cos 76°$

3   Calculate the value of x^2. $x^2 = 145.163247$

4   Take the square root of both sides. $x = 12.05$

Example 14: Using the cosine rule to find an unknown angle   **4G**

Find the value of the angle θ. Answer in degrees, correct to one decimal place.

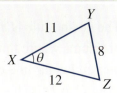

SOLUTION:

1 Write the cosine formula to find an angle. $\cos X = \dfrac{y^2 + z^2 - x^2}{2yz}$

2 Substitute the values for x, y, z and X $\cos \theta = \dfrac{(12^2 + 11^2 - 8^2)}{(2 \times 12 \times 11)}$
   ($x = 8$, $y = 12$, $z = 11$ and $X = \theta$).

3 Calculate the value of $\cos \theta$. $\cos \theta = 0.7613636364$

4 Use your calculator to find θ. $\theta = 40.41543902$

5 Write the answer correct to one decimal place. $= 40.4°$

Example 15: Solving a problem using the cosine rule   **4G**

Samuel shoots for goal when he is
2.5 m from one post and 3.2 m from
the other post. The goal is 2 m wide.
What is the size of the angle θ for
Samuel to score a goal? Answer
correct to the nearest minute.

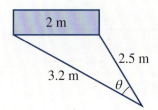

SOLUTION:

1 Write the cosine formula to find an angle. $\cos A = \dfrac{b^2 + c^2 - a^2}{2bc}$

2 Substitute the values for a, b, c and A $\cos \theta = \dfrac{(2.5^2 + 3.2^2 - 2^2)}{(2 \times 2.5 \times 3.2)}$
   ($a = 2$, $b = 2.5$, $c = 3.2$ and $A = \theta$).

3 Calculate the value of $\cos \theta$. $\cos \theta = 0.780625$

4 Use your calculator to find θ. $\theta = 38.68216452°$

5 Use your calculator to convert decimal $= 38°41'$
   degrees to degrees and minutes.

6 Write the answer in words.   The size of the angle for Samuel to score a goal
   is 38°41'.

Exercise 4G

Example 13   **1**   In each triangle, write the cosine rule with x^2 as the subject of the equation.

   a 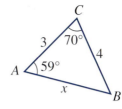   **b** 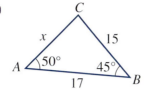   **c**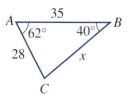

2   Find the value of the x, correct to one decimal place.

   a $x^2 = 3^2 + 4^2 - 2 \times 3 \times 4 \cos 39°$ **b** $x^2 = 7^2 + 10^2 - 2 \times 7 \times 10 \cos 135°$

   c $x^2 = 2^2 + 5^2 - 2 \times 2 \times 5 \cos 45°15'$ **d** $x^2 = 13^2 + 9^2 - 2 \times 13 \times 9 \cos 101°34'$

Example 14   **3**   Find the length of the unknown side x in each triangle, correct to two decimal places.

   a 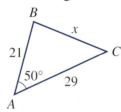   **b** 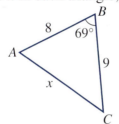   **c**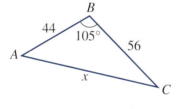

   d 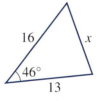   **e** 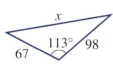   **f**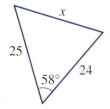

4   Find the length of the unknown side x in each triangle, correct to three decimal places.

   a 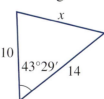   **b** 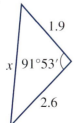   **c**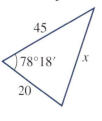

5   In the triangle ABC, $a = 24$, $b = 22$ and $C = 42°$. What is the value of side c? Answer correct to three significant figures.

6 Find the value of the angle A. Answer in degrees correct to two decimal places.

a $\cos A = \dfrac{7^2 + 9^2 - 6^2}{2 \times 7 \times 9}$

b $\cos A = \dfrac{16^2 + 20^2 - 24^2}{2 \times 16 \times 20}$

c $\cos A = \dfrac{4.9^2 + 3.4^2 - 5.7^2}{2 \times 4.9 \times 3.4}$

d $\cos A = \dfrac{3^2 + 4^2 - 6^2}{2 \times 3 \times 4}$

Example 15 **7** Find the size of the unknown angle θ. Answer to the nearest degree.

a
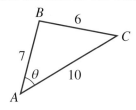

b
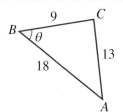

c
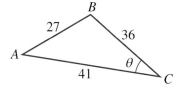

d
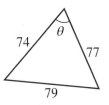

e
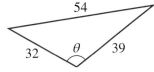

f
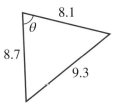

8 In the triangle ABC, $a = 10$, $b = 11$ and $c = 12$. What are the sizes of the following angles? Answer correct to the nearest minute.

a Angle A **b** Angle B **c** Angle C

9 In triangle XYZ, $XY = 8\,\text{cm}$, $YZ = 12\,\text{cm}$ and $XZ = 16\,\text{cm}$. What is the size of angle Y, to the nearest minute?

10 Find the size of the unknown angle θ. Answer to the nearest minute.

a
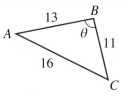

b
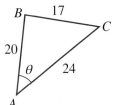

c
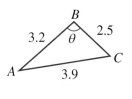

11 In triangle FGH, the length of GH is $14\,\text{cm}$, FH is $9\,\text{cm}$ and FG is $8\,\text{cm}$. Find $\angle HFG$, correct to the nearest minute.

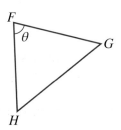

12 *DEF* is a triangle for which *DF* = 37 cm, *EF* = 46 cm and ∠*DFE* = 44°. Use the cosine rule to find the length of *DE*, to the nearest millimetre.

13 A triangle *RST* has ∠*RST* = 51°, ∠*STR* = 63°, *RT* = 40 and *RS* = 48.

   a What is the size of ∠*TRS*?

   b Find the length of *x* using the cosine rule. Answer correct to three significant figures.

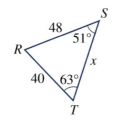

14 Ruby drives a four-wheel drive along a track from point *A* due west to a point *B*, a distance of 14 km. She then turns and travels 19 km to point *C*. Use the cosine rule to calculate the distance Ruby is from her starting point. Answer correct to one decimal place.

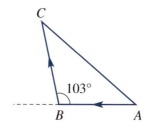

15 Passengers in a car travelling east, along a road that runs west–east, see a castle 10 km away in the direction N65°E. When they have travelled a further 4 km east along the road, what will be the distance to the castle? Answer correct to two decimal places.

16 A stepladder has legs of length 120 cm and the angle between them is 15°. Calculate the distance (to the nearest centimetre) between the legs on the ground.

17 A triangle has sides measuring 4 m, 5 m and 7 m.

   a What is the size of the smallest angle in this triangle? Answer in minutes.

   b What is the size of the largest angle in this triangle? Answer in minutes.

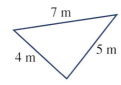

18 A running circuit is in the shape of a triangle with lengths of 6 km, 6.5 km and 7 km. What are the sizes of the angles (in minutes) between each of the sides?

19 The lengths of the sides of triangle *ABC* are in the ratio 7 : 8 : 9. Find the size of each angle, correct to the nearest minute.

Trigonometry is used to solve many practical problems. Use the steps below to solve them.

SOLVING A TRIGONOMETRIC WORD PROBLEM

1 Read the question and underline the key terms.
2 Draw a diagram and label the information from the question.
3 If the triangle is right-angled, use SOH CAH TOA.
4 If the triangle does not have a right angle:
   a use the sine rule if given two sides and two angles.
   b use the cosine rule if given three sides and one angle.
5 Check that the answer is reasonable and units are correct.

Example 16: Solving problems involving non-right-angled triangles   4H

The dimensions of a block of land are shown opposite.
a   What is the length of x, correct to the nearest metre?
b   What is the length of y, correct to the nearest metre?

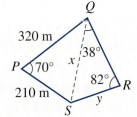

SOLUTION:

1 Looking at ΔPQS, three sides (including x) and one angle are given and the side we want to find (x) is opposite the known angle. Determine which rule fits this situation.

   a   Use the cosine rule in ΔPQS to find x.

2 Write the cosine rule to find a side, changing ABC to PQS to match the triangle in question.

   $$p^2 = q^2 + s^2 - 2qs \cos P$$

3 Substitute the values for p, q, s and P.

   $$x^2 = 210^2 + 320^2 - 2 \times 210 \times 320 \times \cos 70°$$

4 Evaluate to the nearest metre.

   $$x^2 = 100532.4927 \text{ so } x = 317.068 \approx 317\text{m}$$

5 Looking at ΔQRS, two sides (including y, and x is known from part **a**) and two angles are given, and the unknown side is opposite a known angle. Write out the rule that fits this situation.

   b   Use the sine rule to find a side in ΔQRS to find y.

   $$\frac{y}{\sin Y} = \frac{x}{\sin X}$$

6 Substitute the known values.

   $$\frac{y}{\sin 38°} = \frac{317.068}{\sin 82°}$$

7 Multiply both sides by $\sin 38°$.

   $$y = \frac{317.068 \times \sin 38°}{\sin 82°}$$

8 Evaluate to the nearest metre.

   $$= 197.125328 \approx 197 \text{ m}$$

   (Note: Do not use the approximate value from part **a** as it may result in an error.)

Example 17: Solving problems involving a triangle without a right angle 4H

Madison measures the angle of elevation to the top of a wall as 32°. She walks 10 m horizontally towards the wall and measures the angle of elevation as 51°. Find the height of the wall. Answer to the nearest metre.

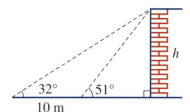

SOLUTION:

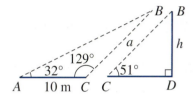

1 Draw a diagram consisting of two triangles.

2 Label each diagram.

3 To find the height of the wall h we need to calculate the value of a.

4 Looking at $\triangle ABC$ there are two sides (including a) and two angles. Determine which rule to use.

5 To calculate $\angle ABC$, use the angle sum of a triangle is 180°.

6 Write the sine rule.

7 Substitute the known values for b, A and B.

8 Multiply both sides of the equation by $\sin 32°$.

9 Evaluate.

10 Determine whether to use a trigonometric ratio or a rule to find h, and which one.

11 Write the ratio for SOH.

12 Substitute the known value of C.

13 Multiply both sides of the equation by a.

14 Evaluate using the exact value of a from step 9.

15 Write the answer correct to the nearest metre.

16 Write the answer in words.

Use the sine rule in $\triangle ABC$ to find a.

$\angle ABC = 180° - (32° + 129°) = 19°$

$$\frac{a}{\sin A} = \frac{b}{\sin B}$$

$$\frac{a}{\sin 32°} = \frac{10}{\sin 19°}$$

$$a = \frac{10 \times \sin 32°}{\sin 19°}$$

$$= 16.276753 \approx 16\text{m}$$

In $\triangle BCD$, D is a right angle. Use a trigonometric ratio SOH to find h.

$$\sin C = \frac{h}{a}$$

$$\sin 51° = \frac{h}{a}$$

$$a \times \sin 51° = h$$

$$h = a \times \sin 51°$$

$$= 12.64941286$$

$$\approx 12\text{m}$$

The wall is 12 m high.

Exercise 4H

1 The bearing of Y from X is 240° and the distance of Y from X is 20 km.

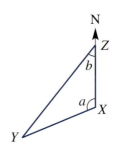

    a What is the value of a?

    b If Z is 18 km due north of X, calculate the distance of Y from Z, correct to the nearest kilometre.

    c What is the value of b to the nearest degree?

2 Andrew plans to build a triangular flower bed in the lower part of a circular garden. The length of TS is 24 m, $\angle TSR$ is 45° and ΔRTS is 40°.

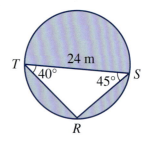

    a What is the size of $\angle SRT$?

    b Use the sine rule to find the length of TR. Answer correct to the nearest metre.

Example 16 **3** The diagram shows information about the locations of towns P, Q and R. Amber takes 2 hours and 30 minutes to walk directly from Town P to Town Q.

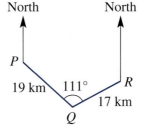

    a What is Amber's walking speed, correct to the nearest km/h?

    b What is the distance from P to R? Answer correct to the nearest kilometre.

    c How long would it take Amber to walk from P to R? Answer to the nearest minute.

4 M is 50 km north of O. The bearing of N from M is 108° and from O it is 061°. Answer the following questions to the nearest kilometre.

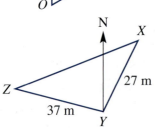

    a What is the distance between M and N?

    b What is the distance between N and O?

5 XYZ represents a triangular area of land. The bearing of X from Y is 041° and the bearing of Z from Y is 305°. The distance XY is 27 m and the distance YZ is 37 m.

    a What is the size of angle XYZ? Answer correct to the nearest degree.

    b Calculate the area of the land to the nearest square metre.

    c What is the length of the boundary XZ, to the nearest metre?

6 A ship is located at *B* and two radar stations 75 km apart are located at *A* and *C* (*C* is east of *A*). The bearing of the ship from one radar station is 038° and from the other radar station it is 306°.

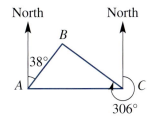

   a How far is the ship from the radar station at *A*, to the nearest kilometre?

   b How far is the ship from the radar station at *C*, to the nearest kilometre?

ample 17 **7** A triangle *DEG* has a right angle at *E* and *DG* is 8 m in length. A line is drawn from *D* to *F* with $\angle DFG = 144°$ and $\angle GDF = 7°$.

   a Find the length of *DF*. Answer correct to two decimal places.

   b Find the size of $\angle DFE$.

   c Find the length of *FE*. Answer correct to two decimal places.

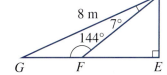

8 Two ladders are the same distance up the wall. The shorter ladder is 4.9 m long and makes an angle of 48° with the ground. The longer ladder is 6.7 m long.

   a How far up the wall do the ladders reach? Answer correct to one decimal place.

   b What is the angle, to the nearest degree, that the longer ladder makes with the ground?

   c Find the distance between the ladders on the ground. Answer correct to one decimal place.

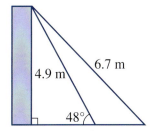

9 The angle of depression from *A* to *D* is 65°. The length of *AB* is 18 m and the length of *BD* is 16 m.

   a What is the size of $\angle ADB$? Answer in minutes.

   b Calculate the angle of elevation from *D* to *B*. Give your answer to the nearest minute.

   c Find the length of *AC*, correct to the nearest metre.

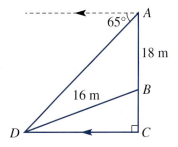

LEVEL 2

10 The diagram shows five roads: *DE*, *DG*, *EF*, *GE* and *GF*. The bearing of *FG* is 304°, *ED* is 292° and *DG* is 040°. The distance from *E* to *F* is 8 km and *E* is due west of *F*.

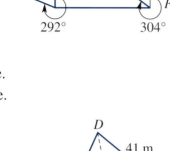

   a Find the size of ∠*GFE*.

   b What is the distance *GE*? Answer correct to one decimal place.

   c What is the size of ∠*DGE*, ∠*GED* and ∠*GDE*? Answer to the nearest degree.

   d What is the distance *DE*? Answer correct to one decimal place.

   e What is the distance *DG*? Answer correct to one decimal place.

11 A survey of a park is shown in the diagram. A path is proposed from *B* to *D* and a fence is required from *B* to *C* to *D*.

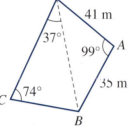

   a What is the length of the path? Answer correct to the nearest metre.

   b Calculate the required length of fencing. Answer correct to the nearest metre.

   c What is the area of the park? Answer correct to the nearest square metre.

LEVEL 3

12 Chris and Dylan are 55 m apart. They both observe a bird in the sky at *B*.

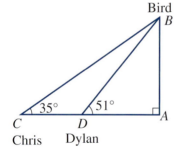

   a Prove that the distance between Dylan and the bird (*BD*) is given by:
$$BD = \frac{55 \sin 35°}{\sin 16°}$$

   b What is the distance between Chris and the bird? Answer correct to three significant figures.

   c How high is the bird above the ground? Answer correct to three significant figures.

13 A boat travels 90 km from point *X* to point *Y* on a bearing of 065°. It then turns and travels on a bearing of 140° from point *Y* to point *Z*. Point *Z* is on a horizontal line from its starting point (*X*).

   a What are the sizes of ∠*XYZ* and ∠*YXZ*?

   b How far is the boat from its starting point (*X* to *Z*)? Answer correct to two decimal places.

14 Investigate navigational methods used by Aboriginal and Torres Strait Islander peoples, and one other culture that uses different methods than those used covered in this chapter. You can use the weblinks provided in the Interactive Textbook.

Write a report outlining the methods used and show how they would be used to navigate from a starting point to a destination.

4I Radial survey

A radial survey is used to create a diagram of a piece of land that is in the shape of a polygon. It involves drawing lines from a central point radiating out to the corners of the polygon. The length of the lines and the angles between them at the central point (usually labelled O for 'origin) are measured.

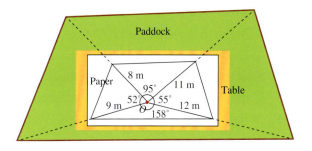

CONDUCTING A COMPASS RADIAL SURVEY

1 A 'plane table' (a surveyor's table) and large sheet of paper are placed in the centre of a field.
2 A point is marked near the middle of the paper and labelled O.
3 A line is drawn on the paper from O to reflect the line of sight to each corner (the radial line).
4 The distance from the O on the paper to the first corner on the land boundary is measured.
5 The length of the line is marked off on the line drawn on the paper using a suitable scale, e.g. 1 m on the ground is 1 cm on the paper.
6 Steps 3–5 are repeated to draw lines from O to every corner of the piece of land.
7 Boundary lines are drawn connecting the ends of the radial lines, representing the land boundary.
8 The angles at O between the radial lines are measured using a compass.

Example 18: Calculating area using a radial survey　　4I

The diagram shows a radial survey of a triangular piece of land.
What is the area of $\triangle ABC$?
Answer in square metres correct to one decimal place.

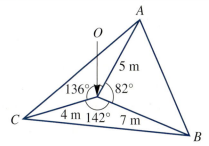

SOLUTION:

1 The three smaller triangles each have known angles between known side lengths. Use the sine rule for area of a triangle.

$$A = \tfrac{1}{2} \times a \times b \times \sin C$$

2 For each triangle, substitute the two sides and the included angle into the area formula, and evaluate.

In $\triangle ABO$:　$A = \dfrac{1}{2} \times 5 \times 7 \times \sin 82° = 17.330\,\text{m}^2$

3 Add up the areas correct to one decimal place.

In $\triangle BCO$:　$A = \dfrac{1}{2} \times 4 \times 7 \times \sin 142° = 8.619\,\text{m}^2$

In $\triangle ACO$:　$A = \dfrac{1}{2} \times 4 \times 5 \times \sin 136° = 6.947\,\text{m}^2$

Total area $= 17.330 + 8.619 + 6.947 = 32.9\,\text{m}^2$

 Example 19: Calculating distance using a compass radial survey **4I**

A compass radial survey for a field is shown opposite.

a What is the size of $\angle POQ$?

b What is the size of $\angle POR$?

c Calculate the length of PQ, correct to two decimal places.

d Calculate the length of PR, correct to two decimal places.

e What is the perimeter of the field? Answer correct to three significant figures.

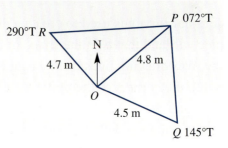

SOLUTION:

1 Subtract the bearing of P from the bearing of Q.

    a $\angle POQ = 145 - 72$

           $= 73°$

2 Calculate the angle between R and the north direction.

    b

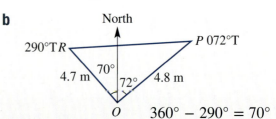

      $360° - 290° = 70°$

3 Identify the angle between P and the north direction from the bearing of P.

    $72°$

4 Add the two angles formed with the north direction ($70°$ and $72°$).

    $\angle POR = 70 + 72$

           $= 142°$

5 In $\triangle POQ$, $\angle POQ$ and two sides are known, so use the cosine formula to find a side (PQ is c).

    c $c^2 = a^2 + b^2 - 2ab \cos C$

6 Substitute the values for a, b, c and C.

    $x^2 = 4.8^2 + 4.5^2 - 2 \times 4.8 \times 4.5 \times \cos 73°$

7 Calculate the value of x^2.

    $x^2 = 30.65954236$

8 Take the square root of both sides.

    $x = 5.54 \, \text{m}$

9 Write the answer to two decimal places.

    Length PQ is 5.54 metres

10 Write the cosine formula to find a side.

    d $c^2 = a^2 + b^2 - 2ab \cos C$

11 Substitute the values for a, b, c and C.

    $x^2 = 4.7^2 + 4.8^2 - 2 \times 4.7 \times 4.8 \times \cos 142°$

12 Calculate the value of x^2.

    $x^2 = 80.6850452$

13 Take the square root of both sides.

    $x = 8.98 \, \text{m}$

14 Write the answer to two decimal places.

    Length PR is 8.98 metres

15 The field has four sides. Perimeter is the sum of the lengths of each side.

    e Perimeter $= 5.54 + 8.98 + 4.5 + 4.7$

             $= 23.72$

16 Write the answer to three sig.figs.

    $= 23.7 \, \text{m}$

Note: Point O, the origin, may be on the boundary of the piece of land, or even outside it.

Exercise 4I

Example 18

1 The diagram below shows a plane table radial survey of a piece of land. All length measurements are in metres.

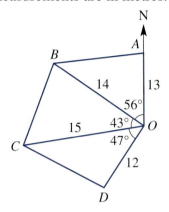

a What is the area of △AOB? Answer correct to two decimal places.

b What is the area of △BOC? Answer correct to two decimal places.

c What is the area of △COD? Answer correct to two decimal places.

d What is the total area of the piece of land? Answer to the nearest square metre.

e Find the length of AB, correct to two decimal places.

f Find the length of BC, correct to two decimal places.

g Find the length of CD, correct to two decimal places.

h Calculate the perimeter of the piece of land. Answer to the nearest metre.

Example 19

2 A radial survey of a triangular field is shown.

a What is the size of ∠AOB?

b What is the size of ∠BOC?

c What is the size of ∠AOC?

d What is the area of △AOB? Answer correct to two decimal places.

e What is the area of △BOC? Answer correct to two decimal places.

f What is the area of △AOC? Answer correct to two decimal places.

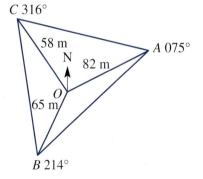

g What is the total area of the triangular field? Answer to the nearest square metre.

h What is the length of AB? Answer correct to two decimal places.

i What is the length of BC? Answer correct to two decimal places.

j What is the length of AC? Answer correct to two decimal places.

k Calculate the perimeter of the piece of land. Answer to the nearest metre.

LEVEL 2

3 A radial survey of land *DEFG* is shown opposite.
  a What is the size of ∠*FOG*?
  b Find the area of triangle *FOG* to the nearest square metre.
  c What is the length of *FG*, correct to the nearest metre?

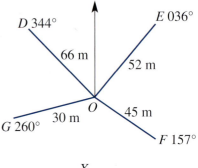

4 The diagram opposite is a compass radial survey of field *VWXYZ*. All distances are in metres. Answer the following questions, correct to one decimal place.
  a What is the length of *XY*?
  b What is the length of *ZY*?
  c What is the length of *VZ*?
  d What is the length of *VW*?
  e What is the length of *XW*?
  f Calculate the perimeter of the field.

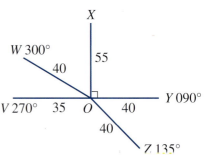

5 A radial survey of land *ABCD* is shown opposite. Answer the following questions correct to the nearest metre.
  a What is the area of Δ*AOB*?
  b What is the area of Δ*BOC*?
  c What is the area of Δ*COD*?
  d What is the area of Δ*AOD*?
  e What is the area of the land?

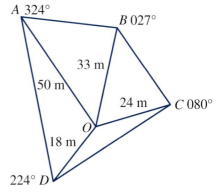

LEVEL 3

6 Alex, Blake and Connor are standing in a field. Connor (*C*) is 15 metres away from Blake (*B*) on a bearing of 032°. Alex (*A*) is 20 metres away from Blake on a bearing of 315°.
  a Draw a diagram to represent the positions *A*, *B* and *C*. Mark the information from the question on the diagram.
  b What is the size of the ∠*ABC* to the nearest degree?
  c What is the area of triangle *ABC*? Answer correct to the nearest square metre.
  d How far is Alex from Connor? Answer correct to the nearest metre.

Summary

Key ideas and chapter summary

Right-angled trigonometry	Use the mnemonic 'SOH CAH TOA'. SOH: **S**ine-**O**pposite-**H**ypotenuse CAH: **C**osine-**A**djacent-**H**ypotenuse TOA: **T**angent-**O**pposite-**A**djacent
Degrees and minutes	One degree is equal to 60 minutes ($1° = 60'$). One minute is equal to 60 seconds ($1' = 60''$).
Angles of elevation and depression	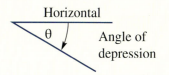
Bearings	Compass bearing A direction given by stating the angle either side of north or south, such as S60°E	True bearing A direction given by measuring the angle clockwise from north, such as 120°T

Bearings	Compass bearing A direction given by stating the angle either side of north or south, such as S60°E	True bearing A direction given by measuring the angle clockwise from north, such as 120°T
Trigonometry with obtuse angles	Acute angle (0 to 90°) $\sin\theta$ – positive $\cos\theta$ – positive $\tan\theta$ – positive	Obtuse angle (90° to 180°) $\sin\theta$ – positive $\cos\theta$ – negative $\tan\theta$ – negative

Area of a triangle	Area of a triangle is half the product of two sides multiplied by the sine of the angle between the two sides (included angle). $\qquad A = \dfrac{1}{2}bc\sin A$
The sine rule	Sine rule is used in a non-right-angled triangle given information about two sides and two angles. • To find a side, use $\dfrac{a}{\sin A} = \dfrac{b}{\sin B} = \dfrac{c}{\sin C}$. • To find an angle, use $\dfrac{\sin A}{a} = \dfrac{\sin B}{b} = \dfrac{\sin C}{c}$.
The cosine rule	Cosine rule is used in a non-right-angled triangle given information about three sides and one angle. • To find a side, use $a^2 = b^2 + c^2 - 2bc\cos A$. • To find an angle, use $\cos A = \dfrac{b^2 + c^2 - a^2}{2bc}$.
Radial surveys	Radial survey involves measuring the angles between radial lines drawn from a central point in the direction of the corners of the land, and measuring the lengths of the radial lines
Navigation by different cultures	Other cultures use different navigation methods relying on the stars, prevailing winds or currents, or landmarks that are recorded in various ways.

Multiple–choice

1 What is the length of a?

    A $14 \cos 63°$ **B** $14 \sin 63°$

    C $\dfrac{14}{\cos 63°}$ **D** $\dfrac{14}{\sin 63°}$

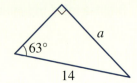

2 What is the correct expression for x?

    A $\dfrac{5 \times \sin 29°}{\sin 39°}$ **B** $\dfrac{5 \times \sin 39°}{\sin 29°}$

    C $\dfrac{5 \times \sin 112°}{\sin 39°}$ **D** $\dfrac{5 \times \sin 112°}{\sin 29°}$

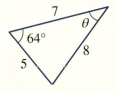

3 How would $\sin \theta$ be calculated?

    A $\dfrac{7 \sin 64°}{8}$ **B** $\dfrac{5 \sin 64°}{8}$

    C $\dfrac{5}{8 \sin 64°}$ **D** $\dfrac{7}{8 \sin 64°}$

4 What is the area of the triangle to the nearest square metre?

    A $115 \, \text{m}^2$ **B** $185 \, \text{m}^2$

    C $205 \, \text{m}^2$ **D** $220 \, \text{m}^2$

5 What is the correct formula for the cosine rule to find angle A?

    A $\cos A = \dfrac{a^2 + c^2 - b^2}{2ac}$ **B** $\cos A = \dfrac{a^2 + b^2 - c^2}{2ab}$

    C $\cos A = \dfrac{b^2 + c^2 - a^2}{2ab}$ **D** $\cos A = \dfrac{b^2 + c^2 - a^2}{2bc}$

6 What is the length of x? Answer correct to two decimal places.

    A 6.93 **B** 6.94

    C 48.14 **D** 48.15

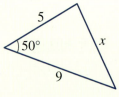

7 The largest angle in the triangle is θ. What is the value of $\cos \theta$?

    A $\cos \theta = \dfrac{6^2 + 7^2 - 5^2}{2 \times 6 \times 7}$ **B** $\cos \theta = \dfrac{5^2 + 7^2 - 6^2}{2 \times 5 \times 7}$

    C $\cos \theta = \dfrac{5^2 + 7^2 - 6^2}{2 \times 5 \times 7}$ **D** $\cos \theta = \dfrac{5^2 + 6^2 - 7^2}{2 \times 5 \times 6}$

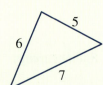

Review

Short-answer

1 Find the value of x, correct to two decimal places.

a
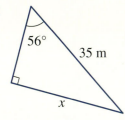
56°
35 m
x

b
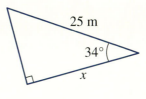
25 m
34°
x

c
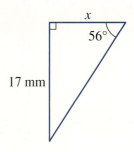
x
56°
17 mm

2 Find the unknown angle θ in each triangle. Answer correct to the nearest minute.

a
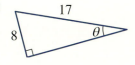
17
8
θ

b
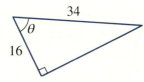
34
θ
16

c
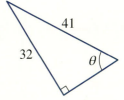
41
32
θ

3 Susan looked from the top of a cliff, 62 m high, and noticed a ship at an angle of depression of 31°. How far was the ship from the base of the cliff? Answer correct to one decimal place.

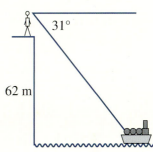
31°
62 m

4 Emma rode for 8.5 km on a bearing of N43°W from her home.

a How far north is Emma from home? Answer correct to one decimal place.

b How far west is Emma from home? Answer correct to one decimal place.

c What is the compass bearing of her home from her current position?

5 Find the value of the following trigonometric ratios, correct to two decimal places.

a $\tan 123°41'$

b $\cos 93°26'$

c $\sin 130°59'$

d $\cos 167°35'$

e $5\sin 134°$

f $7\tan 128°$

g $11\cos 149°$

h $4\tan 137°$

6 Find the value of the obtuse angle θ, to the nearest degree.

  a $\sin \theta = 0.5294$ **b** $\tan \theta = -0.1783$ **c** $\cos \theta = -0.2621$

  d $\cos \theta = -\dfrac{1}{8}$ **e** $\tan \theta = -\dfrac{3}{5}$ **f** $\sin \theta = \dfrac{1}{4}$

7 Find the length of the unknown side x in each triangle, correct to two decimal places.

  a 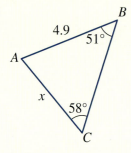   **b** 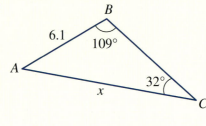   **c**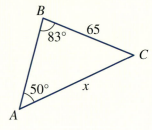

8 Find the length of the unknown side x in each triangle, correct to two decimal places.

  a 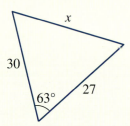   **b** 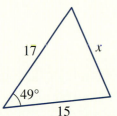   **c**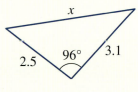

Extended-response

9 A radial survey of land ABC is shown opposite.

  a What is the size of $\angle AOB$?

  b Find the area of triangle AOB to the nearest square metre.

  c What is the length of AB, correct to the nearest metre?

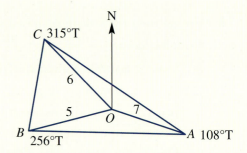

10 A triangle BCE has a right angle at C, $\angle BEC = 24°$ and BE is 20 m in length. A line is drawn from B to D with $\angle DBE = 29°$.

  a Find the length of BD. Answer correct to two decimal places.

  b Find the size of angle BDC. Answer correct to the nearest minute.

  c Find the length of CD. Answer correct to two decimal places.

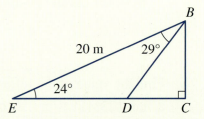

5 Simultaneous linear equations

Syllabus topic — A4.1 Simultaneous linear equations

This topic will develop your understanding of the use of simultaneous linear equations in solving practical problems.

Outcomes

- Graph linear functions.
- Interpret linear functions as models of physical phenomena.
- Develop linear equations from descriptions of situations.
- Solve a pair of simultaneous linear equations using graphical methods.
- Finding the point of intersection between two straight-line graphs.
- Develop a pair of simultaneous linear equations to model a practical situation.
- Solve practical problems by modelling with a pair of simultaneous linear functions.
- Apply break-even analysis to solve simple problems.

Digital Resources for this chapter

In the Interactive Textbook:

- Videos
- Literacy worksheet
- Quick Quiz
- Solutions (enabled by teacher)
- Desmos widgets
- Spreadsheets
- Study guide

In the Online Teaching Suite:

- Teaching Program
- Tests
- Review Quiz
- Teaching Notes

Knowledge check

The Interactive Textbook provides a test of prior knowledge for this chapter, and may direct you to revision from the previous years' work.

5A   Linear functions

A linear function makes a straight line when graphed on a number plane. The linear function $y = 3x - 2$ has two variables y and x. When a number is substituted for a variable, such as $x = 2$, then this variable is called the independent variable. The dependent variable depends on the number substituted for the independent variable. That is, when $x = 2$ (independent) then $y = 3 \times 2 - 2$ or 4 (dependent).

To graph a linear function, construct a table of values with the independent variable as the first row and the dependent variable as the second row. Plot these points on the number plane with the independent variable on the horizontal axis and the dependent variable as the vertical axis. Join the points to make a straight line.

GRAPHING A LINEAR FUNCTION

1   Construct a table of values with the independent variable as the first row and the dependent variable as the second row.
2   Draw a number plane with the independent variable on the horizontal axis and the dependent variable as the vertical axis. Plot the points.
3   Join the points to make a straight line.

Example 1: Drawing a linear function   5A

Draw the graph of $y = -2x - 1$.

SOLUTION:

1   Draw a table of values for x and y.

2   Let $x = -2, -1, 0, 1$ and 2. Find y using the linear function $y = -2x - 1$.

x	−2	−1	0	1	2
y	3	1	−1	−3	−5

3   Draw a number plane with x as the horizontal axis and y as the vertical axis.

4   Plot the points $(-2, 3)$, $(-1, 1)$, $(0, -1)$ and $(1, -3)$. The point $(2, -5)$ has not been plotted as it does not fit the scale of the number plane.

5   Join the points to make a straight line.

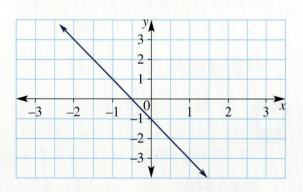

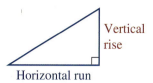

Gradient–intercept formula

When the equation of a straight line is written in the form $y = mx + c$ (or $y = mx + b$) it is called the gradient–intercept formula. The gradient is m or the coefficient of x. It is the slope or steepness of the line. The gradient of a line is calculated by dividing the vertical rise by the horizontal run. Lines that go up to the right (/) have positive gradients and lines that go down to the right (\) have negative gradients.

$$\text{Gradient (or } m) = \frac{\text{Vertical rise}}{\text{Horizontal run}}$$

The intercept of a line is where the line cuts the axis. The intercept on the vertical axis is called the y-intercept and is denoted by the letter c. (Previously in this course, b was used.)

GRADIENT–INTERCEPT FORMULA

Linear equation: $y = mx + c$.
m – Slope or gradient of the line (vertical rise over the horizontal run).
c – y-intercept. Where the line cuts the y-axis or vertical axis.

Example 2: Draw a graph from a table of values, find gradient and y-intercept   5A

Draw the graph of $y = 3x - 2$ from a table of values. Find the gradient and y-intercept of this line, and check that they form a linear equation that is the same as the original one.

SOLUTION:

1 Construct a table of values for x and y.

2 Let $x = -2, -1, 0, 1$ and 2. Find y using the linear function $y = 3x - 2$.

x	-2	-1	0	1	2
y	-8	-5	-2	1	4

3 Draw a number plane with x as the horizontal axis and y as the vertical axis.

4 Plot the points $(-1, -5)$, $(0, -2)$, $(1, 1)$ and $(2, 4)$. The point $(-2, -8)$ has not been plotted as it does not fit the scale of the number plane.

5 Join the points to make a straight line. Calculate the gradient of the line using the 'rise over run formula' and read the value of the y-intecept where the line crosses the vertical axis.

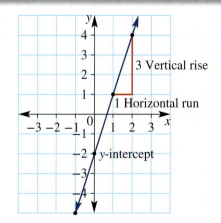

6 Write the values of the gradient and y-intercept.   Gradient m is 3, y-intercept c is -2.

7 Write equation of the line in the form $y = mx + c$. The gradient is the coefficient of x and the y-intercept is -2. $y = 3x - 2$

8 Compare this equation with the question.   The equations are the same.

Sketching a straight line requires at least two points. When an equation is written in gradient–intercept form, one point on the graph is immediately available: the y-intercept. A second point can be quickly calculated using the gradient.

Example 3: Sketching a linear function using the gradient and y-intercept   5A

Sketch the graph of $3y + 6x = 9$.

SOLUTION:

1	Rearrange the equation into gradient form $y = mx + c$.	$3y + 6x = 9$
2	Subtract $6x$ from both sides.	$3y = 9 - 6x$
3	Divide both sides by 3 and simplify.	$y = \dfrac{9 - 6x}{3}$
		$y = 3 - 2x$
4	The equation is now written in the form $y = mx + c$.	$y = -2x + 3$
5	Therefore $m = -2$ and $c = 3$.	Gradient is -2 and y-intercept is 3

6 A gradient of -2 means that for every unit across in the positive x-axis direction, you go down 2 in the negative y-axis direction.

7 Plot the y-intercept $(0, 3)$, then move across 1 (horizontal run) and down 2 (vertical rise) to plot the point $(1, 1)$.

8 Join the points $(0, 3)$ and $(1, 1)$ to make a s traight line.

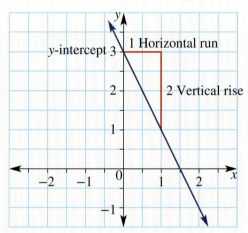

Parallel lines

Consider the linear function $y = 2x + 3$.
It has a gradient of 2 and y-intercept of 3.
Consider the linear function $y = 2x - 4$.
It has a gradient of 2 and y-intercept of -4.
The graph of these linear functions is shown opposite.
They are parallel because they both have the same gradient of $m = 2$.

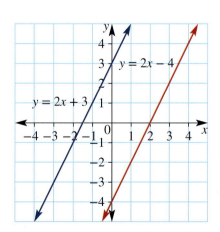

PARALLEL LINES

If the value of m is the same for two linear functions, then the lines are parallel.

Exercise 5A

1 Plot the following points on a number plane and join them to form a straight line.

a

x	−2	−1	0	1	2
y	2	1	0	−1	−2

b

x	−2	−1	0	1	2
y	−3	−1	1	3	5

2 Complete the following table of values and graph each linear function.

a $y = x − 1$

x	0	1	2	3	4
y					

b $y = −2x$

x	0	2	4	6	8
y					

c $y = 2x + 3$

x	−2	−1	0	1	2
y					

d $y = −x + 2$

x	−2	−1	0	1	2
y					

Example 1 3 Draw the graphs of these linear functions by first completing a table of values.

a $y = 2x + 2$

b $y = −x + 3$

c $y = \frac{2}{3}x − 1$

d $y = −\frac{1}{2}x + 1$

e $y = 3x − 1$

f $y = −2x + 3$

Example 2 4 Find the gradient of the following straight lines.

a $y = 5x + 1$

b $y = x − 2$

c $y = −2x$

d $y = \frac{1}{2}x + 4$

e $y = −\frac{2}{3}x + 3$

f $y = \frac{3}{4}x + \frac{1}{2}$

5 Find the y-intercept of the following straight lines.

a $y = 3x − 5$

b $y = −x + 2$

c $y = −4x$

d $y = −\frac{1}{3}x − 1$

e $y = −\frac{2}{5}x + 7$

f $y = \frac{1}{4}x + \frac{3}{5}$

6 Find the equation of the following straight lines defined by:

a gradient 2, passing through (0, 1)

b gradient −3, passing through (0, 4)

c gradient 0.5, passing through (0, −2)

d gradient 0, passing through (0, 6)

e gradient $−\frac{2}{5}$, passing through (0, 4)

f gradient $\frac{1}{3}$, passing through (0, 0).

7 What is the equation of each of the following line graphs?

a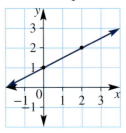

b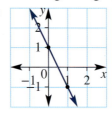

c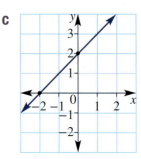

d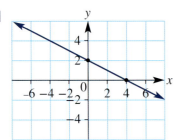

e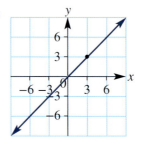

f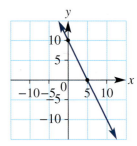

g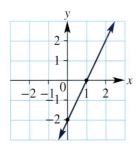

h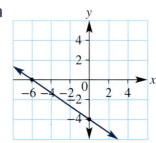

i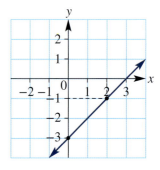

8 Which of the following lines are parallel?

    a $y = 2x + 1$ and $y = x + 2$ **b** $y = -2x + 4$ and $y = 2x + 4$

    c $y = 3x + 1$ and $y = 3x + 2$ **d** $y = -4x + 1$ and $y = -4x$

9 Find the equation of the line passing through each of the following pairs of points.

    a $(0, 3), (3, 0)$ **b** $(-2, 0), (0, 4)$

    c $(2, 0), (0, 2)$ **d** $(1, 0), (0, -1)$

    e $(-1, 0), (0, 3)$ **f** $(0, 4), (4, 2)$

10 Express the following linear equations in gradient–intercept form ($y = mx + c$).

    a $y + 2 = 3x$

    b $x + y - 4 = 0$

    c $y - \frac{1}{2}x = 1$

    d $4x - y + 2 = 0$

    e $\frac{1}{3}x - y = 1$

    f $4 - y = 3x$

11 Draw the graph of the linear functions in question **10** using a table of values.

Example 3   **12** Draw the graphs of these linear functions using the gradient and y-intercept.

    a $y = x + 2$

    b $y = -2x + 1$

    c $y = \dfrac{1}{3}x + 2$

    d $y = -\dfrac{1}{2}x - 1$

    e $y + 2 = x$

    f $3x - y = 0$

13 Consider the equation $2x - y + 5 = 0$.

    a What is the value of y when $x = 3$?

    b What is the value of x when $y = 21$?

    c Does the point $(6, 17)$ lie on the line?

    d What is the gradient and the y-intercept?

    e What is the equation of a line parallel to $2x - y + 5 = 0$ passing through $(0, -2)$?

    f Draw a graph of $2x - y + 5 = 0$.

14 Answer true or false to the following questions.

    a The point $(3, 0)$ lies on the line $y = 3x$.

    b The line $y = x - 7$ passes through the point $(1, -6)$.

    c The point $(1, 4)$ lies on the line $x + 2y = 9$.

    d The line $2x - 3y = 0$ passes through the point $(0, 0)$.

    e The point $(1, -1)$ lies on the line $4x - y + 1 = 0$.

    f The line $3x - 4y + 1 = 0$ passes through the point $(2, 0)$.

15 It is known that y varies directly with x. When $x = 3$ then $y = 12$.

    a Write a linear equation in the form $y = mx$ to describe this situation.

    b Draw the graph of y against x.

16 It is known that y varies directly with x. When $x = 6$ then $y = 2$.

    a Write a linear equation in the form $y = mx$ to describe this situation.

    b Draw the graph of y against x.

17 A motorcyclist is travelling at constant speed. He travels 350 km in 7 hours.

    a Write a linear equation in the form $d = mt$ to describe this situation.

    b Draw the graph of d against t.

5B Linear models

Linear modelling occurs when a practical situation is described mathematically using a linear function. For example, the gradient–intercept form of a straight-line graph can be used to model an iTunes collection. Logan owns 100 songs in his iTunes collection and adds 15 new songs each month. Using this information, we can write a linear equation to model the number of songs in his collection. Letting N be the number of songs and m be the number of months, we can write $N = 15m + 100$.

Note: The number of months (m) must be greater than zero and a whole number.

The graph of this linear model has been drawn opposite. There are two important features of this linear model:

1. Gradient is the rate per month or $15 \left(\dfrac{300}{20} \right)$ songs.

2. The vertical axis intercept is the initial number of songs or 100.

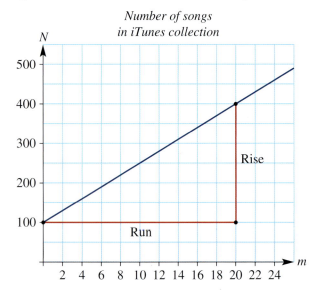

Number of songs in iTunes collection

LINEAR MODELS

Linear models describe a practical situation mathematically using a linear function.

Example 4: Using linear models   5B

The graph opposite is used to convert Australian dollars (AUD) to New Zealand dollars (NZD). Use the graph to convert:

a 40 AUD to NZD

b 25 NZD to AUD.

Australian dollars to New Zealand dollars

SOLUTION:

1 Read from the graph (when AUD = 40, NZD = 50).

a 50 NZD

2 Read from the graph (when NZD = 25, AUD = 20).

b 20 AUD

Example 5: Interpreting linear models 5B

Grace sells insurance. She earns a base salary and a commission on each new insurance policy she sells. The graph shows Grace's weekly income (*I*) plotted against the number of new policies (*n*) she sells in that week. The relationship between *I* and *n* is linear.

a What is Grace's base salary?

b What is Grace's salary in a week in which she sells 8 new policies?

c How many policies does Grace need to sell to earn $700 for the week?

d Find the equation of the straight line in terms of *I* and *n*.

e Use the equation to calculate the weekly income when Grace sells 3 new policies.

f How much does Grace earn for each new policy?

SOLUTION:

1 Read from the graph (when $n = 0$, $I = 400$).   a $400

2 Read from the graph (when $n = 8$, $I = 800$).   b $800

3 Read from the graph (when $I = 700$, $n = 6$).   c 6 new policies

4 Find the gradient by choosing two suitable points. (0, 400) and (8, 800).

d $m = \dfrac{\text{Rise}}{\text{Run}}$, $c = 400$

5 Calculate the gradient (*m*) between these points using the gradient formula.

$$= \frac{800 - 400}{8 - 0}$$
$$= 50$$

6 Determine the vertical intercept (400).

7 Substitute the gradient and *y*-intercept into the gradient–intercept form $y = mx + c$.

$$y = mx + c$$
$$I = 50n + 400$$

8 Use the appropriate variables (*I* for *y*, *n* for *x*).   e $I = 50n + 400$

9 Substitute $n = 3$ into the equation.

$$= 50 \times 3 + 400$$

10 Evaluate.

$$= \$550$$

11 Check the answer using the graph.

12 The gradient of the graph is the commission for each new policy.   f $50

Exercise 5B

1 Complete the following tables of values and graph each linear function.

a $c = d + 5$

c	0	1	2	3	4
d					

b $I = -3n$

I	0	2	4	6	8
n					

2 Draw the graph of these linear functions using a table of values from 1 to 10.

a $C = 2n + 10$ **b** $V = -5t + 30$ **c** $M = \frac{1}{2}n - 10$

Example 4

3 a The conversion graph opposite is used to convert Australian dollars to British pounds. Use the graph to calculate these exchanges.

   i 30 Australian dollars to pounds

   ii 50 Australian dollars to pounds

   iii 20 pounds to Australian dollars

   iv 10 pounds to Australian dollars

b What is the gradient of the conversion graph?

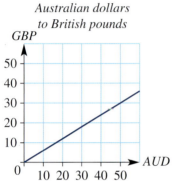

Australian dollars to British pounds

4 The relationship of the age of machinery (a) in years to its value (v) in $1000 is $v = -4a + 20$.

a Construct a table of values for age against value. Use values of a from 0 to 4.

b Draw the graph of age (a) against value (v).

c What is the initial cost of the machinery?

d What is the age of the machinery if its current value is $15000?

e What is the value of the machinery after $3\frac{1}{2}$ years?

f What will be the value of the machinery after 2 years?

g When will the machinery be worth half its initial cost?

Example 5

5 An ultrasound machine was purchased by a medical centre for $150 000. Its value is depreciated each month as shown in the graph.

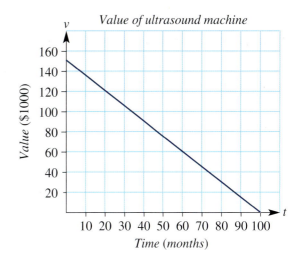

Value of ultrasound machine

a What was the value of the machine after 40 months?

b What was the value of the machine after five years?

c When does the line predict the machine will have no value?

d Find the equation of the straight line in terms of v and t.

e Use the equation to predict the value of the machine after 6 months.

6 A car is travelling at constant speed. It travels 360 km in 9 hours.

a Write a linear equation in the form $d = mt$ to describe this situation.

b Draw the graph of d against t.

7 The cost (C) of hiring a taxi consists of two elements: a fixed flagfall and a figure that varies with the number (n) of kilometres travelled. If the flagfall is $2.60 and the cost per kilometre is $1.50, determine a rule that gives C in terms of n.

8 The weekly wage, w, of a vacuum cleaner salesperson consists of a fixed sum of $350 plus $20 for each cleaner sold. If n cleaners are sold per week, construct a rule that describes the weekly wage of the salesperson.

9 A telecommunications company's rates for local calls from private telephones consist of a quarterly rental fee of $40 plus 25c for every call. Construct a linear rule that describes the quarterly telephone bill. Let C be the cost (in cents) of the quarterly telephone bill and n the number of calls.

10 Blake converted 100 Australian dollars (AUD) to 60 euros (EUR).

a Draw a conversion graph with Australian dollars on the horizontal axis and euros on the vertical axis.

b How many euros is 25 Australian dollars? Use the conversion graph.

c How many Australian dollars is 45 euros? Use the conversion graph.

d Find the gradient and vertical intercept for the conversion graph.

e Write an equation that relates Australian dollars (AUD) to euros (EUR).

11 A car rental company charges $85, plus an additional 24 cents per kilometre.

    a Write a rule to determine the total charge, $C, for hiring a car and travelling x kilometres.

    b What would be the cost to travel 250 kilometres?

12 An electrician charges $50 to call and $80 per hour. Assume that the relationship between charge and time is linear.

    a Find a formula for $C, the charge, in terms of the time spent (t hours).

    b Draw a graph of C against t.

    c Calculate the cost of a job that takes 2 hours 45 minutes to complete.

13 The cost of hiring a taxi is $5 flagfall and $1.50 per kilometre travelled.

    a Construct a table of values using 0, 10, 20, 30 and 40 as values for the kilometres travelled (d). Calculate the cost of the taxi hire (C) for each value of d.

    b Draw the graph of the kilometres travelled (d) against cost of the taxi hire (C).

    c Use the graph to find the cost of the taxi hire after travelling 15 kilometres.

    d Use the graph to find the distance travelled if the cost of the taxi hire was $35.

    e Find the gradient and vertical intercept for this graph.

    f Find the equation of the straight line in terms of d and C.

14 An electronic bank teller registered $775 after it had counted 120 notes and $975 after it had counted 160 notes.

    a Find a formula for the sum registered ($C) in terms of the number of notes (n) counted.

    b Was there a sum already on the register when counting began? If so, how much?

15 A printing firm charges $35 for printing 600 sheets of headed notepaper and $47 for printing 800 sheets.

    a Find a formula, assuming the relationship is linear, for the charge, $C, in terms of number of sheets printed, n.

    b How much would they charge for printing 1000 sheets?

16 The tyres on a racing car had lost 3 mm of tread after completing 250 km of a race and 4 mm of tread after completing 1000 km. Assuming that a linear relationship exists between loss of tread and distance covered, find the total loss of tread, d mm, after s km from the start of the race. What would be the tread loss by the end of a 2000 km race? Give your answer to one decimal place.

5C Simultaneous equations – graphically

Two straight lines will always intersect unless they are parallel. The point at which two straight lines intersect can be found by sketching the two graphs on the one set of axes and reading off the coordinates of the point of intersection. Finding the point of intersection is said to be 'solving the equations simultaneously'. In addition to graphing the straight lines, the point of intersection could be determined by looking at the table of values. If the same value for x and y occurs in both tables it is the point of intersection. See example below.

SOLVING A PAIR OF SIMULTANEOUS EQUATIONS GRAPHICALLY

1. Draw a number plane.
2. Graph both linear equations on the number plane.
3. Read the point of intersection of the two straight lines.
4. Interpret the point of intersection for practical applications.

Example 6: Finding the solution of simultaneous linear equations   5C

Find the simultaneous solution of $y = x + 3$ and $y = -2x$.

SOLUTION:

1. Use the gradient–intercept form to determine the gradient (coefficient of x) and y-intercept (constant term) for each line.

   $y = x + 3$
   Gradient is $+1$, y-intercept is 3.
   $y = -2x$
   Gradient is -2, y-intercept is 0.

2. Draw a number plane.
3. Sketch $y = x + 3$ using the y-intercept of 3 and a gradient of 1.
4. Sketch $y = -2x$ using the y-intercept of 0 and a gradient of -2.

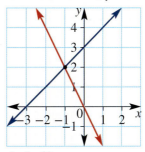

5. Find the point of intersection of the two lines.

   $(-1, 2)$

6. The simultaneous solution is the point of intersection.

   Simultaneous solution is $x = -1$ and $y = 2$, $(-1, 2)$.

7. Alternatively, construct a table of values for x and y. Let $x = -2, -1, 0, 1$ and 2. Find y using the linear function $y = x + 3$.

x	-2	-1	0	1	2
y	1	2	3	4	5

8. Repeat to find y using the linear function $y = -2x$.

x	-2	-1	0	1	2
y	4	2	0	-2	-4

9. The same value of x and y occurs in both tables when $x = -1$ and $y = 2$.

   Simultaneous solution is $x = -1$ and $y = 2$.

Exercise 5C

1 What is the point of intersection for each of these pairs of straight lines?

a

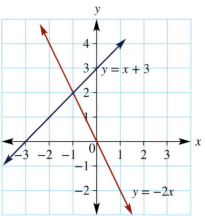

b

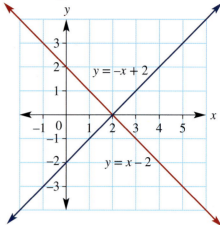

c

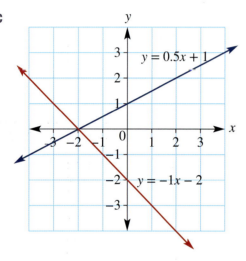

d

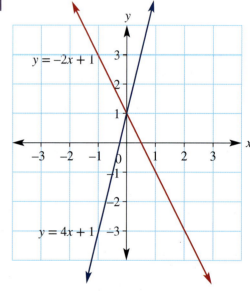

Example 6 **2** Plot the following points on a number plane and join them to form two straight lines. What is the point of intersection of these straight lines?

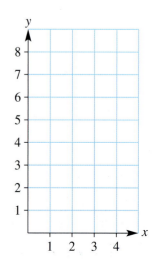

x	0	1	2	3	4
y	0	2	4	6	8

x	0	1	2	3	4
y	6	5	4	3	2

3 Plot the following points on a number plane and join them to form two straight lines. What is the point of intersection of these straight lines?

x	0	1	2	3	4
y	1	3	5	7	9

x	0	1	2	3	4
y	4	3	2	1	0

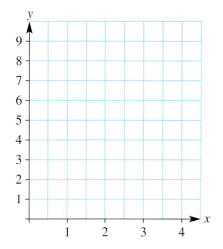

4 Plot the following points on a number plane and join them to form two straight lines. What is the point of intersection of these straight lines?

x	−2	−1	0	1	2
y	−6	−5	−4	−3	−2

x	−2	−1	0	1	2
y	6	3	0	−3	−6

5 Complete the following table of values and plot the points on a number plane. Find the simultaneous solution of these pairs of equations. All solutions are whole numbers.

a $y = 2x + 3$

x	−2	−1	0	1	2
y					

$y = -x$

x	−2	−1	0	1	2
y					

b $y = x + 4$

x	−2	−1	0	1	2
y					

$y = 2x$

x	−2	−1	0	1	2
y					

c $y = 3x + 1$

x	−2	−1	0	1	2
y					

$y = 5x - 3$

x	−2	−1	0	1	2
y					

6 Complete the following table of values and plot the points on a number plane. What is the solution to each pair of simultaneous equations? Some of the solutions are not whole numbers.

a $y = 3x - 3$ $\qquad\qquad\qquad\qquad$ $y = x + 1$

x	-2	-1	0	1	2
y					

x	-2	-1	0	1	2
y					

b $y = 3x - 2$ $\qquad\qquad\qquad\qquad$ $y = -x + 4$

x	-2	-1	0	1	2
y					

x	-2	-1	0	1	2
y					

c $y = x$ $\qquad\qquad\qquad\qquad\qquad$ $y = 4x + 3$

x	-2	-1	0	1	2
y					

x	-2	-1	0	1	2
y					

7 Draw the graphs of the following pairs of equations to find their simultaneous solution. Some of the solutions are not whole numbers.

a $y = -x$ and $y = 4 - 2x$
b $y = 5x + 1$ and $y = 3x - 7$
c $y = x + 1$ and $y = -2x$
d $y = 2x - 4$ and $y = -x + 5$
e $y = x + 1$ and $y = -3x + 2$
f $y = 8x - 10$ and $y = 4x$

8 Estimate the solution to each of the following pairs of simultaneous equations by graphing them on the same number plane. Answer correct to one decimal place.

a $4y = x$ and $x + y = 1$
b $x - y = 2$ and $1 + y = 3x$
c $x + y = 3$ and $y = 4x$
d $x = 2 + y$ and $8x + 4y = 7$
e $x - 2y = 1$ and $4x + 3y = 3$
f $4x + 3y = 4$ and $4x - 6y = 1$

5D [Enrichment] Simultaneous equations – algebraically

A linear equation such as $y = 2x + 3$ has two variables, x and y. It has many solutions; for example, $x = 0$ and $y = 3$ or $x = 1$ and $y = 5$. However, when there are two linear equations there is only one solution unless the two lines are parallel. The two equations are called simultaneous equations. The solution of the simultaneous equations represents the point of intersection of the two lines. There are two algebraic methods of solving simultaneous equations: substitution and elimination.

Method 1: Substitution

When solving simultaneous equations by substitution, the process is to substitute a variable from one equation into the other equation.

SIMULTANEOUS EQUATIONS: SUBSTITUTION METHOD

1. Make one pronumeral the subject in one of the equations.
2. Substitute the expression for this subject into the other equation.
3. Solve this new equation to find the value of one pronumeral.
4. Substitute this value into one of the equations to find the value of the second pronumeral.

Example 7: Solving simultaneous equations by substitution   **5D**

Solve this pair of simultaneous equations: $y = 2x + 3$ and $y = -x$.

SOLUTION:

1 Number the two equations as (1) and (2).	$y = 2x + 3$	(1)
	$y = -x$	(2)
2 Substitute the y-value from equation (2), which is $-x$, into equation (1).	$-x = 2x + 3$	
3 Solve the equation for x by subtracting $2x$ from both sides of the equation.	$-3x = 3$	
4 Divide both sides of the equation by -3.	$x = -1$	
5 To find y, substitute $x = -1$ into equation (2).	$y = -(-1) = 1$	
6 Check the solution by substituting $x = -1$ and $y = 1$ into equation (1).	Check: $y = 2x + 3$ $1 = 2 \times (-1) + 3$ True	
7 Write the answer in words.	Solution is $x = -1$ and $y = 1$, $(-1, 1)$.	

Method 2: Elimination

When solving simultaneous equations by elimination, one of the unknown pronumerals is eliminated by the process of adding or subtracting the two equations. To eliminate a pronumeral requires the coefficients of one pronumeral to be exactly the same or the same but opposite in sign.

SIMULTANEOUS EQUATIONS: ELIMINATION METHOD

1   Make sure that the two coefficients of one pronumeral are the same. This may require multiplying or dividing one or both equations by a number.
2   Eliminate one pronumeral by adding or subtracting the two equations.
3   Solve this new equation to find the value of one pronumeral.
4   Substitute this value into one of the equations to find the value of the second pronumeral.

Example 8: Solving simultaneous equations by elimination   **5D**

Solve the pair of simultaneous equations $y = 2x + 3$ and $y = -x$.

SOLUTION:

1	Number the two equations as (1) and (2).	$y = 2x + 3$ (1) $y = -x$ (2)
2	Subtract equation (2) from equation (1).	$y - y = 2x + 3 - (-x)$
3	To solve the equation for x, eliminate y (since $y - y = 0$) and add the like terms $(2x - (-x) = 3x)$.	$0 = 3x + 3$
4	Subtract $-3x$ from both sides of the equation.	$-3x = 3$
5	Divide both sides of the equation by $-3x$ to give x.	$x = -1$
6	To find y, substitute $x = -1$ into equation (2).	$y = -(-1) = 1$
7	Check the solution by substituting $x = -1$ and $y = 1$ into equation (1).	Check: $y = 2x + 3$ $1 = 2 \times (-1) + 3$ True
8	Write the answer in words.	Solution is $x = -1$ and $y = 1$, $(-1, 1)$.

The elimination method and the substitution method will result in the same solution. This is shown by Examples **7** and **8**. If the simultaneous equations have either x or y as the subject it is often easier to use the substitution method.

Exercise 5D

Example 7

1 Solve the following pairs of simultaneous equations using the substitution method.

a $x + y = 7$
$y = x + 3$

b $x + y = -3$
$y = x + 1$

c $y = 2x$
$x + 5y = 22$

d $x + 3y = -30$
$y = 3x$

e $y = 10 - 3x$
$2x - y = 10$

f $2x + y = 7$
$x = y - 4$

2 Make x or y the subject of one equation and then use the substitution method to solve the equations. Check all solutions.

a $x - y = 7$
$x + 2y = 4$

b $2x - y = 2$
$x + 2y = 11$

c $2x + y = 0$
$2x - y = -8$

d $2x + y = 7$
$x + y = 5$

e $x + 2y = 1$
$3x + y = 13$

f $2x + y = 6$
$2x - 3y = 4$

Example 8

3 Use the elimination method to solve these equations simultaneously by adding the equations.

a $2x - y = 1$
$x + y = 14$

b $x - 2y = 7$
$x + 2y = 3$

c $3x + 2y = 7$
$5x - 2y = 1$

d $-x + y = 6$
$x + 3y = 10$

e $x + 2y = -4$
$-x + 2y = 12$

f $4x + 2y = 9$
$5x - 2y = 0$

4 Use the elimination method to solve these equations simultaneously by subtracting the equations.

a $3x + y = 1$
$5x + y = 7$

b $7x + 2y = -1$
$10x + 2y = 2$

c $2x - y = 2$
$5x - y = 14$

d $5x - 3y = 8$
$5x - y = 16$

e $4x - 2y = 4$
$7x - 2y = 1$

f $3x + 5y = 17$
$2x + 5y = 20$

5 Solve the following pairs of simultaneous equations using the elimination method.

a $4x - 3y = -1$
$2x + 3y = 13$

b $8x + 4y = 4$
$8x - 2y = 34$

c $3x - 2y = 7$
$5x + 2y = 1$

d $x + y = 10$
$x - y = 4$

e $3x - 2y = 15$
$2x + 2y = 20$

f $x + 2y = 8$
$x - 2y = 4$

6 Solve the following pairs of simultaneous equations using the substitution method.

a $3p + 5q = 17$
$4p + 5q = 16$

b $4x - 3y = 6$
$-2x + 5y = 4$

c $3x + 5y = -11$
$-3x - 2y = 8$

d $4a + 3b = 6$
$2a - 6b = 18$

e $3x + 8y = 4$
$3x + 2y = -2$

f $5m - 2n = 20$
$3m - 4n = 12$

7 Multiply one of the equations by a constant and then use the elimination method to solve these pairs of simultaneous equations.

a $2x + 3y = 17$
$x + y = 7$

b $2a + b = 7$
$a + 2b = 11$

c $3x + 2y = 10$
$5x + y = 12$

d $x + 3y = 9$
$4x - y = 10$

e $4m - n = 6$
$3m + 2n = -1$

f $x + 3y = 7$
$5x - 2y = -16$

g $2x - 7y = 19$
$x + 2y = 4$

h $2x + y = 8$
$5x + 2y = -3$

i $x + 3y = 8$
$3x - y = 9$

8 In this question, make sure that the coefficients of x or y are the same in both equations of the pair. This may require multiplying or dividing one or both equations by a number. So for **a**, you could multiply the first equation by 3 to get $3 \times 4x + 3 \times 2y = 3 \times 0$, which becomes $12x + 6y = 0$. (When both sides of an equation are multiplied or divided by the same number, the equation remains true). So now the pair of equations both have 12 as the coefficient of x. As an alternative you could multiply the first equation by 3 and the second equation by 2 so that the coefficient of y is 6 in both equations. Then use the elimination method to solve these pairs of simultaneous equations.

a $4x + 2y = 0$
$12x - 3y = 18$

b $4x + 3y = 15$
$5x + 2y = 10$

c $3a - 7b = 2$
$9x + 5b = 32$

d $5m + 2n = 3$
$7m + 3n = 4$

e $5x + 2y = 28$
$3x + 5y = 51$

f $4x + 3y = -28$
$5x - 6y = -35$

9 Write a pair of simultaneous equations to represent the following problems. Find a solution to the simultaneous equations to solve the problem.

a The sum of two numbers is 38 and their difference is 24. What are the numbers?

b The sum of two numbers is 12, and one of the numbers is three times the other. Find the numbers.

c The sum of x and y is -4. When y is subtracted from $3x$ the result is 16. Find x and y.

d One apple and one orange cost $0.75. Two apples and three oranges cost $1.85. What is the cost of each fruit?

e Jack has twice as much money as Ruby. If I give Ruby $25, she will have three times as much as Jack. How much do Jack and Ruby have altogether?

5E Simultaneous equation models

When two practical situations are described mathematically using a linear function then the point of intersection has an important and often different meaning depending on the situation. For example, when income is graphed against costs the point of intersection represents the point where a business changes from a loss to a profit.

SIMULTANEOUS EQUATIONS AS MODELS

Simultaneous equation models use two linear functions to describe a practical situation and the point of intersection is often the solution to a problem.

Example 9: Using simultaneous equations as models   5E

Zaina buys and sells books. Income received by selling a book is calculated using the formula $I = 16n$. Costs associated in selling a book are calculated using the formula $C = 8n + 24$.

a What is the income when 6 books are sold?

b What is the costs when 6 books are sold?

c Draw the graph of $I = 16n$ and $C = 8n + 24$ on same number plane.

d Use the graph to determine the number of books needed to be sold for the costs to equal the income.

SOLUTION:

1 Substitute 6 for n into the formula for income $I = 16n$.

a $I = 16n = 16 \times 6 = 96$
∴ Income for six books is $96

2 Substitute 6 for n into the formula for costs $C = 8n + 24$.

b $C = 8n + 24 = 8 \times 6 + 24 = \$72$
∴ Costs for six books is $72

3 Draw a number plane.

4 Use the gradient–intercept form to determine the gradient and vertical intercept for each line. Gradient is the coefficient of n. Vertical intercept is the constant term.

5 Sketch $I = 16n$ using the vertical intercept of 0 and gradient of 16.

6 Sketch $C = 8n + 24$ using the vertical intercept of 24 and gradient of 8.

c

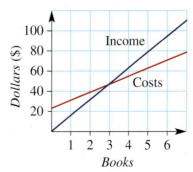

7 Find the point of intersection of the two lines (3, 48).

d Income is equal to costs when $n = 3$
∴ 3 books

Example 10: Solving problems using intersecting graphs   5E

Isabella's Mathematics mark exceeded her English mark by 15. She scored a total of 145 for both tests. Find Isabella's marks in each subject by plotting intersecting graphs.

SOLUTION:

1   Express the relationship between the Mathematics and the English mark as a linear equation.

Let the Mathematics mark be m.
Let the English mark be e.
$m = e + 15$

2   Use the gradient–intercept form to determine the gradient and vertical intercept for the line. Gradient is the coefficient of e. Vertical intercept is the constant term.

Gradient is 1,
vertical intercept is 15.

3   Express the total of the two marks as a linear equation.

$m + e = 145$

4   Use the gradient–intercept form to determine the gradient and vertical intercept for the line.

$m = -e + 145$
Gradient is -1,
vertical intercept is 145.

5   Draw a number plane.

6   Sketch $m = e + 15$ using the vertical intercept of 15 and gradient of 1.

7   Sketch $m = -e + 145$ using the vertical intercept of 145 and a gradient of -1.

8   The simultaneous solution is the point of intersection.

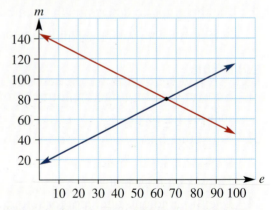

9   Find the point of intersection of the two lines.

Intersection is (65, 80) so $e = 65$ and $m = 80$

10   Write the solution in words using the context of the question.

Isabella scored 65 in English and 80 in Mathematics.

Exercise 5E

1 Matilda and Nathan have wages m and n respectively.
  a Matilda earns $100 more than Nathan. Write an equation to describe this information.
  b The total of Matilda's wages and Nathan's wages is $1200. Write an equation to describe this information.
  c Draw a graph of the two equations on the same number plane. Use n as the horizontal axis and m as the vertical axis.
  d Use the intersection of the two graphs to find Matilda's and Nathan's wages.

2 Let one number be represented by a and the other number by b.
  a The sum of the two numbers is 42. Write an equation to describe this information.
  b The difference of the two numbers is 6. Write an equation to describe this information.
  c Draw a graph of the two equations on the same number plane. Use a as the horizontal axis and b as the vertical axis.
  d Use the intersection of the two graphs to find the two numbers.

3 Let one number be represented by p and another number by q.
  a The sum of the two numbers is 15. Write an equation to describe this information.
  b One of the numbers is twice the other number. Write an equation to describe this information.
  c Draw a graph of the two equations on the same number plane. Use p as the horizontal axis and q as the vertical axis.
  d Use the intersection of the two graphs to find the two numbers.

4 Amy and Nghi work for the same company and their wages are a and b respectively.
  a Amy earns $100 more than Nghi. Write an equation to describe this information.
  b The total of Amy's and Nghi's wages is $1500. Write an equation to describe this information.
  c Draw a graph of the above two equations on the same number plane. Use a as the horizontal axis and b as the vertical axis.
  d Use the intersection of the two graphs to find Amy's and Nghi's wages.

Example 9 **5** A factory produces items whose costs are $1000 plus $10 for every item. The factory receives $60 for every item sold.
  a Write an equation to describe the relationship between the:
    i costs (C) and number of items (n)
    ii income (I) and number of items (n).
  b Draw a graph and find the number of items when income equals costs.

6 Let the cost of an apple be *a* and the cost of a banana be *b*.

  a One apple and one banana cost $1.25. Write an equation (using cents, not dollars) to describe this information.

  b Two apples and three bananas cost $3.25. Write an equation (using cents, not dollars) to describe this information.

  c Draw a graph of the two equations on the same number plane. Use *a* as the horizontal axis and *b* as the vertical axis.

  d Use the intersection of the two graphs to find the cost (in cents) of each fruit.

Example 10 **7** Let Zara's hourly wage rate be *a* and Ryan's hourly wage rate be *b*.

  a Zara's hourly wage rate and Ryan's hourly wage rate equals $70. Write an equation to describe this information.

  b Twice Zara's is the same as three times Ryan's wage rate. Write an equation to describe this information.

  c Draw a graph of the two equations on the same number plane. Use *a* as the horizontal axis and *b* as the vertical axis.

  d Use the intersection of the two graphs to find the wage rates.

8 A business has five times as many junior workers as it does senior workers. If the weekly wage for a senior is $800 and for a junior is $600, find how many of each are employed if the total weekly wage bill is $57 000.

9 A cinema has 2340 seats. All of the rows of seats in the cinema have either 50 seats or 45 seats. If there are three times as many rows with 50 seats as those with 45 seats, find the total number of rows in the cinema.

10 At a birthday party for 20 people each person could order chocolate or strawberry ice-cream. If there were four times as many orders for chocolate as for strawberry, how many orders were taken for chocolate ice-cream? How many people ordered strawberry?

The break-even point is reached when costs or expenses and income are equal. There is no profit or loss at the break-even point. For example, if the break-even point for a business is 100 items per month, the business will make a loss if it sells fewer than 100 items each month; if it sells more than 100 items per month, it will make a profit. A profit (or loss) is calculated by subtracting the costs from the income (Profit = Income – Costs). Income is a linear function of the form $I = mx$, where x is the number of items sold and m is the selling price of each item. Cost is a linear function of the form $C = mx + c$, where x is the number of items sold, m is the cost price per item manufactured and c is the fixed costs of production.

BREAK-EVEN ANALYSIS

Break-even point occurs when costs equal income.

Profit = Income − Costs

Income: $I = mx$

Costs: $C = mx + c$

Example 11: Interpreting the point of intersection of two graphs   **5F**

Grace buys and sells wallets. Income received by selling wallets is calculated using the formula $I = 30x$. Costs associated with selling wallets are calculated using the formula $C = 20x + 30$.

a Use the graph to determine the number of wallets that Grace needs to sell to break even.

b How much profit or loss does she make when four wallets are sold?

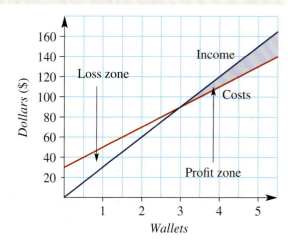

SOLUTION:

1 Consider when the break-even point occurs.	**a** When the income equals the costs.
2 Read the point of intersection of the two linear graphs.	Intersection is at (3, 90). So $x = 3$. Number of wallets $= 3$
3 Profit is determined by subtracting the costs from the income.	**b** Profit = Income − Cost
4 Read from the graph the values of I and C when $x = 4$.	$I = 120$ and $C = 110$
5 Evaluate.	$= 120 - 110$ $= \$10$
6 Write the answer in words.	Profit for selling 4 wallets is \$10.

 Example 12: Break-even analysis   5F

A firm sells its product at \$20 per unit. The cost of production (\$$C$) is given by the rule
$C = 4x + 48$, where x is the number of units produced.

a Find the value of x for which the cost of the production of x units is equal to the income or
revenue received by the firm for selling x units.

b Check your answer algebraically.

SOLUTION:

1 Set up the income equation and determine the gradient and vertical intercept.

a Let the income or revenue for producing x units be \$$I$. Formula is:
$$I = 20x$$
Gradient is 20, vertical intercept is 0

2 Set up the cost of production equation and determine the gradient and vertical intercept.

Cost of production (\$$C$) is given by:
$$C = 4x + 48$$
Gradient is 4, vertical intercept is 48

3 Draw a number plane.

4 Use x as the horizontal axis.

5 Use I and C as the vertical axis.

6 Sketch $I = 20x$ using the vertical intercept of 0 and gradient of 20.

7 Check this line using some valid points such as $(1, 20)$.

8 Sketch $C = 4x + 48$ using the vertical intercept of 48 and gradient of 4.

9 Check this line using some valid points such as $(1, 52)$.

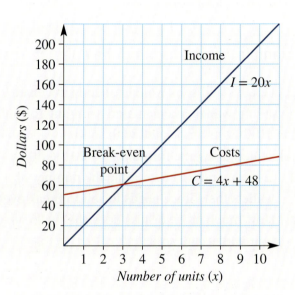

10 Read the value of x at the point of intersection of the two linear graphs.

The point of intersection of the two linear graphs occurs when $x = 3$. This is the break-even point, the value of x for which cost of production is equal to income.

11 Substitute $x = 3$ into the formula $I = 20x$.

12 Substitute $x = 3$ into the formula $C = 4x + 48$.

b Check algebraically.

Income	Costs
$I = 20x$	$C = 4x + 48$
$= 20 \times 3$	$= 4 \times 3 + 48$
$= 60$	$= 60$

13 Check that I is equal to C.

Income equals costs, so answer to **a** is correct.

Exercise 5F

Example 11

1 What is the break-even point for the following graphs?

a

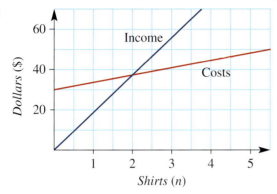

b

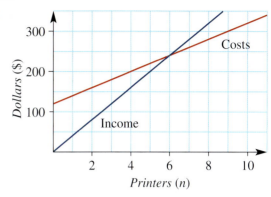

2 The graph on the right shows the cost of producing boxes of chocolates and the income received from their sale.

a Use the graph to determine the number of boxes that need to be sold to break even.

b How much profit or loss is made when 3 boxes are sold?

c How much profit or loss is made when 1 box is sold?

d What are the initial costs?

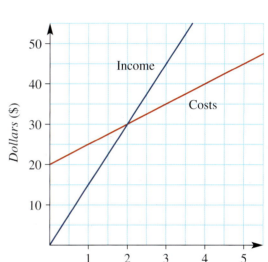

3 The graph on the right shows the cost of producing cartons of soft drinks and the income received from their sale.

a Use the graph to determine the number of cartons that need to be sold to break even.

b How much profit or loss is made when five cartons are sold?

c How much profit or loss is made when two cartons are sold?

d What is the initial cost?

e What is the gradient of the straight line that represents income?

f What is the vertical intercept of the straight line that represents income?

g Write an equation to describe the relationship between income and the number of cartons.

h What is the gradient of the straight line that represents costs?

i What is the vertical intercept of the straight line that represents costs?

j Write an equation to describe the relationship between costs and the number of cartons.

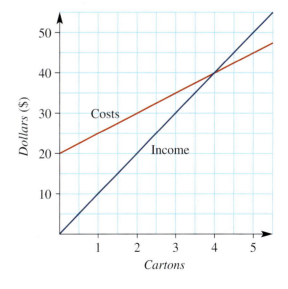

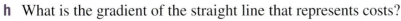

4 The graph on the right shows the cost of producing bottles of wine and the income received from their sale.

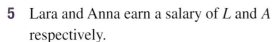
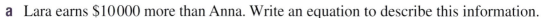

  a Use the graph to determine the number of bottles that need to be sold to break even.
  b Write an equation to describe the relationship between income and the number of bottles.
  c Write an equation to describe the relationship between costs and the number of bottles.

5 Lara and Anna earn a salary of L and A respectively.

  a Lara earns $10 000 more than Anna. Write an equation to describe this information.
  b The total of Lara's salary and Anna's salary is $150 000. Write an equation to describe this information.
  c Draw a graph of the above two equations on the same number plane. Use A ($1000) as the horizontal axis and L($1000) as the vertical axis.
  d Use the intersection of the two graphs to find Lara's and Anna's salaries.

Example 12

6 An industrial plant produces items whose costs are $250 plus $50 for every item. The plant receives $75 for every item sold.

  a Write an equation to describe the relationship between the:
    i costs (C) and number of items (x)
    ii income (I) and number of items (x).
  b Draw a graph to represent the costs and income for producing the item.
  c How many items need to be sold to break even?
  d Check your answer to part **c** algebraically.

7 Laura owns a nursery that grows native plants. It costs Laura $4000 per month to cover costs such as rent, water, electricity and wages. Each plant costs $5 and is sold for $17.50.

  a Write an equation to describe the relationship between:
    i the costs (C) and the number of plants (x)
    ii income (I) and the number of plants (x).
  b Draw a graph to represent the costs and income for producing the plants.
  c How many plants need to be sold each month to break even?
  d Check your answer to part **c** algebraically.

Key ideas and chapter summary

Summary

Linear functions	**1** Construct a table of values with the independent variable as the first row and the dependent variable as the second row. **2** Draw a number plane with the independent variable on the horizontal axis and the dependent variable as the vertical axis. Plot the points. **3** Join the points to make a straight line.
Gradient–intercept formula	Linear equation: $y = mx + c$. m – Slope or gradient of the line (vertical rise over the horizontal run). c – y-intercept Where the line cuts the y-axis or vertical axis.
Linear models	Linear models describe a practical situation mathematically using a linear function.
Simultaneous equations – graphically	**1** Draw a number plane. **2** Graph both linear equations on the number plane. **3** Read the point of intersection of the two straight lines. **4** Interpret the point of intersection for practical applications (break-even point).
[Enrichment] Simultaneous equations – algebraically	Substitution method Make one pronumeral the subject and substitute the expression for this subject into the other equation. Elimination method Eliminate one pronumeral by adding or subtracting the two equations.
Simultaneous equations as models	Simultaneous equation models use two linear functions to describe a practical situation and the point of intersection is often the solution to a problem.
Break-even analysis	Break-even point occurs when costs equals income. Profit = Income − Costs Income: $I = mx$ Costs: $C = mx + c$

Multiple-choice

1   What is the gradient of this line?

   A $-\dfrac{3}{2}$ **B** $-\dfrac{2}{3}$ **C** $\dfrac{2}{3}$ **D** $\dfrac{3}{2}$

2   What is the y-intercept of this line?

   A -2 **B** -1 **C** 1 **D** 2

3   A straight line has the equation of $y = -x - 3$. What is the
   y-intercept?

   A -3 **B** -1 **C** $+1$ **D** $+3$

4   The cost of manufacturing bags (C) is given by the formula $c = 40x + 150$, where x is the
   number of bags sold. What is the cost of manufacturing two bags?

   A $40   **B** $150   **C** $190   **D** $230

5   A car is travelling at a constant speed. It travels 80 km in 4 hours. This situation is described by
   the linear equation $d = mt$. What is the value of m?

   A 0.05   **B** 3   **C** 20   **D** 60

6   What is the point of intersection of the lines $y = x + 2$ and $y = -x + 2$?

   A $(2, 0)$ **B** $(0, 2)$ **C** $(0, -2)$ **D** $(1, 1)$

Use the graph below to answer questions 7–9.

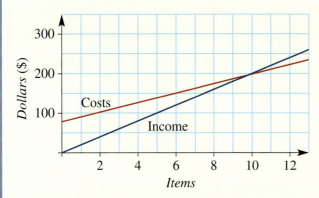

7   What is the profit for selling 12 items?

   A $10   **B** $20   **C** $220   **D** $240

8   What is the break-even point?

   A 10 items   **B** 12 items   **C** 20 items   **D** 80 items

9   What is the loss for selling 5 items?

   A $20   **B** $30   **C** $40   **D** $50

Short-answer

1 Draw the graph of these linear functions.

  a $y = x + 2$ **b** $y = -3x + 1$ **c** $y = 2x - 2$

2 Find the equation of the following straight-line graphs.

  a 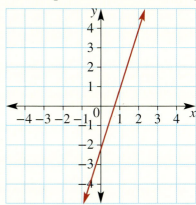   **b**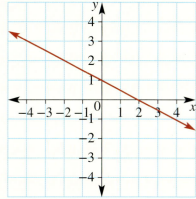

3 The table below shows the speed v (in km/s) of a plane at time t seconds.

Time (t)	1	2	3	4	5
Speed (v)	2.5	4	5.5	7	8.5

  a Draw a number plane with t as the horizontal axis and v as the vertical axis. Plot the points and join them to make a straight line.

  b Determine a linear model in the form $y = mx + c$ to describe this situation.

  c What does the model predict will be the plane's speed when $t = 2.5$ seconds?

  d What does the model predict will be the plane's speed when $t = 6$ seconds?

  e What does the model predict will be the plane's speed when $t = 7$ seconds?

  f What does the model predict will be the plane's speed when $t = 10$ seconds?

4 An internet access plan charges an excess fee of $12 per GB.

Data (d)	1	2	3	4	5	6
Cost (c)	12	24	36	48	60	72

  a Draw a graph of data against cost.

  b Use the graph to find d if c is 30.

  c Use the graph to find c if d is 3.5.

  d Estimate the cost of 7 GB of data.

  e Estimate the cost of 10 GB of data.

  f Estimate the cost of 8.5 GB of data.

5 What is the point of intersection of the lines $y = 3x + 3$ and $y = x - 2$?

6 The graph on the right shows the cost of making picture frames and the income received from their sale.

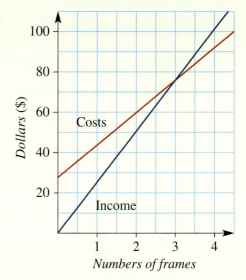

Numbers of frames

   a Use the graph to determine the number of picture frames that need to be sold to break even.

   b How much profit or loss is made when one picture frame is sold?

   c How much profit or loss is made when four picture frames are sold?

   d What is the initial cost?

7 The graph on the right shows the cost of manufacturing tables and the income received from their sale.

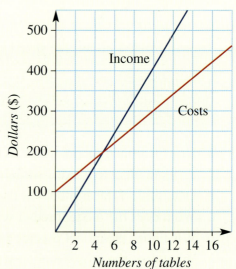

Numbers of tables

   a Use the graph to determine the number of tables which need to be sold to break even.

   b Write an equation to describe the relationship between income and the number of tables.

   c Write an equation to describe the relationship between costs and the number of tables.

   d How much profit or loss is made when 10 tables are sold?

   e How much profit or loss is made when 4 tables are sold?

   f How much profit or loss is made when 16 tables are sold?

Extended-response

8 Let the cost of item A be x and the cost of item B be y.

   a The total cost of both items is $1.80. Write an equation (using cents, not dollars) to describe this information.

   b One item A and two item B's cost $2.75. Write an equation (using cents, not dollars) to describe this information.

   c Draw a graph of the above two equations on the same number plane. Use x as the horizontal axis and y as the vertical axis.

   d Use the intersection of the two graphs to find the cost (in cents) of item A.

6

Bivariate data analysis

Syllabus topic — S4 Bivariate data analysis

This topic will introduce a variety of methods for identifying, analysing and describing associations between pairs of variables.

Outcomes

- Construct bivariate scatterplots to identify patterns in data.
- Use bivariate scatterplots to describe the patterns, features and associations of bivariate datasets.
- Identify the dependent and independent variables within bivariate datasets.
- Calculate and interpret Pearson's correlation coefficient to quantify the strength of a linear association of a sample.
- Model a linear association by fitting an appropriate line of best fit to a scatterplot and using it to describe patterns and associations.
- Model a linear association by fitting a least-squares regression line to the data.
- Use an appropriate line of best fit to make predictions by either interpolation or extrapolation.
- Implement the statistical investigation process that involves two numerical variables.

Digital Resources for this chapter

In the Interactive Textbook:
- Videos
- Literacy worksheet
- Quick Quiz
- Solutions (enabled by teacher)
- Desmos widgets
- Spreadsheets
- Study guide

In the Online Teaching Suite:
- Teaching Program
- Tests
- Review Quiz
- Teaching Notes

Knowledge check

The Interactive Textbook provides a test of prior knowledge for this chapter, and may direct you to revision from the previous years' work.

6A Constructing a bivariate scatterplot

Bivariate data is data that has two variables.

A scatterplot is used to determine if there is a relationship between two numerical variables. Data is collected on the two variables and often displayed in a table of ordered pairs. A scatterplot is a graph of the ordered pairs of numbers. Each ordered pair is a dot on the graph. To illustrate this process, a scatterplot has been constructed to determine the relationship between the height and arm span. The data collected on these variables is shown below in the table of ordered pairs.

Height (in cm)	172	159	178	162	156	174	151	162	165	185	186	176	166	180	158
Arm span (in cm)	172	162	182	164	159	180	151	165	168	189	188	184	167	184	161

Each person has two numerical variables, height and arm span. To construct a scatterplot, draw a number plane with the height on the horizontal axis and arm span on the vertical axis. Plot each ordered pair as a dot. The scatterplot shows there is a relationship between these variables.

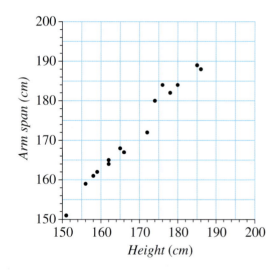

CONSTRUCTING A SCATTERPLOT

1 Draw a number plane.
2 Determine a scale and a title for the horizontal or *x*-axis.
3 Determine a scale and a title for the vertical or *y*-axis.
4 Plot each ordered pair of numbers with a dot.

Example 1: Reading a scatterplot   **6A**

The average numeracy score for year 6 students and their general rate of internet use (%) for 10 countries are displayed in the scatterplot below.

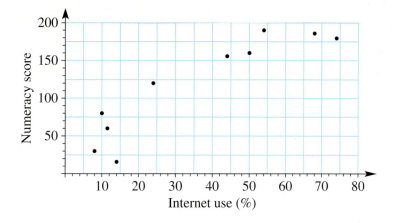

a What is the scale for the vertical axis?
b What is the average numeracy score for the country which has an internet use rate of 24%?
c What is the internet use (%) for the country which has an average numeracy score 160?
d How many countries have internet use of less than 50%?
e How many countries have a numeracy score greater than 100?
f Is there a relationship between these two variables?

SOLUTION:

1 Count the number of divisions between 0 and 50 (5). Therefore 1 unit is 50 divided by 5 (10).

a 1 unit = 10

2 Read from the scatterplot (when internet use is 24% the numeracy score is 120).

b 120

3 Read from the scatterplot (when the numeracy score is 160 the internet use is 50%).

c 50%

4 Count the number of dots less than 50% (left-hand side).

d 6 students

5 Count the number of dots greater than 100 (top-half).

e 6 students

6 Look for any pattern in the dots. In this scatterplot when the internet use is greater than 20%, there is a clear increase in the numeracy score. However, this relationship does not exist when the internet use is less than 20%.

f Yes, there is a relationship. When the internet use is greater than 20%, both the variables are increasing.

Exercise 6A

Example 1 **1** The scatterplot shows the results for 15 students in two tests.

a What is the highest mark in test 2?

b What is the lowest mark in test 1?

c What is the range for test 1?

d What is the mode for test 2

e How many students scored greater than 6 in test 1?

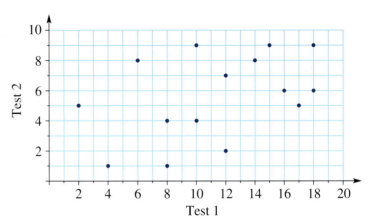

2 The scatterplot shows the head height to age for 10 people.

a What is the head height for the person who is 21 years old?

b What is the age of the person who has a head height of 22 cm?

c What is the largest head height?

d What is the age of the youngest person?

e How many people have a head height greater than 23 cm?

f Is there a clear relationship between these two variables?

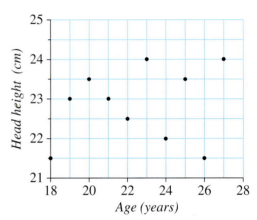

3 The table below shows the height (in cm) of a eucalypt tree seedling as it grows.

Time (in weeks)	0	1	2	3	4	5	6	7	8	9	10
Height (in cm)	0	6.6	8.8	9.0	10.5	12.0	13.5	15.2	15.4	15.8	15.9

a Copy the number plane opposite to construct a scatterplot using the above table.

b What is the increase in the height of the seedling during the first week?

c What is the increase in the height of the seedling during the last week?

d How many weeks does it take for the seedling to increase in height from 9 cm to 12 cm?

e Estimate the height of the seedling after 4.5 weeks.

f Estimate the time taken for the seedling to grow to a height of 14 cm.

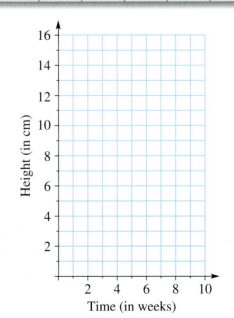

4 Adrian is a political commentator who has been studying the effects of television exposure time on the approval ratings of nine politicians. The data is shown below.

Time (in minutes)	5	15	15	75	25	70	40	55	20
Approval rating (%)	60	30	50	90	25	55	55	45	40

    a Construct a scatterplot of the data given in the table.

    b Are there any conclusions to be drawn from the scatterplot?

5 The table shows the number of runs scored and the number of balls faced by batsmen in a one-day cricket match.

Balls faced	49	29	26	16	19	13	16	10	28	40	6
Runs scored	47	27	10	8	21	3	13	6	15	30	2

    a Construct a scatterplot of the data given in the table.

    b Are there any conclusions to be drawn from the scatterplot?

6 The maximum wind speed and maximum temperature in a location were recorded for 2 weeks. The data is displayed in the table below.

Wind speed (in km/h)	2	6	12	15	19	20	22	25	17	14	5	11	24	13
Temperature (in °C)	28	26	23	22	21	22	19	16	20	24	25	24	19	26

    a Construct a scatterplot of the data given in the table.

    b Are there any conclusions to be drawn from the scatterplot?

7 The table below shows the age (in months) of six cars, and the minimum stopping distance (in metres) when the car is travelling at 60 km/h.

Age of car (in months)	48	12	65	42	98	34
Stopping distance (in metres)	29	28	38	35	36	37

    a Prepare a scatterplot using the above data.

    b Calculate the mean age of the car and the mean stopping distance. Answer correct to one decimal place.

    c Do you agree with the following statement? Justify your answer.

       'As a car gets older, its stopping distance increases.'

    d Are there any limitations when making predictions from this data?

6B   Using a bivariate scatterplot

What are the features in a scatterplot that will identify and describe any relationship? First look for a clear pattern. In the scatterplot opposite, there is no clear pattern in the points: they are just randomly spread on the scatterplot. There is no relationship or association between the variables.

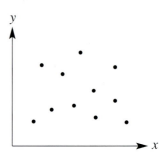

For the three examples below, there is a clear (but different) pattern in each set of points, so we conclude that there is an association in each case.

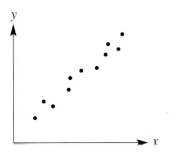 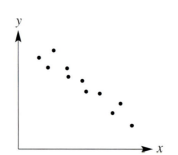 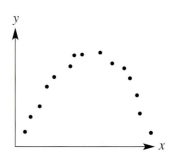

Having found a clear pattern, we need to be able to describe these associations clearly, as they are obviously quite different. There are three things we look for in the pattern of points: form, direction and strength.

Form of an association

If an association exists between the variables then the points in a scatterplot tend to follow a linear pattern or a curved pattern. This is called the form of an association.

Linear form

If the points seem to approximate a straight line, the association is a linear form.

Non-linear form

If the points seem to approximate a curve, the association is a non-linear form.

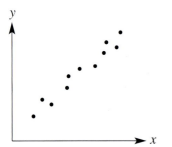 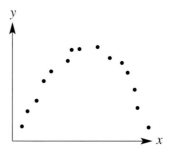

FORM OF AN ASSOCIATION

Linear form – when the points tend to follow a straight line.
Non-linear form – when the points tend to follow a curved line.

Direction of an association

There are two types of direction if the association is in linear form.

Positive

Positive association exists between the variables if the gradient of the line is positive. That is, the dots on the scatterplot tend to go up as we go from left to right.

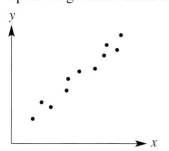

Negative

Negative association exists between the variables if the gradient of the line is negative. That is, the dots on the scatterplot tend to go down as we go from left to right.

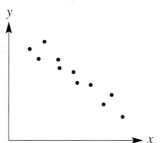

DIRECTION OF AN ASSOCIATION

Positive – gradient of the line is positive.
Negative – gradient of the line is negative.

Strength of an association

The strength of an association is a measure of how much scatter there is in the scatterplot.

Strong

In strong association the dots will tend to follow a single stream. A pattern is clearly seen. There is only a small amount of scatter in the plot.

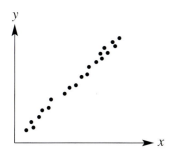

Moderate

In moderate association the amount of scatter in the plot increases and the pattern becomes less clear. This indicates that the association is less strong.

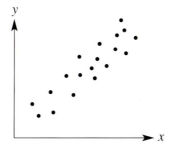

Weak

In weak association the amount of scatter increases further and the pattern becomes even less clear. Linear form is less evident.

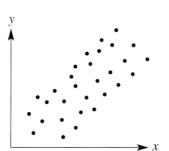

STRENGTH OF AN ASSOCIATION

Strong – small amount of scatter in the plot.
Moderate – modest amount of scatter in the plot.
Weak – large amount of scatter in the plot

Example 2: Describing bivariate datasets   **6B**

The table below shows the height (cm) and weight (kg) of nine people.

Height (*h*)	163	165	170	175	178	180	182	186	190
Mass (*m*)	55	60	64	66	65	70	71	74	78

a Construct a scatterplot using the above table.
b Describe the form of the association.
c Describe the direction of the association.
d Describe the strength of the association.
e Predict the mass of a person who is 173 cm tall using the scatterplot.
f Predict the height of a person who has a mass of 75 kg using the scatterplot.

SOLUTION:

1 Draw a number plane with *h* as the horizontal axis and *m* as the vertical axis.

a

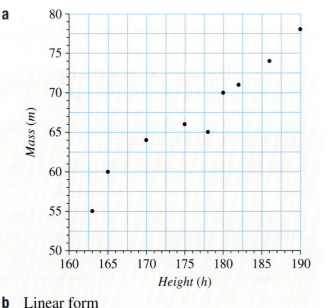

2 Determine a scale for the horizontal axis. Let each unit represent 1 cm.

3 Determine a scale for the vertical axis. Let each unit represent 1 kg.

4 Write titles for the horizontal and vertical axes.

5 Plot the points (163, 55), (165, 60), (170, 64), (175, 66), (178, 65), (180, 70), (182, 71), (186, 74) and (190, 78).

6 Look for a pattern. The points approximate a straight line.

b Linear form

7 Gradient of the line is positive. The dots tend to go up as you move from left to right.

c Positive

8 There is a small amount of scatter in the scatterplot.

d Strong

9 Draw an imaginary vertical line from 173 cm.

10 Try to maintain the linear relationship and guess the weight.

e The person weighs approximately 65 kg.

11 Draw an imaginary horizontal line from 75 kg.

12 Try to maintain the linear relationship and guess the height.

f The person's height is approximately 187 cm.

Independent and dependent variables

Bivariate data has two variables that are often identified as the independent and dependent variables. The independent variable is the input. It is not affected by the other variable and is represented on the horizontal axis of the scatterplot. The dependent variable is the output and is 'dependent' on the independent variable. It is represented on the vertical axis of a scatterplot.

Example 3: Identifying independent and dependent variables   6B

The table below shows the time taken (hours) relative to the distance travelled (km).

Distance (d)	0	10	20	30	40	50
Time (t)	0	0.25	0.38	0.59	0.82	1.00

a   Draw a scatterplot using the above table.
b   Which are the independent and dependent variables?

SOLUTION:

1   Draw a number plane with d as the horizontal axis and t as the vertical axis.

2   Determine a scale for the horizontal axis. Let each unit represent 10 km.

3   Determine a scale for the vertical axis. Let each unit represent 0.2 hours.

4   Write titles for the horizontal and vertical axes.

5   Plot the points $(0, 0)$ $(10, 0.25)$ $(20, 0.38)$ $(30, 0.59)$ $(40, 0.82)$ $(50, 1)$.

a
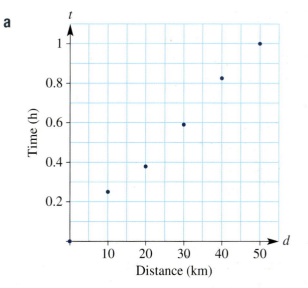

6   The independent variable is the input and represented on the horizontal axis of the scatterplot.

7   The dependent variable is the output and represented on the vertical axis of the scatterplot.

b   Independent variable is distance (d).

Dependent variable is time (t).

Exercise 6B

Example 2 **1** Describe the association in the following scatterplots as:

  i linear or non-linear   **ii** positive or negative

  iii strong, moderate or weak.

a
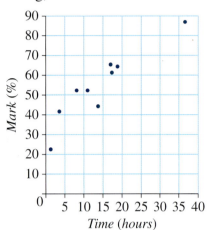

b
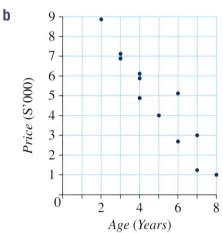

c
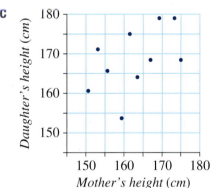

d
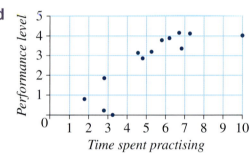

e
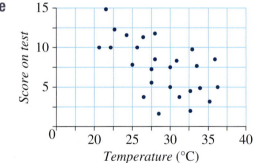

f
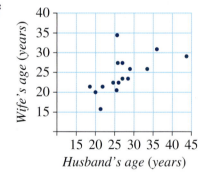

2 For each of the following pairs of variables, indicate whether you expect an association to exist and, if so, whether you would expect the association to be positive or negative.

  a Independent variable: Distance travelled   Dependent variable: Time taken

  b Independent variable: Amount of daily exercise   Dependent variable: Fitness level

  c Independent variable: Foot length of an adult   Dependent variable: Intelligence

  d Independent variable: Number of pages   Dependent variable: Book price

  e Independent variable: Temperature above 30°C   Dependent variable: Comfort level

LEVEL 2

Example 3 **3** Chocolates are sold for $12 per kg. The table below shows weight against cost.

Weight (*w*)	1	2	3	4	5
Cost (*c*)	12	24	36	48	60

 a Which is the independent variable?   **b** Which is the dependent variable?
 c Draw a scatterplot of weight against cost.   **d** Is the form linear or non-linear?
 e Is the direction positive or negative?   **f** Is the strength strong, moderate or weak?

4 The table below shows the drug dosage against reaction time.

Drug dosage (*d*)	0.5	1.0	1.5	2.0	2.5	3.0	3.5	4.0	4.5	5.0	6.0
Reaction time (*t*)	66	48	35	19	18	17	11	15	10	10	11

 a Which is the independent variable?   **b** Which is the dependent variable?
 c Draw a scatterplot of time against cost.   **d** Is the form linear or non-linear?
 e Is the direction positive or negative?   **f** Is the strength strong, moderate or weak?

5 Kayla conducted a science experiment and presented the results in a table.

Mass (*m*)	3	6	9	12	15
Time (*t*)	8.2	6.7	5.2	3.7	2.2

 a Which is the independent variable?   **b** Which is the dependent variable?
 c Draw a scatterplot of mass against time.   **d** Is the form linear or non-linear?
 e Is the direction positive or negative?   **f** Is the strength strong, moderate or weak?

LEVEL 3

6 The table below shows leg length compared to height.

Leg length (in cm)	83	83	85	87	89	89	92	93	94
Height (in cm)	166	167	170	174	179	178	183	185	188

 a Draw a scatterplot using the above table.
 b Describe the association between the leg length and height.

7 The table below shows forearm length and hand length.

Forearm (in cm)	27	28	26	28	29	27	25	26	27
Hand (in cm)	19	18.5	18	19	19.5	18	17.5	18	18.5

 a Draw a scatterplot using the above table.
 b Describe the association between the forearm length and hand length.

6C   Pearson's correlation coefficient

The strength of a linear association is an indication of how closely the points in the scatterplot fit a straight line. If the points in the scatterplot lie exactly on a straight line, we say there is a strong linear association. If there is no fit at all we say there is no association. To measure the strength of a linear association we use Pearson's correlation coefficient (r), which has the following properties:

No linear association
$r = 0$

Positive linear association
$r = +1$

Negative linear association
$r = -1$

Pearson's correlation coefficient r has a value between -1 and $+1$. The closer it is to -1 or $+1$, the stronger the association. The scatterplots below show the approximate values of r for positive linear associations of varying strengths.

Weak positive linear association
$r = +0.3$

Moderate positive linear
association $r = +0.5$

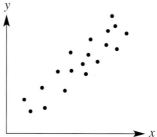

Strong positive linear association
$r = +0.9$

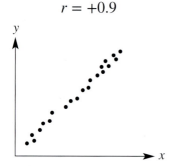

PEARSON'S CORRELATION COEFFICIENT

Pearson's correlation coefficient (r) measures the strength of a linear association ($-1 \leq r \leq +1$).
- Positive correlation (0 to $+1$) – Both quantities increase or decrease at the same time.
- Zero or no correlation (0) – No association between the quantities.
- Negative correlation (-1 to 0) – One quantity increases, the other quantity decreases.
Note: High correlation between two variables does not imply that one causes the other.

Strength of an association using Pearson's correlation coefficient

The table below provides a guideline for classifying the strength of a linear association using Pearson's correlation coefficient.

Association	Pearson's correlation coefficient
Strong positive	$r = +0.75$ to $+0.99$
Moderate positive	$r = +0.50$ to $+0.74$
Weak positive	$r = +0.25$ to $+0.49$
No linear association	$r = -0.24$ to $+0.24$
Weak negative	$r = -0.25$ to -0.49
Moderate negative	$r = -0.50$ to -0.74
Strong negative	$r = -0.75$ to -0.99

Example 4: Calculating Pearson's correlation coefficient   6C

The table below shows foot length and height in centimetres for a group of students.

Foot length (in cm)	24.5	25.6	26.1	25.9	26.2	27.0	27.4	27.5	28.1
Height (in cm)	167	168	170	174	176	180	181	185	187

a Find Pearson's correlation coefficient.

b Classify the strength of the association using Pearson's correlation coefficient.

SOLUTION:

1 Enter the statistics mode of the scientific calculator.

2 Select $\boxed{2:A + BX}$ and enter the data.

3 Select $\boxed{\text{Reg}}$ (regression) and $\boxed{r}$ to view the results.

4 Select the $\boxed{\text{STAT}}$ menu.

5 Enter the foot length data into List1.

6 Enter the height data into List2.

7 To calculate the correlation coefficient, select $\boxed{\text{CALC}}$, $\boxed{\text{REG}}$ (regression) and $\boxed{X}$.

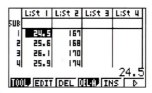

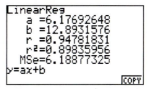

a $r = 0.94781831$

b Strong positive linear association.

8 The value of Pearson's correlation coefficient (r) is between $+0.75$ to $+0.99$, which indicates a strong positive linear association.

Exercise 6C

1 State whether Pearson's correlation coefficient is positive, negative or zero.

a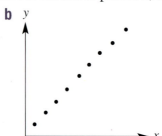

b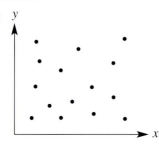

c

d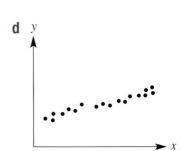

e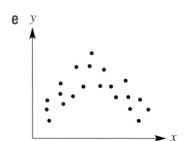

f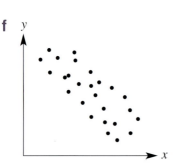

2 Draw a scatterplot that shows:
  a high positive correlation   **b** low positive correlation
  c zero correlation   **d** low negative correlation.

3 Describe the strength of the linear associations with the following Pearson's correlation coefficients.
  a $r = 0.3$ **b** $r = -1$
  c $r = 0.9$ **d** $r = -0.9$
  e $r = -0.3$ **f** $r = 1$

4 The age of a child versus head circumference is shown in the scatterplot.

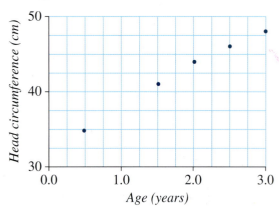

  a State whether the association is positive or negative.
  b Describe the strength of the association as strong, moderate or weak.
  c Estimate the value of Pearson's correlation coefficient.

xample 4 **5** Calculate Pearson's correlation coefficient to three decimal places for each table.

a

x	2	3	4	5	6	7	8	9
y	2	5	7	10	12	16	19	20

b

x	2	3	4	5	6	7	8	9	10	11	12
y	35	31	29	26	20	19	16	14	10	6	3

6 Calculate Pearson's correlation coefficient to three decimal places for each scatterplot.

a
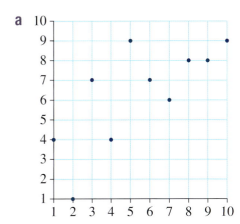

b
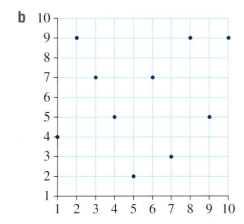

c
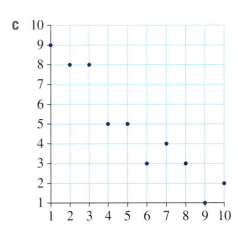

d
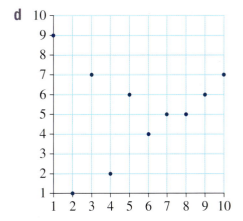

7 The mass (in kg) and body mass index (BMI) of nine
students is shown in the scatterplot.
  a State whether the association is positive or negative.
  b Describe the strength of the association as strong,
    moderate or weak.
  c Calculate the value of Pearson's correlation
    coefficient.
  d Do you think BMI is related to mass?

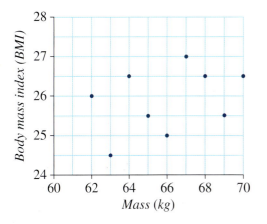

8 A developing nation compared body mass to income. Pearson's correlation coefficient for these quantities was −0.2. What is the meaning of this correlation?

9 Each member of a group of males had his height and foot length measured and recorded. Pearson's correlation coefficient between these variables was 0.9. Describe the association between height and foot length.

10 The table below shows the heart rate (beats per minute) and the score out of 20 in a test.

Heart rate (h)	62	63	66	68	70	72	75	78	79	80
Score on test (s)	19	18	16	18	15	14	11	10	9	8

a Draw a scatterplot using the data in the table.
b State whether the association is positive or negative.
c Describe the strength of the association as strong, moderate or weak.
d Calculate the value of Pearson's correlation coefficient, correct to four decimal places.

11 Rose believes tall women tend to form more associations with taller men than do short women. Do you agree? Explain your view using the data in the table.

Height women (cm)	168	163	168	165	178	165	170	175	169	174
Height men (cm)	183	173	178	173	180	165	168	181	179	175

12 A report found a high positive correlation between the shoe size of primary school students and their reading ability.
  a Does this mean people with big feet are better at reading? Explain your answer.
  b What other factors might explain this relationship?

13 There is a high positive correlation between health and income.
  a This correlation is commonly thought to reflect a causal link running from income to health. Explain how higher income can cause better health.
  b Some experts believe the correlation is a causal link running from health to income. Explain how better health can cause higher income.

If the points on the scatterplot tend to lie on a straight line, then we can fit a line on the scatterplot. The process of fitting a straight line to the data is known as linear regression. Linear regression is completed in many different ways. The simplest method is to draw a line that seems to be a balance of the points above and below the line. The aim of a linear regression is to model the association between two numerical variables by using the equation of a straight line. This equation of the straight line is found using the gradient–intercept formula: $y = mx + c$ where m is the gradient and c is the y-intercept.

LINE OF BEST FIT

A line of best fit is a straight line that approximates a linear association between points.
The equation of the line of best fit is found using the gradient–intercept formula: $y = mx + c$.

The line of best fit is used to make a prediction about one of the variables. When it is used to make a prediction within the data range it is called interpolation. Extrapolation is a prediction outside the data range and must be used carefully, as the line of best fit may not apply: for example, predicting an adult's height based on their increasing height as a child. Interpolation and extrapolation will be examined in detail in section 6E.

Method of least squares

Drawing a line of best fit that seems to balance out the points around the line is not reliable and everyone is likely to come up with a slightly different line. One method of overcoming this problem is to use the method of least squares. First a line of best fit is drawn on the scatterplot. Then the vertical distance (the residual) between each data point and the line is calculated. If the line is a perfect fit, this distance is zero for all the data points. The worse the fit, the larger the differences. Finally, each vertical distance is squared and the squared values are added together. The least-squares line of best fit is the line that minimises the sum of the squares of the vertical distances.

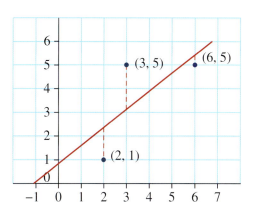

LEAST-SQUARES LINE OF BEST FIT

A line of best fit minimises the sum of the squares of the vertical distances (or residuals).

The equation of least-squares line of best fit

The equation of the least-squares line of best fit is found using a gradient–intercept formula and calculating the gradient and y-intercept by substituting into formulas. These formulas require Pearson's correlation coefficient and the standard deviation and mean of both the x and the y values.

EQUATION OF LEAST-SQUARES LINE OF BEST FIT

The equation is given by $y = mx + c$ where gradient (or slope) is $m = r\dfrac{s_y}{s_x}$

y-intercept is $c = \bar{y} - m\bar{x}$

r Pearson's correlation coefficient

s_x and s_y – Standard deviation of x and y

$\bar{x}$ and $\bar{y}$ – Mean of x and y

Using technology for least-squares line of best fit

Desmos widget 6D Find the line of best fit and its gradient and the y-intercept.

Spreadsheet activity 6D

Use a spreadsheet to find the line of best fit and its gradient and the y-intercept.

Example 5: Using the calculator for least-square line of best fit   **6D**

The heights (x) and masses (y) of 9 people have been recorded and the values of the following statistics determined: $\bar{x} = 176.5556$, $s_x = 8.6681$, $\bar{y} = 67$, $s_y = 6.6833$ and $r = 0.9743$.

a Calculate the gradient of the least-squares line of best fit.

b Calculate the y-intercept of the least-squares line of best fit.

c Write the equation of least-squares line of best fit.

SOLUTION:

1	Write the formula for gradient.	**a**	$m = r\dfrac{s_y}{s_x}$
2	Substitute into the formula.		$= 0.9743 \times \dfrac{6.6833}{8.6681}$
3	Evaluate.		$= 0.751207 \approx 0.75$
4	Write the formula for the y-intercept.	**b**	$b = \bar{y} - m\bar{x}$
5	Substitute into the formula.		$= 67 - 0.751232 \times 176.5556$
6	Evaluate.		≈ -65.63
7	Write the gradient–intercept formula.	**c**	$y = mx + c$
			$= 0.75x - 65.63$
8	Substitute into the formula.		
9	Evaluate.		
10	Express the answer using the names of the variables.		$\text{Weight} = 0.75 \times \text{Height} - 65.63$

Example 6: Using the calculator to find the least-squares line of best fit   **6D**

The table below shows the heights (cm) and masses (kg) of nine people.

Height (h)	163	165	170	175	178	180	182	186	190
Mass (m)	55	60	64	66	65	70	71	74	78

a Find Pearson's correlation coefficient.

b Use a calculator to determine the equation of the least-squares line of best fit.

c Draw a scatterplot showing the least-squares line of best fit.

d Describe the association between height and mass.

SOLUTION:

1 Enter the statistics mode of the scientific calculator.

2 Select 2:A + BX and enter the data.

3 Select Reg (regression) r to view the results.

4 Select Reg (regression) and A and B to view the results.

5 Write the gradient–intercept formula.

6 Substitute into the formula.

7 Evaluate.

8 Draw a number plane with height as the horizontal axis and mass as the vertical axis.

9 Plot the points (163, 55), (165, 60), (170, 64), (175, 66), (178, 65), (180, 70), (182, 71), (186, 74) and (190, 78).

10 Select two heights in the given domain such as 170 and 180.

11 Use $y = 0.75x - 65.63$ and $x = 170$ to calculate a value for y (about 62). Plot (170, 62).

12 Use $y = 0.75x - 65.63$ and $x = 180$ to calculate a value for y (about 69). Plot (180, 69).

13 Draw a line between (170, 62) and (180, 69).

14 The value of Pearson's correlation coefficient (r) is between +0.75 and +0.99.

a $r = 0.9743297568 \ldots$

b $A = -65.63424252 \ldots$
$B = 0.7512323365 \ldots$
$y = mx + c$
$\quad = Bx + A$
$\quad = 0.75x - 65.63$

c

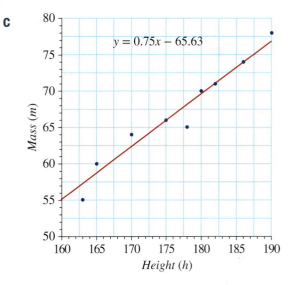

d   Strong positive linear association.

Exercise 6D

1 Draw a scatterplot and a line of best fit by eye for the following points.
   a (0, 0) (10, 30) (20, 67) (30, 93) (40, 126) (50, 158) (60, 178)
   b (5, 20) (10, 42) (15, 73) (20, 94) (25, 122) (30, 150) (35, 165)
   c (0, 6) (2, 24) (3, 39) (4, 44) (5, 59) (6, 64) (7, 79) (8, 84)
   d (10, 55) (12, 45) (14, 20) (16, 40) (18, 30) (20, 28) (22, 25)

2 The scatterplot shows a mother's height (in cm) and her daughter's height (in cm).

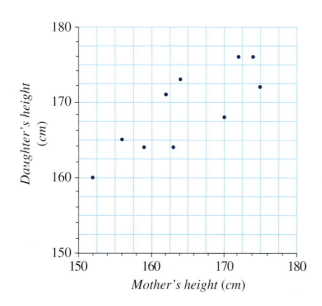

   a Copy the scatterplot and draw a line of best fit by eye.
   b Describe the strength of the relationship as strong, moderate or weak.
   c Estimate the daughter's height if the mother's height is 170 cm.
   d Estimate the mother's height if the daughter's height is 162 cm.

3 The equation relating a person's weight (in kg) to shoe size is given below:
   weight = 2.2 × shoe size + 48.1 (only for shoe sizes between 6 and 12).
   a What is the weight of a person with a shoe size of 7?
   b What is the weight of a person with a shoe size of 5?
   c What is the weight of a person with a shoe size of 11?

Example 5 4 Find the equation of the least-squares line of best fit to two decimal places for each dataset.
   a $\bar{x} = 11.38$, $s_x = 1.87$, $\bar{y} = 230.7$, $s_y = 97.87$ and $r = 0.94$
   b $\bar{x} = 35.54$, $s_x = 5.41$, $\bar{y} = 56.12$, $s_y = 9.58$ and $r = -0.81$
   c $\bar{x} = 5.631$, $s_x = 3.598$, $\bar{y} = 78.135$, $s_y = 40.134$ and $r = 0.946$
   d $\bar{x} = 100.79$, $s_x = 6.43$, $\bar{y} = 59.18$, $s_y = 5.71$ and $r = -0.76$

5 Create the spreadsheet and scatterplot below.

6DQ5

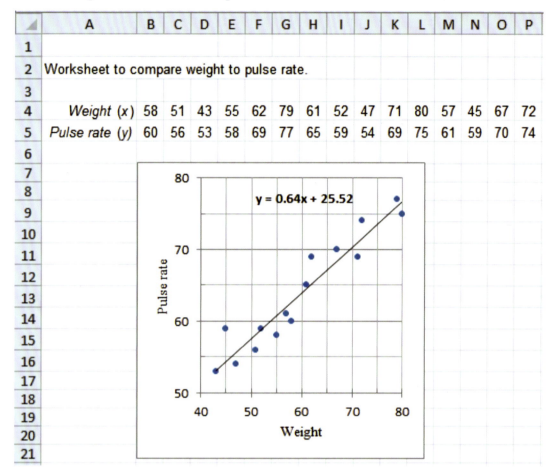

	A	B	C	D	E	F	G	H	I	J	K	L	M	N	O	P
1																
2	Worksheet to compare weight to pulse rate.															
3																
4	Weight (x)	58	51	43	55	62	79	61	52	47	71	80	57	45	67	72
5	Pulse rate (y)	60	56	53	58	69	77	65	59	54	69	75	61	59	70	74

a Use the trendline tool to insert the least-squares line of best fit onto the scatterplot.
b Display the equation of the least-squares line of best fit onto the scatterplot.
c Use the equation to predict the pulse rate when the weight is 65 kg.
d Use the equation to predict the weight when the pulse rate is 60 beats per minute.
e Comment on the reliability of the predictions using the line of best fit.

6 The heights and masses of young children are measured and recorded below.

Height h (cm)	40	45	50	55	60	65	70	75	80	85
Mass m (kg)	1.5	3.1	3.6	5.5	6.0	6.9	7.6	8.6	10.0	11.2

a Determine the equation of the least-squares line of best fit.
b What is the expected mass of a child given their height is 73 cm?
c What is the expected mass of a child given their height is 48 cm?
d What is the expected height of a child given their mass is 4.8 kg?
e What is the expected height of a child given their mass is 9.0 kg?

7 The table below shows the amount of energy (in megajoules, MJ) used per day for 12 people of various mass (in kg).

Energy (MJ)	1.5	1.6	1.7	1.8	1.9	2.0	2.0	2.1	2.2	2.3	2.4	2.5
Mass (kg)	50	54	70	71	78	88	98	101	110	115	119	125

a Draw a scatterplot using energy for the horizontal axis and mass for the vertical axis.
b Calculate Pearson's correlation coefficient. Answer correct to three decimal places.
c Find the equation of the least-squares line of best fit in terms of energy (e) and mass (m).
d Use the equation to predict the mass when 1.55 MJ of energy is used.
e Use the equation to predict the mass when 2.15 MJ of energy is used.
f Use the equation to predict the energy used when the mass is 100 kg.
g Use the equation to predict the energy used when the mass is 80 kg.

8 The table compares a mother's height in centimetres with her son's height in centimetres.

Mother's height (cm)	155	160	165	170	175	180	185
Son's height (cm)	161	167	171	174	179	185	189

a Draw a scatterplot using mother's (m) height as the horizontal axis and son's height (s) as the vertical axis.
b Determine the equation of the least-squares line of best fit.
c Use the equation to predict the son's height if the mother's height is 163 cm.
d Use the equation to predict the mother's height if the son's height is 178 cm.
e Comment on the reliability of the predictions using the line of best fit.

6E | Interpolation and extrapolation

The equation of the line of best fit or regression line can provide important information and be used to make predictions. The gradient (*m*) indicates the change in dependent variable as the independent variable increases by 1 unit. The vertical intercept (*b*) indicates the value of the dependent variable when the independent variable is zero. In addition to this information, the equation of best fit is used for interpolation and extrapolation.

Interpolation

Interpolation is the use of the linear regression line to predict values within the range of the dataset. If the data has a strong linear association then we can be confident our predictions are accurate. However, if the data has a weak linear association, we are less confident with our predictions.

Example 7: Making predictions using interpolation   6E

Life expectancy at birth for females and males is shown below.

Year	1910	1920	1930	1940	1950	1960	1970	1980	1990	2000	2010
Female	58	63	66	68	70	72	74	76	79	82	84
Male	55	59	62	63	65	67	66	68	73	77	79

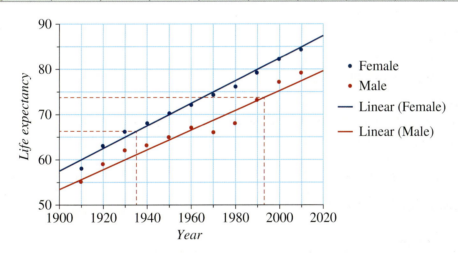

a What was the life expectancy in 1935 for females?
b What was the life expectancy in 1995 for males?

SOLUTION:

1 Draw a vertical line from 1935 until it intersects the blue line. At this point draw a horizontal line until it reaches the vertical axis. Read the value.

2 Draw a vertical line from 1995 until it intersects the red line. At this point draw a horizontal line until it reaches the vertical axis. Read the value.

a Life expectancy for females in 1935 is approximately 67 years.

b Life expectancy for males in 1995 is approximately 74 years.

Extrapolation

Extrapolation is the use of the linear regression line to predict values outside the range of the dataset. Predicted values are either smaller or larger than the dataset. The accuracy of predictions using extrapolation depends on the strength of the linear association similar to interpolation. It may not be reasonable to extrapolate too far as this example shows.

Example 8: Making predications using extrapolation   **6E**

The table below shows the age of a student and their height in centimetres.

Age (in years)	7	8	9	10	11	12	13	14	15	16
Height (in cm)	133	139	144	149	156	163	170	174	177	181

a Construct a scatterplot from the table using age from 0 to 30 and height from 100 to 300.

b Draw the line of best fit and describe the association between age and height.

c Predict the height of the student when they are aged 19 years.

d What are the limitations of this linear model?

SOLUTION:

1 Draw a number plane with age as the horizontal axis and height as the vertical axis.

2 Determine a scale for the horizontal axis. Let each unit represent 1 year.

3 Determine a scale for the vertical axis. Let each unit represent 10 cm.

4 Write a title for the horizontal and vertical axes.

5 Plot the points (7, 133) (8, 139) (9, 144),…

6 There is a small amount of scatter in the scatterplot.

7 Read the height from the scatterplot when age is 19.

8 Extrapolation too far from the dataset needs to be done carefully.

a
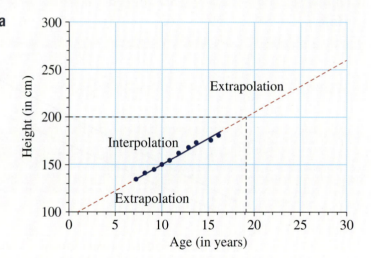

b Strong positive linear association.

c Height of the student is 200 cm when they are 19 years old.

d Adult height does not grow at the same rate as a child. Using the model to extrapolate is flawed, e.g., the prediction is the height will be 260 cm at age 30.

INTERPOLATION	EXTRAPOLATION
Predicting values within the dataset range	Predicting values outside the dataset range

Exercise 6E

1 The scatterplot opposite shows the rainfall (in mm) and the percentage of clear days for each month in 2018.

  a How many months had 10% of clear days?

  b What was the percentage of clear days when the rainfall was 70 mm?

  c Predict the rainfall in the month given the following percentage of clear days:

    i 4%

    ii 22%

    iii 26%.

  d Predict the percentage of clear days in the month given the following rainfall:

    i 80 mm

    ii 90 mm

    iii 100 mm.

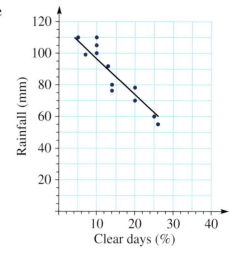

2 The scatterplot shows the average annual female income plotted against average annual male income for 15 countries.

  a What was the average annual female income for a country whose average annual male income was $45 000?

  b How many countries had an average annual female income of $25 000?

  c Predict the female income given the following male income:

    i $20 000

    ii $40 000

    iii $60 000.

  d Predict the male income given the following female income:

    i $25 000

    ii $30 000

    iii $35 000.

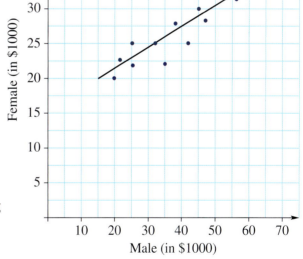

3 In a study of errors made in a test, for times ranging from 5 to 25 seconds, the equation relating the number of errors to time is:

$$errors = -0.53 \times time + 15$$

Use this equation to predict the number of errors (to nearest whole number) with the following times. Are you interpolating or extrapolating?

  a 10 seconds   **b** 20 seconds   **c** 30 seconds

Example 7

4 For minimum temperatures from 5°C to 20°C, the equation relating the maximum and minimum temperature (in °C) at a weather station is shown below:

$$maximum = 0.67 \times minimum + 13$$

Use this equation to predict the maximum temperature given the following minimum temperatures. Are you interpolating or extrapolating?

a 10°C **b** 20°C **c** 30°C

5 The equation relating life expectancy at birth from 1900 to the current year for a particular country is given below:

$$life\ expectancy = 0.21 \times year - 353.78$$

Use this equation to predict a life expectancy in the following years. Are you interpolating or extrapolating?

a 1900

b 1950

c 1870

d 2000

e 2030

f 1970

6 When a person's height is between 160 cm and 190 cm, the equation relating weight (in kg) to the height (in cm) is shown below:

$$weight = 0.75 \times height - 65.63$$

Use this equation to predict a person's weight with the following heights. Are you interpolating or extrapolating?

a 150 cm **b** 175 cm **c** 200 cm

7 When a worker's average pay rate is between \$5 and \$25, the equation relating a country's development index (%) to the average pay rate (in dollars per hour) is shown below:

$$development\ index = 0.272 \times pay\ rate + 81.3$$

Use this equation to predict a country's development index with the following average pay rates. Are you interpolating or extrapolating?

a \$40 per hour **b** \$20 per hour **c** \$10 per hour

8 When the area in a large city is between $1\,km^2$ and $8\,km^2$, the equation relating a population to area (in square kilometres) is shown below:

$$population = 2680 \times area + 5330$$

Use this equation to predict the population with the following areas. Are you interpolating or extrapolating?

a $2.5\,km^2$ **b** $5.0\,km^2$ **c** $7.5\,km^2$

9 A factory produces DVDs. The least-squares regression line for cost of production (C) as a function of the number of DVDs (n) produced is given by:

$C = 7.2n + 500$

Furthermore, this function is deemed accurate when producing between 100 and 1000 DVDs.
a What is the cost to produce 400 DVDs?
b How many DVDs can be produced for $5900?
c What is the cost to produce 10 000 DVDs?
d What are the 'fixed' costs for this production?
e Which of the parts **a** to **c** is an extrapolation?

Example 8   **10** The table below compares the length (in centimetres) for 10 fish and their weight (in grams).

Length (in cm)	30	31	32	33	34	35	36	37	38	39
Weight (in g)	250	310	340	355	445	450	500	520	550	565

a Draw a scatterplot using length as the horizontal axis and weight as the vertical axis.
b Determine the equation of the least-squares line of best fit.
c What is the rate at which the weight is changing relative to the length?
d What is the median weight of the 10 fish?
e Use interpolation to predict a fish's weight if its length is 35.5 cm.
f Use extrapolation to predict a fish's weight if its length is 45 cm.
g What is the length of a fish given it weighs 300 g?

11 The table below compares the literacy score for 10 countries and their internet use (%).

Internet use (%)	9	12	15	22	45	50	60	64	70	73
Literacy score	90	102	131	148	282	295	350	375	390	400

a Draw a scatterplot using internet use as the horizontal axis and literacy as the vertical axis.
b Calculate Pearson's correlation coefficient. Answer correct to four decimal places.
c Describe the association between internet use and literacy score.
d Find the least-squares regression equation.
e Using the least-squares equation, if a country has an internet use of 30% predict the country's literacy score. Answer to the nearest whole number.
f If a country has a literacy score of 300, predict the country's internet use.
g Comment on the internet use for a country with a literacy score of 600.

6F **Statistical investigation**

Statistical investigation is the process of gathering statistics. The information gained from a statistical investigation is a vital part of our society. A statistical investigation involves four steps.

Four steps in a statistical investigation

1. **Collect the data**

   Collecting data involves deciding what to collect, locating it and collecting it. The gathering of statistical data may take the form of a:
   - census – data is collected from the whole population
   - survey – data is collected from a smaller group of the population.

   It is important that procedures are in place to ensure the collection of data is accurate, up-to-date, relevant and secure. If the data collected comes from unreliable sources or is inaccurate, the information gained from it will be incorrect. When taking a sample, the data gathered must be representative of the entire population otherwise the information collected may be biased towards a particular outcome.

2. **Organise the data**

   Organising data is the process of arranging, representing and formatting data. It is carried out after the data is collected. The organisation of the data depends on the purpose of the statistical investigation. For example, to store and search a large amount of data, the data needs to be categorised. Organising gives structure to the data.

3. **Summarise and display the data**

   Displaying data is the presentation of the data and information. Information must be well organised, readable, attractively presented and easy to understand. Information is often displayed using graphs such as scatterplots, dot plots, histograms, line graphs, stem-and-leaf plots and box plots. Data is summarised using statistics such as the mean, median, mode and standard deviation.

4. **Analyse the data**

   Analysing data is the process of interpreting data and transforming it into information. It involves examining the data and giving meaning to it. When analysing bivariate data, the form, direction and strength of the association is determined. Scatterplots and lines of best fit are commonly used to analyse the data. They make it easy to interpret data by making instant comparisons and revealing trends. Predictions and conclusions are completed by interpolating and extrapolating the data.

> **STATISTICAL INVESTIGATION**
>
> A statistical investigation involves four steps: collecting data, organising data, summarising and displaying data and analysing data.

Example 9: Case study of a statistical investigation 6F

James has been asked to complete a statistical investigation on whether the blood glucose level (in mg/100 mL) of an adult can be predicted from their weight (in kg).
James performed the following steps.

1 Collecting the data – James accessed the medical data on 20 adults.

2 Organising the data – James categorised the data into blood glucose levels and weight.

3 Summarising and displaying the data – James presented the bivariate data into the table shown opposite and the scatterplot shown below.

Weight	Glucose	Weight	Glucose
60.2	88.1	71.6	94.9
61.3	91.5	72.0	95.7
63.5	88.7	72.0	95.1
63.7	90.6	72.5	96.4
65.0	90.9	73.7	96.6
66.4	94.0	73.8	97.0
66.9	92.1	74.8	96.3
70.1	96.5	75.9	99.1
70.2	93.9	76.3	98.2
70.5	95.2	78.9	99.9

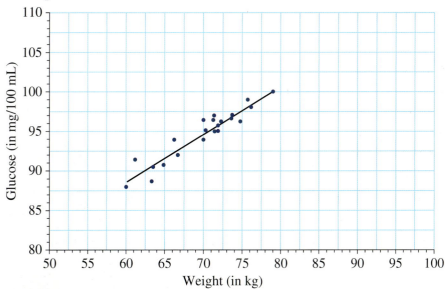

4 Analysing the data –

a James calculated Pearson's coefficient to measure the strength of a linear association.

$r = 0.9507479097 \ldots$
This indicates a strong positive linear association between weight and blood glucose levels.

b James calculated the equation and graphed the least-squares regression line on the scatterplot.

$A = 52.78718161 \ldots$ $B = 0.5966957534 \ldots$
$y = mx + b$
$\quad = Bx + A$
$\quad = 0.60x + 52.79$
$glucose = 0.60 \times weight + 53$

c James applied the results of his statistical investigation to predict the glucose level of a person who weighs 75 kg.

$glucose = 0.60 \times 75 + 53$
$\qquad = 98$
∴ A person weighing 75 kg has a blood glucose level of 98 mg/100 mL.

Issues in a statistical investigation

A statistical investigation raises a number of ethical issues such as bias, accuracy, copyright and privacy.

- Data needs to be free from bias. Bias means that the data is unfairly skewed or gives too much weight to a particular result. For example, if a survey about favourite music was only completed by teenagers, and the results were generalised to the entire population, it would have a bias. Several checks should be made to limit the impact of bias.
- The accuracy of the collected data is a vital ingredient of a statistical investigation. It depends on the source of the data and whether the data has been recorded correctly. The accuracy of the data is often difficult to check in a reasonable time. It is often necessary to compare data from a number of different sources and determine which data is accurate.
- Copyright is the right to use, copy or control the work of authors and artists. It is against the law to infringe copyright. You are not allowed to use or copy the work of another person without their permission. If data is collected from the internet, it should be assumed to be protected by copyright.
- Privacy is the ability of an individual to control personal data. Data collected on individuals is not always accurate. Inaccuracies can be caused by mistakes in gathering or entering the data, by mismatch of the data and the person or by information being out-of-date. Most people give information about themselves to selected parts of the outside world. Often people are quite willing to tell A something but would be shocked if B knew. But what prevents A telling B?

ISSUES IN A STATISTICAL INVESTIGATION

A statistical investigation raises a number of ethical issues such as bias, accuracy, copyright and privacy.

Causation

Causation indicates that one event is the result of the occurrence of another event (or variable). This is often referred to as the cause and effect. That is, one event is the cause of another event happening. For example, the bell at the end of the period is an event that causes students to leave for the next period. When completing a statistical investigation it is important to be aware that two events (or variables) may have a high correlation but be unrelated. That is, high correlation does not imply causation. For

example, the increase in the use of mobile phones has a strong correlation to the increase in life expectancy. However, the use of mobile phones does not cause the increase in life expectancy.

CAUSATION

Causation indicates that one event is the result of the occurrence of another event (or variable).

Exercise 6F

1 Copy and complete the following sentences:

a A statistical _____ involves four steps: collecting data, organising data, summarising and displaying data, and analysing data.

b Census data is collected from the whole _____.

c When taking a _____ the data gathered must be representative of the entire population.

d Displaying data is the _____ of the data and information.

e When analysing _____ data the form, direction and strength of the association is determined.

f Bias means that the data is unfairly _____ or gives too much weight to a particular result.

2 True or false?

a A survey is when data is collected from a smaller group of the population.

b Data collected from unreliable sources results in incorrect information.

c Data is often displayed using graphs such as scatterplots, dot plots, histograms, line graphs, stem-and-leaf plots and box plots.

d Analysing data is the process that interprets data, transforms it into information.

e You are allowed to use or copy the work of another person without their permission.

f Data collected on individuals is always accurate.

3 The Australian Bureau of Statistics collects data for our society. Collecting data is one step in a statistical investigation. List all the four steps involved in a statistical investigation.

4 Explain the difference between a census and a survey.

5 How can you limit the impact of biased data?

6 There is a strong positive correlation between number of car accidents and the number of teachers in cities around the world. Can we conclude from this that teachers are causing car accidents? Give a possible explanation.

7 There is a strong positive correlation between the number of churches in a town and the amount of alcohol consumed by its inhabitants. Does this mean that religion is encouraging people to drink? What common cause might counter this conclusion?

8 Implement a statistical investigation to explore the link between a person's weight and the number of kilometres they run each week. The data below was collected from 15 young adults.

Distance run (km)	0.5	1.0	1.5	2.0	2.5	3.0	3.5	4.0	4.5	5.0	5.5	6.0	6.5	7.0	7.5
Weight (kg)	86.5	87.5	88.0	85.5	86.0	86.5	87.0	85.0	86.5	86.0	85.5	90.0	84.5	84.0	84.0

a Draw a scatterplot to display the data.

b Describe the association between distance run and weight.

c Calculate Pearson's correlation coefficient. Answer correct to four decimal places.

d Find the least-squares regression equation.

e The line graph below was constructed by omitting the value for 6 km. What value for weight would you read from this graph for a person running 6 km?

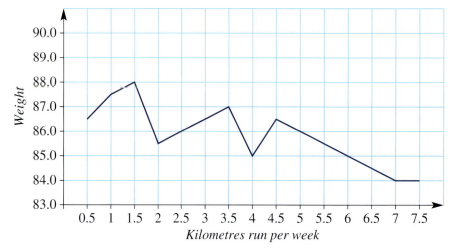

f The graph above was constructed to encourage people to run more kilometres to reduce their weight. Comment on the misrepresentation of the data.

9 The issue of privacy has been a concern for decades. Discuss this statement. What is your view on privacy? Use the internet to find information about privacy. Compare Australian and overseas data.

Example 9 | **10** Implement a statistical investigation to solve these problems.

a Students in Year 12 have decided to have a party after the HSC at a local venue. You have been given the responsibility of choosing the venue. Investigate a number of different venues and collect data such as the name and address of the venue; the cost per head; the initial deposit required; details of meals; and available dates. Design a survey for Year 12 students that will decide on the venue. Students will vote on the venue and if they are committed to attend. The survey should also decide on possible dates and meal arrangements.

b The principal would like to promote the positive features of your school outside the local community. He is presenting these features at a conference centre. Develop a solution for the principal. Design a survey for Year 12 students that will decide on the best five features of your school and use the most appropriate method of presentation.

Key ideas and chapter summary

PPT
STUDY GUIDE

Scatterplot	Constructing a scatterplot: **1** Draw a number plane. **2** Determine a scale and a title for the horizontal or x-axis **3** Determine a scale and a title for the vertical or y-axis **4** Plot each ordered pair of numbers with a dot.

Using a bivariate scatterplot	Form of an association	Linear form – a straight line Non-linear form – a curved line
	Direction of an association	Positive – gradient of the line is positive Negative – gradient of the line is negative
	Strength of an association	Strong – small amount of scatter Moderate – modest amount of scatter Weak – large amount of scatter

Pearson's correlation coefficient	Pearson's correlation coefficient (r) measures the strength of a linear association ($-1 \leq r \leq +1$).

- Positive correlation (0 to +1) — Both quantities increase or decrease at the same time.
- Zero or no correlation (0) — No association between quantities.
- Negative correlation (-1 to 0) — One quantity increases, the other quantity decreases.

Line of best fit	Line of best fit is a straight line that approximates a linear association between points.

Least-squares line of best fit	The equation is given by $y = mx + c$ where: Gradient (or slope) is $m = r\dfrac{s_y}{s_x}$ and y-intercept is $b = \bar{y} - m\bar{x}$. r – Pearson's correlation coefficient. s_x and s_y – Standard deviation of x and y. $\bar{x}$ and $\bar{y}$ – Mean of x and y.

Interpolation	Predicting values within the range of the dataset

Extrapolation	Predicting values outside the range of the dataset

Statistical investigation	Four steps: collecting data, organising data, summarising and displaying data, and analysing data. A statistical investigation raises a number of ethical issues such as bias, accuracy, copyright and privacy.

Multiple-choice

1 Blood pressure levels for women increase as they get older. What is the best description for the association between blood pressure levels and a woman's age?

A Positive correlation.   **B** Zero correlation.

C Negative correlation   **D** Constant correlation

2 What is the correlation between the variables in the scatterplot?

A Strong positive   **B** Weak positive

C Strong negative   **D** Weak negative

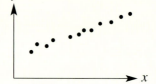

3 Which of the following scatterplots shows weak negative correlation?

A    **B**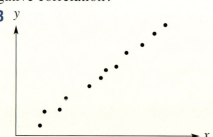

C 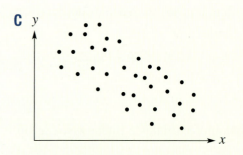   **D**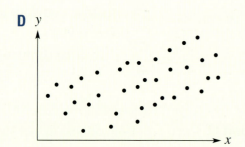

4 The birth weight and weight at age 21 of eight women are given in the table below.

Birth weight	1.9	2.4	2.6	2.7	2.9	3.2	3.4	3.6
Weight at 21	47.6	53.1	52.2	56.2	57.6	59.9	55.3	56.7

What is the value of Pearson's correlation coefficient?

A 0.5360   **B** 0.6182   **C** 0.7863   **D** 0.8232

5 What is the slope of the least-squares regression line given $m = r\dfrac{s_y}{s_x}$, $r = 0.733$, $s_x = 1.871$ and $s_y = 3.391$?

A 0.41   **B** 0.45   **C** 1.33   **D** 1.87

6 The equation of a regression line that enables weekly amount spent on entertainment (in dollars) to be predicted from weekly income is given by: $amount = 0.10 \times income + 40$.

What is the predicted amount spent on entertainment with a weekly income of $600?

A $40   **B** $46   **C** $100   **D** $240

Short-answer

1   The scatterplot shows the navel height and the body height for nine students.

a   Which has been plotted as the independent variable?

b   Which has been plotted as the dependent variable?

c   Is the association between these two variables linear or non-linear?

d   Describe the association as strong, moderate or weak.

e   What is the body height for the student with a navel height of 112 cm?

f   What is the navel height for the student with a body height of 166 cm?

g   Use the scatterplot to predict the body height of a student with a navel height of 110 cm.

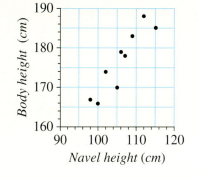

2   The scatterplot shows a student's height (in cm) and their age (in years).

a   What is the age for the student when their height is 120 cm?

b   What is the height for the student whose age is 11 years?

c   State whether the association is positive or negative.

d   Describe the strength of the association as strong, moderate or weak.

e   Estimate the value of Pearson's correlation coefficient. Answer correct to two decimal places.

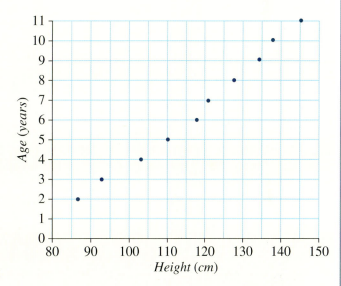

3   The table below shows the length of the right foot (in cm) and body height (in cm).

Length of right foot (cm)	27.5	24.0	22.6	23.7	26.4	27.1	25.5	26.1
Body height (cm)	174.4	156.0	155.3	160.5	170.7	169.3	163.3	164.9

a   Draw a scatterplot using the above table.

b   State whether the association is positive or negative.

c   Describe the strength of the association as strong, moderate or weak.

4   A strong positive linear association exists between the hours spent studying for an exam and the mark achieved. The equation for this association is *mark* = 4.5 × *study hours* + 2.

a   Predict the exam mark if the student studied for 20 hours a week.

b   Predict the amount of study hours required to achieve a mark of 56.

5 The table below shows the age (in months) and the height (in cm) of a young plant.

Age (in months)	1	4	5	8	12	14	15	19	22	24
Height (in cm)	48	65	78	87	114	128	131	159	169	188

  a Find the equation of the least-squares line of best fit. Answer correct to two decimal places.
  b What is the predicted height of the plant after 19 months? Answer to the nearest centimetre.
  c What is the predicted height of the plant after 3 years? Answer to the nearest centimetre.
  d Which of the above questions involves interpolation?

6 The table shows the birth rate (live births per 1000) and the life expectancy (in years).

Birth rate (*br*)	30	38	40	43	34	42	31
Life expectancy (*le*)	66	54	48	42	46	45	64

  a Draw a scatterplot using the above table.
  b State whether the association is positive or negative.
  c Describe the strength of the association as strong, moderate or weak.
  d Calculate the value of Pearson's correlation coefficient. Answer correct to four decimal places.
  e Determine the equation of the least-squares line of best fit.
  f Use the equation to predict the life expectancy when the birth rate is 35.
  g Use the equation to predict the birth rate when the life expectancy is 60.

Extended-response

7 A marketing firm wanted to investigate the relationship between the number of times a song was played on the radio (*played*) and the number of downloads sold the following week (*weekly sales*). The following data was collected from a random sample of ten songs.

Played	47	34	40	34	33	50	28	53	25	46
Weekly sales	3950	2500	3700	2800	2900	3750	2300	4400	2200	3400

  a Construct a scatterplot using the above table.
  b Calculate the value of Pearson's correlation coefficient. Answer correct to four decimal places.
  c Describe the relationship between weekly sales and played in terms of direction, strength and form.
  d Determine the equation of the least-squares line of best fit.
  e Interpret the slope and intercept of the regression line in the context of the problem.
  f Use the equation to predict the number of downloads of a song when it was played on the radio 100 times in the previous week. Are you interpolating or extrapolating?

Practice Paper 2

Section I

Attempt Questions 1–15 (15 marks).

Allow about 20 minutes for this section.

---

1 Which trignometric formula would be most useful in calculating the length of side BC?

A $c^2 = a^2 + b^2 - 2ab \cos C$ **B** $A = \dfrac{1}{2} ab \sin C$

C $\cos C = \dfrac{a^2 + b^2 - c^2}{2ab}$ **D** $\dfrac{a}{\sin A} = \dfrac{b}{\sin B} = \dfrac{c}{\sin C}$

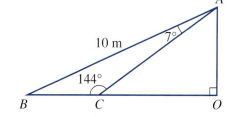

2 The scatterplot shows the weights at age 21 and at birth of 12 women.

How is this association best described?

A Weak positive non-linear

B Weak negative non-linear

C Strong positive linear

D Strong negative linear

3 What is the value of $\sin x$ in the triangle below?

A $\dfrac{b}{c}$

B $\dfrac{a}{b}$

C $\dfrac{b}{a}$

D $\dfrac{a}{c}$

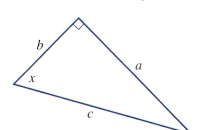

4 What is the value of y predicted by the least-squares regression line $y = -0.78x - 5.6$ when $x = 10$?

A -13.4 **B** -7.2 **C** 2.2 **D** 7.8

5 Which of the following expressions would give the height (h), of the tree in the diagram?

A $42 \times \tan 34°$ **C** $42 \times \cos 34°$

B $\dfrac{42}{\tan 34°}$ **D** $\dfrac{42}{\cos 34°}$

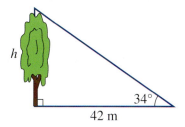

Use the following graph to answer questions 6 to 8.

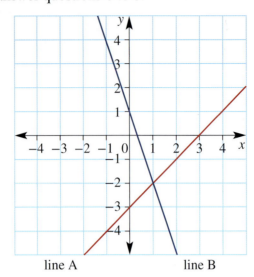

line A   line B

6 What is the slope of line B?

   A −3   **B** 3   **C** $-\dfrac{1}{3}$ **D** $\dfrac{1}{3}$

7 What is the equation of line A?

   A $y - 2x = 3$ **B** $x - y = 3$ **C** $y - x = 3$ **D** $-2y - x = 6$

8 What is the simultaneous solution of line A and line B?

   A $x = -1$ and $y = -2$ **B** $x = -1$ and $y = 2$

   C $x = 1$ and $y = -2$ **D** $x = -3$ and $y = 3$

9 Which of the following equations is closest to the least-squares scatterplot opposite?

   A $y = -0.9x + 8.7$

   B $y = -8.7x + 0.9$

   C $y = 0.9x - 8.7$

   D $y = 8.7x - 0.9$

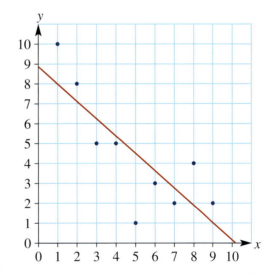

10 What is the approximate length of the side marked with the letter x?

   A 10

   B 31

   C 39

   D 67

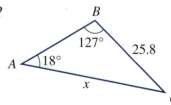

11 The compass bearing of Y from X is S49°W. What is the compass bearing of X from Y?

A S49°W

B S41°W

C N49°E

D N41°E

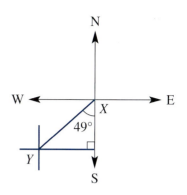

12 For the graph opposite, R is the revenue, in dollars, earned by a mushroom farmer selling n kilograms of mushrooms, and C is the cost, in dollars, of producing n kilograms of mushrooms. To make a profit, how many kilograms of mushrooms should the farmer's production exceed?

A 25   **B** 50

C 100   **D** 250

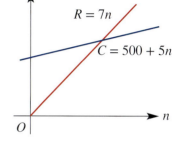

13 Suppose that the least-squares regression line which would enable the amount of money spent at the shopping centre (in dollars) to be predicted from the number of hours spent at the shopping centre is given by:

$$Shopping\ expenditure = 20 + 50 \times Hours\ spent\ shopping$$

The slope of the line can be interpreted as follows.

A On average, for each extra 50 minutes spent shopping an extra $1 is spent.

B On average, for each extra hour spent shopping an extra $50 is spent.

C On average, customers spend $20 per hour at the shopping centre.

D On average, customers spend $50 at the shopping centre.

14 A sailing boat travels due east from A to B.

It then turns and sails on a bearing of 210°.

What is the boat's bearing from A when the boat is closest to A?

A 030°

B 120°

C 150°

D 210°

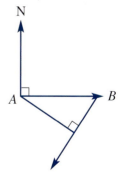

15 If Sue buys three packets of chips and two bottles of cola, it will cost her $13.20. However, if she buys two packets of chips and three bottles of cola it will cost her only $11.80. What is the price of each item?

A cola = $3.20, chips = $1.80

B cola = $2.10, chips = $3

C cola = $1.80, chips = $3.20

D cola = $2, chips = $2.90

Section II

Attempt Questions 16–18 (45 marks).

Allow about 70 minutes for this section.

All necessary working should be shown in every question.

Question 16 (15 marks)   **Marks**

a The cost (C) of hiring a car is given by the formula $C = 2.5x + 65$, where x is the   **2**
number of kilometres travelled. A person is charged $750 for the hire of the car.
What was the number of kilometres travelled?

b Calculate Pearson's correlation coefficient (to three decimal places) for the following table.   **1**

x	22	23	24	25	26	27	28	29	30	31	32
y	32	29	27	24	18	17	14	11	8	4	1

c A radial survey of a park is shown below.   **1**

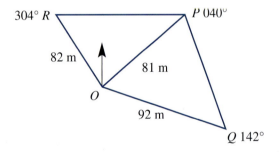

  i   What is the size of $\angle POR$?   **2**

  ii Use the cosine rule to calculate the length of PR, correct to the nearest metre.

d What is the point of intersection of the lines $x + 3y = -4$ and $x + y = 2$?   **3**

e A tower 110 m high stands on the top of a hill. From a point, A, at the foot of the hill, the
angle of elevation of the bottom of the tower is $7°$, and to the top of the tower it is $10°$.

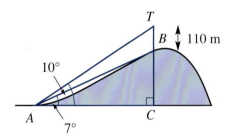

  i   Find the magnitude of angles TAB and ATB.   **2**

  ii Use the sine rule to find the length AB. Answer correct to the nearest metre.   **2**

  iii Find CB, the height of the hill. Answer correct to the nearest metre.   **2**

Question 17 (15 marks)   **Marks**

a The graph shows the cost of growing rose plants and the income received.

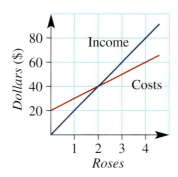

  i Use the graph to determine the number of rose plants that need to be sold to break even.   **1**

 ii How much profit or loss is made when 1 rose is sold?   **1**

iii How much profit or loss is made when 4 roses are sold?   **1**

 iv What are the initial costs?   **1**

b The smallest angle in the triangle below is θ. Find θ to the nearest degree.   **2**

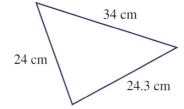

c The cost of preparing meals in a school canteen is linearly related to the number of meals prepared. To help the caterers predict the costs, data were collected on the cost of preparing meals for different levels of demands. The data are shown below.

Number of meals	30	35	40	45	50	55	60	65	70	75	80
Cost (dollars)	138	154	159	182	198	198	214	208	238	234	244

  i Find the equation of the least-squares line of best fit. Answer correct to one decimal place.   **2**

 ii What is the predicted cost of producing 48 meals?   **1**

iii What is the predicted number of meals if the cost is $249.50?   **1**

d A straight line has the equation of $2x + y = -2$.

  i What is the gradient of this line?   **1**

 ii What is the y-intercept?   **1**

iii What is the point of intersection between $2x + y = -2$ and $y = 2$?   **1**

e Each member of a family had their weight and age measured and recorded. Pearson's correlation coefficient between these variables was 0.9. Describe the association between weight and age.   **2**

Question 18 (15 marks)   **Marks**

a The scatterplot shows the average annual female income plotted against average annual male income for 16 countries. A least-squares regression line is fitted to the data.

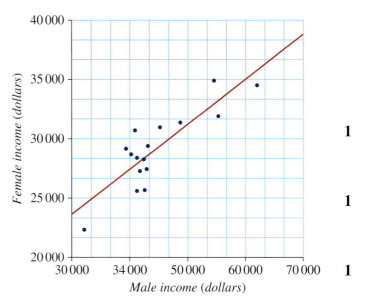

   i What was the female income for a country whose average annual male income was $60 000?   **1**

   ii How many countries had an average annual female income greater than $30 000?   **1**

   iii Find the gradient of the least-squares line of best fit. Answer correct to one decimal place.   **1**

b In the triangle ABC, $AB = 8$ cm, $BC = 5$ cm and $CD = 4$ cm.

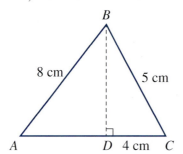

   i Find the size of angle BCD, correct to the nearest degree.   **1**

   ii What is the length of AD? Answer correct to two decimal places.   **2**

   iii Find the area of triangle ABC. Answer correct to two decimal places.   **1**

c Lia sells pillows for $65 each.

   i Write an equation for the revenue, R dollars, that Lia receives from the sale of x pillows.   **1**

   ii The cost, C dollars, of making pillows is given by $C = 500 + 40x$. Find the cost of making 30 pillows.   **1**

   iii Draw the graph of $C = 500 + 40x$ and your equation in part **i** on the same number plane.   **2**

   iv Use the graph to estimate the number of pillows Lia will need to sell to break even.   **1**

d For time ranging from 30 to 60 seconds, the equation relating the number of correct answers to time is:

$$Correct\ answers = 0.72 \times time + 30$$

Use this equation to predict the number of correct answers with the following times. Are you interpolating or extrapolating?

   i 25 seconds   **ii** 50 seconds   **iii** 75 seconds   **3**

7

Annuities

Syllabus topic — F5 Annuities

This topic will develop your appreciation of the use of annuities as an investment.

Outcomes

- Identify an annuity and solve problems involving financial decisions.
- Use technology to model an annuity as a recurrence relation.
- Investigate the effect of changing a variable on an annuity.
- Use a table of future value interest factors to perform calculations.
- Calculate the future value of an annuity.
- Calculate the contribution amount to achieve a given future value.
- Calculate the present value of an annuity.
- Solve problems involving the use of annuities such as loans and superannuation.

Digital Resources for this chapter

In the Interactive Textbook:

- Videos
- Literacy worksheet
- Quick Quiz
- Solutions (enabled by teacher)
- Desmos widgets
- Spreadsheets
- Study guide

In the Online Teaching Suite:

- Teaching Program
- Tests
- Review Quiz
- Teaching Notes

Knowledge check

The Interactive Textbook provides a test of prior knowledge for this chapter, and may direct you to revision from the previous years' work.

7A   Annuity as a recurrence relation

Annuity

Annuity is a form of investment that involves the regular contribution of money. Investments into superannuation or a monthly loan repayment are examples of annuities. The future value of an annuity is the sum of the money contributed, plus the compound interest earned. It is the total value of the investment at the end of a specified term. For example, if $1000 is invested at the end of each year for 4 years at 10% per annum compound interest, then the value of the investment is calculated as follows:

End of first year − Interest = $0 (payment at end of the year)
$$FV = PV(1 + r)^n + 1000$$
$$= 0 \times (1 + 0.10)^1 + 1000$$
$$= \$1000$$

End of second year − Interest = ($1000) × 0.10 × 1 = $100
$$FV = PV(1 + r)^n + 1000$$
$$= 1000 \times (1 + 0.10)^1 + 1000$$
$$= \$2100$$

End of third year − Interest = ($2100) × 0.10 × 1 = $210
$$FV = PV(1 + r)^n + 1000$$
$$= 2100 \times (1 + 0.10)^1 + 1000$$
$$= \$3310$$

End of fourth year − Interest = ($3310) × 0.10 × 1 = $331
$$FV = PV(1 + r)^n + 1000$$
$$= 3310 \times (1 + 0.10)^1 + 1000$$
$$= \$4641$$

These calculations show that the future value of an annuity is $4641 after 4 years. It is the total value of the investment at the end of the fourth year. After 4 years the money contributed was $4000 and the compound interest earned was $641. Be aware that interest received each year has been increasing or compounding. It has not just been increasing by $100 each year.

Recurrence relation

The above calculation to find the future value of an annuity is an example of a recurrence relation. It uses the previous result to obtain the next result. For example, the future value at the end of the first year ($1000) is the present value for the second year and the future value at the end of the second year ($2100) is the present value for the third year. This concept can be represented using a formula where V is the value of the investment and a subscript is used to represent the time period in this case each year. This is shown below.

End of first year $V_1 = V_0(1 + 0.10) + 1000 = \$1000$

End of second year $V_2 = V_1(1 + 0.10) + 1000 = \$2100$

End of third year $V_3 = V_2(1 + 0.10) + 1000 = \$3310$

End of fourth year $V_4 = V_3(1 + 0.10) + 1000 = \$4641$

This recurrence relation can be generalised using a variable (n) to represent a particular year.

End of ($n + 1$) year $V_{n+1} = V_n(1 + 0.10) + 1000$

RECURRENCE RELATION MODELLING AN ANNUITY

A recurrence relation uses the previous result to generate the next value in recurring calculations.
Investment $V_{n+1} = V_n(1 + r) + D$ Loan $V_{n+1} = V_n(1 + r) - D$
V_{n+1} – Value of the investment or loan after $(n + 1)$ payments
V_n – Value of the investment or loan after (n) payments
r – Rate of interest per compounding period expressed as a decimal
D – Payment made per compounding period

Note: If the interest rate is given as a percentage per annum, but the compounding period is monthly, the interest rate needs to be converted to a decimal and then divided by 12. So for an interest rate of 12% per annum, compounding monthly, $r = \dfrac{0.12}{12} = 0.01$. So an annual rate has to be divided by the number of time periods in a year.

Example 1: Modelling an annuity on a loan using a recurrence relation   7A

Alyssa borrows $1000 at an interest rate of 15% per annum, compounding monthly. She will repay the loan by making 4 monthly payments of $257.85.

a Construct a recurrence relation to model this loan, in the form $V_{n+1} = V_n(1 + r) - D$ where V_n is the future value of the loan after n payments.

b Use your calculator to determine recursively the balance of the loan after Alyssa has made each of the four payments.

c What is the balance of the loan (the amount she still owes) after she has made two payments? Give your answer to the nearest cent.

d Is the loan fully paid out after four payments have been made? If not, how much will the last payment have to be to ensure that the loan is fully repaid after four payments?

SOLUTION:

1 Write the recurrence relation.

2 Substitute $r = \frac{0.15}{12} = 0.0125$ (loan is compounding per month) and $D = 257.85$.

Use the calculator recursively to find the balance of the loan each month.

3 Type '1000' and press '='

4 Type '× 1.0125 − 257.85' and press '='

5 Press '=' another 3 times to obtain the result shown opposite.

6 Read balance at end of 2nd month.

7 Read balance at end of 4th month.
Add this balance to the last payment to fully repay the loan.

a $V_{n+1} = V_n(1 + r) - D$
$V_{n+1} = V_n \times 1.0125 - 257.85$

b Substitute recursively into the formula
$V_{n+1} = V_n \times 1.0125 - 257.85$
1st: $1000 \times 1.0125 - 257.85 = 754.65$
2nd: $754.65 \times 1.0125 - 257.85 \approx 506.23$
3rd: $506.23 \times 1.0125 - 257.85 \approx 254.71$
4th: $254.71 \times 1.0125 - 257.85 \approx 0.04$

c After two months Alyssa owes $506.23.

d No. Alyssa still owes 4 cents.
Last payment $= 257.85 + 0.04$
$= \$257.89$

Example 2: Modelling an annuity as an investment using a recurrence relation 7A

Spencer makes an initial deposit of $1000 on an investment taken out over one year at a rate of 7.2% per annum compounded quarterly and an additional deposit of $100 is made each quarter. Complete the table below for the first four deposits and calculate how much interest had been earned over this time.

$n + 1$	V_n	D	V_{n+1}
1			
2			
3			
4			

SOLUTION:

1 Write the recurrence relation.

$$V_{n+1} = V_n(1 + r) + D$$
$$V_1 = 1000(1.018) + 100$$

2 Substitute $r = \frac{0.072}{4} - 0.018$ (loan is compounding per quarter), $D = 100$ and $V_0 = 1000$.

Use the calculator recursively to find the balance of the loan each month.

Substitute recursively into the formula
$V_{n+1} = V_n \times 1.018 + 100$

3 Type '1000' and press '='

1st quarter: $1000 \times 1.018 + 100 = 1118$

4 Type '×1018 + 100' and press '='

2nd quarter: $1118 \times 1.018 + 100 \approx 1238.12$

5 Press '=' another 3 times to obtain the result shown opposite.

3rd quarter: $1238.12 \times 1.018 + 100$
$$\approx 1360.41$$

4th quarter: $1360.41 \times 1.018 + 100$
$$\approx 1484.90$$

6 Complete the table.

$n + 1$	V_n	D	V_{n+1}
1	$V_0 = 1000$	$100	$V_1 = \$1118$
2	$V_1 = \$1118$	$100	$V_2 = \$1238.12$
3	$V_2 = \$1238.12$	$100	$V_3 = \$1360.41$
4	$V_3 = \$1360.41$	$100	$V_4 = \$1484.90$

7 Calculate the interest by subtracting the initial investment ($1000) and the amount deposited (4 × $100) from the amount at the end of the four deposits.

$I = \$1484.90 - \$1000 - (4 \times \$100)$
$= \$84.90$

8 Write answer in words.

$\therefore$ The interest earned in one year is $84.90.

Exercise 7A

Example 1

1 A loan is modelled by the recurrence relation
$$V_{n+1} = V_n \times 1.09 - 600$$
where V_n is the balance of the loan after n payments and $V_0 = 2500$.
Use your calculator to determine recursively the balance of the loan (to nearest cent) after:
a one payment **b** two payments **c** three payments **d** four payments.

2 A loan is modelled by the recurrence relation
$$V_{n+1} = V_n \times 1.0055 - 1500$$
where V_n is the balance of the loan after n payments and $V_0 = 100\,000$. Use your calculator to determine recursively the balance of the loan (to nearest cent) after:
a one payment **b** two payments **c** three payments **d** four payments.

3 An investment is modelled by the recurrence relation
$$V_{n+1} = V_n \times 1.06 + 800$$
where V_n is the balance of the loan after n payments and $V_0 = 5000$. Use your calculator to determine the balance of the investment (to nearest cent) after:
a one payment **b** two payments **c** three payments **d** four payments.

4 An investment is modelled by the recurrence relation
$$V_{n+1} = V_n \times 1.0084 + 2000$$
where V_n is the balance of the loan after n payments and $V_0 = 60000$. Use your calculator to determine the balance of the investment (to nearest cent) after:
a one payment **b** two payments **c** three payments **d** four payments.

5 A loan is modelled by the recurrence relation $V_{n+1} = V_n \times 1.006 - 3200$ where V_n is the balance of the loan after n payments and $V_0 = 500000$. Use your calculator to determine recursively the balance of the loan (to nearest dollar) after six payments.

Example 2

6 Kiara makes an initial deposit of $12000 on an investment taken out over four years at a rate of 7.8% compounding per annum and an additional deposit of $500 is made each year. Complete the table below for the first four years.

$n + 1$	V_n	D	V_{n+1}
1			
2			
3			
4			

7 Gabriel borrows $250 000 at a rate of 4.8% p.a. compounding monthly and makes a repayment of $2000 per month.

  a What is the recurrence relation for this loan?

  b Complete the table below for the first four months. Answer correct to the nearest dollar.

$n + 1$	V_n	D	V_{n+1}
1			
2			
3			
4			

8 Ellie makes an initial deposit of $30 000 on an investment taken out over 6 years at a rate of 8.4% p.a. compounding biannually and an additional deposit of $1500 is made every six months.

  a What is the recurrence relation for this investment?

  b Complete the table below for the first three years. Answer to the nearest dollar.

$n + 1$	V_n	D	V_{n+1}
1			
2			
3			
4			
5			
6			

  c How much interest has been earned over this time?

9 Jett takes out a loan for $2000 at an interest rate of 6% per annum compounding monthly. The loan will be repaid by making 6 monthly payments of $399.

  a What is the recurrence relation for this loan?

  b Use the recurrence relation to determine the balance of the loan after 4 months. Give your answer to the nearest cent.

  c How much extra will the final payment need to be to ensure that the loan is fully repaid after 5 months?

10 Bonnie borrowed $10 000 at an interest rate of 12% per annum compounding quarterly. The loan will be repaid the loan by making 4 quarterly payments of $2690.27. To the nearest cent, does a quarterly payment of $2690.27 ensure that the loan is fully repaid after four payments?

11 Anthony deposits $5000 into an investment account at the beginning of the year. He received interest of $150 after the first quarter.
   a What is the quarterly interest rate?
   b Anthony made an extra deposit of $600 at the end of each quarter for two years. What is the recurrence relation for this investment?
   c Calculate the balance of Anthony's investment account after two years.

12 Indiana takes out a reducing-balance loan of $32 000 whose interest rate is 12% p.a. compounded monthly.
   a What is the monthly interest rate?
   b Indiana makes a monthly repayment of $2500. What is the recurrence relation for this loan?
   c Calculate the balance of the loan after six months. Answer to the nearest dollar.
   d How many months does it take for Indiana to repay the loan?
   e What is the final payment in the last month? Answer to the nearest dollar.

13 Ebony has $3000 in a savings account with an interest rate of 6.5% p.a. compounded annually. She wants to calculate the amount she will receive in 4 years when she plans to buy a car.

   a What amount is available for her car if she deposits $6000 each year into the savings account? Answer to the nearest dollar.
   b Ebony decides to transfer her $3000 into a different savings account with an interest rate of 7.5% p.a. compounded annually. What amount is available for her car if she deposits $6000 each year into this savings account? Answer to the nearest dollar.
   c What is the extra amount saved by investing $6000 each year at 7.5% p.a. compared with $6000 each year at 6.5% p.a.?

7B Using Excel to model an annuity

Excel has several built in functions for working with annuities. Let's consider an annuity where $1000 is invested at the end of each year for 4 years at 10% per annum compound interest. We require the value of the investment after 4 years. The spreadsheet function for this calculation is '= FV(0.10, 4, 1000)' where 0.10 is the rate (10%), 4 is the total number of payment periods and 1000 is the payment per period. The format of the functions in Excel is shown in the table below. The spreadsheet in the Interactive Textbook shows them in action.

Function	Formula	Example
Future value	= FV(rate, nper, pmt, [pv], [type])	= FV(0.10, 4, 1000)
Present value	= PV(rate, nper, pmt, [fv], [type])	= PV(0.10, 4, 1000)
Number of periods	= NPER(rate, nper, pmt, [pv], [type])	= NPER(0.10, 4, 1000)
Payment	= PMT(rate, nper, pv, [fv], [type])	= PMT(0.10, 4, 1000)
Rate	= RATE(nper, pmt, pv, [fv], [type], [guess])	= RATE(0.10, 4, 1000)

Arguments

Rate: interest rate per period expressed as decimal such as 0.10 for 10%.
Nper: the total number of payment periods in an annuity.
Pmt: payment made each period and cannot change over the life of the annuity.
Pv: present value, or amount of money if invested now would equal the future value.
Fv: future value, or sum of the money contributed plus the compound interest earned.
Type: 0 if payments are due at the end of the period or 1 at the beginning of the period.
Guess: guess for what the rate will be.

Example 3: Using Excel to calculate the future value 7B

Ella has decided to save for a cruise to be taken when she finishes her TAFE course. She decides to invest $250 per month, at the end of each month, by placing it into an account earning 6.4% per annum compounded monthly. Ella will do this for three years. How much will Ella have for her cruise? Answer to the nearest cent.

SOLUTION:

1	The function for future value is FV.	Excel function is FV
2	The investment is compounding per month.	Arguments are per month
3	Divide 0.064 by 12 to find the interest rate per month.	RATE = $\dfrac{0.064}{12}$
4	Multiply 3 by 12 to find the number of months in 3 years.	NPER = $3 \times 12 = 36$
5	Express the regular payment per month as a negative.	PMT = -250
6	Start Excel and type the formula into A1.	= FV((0.064/12), 36, −250)
7	Press 'return' or 'enter' to view the answer.	Answer is $9893.09
8	Write answer using appropriate accuracy and in words.	∴ Future value is $9893.09.

Example 4: Using a spreadsheet to calculate the payment
7B

Angus is planning to invest into an annuity at the end of each year that pays 10% per annum compound interest. Use a spreadsheet to calculate the payment Angus needs to make to have $10 000 at the end of 4 years.

SOLUTION:

1 The function for future value is PMT.   Excel function is PMT
2 The investment is compounding per year.   Arguments are per annum
3 Interest rate per year is 10% or 0.10.   RATE = 0.10
4 Number of periods in 4 years is 4.   NPER = 4
5 Express the amount required or future   FV = −10 000
   value as a negative.
6 Start Excel and type the formula into A1.   = PMT(0.10, 4, 0, −10 000)
7 Press 'return' or 'enter' to view the answer. Answer is $2154.71
8 Write answer using appropriate accuracy   ∴ Payment is $2154.71.

7B-2

The spreadsheet below shows this example using values for the arguments.

	A	B	C	D
		Given	*Calculated*	*Formula*
4	*Function*			
5	Future value	-10000		
6	Present value			
7	Number of periods	4		
8	Payment		$2,154.71	=PMT(B9,B7,B6,B5)
9	Rate	0.10		

Example 5: Using Excel to calculate the present value
7B

Find the present value of an annuity in which $1300 is invested at a rate of 5.8% p.a. compounded annually at the end of every year for 6 years.

SOLUTION:

1 The function for present value is PV.   Excel function is PV.
2 The investment is compounding every year.   Arguments are per annum (p.a.).
3 Find interest rate p.a. as a decimal.   RATE = 0.058
4 Number of periods in 6 years is 6.   NPER = 6
5 Enter regular payment p.a. as a negative.   PMT = −1300
6 Start Excel and type the formula into A1.   = PV(0.058, 6, −1300)
7 Press 'return' or 'enter' to view the answer. ∴ Present value is $6432.89.

7B-3

	A	B	C	D
		Given	*Calculated*	*Formula*
4	*Function*			
5	Future value			
6	Present value		$6,432.89	=PV(B9,B7,B8,B5)
7	Number of periods	6		
8	Payment	-1300		
9	Rate	0.06		

Exercise 7B

Example 3 **1** Use Excel to calculate the future value of following investments, to the nearest cent.
   a RATE = 0.05, NPER = 3 and PMT = −700
   b RATE = 0.06, NPER = 5 and PMT = −2000
   c RATE = 10%, NPER = 4 and PMT = −1100
   d RATE = 9%, NPER = 2 and PMT = −5000

2 Use Excel to find the future value to the nearest cent for each of the following annuities.
   a $23 000 at the end of every year for 3 years with an interest rate of 8.5% p.a.
   b $1850 at the end of every year for 5 years with an interest rate of 7.25% p.a.
   c $15 000 at the end of every year for 4 years with an interest rate of $4\frac{1}{2}$% p.a.
   d $7450 at the end of every year for 9 years with an interest rate of $4\frac{2}{3}$% p.a.

3 Linh is planning to invest $2000 at the end of each year at 8% p.a. interest. What will the future value of this annuity be worth after:
   a 5 years?   **b** 10 years?   **c** 15 years?
   d 20 years?   **e** 25 years?   **f** 30 years?

Example 4 **4** Molly's grandparents invest $450 for her at the end of each year. They started the annuity on Molly's first birthday with a rate of interest of 8.2% per annum compounded annually. What is the value of the annuity at the end of the year when Molly turns 15? Answer to the nearest cent.

5 Create the spreadsheet opposite.
   a Cell B8 has a formula that calculates the future value. Enter this formula.
   b Fill down the contents of B8 to B17 using the formula in cell B8.

   Change the annual interest rate to:
   c 10%
   d 15%
   e 20%.

   Change the payment to:
   f $3000
   g $4000
   h $5000.

	A	B	C
1	**Mathematics Standard**		
2	Using Excel to model an annuity		
3			
4	Rate	0.08	
5	Payment	-2600	
6			
7	*Number of periods*	*Future value*	
8	1	$2,600.00	=FV(B4,A8,B5)
9	2	$5,395.00	
10	3	$8,399.62	
11	4	$11,629.60	
12	5	$15,101.82	
13	6	$18,834.45	
14	7	$22,847.04	
15	8	$27,160.56	
16	9	$31,797.61	
17	10	$36,782.43	

Example 5 **6** Use Excel to calculate the present value of following investments, to the nearest cent.
   a RATE = 0.05, NPER = 3 and PMT = −700
   b RATE = 0.06, NPER = 5 and PMT = −2000
   c RATE = 10%, NPER = 4 and PMT = −1100
   d RATE = 9%, NPER = 2 and PMT = −5000

7 Use Excel to find the present value to the nearest cent for each of the following annuities.

   a $23 000 at the end of every year for 3 years with an interest rate of 8.5% p.a.

   b $1850 at the end of every year for 5 years with an interest rate of 7.25% p.a.

   c $15 000 at the end of every year for 4 years with an interest rate of $4\frac{1}{2}$% p.a.

   d $7450 at the end of every year for 9 years with an interest rate of $4\frac{2}{3}$% p.a.

8 Cooper pays $5680 into a managed fund at the end of each year. The fund pays 12% per annum compounding yearly. What is the present value of the annuity if it has 10 years to mature? Answer to the nearest dollar.

9 Mrs Nguyen aims to give Jenny $200 for her birthday for the next 12 years. What lump sum could she invest now, in an account paying 8% per annum, to achieve this goal? Answer to the nearest cent.

7BQ10

10 Create the spreadsheet opposite.

   a Cell B8 has a formula that calculates the future value. Enter this formula.

   b Fill down the contents of B8 to B17 using the formula in cell B8.

Change the interest rate to:

   c 10%

   d 15%

   e 20%.

Change the payment to:

   f $3000

   g $4000

   h $5000.

	A	B	C
1	**Mathematics Standard**		
2	Using Excel to model an annuity		
3			
4	Rate	0.0610	
5	Payment	-900	
6			
7	*Number of periods*	*Present value*	
8	1	$848.26	=PV(B4,A8,B5)
9	2	$1,647.74	
10	3	$2,401.27	
11	4	$3,111.47	
12	5	$3,780.84	
13	6	$4,411.72	
14	7	$5,006.33	
15	8	$5,566.76	
16	9	$6,094.97	
17	10	$6,592.81	

LEVEL 2

11 Use Excel to calculate the future value of following investments, to the nearest cent.

   a $420 at the end of every six months for 3 years at 6% p.a. compounded biannually

   b $960 at the end of every six months for 5 years at 9% p.a. compounded biannually

   c $2000 at the end of every quarter for 9 years at 8% p.a. compounded quarterly

   d $1300 at the end of every quarter for 6 years at 6.4% p.a. compounded quarterly

   e $1200 at the end of every month for 4 years at 4.8% p.a. compounded monthly

   f $360 at the end of every month for 7 years at 7.2% p.a. compounded monthly

   g $680 at the end of every week for 2 years at 5.2% p.a. compounded weekly

   h $840 at the end of every week for 6 years at 7.8% p.a. compounded weekly

   i $320 at the end of every fortnight for 3 years at 4% p.a. compounded fortnightly

   j $560 at the end of every fortnight for 4 years at 10% p.a. compounded fortnightly

12 Hayley's mother invested in an annuity for Hayley when she was born. She invested $230 per month earning 7.8% per annum, compounded monthly.

   a What is the future value of the annuity on Hayley's tenth birthday?

   b On Hayley's tenth birthday they stopped regular payments. However, she left the money in this account earning the same rate of interest. What is the value of the investment on Hayley's eighteenth birthday?

13 Mitch decides to invest $720 per quarter into his superannuation fund. The interest rate quoted is 6.8% per annum, compounded quarterly.

   a What is the future value of his superannuation at the end of 20 years?

   b Calculate the payment needed per quarter to have $40 000 after 10 years.

14 Use Excel to calculate the present value of investments shown in question 11. Answer to the nearest cent.

15 James contributes $860 at the end of each quarter for 15 years into a superannuation fund that earns 9.6% p.a. compounding quarterly.

   a What is the future value of this investment? (Answer to the nearest dollar.)

   b What is the present value of this investment? (Answer to the nearest dollar.)

16 Jake is planning to save for a motorbike in four years' time. Each fortnight he will invest $150 into an annuity earning 5.6% per annum, compounded fortnightly.

   a How much will Jake's investment be worth in four years' time? Answer to the nearest dollar.

   b Calculate the contribution needed per fortnight to have $20 000 after 4 years. Answer to the nearest dollar.

17 Ann aims to have a deposit for a house in 4 years' time by investing in an annuity. The deposit for the house is $80 000. The annuity has an interest rate of 8% p.a. compounded monthly. How much money per month must Ann invest to reach her target? Answer to the nearest cent.

18 Olivia plans to buy a car in 3 years' time by investing in an annuity. The annuity has an interest rate of 6.6% p.a. compounded fortnightly. She estimates that the car will cost $42 000. Calculate the amount of money Olivia must invest at the end of each month to reach her goal. Answer to the nearest cent.

19 Jacob is saving for a holiday, costing $18 000. He has already saved $10 000. He has deposited the $10 000 into a term deposit at 0.75% per month compounded monthly. In addition he is investing $150 per month into an annuity, paid at the end of each month, earning 5.9% p.a., compounding monthly.
  a What is the value of the term deposit after two years?
  b Calculate the future value of the annuity at the end of two years.
  c Does Jacob have enough money for his holiday at the end of two years? Justify.

20 Chelsea will need at least $240 000 to upgrade her hairdressing salon in five years' time. She plans to make regular payments of $4200 into an investment account that pays a rate of interest of 8.4% p.a. compounding monthly.
  a Will Chelsea have enough money to upgrade her salon? Explain your answer by calculation.
  b How much would Chelsea have needed to invest in a lump sum now to have the required $240 000 in five years' time? Assume the same rate of interest.

21 Tyler invests $7500 at 7% per annum compounded monthly for one year. Ava invests $620 at the end of each month at 8% per annum compounded monthly for one year. Which is worth more at the end of the year? Justify your answer.

22 Abbey plans to buy a new car whose present value is $45 000. She decides to take out a loan with an interest rate of 1% per month. The interest on this loan is compounding monthly. What is the monthly contribution required to payout the loan in three years? Answer to the nearest cent.

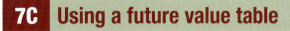

7C | Using a future value table

Investment problems are made easier by using tables. The table below shows the future value of an annuity when $1 is invested at the end of the period at the given interest rate for the given number of periods. The interest is compounded per period. For example, the value of $1 after 6 periods at an interest rate of 6% per period is $6.9753.

Future value of $1						
Period	**1%**	**2%**	**3%**	**4%**	**5%**	**6%**
1	1.0000	1.0000	1.0000	1.0000	1.0000	1.0000
2	2.0100	2.0200	2.0300	2.0400	2.0500	2.0600
3	3.0301	3.0604	3.0909	3.1216	3.1525	3.1836
4	4.0604	4.1216	4.1836	4.2465	4.3101	4.3746
5	5.1010	5.2040	5.3091	5.4163	5.5256	5.6371
6	6.1520	6.3081	6.4684	6.6330	6.8019	6.9753

USING A FUTURE VALUE TABLE

1 Determine the time period and rate of interest.
2 Find the intersection of the time period and rate of interest in the table.
3 Multiply the number in the intersection with the money contributed.

Example 6: Using tables of future values   7C

Use the above table to calculate the future value of:
a $34 000 per year for 3 years at 5% p.a. compounded annually
b $5000 per half-year for 2 years at 6% p.a. compounded six-monthly.

SOLUTION:

1   Find the intersection value from the table for time period 3, interest rate 5%.

2   Multiply intersection value by the money invested.
3   Evaluate.
4   Answer the question in words.
5   Find the intersection value from the table for period 4 $(n = 2 \times 2)$, interest rate 3% $\left(r = \dfrac{6}{2}\%\right)$.

6   Multiply intersection value by the money invested.
7   Evaluate and answer the question in words.

a   Intersection value is 3.1525

$FV = 3.1525 \times 34\,000$
$ = 107\,185$
Future value is $107 185.

b   Intersection value is 4.1836

$FV = 4.1836 \times 5000$
$ = 20\,918$
Future value is $20 918.

Example 7: Using tables of future values

7C

The table shows the future value of an annuity with a contribution of $1. Use the table to answer the following questions.

Future value of $1							
Period	**1.0%**	**1.5%**	**2.0%**	**02.5%**	**3.0%**	**3.5%**	**4.0%**
1	1.000	1.000	1.000	1.000	1.000	1.000	1.000
2	2.010	2.015	2.020	2.025	2.030	2.035	2.040
3	3.030	3.045	3.060	3.076	3.091	3.106	3.122
4	4.060	4.091	4.122	4.153	4.184	4.215	4.246

a   What is the future value of an investment of $300 per month for 3 months at 24% p.a. compounded monthly?

b   What is the future value of an investment of $15000 per quarter for 1 year at 12% p.a. compounded quarterly?

c   Find the payment or contribution per period of an annuity with a future value of $76713 at 3.5% p.a. compounded annually for 4 years.

d   Find the payment or contribution per period of an annuity with a future value of $6105 at 7% p.a. compounded biannually for one year.

SOLUTION:

1   Find the intersection value from the table for period 3 and interest rate 2% ($r = \frac{24}{12}\%$)

2   Multiply intersection value by money invested. Evaluate.

3   Answer the question in words.

4   Find the intersection value from the table for period 4 ($n = 4 \times 1$) and interest rate 3% ($r = \frac{12}{4}\%$).

5   Multiply intersection value by the money invested.

6   Evaluate and answer the question in words.

7   Find the intersection value from the table for period 4 and interest rate 3.5%.

8   Multiply intersection value by the money invested.

9   Divide both sides by the intersection value.

10   Make PMT the subject, evaluate and answer the question in words.

11   Find the intersection value from the table for period 2 ($n = 2 \times 1$) and interest rate 3.5%. ($r = \frac{7.5}{2}\%$)

12   FV ($6105) is intersection value times money invested.

13   Divide both sides by the intersection value.

14   Make PMT the subject, evaluate and answer the question in words.

a   Intersection value is 3.060

$FV = 3.060 \times 300 = 918$
Future value is $918.

b   Intersection value is 4.184

$FV = 4.184 \times 15\,000$
$= 62\,760$
Future value is $62760

c   Intersection value is 4.215.

$FV = 4.215 \times PMT$
$76\,713 = 4.215 \times PMT$
$\frac{76713}{4.215} = PMT$
$PMT = 18\,200$
∴ Payment is $18200.

d   Intersection value is 2.035

$6105 = 2.035 \times PMT$
$\frac{6105}{2.035} = PMT$
$PMT = 3000$
∴ Payment is $3000.

Exercise 7C

Example 6   **1**   The table below shows the future value of an annuity with a contribution of $1.

Future value of $1						
Period	**2%**	**4%**	**6%**	**8%**	**10%**	**12%**
1	1.00	1.00	1.00	1.00	1.00	1.00
2	2.02	2.04	2.06	2.08	2.10	2.12
3	3.06	3.12	3.18	3.25	3.31	3.37
4	4.12	4.25	4.37	4.51	4.64	4.78

Use the table to calculate the future value of the following annuities.
a $2000 per year for 2 years at 12% p.a. compounded annually
b $26000 per year for 3 years at 4% p.a. compounded annually
c $32000 per year for 4 years at 8% p.a. compounded annually
d $7000 per year for 2 years at 6% p.a. compounded annually
e $10000 per year for 3 years at 10% p.a. compounded annually
f $1600 per year for 4 years at 12% p.a. compounded annually

2   Ethan saves $2650 by the end of each year and invests it into an account earning 12% p.a. compound interest. Use the table in question **1** to calculate the future value of the investment after 3 years.

3   The table below shows the future value of an annuity with a contribution of $1.

Future value of $1							
Period	**1%**	**2%**	**3%**	**4%**	**5%**	**6%**	**7%**
1	1.00	1.00	1.00	1.00	1.00	1.00	1.00
2	2.01	2.02	2.03	2.04	2.05	2.06	2.07
3	3.03	3.06	3.09	3.12	3.15	3.18	3.21
4	4.06	4.12	4.18	4.25	4.31	4.37	4.44
5	5.10	5.20	5.31	5.42	5.53	5.64	5.75

Use the above table to calculate the future value of the following annuities.
a $34000 per year for 5 years at 4% p.a. compounded annually
b $18000 per year for 2 years at 6% p.a. compounded annually
c $45000 per year for 4 years at 1% p.a. compounded annually
d $8600 per year for 3 years at 7% p.a. compounded annually
e $14200 per year for 5 years at 5% p.a. compounded annually
f $90000 per year for 2 years at 3% p.a. compounded annually

4 Jacob is saving to buy a car. He deposits $5500 into an account at the end of every year for 3 years. The account pays interest of 6% p.a., compounding annually.

Future value of $1				
End of year	**5%**	**6%**	**7%**	**8%**
1	1.0000	1.0000	1.0000	1.0000
2	2.0500	2.0600	2.0700	2.0800
3	3.1525	3.1836	3.2149	3.2464
4	4.3101	4.3746	4.4399	4.5061

Use the table to calculate the following amounts.
a What is the value of Jacob's investment at the end of the following years?
   i two   **ii** three   **iii** four
b How much interest does Jacob earn on his investment over the following years?
   i two   **ii** three   **iii** four

Example 7   **5** The table below shows the future value of an annuity with a contribution of $1.

Future value of $1						
Period	**1%**	**4%**	**8%**	**12%**	**16%**	**20%**
1	1.0000	1.0000	1.0000	1.0000	1.0000	1.0000
2	2.0100	2.0400	2.0800	2.1200	2.1600	2.2000
3	3.0301	3.1216	3.2464	3.3744	3.5056	3.6400
4	4.0604	4.2465	4.5061	4.7793	5.0665	5.3680
5	5.1010	5.4163	5.8666	6.3528	6.8771	7.4416
6	6.1520	6.6330	7.3359	8.1152	8.9775	9.9299

Use the above table to calculate the future value of the following annuities.
a $7000 per year for 2 years at 1% p.a. compounded annually
b $16 000 per year for 6 years at 12% p.a. compounded annually
c $58 000 per year for 6 years at 4% p.a. compounded annually
d $120 000 per year for 6 years at 1% p.a. compounded annually
e $950 per quarter for 1 year at 16% p.a. compounded quarterly
f $1200 per quarter for 1 year at 4% p.a. compounded quarterly
g $8400 per quarter for 1 year at 16% p.a. compounded quarterly
h $37 000 per half-year for 3 years at 16% p.a. compounded biannually
i $5400 per half-year for 2 years at 8% p.a. compounded biannually
j $12 100 per half-year for 1 year at 8% p.a. compounded biannually

6 The table below shows the future value of an annuity with a contribution of $1.

Future value of $1							
Period	**1.0%**	**1.5%**	**2.0%**	**2.5%**	**3.0%**	**3.5%**	**4.0%**
1	1.000	1.000	1.000	1.000	1.000	1.000	1.000
2	2.010	2.015	2.020	2.025	2.030	2.035	2.040
3	3.030	3.045	3.060	3.076	3.091	3.106	3.122
4	4.060	4.091	4.122	4.153	4.184	4.215	4.246
5	5.101	5.152	5.204	5.256	5.309	5.362	5.416
6	6.152	6.230	6.308	6.388	6.468	6.550	6.633
7	7.214	7.323	7.434	7.547	7.662	7.779	7.898
8	8.286	8.433	8.583	8.736	8.892	9.052	9.214

Use the table to calculate the future value of the following annuities.

a $600 per month for 4 months at 18% p.a. compounded monthly

b $1280 per month for 5 months at 12% p.a. compounded monthly

c $970 per month for 7 months at 42% p.a. compounded monthly

d $11 000 per quarter for 9 months at 4% p.a. compounded quarterly

e $23 000 per quarter for 1 year at 8% p.a. compounded quarterly

f $5000 per quarter for 2 years at 12% p.a. compounded quarterly

g $32 000 per half-year for 18 months at 7% p.a. compounded six-monthly

h $67 000 per half-year for 2 years at 2% p.a. compounded six-monthly

i $14 000 per half-year for 4 years at 8% p.a. compounded six-monthly

7 Create the spreadsheet below.

7CQ7

	FV		fx	=FV(B5,A6,-1)		
	A	**B**	**C**	**D**	**E**	**F**
1	**Mathematics Standard 2**					
2	Tables of future values of $1					
3						
4				Interest rate		
5	Period	1%	2%	3%	4%	5%
6	1	A6,-1)	1.0000	1.0000	1.0000	1.0000
7	2	2.0100	2.0200	2.0300	2.0400	2.0500
8	3	3.0301	3.0604	3.0909	3.1216	3.1525
9	4	4.0604	4.1216	4.1836	4.2465	4.3101
10	5	5.1010	5.2040	5.3091	5.4163	5.5256
11	6	6.1520	6.3081	6.4684	6.6330	6.8019
12	7	7.2135	7.4343	7.6625	7.8983	8.1420
13	8	8.2857	8.5830	8.8923	9.2142	9.5491

a Cell B6 has a formula $= FV(\$B\$5, A6, -1)$ that calculates the future value. Enter this formula.

b Fill down the contents of B6 to B13 using the formula in cell B6.

c Cells C6:F6 have similar formulas to B6. Enter these formulas to calculate the future value.

d Fill down the contents of C6 to F13 using the formulas in cells C6:F6.

8 The table below shows the future value of an annuity with a payment or contribution of $1.

	Future value of $1					
End of year	**3%**	**4%**	**5%**	**6%**	**7%**	**8%**
1	1.0000	1.0000	1.0000	1.0000	1.0000	1.0000
2	2.0300	2.0400	2.0500	2.0600	2.0700	2.0800
3	3.0909	3.1216	3.1525	3.1836	3.2149	3.2464
4	4.1836	4.2465	4.3101	4.3746	4.4399	4.5061
5	5.3091	5.4163	5.5256	5.6371	5.7507	5.8666
6	6.4684	6.6330	6.8019	6.9753	7.1533	7.3359

Using the table find the payment per period of an annuity whose future value is:
a $8242 at 7% p.a. compounded annually for 3 years
b $8780 at 5% p.a. compounded annually for 2 years
c $13 784 at 6% p.a. compounded annually for 4 years
d $20 800 at 8% p.a. compounded annually for 3 years
e $165 000 at 5% p.a. compounded annually for 4 years.

9 Use the table in question **8** to find the annual compound interest rate of an annuity whose future value is:
a $2972.50 when $1450 is invested at the end of each year for 2 years
b $4884.37 when $920 is invested at the end of each year for 5 years
c $12 861.32 when $2940 is invested at the end of each year for 4 years
d $63 743.07 when $20 420 is invested at the end of each year for 3 years
e $8085.50 when $1250 is invested at the end of each year for 6 years.

10 Thomas aims to have a deposit for an apartment of at least $56 000 in 3 years' time by investing in an annuity. The annuity has an interest rate of 8% p.a. compounded biannually. Use the table in question **8** to calculate Thomas's six-monthly contribution to achieve his deposit. Answer correct to the nearest dollar.

11 Use the table in question **8** to answer the following questions, to the nearest dollar.
a What would be the future value of an $820 per quarter annuity at 8% p.a. for 2 years, with interest compounding quarterly?
b What is the value of an annuity that would provide a future value of $98 375 after 6 years at 3% p.a. compound interest?
c An annuity of $3800 per half-year is invested at 4% p.a. compounded six-monthly for 4 years. What will be the amount of interest earned?

7D   Using a present value table

The present value of an annuity is the amount of money that, if invested now, would equal the future value of the annuity. The present value is the principal (P) in the compound interest formula and the future value is the amount (A) or $FV = PV(1 + r)^n$. If the present value is made the subject of this formula, then the present value is the future value divided by $(1 + r)^n$ or $PV = \dfrac{FV}{(1 + r)^n}$.

Calculating the present value is made easy using tables.

USING A PRESENT VALUE TABLE

1   Determine the time period and rate of interest.
2   Find the intersection of the time period and rate of interest in the table.
3   Multiply the number in the intersection by the amount of money contributed.

Example 8: Using tables of present values   7D

Use the table to calculate the present value, if $9600 is contributed per year for 7 years at 4% p.a. compounded annually.

Present value of $1				
End of year	**3%**	**4%**	**5%**	**6%**
6	5.4172	5.2421	5.0757	4.9173
7	6.2303	6.0021	5.7864	5.5824
8	7.0197	6.7327	6.4632	6.2098
9	7.7861	7.4353	7.1078	6.8017

SOLUTION:

1   Find the intersection value from the table for the period 7 and interest rate 4%.   Intersection value is 6.0021.

2   Multiply the intersection value by the money invested. $PV = 6.0021 \times 9600$

3   Evaluate. $= \$57\,620.16$

4   Answer the question in words.   Present value is $57 620.16.

7D Using a present value table   287

Example 9: Using tables of present values   7D

The table shows the present value of an annuity with a contribution of $1.

Use the table to answer the following questions, to the nearest dollar.

	Present value of $1							
Period	**1%**	**2%**	**3%**	**4%**	**6%**	**8%**	**10%**	**12%**
1	0.99	0.98	0.97	0.96	0.94	0.93	0.91	0.89
2	1.97	1.94	1.91	1.89	1.83	1.78	1.74	1.69
3	2.94	2.88	2.83	2.78	2.67	2.58	2.49	2.40
4	3.90	3.81	3.71	3.63	3.47	3.31	3.17	3.04

a   What is the present value of an investment of $500 per month for 2 months at 24% p.a. compounded monthly?

b   What is the present value of an investment of $7000 per quarter for 1 year at 12% p.a. compounded quarterly?

c   Find the payment or contribution per period of an annuity with a present value of $33 240 at 6% p.a. compounded annually for 3 years.

d   Find the payment or contribution per period of an annuity with a present value of $10 000 at 8% p.a. compounded biannually for 1 year.

SOLUTION:

1   Find the intersection value from the table for period 2, and interest rate 2% ($r = 24\% \div 12\%$).

a   Intersection value is 1.94

2   Multiply intersection value by the money invested.

$PV = 1.94 \times 500 = 970$

3   Evaluate and answer the question in words.

∴ Present value is $970.

4   Find the intersection value from the table for period 4 ($n = 4 \times 1$) and interest rate 3% ($r = 12 \div 4\%$).

b   Intersection value is 3.71

5   Multiply intersection value by the money invested.

$PV = 3.71 \times 7000 = 25970$

6   Evaluate and answer the question in words.

∴ Present value is $25 970.

7   Find the intersection value from the table for period 3 and interest rate 6%.

c   Intersection value is 2.67

8 PV ($33 240$) is intersection value times money invested.

$33\,240 = 2.67 \times PMT$

9   Divide both sides by the intersection value.

$\dfrac{33\,240}{2.67} = PMT = 12449$

10   Evaluate and answer the question in words.

∴ Payment is $12 449.

11   Find the intersection value from the table for period 2 ($n = 2 \times 1$) and interest rate 4% ($r = 8 \div 2\%$).

d   Intersection value is 1.89

12 PV ($10 000$) is intersection value times money invested.

$10\,000 = 1.89 \times PMT$

13   Divide both sides by the intersection value.

$\dfrac{10\,000}{1.89} = PMT = 5291$

14   Evaluate and answer the question in words.

∴ Payment is $5291.

Exercise 7D

Example 8   **1**   The table below shows the present value of an annuity with a contribution of $1.

Present value of $1						
Period	**2%**	**4%**	**6%**	**8%**	**10%**	**12%**
1	0.98	0.96	0.94	0.93	0.91	0.89
2	1.94	1.89	1.83	1.78	1.74	1.69
3	2.88	2.78	2.67	2.58	2.49	2.40
4	3.81	3.63	3.47	3.31	3.17	3.04

Use the table to calculate the present value of the following annuities.
  a $8000 per year for 2 years at 10% p.a. compounded annually
  b $35 000 per year for 4 years at 2% p.a. compounded annually
  c $22 000 per year for 2 years at 6% p.a. compounded annually
  d $43 000 per year for 3 years at 12% p.a. compounded annually
  e $6000 per year for 4 years at 8% p.a. compounded annually.

2   Jessica pays $5600 into a managed fund at the end of each year. The fund pays 10% p.a. interest compounding yearly. Use the table in question **1** to calculate the present value of the annuity if it has 3 years to mature.

3   The table below shows the present value of an annuity with a contribution of $1.

Present value of $1				
End of year	**3%**	**4%**	**5%**	**6%**
6	5.4172	5.2421	5.0757	4.9173
7	6.2303	6.0021	5.7864	5.5824
8	7.0197	6.7327	6.4632	6.2098
9	7.7861	7.4353	7.1078	6.8017

Use the table to calculate the present value of the following annuities.
  a $5000 per year for 6 years at 3% p.a. compounded annually
  b $21 000 per year for 9 years at 5% p.a. compounded annually
  c $14 000 per year for 7 years at 6% p.a. compounded annually
  d $1000 per year for 9 year at 4% p.a. compounded annually
  e $8000 per year for 8 years at 6% p.a. compounded annually

4   Use the present value table in question **3** to calculate the present value when $3200 is invested at the end of each year for 9 years at 5% p.a. compound interest. Answer correct to the nearest cent.

5 Hamish would like a new kitchen. He can afford to pay $8400 into an account at the end of every year. The account has an interest rate of 9% p.a. compounded annually. The table below shows the present value of the annuity with a payment of $1.

Present value of $1					
Period	**5%**	**6%**	**7%**	**8%**	**9%**
1	0.9524	0.9434	0.9346	0.9259	0.9174
2	1.8594	1.8334	1.8080	1.7833	1.7591
3	2.7232	2.6730	2.6243	2.5771	2.5313
4	3.5460	3.4651	3.3872	3.3121	3.2397

Use the table to do the following calculations. Answer correct to the nearest dollar.
a What is the present value when the payments are made at the end of the following years?
  i two   ii three   iii four
b Hamish found another account whose interest rate is of 6% p.a. compounded annually. What is the present value when the same payment is made into this account?
  i two   ii three   iii four

xample 9 6 The table below shows the present value of an annuity with a contribution of $1.

Present value of $1							
Period	**1%**	**2%**	**4%**	**6%**	**8%**	**10%**	**12%**
1	0.9901	0.9804	0.9615	0.9434	0.9259	0.9091	0.8929
2	1.9704	1.9416	1.8861	1.8334	1.7833	1.7355	1.6901
3	2.9410	2.8839	2.7751	2.6730	2.5771	2.4869	2.4018
4	3.9020	3.8077	3.6299	3.4651	3.3121	3.1699	3.0373
5	4.8534	4.7135	4.4518	4.2124	3.9927	3.7908	3.6048
6	5.7955	5.6014	5.2421	4.9173	4.6229	4.3553	4.1114

Use the table to calculate the present value of the following annuities. Answer to the nearest dollar.
a $8000 per year for 4 years at 6% p.a. compounded annually
b $11000 per year for 5 years at 10% p.a. compounded annually
c $13000 per year for 6 years at 12% p.a. compounded annually
d $7000 per year for 2 years at 1% p.a. compounded annually
e $51000 per year for 6 years at 4% p.a. compounded annually
f $100000 per year for 6 years at 1% p.a. compounded annually
g $3500 per quarter for 1 year at 8% p.a. compounded quarterly
h $8000 per quarter for 1 year at 4% p.a. compounded quarterly
i $29000 per half-year for 2 years at 2% p.a. compounded biannually
j $6100 per half-year for 3 years at 8% p.a. compounded biannually

7 The table below shows the future value of an annuity with a contribution of $1.

	Present value of $1							
Period	**1%**	**2%**	**4%**	**6%**	**8%**	**12%**	**16%**	**20%**
1	0.9901	0.9804	0.9615	0.9434	0.9259	0.8929	0.8621	0.8333
2	1.9704	1.9416	1.8861	1.8334	1.7833	1.6901	1.6052	1.5278
3	2.9410	2.8839	2.7751	2.6730	2.5771	2.4018	2.2459	2.1065
4	3.9020	3.8077	3.6299	3.4651	3.3121	3.0373	2.7982	2.5887

Use the table to find the present value (to nearest dollar) of the following annuities.

a $8400 per quarter for 1 year at 16% p.a. compounded quarterly

b $950 per quarter for 1 year at 16% p.a. compounded quarterly

c $1200 per quarter for 1 year at 4% p.a. compounded quarterly

d $12 100 per half-year for 1 year at 8% p.a. compounded biannually

e $37 000 per half-year for 1.5 years at 16% p.a. compounded biannually

f $5400 per half-year for 2 years at 8% p.a. compounded biannually

8 The table below shows the value of an annuity with a contribution of $1.

	Present value of $1								
Period	**1.0%**	**1.5%**	**2.0%**	**2.5%**	**3.0%**	**3.5%**	**4.0%**	**4.5%**	**5.0%**
1	0.9901	0.9852	0.9804	0.9756	0.9709	0.9662	0.9615	0.9569	0.9524
2	1.9704	1.9559	1.9416	1.9274	1.9135	1.8997	1.8861	1.8727	1.8594
3	2.9410	2.9122	2.8839	2.8560	2.8286	2.8016	2.7751	2.7490	2.7232
4	3.9020	3.8544	3.8077	3.7620	3.7171	3.6731	3.6299	3.5875	3.5460
5	4.8534	4.7826	4.7135	4.6458	4.5797	4.5151	4.4518	4.3900	4.3295
6	5.7955	5.6972	5.6014	5.5081	5.4172	5.3286	5.2421	5.1579	5.0757
7	6.7282	6.5982	6.4720	6.3494	6.2303	6.1145	6.0021	5.8927	5.7864
8	7.6517	7.4859	7.3255	7.1701	7.0197	6.8740	6.7327	6.5959	6.4632

Use the table to find the present value (to the nearest dollar) of the following annuities.

a $800 per month for 6 months at 30% p.a. compounded monthly

b $630 per month for 7 months at 42% p.a. compounded monthly

c $1520 per month for 5 months at 12% p.a. compounded monthly

d $28 000 per quarter for 1 year at 8% p.a. compounded quarterly

e $11 000 per quarter for 9 months at 4% p.a. compounded quarterly

f $8000 per quarter for 2 years at 16% p.a. compounded quarterly

g $30 000 per half-year for 18 months at 7% p.a. compounded six-monthly

h $19 500 per half-year for 4 years at 8% p.a. compounded six-monthly

i $61 000 per half-year for 2 years at 7% p.a. compounded six-monthly

9 Create the spreadsheet below.

7DQ9

| PV | ⌃⌄ ✕ ✓ *fx* =PV(B5,A6,-1) | | | | | | | | | |

	A	B	C	D	E	F	G	H	I	J	K
1	**Mathematics Standard 2**										
2	Tables of present values of $1										
3											
4						Interest rate					
5	Period	1%	2%	3%	4%	5%	6%	7%	8%	9%	10%
6	1	A6,-1)	0.9804	0.9709	0.9615	0.9524	0.9434	0.9346	0.9259	0.9174	0.9091
7	2	1.9704	1.9416	1.9135	1.8861	1.8594	1.8334	1.8080	1.7833	1.7591	1.7355
8	3	2.9410	2.8839	2.8286	2.7751	2.7232	2.6730	2.6243	2.5771	2.5313	2.4869
9	4	3.9020	3.8077	3.7171	3.6299	3.5460	3.4651	3.3872	3.3121	3.2397	3.1699
10	5	4.8534	4.7135	4.5797	4.4518	4.3295	4.2124	4.1002	3.9927	3.8897	3.7908
11	6	5.7955	5.6014	5.4172	5.2421	5.0757	4.9173	4.7665	4.6229	4.4859	4.3553
12	7	6.7282	6.4720	6.2303	6.0021	5.7864	5.5824	5.3893	5.2064	5.0330	4.8684
13	8	7.6517	7.3255	7.0197	6.7327	6.4632	6.2312	6.0103	5.8000	5.5348	5.4092

a Cell B6 has a formula $= PV(\$B\$5, A6, -1)$ that calculates the present value. Enter this formula.

b Fill down the contents of B6 to B13 using the formula in cell B6.

c Cells C6:K6 have similar formulas to B6. Enter these formulas to find the present value.

d Fill down the contents of C6 to K13 using the formulas in cells C6:K6.

LEVEL 3

10 Use the above spreadsheet table in question **9** to find the payment per period (nearest dollar) of an annuity whose present value is:

a $10 684 at 5% p.a. compounded annually for 2 years

b $5005 at 7% p.a. compounded annually for 3 years

c $139 420 at 5% p.a. compounded annually for 4 years

d $16 860 at 6% p.a. compounded annually for 4 years

e $22 100 at 10% p.a. compounded annually for 3 years.

11 Use the above spreadsheet table in question **9** to find the annual compound interest rate of an annuity whose present value is:

a $25 431.65 when $7850 is invested at the end of each year for 4 years

b $6318.60 when $1500 is invested at the end of each year for 5 years

c $4468.56 when $610 is invested at the end of each year for 8 years

d $70 709.55 when $25 480 is invested at the end of each year for 3 years

e $12 405.39 when $2290 is invested at the end of each year for 6 years.

12 Abbey plans a holiday that has a present value of $3200. She decides to take out a loan with an interest rate of 12% p.a. compounded monthly. What is the monthly contribution required to pay out the loan in 6 months? Use the above spreadsheet table in question **9** and answer to the nearest dollar.

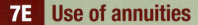
7E   Use of annuities

Loans

The regular loan repayment is an example of an annuity. In a reducing-balance loan, as the payments are made, the balance owing is reduced and therefore the interest charged is reduced. A table (see example below) is often used to summarise the key properties of an annuity. It shows the payment number, the payment received, the interest earned, the principal reduction and the balance of the annuity after each payment has been received.

Example 10: Reading and interpreting an annuity table   7E

Jessica takes out a car loan for $24 000 with an interest rate of 10% p.a. compound interest. She agrees to a regular yearly payment of $5500 over six years. A table for this annuity is shown below.

Payment number	Payment paid	Interest paid	Principal reduction	Balance of annuity
0	0	0.00	0	24 000.00
1	5500.00	2400.00	3100.00	20 900.00
2	5500.00	2090.00	3410.00	17 490.00
3	5500.00	1749.00	3751.00	13 739.00
4	5500.00	1373.90	4126.10	9612.90
5	5500.00	961.29	4538.71	5074.19
6	5500.00	507.42	4992.58	81.61

Determine, to the nearest cent:

a the interest paid when payment 1 is received

b the principal reduction when payment 3 is received

c the balance of the annuity after payment 4 has been received

d the value of the last payment if the balance of the annuity is to be zero after the 6th payment is received

e the total amount of interest paid.

SOLUTION:

1 Read the value in the table.

2 Read the value in the table.

3 Read the value in the table.

4 Add the regular payment and the balance of the annuity.

5 Sum the interest paid column.

a Interest paid is $2400.00

b Principal reduction is $3751.00

c Balance of the annuity is $9612.90

d Payment = $5500 + $81.61
            = $5581.61

e Interest = $2400 + $2090 + …
        = $9081.61

Superannuation

The regular payment into a superannuation fund is an example of an annuity. Superannuation is money invested while you are working, so you can enjoy a regular income later in life when you retire. In Australia your employer must pay 9.5% of your income into a super account. You can also add extra money to increase the amount you have in retirement.

Example 11: Reading and interpreting an annuity table   7E

Michael is aged 60 and is planning to retire at 65 years of age. His current superannuation fund has a balance of $500000 and is delivering 7% p.a. compound interest. Michael is making a payment of $20000 each year into his superannuation fund. A table for this annuity is shown below.

Payment number	Payment received	Interest earned	Principal increase	Balance of annuity
0	0	0.00	0	500000.00
1	20000.00	35000.00	55000.00	555000.00
2	20000.00	38850.00	58850.00	613850.00
3	20000.00	A	B	C
4	20000.00	47377.37	67377.37	744196.87
5	20000.00	52093.78	72093.78	816290.65

What is the value of A, B and C? Answer to the nearest cent.

SOLUTION:

1. Write the future value formula.
2. Substitute $PV = 613850$ (balance of annuity), $r = 0.07$ and $n = 1$. Evaluate.
3. Write the interest formula.
4. Substitute $FV = 656819.50$ and $PV = 613850$
5. Evaluate.
6. Write the answer.
7. Add the interest earned ($42969.50) and the payment ($20000).
8. Write the answer.
9. Add the principal increase ($62969.50) and previous balance of the annuity ($613850.00).
10. Write the answer.

$FV = PV(1 + r)^n$
$= 613850 \times (1.07)^1$
$= \$656819.50$

$I = FV - PV$
$= 656819.50 - 613850.00$
$= \$42969.50$

$\therefore A = \$42969.50$

Increase $= \$42969.50 + \$20000$
$= \$62969.50$

$\therefore B = \$62969.50$

Balance $= \$62969.50 + \$613850$
$= \$676819.50$

$\therefore C = \$676819.50$

ANNUITY TABLE

A table is used to summarise the key properties of an annuity. It shows the payment number, the payment received, the interest earned, the principal reduction and the balance of the annuity after each payment has been received.

Exercise 7E

Example 10   **1**   Sheila is a university student who received a scholarship of $6000 for her first year of study. She invests the money in an annuity paying an interest rate of 3% per annum, compounding monthly. From this annuity, she receives a monthly payment of $508. A table for this annuity is shown below.

Payment number	Payment received	Interest earned	Principal reduction	Balance of annuity
0	0.00	0.00	0.00	6000.00
1	508.00	15.00	493.00	5507.00
2	508.00	13.77	494.23	5012.77
3	508.00	12.53	495.47	4517.30
4	508.00	11.29	496.71	4020.59
5	508.00	10.05	497.95	3522.64
6	508.00	A	B	C
7	508.00	7.56	500.04	2523.01
8	508.00	6.31	501.69	2021.32
9	508.00	5.05	502.95	1518.37
10	508.00	3.80	504.20	1014.17
11	508.00	2.54	505.46	508.70
12	508.00	1.27	506.73	1.97

Determine, to the nearest cent:

a   the monthly interest rate

b   the interest earned when payment 1 is received

c   the principal reduction when payment 3 is received

d   the balance of the annuity after payment 5 has been received

e   the values of A, B and C

f   the value of the last payment if the balance of the annuity is to be zero after the 12th payment is received

g   the total payments received from the annuity

h   the total amount of interest paid.

The interest rate on the annuity has increased to 6% p.a. Determine, to the nearest cent:

i   the monthly interest rate

j   the interest earned when payment 1 is received

k   the principal reduction when payment 1 is received

l   the balance of the annuity after payment 1 has been received

m   the difference in the balance of the annuity after 1 payment with 6% interest compared to the balance with 3% interest.

Example 11 **2** Jennifer is aged 50 and is planning to retire at 60 years of age. Her current superannuation fund has a balance of \$450 000 and is delivering 6% p.a. compound interest. Jennifer is making a payment of \$18 000 each year into her superannuation fund. A table for this annuity is shown below.

Payment number	Payment received	Interest earned	Principal increase	Balance of annuity
0	0.00	0.00	0	450 000.00
1	18 000.00	27 000.00	45 000.00	495 000.00
2	18 000.00	29 700.00	47 700.00	542 700.00
3	18 000.00	32 562.00	50 562.00	593 262.00
4	18 000.00	35 595.72	53 595.72	646 857.72
5	18 000.00	38 811.46	56 811.46	703 669.18
6	18 000.00	42 220.15	60 220.15	763 889.33
7	18 000.00	45 833.36	63 833.36	827 722.69
8	18 000.00	A	B	C
9	18 000.00	53 723.16	71 723.16	967 109.22
10	18 000.00	58 026.55	76 026.55	1 043 135.77
11				
12				
13				

Determine, to the nearest cent:

a the interest earned when payment 1 is received

b the principal increase when payment 3 is received

c the balance of the annuity after payment 5 has been received

d the values of A, B and C

e the final balance of the annuity after payment 10 has been received

f the total payments received by the annuity

g the total amount of interest earned

h the extra interest earned if Jennifer delays retirement for one year (after 11 payments)

i the principal increase if Jennifer delays retirement for one year (after 11 payments)

j the balance of the annuity if Jennifer delays retirement for one year (after 11 payments)

k the interest earned in the twelfth year if Jennifer delays retirement for two years (after 12 payments)

l the principal increase in the twelfth year if Jennifer delays retirement for two years (after 12 payments)

m the balance of the annuity if Jennifer delays retirement for two years (after 12 payments)

n the interest earned in the thirteenth year if Jennifer delays retirement for three years (after 13 payments)

o the principal increase in the thirteenth year if Jennifer delays retirement for three years (after 13 payments)

p the balance of the annuity if Jennifer delays retirement for three years (after 13 payments).

LEVEL 2

3 Adrian borrowed $500 000 for an apartment. The interest rate was 5% p.a. compounding monthly and the monthly repayment is $2500. Copy and complete the annuity table shown below for the first 12 months. Use your calculator answer to complete each cell of the table, not the approximation. Answer correct to the nearest cent.

Payment number	Payment received	Interest earned	Principal reduction	Balance of annuity
0	0.00	0.00	0.00	500 000.00
1	2500.00			
2				
3				
4				
5				
6				
7				
8				
9				
10				
11				
12				

LEVEL 3

4 Stephen is aged 55 and is planning to retire at 65 years of age. His current superannuation fund has a balance of $700 000 and is delivering 4% p.a. compound interest. Stephen is making a payment of $22 000 each year into his superannuation fund.

  a Construct a table to summarise the key properties of this annuity for the next ten years.

  b What is the difference in the balance of the annuity if Stephen retired at 57 years of age?

  c What is the difference in the balance of the annuity if Stephen retired at 62 years of age?

  d What is the difference in the balance of the annuity if Stephen retired at 67 years of age?

Key ideas and chapter summary

Annuity	An annuity is a form of investment that involves the regular contribution of money. Investments into superannuation or a monthly loan repayment are examples of annuities.

Recurrence relation

A recurrence relation occurs when each successive application uses the resultant value of the previous application to generate the next value.

Investment $\qquad V_{n+1} = V_n(1 + r) + D$

Loan $\qquad V_{n+1} = V_n(1 + r) - D$

V_{n+1} — Value of the investment or loan after $(n + 1)$ payments

V_n — Value of the investment or loan after (n) payments

r — Rate of interest per compounding period as a decimal

D — Payment made per compounding period

Excel has several built in functions for working with annuities.

= FV(rate, nper, pmt, [pv], [type]) $\qquad$ = PV(rate, nper, pmt, [fv], [type])

= NPER(rate, nper, pmt, [pv], [type]) $\qquad$ = PMT(rate, nper, pv, [fv], [type])

= RATE(nper, pmt, pv, [fv], [type])

Future value of an annuity

The future value of an annuity is the sum of the money contributed plus the compound interest earned. It is the total value of the investment at the end of a specified term.

Present value of an annuity

The present value of an annuity is the amount of money if invested now would equal the future value of the annuity.

Using a future value or present value table with factors

1 Determine the time period and rate of interest.
2 Find the intersection of the time period and rate of interest.
3 Multiply the number in the intersection with the money contributed.

Use of annuities

A table is used to summarise the key properties of an annuity. It shows the payment number, the payment received, the interest earned, the principal reduction and the balance of the annuity after each payment has been received.

Summary

Multiple-choice

1 A loan is modelled by the recurrence relation $V_{n+1} = V_n \times 1.007 - 400$ where V_n is the balance of the loan after n payments and $V_0 = 25\,000$. What is the balance of the loan after four payments? Answer correct to the nearest whole number.

  A $24\,775   **B** $24\,091   **C** $25\,575   **D** $27\,324

2 An annuity has $250 invested at the end of each month for 4 years. The interest rate is 12% p.a. compounding monthly. What is the future value of the annuity? Use Excel to find the answer correct to the nearest dollar.

  A $1015   **B** $12\,238   **C** $15\,306   **D** $477\,897

3 An annuity consists of quarterly deposits of $400 that are invested at 12% p.a. with interest compounding quarterly. The annuity will mature in 16 years. What is the present value of the annuity? Use Excel to find the answer correct to the nearest dollar.

  A $3331   **B** $5024   **C** $11\,323   **D** $14\,369

Use the table below to answer questions 4 to 7.

Future value of $1							
Period	1.0%	1.5%	2.0%	2.5%	3.0%	3.5%	4.0%
4	4.060	4.091	4.122	4.153	4.184	4.215	4.246
6	6.152	6.230	6.308	6.388	6.468	6.550	6.633
8	8.286	8.433	8.583	8.736	8.892	9.052	9.214

4 Find the future value of an annuity of $3000 per year for 6 years at 4% p.a. compounded annually.

  A $6633   **B** $12\,738   **C** $18\,924   **D** $19\,899

5 Find the future value of an annuity of $800 per month for 4 months at 12% p.a. compounded monthly.

  A $3248   **B** $3347   **C** $4060   **D** $38\,976

6 Find the future value of an annuity of $9000 per quarter for 1 year at 6% p.a. compounded quarterly.

  A $4091   **B** $36\,540   **C** $36\,819   **D** $147\,276

7 William saves $2400 by the end of each year and invests it into an account earning 3.5% p.a. compound interest. What is the future value of the investment after 8 years?

  A $9052.00   **B** $21\,340.80   **C** $21\,724.80   **D** $22\,113.60

Short-answer

1 Let V_n be the balance of a loan after n payments have been made. Write down a recurrence relation model for the balance of a loan of:

a $3500 borrowed at 4.8% per annum, compounding monthly, with payments of $280 per month

b $150000 borrowed at 3.64% per annum, compounding fortnightly, with payments of $650 per fortnight.

2 Use Excel to find the future value to the nearest cent for each of the following annuities.

a $15000 at the end of every year for 4 years with an interest rate of 10% p.a.

b $3950 at the end of every year for 6 years with an interest rate of 9.25% p.a.

3 Sienna decides to invest $980 per quarter into his superannuation fund. The interest rate quoted is 9.2% per annum, compounded quarterly. Use Excel for the following questions.

a What is the future value of his superannuation at the end of 8 years?

b Calculate the contribution needed per quarter to have $50000 after 8 years.

4 Use Excel to find the present value to the nearest cent using the following future values.

a $FV = \$400000$, $r = 6\%$ p.a. compounded biannually and $n = 10$ years

b $FV = \$30000$, $r = 8\%$ p.a. compounded quarterly and $n = 12$ years

5 Lucas invests $1450 per year at 9.8% p.a. compound interest into a 15-year annuity. What lump sum does Ryan need to deposit today to have the same amount as Lucas after 15 years? Ryan's account also pays 9.8% p.a. compounding annually. Use Excel to find the answer correct to the nearest cent.

6 The table below shows the future value of an annuity with a contribution of $1.

Future value of $1							
Period	2%	4%	6%	8%	10%	12%	14%
6	6.31	6.63	6.98	7.34	7.72	8.12	8.54
12	13.41	15.03	16.87	18.98	21.38	24.13	27.27
18	21.41	25.65	30.91	37.45	45.60	55.75	68.39
24	30.42	39.08	50.82	66.76	88.50	118.16	158.66

Use the table to calculate the future value of the following annuities. Answer to the nearest dollar.

a $6000 per year for 18 years at 10% p.a. compounded annually

b $4920 per year for 6 years at 14% p.a. compounded annually

c $2800 per quarter for 6 years at 8% p.a. compounded quarterly

d $11700 per half-year for 12 years at 12% p.a. compounded biannually

e $700 per month for 6 months at 24% p.a. compounded monthly

7 The table below shows the present value of an annuity with a contribution of $1.

			Present value of $1				
Period	**2%**	**3%**	**4%**	**5%**	**6%**	**7%**	**8%**
12	10.58	9.95	9.39	8.86	8.38	7.94	7.54
24	18.91	16.94	15.25	13.80	12.55	11.47	10.53
36	25.49	21.83	18.91	16.55	14.62	13.04	11.72
48	30.67	25.27	21.20	18.08	15.65	13.73	12.19

Use the table to calculate the present value of the following annuities.

a $25 000 per year for 36 years at 3% p.a. compounded annually

b $12 600 per year for 12 years at 8% p.a. compounded annually

c $5700 per year for 24 years at 5% p.a. compounded annually

d $9500 per quarter for 12 years at 8% p.a. compounded quarterly

e $5200 per half-year for 24 years at 6% p.a. compounded biannually

8 Use the table in question **6** to find the contribution per period (to the nearest dollar) of an annuity that has these future values.

a $60 300 at 4% p.a. compounded annually for 6 years

b $342 300 at 10% p.a. compounded annually for 12 years

c $165 200 at 8% p.a. compounded quarterly for 6 years

d $15 600 at 24% p.a. compounded monthly for 1 year

e $19 500 at 12% p.a. compounded biannually for 12 years

9 Use the table in question **7** to find the contribution per period (to the nearest dollar) of an annuity that has these present values.

a $64 600 at 8% p.a. compounded annually for 36 years

b $31 800 at 3% p.a. compounded annually for 12 years

c $87 000 at 12% p.a. compounded quarterly for 6 years

d $150 000 at 8% p.a. compounded biannually for 12 years

e $72 000 at 36% p.a. compounded monthly for 2 years

Extended-response

10 Joel would like $16 000 to go overseas for a holiday in four years' time. The best investment Joel can find pays 10.5% p.a. interest, compounded quarterly.

a Calculate the present value of the investment needed for the holiday. Answer to the nearest cent.

b Joel plans to save for the trip by depositing $80 per week into an annuity at 10.5% p.a. interest, compounded weekly. Will Joel have enough money for the holiday in four years' time? Justify your answer with the appropriate calculations. Answer to the nearest cent.

8

Non-linear relationships

Syllabus topic — A3.2 Non-linear relationships

This topic will develop your understanding of non-linear functions and how they can be used to model and solve a range of practical problems.

Outcomes

- Graph and recognise an exponential function in the form $y = a^x$ and $y = a^{-x}$.
- Construct and analyse an exponential model to solve a practical problem.
- Graph and recognise a quadratic function in the form $y = a^2 + bx + c$.
- Recognise the shape of a parabola and its key features.
- Construct and analyse a quadratic model to solve a practical problem.
- Graph and recognise an reciprocal function in the form $y = \dfrac{k}{x}$.
- Recognise the shape of a hyperbola and its key features.
- Construct and analyse a reciprocal model to solve a practical problem.

Digital Resources for this chapter

In the Interactive Textbook:

- Videos
- Desmos widgets
- Literacy worksheet
- Spreadsheets
- Quick Quiz
- Study guide
- Solutions (enabled by teacher)

In the Online Teaching Suite:

- Teaching Program
- Tests
- Review Quiz
- Teaching Notes

Knowledge check

The Interactive Textbook provides a test of prior knowledge for this chapter, and may direct you to revision from the previous years' work.

8A Exponential functions

Exponential functions have x as the power of a constant (e.g. 3^x). They are defined by the general rule $y = a^x$ and $y = a^{-x}$ where the constant $a > 0$. Their graphs are shown below.

GRAPHS OF EXPONENTIAL FUNCTIONS

Most practical uses of exponential functions have $a > 1$:

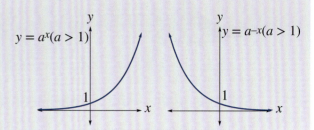

When a is greater than 0 but less than 1, the shape of the curve is reversed horizontally:

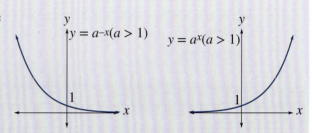

When $a = 1$ the graph is flat line, $y = 1$.

Key features of exponential graphs

- The graph lies wholly above the x-axis because a^x is always positive, regardless of the value of x. It is impossible for the y values to be zero or negative.
- The graph always passes through the point $(0, 1)$ because when $x = 0$ then $y = a^0 = 1$, regardless of the value of a.
- The x-axis is an asymptote. That is, it is a line that the curve approaches by getting closer and closer to it but never reaching it.
- The graph $y = a^{-x}$ is the reflection of the graph $y = a^x$ about the y-axis.
- Increasing the value of a such as changing $y = 2^x$ to $y = 3^x$ affects the steepness of the graph. The y values increase at a greater rate when the x values increase.
- The exponential function $y = a^x$ when $a > 1$ is often referred to as a growth function because as the x values increase, the y values increase.
- The exponential function $y = a^{-x}$ when $a > 1$ is often referred to as a decay function because as the x values increase, the y values decrease.

To graph an exponential function:
1 Construct a table of values.
2 Draw a number plane.
3 Plot the points.
4 Join the points to make a curve.

Example 1: Graphing an exponential function 8A

Draw the graph of $y = 3^x$.

SOLUTION:

1 Construct a table of values for x and y.
2 Let $x = -3, -2, -1, 0, 1, 2$ and 3.
   Find y using the exponential function $y = 3^x$.

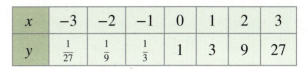

x	-3	-2	-1	0	1	2	3
y	$\frac{1}{27}$	$\frac{1}{9}$	$\frac{1}{3}$	1	3	9	27

3 Draw a number plane with x as the horizontal axis and y as the vertical axis.
4 Plot the points $(-3, \frac{1}{27})$, $(-2, \frac{1}{9})$, $(-1, \frac{1}{3})$, $(0, 1)$, $(1, 3)$, $(2, 9)$ and $(3, 27)$.

5 Join the points to make a curve.

Note: Sometimes it is necessary to rescale the axes to plot the points as some points are impractical to plot, such as $(-3, \frac{1}{27})$.

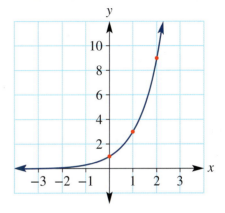

Example 2: Graphing an exponential function 8A

Draw the graph of $y = 3^{-x}$.

SOLUTION:

1 Construct a table of values for x and y.
2 Let $x = -3, -2, -1, 0, 1, 2$ and 3. Find y using the exponential function $y = 3^{-x}$.

x	-3	-2	-1	0	1	2	3
y	27	9	3	1	$\frac{1}{3}$	$\frac{1}{9}$	$\frac{1}{27}$

3 Draw a number plane with x as the horizontal axis and y as the vertical axis.
4 Plot the points $(-3, 27)$, $(-2, 9)$, $(-1, 3)$, $(0, 1)$, $(1, \frac{1}{3})$, $(2, \frac{1}{9})$ and $(3, \frac{1}{27})$.
5 Join the points to make a curve.

Note: The exponential curve $y = 3^{-x}$ is the reflection of $y = 3^x$ about the y-axis. Both curves pass through $(0, 1)$ and have the x-axis as an asymptote.

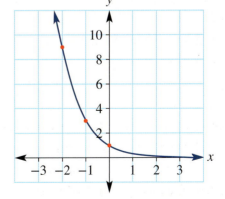

Desmos widget 8A Graphing exponential functions with technology

Spreadsheet activity: Graphing exponential functions

Exercise 8A

Example 1 **1** Complete the following table of values and graph each exponential function.

     a $y = 2^x$ **b** $y = 2^{-x}$

x	-2	-1	0	1	2
y		$\frac{1}{2}$			

x	-2	-1	0	1	2
y					$\frac{1}{4}$

2 Use your graph of $y = 2^x$ in question **1a** to answer these questions.

     a Is it possible for y to have negative values?

     b Is it possible for x to have negative values?

     c Is it possible to calculate y when $x = 0$? If so, what is it?

     d Is it possible to calculate x when $y = 0$? If so, what is it?

     e What is the approximate value of y when $x = 0.5$?

     f What is the approximate value of y when $x = 1.5$?

Example 2 **3** Complete the following table of values by expressing the y values, correct to two decimal places. Graph each exponential function.

     a $y = 4^x$ **b** $y = 4^{-x}$

x	-3	-2	-1	0	1	2	3
y	0.02						

x	-3	-2	-1	0	1	2	3
y						0.06	

4 Use the graph of $y = 4^x$ in question **3a** to answer these questions.

     a Is it possible for y to have negative values?

     b Is it possible for x to have negative values?

     c Is it possible to calculate y when $x = 0$? If so, what is it?

     d Is it possible to calculate x when $y = 0$? If so, what is it?

     e What is the value of y when $x = 1.5$?

     f What is the value of y when $x = 2.5$?

5 Sketch the graph of the following functions on the same set of axes.

     a $y = 2^x$ **b** $y = 3^x$ **c** $y = 4^x$

6 Sketch the graph of the following functions on the same set of axes.

     a $y = 2^{-x}$ **b** $y = 3^{-x}$ **c** $y = 4^{-x}$

7 What is the effect on the graph of changing the value of a in $y = a^x$?

     Hint: Use your graphs in questions **5** and **6**.

8 Complete the following table of values and graph each exponential function.

a $y = 0.5^x$

x	−2	−1	0	1	2
y					$\dfrac{1}{4}$

b $y = 0.5^{-x}$

x	−2	−1	0	1	2
y	$\dfrac{1}{2}$				

9 Use the graph in questions **1** and **8** to answer these questions.

a What are the coordinates on the graph of $y = 0.5^x$ where $x = 1$?

b What are the coordinates on the graph of $y = 2^{-x}$ where $x = -1$?

c What are the coordinates on the graph of $y = 0.5^{-x}$ where $x = 2$?

d What are the coordinates on the graph of $y = 2^x$ where $x = -2$?

e Is the graph of $y = 0.5^x$ the same as $y = 2^{-x}$? Explain your answer.

f Is the graph of $y = 0.5^{-x}$ the same as $y = 2^x$? Explain your answer.

10 Sketch the graph of the following functions on the same set of axes.

a $y = 2^x$ **b** $y = 2^x + 1$ **c** $y = 2^x + 2$

d $y = 2^x - 1$ **e** $y = 2^x - 2$

11 Use the graph in question **10** to answer these questions.

a What is the approximate value of y when $x = 0.5$ on the graph $y = 2^x + 2$?

b What is the approximate value of y when $x = 0.5$ on the graph $y = 2^x + 1$?

c What is the approximate value of y when $x = 0.5$ on the graph $y = 2^x - 1$?

d What is the approximate value of y when $x = 0.5$ on the graph $y = 2^x - 2$?

e What is the effect of adding or subtracting a number to the graph $y = a^x$?

12 Sketch the graph of the following functions on the same set of axes.

a $y = -2^x$

b $y = -3^x$

c $y = -4^x$

d How does multiplying the graph $y = a^x$ by −1 affect the graph?

13 Sketch the graph of the following functions on the same set of axes. Label the y-intercept.

a $y = 2^x$

b $y = 2 \times 2^x$

c $y = \frac{1}{2} \times 2^x$

d How does multiplying the graph $y = a^x$ by a number affect the graph?

14 What does the graph of $y = 1^x$ look like? Why is this graph not exponential?

8B Exponential models

Exponential modelling occurs when a practical situation is described mathematically using an exponential function. The quantity usually experiences fast growth or decay.

EXPONENTIAL MODEL

Exponential growth – Quantity increases rapidly according to the function $y = a^x$ where $a > 1$.

Exponential decay – Quantity decreases rapidly according to the function $y = a^{-x}$ where $a > 1$.

Example 3: Using an exponential model **8B**

The fish population is predicted using the formula, $N = 500 \times 1.5^t$ where N is the number of fish and t is the time in years.

a Construct a table of values for t and N. Use values for t from 0 to 4. Approximate the number of fish to the nearest whole number.

b Draw the graph of $N = 500 \times 1.5^t$.

c How many fish were present after 2 years?

d How many extra fish will be present after 4 years compared to 2 years?

e Estimate the number of fish after 18 months.

SOLUTION:

1 Construct a table of values for t and N.

2 Let $t = 0, 1, 2, 3$ and 4. Find N using the exponential function $N = 500 \times 1.5^t$. Express the values for N as a whole number.

3 Draw a number plane with t as the horizontal axis and N as the vertical axis.

4 Plot the points (0, 500), (1, 750), (2, 1125), (3, 1688) and (4, 2531).

5 Join the points to make the curve.

a

t	0	1	2	3	4
N	500	750	1125	1688	2531

b

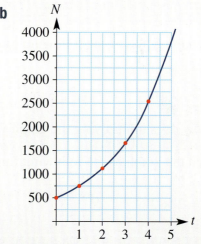

6 Look up $t = 2$ in the table and find N.

7 Subtract the number of fish for 2 years from 4 years.

8 Read the approximate value of N from the graph when $t = 1.5$.

c 1125 fish

d Extra = 2531 − 1125 = 1406

e Approximately 900 fish

Exercise 8B

Example 3

1 The exponential function, $N = 6^t$ is used to model the growth in the number of insects (N) after t days.

a Copy and complete the table of values for t and N.

t	0	1	2	3	4
N					

b Copy and draw the graph of $N = 6^t$ on the number plane below.

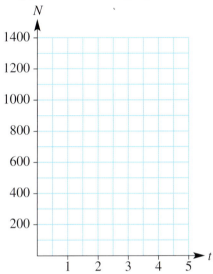

c What was the initial number of insects?

d How many insects were present after 3 days?

e How many extra insects will be present after 4 days compared to 2 days?

f Estimate how many days it took for the number of insects to exceed 1000.

2 The population of an endangered reptile is decreasing exponentially according to the formula, $P = 1.5^{-t} \times 100$ where P is the population of reptiles after t years.

a Copy and complete the table of values for t and P. Express the population of reptiles to the nearest whole number.

t	0	2	4	6	8
N					

b Graph $P = 1.5^{-t} \times 100$ using the table of ordered pairs in part **a**.

c What is the initial population of reptiles?

d Estimate the population of reptiles after 3 years.

e Estimate the population of reptiles after 7 years.

f What is the difference in the population of reptiles after 2 years compared to 6 years?

g Estimate the time taken (to the nearest year) for the population of reptiles to be below 1.

3 The size of a flock of birds, F, after t years is decaying exponentially using the function $F = 200 \times 0.5^t$.

   a Make a table of values for t and F. Use values for t from 0 to 5. Express F correct to the nearest whole number.

   b Draw the graph of $F = 200 \times 0.5^t$.

   c What was the initial flock of birds?

   d How many birds were present after 3 years?

   e How many fewer birds will be present after 4 years compared to 2 years?

   f Estimate how years it will take for the number of birds to fall to less than one bird.

4 The number of bacteria grows exponentially according to the function $b = 30 \times 1.2^t$ where b is the number of bacteria after t hours.

   a Construct a table of ordered pairs using 0, 5, 10, 15 and 20 as values for t. Express the number of bacteria to the nearest whole number.

   b Graph $b = 30 \times 1.2^t$ using the table of ordered pairs in part **a**.

   c What is the initial number of bacteria?

   d What is the number of bacteria after 4 hours?

   e Estimate the time taken for the number of bacteria to reach 120.

5 Tom invested $1000 into a managed fund that appreciated in value for 5 years. The amount of money (A) in the fund for each year (t) is shown below.

t	0	1	2	3	4	5
A	$1000	$1300	$1690	$2197	$2856	$3712

   a Draw a number plane with t as the horizontal axis and A as the vertical axis.

   b Plot the points from the table of values. Join the points to make a curve.
An exponential growth model in the form $y = 1000 \times a^x$ describes this situation.

   c What is the model if x and y are replaced with t and A?

   d Determine the value of a in the model by using $t = 1$.

   e What is the exponential model using t and A?

   f Use the model to find the value (to the nearest dollar) of the fund after $2\frac{1}{2}$ years.

   g Use the model to find the value (to the nearest dollar) of the fund after 7 years.

   h Estimate the time when the value of the fund is approximately $1480.

8C | Quadratic functions

A quadratic function is a curve whose equation has an x squared (x^2). It is defined by the general rule $y = ax^2 + bx + c$ where a, b and c are numbers. Quadratic functions are graphed in a similar method to exponential functions except the points are joined to make a curve in the shape of a parabola.

Key features of a parabola

The basic parabola has the equation $y = x^2$.

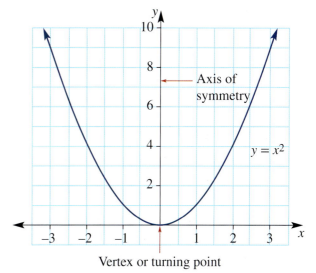

- The vertex (or turning point) is (0, 0).
- It is a minimum turning point.
- Axis of symmetry is $x = 0$ (the y-axis)
- y-intercept is 0 and x-intercept is 0.
- The graph $y = -x^2$ is the reflection of the graph $y = x^2$ about the x-axis.
- Changing the coefficient of the equation such as $y = 2x^2$ or $y = \frac{1}{2}x^2$ affects the height of the parabola.

- Adding or subtracting a number to the equation such as $y = x^2 + 1$ or $y = x^2 - 1$ does not change the shape but moves the parabola up or down.

QUADRATIC FUNCTION

A quadratic function has the form $y = ax^2 + bx + c$ where a, b and c are numbers.

Parabola ($y = x^2$) – Minimum turning point

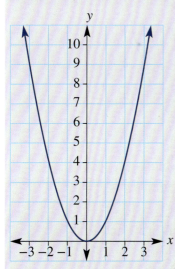

Parabola ($y = -x^2$) – Maximum turning point

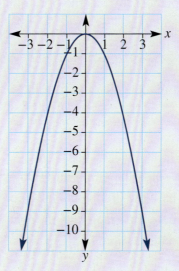

To graph a parabola:

1 Construct a table of values.

2 Draw a number plane.

3 Plot the points.

4 Join the points to make a parabola.

Example 4: Graphing a quadratic function   8C

Draw the graph of $y = x^2 + 1$.

SOLUTION:

1   Construct a table of values for x and y using $x = -3, -2, -1, 0, 1, 2$ and 3. Find y by substituting into $y = x^2 + 1$.

x	−3	−2	−1	0	1	2	3
y	10	5	2	1	2	5	10

2   Draw a number plane with x as the horizontal axis and y as the vertical axis.

3   Plot the points $(-3, 10)$, $(-2, 5)$, $(-1, 2)$, $(0, 1)$, $(1, 2)$, $(2, 5)$ and $(3, 10)$.

4   Join the points to make a curve in the shape of a parabola.

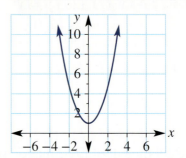

Example 5: Determining the features of a parabola   8C

Draw the graph of $y = x^2 - 4x + 3$ (use $x = -1, 0, 1, 2, 3, 4, 5$) and find the following features.

a   turning point   b   axis of symmetry   c y-intercept

d x-intercepts   e   minimum value

SOLUTION:

1   Construct a table of values for x and y using $x = -1, 0, 1, 2, 3, 4$ and 5. Find y by substituting into $y = x^2 - 4x + 3$.

x	−1	0	1	2	3	4	5
y	8	3	0	−1	0	3	8

2   Draw a number plane with x as the horizontal axis and y as the vertical axis.

3   Plot the points $(-1, 8)$, $(0, 3)$, $(1, 0)$, $(2, -1)$, $(3, 0)$, $(4, 3)$ and $(5, 8)$.

4   Join the points to make a curve in the shape of a parabola.

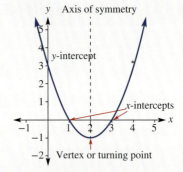

5   Find where the graph changes direction.

6   Find the line that splits the graph into two.

7   Find the point where the graph cuts the y-axis.

8   Find the point where the graph cuts the x-axis.

9   Determine the smallest value of y.

a   Turning point is $(2, -1)$

b   Axis of symmetry is $x = 2$

c y-intercept is 3 $(0, 3)$

d x-intercepts are 1 and 3

e   Minimum value is -1

Desmos widget 8C Graphing a quadratic function with technology

Spreadsheet activity: Graphing a quadratic function with a spreadsheet

Exercise 8C

1 Write the missing features for this graph.

  a The coordinates of the turning point are _____.

  b The y-intercept is _____.

  c The x-intercepts are _____ and _____.

  d The axis of symmetry is _____.

  e The maximum value is _____.

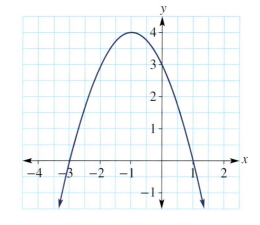

2 Write the missing features for this graph.

  a The coordinates of the turning point are _____.

  b The y-intercept is _____.

  c The x-intercepts are _____ and _____.

  d The axis of symmetry is _____.

  e The minimum value is _____.

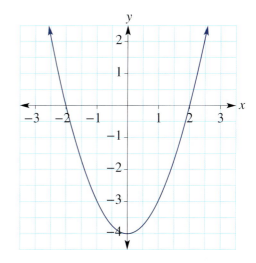

3 Complete the following table of values and graph each quadratic function on the same number plane.

  a $y = x^2$

x	−3	−2	−1	0	1	2	3
y							

  b $y = 2x^2$

x	−3	−2	−1	0	1	2	3
y							

  c $y = 3x^2$

x	−3	−2	−1	0	1	2	3
y							

  d $y = \dfrac{1}{2}x^2$

x	−3	−2	−1	0	1	2	3
y							

  e What is the axis of symmetry for each of the above quadratic functions?

  f Is the turning point for each of the above quadratic functions a maximum or minimum?

  g What is the effect of changing the coefficient of x^2 in the quadratic equation $y = x^2$?

4 Complete the following table of values and graph each quadratic function on the same number plane.

a $y = -x^2$

x	−3	−2	−1	0	1	2	3
y							

b $y = -2x^2$

x	−3	−2	−1	0	1	2	3
y							

c $y = -3x^2$

x	−3	−2	−1	0	1	2	3
y							

d $y = -\dfrac{1}{2}x^2$

x	−3	−2	−1	0	1	2	3
y							

e What is the axis of symmetry for each of the above quadratic functions?

f Is the turning point for each of the above quadratic functions a maximum or minimum?

g What is the effect of changing the coefficient of x^2 in the quadratic equation $y = -x^2$?

Example 4   **5** Complete the following table of values and graph each quadratic function on the same number plane.

a $y = x^2 + 1$

x	−3	−2	−1	0	1	2	3
y							

b $y = x^2 - 1$

x	−3	−2	−1	0	1	2	3
y							

c $y = x^2 + 2$

x	−3	−2	−1	0	1	2	3
y							

d $y = x^2 - 2$

x	−3	−2	−1	0	1	2	3
y							

e What is the axis of symmetry for each of the above quadratic functions?

f Is the turning point for each of the above quadratic functions a maximum or minimum?

g What is the effect of adding or subtracting a number to the quadratic function $y = x^2$?

Example 5   **6** Complete the following table of values and graph each quadratic function on the same number plane.

a $y = x^2 + 2x + 1$

x	−6	−4	−2	0	2	4	6
y							

b $y = x^2 + 4x + 4$

x	−6	−4	−2	0	2	4	6
y							

c $y = x^2 - 2x + 1$

x	−6	−4	−2	0	2	4	6
y							

d $y = x^2 - 4x + 4$

x	−6	−4	−2	0	2	4	6
y							

e What do all of the above quadratic functions have in common?

7 Complete the following table of values and graph each quadratic function on the same number plane.

a $y = x^2 - 4x + 3$

x	−1	0	1	2	3	4	5
y							

b $y = -x^2 + 4x - 3$

x	−1	0	1	2	3	4	5
y							

c $y = 2x^2 - 8x + 6$

x	−1	0	1	2	3	4	5
y							

d $y = -2x^2 + 8x - 6$

x	−1	0	1	2	3	4	5
y							

e What do all of the above quadratic functions have in common?

8 What is the quadratic function for each of these tables of values which form parabolas?

a

x	−3	−2	−1	0	1	2	3
y	10	5	2	1	2	5	10

b

x	−3	−2	−1	0	1	2	3
y	8	3	0	−1	0	3	8

c

x	−3	−2	−1	0	1	2	3
y	−9	−4	−1	0	−1	−4	−9

d

x	−3	−2	−1	0	1	2	3
y	18	8	2	0	2	8	18

e

x	−3	−2	−1	0	1	2	3
y	4	1	0	1	4	9	16

f

x	−3	−2	−1	0	1	2	3
y	16	9	4	1	0	1	4

9 Draw the graph of each quadratic function on the same set of axes for $-5 \le x \le 5$.
  a $y = (x + 1)^2$, $y = (x + 2)^2$ and $y = (x + 3)^2$
  b $y = (x - 1)^2$, $y = (x - 2)^2$ and $y = (x - 3)^2$
  c Explain how the constant k in $y = (x + k)^2$ transforms the graph $y = x^2$.

10 Draw the graph of each quadratic function on the same set of axes for $-5 \le x \le 5$.
  a $y = (x + 1)^2 - 2$, $y = (x + 2)^2 - 3$ and $y = (x + 3)^2 - 5$
  b $y = (x - 1)^2 + 2$, $y = (x - 2)^2 + 3$ and $y = (x - 3)^2 + 5$
  c Explain how the constant h in $y = (x + k)^2 + h$ transforms the graph $y = (x + k)^2$.

8D Quadratic models

Quadratic modelling occurs when a practical situation is described mathematically using a quadratic function.

> ## QUADRATIC MODEL
>
> A quadratic model describes a practical situation using a function in the form $y = ax^2 + bx + c$ where a, b and c are numbers. Quadratic functions are graphed to make a curve in the shape of a parabola.

Example 6: Using a quadratic model 8D

The area (A) of a rectangular garden of length x metres is given by $A = 6x - x^2$.

x	0	1	2	3	4	5	6
A							

a Draw the graph of $A = 6x - x^2$ using the table of ordered pairs.
b Use the graph to estimate the area of the garden when the length of the garden is 4.5 m.
c What is the maximum area of the garden?
d What is the garden length in order to have maximum area?

SOLUTION:

1 Let $x = 0, 1, 2, 3, 4, 5$ and 6 and find A by substituting into the quadratic function $A = 6x - x^2$.

a

x	0	1	2	3	4	5	6
A	0	5	8	9	8	5	0

2 Draw a number plane with x as the horizontal axis and A as the vertical axis.

3 Plot the points (0, 0), (1, 5), (2, 8), (3, 9), (4, 8), (5, 5) and (6, 0).

4 Join the points to make a parabolic curve.

5 Draw a vertical line from $x = 4.5$ on the horizontal axis until it intersects the parabola. At this point draw a horizontal line until it connects with the vertical axis.

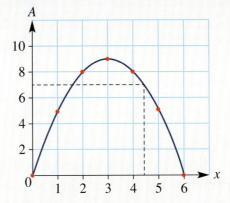

6 Read this value.

b About 7 m². Check your solution algebraically.

$$A = 6x - x^2$$
$$= 6 \times 4.5 - 4.5^2$$
$$= 6.75\,\text{m}^2$$

7 Read the largest value for A.

c Maximum area of the garden is 9.

8 Read the value on the x-axis when the A is largest.

d Maximum area occurs when $x = 3$.

Stopping distance

The stopping distance is the distance a vehicle travels from the time a driver sees an event occurring to the time the vehicle is brought to a stop. It is calculated by adding the reaction distance and the braking distance. Reaction distance (or thinking distance) is the distance travelled by the vehicle when a driver decides to brake to when the driver first commences braking. The reaction time averages 0.75 second for a fit and alert driver. The braking distance is affected by the road surface (wet, slippery, uneven or unsealed), slope of the road (uphill or downhill), weight of the vehicle and condition of the brakes.

STOPPING DISTANCE

Stopping distance = Reaction distance + Braking distance

$$d = \frac{5vt}{18} + \frac{v^2}{170}$$

(formula is an approximation using average conditions)
d – Stopping distance in metres
v – Velocity or speed of the motor vehicle in km/h
t – Time reaction in seconds

Example 7: Using a quadratic model
8D

Tahlia was driving at a speed of 60 km/h and reaction time of 0.80 seconds. Calculate the stopping distance using the formula

$$d = \frac{5vt}{18} + \frac{v^2}{170}$$

Answer correct to the nearest whole metre.

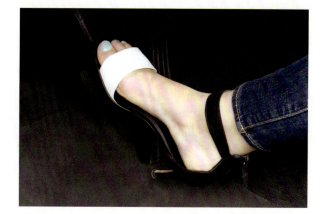

SOLUTION:

1 Write the stopping distance formula.	$d = \dfrac{5vt}{18} + \dfrac{v^2}{170}$
2 Substitute $v = 60$ and $t = 0.80$ into the formula.	$= \dfrac{5 \times 60 \times 0.80}{18} + \dfrac{60^2}{170}$
3 Evaluate.	$= 34.50980 \ldots$
4 Express the answer correct to the nearest whole number.	≈ 35 m
5 Write the answer in words.	$\therefore$ Stopping distance is 35 m.

Exercise 8D

Example 6 **1** The area (A) of a rectangular enclosure of length x metres is given by the formula $A = x(7 - x)$. The graph of this formula is shown on the right.

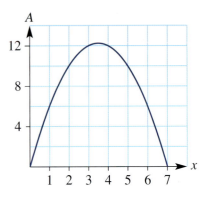

   a What is the area of the enclosure when x is 1 metre?
   b What is the area of the enclosure when x is 5 metres?
   c What is the enclosure's length in order to have maximum area?
   d What is the maximum area of the enclosure?

2 The movement of an object with a velocity v (in metres/second) at time t (seconds) is given by the formula $v = 15t - 5t^2$.
   The graph of this formula is shown on the right.

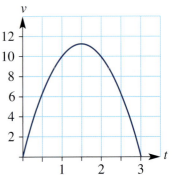

   a What was the initial velocity of the object?
   b What was the greatest velocity reached by the object?
   c How many seconds did it take for the object to reach maximum velocity?
   d Estimate the number of seconds when the velocity is greater than 6 metres per second.

3 The price ($\$P$) of rope depends on the diameter (d), in metres, of the rope when it is rolled into a circle. The quadratic equation $P = 3d^2$ is used to model this situation.
   a Complete the following table of values, correct to the nearest whole number.

d	0	2	4	6	8	10	12	14	16	18	20	22	24
P													

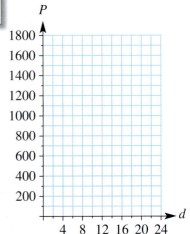

   b Draw the graph of $P = 3d^2$ using the number plane shown opposite.
   c What is the price of the rope when the diameter of the rope is 12 metres?
   d What is the price of the rope when the diameter of the rope is 23 metres?
   e What is the difference between the price of the rope when the diameter of the rope is 5 metres compared to a diameter of 25 metres?

4   A stone falls from rest down a mine shaft. The distance it falls, d metres, at time t seconds is given by the quadratic equation $d = 4.9t^2$.

   a Complete the following table of values, correct to the nearest whole number.

t	0	1	2	3	4	5
d						

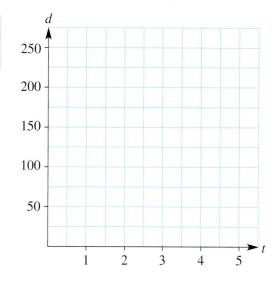

   b Draw the graph of $d = 4.9t^2$ using the number plane shown opposite.

   c What is the distance travelled by the stone after 1 second?

   d What is the distance travelled by the stone after 5 seconds?

   e What is the distance travelled by the stone after 2.5 seconds?

   f How long did it take for the stone to travel 100 metres? Estimate from the graph.

   g How long did it take for the stone to travel 200 metres? Estimate from the graph.

5   The equation $d = 0.005s(s - 1)$ is used to model the stopping distance for a train where d is the stopping distance in metres and s is the train's speed in km/h.

   a Complete the following table of values, correct to the nearest whole number.

s	0	20	40	50	60	80	100
d							

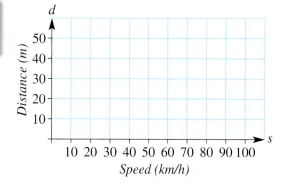

   b Draw the graph of $d = 0.005s(s - 1)$ using the number plane shown opposite.

   c What is the stopping distance when the train is travelling at 20 km/h?

   d What is the stopping distance when the train is travelling 75 km/h?

   e Estimate the maximum speed (km/h) a train could be travelling to stop within 15 m.

   f Estimate the maximum speed (km/h) a train could be travelling to stop within 30 m.

   g What is the difference between the stopping distances when a train is travelling at a speed of 40 km/h compared to travelling at a speed of 80 km/h?

   h What is the difference between the stopping distances when a train is travelling at a speed of 15 km/h compared to travelling at a speed of 95 km/h?

LEVEL 2

Example 7 | **6** Zoe was driving at a velocity of v km/h and reaction time of 0.50 seconds. An approximation between the stopping distance, d (in metres), and the velocity is given using the quadratic equation shown below.

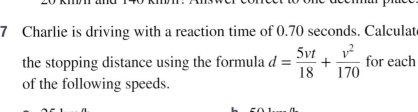

$$d = \frac{5vt}{18} + \frac{v^2}{170} \quad \text{or} \quad d = \frac{5v \times 0.50}{18} + \frac{v^2}{170} \quad \text{or} \quad d = \frac{2.5v}{18} + \frac{v^2}{170}$$

Answer the following questions, correct to the nearest whole number.

a Copy and complete a table of values for v and d.

v	0	10	20	30	40	50	60	70	80	90	100
d											

b Draw the graph of $d = \frac{2.5v}{18} + \frac{v^2}{170}$ using the number plane shown opposite.

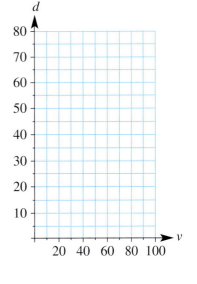

c What is the stopping distance when the velocity is 5 km/h?

d What is the stopping distance when the velocity is 95 km/h?

e What is the stopping distance when the velocity is 125 km/h?

f What is the difference in the stopping distance between 20 km/h and 80 km/h?

g What is the difference in the stopping distance between 20 km/h and 140 km/h? Answer correct to one decimal place.

7 Charlie is driving with a reaction time of 0.70 seconds. Calculate the stopping distance using the formula $d = \frac{5vt}{18} + \frac{v^2}{170}$ for each of the following speeds.

a 25 km/h   **b** 50 km/h

c 75 km/h   **d** 100 km/h

e 125 km/h   **f** 150 km/h

8 Elizabeth was driving her car at 40 km/h through a school zone. A school student ran onto the road 12 metres in front of her. Elizabeth has a reaction time of 0.80 seconds.

a Do you think Elizabeth was able to stop without running over the child? Give a reason for your answer.

b What would have happened if Elizabeth was driving her car at 60 km/h? Explain your answer.

9 Levi uses the freeway to travel to work. Levi has a reaction time of 0.60 seconds and usually drives at the speed limit of 110 km/h.

a What is the stopping distance on the freeway using the formula $d = \frac{5vt}{18} + \frac{v^2}{170}$?

b If Levi is driving at 110 km/h at night, how far ahead does he need to be able to see in order to avoid hitting a stopped car in the road?

10 A ball was dropped from the top of a multistorey building to the ground below. Ignoring air resistance, the relationship between the height, h, above the ground (in metres) and the time, t (in seconds), for it to fall from that height is given by the formula $h = 100 - 4t^2$.

   a Construct a table of values for t and h. Use values for t from 0 to 5.

   b Draw the graph of $h = 100 - 4t^2$.

   c What is the height of the building?

   d How long did it take for the ball to hit the ground?

   e How high above the ground was the ball after 2 seconds?

   f Estimate how long did it take for the ball to fall 64 metres?

   g During which second did the ball fall the greatest distance? Estimate from the graph.

11 A child's circular swimming pool has a depth of 1 metre. The relationship between the volume (V, in m^3) and the radius (r, in m) is given by the formula $V = \pi r^2 h$ (where $h = 1$ m).

   a Complete a table of values for r and V. Use r from 0 to 5 and express V correct to one decimal place.

   b Draw the graph of $V = \pi r^2$ using the table of values.

   c What is the maximum volume of water if the radius is between 0 and 5 metres (correct to one decimal place)?

LEVEL 3

12 The petrol consumption (P, litres per 100 km) and the speed of a car (s, km/h) are modelled by the formula $P = 0.02s^2 - 2s + 55$.

   a Draw the graph of $P = 0.02s^2 - 2s + 55$. Use s from 0 to 100 km/h.

   b What is the petrol consumption at 40 km/h?

   c Estimate the speed of the car which gives the lowest petrol consumption.

13 A rectangular patio is constructed so that the length is 8 metres less than the width.

   a Give an example of a length and width that would be possible for this patio.

   b Write an equation for the area (A) of the patio in terms of its length (x).

   c Construct a graph to compare the area of the patio with its length.

   d Estimate the dimensions of the patio if it had an area of 65 m^2.

8E Reciprocal function

A reciprocal function is a curve whose equation has a variable in the denominator such as $\frac{1}{x}$. It is defined by the general rule $y = \frac{k}{x}$ where k is a number. Reciprocal functions are graphed in a similar method to other non-linear functions and make a curve called a hyperbola.

Key features of a hyperbola

The basic hyperbola has the equation $y = \frac{1}{x}$.

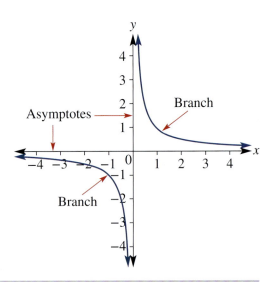

- No value exists for y when $x = 0$.
- The curve has two parts called branches. Each branch is the same shape and size; they are symmetrical and are in opposite quadrants.
- The x-axis and the y-axis are asymptotes of the curve. That is, the curve approaches the x-axis and the y-axis but never touches them.
- The asymptotes are at right angles to each other, so the curve is also called a rectangular hyperbola.

RECIPROCAL FUNCTION

A reciprocal function has the form $y = \frac{k}{x}$ where k is a number.

Hyperbola: $y = \frac{1}{x}$

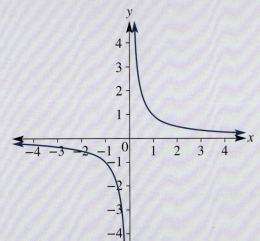

Hyperbola: $y = -\frac{1}{x}$

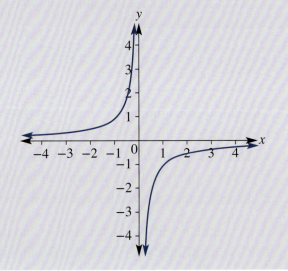

To graph a hyperbola:

1 Construct a table of values.
2 Draw a number plane.
3 Plot the points.
4 Join the points to make a hyperbola.

Example 8: Graphing a reciprocal function   **8E**

Draw the graph of $y = \dfrac{2}{x}$.

SOLUTION:

1 Construct a table of values for x and y.

2 Let $x = -4, -2, -1, -0.5, 0.5, 1, 2$ and 4. Find y using the reciprocal function.

x	−4	−2	−1	−0.5	0.5	1	2	4
y	−0.5	−1	−2	−4	4	2	1	0.5

3 Draw a number plane with x as the horizontal axis and y as the vertical axis.

4 Plot the points $(-4, -0.5)$, $(-2, -1)$, $(-1, -2)$, $(-0.5, -4)$, $(0.5, 4)$, $(1, 2)$, $(2, 1)$ and $(4, 0.5)$.

5 No value exists for y when $x = 0$. This results in the curve having two branches.

6 Join the points to make a curve in the shape of a hyperbola.

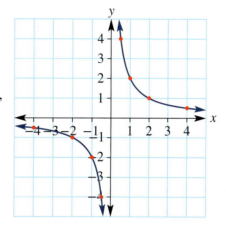

Example 9: Graphing a reciprocal function   **8E**

a Draw the graph of $y = -\dfrac{2}{x}$.

b What are the asymptotes for this graph?

SOLUTION:

1 Construct a table of values for x and y.

2 Let $x = -4, -2, -1, -0.5, 0.5, 1, 2$ and 4. Find y using the reciprocal function.

a

x	−4	−2	−1	−0.5	0.5	1	2	4
y	0.5	1	2	4	−4	−2	−1	−0.5

3 Draw a number plane with x as the horizontal axis and y as the vertical axis.

4 Plot the points $(-4, 0.5)$, $(-2, 1)$, $(-1, 2)$, $(-0.5, 4)$, $(0.5, -4)$, $(1, -2)$, $(2, -1)$ and $(4, 0.5)$.

5 No value exists for y when $x = 0$. This results in the curve having two branches.

6 Join the points to make a curve in shape of a hyperbola.

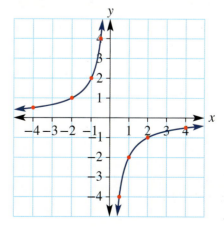

7 The curve approaches the x-axis and the y-axis but never touches them.

b Asymptotes are $x = 0$ and $y = 0$.

Exercise 8E

Example 8

1 A reciprocal function is $y = \dfrac{1}{x}$.

  a Complete the following table of values.

x	-4	-2	-1	$-\dfrac{1}{2}$	$\dfrac{1}{2}$	1	2	4
y								

  b Graph the reciprocal function using the number plane opposite.

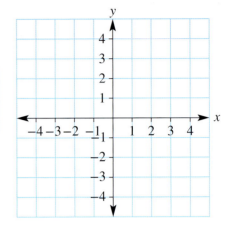

Example 9

2 A reciprocal function is $y = -\dfrac{1}{x}$.

  a Complete the following table of valucs.

x	-4	-2	-1	$-\dfrac{1}{2}$	$\dfrac{1}{2}$	1	2	4
y								

  b Graph the reciprocal function using the number plane opposite.

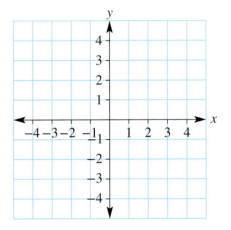

3 Complete the following table of values and graph each reciprocal function on the same number plane.

  a $y = \dfrac{3}{x}$

x	-9	-3	-1	$-\dfrac{1}{3}$	$\dfrac{1}{3}$	1	3	9
y								

  b $y = -\dfrac{3}{x}$

x	-9	-3	-1	$-\dfrac{1}{3}$	$\dfrac{1}{3}$	1	3	9
y								

  c $y = \dfrac{4}{x}$

x	-8	-4	-1	$-\dfrac{1}{2}$	$\dfrac{1}{2}$	1	4	8
y								

  d $y = -\dfrac{4}{x}$

x	-8	-4	-1	$-\dfrac{1}{2}$	$\dfrac{1}{2}$	1	4	8
y								

4 Draw the graph of the following reciprocal functions.

   a $y = \dfrac{6}{x}$ **b** $y = \dfrac{8}{x}$ **c** $y = -\dfrac{5}{x}$ **d** $y = -\dfrac{7}{x}$

5 Find the coordinates on the graph of $y = \dfrac{2}{x}$, where:

   a $x = 2$ **b** $x = 4$ **c** $x = -1$ **d** $x = -8$

6 Find the coordinates on the graph of $y = -\dfrac{5}{x}$, where:

   a $x = 10$ **b** $x = 7$ **c** $x = -5$ **d** $x = -2$

7 What is the reciprocal equation of the following hyperbolas?

   a

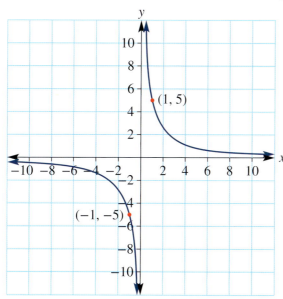

   b

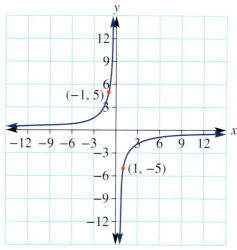

8 Do the following points lie on the hyperbola $y = \dfrac{4}{x}$? Justify your answer.

   a $(1, 4)$ **b** $(-2, -2)$ **c** $(4, 16)$ **d** $(8, 0.5)$

9 Do the following points lie on the hyperbola $y = -\dfrac{10}{x}$? Justify your answer.

   a $(10, 1)$ **b** $(-5, -2)$ **c** $(-20, -0.5)$ **d** $(5, -2)$

10 Draw the graph of the following reciprocal functions.

   a $y = \dfrac{1}{x} + 1$ **b** $y = -\dfrac{1}{x} + 1$ **c** $y = \dfrac{2}{x} - 2$ **d** $y = \dfrac{4}{x} - 3$

   e $xy = 1$ **f** $xy = -2$ **g** $y = \dfrac{x + 2}{x}$ **h** $y = \dfrac{x - 5}{x}$

8F Reciprocal models

Reciprocal modelling occurs when a practical situation is described mathematically using a reciprocal function. The quantity usually experiences fast growth or decay.

RECIPROCAL MODELS

A reciprocal model describes a practical situation using a function in the form $y = \dfrac{k}{x}$ where k is a number. Reciprocal functions are graphed to make a curve in the shape of a hyperbola.

Example 10: Using a reciprocal model   8F

The time taken (t), in hours, for a road trip, at speed (s), in km/h, is given by the reciprocal function $t = \dfrac{2000}{s}$.

a   Construct a table of values for s and t.

b   Draw the graph of $t = \dfrac{2000}{s}$.

c   How long did the road trip take at a speed of 70 km/h?

d   Why is it impossible to complete the road trip in 10 hours?

SOLUTION:

1   Construct a table of values for s and t.   a

2   Choose appropriate values for s, the speed of the car. Let $s = 10, 20, 40, 50, 60, 80$ and 100.

s	10	20	40	50	60	80	100
t	200	100	50	40	33	25	20

3   Find t using the reciprocal function $t = \dfrac{2000}{s}$. Express the values for t as a whole number.

b

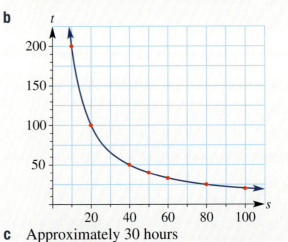

4   Draw a number plane with s as the horizontal axis and t as the vertical axis.

5   Plot the points (10, 200), (20, 100), (40, 50), (50, 40), (60, 33), (80, 25) and (100, 20).

6   Join the points to make a branch of a hyperbola.

7   Read the approximate value of t from the graph when $s = 70$.

c   Approximately 30 hours

8   Read the value of s from the table.

9   Make sense of the result.

d   Speed required to complete the trip in 10 h is 200 km/h, which is above the speed limit on Australian roads.

Example 11: Using a reciprocal model   **8F**

The cost per person of sharing a pizza (C) is dependent on the number of people (n) eating the pizza.

The reciprocal equation $C = \dfrac{24}{n}$ is used to model this situation.

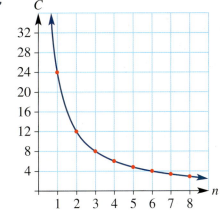

a   Describe the possible values for n.

b   Construct a table of values for n and C.

c   Draw the graph of $C = \dfrac{24}{n}$.

d   What is the cost per person if six people are sharing a pizza?

e   How many people shared a pizza if the cost was $2.40 per person?

SOLUTION:

1   The variable n represents the number of people sharing a pizza.

a n is a positive whole number and likely to be less than 10.

2   Construct a table of values for n and C.

3   Choose appropriate values for n.
Let $n = 1, 2, 3, 4, 5, 6, 7$ and 8.

b

n	1	2	3	4	5	6	7	8
C	24	12	8	6	4.8	4	3.4	3

4   Find C using $C = \dfrac{24}{n}$.

5   Draw a number plane with n as the horizontal axis and C as the vertical axis.

6   Plot the points $(1, 24)$, $(2, 12)$, $(3, 8)$, $(4, 6)$, $(5, 4.8)$, $(6, 4)$, $(7, 3.4)$ and $(8, 3)$.

7   Join the points to make a branch of a hyperbola.

c

8   Read the value of C from the table or graph when $n = 6$.

d   Cost per person is $4.

9   Substitute 2.4 for C into the reciprocal equation.

e $2.4 = \dfrac{24}{n}$

10   Solve the equation for n by rearranging the formula and evaluate.

$n = \dfrac{24}{2.4} = 10$

11   Check that the answer is reasonable.

12   Write the answer in words.

$\therefore$ number of people sharing the pizza was 10

Exercise 8F

Example 10 **1** The time taken (t), in hours, for a road trip, at an
average speed (s), in km/h, is given by the formula
$t = \dfrac{1500}{s}$. The graph of this formula is shown.

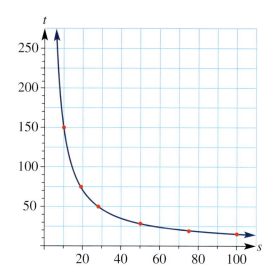

a How long would the road trip take at 50 km/h?

b How long would the road trip take at 75 km/h?

c What is the speed required to complete the road
trip in 25 hours?

d What is the speed required to complete the road
trip in 100 hours?

e Why is it impossible to complete the road trip in
5 hours?

Example 11 **2** The cost per person of hiring a yacht ($\$C$) is
dependent on the number of people (n) sharing the
total cost. The reciprocal equation $C = \dfrac{320}{n}$ is used
to model this situation.

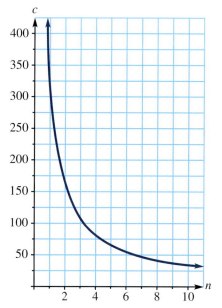

a What is the cost per person of hiring the yacht if
2 people share the total cost?

b What is the cost per person of hiring the yacht if
8 people share the total cost?

c How many people are required to share the cost of
hiring a yacht for $80?

d How many people are required to share the cost of
hiring a yacht for $320?

e Is it possible for the cost per person to be $1?

3 The time taken (t in minutes) to type an essay
depends on the typing speed (s in words per minute).
The reciprocal function $t = \dfrac{150}{s}$ is used to model this
situation.

a Complete the following table of values, correct to
the nearest whole number.

s	5	10	15	25	30	50
t						

b Draw the graph of $t = \dfrac{150}{s}$ using the number plane
shown opposite.

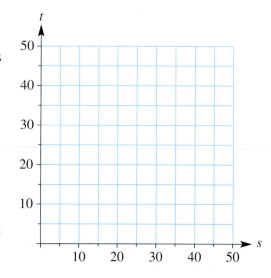

4 The time taken (t in hours) to dig a hole is dependent on the number of people (n) digging the hole. This relationship is modelled using the formula $t = \dfrac{6}{n}$.

a Complete the following table of values, correct to the nearest whole number.

n	1	2	3	4	5	6
t						

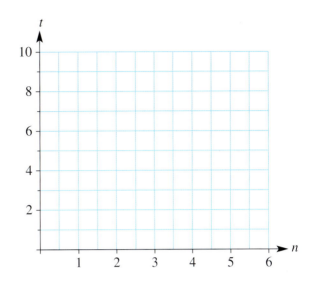

b Draw the graph of $t = \dfrac{6}{n}$ using the number plane shown opposite.

c What is the time taken by one person to dig a hole?

d What is the time taken by 3 people to dig a hole?

e What is the time taken to by 6 people to dig a hole?

f How many people could dig the hole in two hours?

g How many people could dig the hole in 30 minutes?

h How long would it take for 360 people to dig the hole? Is this possible?

5 The maximum number of people (n in 1000's) attending an outdoor concert is dependent on the area (A in m^2) allowed per person. The reciprocal equation $n = \dfrac{1.2}{A}$ models this practical situation.

a Complete the following table of values, correct to the nearest whole number.

A	0.1	0.2	0.3	0.4	0.5	0.6	0.8	0.9	1.0
n									

b Draw the graph of $n = \dfrac{1.2}{A}$ using the number plane shown opposite.

c How many people can attend this concert if the area allowed per person is 0.5 m^2?

d How many people can attend this concert if the area allowed per person is 0.25 m^2?

e What is the area allowed per person if the maximum number of people attending the concert is 2000?

f What is the area allowed per person if the maximum number of people attending the concert is 5000?

g Is it possible for 12 000 people to attend this concert? Justify your answer.

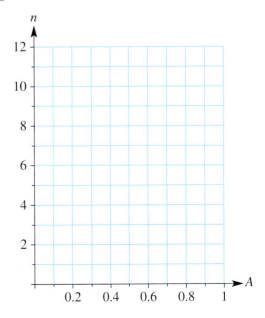

6 The speed in km/h (s) of a truck is given by the formula $s = \dfrac{60}{t}$ where t is the time (hours).

  a Construct a table of ordered pairs using 1, 5, 10, 15, 20 and 60 as values for t.

  b Draw the graph of $s = \dfrac{60}{t}$.

  c What is the speed of the truck if the time taken was 30 hours?

  d What is the time taken if the speed of the truck was 25 km/h?

7 The number of chairs (n) in a row is dependent on the distance $(d$, in metres) between the chairs. This relationship is modelled using the reciprocal equation $n = \dfrac{48}{d}$.

  a Construct a table of ordered pairs using 2, 4, 8, 12, 16, 20 and 24 as values for d.

  b Draw the graph of $n = \dfrac{48}{d}$.

  c How many chairs can be placed in a row if the distance between them is 3 metres?

  d What is the problem with the model if the distance between the chairs is 50 metres?

8 Alex is planning to subdivide his land into rectangular blocks using the formula $l = \dfrac{900}{b}$, where l is the length in metres and b is the breadth in metres.

  a Make a table of values for b and l. Use 5, 10, 30, 50 and 100 for b.

  b Draw the graph of $l = \dfrac{900}{b}$.

  c What is the length of the block if the breadth is 2.5 metres?

  d What is the breadth of the block if the length is 150 metres?

  e If the block were to be a square, what would be its length?

  f Which would cost more to fence, a block that was 60 m wide, or one that was 25 m wide? Justify your answer using relevant calculations.

8G Inverse variation

Inverse variation (or inverse proportion) occurs when one variable increases while the other variable decreases. The variables are dependent on each other but change in opposite directions. For example, the time taken to paint a house depends inversely on the number of people available to paint. The more painters available the less time it would take to paint the house.

SOLVING AN INVERSE VARIATION PROBLEM

1 Write an equation relating the two variables. (k is the constant of variation). y is inversely proportional to x so the equation is $y = \dfrac{k}{x}$.

2 Solve the equation for k by substituting values for x and y.

3 Write the equation with the solution for k (step 2) and solve the problem by substituting a value for either x or y.

Example 12: Solving an inverse variation problem   8G

The cost per person (c) to hire a reception centre is inversely proportional to the number of people attending (n). If there are 50 people, the cost per person is $36.

a What is the cost per person when there are 20 people attending?

b How many people are required for the cost per person to be $25?

SOLUTION:

1 Cost is inversely proportional to the number of people.

2 Use the formula $y = \dfrac{k}{x}$ by replacing the y with c and the x with n.   **a** $c = \dfrac{k}{n}$

3 Substitute 36 for c and 50 for n into the formula. $36 = \dfrac{k}{50}$

4 Evaluate. $k = 1800$

5 Write the formula using the value for the proportionality constant ($k = 1800$). $c = \dfrac{1800}{n}$

6 Substitute 20 for n into the formula. $= \dfrac{1800}{20}$

7 Evaluate. $= \$90$

8 Write the answer in words.   Cost is $90 per person.

9 Write the formula using the value for the proportionality constant ($k = 1800$).   **b** $c = \dfrac{1800}{n}$

10 Substitute 25 for c into the formula. $25 = \dfrac{1800}{n}$

11 Evaluate. $n = 72$

12 Write the answer in words.   72 people required.

Example 13: Solving an inverse variation problem 8G

The number of people (n) waiting at Circular Quay for a ferry is inversely proportional to the time (t, in minutes) until the next ferry arrives. If there are 64 people waiting, the ferry will arrive in $3\frac{1}{2}$ minutes.

a Find the constant of variation.
b Write the inverse variation equation.
c How many people are waiting at Circular Quay 4 minutes before the ferry arrives?
d How long before the ferry arrives if there are 28 people waiting?

SOLUTION:

1	Number of people is inversely proportional to the time.	
2	Use the formula $y = \dfrac{k}{x}$ by replacing the y with n and the x with t.	**a** $n = \dfrac{k}{t}$
3	Substitute 64 for n and 3.5 for t into the formula.	$64 = \dfrac{k}{3.5}$
4	Evaluate.	$k = 224$
5	Substitute 224 for k in the inverse variation equation.	**b** $n = \dfrac{224}{t}$
6	Write the inverse variation equation.	**c** $n = \dfrac{224}{t}$
7	Substitute 4 for t into the formula.	$= \dfrac{224}{4}$
8	Evaluate.	$= 56$
9	Write the answer in words.	56 people are waiting.
10	Write the inverse variation equation.	**d** $n = \dfrac{224}{t}$
11	Substitute 28 for n into the formula.	$28 = \dfrac{224}{t}$
12	Evaluate.	$= 8$
13	Write the answer in words.	Ferry will arrive in 8 minutes.

Exercise 8G

1 y is inversely proportional to x and $y = 4$ when $x = 3$.
   a Write an equation connecting y and x.
   b Calculate the proportionality constant.
   c What is y when x is 6?
   d What is x when y is 12?

2 y is inversely proportional to x and $y = 18$ when $x = 2$.
   a Write an equation connecting y and x.
   b Calculate the proportionality constant.
   c What is y when x is 9?
   d What is x when y is 2?

3 It is known that m varies inversely with n. If $m = 6$ then $n = 8$.
   a Write an equation in the form $m = \dfrac{k}{n}$ to describe this situation.
   b Find the value of m if the value of n is 24.
   c Find the value of n if the value of m is 4.

4 It is known that c varies inversely with d. If $c = 108$ then $d = \dfrac{2}{3}$.
   a Write an equation in the form $c = \dfrac{k}{d}$ to describe this situation.
   b Find the value of c if the value of d is 48.
   c Find the value of d if the value of c is 8.

Example 12 5 The time taken (t), in days, to paint a house varies inversely with the number of painters (p) employed. It takes six painters 5 days to paint a house.
   a Find the constant of variation.
   b Write an inverse variation equation to describe this situation.
   c How long does it take two painters to paint the house?
   d How many painters does it take to paint the house in 3 days?

Example 13 6 Time taken in hours for a trip varies inversely with average speed. It takes five hours to complete a trip travelling at 68 km/h.
   a Find the constant of variation.
   b Write an inverse variation equation to describe this situation.
   c What is the time taken for a trip with an average speed of 34 km/h?
   d What speed is required to complete the trip in 4 hours?

7 The time taken (T), in days, to assemble a shed varies inversely with the number, N, of people employed. It takes three people 2 days to assemble a shed.

  a How long does it take one person to assemble the shed?

  b How many people are required to assemble the shed in 3 days?

  c Is this statement correct? 'If the number of people is doubled then the time taken to assemble the shed is halved.' Give a reason for your answer.

8 The cost ($\$c$) per passenger of hiring a bus is inversely proportional to the number of passengers (n) on the bus. If there were 20 passengers, the cost per passenger is $30.

  a What is the cost per passenger when there are 32 passengers?

  b How many passengers are required for the cost per passenger to be $20?

9 The cost per person (c), in dollars, to attend a formal dance varies inversely with the number of people (n) attending. When 90 people attend, the cost is $60 per person.

  a If only 80 people attend the formal dance, how much will each person have to pay?

  b The organising committee has suggested a cost per ticket of $40. How many people need to attend the formal dance for the tickets to be $40?

10 The number of people (N) who attend a show varies inversely with the amount of floor space (in cm^2) allowed per person (A). A venue can hold 480 people if each person is allowed 2000 cm^2.

  a How many people could the venue hold if each person was allowed 2400 cm^2?

  b What is the space allowed per person to allow 500 to attend the show?

11 Connor uses a microwave oven to reheat a meal. The time taken (in minutes) for heating is inversely proportional to the power setting. The meal takes three minutes at a power setting of 60%. How long would it take at a power setting of 80%?

12 The maximum speed (km/h) of a truck going up an incline is inversely proportional to the square of its weight (tonnes). A truck weighing 5 tonnes can go up the incline at 64 km/h. What is the maximum speed at which a truck weighing 6 tonnes could go up the same incline? Answer to the nearest kilometre per hour.

8H | Miscellaneous problems

Algebraic modelling occurs when a practical situation is described mathematically using an algebraic function. This involves gathering data and analysing the data to determine possible functions. Determining the function is made easier using technology.

ALGEBRAIC MODEL

- Algebraic models are used to describe practical situations.
- Algebraic models may have limitations that restrict their use.

Example 14: Modelling physical phenomena 8H

The mass M kg of a baby orang-utan and its age after x months are given below.

x	0	1	2	3	4	5	6
M	1.5	1.8	2.2	2.6	3.1	3.7	4.5

a   Plot the points from the table onto a number plane.

b   The formula $M = 1.5(1.2)^x$ models the data in the table. Graph $M = 1.5(1.2)^x$ on the same number plane.

c   Use the model to determine the mass of the orang-utan after 2.5 months.

d   This model only applies when x is less than or equal to 6. Why?

SOLUTION:

1   Draw a number plane with x as the horizontal axis and M as the vertical axis.

2   Plot the points $(0, 1.5)$, $(1, 1.8)$, $(2, 2.2)$, $(3, 2.6)$, $(4, 3.1)$, $(5, 3.7)$ and $(6, 4.5)$.

3   The formula $M = 1.5(1.2)^x$ has the same table of values. Join the points to make a curve.

a, b

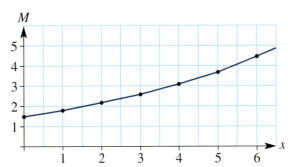

4   Substitute 2.5 for x into the formula.

5   Evaluate, correct to one decimal place.

c $M = 1.5(1.2)^{2.5}$

   $= 2.4$ kg

6   Use the model for x greater than 6. Let x be 48 months or 4 years. Substitute 48 for x into the formula.

7   Evaluate.

8   Write the answer in words.

d $M = 1.5(1.2)^{48}$

   $= 9479.6$ kg

Orang-utans are less than 100 kg in general so the answer of 9479.6 kg is unreasonable.

Exercise 8H

Example 14   **1**   A new piece of equipment is purchased by a business for \$150 000. The value of the equipment (v in thousands of dollars) depreciates each year (t) as shown in the table below.

t	0	1	2	3	4	5	6
v	150	75	38	19	9	5	2

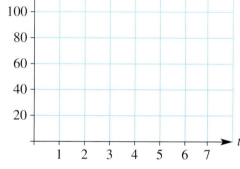

a Draw a number plane as shown opposite.

b Plot the points from the table of values. Join the points.

c An exponential model in the form $y = 2^{-x} \times a$ describes this situation.

    i What is the model if x and y are replaced with t and v?

    ii Determine the value of a in the model by using $t = 0$.

    iii What is the exponential model using t and v?

d Use the model to predict the value of the equipment after 2.5 years.

e Use the model to predict the value of the equipment after 6 months.

f When will the value of the equipment be \$75 000? Answer correct to the nearest thousand.

g Use the model to predict the value of the equipment after 20 years. Explain your answer.

2   The distance (d metres) that an object falls in t seconds is shown in the table below.

t	0	1	2	3	4	5	6
d	0	5	20	45	80	125	180

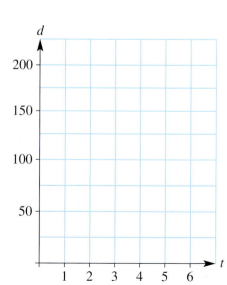

a Plot the points from the table of values on the number plane. Join the points to make a curve.

b A quadratic model in the form $y = ax^2$ describes this situation.

    i What is the model if x and y are replaced with t and d?

    ii Determine the value of a in the model by using $t = 1$.

    iii What is the quadratic model using t and d?

c Use the model to find the distance fallen after $3\frac{1}{2}$ seconds.

d Use the model to find the distance fallen after 10 seconds.

e What is the time taken for an object to fall 320 metres?

f Earth's atmosphere is approximately 1000 km thick. What limitations would you place on this model?

3 The number of tadpoles (*N*) in a pond after *t* months is shown in the table below.

t	0	2	4	6	8	10	14
N	0	24	96	216	384	600	1176

a Draw a number plane with *t* as the horizontal axis and *N* as the vertical axis.
b Plot the points from the table of values. Join the points to make a curve.
c A quadratic model in the form $y = ax^2$ describes this situation.

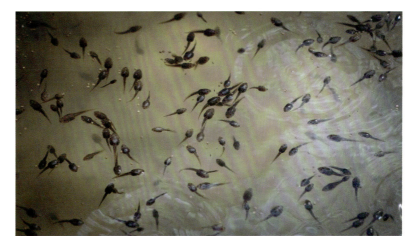

   i What is the model if *x* and *y* are replaced with *t* and *N*?
   ii Determine the value of *a* in the model by using $t = 2$.
   iii What is the quadratic model using *t* and *N*?
d Use the model to find the number of tadpoles after 11 months.
e Use the model to find the time taken for the number of tadpoles to reach 2400.
f Use the model to predict the number of tadpoles after 4.5 months. What limitations would you place on this model?

4 The speed of a car (*s*, in km/h) and the time taken (*t*, in hours) is shown below.

t	1	2	3	4	5	6
s	120	60	40	30	24	20

a Draw a number plane with *t* as the horizontal axis and *s* as the vertical axis.
b Plot the points from the table of values. Join the points to make a curve.

c A hyperbolic model in the form $y = \dfrac{a}{x}$ describes this situation.

   i What is the model if *x* and *y* are replaced with *t* and *s*?
   ii Determine the value of *a* in the model by using $t = 1$.
   iii What is the hyperbolic model using *t* and *s*?
d Use the model to find the speed of the car after 8 hours.
e What is the time taken for a car travelling at a speed of 48 km/h?
f Use the model to predict the speed of the car after 30 minutes. Is this possible? Explain your answer.

5 Lucy invested $100 into a managed fund that appreciated in value for 5 years. The amount of money (A) in the fund for each year (t) is shown below.

t	0	1	2	3	4	5
A	$100	$150	$225	$338	$506	$759

a Draw a number plane with t as the horizontal axis and A as the vertical axis.

b Plot the points from the table of values. Join the points to make a curve.

c An exponential model in the form $y = 100 \times (a)^x$ describes this situation.

   i What is the model if x and y are replaced with t and A?

   ii Determine the value of a in the model by using $t = 1$.

   iii What is the exponential model using t and A?

d Use the model to find the value (to the nearest dollar) of the fund after $2\frac{1}{2}$ years.

e Use the model to find the value (to the nearest dollar) of the fund after 7 years.

f When is the value of the fund approximately $5767?

6 The cost of using a new motorway was initially free and 4500 vehicles used it each day. A toll was introduced that gradually increased.

Let the toll charge be c (in dollars) and the number of vehicles using the toll be n.

a An exponential model in the form $y = b^{-x} \times a$ describes this situation.

   i What is the model if x and y are replaced with c and n?

   ii Determine the value of a in the model by using $c = 0$.

   iii Determine the value of b in the model if there were 3000 vehicles using the toll for a charge of $1.

   iv Determine an exponential model using C and n to describe this situation.

b Construct a table of values by using c (dollars) to represent the value of the toll and (n) for the number of vehicles using the motorway each day.

c Plot the table of values on a number plane.

d How many vehicles use the toll if the charge was $3?

e What is the income received when the toll charge was $3?

f 'A higher toll always means a higher total daily income'. Do you agree with this statement? Explain your answer.

Key ideas and chapter summary

Exponential function	$y = a^x, a > 0$

$y = a^{-x}, a > 0$

Exponential model	Exponential growth	Quantity increases rapidly using $y = a^x$
	Exponential decay	Quantity decreases rapidly using $y = a^{-x}$

Quadratic function

Quadratic function has the form $y = ax^2 + bx + c$ where a, b and c are numbers.

- Parabola ($y = x^2$) Minimum turning point
- Parabola ($y = -x^2$) Maximum turning point

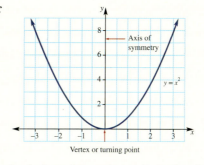

Quadratic model

A quadratic model describes a practical situation using a function in the form $y = ax^2 + bx + c$ where a, b and c are numbers.

Reciprocal function

A reciprocal function has the form $y = \dfrac{k}{x}$ where k is a number.

- Hyperbola: $y = \dfrac{1}{x}$

- Hyperbola: $y = -\dfrac{1}{x}$

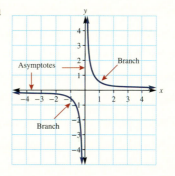

Reciprocal model

A reciprocal model describes a practical situation using a function in the form $y = \dfrac{k}{x}$ where k is a number.

Inverse variation

1 Write an equation relating the two variables. (k is the constant).

y is inversely proportional to x so the equation is $y = \dfrac{k}{x}$.

2 Solve the equation for k by substituting values for x and y.

3 Write the equation with the solution for k (step 2) and solve the problem by substituting a value for either x or y.

Summary

Multiple-choice

1 What is the y-intercept of the exponential function $y = 2^{-x}$?

   A $(0, -1)$ **B** $(0, 0)$ **C** $(0, 1)$ **D** $(0, 2)$

2 Which of the following points lies on the quadratic curve $y = 2x^2 - x + 1$?

   A $(-1, 0)$ **B** $(0, -1)$ **C** $(1, 2)$ **D** $(2, 16)$

3 What is the maximum value of the quadratic function $y = -x^2 + 4x - 3$?

   A -3 **B** 1 **C** 2 **D** 4

4 The equation $d = 0.4(s^2 + s)$ is used to model the stopping distance for a bicycle where d is the stopping distance in metres and s is the bicycle's speed in m/s. What is the stopping distance given a speed of 5 metres per second?

   A 5 m   **B** 10 m   **C** 12 m   **D** 15 m

5 Which of the following points lies on the reciprocal function $y = \dfrac{8}{x}$?

   A $(-2, 8)$ **B** $(-1, 8)$ **C** $(0, 8)$ **D** $(2, 4)$

6 The speed in km/h (s) of a vehicle is given by the formula $s = \dfrac{200}{t}$ where t is the time in hours. What is the time taken if the average speed was 80 km/h?

   A 0.4 h   **B** 2.5 h   **C** 120 h   **D** 280 h

7 If the temperature (t) varies inversely with the cost (c), which formula correctly expresses t in terms of c and k, where k is the constant of variation?

   A $t = \dfrac{k}{c}$ **B** $t = \dfrac{c}{k}$ **C** $t = k^c$ **D** $t = kc^2$

8 The graph opposite shows the insect population (N) plotted against the time (t) in days.

t	0	1	2	3	4
N	0	2	8	18	32

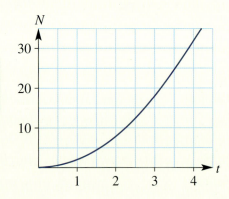

What type of function would model this data?

   A Exponential

   B Hyperbolic

   C Quadratic

   D Reciprocal

Short-answer

1 Complete the following table of values by expressing the y values correct to one decimal place. Graph each exponential function.

a $y = 1.5^x$

x	−3	−2	−1	0	1	2	3
y							

b $y = 0.5^x$

x	−3	−2	−1	0	1	2	3
y							

2 The height, h cm, of a plant and its age after x months is given below.

x	0	1	2	3	4	5	6
h	1.1	2.4	5.3	11.7	25.8	56.7	124.7

a Plot the points from the above table onto a number plane.

b The formula $h = 2.2^x \times 1.1$ models the data in the table. Draw this function.

c Use the model to determine the height of a plant after 1.5 months. Answer correct to one decimal place.

d Use the model to determine the height of a plant after 3.5 months. Answer correct to one decimal place.

3 The population of earthworms grows exponentially according to the formula $w = 1.1^t \times 25$ where w is the number of earthworms after t days.

a Construct a table of ordered pairs using 0, 5, 10, 15 and 20 as values for t. Express the number of earthworms to the nearest whole number.

b Graph $w = 1.1^t \times 25$ using the table of ordered pairs in part **a**.

c What is the initial number of earthworms?

d What is the number of earthworms after 3 days?

e Estimate the time taken for the earthworms to reach a population of 75.

4 Complete the following table of values and graph each quadratic function.

a $y = 3x^2$

x	−3	−2	−1	0	1	2	3
y							

b $y = -\dfrac{1}{3}x^2$

x	−9	−3	−1	0	1	3	9
y							

c $y = x^2 + 3$

x	−3	−2	−1	0	1	2	3
y							

d $y = x^2 - 5x - 4$

x	0	1	2	3	4	5	6
y							

5 Abbey throws a rock and it takes 6 seconds to reach the ground. The height it reaches is given by the formula $h = -t^2 + 6t$ where h is the height (in metres) and t is the number of seconds after it has been thrown.

a Complete the following table of values.

t	0	1	2	3	4	5	6
h							

b Draw the graph of $h = -t^2 + 6t$.
c What was the maximum height reached by the rock?
d When was the maximum height reached?

6 Complete the following table of values and graph each reciprocal function on the same number plane.

a $y = \dfrac{7}{x}$

x	-7	-1	$-\dfrac{1}{7}$	$\dfrac{1}{7}$	1	7
y						

b $y = -\dfrac{7}{x}$

x	-7	-1	$-\dfrac{1}{7}$	$\dfrac{1}{7}$	1	7
y						

7 The number of chairs (c) in a row varies inversely with the distance (d in metres) between them. When the chairs are 2 m apart the row can accommodate 60 chairs.

a How many chairs can be placed in a row if the distance between them is 1.5 m?
b What is the distance between the chairs if the number of chairs is 40?

8 The cost per person (c) to use a conference centre is inversely proportional to the number of people attending (n) the conference. If there were 20 people, the cost per person is $60. How many people are required for the cost per person to be $40?

Extended-response

9 A rectangular patio has a length of x metres and a breadth of $(4 - x)$ metres.

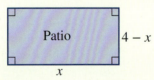

a Find a quadratic equation for the area (A) of the patio in terms of the length (x).
b Complete the table of values and draw the graph of this quadratic equation.

x	0	0.5	1	1.5	2	2.5	3	3.5	4
A									

c What is the maximum area of the patio?
d What is the patio length in order to have maximum area?

PDF
LITERACY

9 The normal distribution

Syllabus topic — S5 The normal distribution

This topic will develop an understanding of the properties of the normal distribution and how it can be used to analyse data and make judgments about the reasonableness of a solution.

Outcomes

- Recognise data that is normally distributed.
- Understand that the mean and the median are approximately equal for normally distributed data.
- Calculate the z-score using the formula.
- Describe the z-score in terms of standard deviations.
- Use z-scores to compare scores from different datasets.
- Use collected data from a normal distribution to make judgments.
- Use z-scores to identify probabilities of a given event.

Digital Resources for this chapter

In the Interactive Textbook:

- Videos
- Literacy worksheet
- Quick Quiz
- Solutions (enabled by teacher)
- Desmos widgets
- Spreadsheets
- Study guide

In the Online Teaching Suite:

- Teaching Program
- Tests
- Review Quiz
- Teaching Notes

Knowledge check

The Interactive Textbook provides a test of prior knowledge for this chapter, and may direct you to revision from the previous years' work.

9A | Normally distributed data

A normal distribution has the same mean, mode and median. It is symmetrical about the mean. The graph of a normal distribution is often called a 'bell curve' (or 'normal curve') due to its shape, as shown to the right.

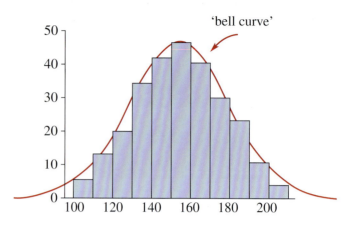

Mean and median in a normal distribution

The mean is a measure of the centre. It is calculated by summing all the scores and dividing by the number of scores. The mean of a set of data is what most people call the 'average'. The median is the middle score or value. To find the median, list all the scores in increasing order and select the middle one. The mean and median are approximately equal for normally distributed data.

For example, consider the set of data: 2 3 3 4
The mean of this set of data is given by:

$$\text{mean } \bar{x} = \frac{\sum x}{n} = \frac{2 + 3 + 3 + 4}{4}$$

$$= \frac{12}{4} = 3$$

Data is ordered: 2 3 3 4
Median = 3

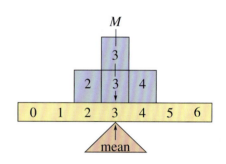

This data is normally distributed. Both the mean and median are equal to 3. The balance point of the distribution is also the point that splits the distribution in half; that is, there are two data points to the left of the mean and two to the right. This is a general characteristic of a normal distribution. However, consider the set of data: 2 3 3 8
The mean of this set of data is given by:

$$\text{mean} = \frac{\sum x}{n} = \frac{2 + 3 + 3 + 8}{4}$$

$$= \frac{16}{4} = 4$$

Data is ordered: 2 3 3 8
Median = 3

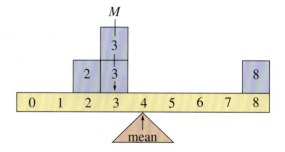

This data is skewed. The mean is 4 and is not equal to median of 3. The mean is affected by changing the largest data value but the median is not.

Characteristics of a normal distribution

The normal distribution is arguably the most important distribution in statistics. There are many datasets that arise in practice that are roughly symmetrical and have an approximate bell shape, as shown below.

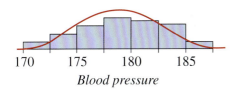

Blood pressure

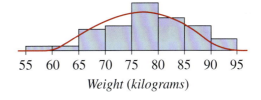

Weight (kilograms)

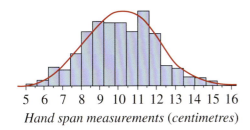

Hand span measurements (centimetres)

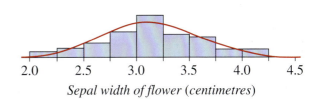

Sepal width of flower (centimetres)

Normal distributions can differ in their means and in their standard deviations. The diagram opposite shows three normal distributions. The blue distribution has a mean of −3 and a standard deviation of 0.5, the distribution in red has a mean of 0 and a standard deviation of 1, and the distribution in black has a mean of 2 and a standard deviation of 3. All of these line graphs represent a normal distribution. Notice that all these three graphs are symmetrical about the centre and most of the data is at the centre.

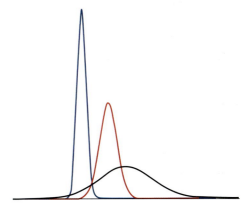

There are five important characteristics of a normal distribution.
- A normal distribution is symmetrical about the mean.
- The mean, median and mode (the score that occurs the most) are equal.
- The majority of the data is located at the centre with less data at the tails.
- A normal distribution has an asymptote on both ends of the *x*-axis.
- Mean and standard deviation of the dataset is used to define the normal distribution.

NORMAL DISTRIBUTION

A normal distribution has the same mean, mode and median. It is symmetrical about the mean. The graph of a normal distribution is called a 'bell curve'.

 Example 1: Drawing a 'bell-shaped' to represent normally distributed data **9A**

The heights (in cm) of 11 women are shown below.

163, 164, 165, 165, 166, 166, 166, 167, 167, 168, 169

a Construct a frequency table

b Find the mean and median.

c What is the population standard deviation, correct to two decimal places?

d Draw a dot plot and bell-shaped curve to show this distribution.

SOLUTION:

1 Draw a table with three columns and label them score, tally and frequency.

2 List the temperatures in the score column from the lowest (163) to the highest (169).

3 Record a mark in the tally column for each temperature.

4 Count the tally marks and write the total in the frequency column.

a Frequency table

Score	Tally	Frequency
163	I	1
164	I	1
165	II	2
166	III	3
167	II	2
168	I	1
169	I	1

5 Sum all of the scores and divide by the number of scores.

6 Evaluate.

b Mean $= \dfrac{\sum x}{n} = \dfrac{163 + 164 + \ldots + 169}{11}$

$= \dfrac{1826}{11}$

$\bar{x} = 166$

7 Write the scores in increasing order.

163, 164, 165, 165, 166, **166**, 166, 167, 167, 168, 169

8 Count the total number of scores. There are 11 scores.

9 Median is the middle or 6th score.

Median $= 166$

10 Enter the statistics mode of the calculator.

11 Clear memory and enter the data into the calculator.

12 Select the σ_x to view the results.

c Population standard deviation $\sigma_x \approx 1.65$

13 Draw a number line, scaled to all the data values.

14 Plot each data value by marking a dot above the corresponding value on the number line.

15 Draw a 'bell-shaped' curve to match the dot plot.

d Dot plot and bell-shaped curve

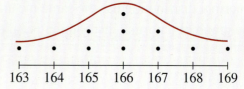

Exercise 9A

1 Copy and complete the following sentences.

  a A normal distribution has the same mean, mode and _____.

  b A normal distribution is symmetrical about the _____.

  c The graph of a _____ distribution is often called a 'bell-shaped' curve.

  d Mean is calculated by summing all the _____ and dividing by the number of scores

  e To find the median, list all the scores in increasing order and select the _____ one.

  f Normal distributions can differ in their means and in their _____ deviations.

  g The majority of the data in a normal distribution is located at the _____.

  h A normal distribution has an _____ on both ends of the x-axis.

2 Find the mean and median for each normally distributed dataset.
Answer correct to the nearest whole number.

  a 5, 8, 9, 9, 10, 11, 11, 13

  b 37, 38, 38, 39, 40, 40, 40, 40, 40, 40, 41, 41, 41, 41, 42, 42

  c 65, 70, 71, 71, 72, 73, 75, 75, 77, 77, 78

  d 33, 23, 31, 24, 30, 32, 26, 32, 29, 30, 40

  e 117, 127, 116, 119, 122, 123, 120, 125, 120, 106, 125

  f 95, 93, 94, 95, 94, 98, 95, 93, 96, 101, 93, 94, 100, 92, 98, 87, 91, 88, 89

Example 1

3 The time (in minutes) it takes Layla to travel to
work is shown below.
60, 61, 62, 62, 63, 63, 63, 64, 64, 64, 64, 65,
65, 65, 66, 66, 67, 68

  a Construct a frequency table.

  b Find the mean and median.

  c What is the population standard deviation?

  d Draw a dot plot and 'bell-shaped'
    curve to show this distribution.

4 The weight (in grams) of Henry's oranges is
shown below.
149, 150, 146, 148, 150, 149, 150, 147, 148,
152, 153, 154, 151, 152, 151

  a Construct a frequency table.

  b Find the mean and median. Answer to the
    nearest whole number.

  c What is the population standard deviation?
    Answer correct to two decimal places.

  d Draw a dot plot and 'bell-shaped' curve to
    show this distribution.

5 Create the spreadsheet below.

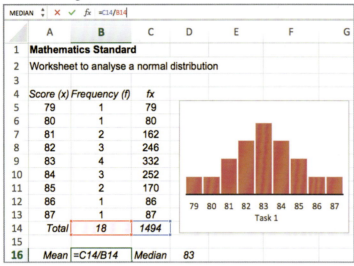

a   Cell B14 has a formula that calculates the total using the frequency table.

b   Cell C14 has a formula that calculates the mean using the frequency table.

c   Column chart is created using horizontal (x-values) A5:A13 and y-values B5:B13.

d   Change the scores by adding 2 to each score.

e   Change the frequency by adding these scores: 79, 82, 83, 84 and 87.

6 A sample of 11 students were given a general knowledge test with the following results.

20, 20, 19, 21, 21, 18, 20, 22, 23, 17, 19

a   Calculate the mean and population standard deviation of the test scores, correct to one decimal place.

b   The median test score is 20, which is similar in value to the mean. What does this tell you about the distribution of test scores?

c   Draw a column graph to show the distribution of test scores.

7 The stem plot shows the distribution of weights (in kg) of 23 footballers.

a   What is the mean and median for this distribution?

b   Is this a normal distribution? Give a reason for your answer.

c   Which measure of centre, the mean or the median, do you think would best indicate the typical weight of these footballers?

Weight (kg)

6	9
7	0 2
7	6 6 7 8
8	0 0 1 2 3 3 4
8	5 5 5 6 9
9	1 2
9	8
10	3

A normal distribution has the same mean, mode and median. It is symmetrical about the mean. The percentage of data that lie within a certain number of standard deviations (or z-scores) is always the same for a normal distribution. That is, 68% are within one standard deviation, 95% are within two standard deviations and 99.7% are within three standard deviations. This gives rise to what is known as the 68–95–99.7% rule.

THE 68–95–99.7 RULE AND STANDARD DEVIATION

For a normal distribution, approximately:
- 68% of data lie within one standard deviation of the mean.
- 95% of data lie within two standard deviations of the mean.
- 99.7% of data lie within three standard deviations of the mean.

Note: 50% of data will lie above the mean and 50% of data will lie below the mean.

Graphical form of the 68–95–99.7 rule

If a data distribution is approximately normal, then:

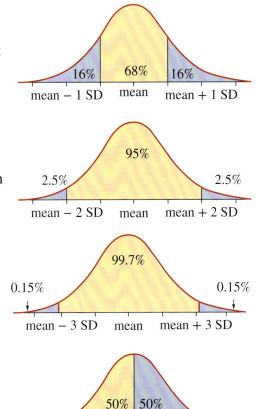

- around 68% of data will lie within one standard deviation (SD) of the mean ($\bar{x} \pm s$). This also means that 32% of data lie outside this region. As the distribution is symmetric, we can also say that around 16% of data lie in each of the tails (shaded blue, opposite).
- around 95% of data will lie within two standard deviations (SD) of the mean ($\bar{x} \pm 2s$). This also means that 5% of data lie outside this region. As the distribution is symmetric, we can also say that around 2.5% of data lie in each of the tails (shaded blue, opposite).
- around 99.7% of data will lie within three standard deviations (SD) of the mean($\bar{x} \pm 3s$). This also means that 0.3% of data lie outside this region. As the distribution is symmetric, we can also say that around 0.15% of data lie in each of the tails (shaded blue, opposite).

Finally, because the normal distribution is symmetric, the mean and the median coincide. Therefore, 50% of data will lie above the mean and 50% of data will lie below the mean.

Example 2: Applying the 68–95–99.7% rule   **9B**

A normal distribution of scores has a mean of 75 and standard deviation (SD) of 5. Complete the information about these percentages of the scores:

a 50% lie above _____   **b** 68% lie between _____ and _____

c 95% lie between _____ and _____   **d** 99.7% lie between _____ and _____

SOLUTION:

1 The normal distribution is symmetrical about the mean. Therefore, 50% of the scores lie above the mean or 75.	**a** 75 ∴ 50% lie above 75
2 68% of the scores lie within one SD of the mean.	**b** $75 - 1 \times 5 = 70$ $75 + 1 \times 5 = 80$
3 Write the answer in words.	∴ 68% lie between 70 and 80
4 95% of the scores lie within two SDs of the mean.	**c** $75 - 2 \times 5 = 65$ $75 + 2 \times 5 = 85$
5 Write the answer in words.	∴ 95% lie between 65 and 85
6 99.7% of the scores lie within three SDs of the mean.	**d** $75 = 75 - 3 \times 5 = 60$ $75 = 75 + 3 \times 5 = 90$
7 Write the answer in words.	∴ 99.7% lie between 60 and 90

Example 3: Applying the 68–95–99.7% rule   **9B**

In a normal distribution, the mean recovery time after contracting a certain disease is 12 days with a standard deviation (SD) of 2 days.

a How long would it take for half the patients to recover?

b What percentage of patients would recover within 8 to 16 days?

c What percentage of patients would recover within 10 days?

d If 400 patients contracted the disease last year, how many recovered within 16 days?

SOLUTION:

1 The normal distribution is symmetrical about the mean, 50% of scores lie above the mean (12).	**a** 12 days
2 8 days is two SDs below the mean and 16 days is two SDs above the mean.	**b** $12 - 2 \times 2 = 8$ days $12 + 2 \times 2 = 16$ days
3 Write the answer in words.	∴ 95% recover within 8 to 16 days
4 10 days is one SD below the mean. The percentage below one SD is 16%.	**c** $12 - 1 \times 2 = 10$ days
5 Write the answer in words.	∴ 16% recover within 10 days
6 16 days is two SDs above the mean. The percentage above two SDs is 2.5%, so 97.5% recovered in 16 days.	**d** $12 + 2 \times 2 = 16$ days
7 Number of patients is 97.5% of 400.	Patients $= \dfrac{97.5}{100} \times 400 = 390$
8 Write the answer in words.	∴ 390 patients recover in 16 days.

Example 4: Applying the 68–95–99.7% rule   **9B**

The distribution of delivery times for pizzas made by House of Pizza is approximately normal, with a mean of 25 minutes and a standard deviation (SD) of 5 minutes.

a What percentage of pizzas have delivery times of between 15 and 35 minutes?

b What percentage of pizzas have delivery times of greater than 30 minutes?

c In 1 month, House of Pizza delivers 2000 pizzas. How many of these pizzas are delivered in less than 10 minutes?

SOLUTION:

1 Draw, scale and label a normal distribution curve with a mean of 25 and an SD of 5.

a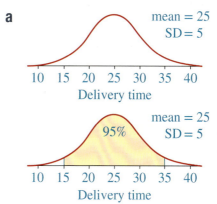

2 Shade the region under the normal curve representing delivery times of between 15 and 35 minutes.

3 Note that delivery times of between 15 and 35 minutes lie within two SDs of the mean. ($15 = 25 - 2 \times 5$ and $35 = 25 + 2 \times 5$)

4 95% of values are within two SDs of the mean. Write answer in words

∴ 95% of pizzas will have delivery times of between 15 and 35 minutes.

5 Draw, scale and label a normal distribution curve with a mean of 25 and an SD of 5. Shade the region under the normal curve representing delivery times of greater than 30 minutes.

b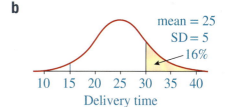

6 Delivery times of greater than 30 minutes are more than one SD above the mean. ($30 = 25 + 1 \times 5$)

7 16% of values are more than one SD above the mean. Write your answer.

∴ 16% of pizzas will have delivery times of greater than 30 minutes.

8 Write down the number of pizzas delivered.

c Number = 2000

9 Delivery times of less than 10 minutes are more than three SDs below the mean. ($10 = 25 - 3 \times 5$).

10 0.15% of values are more than three SDs below the mean.

Percentage delivered in less than 10 minutes = 0.15%

11 Multiply total number of pizzas delivered by 15% and evaluate.

$= 2000 \times 15\% = \dfrac{0.15}{100} \times 2000 = 3$

12 Write the answer in words.

∴ Number of pizzas delivered in less than 10 minutes is 3.

Exercise 9B

1 What percentage of data in a normal distribution lie:

   a above the mean?

   b within one standard deviation of the mean?

   c outside one standard deviation of the mean?

   d within two standard deviations of the mean?

   e outside two standard deviations of the mean?

   f within three standard deviations of the mean?

   g outside three standard deviations of the mean?

Example 2   **2** Scores in a class test are normally distributed with a mean of 60 and standard deviation of 10. Given this information it can be concluded that:

   a 50% of the scores lie above _____

   b 68% of the scores lie between _____ and _____

   c 95% of the scores lie between _____ and _____

   d 99.7% of the scores lie between _____ and _____.

3 The lifetimes of batteries used in a toy have a mean of 12 hours and a standard deviation of 3 hours. The battery lifetimes are normally distributed. Given this information it can be concluded that:

   a 50% of the batteries have lifetimes above _____

   b 68% of the batteries have lifetimes between _____ and _____

   c 95% of the batteries have lifetimes between _____ and _____

   d 99.7% of the batteries have lifetimes between _____ and _____.

4 The monthly rainfall at Georgetown follows a 'bell-shaped' curve with a mean of 55 mm and a standard deviation of 2.5 mm. Given this information it can be concluded that:

   a 50% of the monthly rainfall measurements lie above _____

   b 68% of the monthly rainfall measurements lie between _____ and _____

   c 95% of the monthly rainfall measurements lie between _____ and _____

   d 99.7% of the monthly rainfall measurements lie between _____ and _____.

5 The weight of coffee in a glass jar is normally distributed with a mean of 101.5 g and a standard deviation of 0.7 g. Given this information it can be concluded that:

   a 50% of the weights lie above _____

   b 68% of the weights lie between _____ and _____

   c 95% of the weights lie between _____ and _____

   d 99.7% of the weights lie between _____ and _____.

Example 3   **6**   The blood pressure readings for executives are normally distributed with a mean systolic blood pressure of 134 and a standard deviation of 20. Given this information it can be concluded that:

a 68% of the executives have blood pressures between _____ and _____

b 95% of the executives have blood pressures between _____ and _____

c 99.7% of the executives have blood pressures between _____ and _____

d 16% of the executives have blood pressures above _____

e 2.5% of the executives have blood pressures below _____

f 0.15% of the executives have blood pressures below _____

g 50% of the executives have blood pressures above _____.

7   The mean length of 1000 garden stakes is 180 cm. The standard deviation of the lengths is 3 cm. The length of the garden stakes is normally distributed. What percentage of the garden stakes lie between:

a 177 cm and 183 cm?

b 174 cm and 186 cm?

c 171 cm and 189 cm?

Example 4   **8**   The weights of packets of potato chips are normally distributed. The mean is 200 grams and the standard deviation is 8 grams.

a What percentage of packets will have a weight between 184 grams and 216 grams?

b What percentage of packets will have a weight between 192 grams and 208 grams?

c What percentage of packets will have a weight between 176 grams and 224 grams?

d What percentage of packets will have a weight greater than 200 grams?

9   The time taken for 2000 bus trips between two towns is normally distributed with a mean of 78 minutes and a standard deviation of 4 minutes. What percentage of bus trips take:

a 78 minutes or more?

b less than 78 minutes?

c between 66 and 90 minutes?

d between 74 and 82 minutes?

e between 70 and 86 minutes?

f more than 82 minutes?

g less than 82 minutes?

h more than 86 minutes?

10   An assessment task has a normal distribution with a mean of 67 and a standard deviation of 7. What percentage of scores lie between:

a 46 and 88?

b 53 and 81?

c 60 and 74?

d 60 and 67?

e 67 and 74?

f 67 and 81?

11 The average weight of a bag of 10 blood plums picked at U-Pick Orchard is normally distributed with a mean of 1.88 kg and a standard deviation of 0.20 kg. What percentage of the bags of 10 plums weigh:

a between 1.68 and 2.08 kg? b between 1.28 and 2.48 kg?

c between 1.48 and 2.28 kg? d between 1.88 and 2.08 kg?

e more than 2.08 kg? f more than 2.28 kg?

g less than 1.28 kg? h less than 1.88 kg?

12 The distribution of times taken for walkers to complete a circuit in a park is normal, with a mean time of 14 minutes and a standard deviation of 3 minutes. What percentage of walkers complete the circuit in:

a between 11 and 14 minutes? b between 14 and 23 minutes?

c between 14 and 20 minutes? d between 5 and 14 minutes?

e more than 17 minutes? f more than 23 minutes?

g less than 8 minutes? h less than 5 minutes?

13 The distribution of heights of 19-year-old women is approximately normal, with a mean of 170 cm and a standard deviation of 5 cm.

a What percentage of these women have heights:

 i between 155 and 185 cm?

 ii greater than 180 cm?

 iii between 160 and 180 cm?

b In a sample of 5000 of these women, how many have heights:

 i between 155 and 185 cm?

 ii greater than 180 cm?

 iii between 160 and 180 cm?

14 The distribution of resting pulse rates of 20-year-old men is approximately normal, with a mean of 66 beats/minute and a standard deviation of 4 beats/minute.

a What percentage of these men have pulse rates of:

 i higher than 66?

 ii between 66 and 70?

 iii between 58 and 74?

b In a sample of 2000 of these men, how many have pulse rates:

 i higher than 66?

 ii between 66 and 70?

 iii between 58 and 74?

15 A cake mix should contain 65 mg of sodium per 100 g of the product with a standard deviation of 4.3 mg. However, Madison analysed a sample cake mix and found it contained 77.9 mg of sodium. What conclusions could Madison draw assuming the data is normally distributed?

16 The heights (to the nearest 5 cm) of a number of children are given below.

Heights (m)	1.30	1.35	1.40	1.45	1.50	1.55	1.60	1.65
Frequency	6	18	22	32	31	20	17	6

a How many children were measured?

b What is the mean for this data? Answer correct to two decimal places.

c What is the median for this data?

d Find the sample standard deviation. Answer correct to two decimal places.

e Is this data normally distributed or skewed? Justify your answer.

f Find the range of values (correct to two decimal places) for:

  i $\bar{x} \pm s$ **ii** $\bar{x} \pm 2s$ **iii** $\bar{x} \pm 3s$

g Ignoring rounding and assuming all children have exactly the heights shown in the table, how many children have a height that corresponds to:

  i at least one standard deviation below the mean?

  ii at least one standard deviation above the mean?

17 The results of a numeracy test are normally distributed and shown below.

Score	0	1	2	3	4	5	6	7	8	9	10
Frequency	5	20	50	125	200	250	200	125	50	20	5

a How many scores are there?

b What is the mean for this data?

c What is the median for this data?

d Find the population standard deviation? Answer correct to one decimal place.

e Find the range of values (correct to one decimal place) for:

  i $\mu \pm \sigma$ **ii** $\mu \pm 2\sigma$ **iii** $\mu \pm 3\sigma$

f How many scores correspond to:

  i at least two standard deviations above the mean?

  ii at least two standard deviations below the mean?

9C   z-scores

A z-score is a statistical measure of how many standard deviations a raw score is above or below the mean. A z-score can be positive or negative, indicating whether it is above or below the mean, or zero. The z-score, or standardised score, is used to compare scores in a normal distribution. The z-score is calculated by subtracting the mean from the score and dividing the result by the standard deviation. The z-score is the number of standard deviations the score is from the mean.

Z-SCORE OR STANDARDISED SCORE

z-score is the number of standard deviations the score is from the mean: $z = \dfrac{x - \bar{x}}{s}$

z – z-score or standardised score x – Score $\bar{x}$ – Mean of a set of scores

s – Standard deviation ($s = \sigma_n$ for population standard deviation)

A z-score of 0 indicates the score is equal to the mean. A positive z-score is above the mean and a negative z-score is below the mean. A z-score of 1 is one standard deviation above the mean and a z-score of -1 is one standard deviation below the mean. The larger the z-score (ignoring the positive or negative), the further away it is from the centre of the data.

Example 5: Calculating the z-score   9C

For a normal distribution, the mean is 62 and the standard deviation is 11.
Find the z-score for 84 and interpret this result.

SOLUTION:

1   Write the z-score formula, and substitute $x = 84$, $\bar{x} = 62$ and $s = 11$, and evaluate. $z = \dfrac{x - \bar{x}}{s} = \dfrac{84 - 62}{11} = 2$

2   Interpret the z-score of 2.   The z-score of 2 tells us that 84 is two standard deviations above the mean.

Example 6: Calculating the z-score   9C

Ruby gained a mark of 70 for a class test. What is her z-score if the class mean was 78 and the standard deviation was 6? Answer correct to one decimal place.

SOLUTION:

1   Write the z-score formula, and substitute $x = 70$, $\bar{x} = 78$ and $s = 6$. $z = \dfrac{x - \bar{x}}{s} = \dfrac{70 - 78}{6}$

2   Evaluate, correct to one decimal place. $= -1.3333333 \cong -1.3$

3   Write the answer in words. $\therefore$ Ruby's z-score is -1.3

Desmos widget 9C The set of z-scores from a normally distributed dataset has a mean of 0 and a standard deviation of 1.

Example 7: Calculating standard scores   9C

The heights of a group of young women have a mean of $\bar{x} = 160\,\text{cm}$ and a standard deviation of $s = 8\,\text{cm}$. Determine the standard z-scores of a woman who is:

a 172 cm tall   **b** 150 cm tall   **c** 160 cm tall.

SOLUTION:

1 Write the z-score formula and substitute $x = 172$, $\bar{x} = 160$, $s = 8$.

2 Evaluate.

a $z = \dfrac{x - \bar{x}}{s} = \dfrac{172 - 160}{8}$
$= 1.5$

3 Write the z-score formula and substitute $x = 150$, $\bar{x} = 160$, $s = 8$.

4 Evaluate.

b $z = \dfrac{x - \bar{x}}{s} = \dfrac{150 - 160}{8}$
$= -1.25$

5 Write the z-score formula and substitute $x = 160$, $\bar{x} = 160$, $s = 8$.

6 Evaluate.

c $z = \dfrac{x - \bar{x}}{s} = \dfrac{160 - 160}{8}$
$= 0$

Example 8: Describing the z-score   9C

What is the z-score that corresponds to a score that is:

a the mean?   **b** one standard deviation above the mean?
c one standard deviation below the mean?

SOLUTION

1 The score is equal to the mean.

a $x = \bar{x}$

2 Write the z-score formula and substitute $x = \bar{x}$.

$z = \dfrac{x - \bar{x}}{s} = \dfrac{\bar{x} - \bar{x}}{s}$

3 Simplify.

$= 0$

4 The score is equal to the mean plus the SD.

b $x = \bar{x} + s$

5 Write the z-score formula and substitute $x = \bar{x} + s$.

$z = \dfrac{x - \bar{x}}{s} = \dfrac{(\bar{x} + s) - \bar{x}}{s}$

6 Simplify.

$= \dfrac{s}{s} = 1$

7 The score is equal to the mean minus the SD.

c $x = \bar{x} - s$

8 Write the z-score formula and substitute $x = \bar{x} - s$ into the formula.

$z = \dfrac{x - \bar{x}}{s} = \dfrac{(\bar{x} - s) - \bar{x}}{s}$

9 Simplify.

$= \dfrac{-s}{s} = -1$

Exercise 9C

1 Calculate the z-score, correct to one decimal place, for each of the following:

    a $x = 60$, $\bar{x} = 75$ and $s = 9$ **b** $x = 73$, $\bar{x} = 64$ and $s = 5$

    c $x = 22$, $\bar{x} = 27$ and $s = 2$ **d** $x = 134$, $\bar{x} = 120$ and $s = 30$

    e $x = 10$, $\bar{x} = 5$ and $s = 4$ **f** $x = 93$, $\bar{x} = 78$ and $s = 6$

Example 5   **2** In a common test the mean was 50 and the standard deviation was 10. Find the z-scores for the following test scores.

    a   60   **b**   70   **c**   80   **d**   90

    e   40   **f**   30   **g**   20   **h**   10

    i   55   **j**   45   **k**   65   **l**   35

3 A set of scores has a mean of 100 and a standard deviation of 20. Standardise the following scores.

    a   120   **b**   140   **c**   80

    d   100   **e**   40   **f**   110

Example 7   **4** The mean number of hours spent on the internet each week by students is 12 hours with a standard deviation of 3 hours. Complete the table, which shows the hours spent on the internet by five students.

Student	Hours	z-score
a Amber	12	
b Bailey	6	
c Chloe	18	
d Dylan	0	
e Ella	15	

5 Packets of pasta are each labelled as having a mass of 500 g. The mass of these packets has a mean of 510 g with a standard deviation of 5 g. What are the z-scores for the packets of pasta with the following masses?

    a   500 g   **b**   505 g   **c**   510 g   **d**   515 g

6 The mean height for a group of students is 180 cm with a standard deviation of 6 cm. What is Julie's standardised score (z-score) if her height is 171 cm?

Example 8   **7** What is the z-score that corresponds to a score that is two standard deviations:

    a   above the mean?   **b**   below the mean?

8 What is the z-score that corresponds to a score that is three standard deviations:

    a   above the mean?   **b**   below the mean?

9CQ9

9 Create the spreadsheet below.

	STDEV	▼	✕ ✓ *fx*	=STANDARDIZE(A6,D5,D6)	
	A	B	C	D	E
1					
2	Worksheet to calculate the z-score				
3					
4					
5	*Score*	*z-score*	*Mean*	60.00	
6	80	=STANDARDIZE	*Standard deviation*	13.69	
7	75	1.10			
8	70	0.73			
9	65	0.37			
10	60	0.00			
11	55	-0.37			
12	50	-0.73			
13	45	-1.10			
14	40	-1.46			
15					

a Cell D5 has a formula that calculates the mean. Enter this formula.

b Cell D6 has a formula that calculates the standard deviation. Enter this formula.

c Cell B6 has a formula that calculates the z-score. Enter this formula.

d Fill down the contents of B6 to B14 using the formula in cell B6.

e Change the scores by adding 2 to each score.

f Delete the last 6 scores.

10 Emily scored 70 in a Science test. The test mean was 60 and the standard deviation was 4.

a What was Emily's z-score?

b There was a mistake calculating the mean. It should have been a mean of 65. What is Emily's new z-score?

c There was a mistake calculating the mean and standard deviation. It should have been a mean of 65 and a standard deviation of 10. What is Emily's new z-score?

d What z-score corresponds to a score of 3 standard deviations above the updated mean and standard deviations?

e What z-score corresponds to a score of 3 standard deviations below the updated mean and standard deviations?

11 Daniel's class achieved the following results in a Mathematics test: 29, 78, 55, 39, 96, 55, 74, 46, 63, 65, 49, 61, 57 and 73.

a What is the mean and population standard deviation? (Answer to one decimal place.)

b What is the z-score for the highest score? (Answer to one decimal place.)

c What is the z-score for the lowest score? (Answer to one decimal place.)

d Daniel usually achieves a score two standard deviations above the mean. What is Daniel's z-score and expected mark?

9D | Converting *z*-scores into actual scores

Having learnt how to calculate *z*-scores, you also need to be able to convert *z*-scores back into actual scores. The rule for converting a *z*-score into an actual score involves making x the subject of the *z*-score formula. This is shown below.

$$z = \frac{x - \bar{x}}{s}$$
$$z \times s = x - \bar{x}$$
$$x = \bar{x} + z \times s$$

In other words, the actual score can be calculated by adding the mean to the product of the *z*-score and the standard deviation.

CONVERTING *Z*-SCORES INTO ACTUAL SCORES

z-score is the number of standard deviations the score is from the mean.

$x = \bar{x} + z \times s$ or make x the subject of $z = \dfrac{x - \bar{x}}{s}$

z – *z*-score or standardised score

x – Score

$\bar{x}$ – Mean of a set of scores

s – Standard deviation

Example 9: Converting *z*-scores into actual scores | 9D

In a normal distribution the mean was 30 and the standard deviation was 3.5. Blake achieved a standardised score of 2. Calculate Blake's actual score by:

a using the formula $x = \bar{x} + z \times s$ **b** making x the subject of $z = \dfrac{x - \bar{x}}{s}$.

SOLUTION:

1 Write the formula $x = \bar{x} + z \times s$.	**a** $x = \bar{x} + z \times s$
2 Substitute $\bar{x} = 30$, $z = 2$, and $s = 3.5$ into the formula.	$= 30 + 2 \times 3.5$
3 Evaluate.	$= 37$
4 Write the *z*-score formula.	**b** $z = \dfrac{x - \bar{x}}{s}$
5 Substitute $z = 2$, $\bar{x} = 30$ and $s = 3.5$ into the formula.	$2 = \dfrac{x - 30}{3.5}$
6 Solve the equation.	$2 \times 3.5 = x - 30$
7 Multiply both sides of the equation by 3.5.	
8 The opposite operation to subtracting 30 is adding 30. Add 30 to both sides of the equation.	$(2 \times 3.5) + 30 = x - 30 + 30$
9 Make x the subject and evaluate.	$x = (2 \times 3.5) + 30$
10 Write the answer in words.	$= 37$
	Blake scored 37.

Example 10: Converting *z*-scores into actual scores   9D

A class test (out of 50) has a mean mark of $\bar{x} = 34$ and a standard deviation of $s = 4$.
Mary's standardised test mark was $z = -1.5$. What was Mary's actual mark?

SOLUTION:

1 Write the formula and substitute $\bar{x} = 34$, $z = -1.5$, $s = 4$.

$x = \bar{x} + z \times s = 34 + (-1.5) \times 4$

2 Evaluate.

$= 28$

3 Alternatively, write the *z*-score formula and substitute $z = -1.5$, $\bar{x} = 34$, $s = 4$.

$z = \dfrac{x - \bar{x}}{s} = -1.5 = \dfrac{x - 34}{4}$

4 To solve the equation, multiply both sides by 4.

$-1.5 \times 4 = x - 34$

5 The opposite operation to subtracting 34 is adding 34. Add 34 to both sides of the equation.

$(-1.5 \times 4) + 34 = x - 34 + 34$

6 Make x the subject of the equation and evaluate.

$x = (-1.5 \times 4) + 34$
$= 28$

7 Write the answer in words.

Mary scored 28.

Example 11: Converting *z*-scores into actual scores   9D

Jordan achieved a *z*-score of 2.5 for a reading test. The state mean for this reading test was 71.5 and the standard deviation (SD) was 6.4.
a Explain the meaning of Jordan's *z*-score of 2.5.
b What mark did Jordan score in the reading test? Answer correct to the nearest whole number.

SOLUTION:

1 A positive *z*-score indicates the score is above the mean. *z*-score is the number of SDs the score is from the mean.

a *z*-score of 2.5 is an excellent mark as it is 2.5 times the SD above the mean.

2 Write the formula $x = \bar{x} + z \times s$ and substitute $\bar{x} = 71.5$, $z = 2.5$, $s = 6.4$.

b Using $x = \bar{x} + z \times s$
$= 71.5 + 2.5 \times 6.4$

3 Evaluate.

$= 87.5 \approx 88$

4 Alternatively, write the *z*-score formula and substitute $z = 2.5$, $\bar{x} = 71.5$, $s = 6.4$.

$z = \dfrac{x - \bar{x}}{s} = 2.5 = \dfrac{x - 71.5}{6.4}$

5 To solve the equation, multiply both sides by 6.4.

$2.5 \times 6.4 = x - 71.5$

6 Add 71.5 to both sides (opposite operation to -71.5).

$(2.5 \times 6.4) + 71.5$
$= x - 71.5 + 71.5$

7 Make x the subject and evaluate, correct to the nearest whole number.

$x = (2.5 \times 6.4) + 71.5$
$= 87.5 \approx 88$

8 Write the answer in words.

Jordan scored 88.

Exercise 9D

Example 9   **1**   Find the actual score by using the formula $x = \bar{x} + z \times s$

    a $\bar{x} = 60$, $z = 2.0$, and $s = 5$ **b** $\bar{x} = 60$, $z = -2.0$, and $s = 5$

    c $\bar{x} = 50$, $z = -1.5$, and $s = 8$ **d** $\bar{x} = 50$, $z = -1.5$, and $s = 16$

    e $\bar{x} = 70$, $z = 3$, and $s = 2$ **f** $\bar{x} = 70$, $z = -3$, and $s = 2$

    g $\bar{x} = 80$, $z = -2.5$, and $s = 6$ **h** $\bar{x} = 80$, $z = 0.5$, and $s = 6$

2   The mean number of the accidents at an intersection is 25 with a standard deviation of 8. Find the score that corresponds to each of the following z-scores.

    a $z = 1$ **b** $z = 3$ **c** $z = -1$

    d $z = 2$ **e** $z = 0$ **f** $z = -2$

    g $z = -3$ **h** $z = 1.5$ **i** $z = -2.5$

    j $z = 0.5$ **k** $z = -0.25$ **l** $z = 2.5$

3   In a common test the mean was 60 and the standard deviation was 5. What score corresponds to the following standardised scores?

    a   1.4   **b**   2.8   **c**   3.1

    d   0.2   **e**   0.9   **f**   2.1

    g   −0.6   **h**   −1.3   **i**   −2.7

    j   −2.5   **k**   −0.8   **l**   −1.8

4   The concentration span on a reading task has a mean of 47 seconds and a standard deviation of 12 seconds. What is the concentration span on the following z-scores?

    a $z = 1$ **b** $z = 2$ **c** $z = 3$

    d $z = 0.8$ **e** $z = 1.4$ **f** $z = 2.6$

    g $z = -1$ **h** $z = -2$ **i** $z = -3$

    j $z = -0.3$ **k** $z = -1.8$ **l** $z = -2.5$

5   The mean time spent on the internet each week by students is 12 hours with standard deviation of 3 hours. The table shows the z-scores of hours spent on the internet by five students. Complete the table by finding the number of hours spent on the internet by each student. Answer correct to one decimal place.

Student	z-score	Hours
a Alexis	1.5	
b Ben	2.2	
c Chris	0.9	
d Debbie	−1.6	
e Evan	−2.3	

Example 10   **6**   The monthly rainfall in Rockwaters has a mean of 55 mm and a standard deviation of 1.8 mm. What is the monthly rainfall if the standardised score was 3.2?

Example 11   **7**   Holly gained a standardised score (z-score) of −3 for a fitness test.
    a   Describe Holly's results in terms of the mean and standard deviation of the test.
    b   The fitness test has a mean of 75 and a standard deviation of 7. What is the actual mark scored by Holly?

8   An assessment task is marked out of 20. The results of the test are shown below.

| 10 | 11 | 19 | 17 | 14 | 15 | 17 | 11 |
| 12 | 14 | 8 | 16 | 18 | 20 | 14 | 13 |

    a   Calculate the mean and population standard deviation for these scores. Answer correct to one decimal place.
    b   Aiden scored the lowest mark in the task. What is his z-score?
    c   Mason was absent for this task, but his mark is usually 1.5 standard deviations above the mean. What mark should his teacher give him?

9   An assessment task is marked out of 100. The results of the test are shown below.

| 75 | 80 | 65 | 66 | 79 | 83 | 61 | 77 |
| 87 | 88 | 67 | 74 | 79 | 75 | 80 | 81 |

    a   Calculate the mean and population standard deviation for these scores. Answer correct to one decimal place.
    b   Hannah scored the highest mark in the task. What is her z-score?
    c   Lucy was absent for this task, but her mark is usually 1.9 standard deviations below the mean. What mark should her teacher give her?

10   Chris's factory produces 200-gram packets of biscuits. In the past week the factory has produced packets with a mean weight of 201.5 grams and a standard deviation of 3 grams.

    a   Quality control requires any packet with a z-score of less than −1 to be rejected. What is the minimum weight that will be accepted?
    b   Packets of biscuits with a z-score greater than 3 are also rejected. What is the maximum weight that will be accepted?

11   Max was given his numeracy test result in the form of a z-score. He gained a z-score of 1.8.
    a   Explain the meaning of Max's result in terms of the mean and standard deviation.
    b   Calculate Max's mark if the mean mark is 61 and the standard deviation is 7.2. Answer correct to the nearest whole mark.

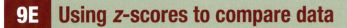

9E Using *z*-scores to compare data

It is often difficult to compare two sets of data because they have different distributions. For example, if two tests have different means and standard deviations how do we compare a student's marks in these tests? Using the *z*-score allows us to determine the number of standard deviations the mark is above or below the mean. The larger the *z*-score (ignoring the positive or negative) the further away it is from the centre of the data. It makes comparisons easier between two sets of data.

USING *Z*-SCORES TO COMPARE DATA

z-scores are used to compare scores from different datasets.
1   Read the question carefully to determine whether a higher or lower *z*-score is better.
2   The larger the *z*-score (ignoring the positive or negative), the further away it is from the centre of the data.

Example 12: Comparing data using *z*-scores   9E

David compares his swimming times in freestyle and butterfly. In freestyle, David swam 35 s and the club average was 43 s with a standard deviation of 4. In butterfly, David swam 37 s and the club average was 46 s with a standard deviation of 3. In which event did David do better, relative to other swimmers in his club? Justify your answer.

SOLUTION:

1   Calculate the *z*-score for freestyle.

2   Write the *z*-score formula.

3   Substitute $x = 35$, $\bar{x} = 43$ and $s = 4$ into the formula.

4   Evaluate.

5   Calculate the *z*-score for butterfly.

6   Write the *z*-score formula.

7   Substitute $x = 37$, $\bar{x} = 46$ and $s = 3$ into the formula.

8   Evaluate.

9   Justify the answer in words using the *z*-scores. The lower the relative time in swimming the better.

Freestyle

$$z = \frac{x - \bar{x}}{s}$$
$$= \frac{35 - 43}{4}$$
$$= -2$$

Butterfly

$$z = \frac{x - \bar{x}}{s}$$
$$= \frac{37 - 46}{3}$$
$$= -3$$

Butterfly is the better result as it is further from the mean ($z = -3$) than the freestyle result ($z = -2$). Lower relative time.

Example 13: Comparing data using z-scores 9E

The mean and standard deviation of Algebra and
Finance exams are shown in the table.

Topic	Mean	Standard deviation
Algebra	72	8
Finance	67	10

Kayla scored 76 in Algebra and 74 in Finance.

a What is Kayla's z-score for her result in Algebra?

b What is Kayla's z-score for her result in Finance?

c Kayla was very pleased with her result in Algebra.
Did she do better in Algebra or Finance, relative to the others who took the exams? Justify
your answer.

SOLUTION:

1 Write the z-score formula and substitute
$x = 76$, $\bar{x} = 72$, $s = 8$.

2 Evaluate, correct to one decimal place.

3 Write the z-score formula and substitute
$x = 74$, $\bar{x} = 67$ and $s = 10$.

4 Evaluate, correct to one decimal place.

5 Justify the answer in words using the z-scores.
Finance result is further from the mean ($z = 0.7$)
than the Algebra result ($z = 0.5$).

a $z = \dfrac{x - \bar{x}}{s} = \dfrac{76 - 72}{8}$

$= 0.5$

b $z = \dfrac{x - \bar{x}}{s} = \dfrac{74 - 67}{10}$

$= 0.7$

c Kayla's z-score of 0.7 for Finance
shows she did better relative to
others who took the exam than her
z-score of 0.5 for Algebra.

Example 14: Comparing data using z-scores 9E

Xavier scored 65% in his English test (mean 52, standard deviation 9.5) while scoring 61% in
Mathematics (mean 47, standard deviation 7.5). In which subject did he perform better?

SOLUTION:

1 English test: Write the z-score formula and substitute
$x = 65$, $\bar{x} = 52$, $s = 9.5$.

2 Evaluate.

3 Maths test: Write the z-score formula and substitute
$x = 61$, $\bar{x} = 47$ and $s = 7.5$.

4 Evaluate.

5 Justify answer in words using the z-scores.

$z = \dfrac{x - \bar{x}}{s} = \dfrac{65 - 52}{9.5}$

≈ 1.37

$z = \dfrac{x - \bar{x}}{s} = \dfrac{61 - 47}{7.5}$

≈ 1.87

$\therefore$ Xavier performed better in
Maths as his z-score is higher.

Exercise 9E

Example 12 **1** Ebony's z-scores obtained in her examinations for three subjects are shown below.

English ($z = 0.5$)   Maths ($z = 1$)   Science ($z = -2$)

   a Ebony scored the mean mark in History. What is the z-score for History?

   b What is Ebony's best result in these examinations?

   c What is Ebony's worst result in these examinations?

   d Order Ebony's results from best to worst.

Example 13 **2** The table shows the mean and standard deviation of the results in a Chinese and a Vietnamese exam.

Subject	Mean	Standard deviation
Chinese	72	6
Vietnamese	61	8

Hoang scored 81 in Chinese and 77 in Vietnamese.

   a What is Hoang's z-score for his result in Chinese?

   b What is Hoang's z-score for his result in Vietnamese?

   c In which of the two exams was his result better? Justify your answer.

3 The results of two class tests are normally distributed. The mean and standard deviation of the tests are displayed in the table.

	Test 1	Test 2
Mean	68	66
Standard deviation	12.40	12.00

Ava scored 71 in test 1 and 70 in test 2.

   a What is Ava's z-score for her result in test 1? Answer correct to two decimal places.

   b What is Ava's z-score for her result in test 2? Answer correct to two decimal places.

   c Ava thinks she has performed better in test 1. Do you agree? Justify your answer.

Example 14 **4** Michael scored 82 in task 1 in which the mean was 72 and the standard deviation was 6. He scored 75 in task 2 in which the mean was 63 and the standard deviation was 9. In which task did Michael perform better? Give reasons for your answer.

5 Joel scored 68% in his TAFE course for semesters 1 and 2. In semester 1, the class mean was 70% and the standard deviation was 4, and in semester 2 the class mean was 72% and the standard deviation was 6. Which semester was Joel's better result? Justify your answer using appropriate calculations.

6 Lachlan scored 75% in this Mathematics test (mean 57, standard deviation 11.5) while scoring 72% in Chemistry (mean 53, standard deviation 9.6). In which subject did he perform better? Justify your answer using appropriate calculations.

7 Grace has received her first two assessment results for this term. The details are shown below.

Sports coaching: mark 66, mean 58.6, standard deviation 5.1

Modern history: mark 74, mean 67.1, standard deviation 8.1

a What is Grace's z-score for her result in sports coaching?

b What is Grace's z-score for her result in modern history?

c In which of the two assessment tasks was her result better? Justify your answer.

d Grace's best performing subject is usually economics. She achieved a mark of 82 in economics whose mean was 76 and standard deviation of 6.5. Is economics still the better performing subject compared to sports coaching and modern history?

8 The table below contains the scores a student obtained in the Trial HSC. Also shown is the mean and standard deviation for each subject.

Subject	Mark	Mean	Standard deviation
English	55	55	6
Mathematics	73	82	4
Biology	69	60	4
Business studies	75	60	5
Legal studies	55	44	10

a Calculate their z-score for each subject.

b Use the z-score to rate their performance in each subject from the best performing subject to the worst performing subject.

c The Mathematics result was entered incorrectly. The mean was 62 not 82. What is the new z-score for Mathematics?

d How does the above error affect the rating of Mathematics? Give reasons for your answer.

9 Michael compared his recent marks in two subjects:

Construction: mark 77, mean 64.6, standard deviation 10.1

Legal studies: mark 74, mean ☐, standard deviation 12.5

a What is Michael's z-score (correct to two decimal places) for his mark in Construction?

b Michael achieved the same z-score in both Construction and Legal studies. What is the mean for Legal studies? Answer correct to one decimal place.

c What mark does Michael require in Construction to achieve a z-score of 2?

d What mark does Michael require in Legal studies to achieve a z-score of 2?

10 Amelia's assessment task results are recorded in the table below.

Topic	Mean	Standard deviation	Amelia's result
Task 1	62	8	74
Task 2	62	12	76
Task 3	63	15	80
Task 4	60	10	73

  a Standardise Amelia's results for each task. Answer correct to two decimal places.

  b Rank her tasks in order of relative performance.

  c Describe Amelia's performance in these assessment tasks.

  d All the tasks are moderated so that the mean mark is 60 and the standard deviation is 12. What will be Amelia's moderated mark on these tasks if the z-score is maintained? Answer to the nearest whole number.

11 The scores of three students on their Multimedia and Technology projects are given below. The Multimedia mean was 63 and the standard deviation 15. The Technology mean was 58 and the standard deviation 11.

Student	Multimedia	Technology
Anthony	69	75
Irene	75	70
Katherine	88	66

  a Convert Anthony's Multimedia and Technology marks to z-scores. Which result was better in comparison to the other students in the course?

  b Convert Irene's Multimedia and Technology marks to z-scores. Which result was better in comparison to the other students in the course?

  c Convert Katherine's Multimedia and Technology marks to z-scores. Which result was better in comparison to the other students in the course?

  d Students on each assessment task are given a merit award if their result is one standard deviation above the mean. Which students would receive the award, and on which result would their award be based?

9F Further applications of normal distributions

A normal distribution has the same mean, mode and median. It is symmetrical about the mean. The percentage of scores that lie within a certain number of standard deviations (or *z*-score) is always the same for a normal distribution. That is, 68% are within one standard deviation, 95% are within 2 standard deviations and 99.7% are within 3 standard deviations.

z-score between 1 and −1   z-score between 2 and −2   z-score between 3 and −3

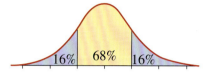  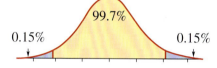

THE 68–95–99.7 RULE AND Z-SCORES

In a normal distribution:
- 68% of scores have a *z*-score between 1 and −1 (*mostly* in this range).
- 95% of scores have a *z*-score between 2 and −2 (*very probably* in this range).
- 99.7% of scores have a *z*-score between 3 and −3 (*almost certainly* in this range).

A bell-shaped curve represents a normal distribution. The *z*-scores on either side of the mean have the same percentage of the scores (symmetrical). These percentages are calculated using 68%, 95% and 99.7%.

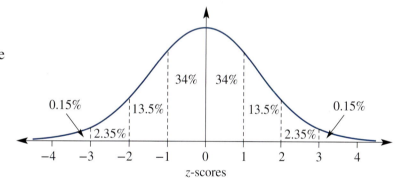

Example 15: Applying the 68–95–99.7% rule and *z*-scores   9F

The heights of children are normally distributed. The mean is 150 cm and the standard deviation is 5 cm. What percentage of children lie between 145 cm and 155 cm in height?

SOLUTION:

1. Calculate the *z*-score for each height.

2. Write the *z*-scores formula for each height.

3. Substitute $x = 145$ (left) and $x = 155$ (right), $\bar{x} = 150$ and $s = 5$ into the formulas.

4. Evaluate.

5. Use the *z*-scores of −1 and 1 to determine the percentage of children within this range (68%).

For 145 cm:

$$z = \frac{x - \bar{x}}{s}$$

$$= \frac{145 - 150}{5}$$

$$= -1$$

For 155 cm:

$$z = \frac{x - \bar{x}}{s}$$

$$= \frac{155 - 150}{5}$$

$$= 1$$

The percentage of children in this range is 68%.

Example 16: Applying 68–95–99.7% rule and z-scores   9F

The mass of 700 jars of jam is normally distributed. The mean is 420 grams and standard deviation 3 grams.

a What percentage of the jars are:
  i more than 426 grams?
  ii less than 423 grams?

b What percentage of jars are predicted to have a weight between 414 and 429 grams?

SOLUTION:

1 Write the z-scores formula.

a i $z = \dfrac{x - \bar{x}}{s}$

$= \dfrac{426 - 420}{3} = 2$

2 Substitute $x = 426$, $\bar{x} = 420$ and $s = 3$ into the formula, and evaluate.

3 95% of z-scores lie between -2 and 2. Calculate how many of the scores lie outside this range.

Scores outside range $= 100\% - 95\%$
$= 5\%$

4 Half of the 5% are more than 2 (symmetrical).

$5\% \div 2 = 2.5\%$ are more than 426 g.

5 Write the z-scores formula.

ii $z = \dfrac{x - \bar{x}}{s}$

$= \dfrac{423 - 420}{3} = 1$

6 Substitute $x = 423$, $\bar{x} = 420$ and $s = 3$ into the formula, and evaluate.

7 68% of z-scores lie between -1 and 1. Hence half of the 68% of scores lie between 0 and 1.

Scores between 0 and 1 $= \dfrac{68\%}{2} = 34\%$

8 Percentage of z-scores that are less than 0:

50%

9 Add the z-scores between 0 and 1, and less than 0.

$34\% + 50\% = 84\%$ are less than 423 g.

10 Write the z-scores formula.

b $z = \dfrac{x - \bar{x}}{s}$

$= \dfrac{414 - 420}{3} = -2$

11 Substitute $x = 414$, $\bar{x} = 420$ and $s = 3$ into the formula, and evaluate.

12 Write the z-scores formula.

$z = \dfrac{x - \bar{x}}{s}$

$= \dfrac{429 - 420}{3} = 3$

13 Substitute $x = 429$, $\bar{x} = 420$ and $s = 3$ into the formula, and evaluate.

14 95% of z-scores lie between -2 and 2. Hence half of the 95% of the z-scores lie between -2 and 0.

$95\% \div 2 = 47.5\%$

15 99.7% of z-scores lie between -3 and 3. Hence half of the 99.7% of z-scores lie between 0 and 3.

$99.7\% \div 2 = 49.85\%$

16 Add the percentages for the z-scores between -2 and 0, and the z-scores between 0 and 3.

$47.5\% + 49.85\% = 97.35\%$

17 Write the answer.

97.35% of jars are predicted to have a weight between 414 and 429 g.

Exercise 9F

1 What percentage of scores in a normal distribution have a z-score:

a between −1 and 1?   b between −2 and 2?   c between −3 and 3?

d between 0 and 1?   e between −1 and 0?   f between 0 and 2?

g between −2 and 0?   h between 0 and 3?   i between −3 and 0?

Example 15

2 A normal distribution of scores has a mean of 240 and a standard deviation of 20. What percentage of scores lie between:

a 220 and 260?   b 200 and 280?   c 180 and 300?

3 The lengths of timber are normally distributed with a mean of 1.80 m and a standard deviation of 0.05 m. What percentage of length of timber lies between:

a 1.75 m and 1.85 m?   b 1.70 m and 1.90 m?   c 1.65 m and 1.95 m?

4 The weights of boxes of chocolates are normally distributed. The mean is 748 grams and the standard deviation is 5 grams.

a A box of chocolates has a weight of 738 grams. What is the z-score?

b What percentage of boxes will have a weight between 743 grams and 753 grams?

c What percentage of boxes will have a weight between 738 grams and 758 grams?

5 The ages of the community members are normally distributed. The mean is 42 years and the standard deviation is 12 years. What percentage of the community members are aged between:

a 18 and 66 years?   b 30 and 54 years?   c 6 and 78 years?

d 42 and 54 years?   e 42 and 66 years?   f 42 and 78 years?

g 30 and 42 years?   h 18 and 42 years?   i 6 and 42 years?

6 An assessment task has a normal distribution with a mean of 72 and a standard deviation of 8. What percentage of scores lie between:

a 48 and 96?   b 64 and 80?   c 56 and 88?

d 48 and 72?   e 72 and 96?   f 64 and 72?

Example 16
7 What percentage of scores in a normal distribution have a z-score:

   a greater than 1?   **b** greater than 2?   **c** greater than 3?

   d less than -1?   **e** less than -2?   **f** less than -3?

8 What percentage of scores in a normal distribution have a z-score:

   a between 1 and 2?   **b** between -1 and -2?   **c** between 2 and 3?

   d between -3 and -1?   **e** between -1 and 2?   **f** between -1 and 3?

9 A set of scores with a normal distribution has a mean of 68 and a standard deviation of 8. What percentage of scores lie:

   a above 68?   **b** above 76?   **c** above 84?

   d below 68?   **e** below 76?   **f** below 84?

10 Kumar is a company that produces packets of tea. The mass of the packets is normally distributed, with a mean of 200 grams and a standard deviation of 10 grams.

   a In what range of mass should 68% of the packets lie?

   b In what range of mass should 95% of the packets lie?

11 Caitlin achieved a z-score of 2 in a general knowledge quiz. The results of the quiz are normally distributed.

   a Between which two z-scores will people sitting the quiz mostly lie?

   b Between which two z-scores will people sitting the quiz almost certainly lie?

   c Between which two z-scores will people sitting the quiz very probably lie?

12 Nathan sells a diet plan with a money-back guarantee if the customer does not lose 9 kg in the first three months. The weight loss after three months is normally distributed with a mean loss of 13.2 kg and a standard deviation of 1.4 kg.

   a What is the z-score corresponding to a weight loss of 9 kg?

   b What percentage of customers will not reach the 9 kg in three months?

   c Nathan has sold 2000 diet plans. How many refunds are expected?

13 A CityRail train is timetabled to arrive at Central station at 8:44 am each day of the week. After 3 months the mean arrival time was 8:44 am with a standard deviation of 3 minutes. The data has been normally distributed.

   a What percentage of times will the train arrive between 8:38 am and 8:50 am?

   b What percentage of times will the train arrive between 8:35 am and 8:47 am?

   c What percentage of times will the train arrive before 8:38 am?

   d What percentage of times will the train arrive after 8:47 am?

   e What percentage of times will the train arrive on time or earlier?

   f CityRail does not classify a train as late unless it arrives 6 minutes later than the scheduled time. What percentage of times will the train arrive late according to CityRail?

   g How often will this train run late according to CityRail, in 200 days?

   h How often will this train run late according to CityRail, if it runs every day of the year?

14 The marks in an examination are expressed as a percentage and normally distributed with a mean of 60 and a standard deviation of 12.5.

   a What are the boundaries between which you would mostly expect the marks to lie?

   b What are the boundaries between which you would very probably expect the marks to lie?

   c What are the boundaries between which you would almost certainly expect the marks to lie?

   d What percentage of students will get a mark of 85 or higher?

   e What percentage of students will get a mark of 35 or higher?

   f What percentage of students will get a mark of less than 72.5?

   g If there were 80 000 students who sat for this examination, how many students are expected to get a mark of 35 or higher?

   h If there were 60 000 students who sat for this examination, how many students are expected to get a mark of less than 72.5?

15 The mean height of an Irish wolfhound is 82 cm with a standard deviation of 1.5 cm. The data has been normally distributed.

   a In what height range should 68% of Irish wolfhounds lie?

   b In what height range should 95% of Irish wolfhounds lie?

   c What height are 84% of Irish wolfhounds more than?

   d What height are 97.5% of Irish wolfhounds less than?

   e What percentage of Irish wolfhounds have a height greater than 86.5 cm?

   f What percentage of Irish wolfhounds have a height less than 80.5 cm?

   g If there are 800 Irish wolfhounds, how many Irish wolfhounds are expected to have a height of greater than 86.5 cm?

   h If there are 500 Irish wolfhounds, how many Irish wolfhounds are expected to have a height of less than 80.5 cm?

16 The normal distribution below represents the masses of 200 students. They have a mean of 70 and a standard deviation of 10.

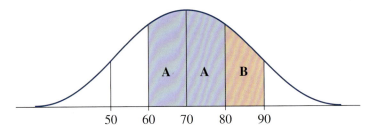

a What percentage of the students will have a mass that lies in the region marked with the letter A?

b How many students will have a mass in the region marked with the letter A?

c What percentage of the students will have a mass that lies in the region marked with the letter B?

d How many students will have a mass in the region marked with the letter B?

e How many students will have a mass between 50 and 60?

f How many students will have a mass between 60 and 90?

g How many students will have a mass greater than 50?

17 The maximum temperature for 600 summer days in Katoomba was recorded. The mean was 21.9°C and the standard deviation is 3.6°C. The maximum temperatures were normally distributed.

a What percentage of summer days in Katoomba would have maximum temperatures between:

  i 18.3°C and 25.5°C?   **ii** 29.1°C and 32.7°C?

  iii 11.1°C and 29.1°C?   **iv** 14.7°C and 18.3°C?

b How many summer days will have a maximum temperature less than 18.3°C?

c How many summer days will have a maximum temperature less than 14.7°C?

d How many summer days will have a maximum temperature greater than 21.9°C?

e How many summer days will have a maximum temperature greater than 29.1°C?

PPT

STUDY GUIDE

Key ideas and chapter summary

Summary

Normally distributed data	A normal distribution has the same mean, mode and median. The graph of a normal distribution is called a 'bell curve'.

- A normal distribution is symmetrical about the mean.
- The mean, median and mode are equal.
- The majority of the data is located at the centre
- A normal distribution has the *x*-axis as an asymptote.
- Mean and standard deviation define a normal distribution.

The 68–95–99.7 rule

In a normal distribution:

- 68% of data lie within 1 standard deviation of the mean.
- 95% of data lie within 2 standard deviations of the mean.
- 99.7% of data lie within 3 standard deviations of the mean.
- 50% of data lie above the mean and 50% of data lie below the mean.

z-score or standardised score

z-score is the number of standard deviations from the mean.

$$z = \frac{x - \bar{x}}{s}$$

z: *z*-score   *x̄*: Mean of a set of scores
x: Score   *s*: Standard deviation

Converting z-scores into actual scores

$x = \bar{x} + z \times s$ or make *x* the subject of the above formula.

Using z-scores to compare data

z-scores are used to compare scores from different datasets.

- Read the question carefully to determine whether a higher or lower *z*-score is better.
- The larger the *z*-score (ignoring the positive or negative) the further away it is from the centre of the data.

Further applications of normal distributions

In a normal distribution:

- 68% of scores have a *z*-score *mostly* between 1 and −1
- 95% of scores have a *z*-score *very probably* between 2 and −2
- 99.7% of scores have a *z*-score *almost certainly* between 3 and −3.

A bell-shaped curve represents a normal distribution.

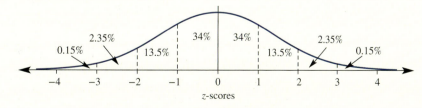

Multiple-choice

1 A normal distribution is symmetrical about the:

    A mean   **B** standard deviation   **C** maximum   **D** z-score

2 The ages of the citizens who live in Bishop are normally distributed. The mean age is 53 years and the standard deviation is 14. What percentage of the citizens is younger than 67?

    A 34%   **B** 68%   **C** 84%   **D** 95%

3 Zoe scored 76 in a science test. The science test had a mean of 60 and a standard deviation of 8. A recent history test had a mean of 56 and a standard deviation of 12. What mark in the history test would have been equivalent to Zoe's science mark?

    A 68   **B** 72   **C** 76   **D** 80

4 What is the z-score if $x = 20$, $\bar{x} = 16$ and $s = 4$?

    A -2 **B** -1 **C** 1   **D** 2

5 A student's mark on a test is 50. The mean mark for their class is 55 and the standard deviation is 2.5. Their standard score is:

    A -2.0 **B** -1.5 **C** 2.0   **D** 2.5

6 Aaron's class achieved the following results in a topic test: 44, 91, 78, 55, 65, 49, 61, 55, 74, 46, 73, 63, 57 and 29. Using the population standard deviation, how many scores have a z-score greater than 2?

    A 0   **B** 1   **C** 2   **D** 3

7 Susan scored 80 in a maths test. The test mean was 70 and the standard deviation was 5. This test is being rescaled to a mean of 60 and a standard deviation of 8 without changing Susan's z-score. What is Susan's new score?

    A 64%   **B** 70%   **C** 76%   **D** 80%

8 Benjamin achieved a z-score of 2.5 on his last assessment task. The class mean was 58% and standard deviation 6%. What was Benjamin's mark?

    A 60.5%   **B** 61%   **C** 67%   **D** 73%

9 What percentage of scores in a normal distribution has a z-score between 0 and 3?

    A 0.15%   **B** 0.30%   **C** 49.85%   **D** 97%

10 The results of a literacy exam were normally distributed. Samuel gained a z-score of -1. What percentage of students scored better than Samuel?

    A 16%   **B** 34%   **C** 68%   **D** 84%

Short-answer

1 A normal distribution of scores has a mean of 136.5 and a standard deviation of 18.9. In what range of values would you expect to find:

   a 68% of the scores?   **b** 95% of the scores?   **c** 99.7% of the scores?

2 A normally distributed set of data has a mean of 9.9 and a standard deviation of 0.8. Find the percentage of data that lies between these ranges.

   a 9.1 and 10.7   **b** 7.5 and 12.3   **c** 8.3 and 11.5

   d 11.5 and 12.3   **e** 8.3 and 9.1   **f** 9.9 and 12.3

3 Boxes of breakfast cereal are labelled as having a mass of 2 kg. The mass of these boxes is normally distributed with a mean of 2.02 kg and a standard deviation of 0.02 kg. What percentage of the boxes are:

   a greater than 2.06 kg?

   b less than 1.98 kg?

   c between 1.96 kg and 2.04 kg?

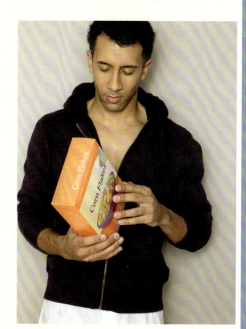

4 A set of scores has a mean of 20 and a standard deviation of 3.2. Find the z-score for each of the following scores.

   a 26.4   **c** 27.2

   b 15.2   **d** 16.8

5 Adam scored 72 in an assessment task. The mean for this task was 65 with a standard deviation of 14. What is Adam's z-score?

6 In a university exam, the mean mark was 59%. Kayla scored 68% in this exam and it gave her a z-score of 1.5. What is the standard deviation of this exam?

7 Patrick's mark on his exam paper was converted to a z-score of -1.5. The mean of this exam paper was 74 and the standard deviation was 4. What was Patrick's exam mark?

8 A quiz has these results: 11, 15, 19, 12, 9, 16, 14, 10, 13, 7, 17, 13, 10, 18, 13 and 16.

   a Calculate the mean and population standard deviation for these marks. Answer correct to two decimal places.

   b Jade scored the lowest mark in the class. What is her z-score? (Answer correct to one decimal place.)

   c Lucas was absent for this quiz. He usually scores 2.3 standard deviations above the mean. What mark would you expect Lucas to achieve on this quiz?

9 Lily scored 78 in English, 75 in Mathematics and 77 in Science. The class mean and standard deviations are shown in the table below.

Subject	Mean	Standard deviation
English	66	15
Mathematics	65	10
Science	68	6

a What was Lily's z-score for English?   **b** What was Lily's z-score for Maths?

c What was Lily's z-score for Science?   **d** What was Lily's best result?

e The Science result is moderated so that the new mean is 72 and standard deviation is 8. What will be Lily's mark for Science if she maintains the same z-score?

10 Riley scored a mark of 74 in a literacy test whose mean was 67.6 and standard deviation was 5.1. In a numeracy test with a mean of 74.1 and standard deviation of 8.1, he scored 80. On which test did Riley perform better? Justify your answer with appropriate calculations.

11 The blood pressures of 200 people are found to be normally distributed with a mean of 110 and a standard deviation of 5.

a Find the number of people whose blood pressure is between 100 and 120.

b Find the number of people whose blood pressure is between 105 and 120.

c How many people have blood pressure less than 100?

d How many people have blood pressure more than 115?

12 The body weights of a large group of 14-year-old girls have a mean of 54 kg and a standard deviation of 10 kg.

a Kate weighs 56 kg. Determine her standardised weight.

b Lani has a standardised weight of −0.75. Determine her actual weight.

Assuming the girls' weights are approximately normally distributed with a mean of 54 kg and a standard deviation of 10 kg, determine the:

c percentage of these girls who weigh more than 74 kg

d percentage of these girls who weigh between 54 and 64 kg.

Extended-response

13 A factory makes car pistons with an average diameter of 70 mm and standard deviation of 0.002 mm. The diameter of the pistons is normally distributed.

a In what range of diameters should 99.7% of the pistons lie?

b What percentage of pistons will have a diameter greater than 70.002 mm?

c What percentage of pistons will have a diameter less than 69.994 mm?

d If the factory made 600 pistons, how many would you expect to be undersized by at least 0.004 mm?

10

Critical path analysis

Syllabus topic — N3 Critical path analysis

This topic will develop your awareness of critical path analysis in the optimisation of real-life problems.

Outcomes

- Construct an activity chart to represent a particular project.
- Draw a network diagram to represent the activities to be completed during a project.
- Use critical path analysis to determine the minimum time for a project to be completed.
- Use forward and backward scanning to determine the earliest starting times (EST) and latest starting times (LST) for each activity in a project.
- Calculate float times of non-critical activities.
- Use ESTs and LSTs to locate the critical path for the project.
- Solve small-scale network flow problems.
- Use the 'maximum-flow minimum-cut' theorem to solve a flow problem.
- Convert information presented in a table into a network diagram.
- Determine the flow capacity of a network.

Digital Resources for this chapter

In the Interactive Textbook:

- Videos
- Desmos widgets
- Literacy worksheet
- Spreadsheets
- Quick Quiz
- Study guide
- Solutions (enabled by teacher)

In the Online Teaching Suite:

- Teaching Program
- Tests
- Review Quiz
- Teaching Notes

Knowledge check

The Interactive Textbook provides a test of prior knowledge for this chapter, and may direct you to revision from the previous years' work.

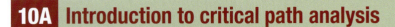

10A Introduction to critical path analysis

This chapter will develop your awareness of critical path analysis. Critical path analysis is a technique that identifies the activities required to complete a project or task, including identifying the time necessary to complete each activity and the relationships between the activities. Critical path analysis helps to predict if a project will finish on time.

For example, building a house, manufacturing a product, organising a wedding and other similar projects all require many individual activities to be completed before the project is finished. The individual activities often rely upon each other and some can't be performed until other activities are complete. In the organisation of a wedding, invitations would be sent out to guests, but a plan for seating people at the tables during the reception can't be completed until the invitations are accepted. When building a house, the plastering of the walls can't begin until the house is sealed from the weather.

CRITICAL PATH ANALYSIS

Critical path analysis is a technique that identifies the activities required to complete a project, the time necessary to complete each activity and the relationships between the activities.

Activity chart

An activity chart or precedence table is used to describe the activities in a project. It consists of a table containing the activities of a project, their duration and their immediate predecessors. Let's consider some simple projects and their activity chart.

Project: To make a phone call

Activity	Task	Duration (in min)	Immediate predecessors
A	Look up the number	1	–
B	Dial the number and wait for answer	1	A
C	Deliver the message	10	B
D	Hang up the phone	1	C

Project: To make old-style lemonade

Activity	Task	Duration (in min)	Immediate predecessors
A	Fill a tall glass with cracked ice	3	–
B	Add lemon juice and sugar	2	A
C	Stir well	2	B
D	Top with water	1	C
E	Add a slice of lemon	1	D
F	Serve with drinking straws	2	E

ACTIVITY CHART

A table containing the activities of a project, their duration and their immediate predecessors.

Immediate predecessors and scheduling

For any project, if activity A must be completed before activity B can begin then activity A is said to be an immediate predecessor of activity B. The activities within a project can have multiple immediate predecessors. A time schedule indicates the length of time or duration of each activity. Allocating time to the completion of activities in a project is called scheduling. It shows the immediate predecessors and duration for each activity. Notice that checking email can only be completed after Sandra gets out of bed, has breakfast, and gets dressed.

Activity	Task	Duration (in min)	Immediate predecessors
A	Get out of bed	1	–
B	Cook breakfast	6	A
C	Eat breakfast	5	B
D	Brush teeth	3	C
E	Have shower	4	A
F	Get dressed	6	E
G	Check email	5	C, F

Example 1: Constructing an activity chart   10A

Project: To catch a train.
The tasks shown below are to catch a train. However, they are in the wrong sequence.

Wait for train (8 minutes)
Go to the correct platform (2 minutes)
Scan your Opal card (1 minute)
Board the train (1 minute)
Travel to the train station (5 minutes)

Correctly sort the above tasks and construct an activity chart for this project with the four headings: Activity, Task, Duration and Immediate predecessors.

SOLUTION:

1 Analyse the tasks and sort into a logical sequence.

Correct sequence of tasks: Travel to the train station, scan your Opal card, go to the correct platform, wait for train and board the train.

2 Draw an activity chart with 4 columns.

3 Label the 5 activities (A to E).

4 Write the sorted tasks in the task column.

5 Record the duration for each activity.

6 Determine the predecessor for each activity.

Activity	Task	Duration (in min)	Immediate predecessors
A	Travel to train station	5	–
B	Scan your opal card	1	A
C	Go to platform	2	B
D	Wait for train	8	C
E	Board the train	1	D

Example 2: Reading an activity chart   **10A**

Joshua wants to create a patio in his garden. The activity chart for this project is shown below.

Activity	Task	Duration (in hours)	Immediate predecessors
A	Clean up garden	3	–
B	Measure area of patio	1	–
C	Plan the patio	2	B
D	Buy fencing	1	B
E	Buy plants and pots	3	A, C
F	Insert plants in pots	1	E
G	Buy paving	1	C
H	Make garden	5	D, F, G

Note: Activity A (clean up garden) is an immediate predecessor of activity E (buy plants and pots) as it determines the number plants required to fill the space.

a How many activities in the project?
b What are the first activities?
c Which activity has the longest time interval?
d What is the total time for Joshua to complete this project?
e What is the immediate predecessor for activity C?
f What is the immediate predecessor for activity G?
g Why are there three immediate predecessors for activity H?

SOLUTION:

1 Count the number of activities (A to H).

a There are 8 activities.

2 List the activities with no immediate predecessor.

b A to B are the first activities.

3 Find the largest number in the duration column.

c Making the garden (H) takes 5 hours.

4 Add the time listed in the duration column.

d Total time = 3 + 1 + 2 + 1 + ... + 5
= 17 h

5 List the activity in the predecessor column.

e Immediate predecessor of C is B.

6 List the activity in the predecessor column.

f Immediate predecessor of G is C.

7 Look for the 3 immediate predecessors of activity H.

g Activity H cannot be completed until Joshua buys the materials (fencing, plants, pots and paving).

Exercise 10A

1 Copy and complete the following sentences.
   a Critical path analysis identifies the _____ required to complete a project.
   b Activity chart contains the activities, _____ and their immediate predecessors.
   c If activity A must be completed before activity B can begin then activity A is said to be an _____ of activity B.
   d Allocating time to the completion of activities in a project is called _____.

Example 2 2 An incomplete activity chart for washing your hands is shown below.

Activity	Task	Duration (in min)	Immediate predecessors
	Turn on water	1	–
B	Wet hands	1	
	Clean hands with soap	3	B
D	Rinse off soap	2	
	Dry hands	3	D

   a Copy and complete the activity chart shown above.
   b How many activities in the project?
   c Which activity has the longest time interval?
   d What is the total time for this project?
   e What is the immediate predecessor for activity C?
   f What activities precede activity B?

3 An incomplete activity chart for preparing a meal is shown below.

Activity	Task	Duration (in min)	Immediate predecessors
A	Find recipe	2	
	Prepare ingredients	10	A
C	Cook meal	25	
	Serve meal	3	C
	Clean up	10	D

   a Copy and complete the activity chart shown above.
   b How many activities in the project?
   c Which activity has the shortest time interval?
   d What is the total time for this project?

Example 1   **4**   The tasks for each of the following projects have errors in their sequence. Find these errors and construct an activity chart for each project with the four headings: Activity, Task, Duration and Immediate predecessor.

a   Project: To watch your favorite television show
Turn television off (1 minute)
Turn television on (1 minute)
Find remote control (2 minutes)
Watch television show (30 minutes)
Select television show (1 minute)

b   Project: To listen to a music playlist
Select play (1 minute)
Turn off phone (1 minute)
Unlock phone (1 minute)
Select the music app (1 minute)
Turn on phone (2 minutes)
Select playlist (3 minutes)
Listen to music (50 minutes)

c   Project: To plant a tree in the garden
Water the tree (5 minutes)
Decide on the tree required (10 minutes)
Purchase the tree (8 minutes)
Dig the hole (12 minutes)
Plant the tree (5 minutes)
Mulch the tree (3 minutes)

d   Project: To bake a cake
Mix the icing (4 minutes)
Cool the cake (30 minutes)
Bake the cake (35 minutes)
Put cake mixture in cake tin (3 minutes)
Heat oven (10 minutes)
Mix ingredients (6 minutes)
Ice the cake (8 minutes)

e   Project: To install a smoke alarm
Select a section of the ceiling (2 minutes)
Screw the mounting plate into the ceiling (5 minutes)
Install the batteries into the alarm (3 minutes)
Remove the mounting plate from the alarm (2 minutes)
Choose a room (2 minutes)
Connect the alarm body to the mounting plate (4 minutes)

5   Jayden is required to organise a birthday party. He has estimated the following time for these tasks: buying the food – 2 hours; preparing the food – 3 hours; serving the meal – 1 hour; cleaning up – 2 hours. Construct an activity chart for this project.

6   Hayley needs her new laptop operating in less than a day. She has estimated the following time for these tasks: buying the laptop – 1 hour; unpacking the laptop – 0.5 hours; installing the software – 4 hours; copying the data – 3 hours; testing the software with the data – 1 hour. Construct an activity chart for this project.

7   Consider each of the following tasks as projects and construct an activity chart. Use the four headings: activity, task, duration and immediate predecessor.
   a   Make buttered toast
   b   Pump up a bicycle tyre
   c   Make a cheese sandwich

8   Sophie is renovating her lounge room. She has organised this project into six unordered tasks.

   Arrange new furniture – 1 day.
   Remove furniture and curtains – 1 day;
   Lay new carpet – 1 day;
   Hang new curtains – 1 day;
   Paint walls – 4 days;
   Prepare walls – 2 days;

   a   What is the first task? Give a reason for your answer.
   b   What is the immediate predecessor to the following tasks?
   i   Prepare walls   **ii**   Paint walls
   iii   Lay new carpet   **iv**   Hang new curtains
   c   List the two immediate predecessors for 'arranging new furniture'.
   d   Construct an activity chart for this project.

9   Samuel is cooking a pizza for dinner. He has divided this project into five tasks: Defrost the pizza base – 5 min; prepare the toppings – 10 min; place the sauce and topping on pizza – 2 min; heat oven – 10 min; cook pizza – 25 min.
   a   What tasks can be performed at the same time?
   b   Which tasks are predecessor tasks for cooking the pizza?
   c   Construct an activity chart for this project.

A network diagram is often used for critical path analysis. It can represent the activities required to complete a project, the time necessary to complete each activity and the relationships between the activities. In critical path analysis a network diagram does not have labelled vertices. The activities in the project are represented by the edges of the diagram and so it is the edges that must be labelled, not the vertices. Drawing a network diagram from the activity chart opposite, is shown below.

Activity	Immediate predecessors
A	–
B	–
C	A
D	B
E	B
F	C, D
G	E, F

1. Activities A and B have no immediate predecessors. These activities can start immediately and can be completed at the same time.

2. Activity A is an immediate predecessor of activity C, so activity C must follow immediately after activity A. Activity C is an immediate predecessor of activity F, so activity F must follow immediately after activity C.

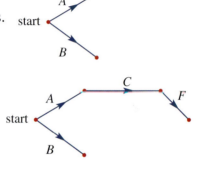

3. Activity D has immediate predecessor activity B so it follows immediately after activity B. Activity D is also an immediate predecessor of activity F so activity F must follow immediately after activity D.

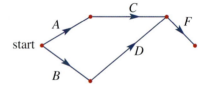

4. Activity E has immediate predecessor activity B so it will follow immediately after activity B. Activity G has immediate predecessor activity F and activity E and so it must follow immediately after both of these activities.

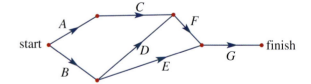

5. Activity G is not an immediate predecessor for any activity and so the project is finished after this activity is complete.

CONSTRUCTING A NETWORK DIAGRAM GIVEN AN ACTIVITY CHART

Activities that have no immediate predecessors follow from the start vertex.
Activities that are not immediate predecessors for other activities lead to the finish vertex.
For every other activity, look for:
- the activities for which it is an immediate predecessor
- the activities it has as immediate predecessors.

Example 3: Constructing a network diagram given an activity chart — 10B

Draw a network diagram from the activity chart shown on the right. In this solution, the network diagram will be drawn from the finish back to the start.

Activity	Immediate predecessors
A	–
B	A
C	A
D	A
E	B
F	C
G	D
H	E, F, G

SOLUTION:

1 H is not an immediate predecessor for any other activity so it will lead to the finish of the project.

2 H has immediate predecessors E, F and G and so these three activities will lead into activity H.

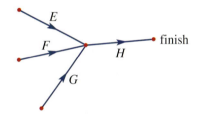

3 Activity D is an immediate predecessor of activity G and has immediate predecessor activity A. There will be a path through activity A, activity D and then activity G.

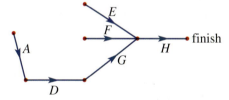

4 Activity C is an immediate predecessor of activity F and has immediate predecessor activity A. There will be a path through activity A, activity C and then activity F.

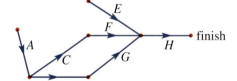

5 Activity B is an immediate predecessor of activity E and has immediate predecessor activity A. There will be a path through activity A, activity B and then activity E.

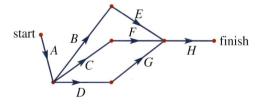

6 Activity A has no immediate predecessors, so it is the start of the project.

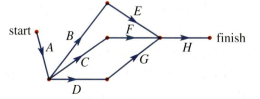

Exercise 10B

1   Answer the following questions for each network diagram in parts **a** to **d**.
   i   How many activities in the project?
   ii What is the beginning activity?
   iii What is the ending activity?
   iv Which activity is the immediate predecessor to activity D?
   v   Which activities have no predecessors?

   a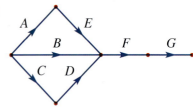

   b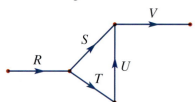

   c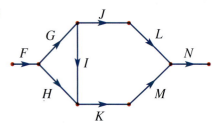

   d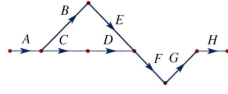

2   Construct an activity chart for each of the following network diagrams.

   a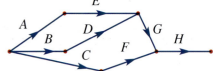

   b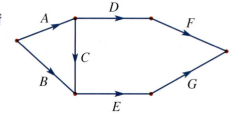

   c

   d

   e

   f

Example 3 | **3** Construct a network diagram for each of the activity charts below.

a

Activity	Immediate predecessors
P	–
Q	–
R	Q
S	R

b

Activity	Immediate predecessors
D	–
R	D
F	R
G	F

c

Activity	Immediate predecessors
D	–
E	–
F	D, E
G	F

d

Activity	Immediate predecessors
W	–
X	W
Y	W
Z	W

e

Activity	Immediate predecessors
A	–
B	A
C	A
D	B

f

Activity	Immediate predecessors
P	–
Q	–
R	P
S	Q

g

Activity	Immediate predecessors
C	–
D	–
E	–
F	C, D, E
G	F

h

Activity	Immediate predecessors
H	–
I	H
J	H
K	I
L	K

i

Activity	Immediate predecessors
A	–
B	A
C	A
D	B
E	C

j

Activity	Immediate predecessors
P	–
Q	–
R	P
S	Q
T	R, S

4 Construct an activity chart for each of the following network diagrams.

a

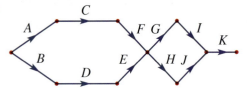

b

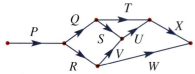

c

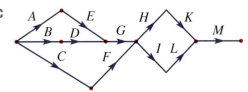

d

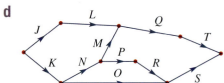

5 Construct a network diagram for each of the activity charts below.

a

Activity	Immediate predecessors
T	–
U	–
V	U
W	T
X	V, W
Y	X
Z	Y

b

Activity	Immediate predecessors
F	–
G	–
H	–
I	F
J	G, I
K	H, J
L	K

c

Activity	Immediate predecessors
K	–
L	–
M	K
N	M
O	N, L
P	O
Q	P
R	M
S	R, Q

d

Activity	Immediate predecessors
A	–
B	–
C	–
D	B
E	A, D
F	E, C
G	F
H	G
I	E, C
J	G
K	H, I

10C Dummy activities

Sometimes two activities will have some of the same immediate predecessors, but not all of them. In this activity chart, activity D and activity E share the immediate predecessor activity B, but they both have an immediate predecessor activity that the other does not. This overlap of predecessors presents some difficulty when constructing the network diagram. That is, you cannot have an edge that represents activity B being drawn to both the edge for activity D and the edge for activity E. This difficulty is easily overcome.

Activity	Immediate predecessors
A	–
B	–
C	–
D	A, B
E	B, C

Activity D and activity E are not immediate predecessors for any other activity, so they will lead directly to the finish vertex of the project. Activities A, B and C have no immediate predecessors, so they will be the starting vertex of the project.

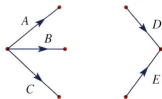

We need to use the precedence information for activity D and activity E to join these two parts together. Activity D needs to follow directly from activity A and activity B, but we can only draw one edge for activity D. Activity E needs to follow directly from both activity B and activity C, but again we only have one edge for activity E, not two.

The solution is to draw the diagram with activity D starting after one of its immediate predecessors, and using a dummy activity for the other. The dummy activities are represented by dotted edges and are, in effect, imaginary. They are not real activities, but they allow all of the predecessors from the table to be correctly represented.

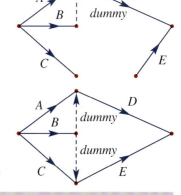

The dummy activity for D allows activity D to directly follow both activity A and B. A dummy activity is also needed for activity E because it, too, has to start after two different activities, activity B and C.

DUMMY ACTIVITIES

- A dummy activity is required if two activities share some, but not all, of their immediate predecessors.
- A dummy activity will be required from the end of each shared immediate predecessor to the start of the activity that has additional immediate predecessors.
- A dummy activity is not real but imaginary, and so it takes no time (its duration is 0).
- Dummy activities are represented in the network diagram using dotted lines so the label 'dummy' on the diagram is not actually needed, and won't be used from now on, but you can include it on your own network diagrams for emphasis.

If two activities share the same immediate predecessor and end at the same node, a dummy activity is not required. Instead use multiple lines between the two nodes.

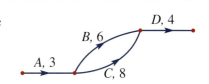

Example 4: Using a dummy activity in a network diagram　10C

Draw a network diagram from the activity chart shown on the right.

Activity	Immediate predecessors
A	–
B	–
C	A
D	B
E	C, D
F	C
G	E, F

SOLUTION:

1　A and B will lead from the start vertex.

2　G will lead to the end vertex.

3　A dummy will be required the end of activity C (shared immediate predecessor) to the start of activity E (the activity with an additional immediate predecessor).

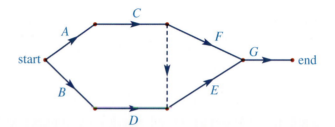

Example 5: Creating an activity chart from a network diagram　10C

Construct an activity chart for the network diagram shown on the right.

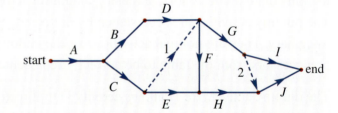

SOLUTION:

1　Create a table with a row for each activity.

2　Look at the start of an activity. Write down all of the activities that lead directly to this activity in the immediate predecessor column.

3　The dummy activity 1 makes activity C a predecessor of activities F and G as well as E.

4　The dummy activity 2 makes activity G a predecessor of activity J as well as I.

Activity	Immediate predecessors
A	–
B	A
C	A
D	B
E	C
F	D, C
G	D, C
H	E, F
I	G
J	G, H

Scheduling on a network diagram

Activity charts often include a duration to indicate the length of time of each activity. You will recall that allocating time to the completion of activities in a project is called scheduling. Knowing how long individual activities within a project are likely to take allows managers of such projects to hire staff, book equipment and also to estimate overall costs of the project. Scheduling on a network diagram is shown using a weighted edge. The number or weight on the edge indicates the duration of the activity. The weight of dummy activities is always zero.

GLOBAL NETWORK

Example 6: Scheduling on a network diagram   10C

Draw a network diagram from the activity chart shown on the right.

Activity	Duration (in days)	Immediate predecessors
A	8	–
B	6	–
C	1	A
D	2	B
E	3	C
F	1	C, D
G	2	E, F
H	1	G

SOLUTION:

1 A and B will lead from the start vertex. Indicate the time as a weight edge.

2 H will lead to the end vertex. Indicate the time as a weighted edge.

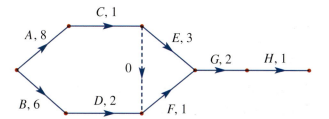

3 Both F and G have two predecessors. F shares one of its predecessors (C) with activity E, but F and E do not have exactly the same predecessors. Activity G's immediate predecessors E and F are not shared with any other activity. So a dummy activity is required from the end of activity C to the start of activity F to show that E and F share an immediate predecessor, C.

SCHEDULING ON A NETWORK DIAGRAM

Scheduling on a network diagram is shown using a weighted edge. The number on the edge indicates the duration of the activity. The weight of dummy activities is always zero.

Exercise 10C

Example 4   **1**   Complete each network diagram by inserting a dummy activity for each activity chart.

a

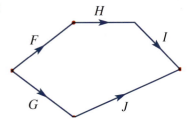

Activity	Immediate predecessors
F	–
G	–
H	F
I	H, G
J	G

b

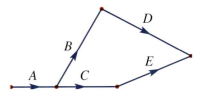

Activity	Immediate predecessors
A	–
B	A
C	A
D	B
E	B, C

Example 6   **c**

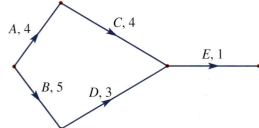

Activity	Duration (in days)	Immediate predecessors
A	4	–
B	5	–
C	4	A, B
D	3	B
E	1	C, D

d

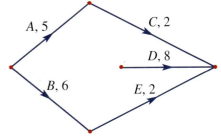

Activity	Duration (in hrs)	Immediate predecessors
A	5	–
B	6	–
C	2	A
D	8	A, B
E	2	B

e

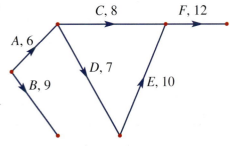

Activity	Duration (in mins)	Immediate predecessors
A	6	–
B	9	–
C	8	A, B
D	7	A, B
E	10	D
F	12	C, E

Example 5 **2** Complete each activity chart for the network diagrams shown below.

a

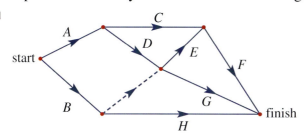

Activity	Immediate predecessors
A	
	–
C	
D	
E	D, B
F	
G	
	B

b

Activity	Immediate predecessors
P	–
R	
S	
	Q
U	
W	
	U
Y	
Z	

c

Activity	Duration (in mins)	Immediate predecessors
A	3	
B		
C		
D		A
E		
F		
G	7	

d

Activity	Duration (in hrs)	Immediate predecessors
A		
B	4	
C		
D		
E		
F		C
G		
H		

3 Draw an activity chart for each network diagram.

a

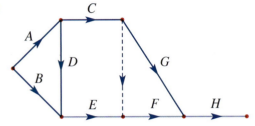

b

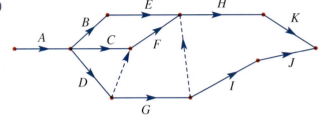

4 The following network diagram shows the activities in a project to repair a dent in a car panel. The activities are listed in the table on the right.

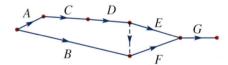

Activity	Description
A	Remove panel
B	Order component
C	Remove broken component
D	Pound out dent
E	Repaint
F	Install new component
G	Replace panel

a Which activity or activities are the immediate predecessors of the event 'remove broken component'?

b Which activities are the immediate predecessors of the activity 'install new component'?

5 Construct a network diagram for each of the activity charts below.

a

Activity	Immediate predecessors
P	–
Q	–
R	P
S	Q
T	Q
U	R, S
V	R, S, T

b

Activity	Immediate predecessors
A	–
B	A
C	A
D	B, C
E	C
F	E
G	D
H	F, G

10D Forward and backward scanning

Forward scanning

For a project to be completed in the shortest time possible, it is important to be aware of each activity's earliest starting time (EST) after the start of the entire project. An EST of 8 means an activity cannot start until 8 hours (or whatever time unit is given) after the start of the project. The EST for each activity is found by a process called forward scanning, described below.

Example 7: Finding the earliest starting time using forward scanning   10D

Find the earliest starting time (EST) for the project represented in the network diagram opposite. The duration of each activity is in days.

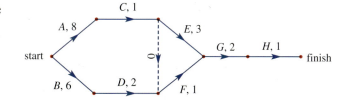

SOLUTION:

1   Draw a box, split into two cells, next to each vertex of the network diagram, as shown in the diagram opposite. If more than one activity begins at a vertex, draw a box for each of these activities.

2   Activity A and B start the project and have an EST of zero. Write zero in the left box (shaded yellow).

3   Activity C has an EST of 8 (add the EST of the immediate predecessor to the duration of the activity).

4   Repeat step 3 for each activity. However, if an activity has more than one predecessor, calculate the EST using each of the predecessors and choose the largest value.

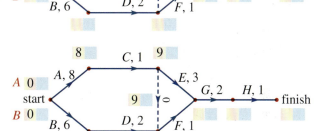

Note: EST of F = 6 + 2 = 8 or EST of F = 9 + 0 = 9. Use 9.
        EST of G = 9 + 1 = 10 or EST of G = 9 + 3 = 12. Use 12.

5   The EST value at the finish of the project is the minimum time it takes to complete the project.

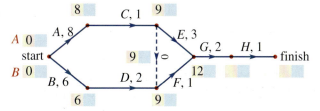

6   Write the answer in words.   ∴ EST of the project is 15 days.

Backward scanning

Some activities have some flexibility around the time they can start. The latest start time, or LST, for each activity is the latest time after the start of the project that the individual activity can start for the project to still be completed in the minimum time. LSTs for each activity are calculated using the reverse of the process used to calculate the ESTs. This process is called backward scanning and is demonstrated below.

Example 8: Finding the latest starting time using backward scanning   10D

Find the latest starting time (LST) for each activity using the network diagram and completed forward scanning from the previous example. The duration of each activity is in days.

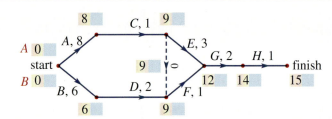

SOLUTION:

1   Copy the minimum time to complete the project into the right cell shown shaded blue in the diagram.

2   Calculate the LST for each activity by subtracting the duration of the activity from the LST of the following activity.

3   If more than one activity has the same predecessor, calculate the LST using each of the activities that follow and choose the smallest value.

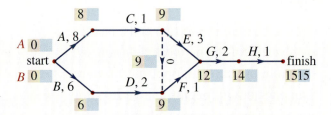

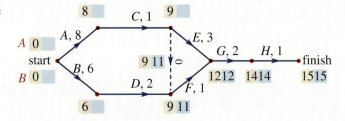

4   The LST for each activity is shown in shaded blue cell in the diagram opposite.

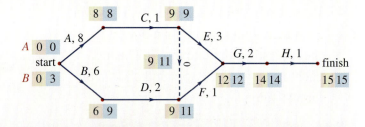

EARLIEST STARTING TIME (EST)	LATEST STARTING TIME (LST)
The earliest time any activity can be started after all prior activities have been completed. The EST of an activity is zero if there are no prior activities, otherwise it is greater than zero.	The latest time any activity can be started before delaying the entire project after all prior activities have been completed.

Exercise 10D

mple 7, 8 **1** A section of a network diagram is shown below.

  a What are the earliest start times for each of these activities?

    i A   **ii** B

    iii C   **iv** D

  b What are the latest start times for each of these activities?

    i A   **ii** B

    iii C   **iv** D

  c Find the duration of the four activities.

2 A section of a network diagram is shown on the right.

  a What are the earliest start times for each of these activities?

    i A   **ii** B

    iii C   **iv** D

    v F   **vi** G

  b What are the latest start times for each of these activities?

    i A   **ii** B

    iii C   **iv** D

    v F   **vi** G

3 Write down the value of each pronumeral in the sections of network diagrams below.

a

b

c

d

e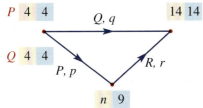

f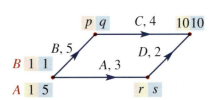

4 What are the values of f and g in the section of a network diagram shown opposite?

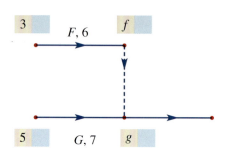

5 Consider the section of a network diagram shown in the diagram on the right.
  a What is the duration of activity B?
  b What is the latest start time for activity E?
  c What is the earliest time that activity E can start?

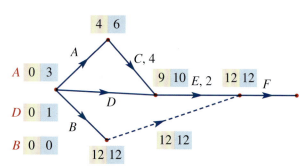

6 Find the earliest starting times (EST) and latest start times (LST) for all activities given the activity charts and network diagrams below.

a

Activity	Duration (in hrs)	Immediate predecessors
A	1	–
B	2	–
C	1	A
D	1	B, C
E	2	D

b

Activity	Duration (in hrs)	Immediate predecessors
A	5	–
B	7	–
C	4	–
D	2	C
E	3	C
F	15	A
G	8	E

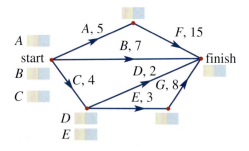

c

Activity	Duration (in days)	Immediate predecessors
A	4	–
B	5	A
C	2	A
D	1	B
E	6	D

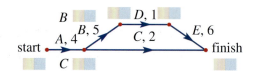

7 Determine the earliest starting times (EST) and latest starting time (LST) for each activity in the network diagram.

a

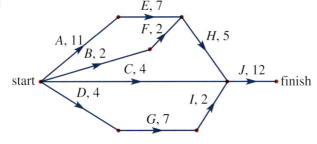

b

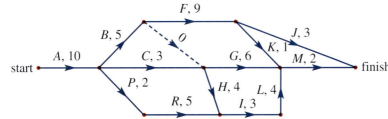

8 The activity chart for a project is shown opposite.

a Construct a network diagram using the above activity chart.

b Show the earliest starting times (EST) for each activity on the network diagram.

c Show the latest starting times (LST) for each activity on the network diagram.

Activity	Duration (in min)	Immediate predecessors
A	4	–
B	5	–
C	7	A
D	7	B
E	3	B, C
F	6	D, E

9 The activity chart for a project is shown opposite.

a Construct a network diagram using the above activity chart.

b Show the earliest starting times (EST) for each activity on the network diagram.

c Show the latest starting times (LST) for each activity on the network diagram.

Activity	Duration (in min)	Immediate predecessors
A	5	–
B	6	A
C	4	A
D	2	B
E	7	A
F	6	C
G	1	C
H	3	D
I	2	G

10E Float times and the critical path

The diagram below shows a small section of a network diagram. There are three activities shown, with their individual durations, in hours.

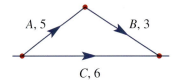

Activity B and activity C are both immediate predecessors to the next activity, so the project cannot continue until both of these tasks are finished. Activity B cannot begin until activity A is finished.

Activity C can be completed at the same time as activity A and activity B. Activity A and B will take a total of $5 + 3 = 8$ hours, while activity C only requires 6 hours. There is therefore some flexibility around when activity C needs to start. There are $8 - 6 = 2$ hours spare for the completion of activity C. This value is called the float time (or slack time) for activity C. The flexibility around the starting time for activity C can be demonstrated with the following diagram.

Hours:	1st	2nd	3rd	4th	5th	6th	7th	8th
	A	A	A	A	A	B	B	B
Start at same time	C	C	C	C	C	C	Float	Float
Delay C by 1 hour	Float	C	C	C	C	C	C	Float
Delay C by 2 hour	Float	Float	C	C	C	C	C	C

- The five red squares represent the 5 hours it takes to complete activity A.
- The three green squares represent the 3 hours it takes to complete activity B.
- The six yellow squares represent the 6 hours it takes to complete activity C.

Activity C does not have to start at the same time as activity A because it has some float time available (2 hours). Activity C should not be delayed by more than 2 hours because this would cause delays to the project and would affect the EST of the next activity. The next activity requires B and C to be complete before it can begin.

FLOAT TIMES

- Float time is the amount of time that a task in a project network can be delayed without causing a delay to subsequent tasks.
- Float time is calculated by subtracting the earliest start time from the latest start time.
  Float time = LST − EST

Identifying float times

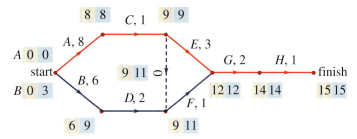

The boxes at the vertices in the network diagram above give the EST and LST for the activity that begins at that vertex.

The EST for activity D is 6 and the LST for activity D is 9. This means activity D has a float time of $9 - 6 = 3$ hours.

Activity D can be delayed by 3 hours without delaying the rest of the project.

The EST for activity C is 8 and the LST for activity C is 8. This means activity C has a float time of $8 - 8 = 0$ hours.

Activity C has no flexibility around its starting time at all. Any delay to the start of this activity will delay the whole project and extend the minimum time for completion. This means that activity C is a critical activity.

Critical path

All activities that have no float time are critical activities for completion of the project. Tracking through the network diagram along the edges of critical activities gives the critical path for the project. The critical path for the previous project is highlighted in red on the diagram below.

We say the critical path is A → C → E → G → H, and that activities A, C, E, G and H are all critical activities.

The process for determining the critical path is called critical path analysis. The steps involved in critical path analysis are outlined below.

1   Draw a box with two cells next to the start of each edge of the network diagram and at the finish.
2   Calculate the EST for each activity by forward scanning:
    EST = EST of predecessor + duration of predecessor.
3   If an activity has more than one predecessor, the EST is the largest of the alternatives.
4   The minimum overall completion time of the project is the EST value at the finish.
5   The LST of the finish is the same as the EST of the finish. Calculate the LST for each activity by backward scanning:
    LST = LST of following activity − duration of activity.
6   If an activity has more than one following activity, the LST is the smallest of all the alternative following activities.
7   Float time of an activity = LST − EST.
8   If the float time = 0, the activity is on the critical path.

CRITICAL PATH	MINIMUM TIME
The critical path is the sequence of the critical activities. Critical activities are ones that cannot be delayed without affecting the overall completion time of the project.	The minimum overall completion time of the project is the EST value at the finish.

Example 9: Locating the critical path   10E

What is the critical path in the network diagram shown below?

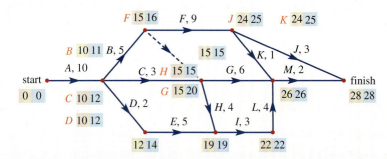

SOLUTION:

1   The critical path has activities with a zero float time.

2   Look for
Float = LST − EST = 0.
These instances are highlighted by the red boxes.

3   The critical path is highlighted in red. The dummy activity is not included in the critical path.

4   Write the answer in words.

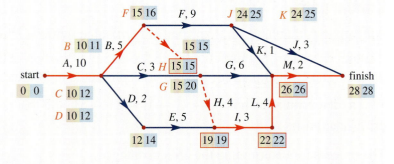

The critical path of this project is A→B→H→I→L→M.

Example 10: Finding the float time and the critical path 10E

A project has six activities as shown in the activity chart opposite.

a Draw a network diagram for this project.

b Calculate the EST and LST for each activity.

c What is the float time for each activity?

d Write down the critical path of this project.

e What is the minimum time required to complete the project?

Activity	Estimated completion time (days)	Immediate predecessors
A	6	–
B	9	–
C	8	A, B
D	7	A, B
E	10	D
F	12	C, E

SOLUTION:

1 A and B have no predecessors and so can begin at the same time. Since A and B are predecessors of C and D, a dummy activity will be required.

a

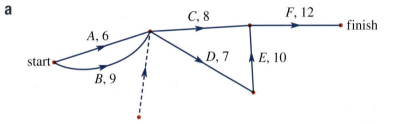

2 Forward scan to determine the EST (yellow box) and backward scan to determine the LST (blue box).

b

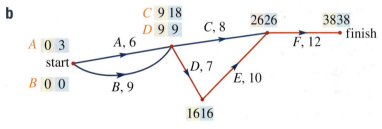

3 Subtract the earliest start time from the latest start time for each activity to calculate their float time.

c A: Float time = 3 − 0 = 3 days
B: Float time = 0 − 0 = 0 days
C: Float time = 18 − 9 = 9 days
D: Float time = 9 − 9 = 0 days
E: Float time = 16 − 16 = 0 days
F: Float time = 26 − 26 = 0 days

4 Look for activities with a zero float time to find the critical path.
(Float = LST − EST = 0)

d The dummy is not included in the critical path. Activities with a float time of zero are in the critical path.

The critical path of this project is B→D→E→F.

5 The critical path is highlighted in red in answer **b**.

6 The minimum completion time is in EST of the end box.

e The minimum completion time of this project is 38 days.

Exercise 10E

1 Find the float time for all activities (measured in minutes) in the network diagrams below.

a

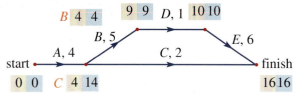

b

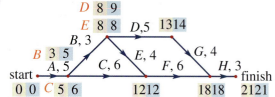

2 Identify the critical path in the network diagrams below.

a

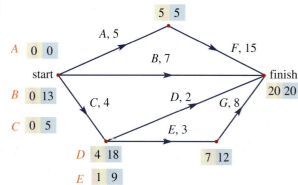

b

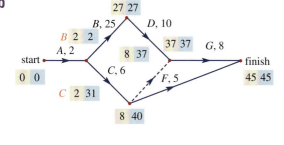

3 The network diagram shows the time (in days) for all activities, EST and LST.

  a Calculate the float times for all the activities.

  b Write down the critical path for this project.

  c What is the minimum time for the project to be completed?

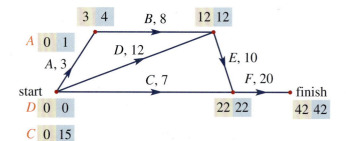

4 The network diagram shows the time (in hours) for all activities, EST and LST.

  a Calculate the float times for all the activities.

  b Write down the critical path for this project.

  c What is the minimum time for the project to be completed?

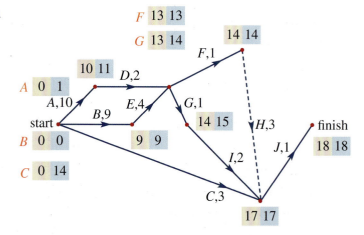

5 An incomplete activity chart and network diagram for a project are shown below.

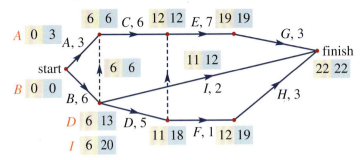

Activity	Duration (in weeks)	Immediate predecessors
A	3	–
B	6	–
C	6	
D		B
E	7	
F	1	D
G		E
H	3	
I	2	B

a Complete the activity chart.

b Find the float times for all activities.

c What is the critical path of this project?

d What is the minimum completion time for the project?

6 The activity chart for a project is shown.

a Draw a network diagram for this project.

b Complete the critical path analysis to calculate the EST and LST for each activity.

c Write down the critical path of this project.

d What is the minimum time required to complete the project?

Activity	Duration (weeks)	Immediate predecessors
P	4	–
Q	5	–
R	12	–
S	3	P
T	6	Q
U	3	S
V	4	R
W	8	R, T, U
X	13	V
Y	6	W, X

7 The activity chart for a project is shown.

a Draw a network diagram for this project.

b Complete the critical path analysis to calculate the EST and LST for each activity.

c Write down the critical path of this project.

d What is the minimum time required to complete the project?

Activity	Duration (weeks)	Immediate predecessors
I	2	–
J	3	–
K	5	–
L	4	I
M	8	J, N
N	1	K
O	6	L, M
P	6	J, N
Q	7	J, N
R	5	K
S	1	O
T	9	Q, R

10F   Minimum completion time

The minimum time it takes to complete a project depends upon the time it takes to complete the individual activities of the project, and upon the predecessors for each activity. Critical path analysis can be completed to find the overall minimum completion time.

Completing activities in a shorter time

Sometimes, the managers of a project might arrange for one or more activities within the project to be completed in a shorter time than originally planned. Changing the conditions of an activity within a project, and recalculating the minimum completion time for the project, is sometimes called crashing. An individual activity could be crashed by employing more staff, sourcing alternative materials or simply because weather or other factors allow the activity to be completed in a shorter time than usual.

Example 11: Finding the minimum completion time   **10F**

The network diagram below shows the time (in hours) for all activities, EST and LST. The critical path is shown in red.

a What is the minimum completion time for the project?

b Which of these activities, if reduced in time individually, would not result in an earlier completion of the project?

c Activity D was reduced in time to 4 hours. What is the new minimum completion time?

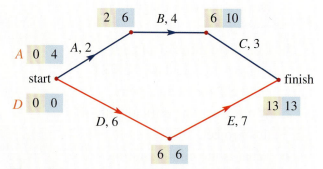

SOLUTION:

1 The minimum completion time is the EST of the end box.

2 The activities not on the critical path will not shorten the time taken to complete the project.

3 Decrease the weighted edge for activity D from 6 to 4 hours.

4 Recalculate the EST and LST for each activity.

a The minimum completion time of this project is 13 hours.

b Activities A, B or C

c

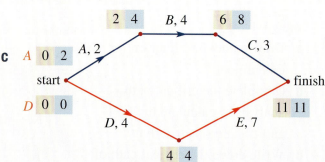

5 The minimum completion time is the EST of the end box.

The minimum completion time is now 11 hours.

Example 12: Finding the minimum completion time 10F

A community centre is being built. Nine activities have been identified for a building project. The network diagram on the right shows the activities, completion times in weeks, ESTs and LSTs.

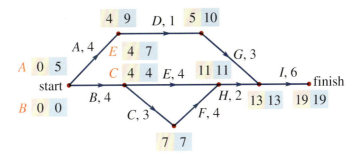

a What is the critical path and the minimum time, in weeks, to complete this project?
b The builders of the community centre are able to speed up the project. Activities A, C, F and G can be reduced in time at an additional cost. Which of these activities, if reduced in time individually, would not result in an earlier completion of the project?
c The owner of the estate is prepared to pay the additional cost to achieve early completion. The cost of reducing the time of each activity is $5000 per week. The maximum reduction in time for each one of the five activities, A, C, F and G is 2 weeks. Find the minimum time, in weeks, for the project to be completed given these activities are reduced in time.

SOLUTION:

1 Look for activities with a zero float time to find the critical path.

a Critical path is B → C → F → H → I

2 The minimum completion time is the EST of the end box.

∴ Minimum completion time is 19 weeks.

3 Look for activities not on the critical path. Reducing their time will not affect the overall time for the project.

b Activities A, G, D and E are not on the critical path. These activities would not result in an earlier completion of the project.

4 Activities C and F are on the critical path. Reduce the time of each activity by 2 weeks.

c C can now be completed in 1 week.
F can now be completed in 2 weeks.
Update the network diagram (see below).

5 Recalculate the EST and LST.

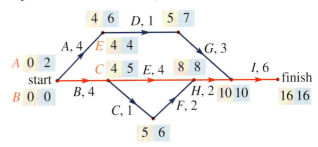

6 Check for change in the critical path.
7 Look for activities with a zero float time to find the critical path.

New critical path is B→E→ H→I
∴ Minimum completion time is now 16 weeks.

Exercise 10F

Example 11 **1** The network diagram below shows the time (in days) for all activities, EST and LST. The critical path is shown in red.

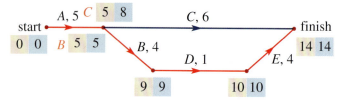

a What is the minimum completion time?

b Reducing the time taken in which activities would not result in a reduction in the minimum completion time?

c Activity A was reduced in time to 3 days. What is the new minimum completion time?

2 The network diagram below shows the time (in weeks) for all activities, EST and LST. The critical path is shown in red.

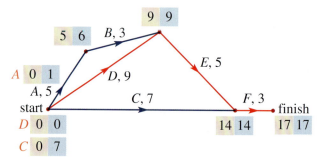

a What is the minimum completion time for the project?

b Reducing the time taken in which activities would not result in a reduction in the minimum completion time?

c Activity E was reduced in time to 1 hour. What is the new minimum completion time?

3 The network diagram below shows the time (in hours) for all activities, EST and LST. The critical path is shown in red.

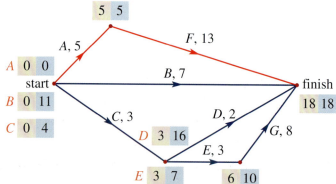

a What is the minimum completion time for the project?

b Reducing the time taken in which activities would result in a reduction in the minimum completion time?

c Activity B was reduced in time to 5 hours. What is the new minimum completion time?

4 The network diagram below shows the time (in minutes) for all activities, EST and LST. The critical path is shown in red.

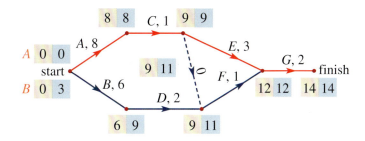

a What is the minimum completion time?

b Reducing the time taken in which activities would result in a reduction in the minimum completion time?

c Both activities A and E are reduced by 2 minutes. What is the new minimum completion time?

LEVEL 2

Example 12   **5** The network diagram for a project is shown in the diagram below. The duration for each activity is in hours.

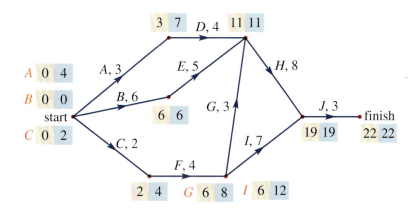

a Identify the critical path for this project.

b What is the minimum completion time for the project?

c What is the maximum number of hours that the completion time for activity E can be reduced without changing the critical path of the project?

d What is the maximum number of hours that the completion time for activity H can be reduced without affecting the critical path of the project?

e If activity B is reduced from 6 hours to 4 hours, what is the minimum completion time for the project?

6   The network diagram for a project is shown in the diagram below. The duration for each activity is in hours.

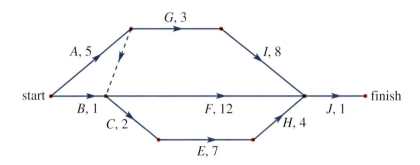

  a   Find the earliest starting times (EST) and latest start times (LST) for all activities.

  b   Identify the critical path for this project.

  c   How much time overall is saved if activity F is reduced in duration by 2 hours?

  d   If only one activity can have its duration reduced, what is the maximum possible reduction in the completion time of the project?

7   The network diagram for a project is shown in the diagram below. The duration for each activity is in hours.

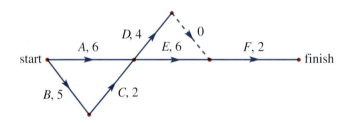

  a   Find the earliest starting times (EST) and latest start times (LST) for all activities.

  b   Determine the shortest time in which this project can be completed.

  c   Write down the critical path for this project.

  d   The time it takes to complete activity A can be reduced by one hour at a cost of $50. Explain why this will not affect the completion time of this project.

  e   Activity B can be reduced in time at a cost of $100 per hour. Activity E can be reduced in time at a cost of $50 per hour. What is the cost of reducing the completion time of this project as much as possible?

10G Network flow problems

One of the applications of directed graphs to real-life situations is network flow problems which involve the transfer or flow of material from one point, called the source, to another point called the sink. Examples of this include water flowing through pipes, or traffic flowing along one-way roads.

> source → flow through network → sink

The source is like the start, and the sink is like the finish, in the critical path analysis section.

Water flows through pipes in only one direction. In a directed graph representing water flow, the vertices are the origin and destination of the water and the edges represent the pipes connecting them. The weights on the edges would be the amount of water that can flow through the pipe in a given time. The weights of flow problem directed graphs are called capacities.

The diagram on the right shows two pipes that are joined together, connecting the source of water to the sink. There is a small pipe with capacity 25 litres per minute joined to a large pipe with capacity 58 litres per minute. When an edge is at its maximum flow we say it is saturated.

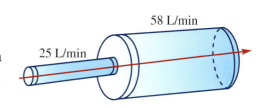

Even though the large pipe has a capacity greater than 25 litres per minute, the small pipe will only allow 25 litres of water through each minute. The flow through the large pipe will never be more than 25 litres per minute. The large pipe will experience flow below its capacity. We say that it has an excess flow capacity, which is like the the float time from the critical path analysis section.

If we reverse the connection and direct water through the large capacity pipe into the smaller capacity pipe, there will be a 'bottleneck' of flow at the junction.

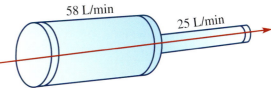

The large capacity pipe is delivering 58 litres of water every minute to the small pipe, but the small pipe will only allow 25 litres per minute to pass.

In both of these situations, the flow through the entire pipe system (both pipes from source to sink) is restricted to a maximum of 25 litres per minute. This is the capacity of the smallest pipe in the connection.

If we connect more pipes together, one after the other, we can calculate the overall flow capacity or maximum flow of the pipe system by looking for the smallest capacity pipe in that system.

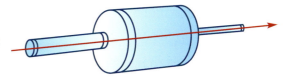

MAXIMUM FLOW

If pipes of different capacities are connected one after the other, the maximum flow (or flow capacity) through the pipes is equal to the maximum capacity of the individual smallest pipe.

Example 13: Calculating the maximum flow   10G

In the directed graph shown on the right, the vertices A, B, C, D and E represent towns. The edges of the graph represent roads and the weights of these edges are the maximum number of cars that can travel on the road each hour. The roads allow only one-way travel.

a Find the maximum traffic flow from A to E through town C.

b Find the maximum traffic flow from A to E overall.

c A new road is being built to allow traffic from town D to town C. This road can carry 500 cars per hour.

   i Add this road to the directed graph.

   ii Find the maximum traffic flow from A to E overall after this road is built.

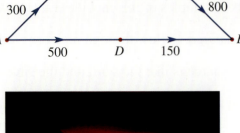

SOLUTION:

1 Look at the path A→B→C→E. The smallest capacity of the individual roads is 300 cars per hour. This will be the maximum flow through this path. Note that at maximum flow, the path A→B is saturated, and path B→C and C→E have excess flow capacity.

a

2 Write the maximum flow (300) for this path near the edge's weight.

3 Write answer in words.

The maximum flow is 300 cars per hour.

4 Look at the path A→D→E. The smallest capacity of the individual roads is 150 cars per hour. This will be the maximum flow through this path.

b

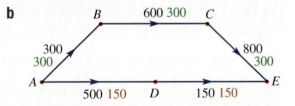

5 Write the maximum flow (150) for this path near the weight edge.

6 Add the maximum flow for path A→B→C→E and path A→D→E.

The maximum flow from A to E overall is: 300 + 150 = 450 cars per hour.

7 Add the edge to the network diagram.

ci

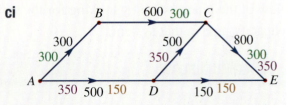

8 Look at the path A→D→C→E. The smallest capacity of the individual roads is 350 cars per hour. This will be the maximum flow through this path.

9 Write the maximum flow (350) for this path near the weight edge.

10 Add the maximum flow for path A→B→C→E, path A→D→E and path A→D→C→E.

ii The new maximum flow is:
300 + 150 + 350 = 800 cars per hour.

Cuts

It is difficult to determine the maximum flow by inspection for directed networks that involve many vertices and edges. We can simplify the search for maximum flow by searching for cuts within the directed graph.

A cut divides the network into two parts, completely separating the source from the sink. It is helpful to think of cuts as imaginary breaks within the network that completely block the flow through that network. For the network or water pipes shown in this diagram, the dotted line is a cut. This cut completely blocks the flow of water from the source (S) to the sink (A).

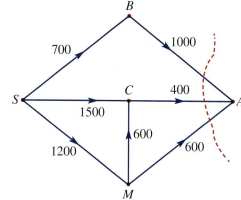

Cut

The dotted line on the graph below is a cut because it separates the source and the sink completely. No material can flow from the source to the sink.

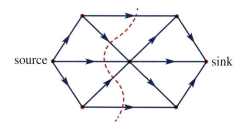

Not a cut

The dotted line on the graph below is not a cut because material can still flow from the source to the sink. Not all of the pathways from source to sink have been blocked by the cut.

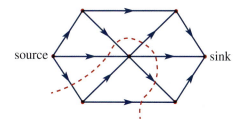

CUTS

- A cut is an imaginary line across a directed graph that completely separates the source (start of the flow) from the sink (destination of the flow).
- Cut capacity is the sum of all the capacities of the edges that the cut passes through, taking into account the direction of flow. The capacity of an edge is only counted if it flows from the source side to the sink side of the cut.
- A cut is like a snapshot across the system of the flow at that time.

In the simple network shown, the cut passes through three edges. The edge B to A is not counted in the capacity of the cut because the flow for that edge is from the sink side to the source side of the cut.

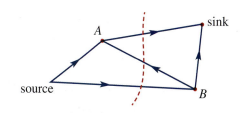

Example 14: Calculating the cut capacity

Calculate the capacity of the four cuts shown in the network on the right. The source is vertex S and the sink is vertex T.

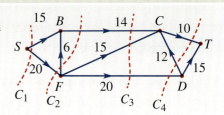

SOLUTION

1	All edges in C_1 are counted.	The capacity of $C_1 = 15 + 20 = 35$.
2	In C_2 the edge from F to B is not counted.	The capacity of $C_2 = 14 + 20 = 34$.
3	All edges in C_3 are counted.	The capacity of $C_3 = 14 + 15 + 20 = 49$.
4	In C_4 the edge from D to C is not counted.	The capacity of $C_4 = 20 + 10 = 30$.

Maximum-flow minimum-cut theorem

The capacity of a cut is important to help determine the maximum flow through any directed graph. Look for the smallest, or minimum, cut capacity that exists in the graph. This will be the same as the maximum flow that is possible through that graph. This is known as the maximum-flow minimum-cut theorem.

MAXIMUM-FLOW MINIMUM-CUT THEOREM

The flow through a network cannot exceed the value of any cut in the network and the maximum flow equals the value of the minimum cut.

Example 15: Calculating the maximum flow

The table shows the flow capacities (FC) of the edges of a network. Determine the maximum flow from S to T.

From	To	FC	From	To	FC
S	A	8	B	T	5
S	C	11	C	B	3
A	T	3	C	T	1
B	A	5			

SOLUTION:

1 Construct a network graph using the values in the cells as the flow capacity of the edges.

2 Mark the possible paths and their capacity (trial and error process). These are: Green — 3; brown — 3; purple — 1. Purple path has a capacity of 1.

3 Identify the minimum cut (red dotted line).

4 Find the minimum cut capacity.

5 Find the maximum flow capacity.

6 Write the answer in words.

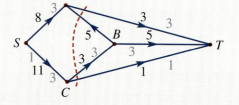

Minimum cut capacity $= 3 + 3 + 1 = 7$.

Maximum flow $= 3 + 3 + 1 = 7$.

Therefore the maximum flow is 7.

Note: The maximum flow must equal the minimum cut.

Exercise 10G

Example 13 | **1** Find the maximum flow for each of the following network diagrams. Each colour on the weighted edge represents the flow capacity of a path from the source (S) to the sink (T).

a

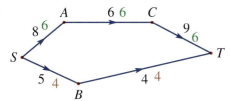

b

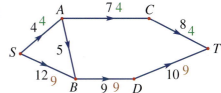

c

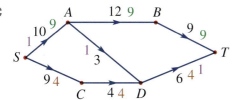

d

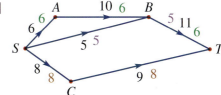

e

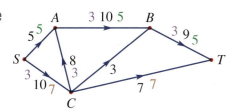

f

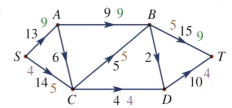

Example 14 | **2** Find the capacity of each of the cuts in the following network diagrams. The source is vertex S and the sink is vertex T.

a

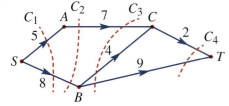

b

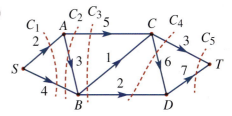

c

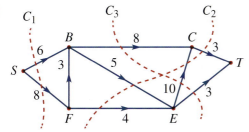

d

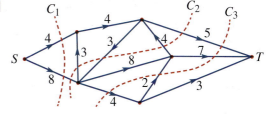

Example 15 **3** Find the maximum flow for each of the following network diagrams. The source is vertex S and the sink is vertex T. Check your answer by finding the minimum cut.

a
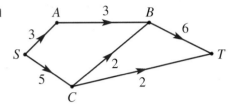

b
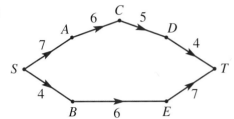

c
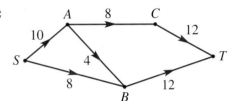

d
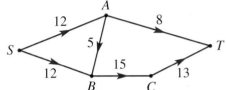

e
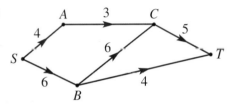

f
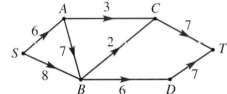

g
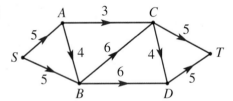

h
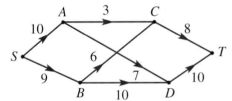

i
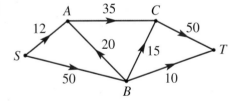

j
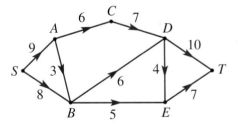

k
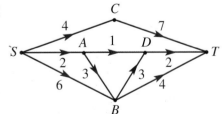

l
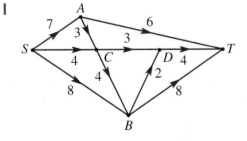

4   The table opposite shows the flow capacities of the edges of a
    network.
    a Construct a network diagram showing the direction and quantity
       of the flow. The source is vertex A and the sink is vertex E.
    b Find the maximum flow through the network. Check your
       answer by finding the minimum cut.
    c Find one example of the maximum flow through the network.

From	To	Capacity
A	B	5
B	C	4
C	D	2
C	E	2
D	E	1

5   The table opposite shows the flow capacities of the edges of a
    network.
    a Construct a network diagram showing the direction and
       quantity of the flow. The source is vertex C and the sink is
       vertex H.
    b Find the maximum flow through the network. Check your
       answer by finding the minimum cut.
    c Find one example of the maximum flow through the network.

From	To	Capacity
C	D	9
C	E	9
D	G	7
D	F	3
E	F	6
E	G	4
F	H	9
G	H	9

6   The table opposite shows the flow capacities of the edges of a
    network.
    a Construct a network diagram showing the direction and
       quantity of the flow. The source is vertex A and the sink is
       vertex E.
    b Find the maximum flow through the network. Check your
       answer by finding the minimum cut.
    c Find one example of the maximum flow through the network.

From	To	Capacity
A	B	14
B	C	8
B	D	6
C	E	6
C	F	4
D	F	5
E	G	7
F	G	8
G	H	14

7   The table opposite shows the flow capacities of the edges of a
    network.
    a Construct a network diagram showing the direction and
       quantity of the flow. The source is vertex P and the sink is
       vertex V.
    b Find the maximum flow through the network. Check your
       answer by finding the minimum cut.
    c Find one example of the maximum flow through the network.

From	To	Capacity
P	Q	5
P	R	8
P	S	9
Q	R	5
Q	U	4
R	U	7
R	T	4
S	R	5
S	T	3
U	V	10
T	V	12

8 A plane journey consists of a connected sequence of stages formed by edges on the following directed network from city A to city B. The number of available seats for each stage is indicated beside the corresponding edge, as shown on the diagram on the right.

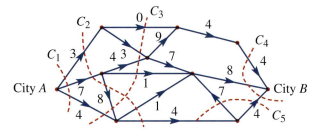

  a What is the capacity of each of the five cuts shown?

  b Explain why cut 5 is not a valid cut when trying to find the minimum cut between city A and city B.

  c Find the maximum number of available seats for a plane journey from city A to city B.

  d Find one example of the maximum number of available seats for a plane journey from city A to city B.

9 Water pipes of different capacities are connected to two water sources and two sinks. Network of water pipes is shown in the diagram opposite. The numbers on the edges represent the capacities, in kilolitres per minute, of the pipes. Find the maximum flow, in kilolitres per minute, to each of the sinks in this network.

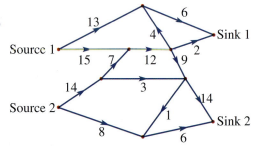

10 Storm water enters a network of pipes at either Dunlop North (Source 1) or Dunlop South (Source 2) and flows into the ocean at either Outlet 1 or Outlet 2. On the network diagram below, the pipes are represented by straight lines with arrows that indicate the direction of the flow of water. Water cannot flow through a pipe in the opposite direction. The numbers next to the arrows represent the maximum rate, in kilolitres per minute, at which storm water can flow through each pipe.

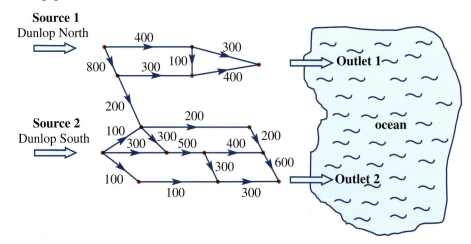

Determine the maximum rate, in kilolitres per minute, at which water can flow from these pipes into the ocean at Outlet 1 and Outlet 2.

Key ideas and chapter summary

Critical path analysis	Critical path analysis is a technique that identifies the activities required to complete a project, the time necessary to complete each activity and the relationships between the activities.
Activity chart	A table containing the activities of a project, duration and their immediate predecessors.
Constructing a network diagram given an activity chart	Activities that have no immediate predecessors follow from the start vertex. Activities that are not immediate predecessors for other activities lead to the finish vertex. For every other activity, look for: • the activities for which it is an immediate predecessor • the activities it has as immediate predecessors.
Dummy activities	A dummy activity is required if two activities share some, but not all, of their immediate predecessors.
Scheduling on a network diagram	Scheduling on a network diagram is shown using a weighted edge. The number on the edge indicates the duration of the activity. The weight of dummy activities is always zero.
Earliest starting time (EST)	The earliest time any activity can be started after all prior activities have been completed.
Latest starting time (LST)	The latest time any activity can be started after all prior activities have been completed.
Float times	Float time is the amount of time that a task in a project network can be delayed without causing a delay to subsequent tasks. $$\text{Float time} = \text{LST} - \text{EST}$$
Critical path	The critical path is the sequence of activities that cannot be delayed without affecting the overall completion time of the project.
Minimum time	The minimum overall completion time of the project is the EST value at the end vertex.
Crashing	Crashing involves recalculating the minimum completion time for the project after the conditions of an activity within a project have changed.
Maximum flow	If pipes of different capacities are connected one after the other, the maximum flow (or flow capacity) through the pipes is equal to the minimum capacity of the individual pipes.
Cuts	A cut is an imaginary line across a directed graph that completely separates the source (start of the flow) from the sink (destination of the flow).
Maximum-flow minimum-cut theorem	The flow through a network cannot exceed the value of any cut in the network and that the maximum flow equals the value of the minimum cut.

Multiple-choice

1 The network diagram represents a manufacturing process with activities and their duration (in hours) listed on the edges of the graph. What is the earliest time (in hours) after the start that activity G can begin?

   A 3   **B** 6   **C** 7   **D** 8

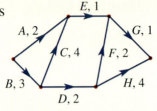

2 The table opposite lists the six activities in a project and the earliest start time, in hours, and the predecessor(s) of each task. The time taken for activity E is two hours. Without affecting the time taken for the entire project, how much could the time taken for activity C be increased by?

   A 0 hours   **B** 8 hours

   C 11 hours   **D** 22 hours

Activity	Immediate predecessors	EST
A	–	0
B	–	0
C	A	8
D	B	15
E	C	22
F	D, E	35

3 The edges in this network diagram correspond to the tasks involved in the preparation of an examination. The numbers indicate the time, in weeks, needed for each task. What is the minimum completion time to prepare this examination?

   A 14   **B** 15   **C** 16   **D** 17

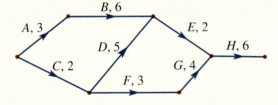

4 This network diagram is for a project where the component times are shown in days. The critical path for the network of this project is given by:

   A A–B–E–I–K   **B** A–D–H–I–K

   C A–C–G–H–I–K   **D** A–C–F–J–K

5 For the network shown on the right, the capacity of the cut is:

   A 3

   B 7

   C 10

   D 15

6 The maximum flow in the network diagram opposite is:

   A 10

   B 11

   C 12

   D 13

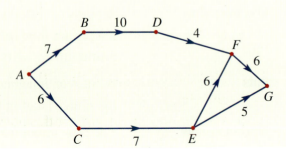

Short-answer

1   Jake is renovating his family room. He has organised this project into six tasks.

Buy hardware –1 day
Prepare walls – 1 day
Paint walls – 4 days
Sand timber floor – 3 days
Seal floor – 2 days
Put furniture in the room – 1 day.

   a Which task has no immediate predecessor? Give a reason for your answer.
   b What is the immediate predecessor to the following tasks?
      i   Buy hardware   ii Prepare walls
      iii Paint walls   iv Sand timber floor
      v   Seal floor   vi Put furniture in the room
   c Construct an activity chart for this project. Use the headings; Activity, Task, Duration (in
      days) and Immediate predecessors. Label the above tasks as activities A to F respectively.
   d Draw a network diagram from this activity chart.

2   Draw an activity chart for the network diagram shown
    opposite.

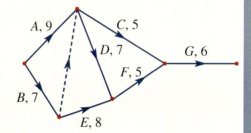

3   Jet 12 makes light aircraft for the civil aviation industry.
    They have identified 10 activities required for
    production of their new aircraft. These activities and
    their durations are given in the table opposite.

   a Copy and complete the network diagram shown
      below for this project by inserting and labelling
      activity D.

	Duration	Immediate
Activity	(weeks)	predecessors
A	4	–
B	5	A
C	7	B
D	6	B
E	7	B
F	4	C
G	2	E, F
H	4	E, F
I	2	D, G
J	1	H, I

   b Find the earliest starting times (EST) for all
      activities.
   c Find the latest starting times (LST) for all
      activities.
   d What is the critical path for this network?

4 A network diagram for project is shown. The duration for each activity is in hours.

a Calculate the float times for all the activities.

b Identify the critical path for this project.

c What is the minimum completion time for the project?

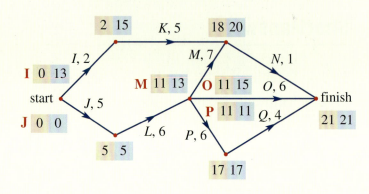

5 In the network opposite, the values on the edges give the maximum flow possible between each pair of vertices. The arrows show the direction of flow in the network. Also shown is a cut that separates the source (S) from the sink (T).

a Find the capacity of the cut shown.

b Determine the maximum flow through this network.

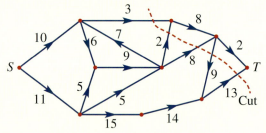

6 Determine the maximum flow from S to T for the network graph shown on the right. Check your answer by finding the minimum cut.

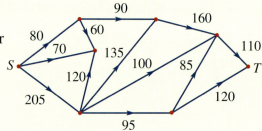

Extended-response

7 A development project involves completing a number of activities as shown in the table. Each activity is shown with its duration. Time is measured in days.

a Construct a network diagram for this project, labelling the activities on the edges with their associated shortest durations.

b Determine the earliest start time for each activity from your graph.

c Determine the latest start time for each activity from your graph.

d State the critical path.

e How long is the estimated project time under this set of activity durations?

f If the final activity, K, had to be delayed, how many days could this delay take before the project schedule was disrupted?

Activity	Duration (days)	Immediate predecessors
A	4	–
B	2	–
C	1	A
D	6	B
E	5	B
F	7	B
G	5	C, D
H	1	E
I	2	F
J	10	G, H
K	6	I

PDF

LITERACY

Practice Paper 3

Section I

Attempt Questions 1–15 (15 marks).
Allow about 20 minutes for this section.

---

1 The maximum flow in the network diagram opposite is:

A 4

B 10

C 14

D 21

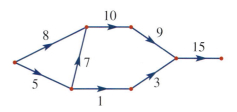

2 The amount of money in a fund is given by $A = 800(1.1)^t$ where A is the amount of money and t is the time in years. What is the initial amount of money invested in the fund?

A $800

B $880

C $1000

D $1100

3 In a normally distributed set of scores, the mean is 70 and the standard deviation is 6. Approximately what percentage of the scores will lie between 58 and 82?

A 34%

B 68%

C 95%

D 99.7%

4 An investment is modelled by the recurrence relation

$$V_{n+1} = V_n \times 1.09$$

where V_n is the balance of the loan after n payments and $V_0 = 2000$.

After how many years will the value of the investment first exceed $2500?

A 1   **B** 2

C 3   **D** 4

5 The graph of $y = 3x^2 - 6x + 7$ meets the y-axis at:

A (0, 1)   **B** (0, 7)

C (7, 0)   **D** (1, 0)

6 Which graph best represents $y = 2^x$?

A

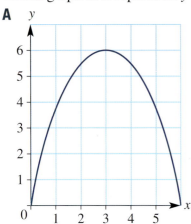

B

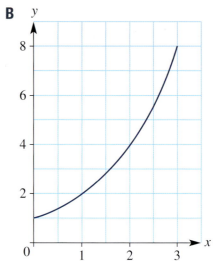

C

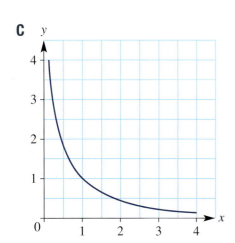

D

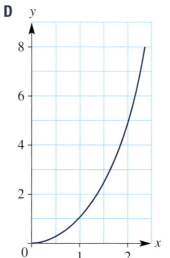

Use the table below to answer questions 7 to 8.

7 A reducing-balance loan of $8000 will be repaid with quarterly payments. The table for this annuity is shown below.

Payment number	Payment paid	Interest paid	Principal reduction	Balance of annuity
0	0	0.00	0.00	8000
1	2043.94	70.00	1973.94	6026.06
2	2043.94	52.73	1991.21	4034.85

The annual percentage interest rate on this loan is:

A 1.2% **B** 3.42% **C** 3.5% **D** 8.75%

8 What is the reduction in the above loan after 6 months?

A $2043.94 **B** $3965.15 **C** $4034.85 **D** $6016.06

9 Emma's class achieved a standardised score of $z = 2.1$. This result is:

A well below average

B around average

C exactly average

D well above average

10 The balance of a reducing-balance loan after n monthly payments can be modelled by the recurrence relation $V_{n+1} = V_n \times 1.0125 - 1300$ where V_n is the balance of the loan after n payments. This loan has:

A monthly interest rate 12.5% and monthly payments of $1300

B monthly interest rate 15% and monthly payments of $1300

C monthly interest rate 12.5% and yearly payments of $1300

D annual interest rate 15% and monthly payments of $1300

11 For the network shown on the right, the capacity of the cut is 30. What is the value of x?

A 0

B 7

C 10

D 14

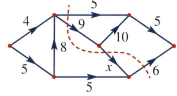

12 The time taken to make a bus trip between the two towns is normally distributed with a mean of 78 minutes and a standard deviation of 4 minutes. A standardised time for a trip is $z = -0.25$. The actual time (in minutes) is:

A 77   **B** 77.25

C 77.75   **D** 78.25

13 The cost per person of hiring a yacht (c) varies inversely with the number of people sharing the total cost (n). Which formula correctly expresses c in terms of n and k, where k is the constant of variation?

A $c = k^N$ **B** $c = kn^2$

C $c = \dfrac{n}{k}$ **D** $c = \dfrac{k}{n}$

14 A student's mark on a test is 64. The mean mark for their class is 73 and the standard deviation is 4.5. Their standard score is:

A -2.0 **B** -1.5

C 2.0   **D** 2.5

15 The network diagram shows the activities and their duration (in hours) listed on the edges of the graph. The earliest time (in hours) after the start that activity H can begin is:

A 4

B 10

C 11

D 13

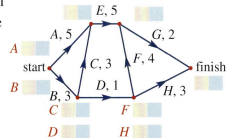

Section II

Attempt Questions 16–18 (45 marks).

Allow about 70 minutes for this section.

All necessary working should be shown in every question.

Question 16 (15 marks)   **Marks**

a A factory produces bags of sultanas. The weights of the bags are normally distributed,   **2**
with a mean of 900 g and a standard deviation of 50 g. What percentage of bags
weigh more than 1000 g?

b Jake borrows $14 000 to build fishing platforms and shelters around his lake. Interest
will be charged at the rate of 9.6% per annum, compounding monthly. Jake will repay
the loan with monthly payments of $760.

   i What is a recurrence relation model for the balance of this loan?   **2**

   ii Find the value of the loan after 1 month.   **1**

   iii How much interest did Jake pay with the first payment of $760?   **1**

   iv By how much has the balance of the loan been reduced by the first payment   **1**
of $760?

   v Find the value of the loan after five months, correct to the nearest cent.   **1**

   vi Show that Jake paid a total of $507.74 interest, correct to the nearest cent, after   **1**
five months.

c The number of people (N) who attend a show varies inversely with the amount of
floor space (in cm^2) allowed per person (A). A venue can hold 4800 people if each
person is allowed 200 cm^2.

   i How many people could the venue hold if a person was allowed 2400 cm^2?   **2**

   ii What is the space allowed per person for 5000 to attend the show?   **1**

d A network diagram with six activities is shown below.

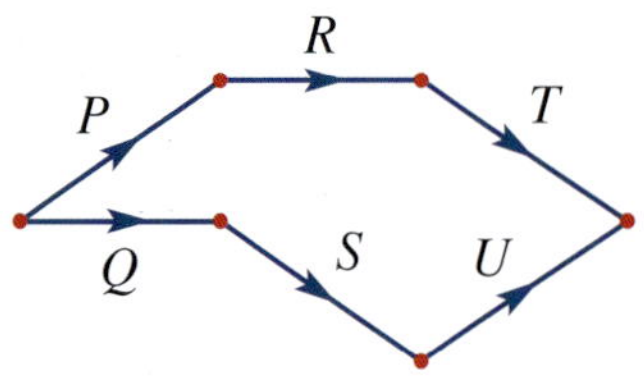

   i What activities have no predecessor?   **1**

   ii Construct an activity chart for this network diagram.   **2**

Question 17 (15 marks)   **Marks**

a i Complete the table of values for the equation $y = x^2 - 4$.   1

x	−3	−2	−1	0	1	2	3
y							

ii Draw the graph of the quadratic function $y = x^2 - 4$.   1

iii Complete the table of values for the equation $y = -x^2 + 2x + 8$.   1

x	−2	−1	0	1	2	3	4
y							

iv Draw the graph of the quadratic function $y = -x^2 + 2x + 8$.   1

b The table below shows the future value of an annuity with a contribution of $1.

Future value of $1						
Period	**1%**	**2%**	**3%**	**4%**	**5%**	**6%**
1	1.0000	1.0000	1.0000	1.0000	1.0000	1.0000
2	2.0100	2.0200	2.0300	2.0400	2.0500	2.0600
3	3.0301	3.0604	3.0909	3.1216	3.1525	3.1836
4	4.0604	4.1216	4.1836	4.2465	4.3101	4.3746

Use the above table to calculate the future value of the following annuities.

i $12 000 per year for 3 years at 2% p.a. compounded annually.   1

ii $8 900 per half-year for 2 years at 6% p.a. compounded six-monthly.   1

c Results for a class test are given as z-scores. In this test, Noah gained a z-score equal to −2.

i Interpret this z-score in terms of the mean and standard deviation of the test.   1

ii If the test has a mean of 67 and a standard deviation of 7, calculate the actual mark scored by Noah.   1

d The network diagram shows the time (in days) for all activities, EST and LST.

i Find the float times for all the activities.   2

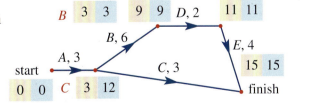

ii What is the critical path for this project?   1

e The weights of boxes of muesli are normally distributed. The mean is 756 grams and the standard deviation is 4 grams.

i A box of muesli has a weight of 748 grams. What is the z-score?   1

ii What is the weight of a box that has a z-score of 3?   1

iii What percentage of boxes will have a weight between 752 grams and 760 grams?   2

Question 18 (15 marks)   **Marks**

a The table shows the present value of a $1 annuity.

Present value of $1						
Period	**1%**	**2%**	**4%**	**6%**	**8%**	**10%**
1	0.9901	0.9804	0.9615	0.9434	0.9259	0.9091
2	1.9704	1.9416	1.8861	1.8334	1.7833	1.7355
3	2.9410	2.8839	2.7751	2.6730	2.5771	2.4869
4	3.9020	3.8077	3.6299	3.4651	3.3121	3.1699
5	4.8534	4.7135	4.4518	4.2124	3.9927	3.7908
6	5.7955	5.6014	5.2421	4.9173	4.6229	4.3553

  i What would be the present value of an $11 000 per year annuity at 10% per   **1**
annum for 5 years, with interest compounding annually?

  ii An annuity of $8000 each three months is invested at 4% per annum,   **1**
compounded quarterly for 1 year. What is the present value of the annuity?

  iii What is the value of an annuity that would provide a present value of $47 934   **2**
after 3 years at 8% per annum compound interest? Answer to the nearest dollar.

b The ages of the residents in Green Hill are normally distributed. The mean age is 42
years and the standard deviation is 11 years. Determine the:

  i percentage of residents younger than 42 years   **1**

  ii percentage of residents younger than 53 years   **1**

  iii percentage of residents older than 9 years.   **1**

c The number of bacteria grows exponentially according to the formula $b = 30(1.2)^t$,
where b is the number of bacteria after t hours.

  i What is the initial number of bacteria?   **1**

  ii Copy and complete the table of ordered pairs. Express the number of bacteria to **2**
the nearest whole number.

t	0	5	10	15
b				

  iii Draw a graph of the formula $b = 30(1.2)^t$.   **1**

  iv Estimate the time taken for the number of bacteria to reach 120.   **1**

d Determine the maximum flow   **3**
from S to T for the network graph
shown on the right. Check your
answer by finding the minimum cut.

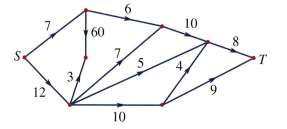

2019 Higher School Certificate Examination Mathematics Standard 1/2 Reference sheet

Measurement

Precision

Absolute error $= \dfrac{1}{2} \times$ precision

Upper bound $=$ measurement $+$ absolute error

Lower bound $=$ measurement $-$ absolute error

Length, area, surface area and volume

$$l = \dfrac{\theta}{360} \times 2\pi r$$

$$A = \dfrac{\theta}{360} \times \pi r^2$$

$$A = \dfrac{h}{2}(x + y)$$

$$A \approx \dfrac{h}{2}(d_f + d_l)$$

$$A = 2\pi r^2 + 2\pi rh$$

$$A = 4\pi r^2$$

$$V = \dfrac{1}{3} Ah$$

$$V = \dfrac{4}{3} \pi r^3$$

Trigonometry

$$A = \dfrac{1}{2} ab \sin C$$

$$\dfrac{a}{\sin A} = \dfrac{b}{\sin B} = \dfrac{c}{\sin C}$$

$$c^2 = a^2 + b^2 - 2ab \cos C$$

$$\cos C = \dfrac{a^2 + b^2 - c^2}{2ab}$$

Financial Mathematics

$$FV = PV(1 + r)^n$$

Straight-line method of depreciation

$$S = V_0 - Dn$$

Declining-balance method of depreciation

$$S = V_0(1 - r)^n$$

Statistical Analysis

$$z = \dfrac{x - \bar{x}}{s}$$

An outlier is a score

    less than $Q_1 - 1.5 \times IQR$

    or

    more than $Q_3 + 1.5 \times IQR$

Normal distribution

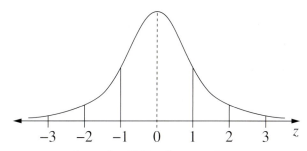

- approximately 68% of scores have z-scores between -1 and 1
- approximately 95% of scores have z-scores between -2 and 2
- approximately 99.7% of scores have z-scores between -3 and 3

Glossary

A

Absolute error – The difference between the actual value and the measured value indicated by an instrument. It is also calculated by finding half the smallest unit on the measuring device.

Account servicing fee – Ongoing account keeping fees.

Activity chart – A table containing the activities of a project, duration and their immediate predecessors.

Adjacent side – A side in right-angled triangle next to the reference angle but not the hypotenuse.

Algebraic modelling – When a practical situation is described mathematically using an algebraic function.

Allowable deduction – Deductions allowed by the Australian Taxation Office such as work-related, self-education, travel, car or clothing expenses.

Analysing data – A process that interprets data and transforms it into information.

Angle of depression – The angle between the horizontal and the direction below the horizontal.

Angle of elevation – The angle between the horizontal and the direction above the horizontal.

Annual leave loading – A payment calculated as a fixed percentage of the normal pay over a fixed number of weeks. Annual leave loading is usually at the rate of $17\frac{1}{2}\%$.

Annually – Once a year.

Annuity – A form of investment that involves the regular contribution of money.

Annuity table – A table is used to summarise the key properties of an annuity.

Annulus – Area between a large and a small circle.

Appreciation – An increase in value of an item over time. It is often expressed as the rate of appreciation.

Arc – See *Edge*.

Area – The amount of surface enclosed by the boundaries of the shape.

Asset – Item that is of value to the owner.

Association – A connection or relationship between the variables of function.

Asymptote – A line that the curve approaches by getting closer and closer to it but never reaching it.

Axis of symmetry – A vertical line that divides the shape into two congruent or equal halves.

B

Backward scanning – The process of calculating the latest starting time (LST).

BASIX – Building Sustainability Index (BASIX) is a scheme to regulate the energy efficient of residential buildings.

Bearing – The direction one object is from another object. See *Compass bearing* and *True bearing*.

Biannually – Every six months or twice a year.

Bias – When events are not equally likely.

Bimodal – Data with two modes or peaks.

Bivariate data – The data relating to two variables that have both been measured on the same set of items or individuals.

Blood alcohol content (BAC) – A measure of the amount of alcohol in your blood.

Bonus – An extra payment or gift earned as reward for achieving a goal.

Book value – See *Salvage value*.

Box plot – See *Box-and-whisker plot*.

Box-and-whisker plot – A graph that uses five-number summary of a numerical dataset.

Braking distance – The distance travelled by the vehicle after the driver presses the brake.

Break-even point – The point of intersection when income equals costs in some practical problems.

Budget – A plan used to manage money by listing a person's income and expenditure.

Building plan – See *House plan*.

C

Calorie – A measurement for food energy.

Capacity – The amount of liquid within a solid figure or the weights on a directed graph of a flow problem.

Car running costs – Car costs such as maintenance, repairs, fuel, improvements, parking, tolls, car washes and fines.

Casual rate – An amount paid for each hour of casual work.

Categorical data – The data that is divided into categories such as hair colour. It uses words not numbers.

Causation – Indicates that one event is the result of the occurrence of another event (or variable).

Census – Collecting data from the whole population.

Circuit – A walk with no repeated edges that starts and ends at the same vertex.

Class centre – Median or middle score of a class in a grouped frequency distribution.

Closed cylinder – A cylinder with both circular bases. See *Open cylinder*.

Coefficient – The number in front of a particular letter in an algebraic expression. For example, the term $3y$ has a coefficient of 3.

Collecting data – A process that involves deciding what to collect, locating it and collecting it.

Commission – A payment for services, mostly as a percentage of the value of the goods sold.

Compass bearing – A bearing that uses the four directions of the compass (north, south, east and west) such as N37°E.

Compass radial survey – See *Radial survey*.

Complementary event – The outcomes that are not members of the event.

Composite shape – Two or more plane shapes.

Composite solid – Two or more common solids.

Compound interest – Interest calculated from the initial amount borrowed or principal plus any interest that has been earned. It calculates interest on the interest.

Compounding period – The length of time between interest payments in a compound interest investment.

Cone – A solid figure, with a circular base, that tapers to a point.

Connected graph – A graph is connected if every vertex in the graph is accessible from every other vertex in the graph along a path formed by the edges of the graph.

Connector problem – Problems using the minimal spanning tree to the find least cost to link locations or objects.

Constant of variation – The rate at which two quantities vary.

Continuous data – Numerical data obtained when quantities are measured rather than counted.

Conversion graph – A graph used to change one quantity from one unit to another unit.

Coordinated universal time (UTC) – See *Greenwich Mean Time*.

Correlation – Strength of the relationship between two variables.

Correlation coefficient – See *Pearson's correlation coefficient*.

Cosine ratio – The ratio of the adjacent side to the hypotenuse in a right-angled triangle.

Cosine rule – Trigonometric rule that relates the sides and angles in a triangle. It is used to solve triangle problems involving three sides and one angle.

Crashing – The recalculation of the minimum completion time for the project after the conditions of an activity within a project have changed.

Credit card – A small plastic card used to buy goods and services and pay for them later.

Credit card statement – Information sent to the credit card user each month. It includes an account number, opening balance, new charges, payments, refunds, reward points, payment due data, minimum payment and closing balance.

Critical path – The sequence of activities that cannot be delayed without affecting the overall completion time of the project.

Critical path analysis – A technique that identifies the activities required to complete a project, the time necessary to complete each activity and the relationships between the activities.

Cross-section – The intersection of a solid with a plane.

Cumulative frequency – The frequency of the score plus the frequency of all the scores less than that score. It is the progressive total of the frequencies.

Cumulative frequency histogram – A histogram with equal intervals of the scores on the horizontal axis and the cumulative frequencies associated with these intervals shown by vertical rectangles.

Cumulative frequency polygon – A line graph constructed by joining the top right-hand corner of the rectangles in a cumulative frequency histogram.

Cut – An imaginary line across a directed graph that completely separates the source from the sink.

Cycle – A walk with no repeated vertices that starts and ends at the same vertex.

Cylinder – A prism with a circular base. See *Open cylinder* and *Closed cylinder*.

D

Data – Raw scores. Information before it is organised.

Dataset – Collection or group of scores.

Decile – Divides an ordered dataset into 10 equal groups.

Declining-balance depreciation – A method of depreciation when the value of an item. decreases by a fixed percentage each time period.

Deduction – A regular amount of money subtracted from a person's wage or salary.

Degree – A unit for measuring angles or the number of edges that are connected to a vertex in a network diagram.

Dependent variable – A variable that depends on the number substituted for the independent variable.

Direct proportion – See *Direct variation*.

Direct variation – Relationship between two variables when one variable depends directly on another variable.

Directed network – A network whose edges have arrows and travel is only possible in the direction of the arrows.

Discrete data – The data obtained when a quantity is counted. It can only take exact numerical values.

Displaying data – A process that involves the presentation of the data and information.

Distributive law – A rule for expanding grouping symbols by multiplying each term inside the grouping symbol by the number or term outside the grouping symbol.

Dividend – A payment given as an amount per share or a percentage of the issued price.

Dividend yield – The annual dividend by the share's market price and expressed as a percentage.

Dot plot – A graph that consists of a number line with each data point marked by a dot. When several data points have the same value, the points are stacked above each other.

Double stem-and-leaf plot – A stem-and-leaf plot that uses two sets of similar data together.

Double time – A penalty rate that pays the employee twice the normal hourly rate.

Dummy activity – An imaginary activity that is required if two activities share some, but not all, of their immediate predecessors.

Duration – The length of time for an activity or task.

E

Earliest starting time (EST) – The earliest time any activity can be started after all prior activities have been completed.

Edge – The line that connects the vertices in a network diagram.

Elevation – A view of an object from one side such as a front elevation or side elevation.

Elimination method – A process to solve simultaneous equations by eliminating one of the unknown pronumerals by adding or subtracting the two equations.

Energy – The capacity or power to do work.

Energy consumption – The amount of energy consumed per unit of time.

Enlargement – A similar figure drawn larger than the original figure.

Equally likely outcomes – The outcomes of an event that have the same chance of occurring.

Equation – A mathematical statement that says that two things are equal.

Equator – Imaginary horizontal line that divides the earth into two hemispheres. Latitude of the equator is $0°$.

Eulerian circuit – A circuit that uses every edge of a network graph exactly once.

Eulerian trail – A trail that uses every edge of a graph exactly once.

Evaluate – Work out the exact value of an expression.

Expand – Remove the grouping symbols.

Expected frequency – The number of times that a particular event should occur.

Exponential decay – Quantity decreases rapidly according to the function $y = a^{-x}$.

Exponential function – A curve whose equation has an x as the power (e.g. 3^x). It is defined by the general rule $y = a^x$ and $y = a^{-x}$ where $a > 0$.

Exponential growth – Quantity increases rapidly according to the function $y = a^x$.

Exponential model – A practical situation described mathematically using an exponential function. The quantity usually experiences fast growth or decay.

Expression – A mathematical statement written in numbers and symbols.

Extrapolation – Predicting values outside the range of the dataset.

F

Factorise – To break up an expression into a product of its factors.

Field diagram – A diagram used to calculate the area of irregularly shaped blocks of land.

Five-number summary – A summary of a dataset consisting of the lower extreme, lower quartile, median, upper quartile and upper extreme.

Flat interest – See *Simple interest*.

Flat rate loan – A loan that uses simple interest.

Float time – The amount of time that a task in a project network can be delayed without causing a delay to subsequent tasks. It is calculated by subtracting the earliest start time from the latest start time.

Flow capacity – See *Maximum flow*.

Flow problem – A problem that involves the transfer or flow of material from one point (source) to another point (sink).

Formula – A mathematical relationship between two or more variables.

Fortnight – Two weeks or 14 days.

Forward scanning – The process of calculating the earliest starting time (EST).

Frequency – The number of times a certain event occurs.

Frequency distribution – See *Frequency table*.

Frequency histogram – A histogram with equal intervals of the scores on the horizontal axis and the frequencies associated with these intervals shown by vertical rectangles.

Frequency polygon – A line graph constructed by joining the midpoints at the tops of the rectangles of a frequency histogram.

Frequency table – A table that lists the outcomes and how often (frequency) each outcome occurs.

Fuel consumption – The number of litres of fuel a motor vehicle uses to travel 100 kilometres.

Fuel consumption rate – The number of litres of fuel a vehicle uses to travel 100 kilometres.

Future value – The sum of money contributed plus the compound interest earned.

G

General form – A linear equation written in the form $ax + by + c = 0$.

Goods and Services Tax (GST) – A tax added to the purchase price of each item. The GST rate in Australia is 10% of the purchase price of the item except for basic food items and some medical expenses.

Gradient – The steepness or slope of the line. It is calculated by dividing the vertical rise by the horizontal run.

Gradient-intercept formula – A linear equation written in the form $y = mx + c$.

Greenwich Mean Time – Time at the Greenwich meridian.

Greenwich meridian – An imaginary vertical line that passes through the town of Greenwich (London). The longitude of the Greenwich meridian is $0°$.

Gross income – The total amount of money earned from all sources. It includes interest, profits from shares or any payment received throughout the year.

Gross pay – The total of an employee's pay including allowances, overtime pay, commissions and bonuses.

Grouped data – Data organised into small groups rather than as individual scores.

Grouping symbol – Symbols used to indicate the order of operations such as parentheses ( ) and brackets [ ].

H

Hamiltonian cycle – A Hamiltonian path that starts and finishes at the same vertex.

Hamiltonian path – A path that passes through every vertex of a graph once and only once.

Heart rate – The number of heart beats per minute (bpm).

Heron's formula – A rule used to find the area of a triangle given the lengths of three sides.

Histogram – A graph using columns to represent frequency or cumulative frequency. See *Frequency histogram* and *Cumulative frequency histogram*.

House plan – A horizontal section cut through the building showing the walls, windows, door openings, fittings and appliances.

Hyperbola – A curve graphed from a reciprocal function.

Hyperbolic function – See *Reciprocal function*.

Hypotenuse – A side in right-angled triangle opposite the right angle. It is the longest side.

I

Immediate predecessor – The activity or task coming immediately before the current task or activity.

Income tax – A tax paid on income received.

Independent variable – A variable that does not depend on another variable for its value.

Index form – See *Index notation*.

Index notation – A method to write expressions in a shorter way such as $a \times a = a^2$.

Inflation – A rise in the price of goods and services or Consumer Price Index (CPI). It is often expressed as annual percentage.

Inflation rate – The annual percentage change in the Consumer Price Index (CPI).

Intercept – The position where the line cuts the axes.

Interest – The amount paid for borrowing money or the amount earned for lending money.

Interest rate – The rate at which interest is charged or paid. It is usually expressed as a percentage.

International date line – An imaginary line through the Pacific ocean that corresponds to 180° longitude.

Interpolation – Predicting values within the range of the dataset.

Interquartile range – The difference between the first quartile and third quartile.

Inverse proportion – See *Inverse variation*.

Inverse variation – Relationship between two variables when one variable increases while the other variable decreases.

Isomorphic graphs – Two or more different-looking graphs that can contain the same information.

K

Kilojoules (kJ) – Internationally accepted measurement for food energy.

Königsberg bridge problem – A network problem to determine if the seven bridges in Königsberg could all be crossed only once during a single trip that starts and finishes at the same place.

L

Latest starting time (LST) – The latest time any activity can be started after all prior activities have been completed.

Latitude – The angle or angular distance north or south of the equator.

Legal fee – Costs in the legal processing of a property.

Like term – Terms with exactly the same pronumerals such as $3a$ and $6a$.

Limit of reading – The smallest unit on measuring instrument.

Line of best fit – A straight line used to approximately model the linear relationship between two variables.

Linear association – A connection between the variables of function that results in the points on a scatterplot following a linear pattern.

Linear equation – An equation whose variables are raised to the power of 1.

Linear function – A function that when graphed on a number plane is a straight line.

Linear modelling – A mathematical description of a practical situation using a linear function.

Linear regression – The process of fitting a straight line to the data.

Loan application fee – Initial costs in processing a loan application.

Loan establishment fee – See *Loan application fee*.

Loan repayment – The amount of money to be paid at regular intervals over the time period.

Longitude – The angle or angular distance east or west of the Greenwich meridian.

Loop – Edge that starts and ends at the same vertex.

Lower extreme – Lowest score in the dataset.

Lower quartile – The lowest 25% of the scores in the dataset.

M

Mass – The amount of matter within an object.

Maximum flow – The largest amount of material that can be transferred from one point to another.

Maximum-flow minimum-cut theorem – The flow through a network cannot exceed the value of any cut in the network and that the maximum flow equals the value of the minimum cut.

Mean – A measure of the centre. It is calculated by summing all the scores and dividing by the number of scores.

Measurement – Determining the size of a quantity.

Measures of central tendency – Also known as measures of location. The most common measures are mean, median and mode.

Measures of spread – Measures of spread include range, interquartile range and standard deviation.

Median – The middle score or value. To find the median, list all the scores in increasing order and select the middle one.

Medicare levy – An additional charge to support Australia's universal health care system.

Meridians of longitude – Great imaginary circles east and west of the Greenwich meridian.

Method of least squares – A line of best fit that minimises the sum of the squares of the vertical distance (or residual).

Minimum completion time – The least amount of time it takes to complete a project.

Minimum spanning tree – A spanning tree of minimum length. It connects all the vertices together with the minimum total weighting for the edges.

Minute – A measure of time or an angle. There are sixty minutes in one hour and one degree.

Modality – The number of modes occurring in a set of data.

Mode – The score that occurs the most. It is the score with the highest frequency.

Modelling – See *Algebraic modelling*.

Monthly – Every month or twelve times a year.

Mortgage – A loan given to buy a house or unit.

Multi-stage event – Two or more events such as tossing a coin and rolling a die.

Multimodal – Data with many modes or peaks.

N

Negative association – Linear association between the variables with a negative gradient.

Negatively skewed – Data more on the right side. The long tail is on the left side (negative side).

Net of a solid – A drawing consisting of plane shapes that can be folded to form the solid.

Net pay – The amount remaining after deductions have been subtracted from the gross pay.

Network – A term to describe a group or system of interconnected objects. It consists of vertices and edges that indicate a path or route between two objects.

Network diagram – A representation of a group of objects called vertices that are connected together by line.

Nominal data – Categorical data whose name does not indicate order.

Non-linear association – A connection between the variables of function that results in the points on a scatterplot following a curved pattern.

Non-traversable graph – A network diagram that is not traversable. (See *Traversable graph*)

Normal distribution – Data with the same mean, mode and median.

Number pattern – A sequence of numbers formed using a rule. Each number in the pattern is called a term.

O

Offset survey – A survey involving the measurement of distances along a suitable diagonal or traverse. The perpendicular distances from the traverse to the vertices of the shape are called the offsets.

Open cylinder – A cylinder without a circular base. It is the curved part of the cylinder.

Opposite side – A side in right-angled triangle opposite the reference angle.

Ordinal data – Categorical data whose name does indicate order.

Organising data – A process that arranges, represents and formats data. It is carried out after the data is collected.

Outcome – A possible result in a probability experiment.

Outlier – Data values that appear to stand out from the main body of a dataset.

Overtime – Extra payments when a person works beyond the normal working day.

P

Parallel box-and-whisker plot – A box-and-whisker plot that uses two sets of similar data together.

Parallel lines – Two or more straight lines that do not intersect. The gradient of parallel lines are equal.

Parallel of latitude – Small imaginary circles north and south of the equator.

Pareto chart – A graph that combines a frequency histogram and cumulative frequency line graph.

Path – A walk with no repeated vertices.

Pay As You Go (PAYG) – Tax deducted from a person's wage or salary throughout the year.

Pearson's correlation coefficient (r) – A measure of the correlation. It is a number between -1 and $+1$.

Per annum – Per year.

Percentage change – The increase or decrease in the quantity as a percentage of the original amount of the quantity.

Percentage error – The maximum error in a measurement as a percentage of the measurement given.

Percentile – Divides an ordered dataset into 100 equal groups.

Piecework – A fixed payment for work completed.

Plan – A view of an object from the top.

Plane-table radial survey – See *Radial survey*.

Population – The entire dataset.

Population – The entire dataset.

Population standard deviation – A calculation for the standard deviation that uses all the data or the entire population. (σ_n)

Positive association – Linear association between the variables with a positive gradient.

Positively skewed – Data more on the left side. The long tail is on the right side (positive side).

Power – The rate at which energy is generated or consumed.

Precedence table – See *Activity chart*.

Prefix – The first part of a word. In measurement it is used to indicate the size of a quantity.

Present value – The amount of money if invested now would equal the future value of the annuity.

Prim's algorithm – A set of rules to determine a minimum spanning tree for a graph.

Principal – The initial amount of money borrowed.

Prism – A solid shape that has the same cross-section for its entire height.

Probability – The chance of something happening. The probability of the event is calculated by dividing the number of favourable outcomes by the total number of outcomes.

Pronumeral – A letter or symbol used to represent a number.

Pyramid – A solid shape with a plane shape as its base and triangular sides meeting at an apex.

Pythagoras theorem – The square of the hypotenuse is equal to the sum of the squares of the other two sides. $h^2 = a^2 + b^2$

Q

Quadrant – Quarter of a circle. The arc of a quadrant measures 90°.

Quadratic function – A curve whose equation has an x squared (x^2). It is defined by the general rule $y = ax^2 + bx + c$ where a, b and c are numbers.

Quadratic model – A practical situation using a function in the form $y = ax^2 + bx + c$ where a, b and c are numbers. Quadratic functions are graphed to make a curve in the shape of a parabola.

Quantile – A set of values that divide an ordered dataset into equal groups.

Quantitative data – Numerical data. It is data that has been measured.

Quarterly – Every three months or four times a year.

Quartile – Divides an ordered dataset into 4 equal groups. See *Upper quartile* and *Lower quartile*.

Questionnaire – A series of questions to gather specific information.

R

Radial survey – A survey that involves measuring the angles and sides from a central point.

Random sample – A sample that occurs when members of the population have an equal chance of being selected.

Range – The difference between the highest and lowest scores. It is a simple way of measuring the spread of the data.

Rate – A comparison of different quantities in definite order.

Rate of interest – See *Interest rate*.

Ratio – A number used to compare amounts of the same units in a definite order such as 3:4.

Reaction distance – The distance travelled by the vehicle when a driver decides to brake to when the driver first commences braking.

Reciprocal function – A curve whose equation has a variable in the denominator such as $\frac{1}{x}$. It is defined by the general rule $y = \frac{k}{x}$ where k is a number.

Reciprocal model – A practical situation using a function in the form $y = \frac{k}{x}$ where k is a number. Reciprocal functions are graphed to make a curve in the shape of a hyperbola.

Recurrence relation – When each successive application uses the resultant value of the previous application to generate the next value.

Reducing-balance loan – A loan calculated on the balance owing not on the initial amount of money borrowed.

Reduction – A similar figure drawn smaller than the original figure.

Relative error – A measurement calculated by dividing the limit of reading (absolute error) by the actual measurement.

Relative frequency – The frequency of the event divided by the total number of frequencies. It estimates the chances of something happening or the probability of an event.

Retainer – A fixed payment usually paid to a person receiving a commission.

Royalty – A payment for the use of intellectual property such as book or song. It is calculated as a percentage of the revenue or profit received from its use.

S

Salary – A payment for a year's work which is divided into equal monthly, fortnightly or weekly payments.

Salvage value – The depreciated value of an item.

Sample – A part of the population.

Sample space – The set of all possible outcomes.

Sample standard deviation – A calculation for the standard deviation when the dataset is a sample (σ_{n-1}).

Scale drawing – A drawing that represents the actual object.

Scale factor – The ratio of the size of the drawing to the actual size of the object.

Scatterplot – A graph of the ordered pairs of numbers. Each ordered pair is a dot on the graph.

Scheduling – Allocating time to the completion of activities in a project and determining the order of those activities.

Scientific notation – See *Scientific notation*.

Sector – Part of a circle between two radii and an arc.

Self-selected sample – Members of the population volunteer themselves.

Semicircle – Half a circle. The arc of a semicircle measures 180°.

Share – A part ownership in a company.

Shortest path – A path between two vertices in a network where the sum of the weights of its edges is minimised.

Significant figures – A statement to specify the accuracy of a number. It is often used to round a number.

Similar figure – Figures that have exactly the same shape but they are different sizes.

Simple interest – A fixed percentage of the amount invested or borrowed and is calculated on the original amount.

Simulation – A mathematical model that represents a real experiment or situation.

Simultaneous equations – Two or more equations whose values are common to all the equations. It is the point of intersection of the equations.

Sine ratio – The ratio of the opposite side to the hypotenuse in a right-angled triangle.

Sine rule – Trigonometric rule that relates the sides and angles in a triangle. It is used to solve triangle problems involving two sides and two angles.

Sink – Ending point of a flow problem.

Skewed data – Data that is not symmetrical. See *Symmetrical*, *Positively skewed* and *Negatively skewed*.

Slope – See *Gradient*.

Smoothness – Data whose graph has no breaks or jagged sections.

Source – Starting point of a flow problem.

Spanning tree – A tree that connects all of the vertices in the graph.

Speed – A rate that compares the distance travelled to the time taken.

Sphere – A perfectly round object such as a ball.

Stamp duty – Tax paid to the government when registering or transferring a motor vehicle.

Standard deviation – A measure of the spread of data about the mean. It is an average of the squared deviations of each score from the mean.

Standard drink – Any drink containing 10 grams of alcohol.

Standard form – A number between 1 and 10 multiplied by a power of ten. It is used to write very large or very small numbers more conveniently.

Standard notation – See *Scientific notation*.

Standardised score – See *z-score*.

Statistical investigation – A process of gathering statistics. It involves four steps: collecting data, organising data, summarising and displaying data, and analysing data.

Stem-and-leaf plot – A method of displaying data where the first part of a number is written in the stem and the second part of the number is written in the leaves.

Stopping distance – The distance a vehicle travels from the time a driver sees an event occurring to the time the vehicle is brought to stop.

Straight-line depreciation – The value of an item decreases by the same amount each period.

Strata – A group within a population that reflects the characteristics of the entire population.

Stratified sample – A sample using categories or strata of a population. Members from each category are randomly selected. For example, one student is selected from each Year 7, 8, 9, 10, 11 and 12.

Strength of an association – A measure of how much scatter there is in the scatterplot.

Subject of the formula – When a formula or equation has a pronumeral with no numbers on the left-hand side of the equal sign, such as $C = 40n + 75$, then C is the subject of the formula.

Substitution – Involves replacing the pronumeral in an algebraic expression with one or more numbers.

Substitution method – A process to solve simultaneous equations by substituting one variable from one equation into the other equation.

Summary statistic – A number such as the mode, mean or median that describes the data.

Superannuation – Money invested while you are working, so you can enjoy a regular income later in life when you retire.

Superannuation fund – Type of annuity where money is invested for a person's retirement.

Surface area – The sum of the area of each surface of the solid.

Symmetrical – Data that forms a mirror image of itself when folded in the 'middle' along a vertical axis.

Symmetry – Data evenly balanced about the centre.

Systematic sample – A sample that divides the population into a structured sample size. For example, sorting the names of people in alphabetical order and selecting every 5th person.

T

Tangent ratio – The ratio of the opposite side to the adjacent side in a right-angled triangle.

Taxable income – The gross income minus any allowable deductions.

Time, 24-hour – Time of day written in form hh:mm (hours:minutes).

Time zone – A region of the earth that has a uniform standard time or local time.

Time-and-a-half – A penalty rate that pays the employee one and half times the normal hourly rate.

Timetable – A list of times at which possible events or actions are intended to take place.

Trail – A walk with no repeated edges.

Trapezoidal rule – A formula to estimate the area of a shape with an irregular boundary.

Traversable graph – A network diagram with a trail that includes every edge.

Traverse survey – See *Offset survey*.

Tree – A connected graph that contains no cycles, multiple edges or loops.

Tree diagram – A technique used to list the outcomes in a probability experiment. It shows each event as a branch of the tree.

Trigonometry – A branch of mathematics involving the measurement of triangles.

True bearing – A bearing using the angle measured clockwise from the north, around to the required direction, such as 120°.

U

Undirected network – A network whose edges have no arrows and travel is possible in both directions.

Unimodal – Data with only one mode or peak.

Unitary method – A technique used to solve a problem that involves finding one unit of an amount by division.

Upper extreme – Highest score in the dataset.

Upper quartile – The highest 25% of the scores in the dataset.

V

Valuation fee – Costs in the assessment of the market value of a property.

Value Added Tax (VAT) – A tax added to the purchase price of each item. VAT is used in many countries with the rate ranging from 2% to 25%.

Variable – A symbol used to represent a number or group of numbers.

Vertex – A point (or dot) in a network diagram at which lines of pathways intersect or the turning point of a parabola.

Volume – The amount of space occupied by a three-dimensional object.

W

Wage – A payment for work that is calculated on an hourly basis.

Walk – A connected sequence of the edges showing a route between vertices where the edges and vertices may be visited multiple times.

Watt (W) – The International System of Units (SI) unit of power and is equal to one joule per second.

Weighted edge – The edge of a network diagram that has a number assigned to it that implies some numerical value such as cost, distance or time.

Weighted graph – A network diagram that has weighted edges.

X

x-intercept – The point at which a graph cuts the x-axis.

Y

y-intercept – The point at which a graph cuts the y-axis.

Z

z-score – A standardised score used to compare scores in a normal distribution.

Answers

Chapter 1

Exercise 1A

1a $25/h **b** 12 m/s
c 70 L/h **d** $3.25/h
e 60 c/kg **f** 10.5 km/L
g 300 rev/min **h** 5°/h
2a 5 km/L **b** 1.5 m/s
c $128 /m **d** 112 L/min
e 6 mg/g **f** 14 g/L
g 2.5 g/m² **h** 15 mL/min
3a $12.50 **b** $196
c $175 **d** $195
e $2.90 **f** 36 km
g 12 mL **h** 20 mL
4a 20 km **b** 200 km
c 300 km **d** 95 km/h
e 16.96 km/h **f** 140 h
5a 654 m/s **b** 200 cm/s
c 880 mm/h **d** 920 m/min
e 400 m/s **f** 0.0575 km/s
g 6090 mg/mL
h 4 800 000 mL/kL
6a $337.50 **b** 32
c $78 000
7 6 h
8 120 L
9 18 overs
10 2.5 h
11 17.5 km
12 25 weeks
13 6.25 kg
14 200 s
15a 3 km **b** 180 km
16a 17 m/s **b** 72 m/s
17 36 km/h
18a $183 **b** 11 000 MJ
19a $11/$1000 **b** $10.80/$1000
20a $13.50 **b** 370 km
21a 40 212 km **b** 1676 km/h
c 129 s

22a 600 km **b** 6.5 L/100 km
23a 893 km/h **b** 171 kL

Exercise 1B

1a 200 **b** 190 **c** 180
d 170 **e** 160 **f** 150
g 140 **h** 130 **i** 120
2a-c

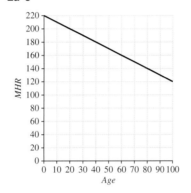

d 195 **e** 182
f 65 **g** 45
3a 130–170
b 123.5–161.5
c 117–153
d 110.5–144.5
e 104–136
f 97.5–127.5
g 91–119
h 84.5–110.5
i 78–102
4a 77–82 **b** 60–64
c Below average **d** Athlete
5 Investigation
6 Investigation
7a 91 **b** 55 **c** 1406
d 70.3 **e** 10.5 **f** 8.1

Exercise 1C

1a 46.2 kWh **b** $13.02
2a $49.63 **b** $50.48 **c** $68.85
3a 4.2 kWh **b** $1.26
4 $2.03

5a $160.02 **b** $171
c $331.02
6a 43.8 kWh **b** $10.98
7 $5.48
8a 5% **b** 69%
c $202 860 000 **d** $64 680 000
e $14 700 000
9a 21 723
b

Type	Number	Percentage
No active heating system	6332	29%
Gas fixed flued heater	2333	11%
Gas hydronic system	327	2%
1-phase air-conditioning	3357	15%
3-phase air-conditioning	6867	32%
Air-conditioning ducted	872	4%
Wood heating	1635	8%

c 3-phase air-conditioning
d 11 096
e

- No active heating system
- Gas fixed flued heater
- Gas hydronic system
- 1-phase air-conditioning
- 3-phase air-conditioning
- Air-conditioning ducted
- Wood heating

10a 10.8 kWh **b** 1750 Wh
c 32 h **d** 40 h
11a $122.76 **b** $147.04
c 8.3% **d** 4200 MJ
e 2508 MJ **f** $150.34
12 Investigation

Exercise 1D

1a 8.75   **b** 6.15   **c** 5.8
d 11.4   **e** 6.7   **f** 3.8
2a 316 L   **b** 77 L   **c** 212 L
d 51 L   **e** 57 L   **f** 24 L
g 267 L
3a 450 km   **b** 36 L   **c** $43.20
4 480 km
5 Once. Distance required is 840 km. Distance travelled on one tank of petrol is 562.5 km.
6a $18.28   **b** $23.87   **c** $5.59
7a 1935.84   **b** $2688
   c $4623.84   **d** $6177.60
8a 44.55
   b 66.6
   c Eden 2316.6 L, Toby 3463.2 L
   d $3474.90
   e $2943.72
   f 5
9 Research

Exercise 1E

1a 5:1   **b** 1:4   **c** 3:2
   d 7:15   **e** 2:3   **f** 7:2
   g 3:1   **h** 3:2   **i** 1:3
   j 1:2:1   **k** 1:2:4   **l** 9:3:1
2a 4:3   **b** 1:4   **c** 7:2
3a 2:5   **b** 1:8   **c** 1:5
   d 4:1   **e** 6:1   **f** 20:1
   g 10:3   **h** 1:6   **i** 40:9
4a 7:5   **b** 5:7   **c** 7:12
5 1:5
6 9:5
7 2:5
8a $2.56   **b** $25.60
   c $35.84   **d** $15.36
9a $14.20   **b** $56.80
   c $85.20   **d** $142.00
10 1:4
11a 5:2   **b** 14:9   **c** 3:4
   d 5:1   **e** 1:2   **f** 10:9
   g 4:3   **h** 2:3   **i** 9:10
12a 2:1   **b** 1:3   **c** $2a$:1
   d 1:2   **e** y:4   **f** $7m$:1
   g 1:5   **h** 2:3y **i** $8a$:b
13 10:7:5

14a 3:2   **b** $900   **c** $1740
15a 1.5:1   **b** 3.2:1
   c $\frac{4}{3}$:1   **d** 0.25:1
16a 1:0.5   **b** 1:1.875
   c 1:4   **d** 1:3.5
17 $6.95

Exercise 1F

1a $70:$30   **b** $40:$60
   c $55:$45   **d** $28:$32:$40
2a 160:80   **b** 144:96
   c 40:200   **d** 140:100
3a $16:$4   **b** $14:$6   **c** $5:$10
   d 33 drinks:44 drinks
   e 35 lollies:65 lollies
   f 20 kg:25 kg
   g 100 books:60 books
   h 80 pencils:280 pencils
   i 12.5 g:37.5 g
   j 32 km:28 km
4 150 g
5 5026
6a $120 000   **b** $100 000
   c $20 000
7 6 km^2
8 $150
9 4200
10a 3/5 L or 0.6 L   **b** 7.5 L
11a $218 750   **b** $156 250
   c $125 000
12 150 g of flour and 100 g of sugar
13 3 t and 5.5 t
14 A–230 t, B–322 t, C–230 t
15 $3\frac{1}{8}$ or 3.125 kg
16a 15 cm   **b** 6 cm
17 $45
18 29.16 mm
19 4 mL
20 A–19 575, B–52 200, C–20 880

Exercise 1G

1a 2 m   **b** 1 m   **c** 3.4 m
   d 2.8 m   **e** 8.5 m   **f** 4.9 m
2a 80 mm   **b** 30 mm
   c 1.6 mm   **d** 140 mm
   e 2 mm   **f** 55 mm

3a 1:2   **b** 1:50
   c 1:300 000
4a 200 m   **b** 100 m   **c** 50 m
   d 10 m   **e** 34 m   **f** 80 m
5a 37.5 km   **b** 675 km
6a 10 mm   **b** 16 mm   **c** 20 mm
   d 24 mm   **e** 30 mm   **f** 48 mm
7 Map distance is 7 mm
8a 1125 mm or 1.125 m
   b 0.04 m or 40 mm
9a 5:6400 or 1:1280 (approximation)
   b Height of the antenna is approximately 32 m
10a 10 mm   **b** 24 mm
   c 40 mm   **d** 600 mm
   e 80 mm   **f** 480 mm
11a 1:1000   **b** 28 m
   c 13 m   **d** 10 m
12a 1:1000   **b** 200 m
   c 15 m

Exercise 1H

1a Plan

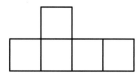

Front elevation

Side elevation

b Plan

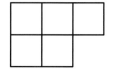

Front elevation

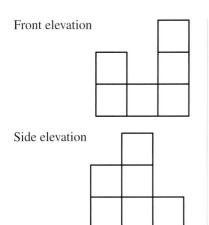

Side elevation

2a Triangular prism
 b Square pyramid
 c Cylinder
 d Cube
 e Cone

3

	Plan	Front elevation	Side elevation
a	▭ (rectangle divided)	△	▭
b	◯	▭	▭
c	⊠	△	△
d	◯	◯	◯
e	◯	▽	▽
f	□	□	□

4a Ensuite or bathroom
 b
 c
 d Walk In Robe
5a 3150 × 3700 or 3.15 m by 3.7 m
 b (diagram)
 c (diagram)

d Refrigerator   **e** Pantry
6a 3300 × 2800 or 3.3 m by 2.8 m
 b (diagram)
 c Built In Wardrobe
 d 3.3 m
 e 1:70
7a 4.15 × 3.80 m   **b**
 c 4.15 m   **d** 1:80
 e 1.12 × 0.72   **f** 15.77 m²
8a 3.6 m by 2.99 m
 b 4.94 m by 4.13 m
 c 1:165   **d** 7.92 m
 e 3 m²   **f** 9 m²
9a 2585 mm²
 b 2 585 000 000 mm³
 c 5 170 000 000 mm³
10a 14 m
 b 9 m
 c 1 m by 2 m
 d 200 cm by 160 cm
 e 32 000 cm²
 f 207 000 cm²
 g 300 000 cm²
11a 2.44 m   **b** 2.698 m
 c 22.5°   **d** 6
12a 14 m by 9 m
 b 126 m²
 c 25 m³
13a 1:250
 b 2.5 m by 5.0 m
 c 6.8 m by 7.5 m
 d 3.8 m by 3.8 m
 e 25 m²
 f $3500
14a 1:175   **b** 13.5 m
 c 90 m²   **d** 1000
 e Tiles will fit exactly into the
  three rooms and no breakage
  will occur.
 f 13.5 m³

Exercise 1I

1a 1.5 cm to 5000 cm or 1:333.33…
 b 183 m by 208 m
 c 153 m
 d 60 m
 e 137 m

 f 350 m
 g 4110 m²
2a 77 m   **b** 133 m
 c 83 m   **d** 432 m
 e 11 039 m²   **f** 157 m
3a 33 m
 b 10 m
 c 209 m
 d 3421 m²(3484 m²)
 e 5 m
 f 31 m
4 Student investigation
5a 25 500 m²
 b 6400 m²
 c 47 000 m²
6a 3584 m³   **b** 1890 m³
7 162 m³
8a 3600 m   **b** 1866 m
 c 2134 m   **d** 3734 m
 e 720 000 m²   **f** 213 200 m²
 g 266 800 m²
9a 1 m²   **b** 6 m²
 c 5 m²   **d** 13 m²
 e 10 m²
10a 16 800 m²   **b** 84 000 m³
11a 86 520 m³   **b** 893 mm

Review 1

Multiple-choice

1 A	**2** C	**3** D	**4** C	**5** B
6 C	**7** D	**8** A	**9** D	**10** A

Short-answer

1a $0.015/g
 b 240 m/min
 c 72 000 mm/min
 d 4.8 kg/mg
 e 14 000 000 mL/kg
 f 360 c/mg
2 $1015
3 350 km
4a $18.40   **b** $73.60
 c $5.52   **d** $12.88
 e $920   **f** $460
5 198
6 640 km

7a 5:1   **b** 2:3

c 4:1   **d** 2:3:6

e 4:3   **f** 7:11

g 3:1   **h** 3:2

8a $1473   **b** $1408

9 12.5 buckets of sand

10 154 cm

11a 1:300   **b** 1:60   **c** 1:2500

12 23 km

13a 80 mm   **b** 25 mm

c 1 mm   **d** 130 mm

e 0.4 mm   **f** 42.5 mm

14a 720 m   **b** 80 m

c 20 m   **d** 84 m

e 248 m   **f** 24 m

15a 1:120

b

c water closet or toilet

d 3 m by 2.4 m (approx.)

16a 450 m^3 **b** 1.62 m^3

Extended-response

17 Passengers have 16 boats and the crew have 6 boats.

18 $3\frac{1}{3}$ minutes

Chapter 2

Exercise 2A

1a interconnected

b edges or arcs

c vertex

d degree

e arrows

2a True   **b** False

c True   **d** True

e False   **f** False

g True

3a 5   **b** 6   **c** 2

d 3   **e** 3   **f** 1

g 3

4a 4   **b** 7   **c** 3

d 3   **e** 4   **f** 4

5a 2   **b** 3   **c** 2

d 3   **e** 10   **f** 5

6a 3   **b** 3

c 2   **d** 3

e 14   **f** 7

7a 2   **b** 3

c 3   **d** 2

e 10   **f** 5

8a 3   **b** 2

c 4   **d** 4

9a B   **b** A, D & E

c A, B, D & E   **d** C & F

10a A & B   **b** C, D & E

c C, D & E   **d** A & B

11a All vertices have a degree of 4

b All vertices have a degree of 4

c All 5 vertices have even degrees

d No vertices with odd degrees

12a 4   **b** 6

c 4   **d** 4

13a 4   **b** 7

c 6   **d** 2

e There are two vertices with odd degrees (A & C)

f There are two vertices with even degrees (B & D)

14a 8   **b** 14

c 3   **d** 5

e 3   **f** 2

g All 8 vertices have odd degrees

h No vertices with even degrees

15a 4   **b** 8

c Increase by two

d Increase by one

16

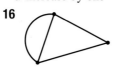

17 Because each edge must start and end at a vertex. It is a bit like shaking hands, there must be two hands at the end of each shake, even if you are shaking with yourself (a loop)

Exercise 2B

1a path   **b** trail

c path   **d** walk

e trail   **f** path

2a walk   **b** cycle

c path   **d** walk

e path   **f** walk

3a ii *G-K-L-S-E-K-M*

b i *K-E-G-M-L*

  ii *E-K-L-M*

c ii *E-S-K-L-M-K-E*

d i *K-E-G-K*

  iii *L-S-E-K-L*

4a Trail   **b** Cycle.

5a i traversable

  ii

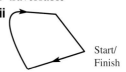

b i traversable

  ii

c i not traversable

  ii no circuit

6a i traversable

  ii

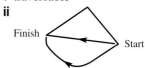

b i traversable

  ii

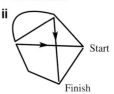

c i traversable

  ii

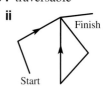

Exercise 2C

1a Graph 1 and 3 are connected. Graphs 2 and 4 are not connected.

b Graph 2 and 3 are connected. Graphs 1 and 4 are not connected.

2 There are many possible answers to this question. An example for each question is shown below.

a

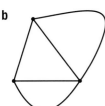

b

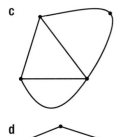

c

d

3 There are many possible answers to this question. An example for each question is shown below.

a

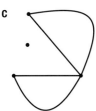

b

c

d

4a Graph 1 (Vertex C has degree 3 in graphs 2, 3 and 4 but degree 2

in graph 1. Graphs 2, 3, and 4 have the same edges.)

b Graph 2 (Vertex C has degree 2 in graphs 1, 3 and 4 but degree 3 in graph 2. Graphs 1, 3, and 4 have the same edges.)

5a Vertices are the train stations.

b Edges are the rail lines that connect the train stations.

c Yes. Every vertex in the graph is accessible from every other vertex.

d City circle – Central, Town hall, Wynyard, Circular Quay, St James, Museum and Martin Place.

e

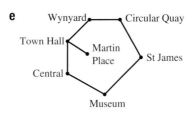

6a Vertices are the regional towns and cities, and other places where roads meet.

b Edges are the main roads.

c Yes. Every vertex in the graph is accessible from every other vertex.

d

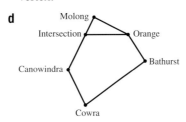

7a

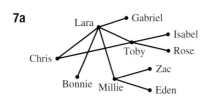

b The edges represent whether there is a friendship between the two students.

c Yes. Every vertex in the graph is accessible from every other vertex.

d Bonnie to Lara to Toby to Rose

8a

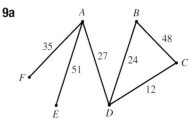

b Vertices are the names of the friends.

c Edges indicate time in minutes to walk between friends' homes.

d Alex and Max do not have a direct path between each others' homes.

e $1 + 2 + 4 + 2 = 9$ minutes

9a

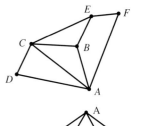

b Vertices are the cities A to F.

c Edges are the motorways.

d B and C are not linked to A.

e Travel from F to A and then from A to D.

f $35 + 27 = 62$ km

10 Different answers are possible. A possible solution is given below.

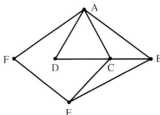

11

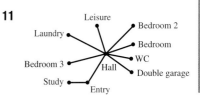

12

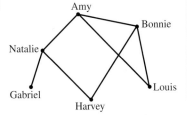

13

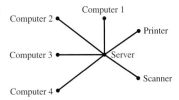

Exercise 2D

1a $\deg(A) = 3$, $\deg(B) = 4$, $\deg(C) = 2$, $\deg(D) = 4$, $\deg(E) = 3$

b Eulerian trails exist if the graph is connected and has exactly two vertices with an odd degree. Vertices A and E are the only vertices with odd degrees.

c Example: $A–B–E–D–B–C–D–A–E$

2a $\deg(A) = 2$, $\deg(B) = 2$, $\deg(C) = 4$, $\deg(D) = 2$, $\deg(E) = 2$

b Eulerian circuits exist if the graph is connected and every vertex of the graph has an even degree. All vertices are even.

c Example: $A–B–C–E–D–C–A$

3a Eulerian circuit: all vertices are even

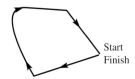

b Neither: more than two odd vertices

c Eulerian trail: two odd vertices, rest even

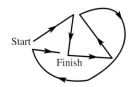

d Eulerian trail: two odd vertices, rest even

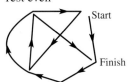

e Eulerian circuit: all vertices are even

f Eulerian trail: two odd vertices, rest even

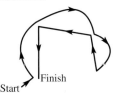

g Eulerian circuit: all vertices are even

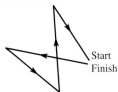

h Eulerian trail: two odd vertices, rest even

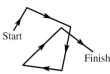

i Neither: more than two odd vertices

4a Yes, all vertices are even.

b Other routes are possible.

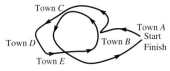

5a $A–B–D–C$

b Yes.　　**c** No

d A Hamiltonian path passes through every vertex of a graph once and only once.

e $A–D–B–C$

6a $A–C–F–E–D–B–A$

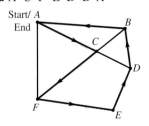

b Yes　　**c** No

d A Hamiltonian cycle is a Hamiltonian path that starts and finishes at the same vertex.

e $A–F–E–D–C–B–A$

7 Other answers are possible.

a $A–B–C–D–E–F–A$

b $A–B–C–D–E–A$

c $A–B–C–F–I–H–E–G–D–A$

d $F–E–D–A–B–C–F$

e $A–E–F–D–C–B–A$

f $A–F–E–D–C–B–G–A$

8a $C–D–E–B–A$. Hamiltonian path

b $E–A–B–C–D–E$. Hamiltonian cycle

9a Eulerian circuit: graph is connected and all vertices are even

b $K–M–G–D–E–G–K–E–S–K$.

10a $K–M–T–L–S–E–D–G–K$. Hamiltonian cycle

b $D–E–S–L–T–M–G–K$. Hamiltonian path

11a No, not all the vertices are even

b Several routes are possible. One is shown below.

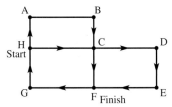

12 Several answers are possible. $W–A–F–E–D–B–C$

Exercise 2E

1a

b See graph bottom on previous page – the odd degree vertices are *B* and *A*

c Yes. Eulerian trails exist if the graph is connected and two of the vertices are odd.

d Multiple solutions exist. One example is:

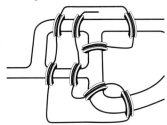

2a

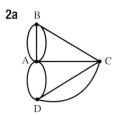

b There are no odd vertices.

c Yes. An Eulerian circuit exists if the graph is connected and every vertex is even.

d Many solutions exist. One example is:

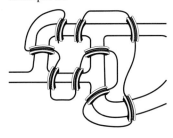

3a There are no odd vertices.

b Yes. An Eulerian circuit exists if every vertex is even.

c Many solutions exists. One example is:

A–B–C–D–B–H–D–E–F–G–A

d One example is:

A–B–H–D–B–C–D–E–F–G–A

4a i 9 min   **ii** 16 min

  iii 10 min   **iv** 11 min

  v 11 min

b *A–F–E–C–D*

c *A–F–E–D*

5a 9 flights   **b** 116

  c 950   **d** 6630

e Perth–Sydney–Melbourne

Perth–Sydney–Adelaide–Melbourne

Perth–Adelaide–Melbourne

Perth–Adelaide–Sydney–Melbourne

f 1680

g Sydney–Adelaide–Melbourne

Sydney–Adelaide–Perth–Melbourne

Sydney–Perth–Melbourne

Sydney–Perth–Adelaide–Melbourne

h 6630

6a

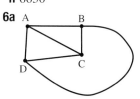

b An Eulerian trail does not exist. The graph has more than two odd vertices.

c One possible solution is circled.

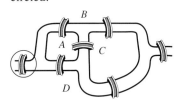

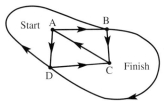

d The bridges can now be crossed only once in a single walk because an Eulerian trail now exists. The graph has two odd vertices and the rest are even. See the graph for a possible route.

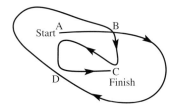

Exercise 2F

1a edges

  b length

  c spanning

  d eight

  e nine

2a 14

  b 6

  c Four vertices

  d Five vertices

3a Tree   **b** Tree

  c Not a tree   **d** Tree

  e Not a tree

  f Not a tree as it has a loop

4 Other answers are possible.

a

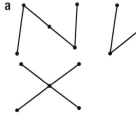

b

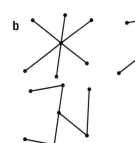

c

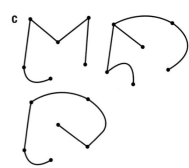

5a

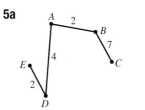

15 units

b

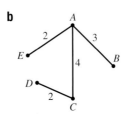

11 units

c

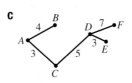

22 units

d

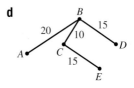

60 units

e

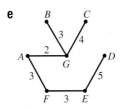

20 units

f

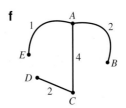

9 units

g

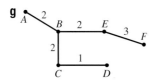

10 units

h

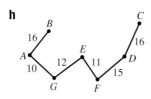

80 units

i

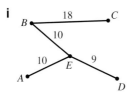

47 units

6

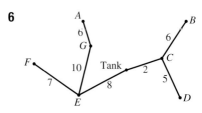

44 m

7

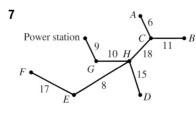

94 km

Exercise 2G

1a Town *B*, 7 km

  b Town *D*, 6 km

  c Town *C*, 8 km

  d Either town *E* or *F*, 9 km

  e Either town *E* or *F* (whichever was not selected for 1d), 7 km

  f 37 km

2a Town *C*, $8 million

  b Town *D*, $4 million

  c Town *B*, $5 million

  d Town *E*, $20 million

  e Town *F*, $8 million

  f Town *G*, $11 million

  g $56 million

3a Town *F*, 90 km.

  b Town *E*, 90 km.

  c Town *C*, 100 km.

  d Town *H*, 70 km.

  e Town *B*, 80 km.

  f Town *D*, 100 km.

  g Town *G*, 200 km.

  h 730 km

4a

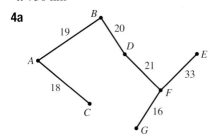

b 127 km

5a

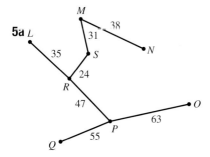

b 293 km

6a

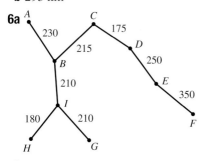

b 1820 m

Exercise 2H

1a 8 h	**b** 11 h
c 15 h	**d** 12 h
2a 20 m	**b** 30 m
c 35 m	**d** 25 m
3a $8	**b** $6
c $10	**d** $6
e $9	**f** $4
g $6	**h** $9

4a 5 min   **b** 5 min
c 10 min   **d** 7 min
e 8 min   **f** 8 min
5a 17 m   **b** 19 m
c 19 m   **d** 16 m
e 18 m   **f** 26 m
6a 34 km   **b** 37 km
c 56 km   **d** 64 km
e 22 km   **f** 28 km
g *A–E–F–G–I* or
A–C–F–G–I, 26 km
h *C–A–B–D* or *D–B–A–C*, 17 km
7a 64 min
b 64 min
c 77 min
d *A–B–C–E–F–D–A*, 63 min
e The shortest average time
may not be the best path for a
competitor. For example, if a
particular competitor is faster than
the average going uphill then they
could be quicker going through
the checkpoints with hills.
8a 145 min
b 220 min
c *A–D–E–F–G*, 110 min
d The shortest time in a train
journey may not be the best path
if the train is crowded and you
do not get a seat. The best path
could be to catch a train that
takes longer but you have a seat
on the train.
e 135 minutes, using the route
A–B–F–G

Review 2

Multiple-choice

1 *A*
2 C
3 D
4 B
5 C
6 B
7 A
8 A

Short-answer

1a 2
b 5
c 3
d 4
e 4
f 2
2a deg(*A*) = 1, deg(*B*) = 2,
deg(*C*) = 4, deg(*D*) = 2,
deg(*E*) = 4, deg(*F*) = 1
b Eulerian trails exist if the graph
is connected and has exactly
two vertices with an odd degree.
Vertices *A* and *F* are the only
vertices with odd degrees.
c *A–C–B–D–E–C–E–F* (other
solutions exist)
3a deg(*A*) = 2, deg(*B*) = 4,
deg(*C*) = 2, deg(*D*) = 4,
deg(*E*) = 4, deg(*F*) = 2
b Eulerian circuits exist if the
graph is connected and every
vertex has an even degree. All
vertices are even.
c *A–B–C–D–E–F–D–B–E–A*
(other solutions exist)
4a

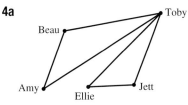

b Vertices are the names of the
players
c Amy & Ellie, Amy & Jett,
Beau & Ellie, Beau & Jett
5 24
6 56
7a 11 km
b 17 km
8 12

Extended-response

9a 750 m
b Yes, all vertices are even.
c 1270 m

Chapter 3

Exercise 3A

1a $424.36   **b** $35 372.71
c $70 710.87   **d** $3920.88
e $22 843.06   **f** $78 311.44
g $388 543.35   **h** $16 634.84
2 $17 640
3 $18 281.70
4 $7378
5a $9289.92   **b** $13 968.61
c $44 799.23
6 $101 011.72
7a $2800   **b** $3591
c $5600   **d** $9263
8 Investment B
9a $29 063.34   **b** $48 444.86
c $121 953.77   **d** $112 227.23
e $3243.49   **f** $55 621.16
g $189 862.19   **h** $46 543.55
10 $3542
11a $828.51   **b** $7147.51
c $1587.65   **d** $1272.62
e $583.20
12 Investment E
13a $925   **b** $5964
c $1304   **d** $15 421
e $2679
14 $4588.29
15a $25 531.63   **b** $9131.63
16 $57 747.51
17 $15 917.61
18 $7706.23
19a $362 803.68
b $363 879.35
c Interest is compounded monthly
compared with quarterly.

Exercise 3B

1a $I = 120n$
b

n	0	1	2	3	4	5
I	0	120	240	360	480	600

c,d Simple interest on $2000 at 6% p.a.

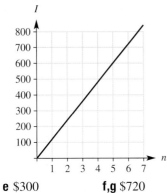

e $300   **f,g** $720

2a $I = 56n$

b

n	0	1	2	3	4	5	6
I	0	56	112	168	224	280	336

c,d Simple interest on $800 at 7% p.a.

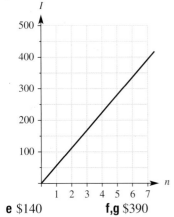

e $140   **f,g** $390

3a Simple interest on $1000

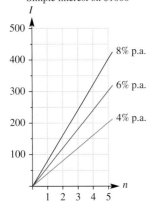

b i $200   **ii** $300   **iii** $400

c i $140   **ii** $210   **iii** $280

d i 5 years   **ii** 3.3 years

iii 2.5 years

4a $FV = 2000 \times (1.06)^n$

b $I = 2000(1.06)^n - 2000$

c

n	0	1	2	3	4	5
FV	2000	2120	2247	2382	2525	2676
I	0	120	247	382	525	676

d,e Compound interest on $2000 at 6% p.a.

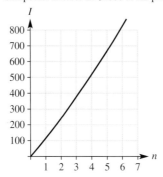

f $840

g Harvey earned $600 (simple interest) and Ava earned $676 (compound interest).

5a $FV = 800 \times (1.07)^n$

b $I = 800(1.07)^n - 800$

c

n	0	1	2	3	4	5	6
FV	800	856	916	980	1049	1122	1201
I	0	56	116	180	249	322	401

d,e Compound interest on $800 at 7% p.a.

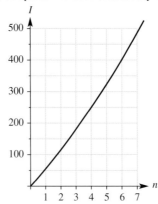

f $150

g Olive earned $336 (simple interest) and Dylan earned $401 (compound interest).

6a Compound interest on $1000

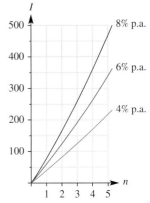

b i $217   **ii** $338   **iii** $469

c i $150   **ii** $220   **iii** $310

d i 4.6 years

ii 3.1 years

iii 2.3 years

e Ellie earned $400 (simple interest) and Bailey earned $469 (compound interest).

7 Compound interest on $1000 at 10% p.a.

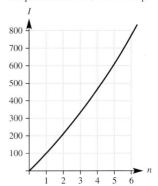

Interest is about $690.

8a Simple interest on $100 000 for 6 months

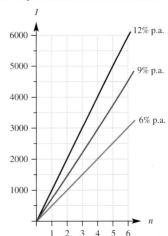

b i $1000

  ii $1500

  iii $2000

c i $3000

  ii $4500

  iii $6000

d i 6 months

  ii 4 months

  iii 3 months

9a

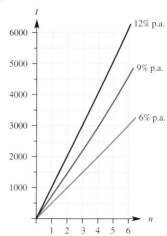

Compound interest on $100 000

b i $101 003

  ii $101 506

  iii $102 010

c i $3038

  ii $4585

  iii $6152

d i 6 months

  ii 4 months

  iii 3 months

10a

Compound interest on $50 000

b $56 320

c About $56 300

d Just under 2 years

Exercise 3C

1 $88 373.39

2 $535 092.25

3a $5151.43   **b** $7543.25

  c $1764.48

4 $2360.28

5 $1900

6a $4.14   **b** $3.83

  c $5.22   **d** $6.03

7a $340 342   **b** $923 785

  c $393 824   **d** $704 994

  e $1 531 538   **f** $1 162 024

8a $150   **b** $50   **c** $25

  d $V = 25n + 50$

9a 7.32%   **b** 8.59%

10a $1215.32   **b** $515.32

11a $29 386.56   **b** $9386.56

  c 10 years

12 5%

Exercise 3D

1a $2988   **b** $852.40

  c $5574   **d** $3393

  e $10 351.88   **f** $219 330

2 $18 622.50

3a 2.49%   **b** 7.38%   **c** 4.86%

  d 5.59%   **e** 6.30%   **f** 2.50%

4 6.67%

5a $124.80   **b** $310.11   **c** $1282.95

  d $377.09   **e** $8805.32   **f** $794.80

6 $0.12

7a $1330   **b** 37.02%

8a $14 155   **b** $900   **c** $1275

9 $120

10a $7.30   **b** $1.90   **c** 22.62%

11 Answers will vary.

12 $0.64

13 $252.40

Exercise 3E

1a $18 480.00   **b** $15 523.20

  c $13 039.49

2 $4740

3a $6532   **b** $10 968

4 $32 752

5a $5046   **b** $14 854

6a $4000   **b** $1000

  c 2.5 years   **d** 3.5 years

  e About $1250   **f** About $2600

7 $24 414

8 17.27%

9a 27.143%   **b** $13 536

10 8.9%

11 After 4 years

12a $5120

  b

Year	Current value	Depre-ciation	Depre-ciated value
1	$32 000	$5120	$26 880
2	$26 880	$4301	$22 579
3	$22 579	$3613	$18 966
4	$18 966	$3035	$15 931
5	$15 931	$2549	$13 382

  c

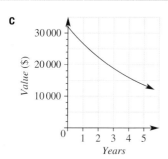

Exercise 3F

1a $801   **b** $1974

  c $2120   **d** $534

  e $2650

2a $1590   **b** $95 400

  c $20 400

3a $5096.40   **b** $1966.80

  c $7911   **d** $2856.60

4a $573.65   **b** $33 838

5a $3655   **b** $657 900

  c $317 900   **d** $118 524

6a $420 960   **b** $240 960

7a $100 000   **b** $84 000

  c $68 000   **d** $48 000

  e about 84 months

  f about 48 months

  g 96–97 months

8a $3344   **b** $802 560

  c $402 560   **d** $114 240

  e $220 320   **f** 5.03% p.a

9a $332 800   **b** $172 800

  c 13.5% p.a.

10a 23.35%   **b** 16.72%

  c 16.94%   **d** 20.00%

  e 21.12%   **f** 30.40%

  g 28.80%

Exercise 3G

1a $5.05   **b** $7.46

  c $85.82   **d** $1.16

  e $0.72   **f** $10.91

2a $983.93   **b** $987.87

  c $991.83   **d** $995.80

  e $999.79   **f** $1003.80

3a $392.65   **b** $501.71

  c $15.57   **d** $3369.85

  e $61.15   **f** $573.23

4 $7.14

5 $4.47

6 $6899.88

7a $543.12   **b** $270.73

  c $1415.27   **d** $483.80

  e $681.68

8a $5.61   **b** $3.17   **c** $27.57

  d $16.67   **e** $28.55

9a 0.05%   **b** $73.88

10a 0.042%   **b** $650

  c $0.94   **d** $1.03

11 $6.53

12a $144.75   **b** $146.94

  c $2.19   **d** $5.53

13a $423.54   **b** $412.60

14a $4355   **b** $69.68

  c $132.74   **d** $4229.79

Exercise 3H

1a 21 Apr 2020   **b** $172.91

  c $172.91   **d** $10.00

  e $743.42   **f** $0.00

  g $743.42   **h** $4511.88

2a $19 500.00   **b** $3 950.82

  c 5   **d** $15 549.18

  e $89.66   **f** $72.53

  g Myer   **h** WW petrol

  i 7 Dec   **j** $57.00

3a 5   **b** $38.95

  c 30 days   **d** $4892.08

  e $4902.08   **f** $0.06

4a $5821.31   **b** $12 000

  c $6361   **d** $5638.25

  e $511.93   **f** $86.26

  g i $2.82   **ii** $1128.55

5a $5246.84   **b** $1371.50

  c $23 381.66   **d** 2

  e 10   **f** General pants

  g 23 Nov   **h** $6618.34

  i $493.94

6a $5492.29   **b** $171.87

Exercise 3I

1a $457.50   **b** $640   **c** $595

  d $590   **e** $600   **f** $350

2a $2.20   **b** $16

  c Bank B   **d** Bank B

  e $4   **f** $0.40

  g $228.75   **h** $15.75

  i i $300   **ii** $286

    iii $316   **iv** $313

  j i $515   **ii** $540

    iii $502   **iv** $526

3 $522

4a $20   **b** $25   **c** $500

  d $35.80   **e** $86.20   **f** $100

  g $85   **h** $400   **i** $300

5a $118.19   **b** $94.98

  c $71.56   **d** $47.93

  e $24.09   **f** $0.04

6a $525.19   **b** $439.85

  c $353.66   **d** $266.60

  e $178.67   **f** $89.87

7a $3505   **b** $5355

  c $160.65   **d** $78.48

Review 3

Multiple-Choice

1 D   **2** D   **3** D   **4** C

5 C   **6** D   **7** C   **8** B

Short-answer

1a $1118.27   **b** $2520.54

2a $22 524.07   **b** $6664.49

3 $62 360.95

4a $710 517   **b** $230 517

5a $3.02   **b** $4.95   **c** $6.46

  d $1.72   **e** $4.85   **f** $9.58

6 $722.95

7 4.96%

8 $273.50

9a $5046   **b** $14 854

10a $27 123   **b** 9.7%

11 6.61% p.a.

12 $172.07

13a $436   **b** $500

Extended-response

14a $3.26   **b** $0.98   **c** $1.45

  d $0.67   **e** $2.10   **f** $1.22

Practice paper 1

1 B   **2** D   **3** A   **4** D

5 C   **6** A   **7** C   **8** D

9 A   **10** D   **11** C   **12** B

13 B   **14** A   **15** C

16a $375, $225, $600

  b i 148 m^2 **ii** 38.5%   **iii** 25.6 m^2

    iv 1536   **v** $3000

  c $1152

  d i $200   **ii** $87.50   **iii** $230

17a i No. An Eulerian circuit only exists if all vertices have even degree.

    ii 21   **iii** 16   **iv** 20

    v *E–F–C–D–A–B–E* or *E–B–A–D–C–F–E* length is 44

  b i 8 cm by 5 cm

    ii Any two features: renewable energy, north facing, insulation, overhanging eaves, good ventilation, …

  c $1620

  d i $\frac{2}{3}$ **ii** 7.5 cm

18a i 5

    ii One example is A–B–D–E–C

  b i $5861.82   **ii** $863.87

  c i 2 kWh   **ii** $2.14

  d Between 9 and 10 years

  e i Eulerian circuit

    ii All vertices in the network graph are even and the network is connected.

    iii One possible route: Reservoir–B–A–C–D–E–C–B–E–F–Reservoir

    iv 32 km

Chapter 4

Exercise 4A

1a 0.54   **b** 0.34   **c** 2.47
d 2.85   **e** 0.74   **f** 1.45
g 0.91   **h** 2.16
2a 28°   **b** 70°   **c** 20°
d 32°   **e** 30°   **f** 76°
3a 6.57   **b** 20.48   **c** 15.95
d 3.46   **e** 17.88   **f** 62.20
4a 46°57′   **b** 42°8′   **c** 20°45′
d 41°49′   **e** 59°8′   **f** 51°51′
5a 30.79   **b** 22.99   **c** 88.91
6a 53°   **b** 62°   **c** 44°
7 Height is 15.0 m
8 Pole is 4.50 m high
9 River is 40 m wide
10 Depth is 40.2 m
11 Pole is 4 m high
12 Angle is 34°
13 Angle the ladder makes is 60°
14 Angle is 1°26′
15 Length of the rope is 6.6 m
16 Ramp is 8.77 m
17a Horizontal distance is 3.8 km
  b Height is 1.3 km
18a Ladders reach 3.83 m
  b Angle is 33°
19 Angle is 38°

Exercise 4B

1 Height is 752 m
2 Height of the tower is 116 m
3 Boat is 107.23 m from the base of the cliff.
4 Plane was 17326 m from the airport
5 Height of the tree is 55.6 m
6 Depth of the shaft is 74 m
7 Height of tree is 35 m
8 Angle of depression is 9°
9 Angle of elevation is 23°
10 Angle of elevation is 34°
11 Angle of depression is 2.5°
12 Angle of elevation is 3°
13 Angle of elevation is 34°
14 Angle of depression is 47°

15 Height of the tree is 10 m.
16 Angle of depression is 20°58′
17 Launching pad is 45 m in height.
18a Height of hill is 210 m
  b Height of hill and tower is 281 m
  c Height of tower 71 m
19a $x = 53$ **b** $y = 113$
  c Man is 60 m from the boat
20 Height of the lighthouse is 22 m
21a Plane has flown 1569 m
  b Speed is 226 km/h.
22 Boat travels 500 m towards the cliff.

Exercise 4C

1a N45°E, 045°   **b** N45°W, 315°
c S45°E, 135°   **d** S45°W, 225°
2a N52°E, 052°   **b** N63°W, 297°
c S55°E, 125°   **d** S57°W, 237°
e N70°E, 070°   **f** N55°W, 305°
g N59°E, 059°   **h** N78°W, 282°
i S82°E, 098°   **j** S60°W, 240°
k N77°W, 283°   **l** S70°E, 110°

3a
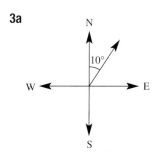

b
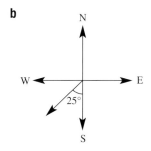

c
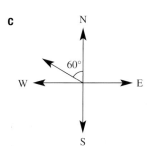

d
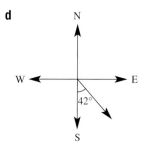

e   **f**
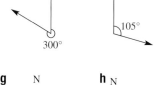

g   **h**
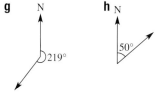

4 Aaron has ran 5.1 km
5a N30°E   **b** 210°   **c** S30°W
6a 045°   **b** 315°   **c** 200°
7a $x = 52$ and $y = 41$
  b N49°W   **c** 311°
8a 106 km   **b** 66 km
9a 58°   **b** 212°   **c** S32°W
10a 124.2 km   **b** 57.9 km
11a S45°W   **b** 225°
12a 4.25 km   **b** 7.36 km
  c N30°E
13a 5.1 km   **b** 14.1 km   **c** 110°T
14a 5.00 km   **b** 3.15 km
  c 6.85 km   **d** 3.89 km
  e 7.88 km   **f** N30°W
15a 247.49 km   **b** 247.49 km
  c 252.51 km   **d** 44°
  e 316°T
16 Oscar is 164 km east of starting point.

Exercise 4D

1a Negative   **b** Positive
  c Negative   **d** Negative
  e Negative   **f** Positive
  g Negative   **h** Negative
2a 0.64   **b** −0.02   **c** −2.14
  d −0.63   **e** −6.31   **f** 0.10
  g −0.91   **h** −0.21

3a 1.0   **b** −0.8   **c** −0.1

d −0.2   **e** 1.0   **f** −1.5

g −0.6   **h** −0.3

4a −3.00   **b** 2.90   **c** −1.91

d −19.20   **e** −2.23   **f** 7.13

g 2.14   **h** 2.78

5a 118   **b** 147   **c** 141

d 143   **e** 112   **f** 150

6a 119°57′   **b** 121°18′   **c** 139°47′

d 101°32′   **e** 126°52′   **f** 145°9′

7a 117°   **b** 118°   **c** 124°

d 171°   **e** 136°   **f** 166°

8 134°26′

9a 2.97   **b** 4.42   **c** 2.91

d 15.37   **e** 33.31   **f** 4.82

g 2.77   **h** 2.92

10a 150°   **b** 106°   **c** 120°

d 150°   **e** 104°   **f** 135°

11a 129°14′   **b** 121°5′   **c** 146°1′

d 150°0′   **e** 154°46′   **f** 156°43′

12a 146°   **b** 102°   **c** 132°

d 103°   **e** 153°   **f** 146°

13a 143°   **b** −0.75   **c** 0.6

14a 113°30′   **b** −0.399   **c** 0.9171

Exercise 4E

1a 22.4 sq units   **b** 177.7 sq units

c 312.0 sq units   **d** 9.1 m^2

e 295.6 cm^2 **f** 97.1 mm^2

2 801.09 cm^2

3 7.83 m^2

4 10 cm^2

5a 204.9 sq units   **b** 864.4 sq units

c 8.6 sq units   **d** 209.0 mm^2

e 565.4 cm^2 **f** 2.3 m^2

6 281 cm^2

7a 6.4 cm^2 **b** 12.9 cm^2

8a 27.8 km^2 **b** 17.1 km^2 **c** 45 km^2

9 19.9 m

10 153 cm^2 **11** 12 cm

Exercise 4F

1a $a = 11$, $b = 12$ and $c = 14$

b $a = 19$, $b = 15$ and $c = 26$

c $a = 6$, $b = 5$ and $c = 7$

2a 6.30   **b** 22.96   **c** 9.56

d 5.82   **e** 3.47   **f** 12.00

3a 45.14   **b** 2.00   **c** 7.99

d 23.68   **e** 22.18   **f** 14.44

4a 8.01   **b** 24.55   **c** 9.39

5a 39°5′   **b** 45°5′   **c** 35°47′

d 38°6′   **e** 49°26′   **f** 49°2′

6a 33°   **b** 37°   **c** 49°

d 44°   **e** 38°   **f** 51°

7a 62°49′   **b** 47°5′   **c** 30°34′

8a 17.48   **b** 22.18   **c** 37.68

9a 21°   **b** 45°   **c** 30°

10a 28.13   **b** 5.31   **c** 108.11

d 9.59   **e** 6.72   **f** 2.38

11 The size of $\angle RPQ$ is 74°.

12a 6.9   **b** 10.1

13a 86°   **b** 37 cm

14 Longest side is 12.8 cm.

15a 5.0 km   **b** 7.5 km

16a $\angle PQR = 35°42′$, $\angle PRQ = 9°33′$, $\angle QPR = 134°45′$

b 52.8 km   **c** 64.2 km

17a $\angle CAB = 50°$ and $\angle CBA = 45°$

b 33 km   **c** 20 km

18 Harrison is 254 m in a straight line to the top of the mountain.

19a 22.4 km   **b** 18.1 km   **c** 54 min

Exercise 4G

1a $x^2 = 3^2 + 4^2 − 2 \times 3 \times 4 \cos 70°$

b $x^2 = 15^2 + 17^2 − 2 \times 15 \times 17 \cos 45°$

c $x^2 = 28^2 + 35^2 − 2 \times 28 \times 35 \cos 62°$

2a 2.5   **b** 15.7

c 3.9   **d** 17.2

3a 22.34   **b** 9.66

c 79.67   **d** 11.66

e 138.65   **f** 23.77

4a 9.635   **b** 3.270   **c** 45.387

5 16.6

6a 41.75°   **b** 82.82°

c 84.70°   **d** 117.28°

7a 36°   **b** 43°   **c** 40°

d 63°   **e** 99°   **f** 67°

8a 51°19′   **b** 59°10′   **c** 69°31′

9 104°29′

10a 83°10′   **b** 44°18′   **c** 85°25′

11 $\angle HFG = 110°45′$

12 32.2 cm or 322 mm

13a 66°   **b** 48.4

14 Ruby is 26.0 km from starting point.

15 Distance to the castle is 6.60 km.

16 Distance between the legs is 31 cm.

17a 34°3′   **b** 101°32′

18 Angles are 67°59′, 59°24′ and 52°37′.

19 Angles are 73°24′, 58°25′ and 48°11′.

Exercise 4H

1a 120°   **b** 33 km   **c** 32°

2a 95°   **b** 17 m

3a 8 km/h   **b** 30 km   **c** 3 h 54 min

4a 60 km   **b** 65 km

5a 96°   **b** 497 m^2 **c** 48 m

6a 44 km   **b** 59 km

7a 6.60 m   **b** 36°   **c** 5.34 m

8a 3.6 m   **b** 33°   **c** 2.3 m

9a 28°23′   **b** 36°37′   **c** 28 m

10a 34°   **b** 5.4 km

c $\angle DGE = 40°$, $\angle GED = 68°$ and $\angle GDE = 72°$

d 3.6 km   **e** 5.3 km

11a 58 m   **b** 93 m   **c** 1689 m^2

12a $\angle CBD + 35 = 51$ (exterior angle theorem)

$\angle CBD = 16°$

$$\frac{BD}{\sin 35} = \frac{55}{\sin 16°}$$

$$BD = \frac{55 \sin 35°}{\sin 16°}$$

b 155 m   **c** 88.9 m

13a $\angle XYZ = 105°$ and $\angle YXZ = 25°$

b 113.48 km

Exercise 4I

1a 75.44 m^2 **b** 71.61 m^2

c 65.82 m^2 **d** 213 m^2 **e** 12.71 m

f 10.67 m   **g** 11.11 m   **h** 59 m

2a 139°   **b** 102°   **c** 119°

d 1748.40 m^2 **e** 1843.81 m^2

f 2079.85 m^2 **g** 5672 m^2

h 137.82 m   **i** 95.69 m

j 121.24 m   **k** 355 m

3a $103°$ **b** 658 m^2 **c** 59 m

4a 68.0 m **b** 30.6 m **c** 69.3 m
d 20.0 m **e** 49.2 m **f** 237.1 m

5a 735 m^2 **b** 316 m^2 **c** 127 m^2
d 443 m^2 **e** 1621 m^2

6a

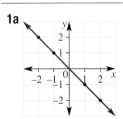

b $77°$ **c** 146 m^2 **d** 22 m

Review 4

Multiple-choice

1 B	**2** D	**3** B	**4** B
5 D	**6** B	**7** D	

Short-answer

1a 29.02 m **b** 20.73 m
c 11.47 mm

2a $28°4'$ **b** $61°56'$ **c** $51°18'$

3 Ship is 103.2 m from the base of the cliff.

4a 6.2 km **b** 5.8 km **c** S47E

5a -1.50 **b** -0.06 **c** 0.75
d -0.98 **e** 3.60 **f** -8.96
g -9.43 **h** -3.73

6a $148°$ **b** $170°$ **c** $105°$
d $97°$ **e** $149°$ **f** $166°$

7a 4.49 **b** 10.88 **c** 84.22

8a 29.89 **b** 13.39 **c** 4.18

Extended-response

9a $148°$ **b** 9 m^2 **c** 12 m
10a 10.19 m **b** $53°$ **c** 6.13 m

Chapter 5

Exercise 5A

1a

b

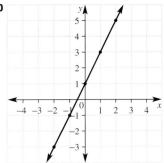

2a

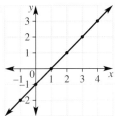

b

c

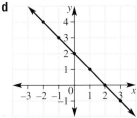

d

3a

b

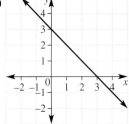

c

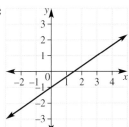

d

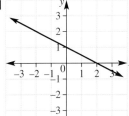

e

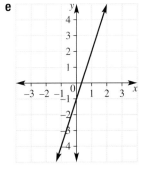

Answers

f
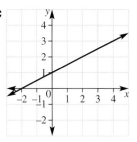

4a 5   **b** 1   **c** −2

d $\dfrac{1}{2}$ **e** $\dfrac{-2}{3}$ **f** $\dfrac{3}{4}$

5a −5   **b** 2   **c** 0

d −1   **e** 7   **f** $\dfrac{3}{5}$

6a $y = 2x + 1$ **b** $y = -3x + 4$

c $y = 0.5x - 2$ **d** $y = 6$

e $y = -\dfrac{2}{5}x + 4$ **f** $y = \dfrac{1}{3}x$

7a $y = \dfrac{1}{2}x + 1$ **b** $y = -2x + 1$

c $y = x + 2$ **d** $y = -\dfrac{1}{2}x + 2$

e $y = x$ **f** $y = -2x + 10$

g $y = 2x - 2$ **h** $y = -\dfrac{2}{3}x - 4$

i $y = x - 3$

8a Not parallel   **b** Not parallel

c Parallel   **d** Parallel

9a $y = -x + 3$ **b** $y = 2x + 4$

c $y = -x + 2$ **d** $y = x - 1$

e $y = 3x + 3$ **f** $y = -\dfrac{1}{2}x + 4$

10a $y = 3x - 2$ **b** $y = -x + 4$

c $y = \dfrac{1}{2}x + 1$ **d** $y = 4x + 2$

e $y = \dfrac{1}{3}x - 1$ **f** $y = -3x + 4$

11a
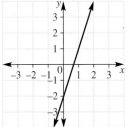

b
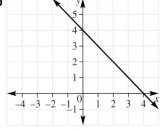

c
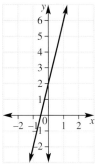

d

e
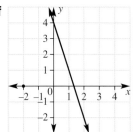

f
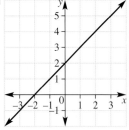

12a

b
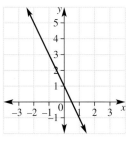

c

d

e
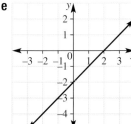

f
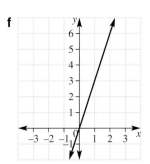

13a 11   **b** 8   **c** Yes

d gradient = 2; y−int = 5

e $y = 2x - 2$

f
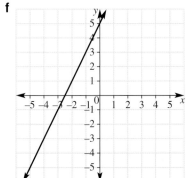

14a False   **b** True   **c** True

d True   **e** False   **f** False

15a $y = 4x$

b
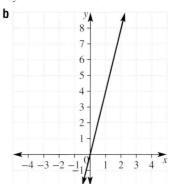

16a $y = \dfrac{1}{3}x$

b
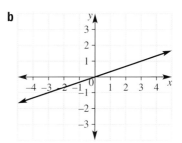

17a $d = 50t$

b
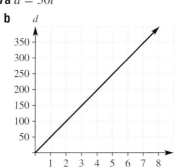

Exercise 5B

1a
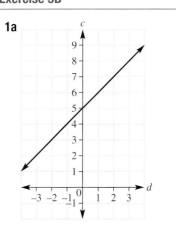

b
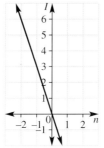

2a
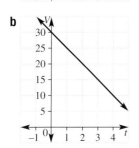

b
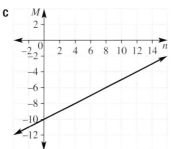

c

3a i 18 GBP   **ii** 30 GBP
iii 33 AUD   **iv** 17 AUD

b $m = \dfrac{3}{5}$ or 0.6

4a

a	0	1	2	3	4
v	20	16	12	8	4

b
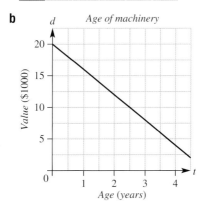

Age of machinery

c $20\,000$ **d** 1.25 years
e 6000 **f** $12\,000$
g 2.5 years
5a $90\,000$ **b** $60\,000$
c 100 months
d $v = -1.5t + 150$ **e** $141\,000$
6a $d = 40t$

b
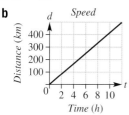

7 $C = 1.5n + 2.6$
8 $w = 20n + 350$
9 $C = 25n + 4000$
10a
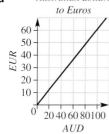

b 15 EUR   **c** 75 AUD
d Gradient is 0.6 and the vertical
intercept is 0.
e $EUR = 0.6 \times AUD$
11a $C = 0.24x + 85$ **b** 145
12a $C = 80t + 50$

b
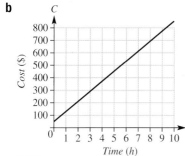

c 270

13a

d	0	10	20	30	40
C	5	20	35	50	65

b
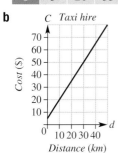

c $27.50

d 20 km

e Gradient is 1.5 and the vertical intercept is 5

f $c = 1.5d + 5$

14a $C = 5n + 175$ **b** Yes. $175

15a $C = 0.06n - 1$ **b** $59

16 $d = 2\frac{2}{3} + \frac{s}{750}$; tread loss after 2000 km is 5.3 mm

Exercise 5C

1a $(-1, 2)$ **b** $(2, 0)$

c $(-2, 0)$ **d** $(0, 1)$

2

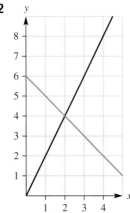

The point of intersection is $(2, 4)$

3

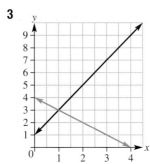

The point of intersection is $(1, 3)$

4

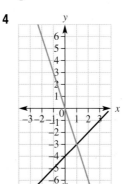

The point of intersection is $(1, -3)$

5a

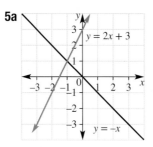

∴ Simultaneous solution is $x = -1$ and $y = 1$

b

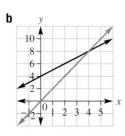

∴ Simultaneous solution is $x = 4$ and $y = 8$

c

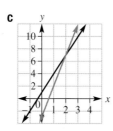

∴ Simultaneous solution is $x = 2$ and $y = 7$

6a

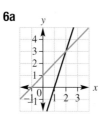

∴ Simultaneous solution is $x = 2$ and $y = 3$

b

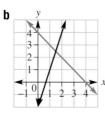

∴ Simultaneous solution is $x = 1\frac{1}{2}$ and $y = 2\frac{1}{2}$

c

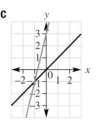

∴ Simultaneous solution is $x = -1$ and $y = -1$

7a

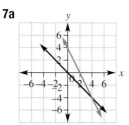

∴ Simultaneous solution is $x = 4$ and $y = -4$

b

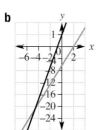

∴ Simultaneous solution is $x = -4$ and $y = -19$

c

∴ Simultaneous solution is $x = -\frac{1}{3}$ and $y = \frac{2}{3}$

d

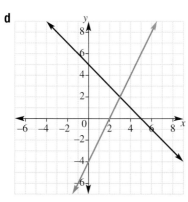

∴Simultaneous solution is $x = 3$ and $y = 2$

e

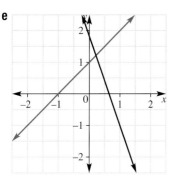

∴ Simultaneous solution is $x = \frac{1}{4}$ and $y = \frac{5}{4}$

f

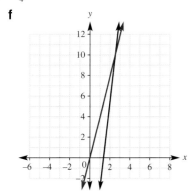

∴ Simultaneous solution is $x = \frac{5}{2}$ and $y = 10$

8a $(0.8, 0.2)$ **b** $(-0.5, -2.5)$
c $(0.6, 2.4)$ **d** $(1.3, -0.8)$
e $(0.8, -0.1)$ **f** $(0.8, 0.3)$

Exercise 5D

1a $(2, 5)$ **b** $(-2, -1)$
c $(2, 4)$ **d** $(-3, -9)$
e $(4, -2)$ **f** $(1, 5)$
2a $(6, -1)$ **b** $(3, 4)$
c $(-2, 4)$ **d** $(2, 3)$
e $(5, -2)$ **f** $(2.75, 0.5)$
3a $(5, 9)$ **b** $(5, -1)$
c $(1, 2)$ **d** $(-2, 4)$
e $(-8, 2)$ **f** $(1, 2.5)$
4a $(3, -8)$ **b** $(1, -4)$
c $(4, 6)$ **d** $(4, 4)$
e $(-1, -4)$ **f** $(-3, 5.2)$
5a $(2, 3)$ **b** $(3, -5)$
c $(1, -2)$ **d** $(7, 3)$
e $(7, 3)$ **f** $(6, 1)$
6a $(-1, 4)$ **b** $(3, 2)$
c $(-2, -1)$ **d** $(3, -2)$
e $(-1\frac{1}{3}, 1)$ **f** $(4, 0)$

7a $(4, 3)$ **b** $(1, 5)$
c $(2, 2)$ **d** $(3, 2)$
e $(1, -2)$ **f** $(-2, 3)$
g $(6, 1)$ **h** $(-19, 46)$
i $(3\frac{1}{2}, 1\frac{1}{2})$
8a $(1, -2)$ **b** $(0, 5)$
c $(3, 1)$ **d** $(1, -1)$
e $(2, 9)$ **f** $(-7, 0)$
9a 7 and 31 **b** 3 and 9
c 3 and -7
d Apple is \$0.40 and orange is \$0.35
e Jack has \$10 and Ruby \$5; altogether they have \$15.

Exercise 5E

1a $m = n + 100$
b $m + n = 1200$
c

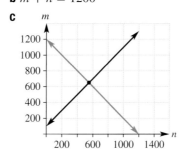

d Matilda's wage is \$650 and Nathan's wage is \$550.
2a $a + b = 42$
b $a - b = 6$
c

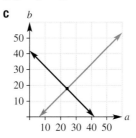

d The numbers are 18 and 24
3a $p + q = 15$
b $p = 2q$
c

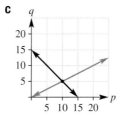

d The numbers are 5 and 10

4a $a = 100 + b$
b $a + b = 1500$
c

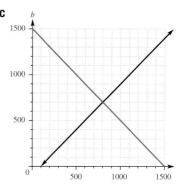

d Amy's wage is \$800 and Nghi's wage is \$700.
5a i $C = 1000 + 10n$
ii $I = 60n$
b 20 items
6a $a + b = 125$
b $2a + 3b = 325$
c

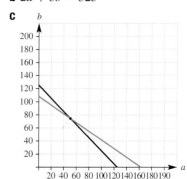

d An apple costs \$0.50 and a banana costs \$0.75
7a $a + b = 70$ **b** $2a = 3b$
c

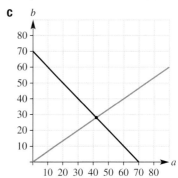

d Zara's wage rate is \$42 and Ryan's wage rate is \$28
8 There are 15 senior workers and 75 junior workers.
9 48 rows
10 16 order chocolate, 4 order strawberry

Exercise 5F

1a 2 shirts **b** 6 printers

2a 2 boxes **b** $10 profit

c $10 loss **d** $20

3a 4 cartons to break even

b Profit of $5

c Loss of $10

d Initial costs are $20

e Gradient is 10

f Vertical intercept is $0

g $I = 10n$

h Gradient is 5

i Vertical intercept is $20

j $C = 5n + 20$

4a 5 bottles to break even.

b $I = 20n$

c $C = 10n + 50$

5a $L = A + 10000$

b $L = -A + 150000$

c
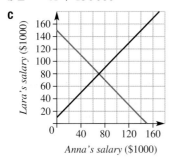

d Anna's salary is $70000 and Lara's salary is $80000.

6a i $C = 50x + 250$

ii $I = 75x$

b
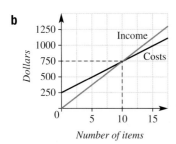

c 10 items need to sold to break even.

d $I = 75x = 75 \times 10 = \$750$
$C = 50x + 250 = 50 \times 10 + 250$
$= \$750$

7a i $C = 5x + 4000$

ii $I = 17.5x$

b
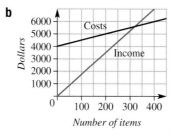

c 320 plants need to be sold to break even.

d $I = 17.5x = 17.5 \times 320 = \$5600$
$C = 5x + 4000 = 5 \times 320 + 4000$
$= \$5600$

Review 5

Multiple-choice

1 A **2** C **3** A **4** D **5** C
6 B **7** B **8** A **9** C

Short-answer

1a
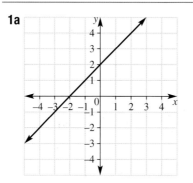

b
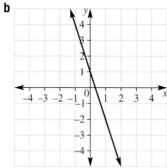

c
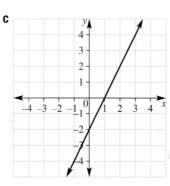

2a $y = 3x - 2$ **b** $y = -\dfrac{1}{2}x + 1$

3a
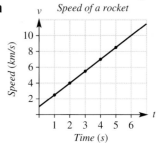

b $v = 1.5t + 1$ **c** 4.75 km/s

d 10 km/s **e** 11.5 km/s

f 16 km/s

4a
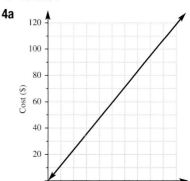

b 2.5 GB **c** $42 **d** $84

e $120 **f** $102

5 $(-2.5, -4.5)$

6a 3

b loss of about $17

c profit of about $8

d About $28

7a 5 **b** $I = 40n$

c $C = 20n + 100$ **d** $100 profit

e $20 loss **f** $220 profit

Extended-response

8a $x + y = 180$

b $x + 2y = 275$

c
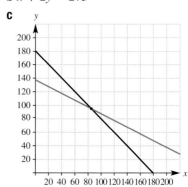

d $0.85 (85 cents)

462

Chapter 6

Exercise 6A

1a 9 **b** 2 **c** 16 **d** 9 **e** 12
2a 23 cm **b** 24 **c** 24 cm
d 18 **e** 4
f No clear relationship

3a

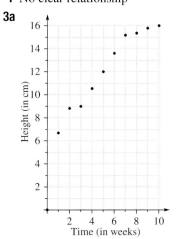

b 6.6 cm **c** 0.1 cm **d** 2 weeks
e 11 cm **f** 6.5 weeks

4a

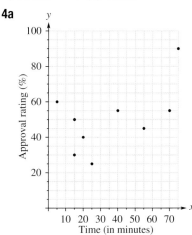

b There is no clear relationship. However it could be argued that the more a politician appears on television the greater the approval rating.

5a

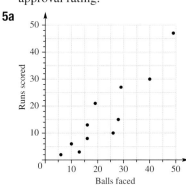

b As the balls faced increased the number of runs increased.

6a

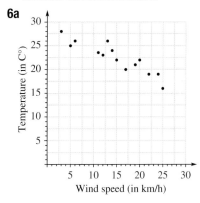

b As the wind speed increases the temperature decreases.

7a

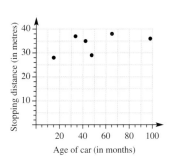

b Age of car: Mean = 49.8 months
Stopping distance:
Mean = 33.8 m

c Disagree with this statement. The stopping distances of cars whose age is 34, 42, 65 and 98 months is about the same (37, 35, 38 and 36 metres). Stopping distances are dependent on the servicing of the car.

d Data is only provided for six cars which makes predictions unreliable. Furthermore other factors affect the result such as the type of car, road conditions and car servicing.

Exercise 6B

1a i Linear **ii** Positive
iii Strong
b i Linear **ii** Negative
iii Strong

c i Linear **ii** Positive
iii Moderate or weak
d i Non-linear **ii** Positive
iii Moderate
e i Linear **ii** Negative
iii Weak
f i Linear **ii** Positive
iii Moderate
2a Positive associated
b Positively associated
c No association
d Positively associated
e Negatively associated.
3a Weight (w) **b** Cost (c)
c

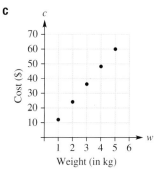

d Linear **e** Positive
f Strong.
4a Drug dosage (d)
b Reaction time (t)
c

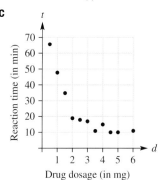

d Non-linear
e Negative
f Moderate.
5a Mass (m) **b** Time (t)
c

d Linear
e Negative
f Strong.

6a

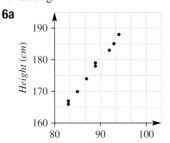

Leg length (cm)

b Strong positive linear association

7a

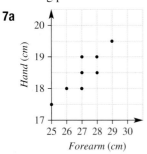

Forearm (cm)

b Moderate positive linear association

Exercise 6C

1a negative   **b** positive
 c zero   **d** positive
 e zero   **f** negative

2a

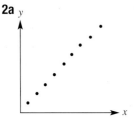

b

c

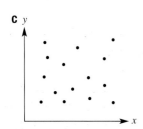

d

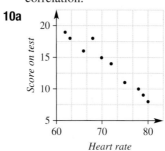

3a Weak positive
 b Perfect negative
 c Strong positive
 d Strong negative
 e Weak negative
 f Perfect positive

4a positive   **b** strong
 c 0.99

5a 0.996   **b** −0.996

6a 0.731   **b** 0.185
 c −0.951   **d** 0.107

7a Positive   **b** Weak
 c 0.362
 d Yes. An increase in mass results in an increase in the BMI.

8 Body mass decreases as the income increases. Weak negative correlation. Not a strong relationship.

9 Height increases as the foot length increases. Strong positive correlation.

10a

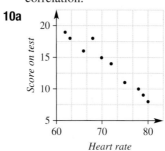

Heart rate

b negative   **c** strong
 d −0.9727

11 Weak positive correlation. Student opinion.

12a No. Strong positive correlation is not sufficient to imply causation.
 b Students with big feet may be older and at a later stage of development than students with small feet.

13a Higher income allows people to afford better healthcare, more nutritious food and better living conditions. This results in better health.
 b Better health allows people to perform at a higher level and to be more productive. This results in higher income.

Exercise 6D

1a

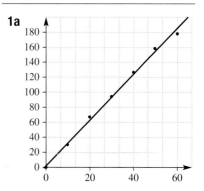

b

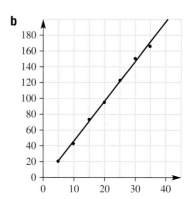

c

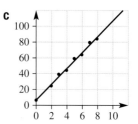

d

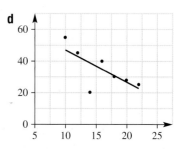

2a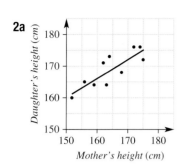

b strong   **c** 172 cm   **d** 154 cm

3a 63.5 kg   **b** 59.1 kg   **c** 72.3 kg

4a $y = 49.20x - 329.16$

   b $y = -1.43x + 107.10$

   c $y = 10.55x + 18.72$

   d $y = -0.67x + 127.20$

5a Shown on spreadsheet

   b Shown on spreadsheet

   c 67.12 beats per minute

   d 53.875 kg

   e A strong positive correlation indicates the predictions are reliable.

6a $m = 0.2034h - 6.3121$

   b 8.5 kg   **c** 3.5 kg

   d 54.6 cm   **e** 75.3 cm

7a

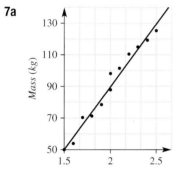

   b 0.987

   c $w = 79.182e - 68.447$

   d 54.285 kg   **e** 101.794 kg

   f 2.127 MJ   **g** 1.875 MJ

8a

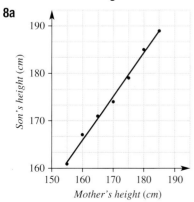

   b $s = 0.9143m + 19.714$

   c 168.7 cm

   d 173.1 cm

   e A strong positive correlation indicates the predictions are reliable.

Exercise 6E

1a 3 months   **b** 20%

   c **i** 110 mm

     ii 70 mm

    iii 60 mm

   d **i** 17%

     ii 13%

    iii 8%

2a $30 000   **b** 3 countries

   c **i** $22 000

     ii $27 500

    iii $33 000

   d **i** $32 000

     ii $49 000

    iii $65 000

3a 10 errors (interpolation)

   b 4 errors (interpolation)

   c −1 error (extrapolation)

4a 19.7°C (interpolation)

   b 26.4°C (interpolation)

   c 33.1°C (extrapolation)

5a 45.22 (interpolation)

   b 55.72 (interpolation)

   c 38.92 (extrapolation)

   d 66.22 (interpolation)

   e 72.52 (extrapolation)

   f 59.92 (interpolation)

6a 46.87 kg (extrapolation)

   b 65.62 kg (interpolation)

   c 84.37 kg (extrapolation)

7a 92.18% (extrapolation)

   b 86.74% (interpolation)

   c 84.02% (interpolation)

8a 12 030 (interpolation)

   b 18 730 (interpolation)

   c 25 430 (interpolation)

9a $3380

   b 750 DVDs

   c $72 500

   d $500

   e part c

10a

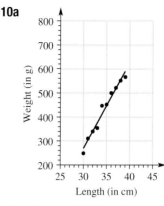

   b $weight = 35.485 \times length - 795.73$

   c 35.485   **d** 447.5 g   **e** 464 g

   f 801 g   **g** 31 cm

11a

   b 0.9981

   c Strong positive correlation

   d $literacy = 4.9702$ $internet\ use + 47.55$

   e 197

   f 51%

   g The model predicts an Internet use of 111% for literacy score of 600. This is clearly incorrect. Care needs to be taken when extrapolating.

Exercise 6F

1a investigation   **b** population

   c sample   **d** presentation

   e bivariate   **f** skewed

2a true   **b** true   **c** true

   d true   **e** false   **f** false

3 A statistical investigation involves four steps: collecting data, organising data, summarising and displaying data and analysing data.

4 Census is data is collected from the whole population. A survey is data is collected from a smaller group of the population.

5 Several checks should be made to limit the impact of bias. This includes how the data is collected and whether this is likely to influence who responds and how they respond. Also compare the demographics of survey respondents to the general population to check whether the sample is representative.

6 Since the number of car accidents and the number of school teachers will both increase with the size of the city, then the size of the city is likely to explain this correlation.

7 Not necessarily. While one possible explanation is that religion is encouraging people to drink, a better explanation is that towns with a large numbers of churches also have large populations, thus explaining that larger amount of alcohol consumed. Town size is the probable common cause for this association.

8a

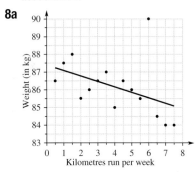

b Weak negative linear association
c $r = -0.4122$
d $weight = -0.29 \times distance + 87.34$
e 85 kg
f Omitting the data gives the impression that increasing the number of kilometres resulted in a steady decline in the

person's weight. It increased the correlation between the two variables.

9 Student opinion.
10 Student investigation.

Review 6

Multiple-choice

1	A	**2**	A
3	C	**4**	C
5	C	**6**	C

Short-answer

1a navel height   **b** body height
 c linear   **d** moderate
 e 188 cm   **f** 100 cm
 g 182 cm
2a 7 years   **b** 145 cm
 c positive   **d** strong
 e 0.99

3a

Body height (cm) vs Length of right foot (cm) scatter plot.

b positive   **c** Strong
4a 92   **b** 12
5a $height = 5.95 \times age + 42.91$
 b 156 cm
 c 257 cm
 d part b
6a

Life expectancy vs Birth rate scatter plot.

b negative
c strong
d -0.8570
e $e = -1.56r + 109.57$
f 55   **g** 32

Extended-response

7a

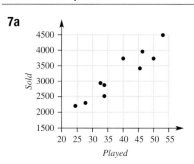

b $r = 0.9458$
c Strong positive linear association
d $weekly\ sales = 74.3 \times played + 293$
e Slope: on average, the number of downloads increases by 74.3 for each additional time the song is played on the radio in the prevous week. Intercept: predicts 293 downloads of the song if it is not played on the radio in the previous week.
f 7723 (Extrapolating)

Practice paper 2

1	D	**2**	C	**3**	D
4	A	**5**	A	**6**	A
7	B	**8**	C	**9**	A
10	D	**11**	C	**12**	D
13	B	**14**	B	**15**	C

16a 274 km
 b -0.997
 c i 96°   **ii** 121 m
 d $(5, -3)$
 e i $\angle TAB = 3°$, $\angle ATB = 80°$,
 ii 2070 m
 iii 252 m
17a i 2
 ii Loss of $10

iii Profit of $20

iv $20

b 45°

c i cost = 2.1 × number of meals + 81.5

ii $182.30

iii 80

d i −2 ii −2 iii (−2, 2)

e Weight increases as the age increases. Strong positive correlation.

18a i $35000

ii 6

iii 0.4

b i 37°

ii 7.42 cm

iii 17.12 cm²

c i R = 65x

ii $1700

iii

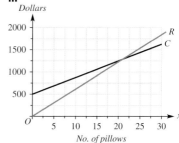

Dollars / No. of pillows

iv 20 pillows

d i 48 Extrapolation

ii 66 Interpolation

iii 84 Extrapolation

Chapter 7

Exercise 7A

1a $2125 b $1716.25

c $1270.71 d $785.08

2a $99050 b $98094.78

c $97134.30 d $96168.53

3a $6100 b $7266

c $8501.96 d $9812.08

4a $62504 b $65029.03

c $67575.28 d $70142.91

5 498782

6

	V_n	D	V_{n+1}
1	$V_0 = 12000$	$500	$V_1 = \$13\,436$
2	$V_1 = \$13\,436$	$500	$V_2 = \$14\,984.01$
3	$V_2 = \$14\,984.01$	$500	$V_3 = \$16\,652.76$
4	$V_3 = \$16\,652.76$	$500	$V_4 = \$18\,451.68$

7a $V_{n+1} = V_n \times 1.004 - 2000$

b

	V_n	D	V_{n+1}
1	$V_0 = 250000$	$2000	$V_1 = \$249\,000$
2	$V_1 = \$249\,000$	$2000	$V_2 = \$247\,996$
3	$V_2 = \$247\,996$	$2000	$V_3 = \$246\,988$
4	$V_3 = \$246\,988$	$2000	$V_4 = \$245\,976$

8a $V_{n+1} = V_n \times 1.042 + 1500$

b

	V_n	D	V_{n+1}
1	$V_0 = 30000$	$1500	$V_1 = \$32\,760$
2	$V_1 = \$32\,760$	$1500	$V_2 = \$35\,636$
3	$V_2 = \$35\,636$	$1500	$V_3 = \$38\,633$
4	$V_3 = \$38\,633$	$1500	$V_4 = \$41\,755$
5	$V_4 = \$41\,755$	$1500	$V_5 = \$45\,009$
6	$V_5 = \$45\,009$	$1500	$V_6 = \$48\,399$

c $9399

9a $V_{n+1} = V_n \times 1.005 - 399$

b $432.29

c $35.45

10 Yes. Balance after 4 payments is zero rounded to the nearest cent.

11a 3%

b $V_{n+1} = V_n \times 1.03 + 600$

c $11669.30

12a 1%

b $V_{n+1} = V_n \times 1.01 - 2500$

c $18589

d 14

e $1895

13a $30302 b $30844

c $542

Exercise 7B

1a $2206.75 b $11274.19

c $5105.10 d $10450

2a $75031.18 b $10692.07

c $64172.87 d $81028.85

3a $11733.20 b $28973.12

c $54304.23 d $91523.93

e $146211.88 f $226566.42

4 $12410.32

5 Computer application

6a $1906.27 b $8424.73

c $3486.85 d $8795.56

7a $58742.51 b $7534.86

c $53812.89 d $53748.22

8 $32093

9 $1507.22

10 Computer application

11a $2716.73 b $11796.68

c $103988.73 d $37674.78

e $63361.97 f $39170.30

g $74489.10 h $333893.05

i $26497.72 j $71443.08

12a $41611.35 b $66344.35

13a $120786.82 b $706.40

14a $2275.22 b $7596.21

c $50977.68 d $25739.60

e $52313.10 f $23698.81

g $67134.95 h $209175.03

i $23503.54 j $47926.49

15a $112858 b $27198

16a $17464 b $172

17 1419.70 18 $487.59

19a $11 964.14

  b $3811.08

  c Jacob will have saved
$15 775.22. This is not enough
for a holiday costing $18 000.

20a $311 842 (This is enough money
to upgrade the salon)

  b $157 922.14

21 Tyler's investment is $8042.18
Ava's investment is $7718.95
∴ Tyler's is worth more at the
end of the year.

22 $1494.64

Exercise 7C

1a $4240

  b $81 120

  c $144 320

  d $14 420

  e $33 100

  f $7648

2 8930.50

3a $184 280

  b $37 080

  c $182 700

  d $27 606

  e $78 526

  f $182 700

4a i $11 330

   ii 17 509.80

   iii 24 060.30

  b i $330

   ii $1009.80

   iii 2060.30

5a $14 070   **b** 129 843.20

  c $384 714   **d** 738 240

  e $4034.18   **f** $4872.48

  g $35 670.60 **h** 271 428.30

  i $22 931.10 **j** $24 684

6a $2454.60   **b** $6529.28

  c $7545.63   **d** $33 330

  e $94 806   **f** $44 460

  g $99 392   **h** $272 020

  i $128 996

7 Computer investigation

8a $2563.69

  b $4282.93

  c $3150.92

  d $6407.10

  e $38 282.17

9a 5%   **b** 3%

  c 6%   **d** 4%

  e 3%

10 $8443

11a $7038   **b** $15 209 **c** $2215

Exercise 7D

1a $13 920

  b $133 350

  c $40 260

  d $103 200

  e $19 860

2 $13 944

3a $27 086

  b $149 264

  c $78 154

  d $7435

  e $49 678

4 $22 744.96

5a i $14 776

   ii $21 263

   iii $27 213

  b i $15 401

   ii $22 453

   iii $29 107

6a $27 721   **b** $41 699

  c $53 448   **d** $13 793

  e $267 347 **f** $579 550

  g $13 327   **h** $31 216

  i $113 158   **j** $31 977

7a $30 491   **b** $3448

  c $4682   **d** $22 822

  e $95 353   **f** $19 601

8a $4406   **b** $3852

  c $7377   **d** $106 616

  e $32 351   **f** $53 862

  g $84 048   **h** $131 288

  i $224 059

9 Computer investigation

10a $5746

  b $1907

  c $39 318

  d $4866

  e $8887

11a 9%

  b 6%

  c 2%

  d 4%

  e 3%

12 $552

Exercise 7E

1a 0.25%

  b $15.00

  c $495.47

  d $3522.64

  e A = $8.81, B = $499.19,
C = $3023.45

  f $509.97

  g $6097.97

  h $97.97

  i 0.5%

  j $30.00

  k $478.00

  l $5522.00

  m $15.00

2a $27 000.00   **b** $50 562.00

  c $703 669.18

  d A = $49 663.36, B = $67 663.36,
C = $895 386.05

  e $1 043 135.77

  f $180 000.00

  g $413 135.77

  h $62 588.15

  i $80 588.15

  j $1 123 723.92

  k $67 423.44

  l $85 423.44

  m $1 209 147.36

  n $72 548.84

  o $90 548.84

  p $1 299 696.20

3

Payment number	Payment received	Interest earned	Principal reduction	Balance of annuity
0	0	0.00	0	500000.00
1	2500.00	2083.33	416.67	499583.33
2	2500.00	2081.60	418.40	499164.93
3	2500.00	2079.85	420.15	498744.78
4	2500.00	2078.10	421.90	498322.89
5	2500.00	2076.35	423.65	497899.23
6	2500.00	2074.58	425.42	497473.81
7	2500.00	2072.81	427.19	497046.62
8	2500.00	2071.03	428.97	496617.65
9	2500.00	2069.24	430.76	496186.89
10	2500.00	2067.45	432.55	495754.33
11	2500.00	2065.64	434.36	495319.98
12	2500.00	2063.83	436.17	494883.81

4a

Payment number	Payment received	Interest earned	Principal increase	Balance of annuity
0(55)	0	0.00	0	700000.00
1(56)	22000.00	28000.00	50000.00	750000.00
2(57)	22000.00	30000.00	52000.00	802000.00
3(58)	22000.00	32080.00	54080.00	856080.00
4(59)	22000.00	34243.20	56243.20	912323.20
5(60)	22000.00	36492.93	58492.93	970816.13
6(61)	22000.00	38832.65	60832.65	1031648.77
7(62)	22000.00	41265.95	63265.95	1094914.72
8(63)	22000.00	43796.59	65796.59	1160711.31
9(64)	22000.00	46428.45	68428.45	1229139.77
10(65)	22000.00	49165.59	71165.59	1300305.36
11(66)	22000.00	52012.21	74012.21	1374317.57
12(67)	22000.00	54972.70	76972.70	1451290.27

b $498305.36

c $205390.63

d $150984.92

Review 7

Multiple-choice

1 B
2 C
3 C
4 D
5 A
6 C
7 C

Short-answer

1a $V_{n+1} = V_n \times 1.004 + 280$
  b $V_{n+1} = V_n \times 1.0014 + 650$
2a $69615.00
  b $29905.22
3a $45601.45
  b $1074.53
4a $221470.30
  b $11596.13
5 $11155.87
6a $273600
  b $42017
  c $85176
  d $594594
  e $4417
7a $545750
  b $95004
  c 78660
  d $291365
  e $131404
8a $9095
  b $16010
  c $5431
  d $1163
  e $384
9a $5512
  b $3196
  c $5136
  d $9836
  e $4250

Extended-response

10a $10569.86
  b Joel will have saved $20654 at the end of four years. This is enough for his holiday.

Chapter 8

Exercise 8A

1a

x	−2	−1	0	1	2
y	$\frac{1}{4}$	$\frac{1}{2}$	1	2	4

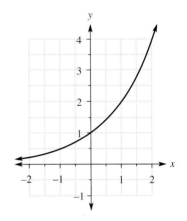

b

x	−2	−1	0	1	2
y	4	2	1	$\frac{1}{2}$	$\frac{1}{4}$

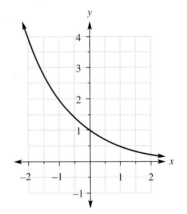

2a No
 b Yes
 c Yes. The value of y is 1 when x equals 0.
 d No. The x-axis (y = 0) is an asymptote.
 e 1.4
 f 2.8

3a

x	−3	−2	−1	0	1	2	3
y	0.02	0.06	0.25	1	4	16	64

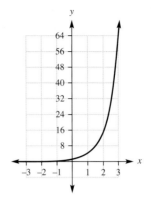

b

x	−3	−2	−1	0	1	2	3
y	64	16	4	1	0.25	0.06	0.02

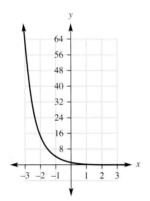

4a No
 b Yes
 c Yes. The value of y is 1 when x equals 0.
 d No. The x-axis (y = 0) is an asymptote.
 e 8
 f 32

5

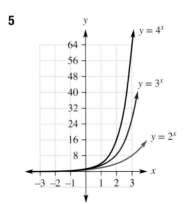

6

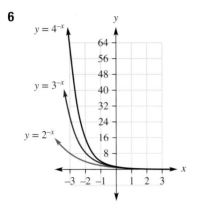

7 When the value of a changes it affects the steepness of the graph. That is, the y values increase or decrease at a greater rate when the x values change.

8a

x	−2	−1	0	1	2
y	4	2	1	$\frac{1}{2}$	$\frac{1}{4}$

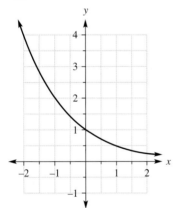

b

x	−2	−1	0	1	2
y	$\frac{1}{4}$	$\frac{1}{2}$	1	2	4

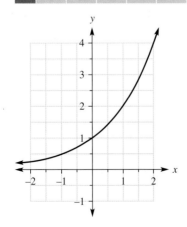

9a $(1, 0.5)$ **b** $(-1, 2)$
c $(2, 4)$ **d** $(-2, 0.25)$
e Yes.
$$\left(y = 0.5^x = \left(\frac{1}{2}\right)^x = (2^{-1})^x = 2^{-x}\right)$$
f Yes.
$$\left(y = 0.5^{-x} = \left(\frac{1}{2}\right)^{-x} = (2^{-1})^{-x} = 2^x\right)$$

10

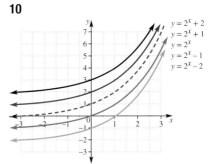

11a 3.4 **b** 2.4 **c** 0.4 **d** -0.6
e Adding or subtracting a number to the graph $y = a^x$ moves the graph up or down.

12abc

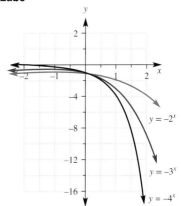

d Multiplying the graph $y = a^x$ by -1 reflects the graphs about the x-axis. The y values are now negative instead of being positive.

13abc

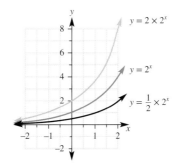

d Multiplying the graph $y = a^x$ by a whole number increases the y values (graph is stretched). Multiplying the graph $y = a^x$ by a fraction decreases the y values (graph is dilated).

14 Horizontal line $y = 1$. It is not an exponential graph as $1^x = 1$ for all x.

Exercise 8B

1a

t	0	1	2	3	4
N	1	6	36	216	1296

b

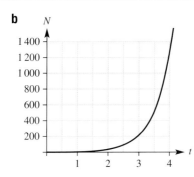

c 1 **d** 216 **e** 1260
f Approximately 3.8 days

2a

t	0	2	4	6	8
N	100	44	20	9	4

b

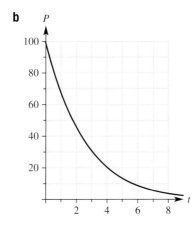

c 100 **d** 30 **e** 6 **f** 35 **g** 12

3a

t	0	1	2	3	4	5
F	200	100	50	25	13	6

b

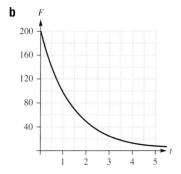

c 200 **d** 25 **e** 37 **f** 8

4a

t	0	5	10	15	20
b	30	75	186	462	1150

b

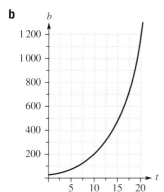

c 30 **d** About 60
e About 7.5 h

5ab

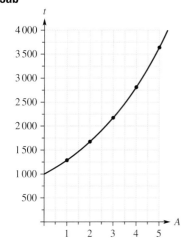

c $A = 1000 \times a^t$ **d** 1.3
e $A = 1000 \times 1.3^t$ **f** $1927
g $6275 **h** 1.5 years

Exercise 8C

1a $(-1, 4)$ **b** $(0, 3)$
c $(-3, 0)$ and $(1, 0)$ **d** $x = -1$
e 4

2a $(0, -4)$ **b** $(0, -4)$
c $(-2, 0)$ and $(2, 0)$ **d** $x = 0$
e -4

3a

x	−3	−2	−1	0	1	2	3
y	9	4	1	0	1	4	9

b

x	−3	−2	−1	0	1	2	3
y	18	8	2	0	2	8	18

c

x	−3	−2	−1	0	1	2	3
y	27	12	3	0	3	12	27

d

x	−3	−2	−1	0	1	2	3
y	4.5	2	0.5	0	0.5	2	4.5

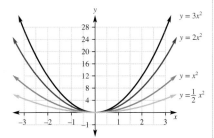

e $x = 0$
f Minimum
g Affects the shape of the parabola. A larger coefficient makes the sides of the parabola steeper.

4a

x	−3	−2	−1	0	1	2	3
y	−9	−4	−1	0	−1	−4	−9

b

x	−3	−2	−1	0	1	2	3
y	−18	−8	−2	0	−2	−8	−18

c

x	−3	−2	−1	0	1	2	3
y	−27	−12	−3	0	−3	−12	−27

d

x	−3	−2	−1	0	1	2	3
y	−4.5	−2	−0.5	0	−0.5	−2	−4.5

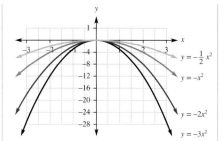

e $x = 0$ **f** Maximum
g Affects the shape of the parabola. A larger coefficient makes the sides of the parabola steeper.

5a

x	−3	−2	−1	0	1	2	3
y	10	5	2	1	2	5	10

b

x	−3	−2	−1	0	1	2	3
y	8	3	0	−1	0	3	8

c

x	−3	−2	−1	0	1	2	3
y	11	6	3	2	3	6	11

d

x	−3	−2	−1	0	1	2	3
y	7	2	−1	−2	−1	2	7

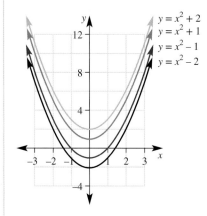

e $x = 0$
f Minimum
g Adding or subtracting a number to the quadratic function $y = x^2$ moves the parabola up or down.

6a

x	−6	−4	−2	0	2	4	6
y	25	9	1	1	9	25	49

b

x	−6	−4	−2	0	2	4	6
y	16	4	0	4	16	36	64

c

x	−6	−4	−2	0	2	4	6
y	49	25	9	1	1	9	25

d

x	−6	−4	−2	0	2	4	6
y	64	36	16	4	0	4	16

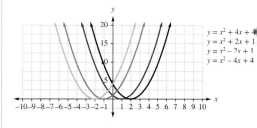

$y = x^2 + 4x + 4$
$y = x^2 + 2x + 1$
$y = x^2 - 2x + 1$
$y = x^2 - 4x + 4$

e All these graphs have a minimum turning point that touches the x-axis.

7a

x	−1	0	1	2	3	4	5
y	8	3	0	−1	0	3	8

b

x	−1	0	1	2	3	4	5
y	−8	−3	0	1	0	−3	−8

c

x	−1	0	1	2	3	4	5
y	16	6	0	−2	0	6	16

d

x	−1	0	1	2	3	4	5
y	−16	−6	0	2	0	−6	−16

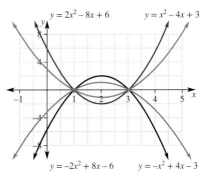
$y = 2x^2 - 8x + 6$ $y = x^2 - 4x + 3$

$y = -2x^2 + 8x - 6$ $y = -x^2 + 4x - 3$

e All the quadratic functions have
   x-intercepts of 1 and 3, and
   $x = 2$ as an axis of symmetry.

8a $y = x^2 + 1$ **b** $y = x^2 - 1$
   c $y = -x^2$ **d** $y = 2x^2$
   e $y = (x + 1)^2$ **f** $y = (x - 1)^2$

9a

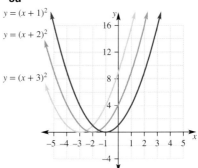
$y = (x + 1)^2$
$y = (x + 2)^2$
$y = (x + 3)^2$

b

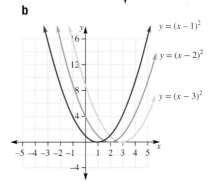
$y = (x - 1)^2$
$y = (x - 2)^2$
$y = (x - 3)^2$

c Positive k shifts the graph to the
   left; negative k shifts the graph
   to the right.

10a

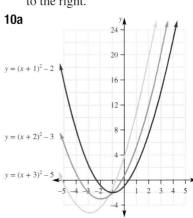
$y = (x + 1)^2 - 2$
$y = (x + 2)^2 - 3$
$y = (x + 3)^2 - 5$

b

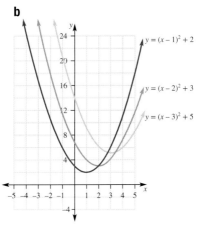
$y = (x - 1)^2 + 2$
$y = (x - 2)^2 + 3$
$y = (x - 3)^2 + 5$

c Adding or subtracting a number
   to the quadratic function
   $y = (x + k)^2$ moves the parabola
   up or down.

Exercise 8D

1a 6 m²   **b** 10 m²
   c 3.5 m   **d** 12.25 m²
2a 0 m/s   **b** 11.25 m/s
   c 1.5 s   **d** 2

3a

d	0	2	4	6	8	10	12
P	0	12	48	108	192	300	432

d	14	16	18	20	22	24
P	588	768	972	1200	1452	1728

b

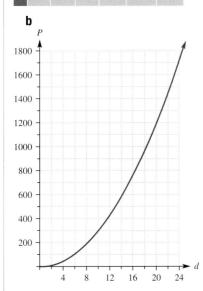

c $432   **d** $1587   **e** $1800

4a

t	0	1	2	3	4	5
d	0	5	20	44	78	123

b

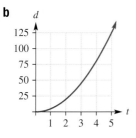

c 5 m   **d** 123 m   **e** 31 m
f 4.5 s   **g** 6.4 s

5a

s	0	20	40	50	60	80	100
d	0	2	8	12	18	32	50

b

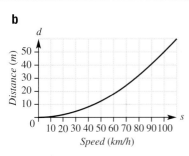

c $d = 2$ m   **d** $d = 28$ m
e About 55 km/h
f About 78 km/h
g 24 m   **h** 44 m

6a

v	0	10	20	30	40	50	60	70
d	0	2	5	9	15	22	30	39

v	80	90	100
d	49	60	73

b

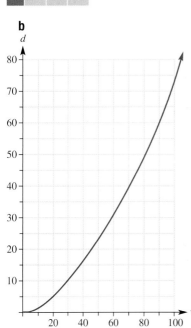

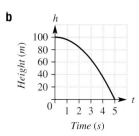
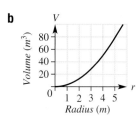
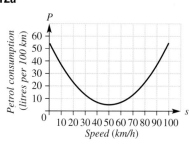
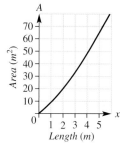
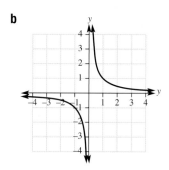
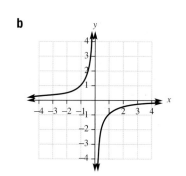
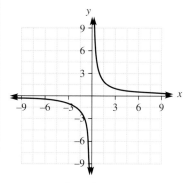
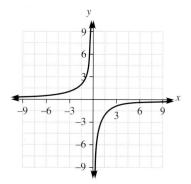
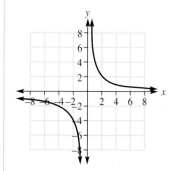

d $y = -\dfrac{4}{x}$

x	-8	-4	-1	$-\dfrac{1}{2}$	$\dfrac{1}{2}$	1	4	8
y	$\dfrac{1}{2}$	1	4	8	-8	-4	-1	$-\dfrac{1}{2}$

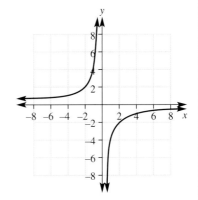

4a

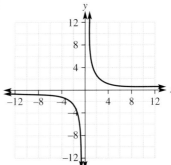

b

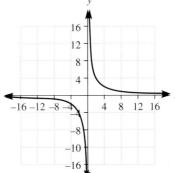

c

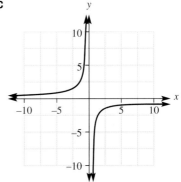

d

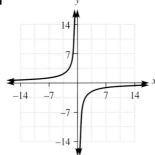

5a $(2, 1)$ **b** $(4, 0.5)$

  c $(-1, -2)$ **d** $(-8, -0.25)$

6a $(10, -0.5)$ **b** $\left(7, -\dfrac{5}{7}\right)$

  c $(-5, 1)$ **d** $(-2, 2.5)$

7a $y = \dfrac{5}{x}$ **b** $y = -\dfrac{5}{x}$

8a $(1, 4)$ lies on the hyperbola.

  b $(-2, -2)$ lies on the hyperbola.

  c $(4, 16)$ does not lie on the hyperbola.

  d $(8, 0.5)$ lies on the hyperbola.

9a $(10, 1)$ does not lie on the hyperbola.

  b $(-5, -2)$ does not lie on the hyperbola.

  c $(20, -0.5)$ does not lie on the hyperbola.

  d $(5, -2)$ lies on the hyperbola.

10a

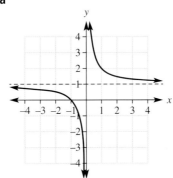

b

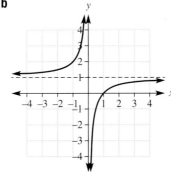

c

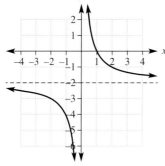

d

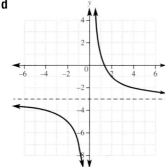

e

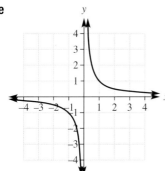

f

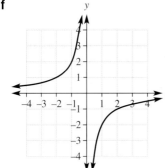

g

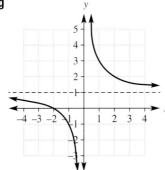

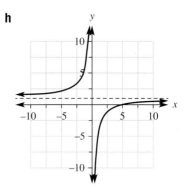

h

Exercise 8F

1a 30 h **b** 20 h
c 60 km/h **d** 15 km/h
e Road trip taking 5 hours requires a speed of 300 km/h. This is not possible on Australian roads.
2a $160 **b** $40 **c** 4 **d** 1
e Yacht would have to be able to accommodate 320 people if the cost per person is $1.

3a

s	5	10	15	25	30	50
t	30	15	10	6	5	3

b

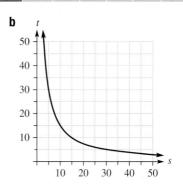

4a

n	1	2	3	4	5	6
t	6	3	2	1.5	1.2	1

b

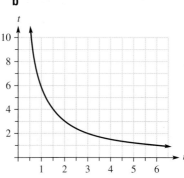

c 6 h **d** 2 h **e** 1 h
f 3 **g** 12
h It would take 1 minute for 360 people to dig the hole. Coordinating 360 people to dig a hole in 1 minute is impractical.

5a

A	0.1	0.2	0.3	0.4	0.5	0.6	0.8	0.9	1.0
n	12	6	4	3	2.4	2	1.5	1.3	1.2

b

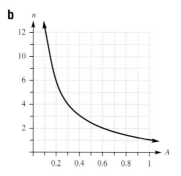

c 2400
d 4800
e 0.6 m²
f About 0.24 m²
g When 12 000 attend the concert then 0.1 m² is allowed per person. This is insufficient room for each person.

6a

b	1	5	10	15	20	60
l	60	12	6	4	3	1

b

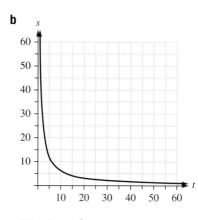

c 2 km/h **d** 2.4 h

7a

d	2	4	8	12	16	20	24
n	24	12	6	4	3	2.4	2

b

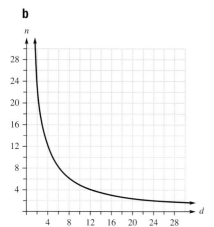

c 16
d The number of chairs is less than 1 which is an unreasonable answer.

8a

b	5	10	30	50	100
l	180	90	30	18	9

b

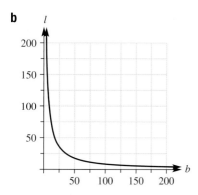

c 360 m **d** 6 m **e** 30 m
f Block 60 m wide
Dimensions are 15 m and 60 m
$P = 2 \times (15 + 60) = 150$ m
Block 25 m wide
Dimensions are 36 m and 25 m
$P = 2 \times (36 + 25) = 122$ m
∴ 60 m wide block would cost more.

Exercise 8G

1a $y = \dfrac{k}{x}$ **b** 12 **c** 2 **d** 1

2a $y = \dfrac{k}{x}$ **b** 36 **c** 4 **d** 18

3a $m = \dfrac{48}{n}$ **b** 2 **c** 12

4a $c = \dfrac{72}{d}$ **b** 1.5 **c** 9

5a 30	**b** $t = \dfrac{30}{p}$

  c 15 days	**d** 10

6a 340	**b** $t = \dfrac{340}{s}$

  c 10 h	**d** 85 km/h

7a 6 days	**b** 2 people

  c Let the number of people be N

$$T = \frac{6}{N}$$

   Doubling the number of people or $2N$

$$T = \frac{6}{2N} = \frac{1}{2} \times \frac{6}{N}$$

   $\therefore$ statement is correct.

8a $18.75	**b** 30

9a $67.50	**b** 135 people

10a 400	**b** 1920 cm^2

11 2.25 minutes	**12** 44 km/h

Exercise 8H

1a, b

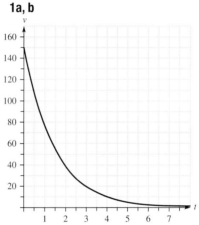

 ci $v = 2^{-t} \times a$	**ii** 150

 iii $v = 2^{-t} \times 150$

 d $27 000	**e** $106 000	**f** 1

 g $0.14. Equipment is worth no value after 20 years.

2a

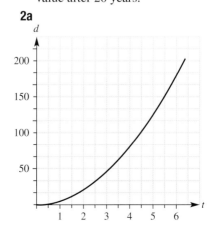

 b i $d = at^2$	**ii** 5	**iii** $d = 5t^2$

 c 61.25 m	**d** 500 m	**e** 8 s

 f Model is not appropriate for distances greater than 1000 km

3a, b

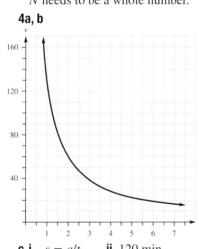

 ci $N = at^2$	**ii** 6	**iii** $N = 6t^2$

 d 726

 e 20 months

 f 121.5 tadpoles. Not possible to have half a tadpole. The variable N needs to be a whole number.

4a, b

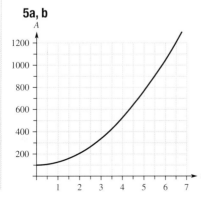

 c i $s = a/t$	**ii** 120 min

 iii $s = 120/t$

 d 15 km/h	**e** 2.5 h

 f 240 km/h

  This speed exceeds the speed limits on Australian roads.

5a, b

 c i $A = 100 \times (a)^t$

  ii 1.5

  iii $A = 100 \times 1.5^t$

 d $276

 e $1709

 f 10 years

6a i $n = b^{-c} \times a$

  ii 4500

  iii 1.5

  iv $n = 1.5^{-c} \times 4500$

 b

c	0	1	2	3	4	5	6
n	4500	3000	2000	1333	889	593	395

 c

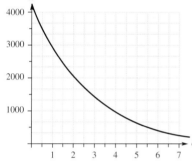

 d Approximately 1333

 e $4000

 f Toll of $1 has an income of $3000

  Toll of $2 has an income of $4000

  Toll of $3 has an income of $4000

  Toll of $4 has an income of $3556

  Toll of $5 has an income of $2963

  Toll of $6 has an income of $2370

  $\therefore$Disagree with this statement. Toll decreases when the charge is greater than $3

Review 8

Multiple-choice

1 C	**2** C	**3** B	**4** C
5 D	**6** B	**7** A	**8** C

Short-answer

1a

x	−3	−2	−1	0	1	2	3
y	0.3	0.4	0.7	1	1.5	2.3	3.4

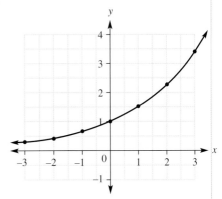

b

x	−3	−2	−1	0	1	2	3
y	8	4	2	1	0.5	0.3	0.1

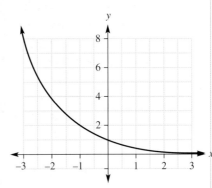

2 a, b

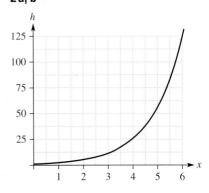

c 3.6 cm   **d** 17.4 cm

3a

t	0	5	10	15	20
w	25	40	65	104	168

b

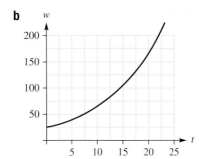

c 25 earthworms

d 33

e About 11.5

4a

x	−3	−2	−1	0	1	2	3
y	27	12	3	0	3	12	27

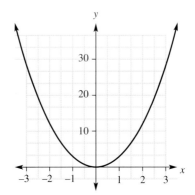

b

x	−9	−3	−1	0	1	3	9
y	−27	−3	$\frac{1}{3}$	0	$-\frac{1}{3}$	−3	−27

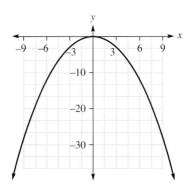

c

x	−3	−2	−1	0	1	2	3
y	12	7	4	3	4	7	12

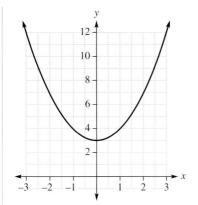

d

x	0	1	2	3	4	5	6
y	−4	−8	−10	−10	−8	−4	2

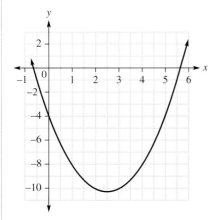

5a

t	0	1	2	3	4	5	6
h	0	5	8	9	8	5	0

b

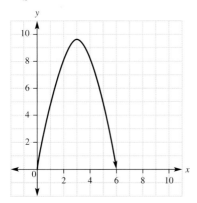

c 9 m   **d** 3 s

6a

x	−7	−1	$-\frac{1}{7}$	$\frac{1}{7}$	1	7
y	−1	−7	−49	49	7	1

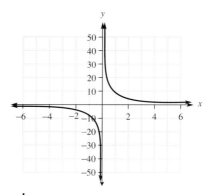

b

x	-7	-1	$-\dfrac{1}{7}$	$\dfrac{1}{7}$	1	7
y	1	7	49	-49	-7	-1

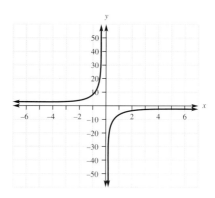

7a 80   **b** 3 m

8 30

Extended-response

9a $A = 4x - x^2$

b

x	0	0.5	1	1.5	2	2.5	3	3.5	4
A	0	1.8	3	3.8	4	3.8	3	1.8	0

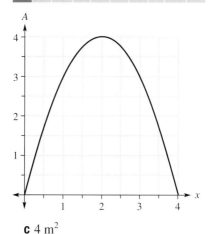

c 4 m²

d 2 m

Chapter 9

Exercise 9A

1a median
b mean   **c** normal   **d** scores
e middle   **f** standard
g centre   **h** asymptote

2a Mean = 10   Median = 10
b Mean = 40   Median = 40
c Mean = 73   Median = 73
d Mean = 30   Median = 30
e Mean = 120   Median = 120
f Mean = 94   Median = 94

3a

Score	Tally	Frequency
60	I	1
61	I	1
62	II	2
63	III	3
64	IIII	4
65	III	3
66	II	2
67	I	1
68	I	1

b Mean = 64   Median = 64

c 2.06

d

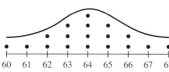

4a

Score	Tally	Frequency
146	I	1
147	I	1
148	II	2
149	II	2
150	III	3
151	II	2
152	II	2
153	I	1
154	I	1

b Mean = 150   Median = 150

c 2.16

---

d

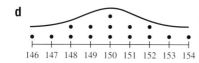

5 Computer investigation

6a $\bar{x} = 20.0$ $\sigma_x \approx 1.7$
b The distribution is symmetric and likely to be a normal distribution.

c

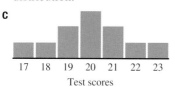

7a Mean = 82.8 median = 83
b The distribution is very close to being a normal distribution. It is symmetric about the mean (82.8), the mean and median are close together and the majority of the data is located at the centre with less data at the tails.
c The distribution is symmetric so either the mean or the median is a good measure of the centre.

Exercise 9B

1a 50%   **b** 68%   **c** 32%
d 95%   **e** 5%   **f** 99.7%
g 0.3%

2a 60   **b** 50 and 70
c 40 and 80   **d** 30 and 90

3a 12 h   **b** 9 h and 15 h
c 6 h and 18 h   **d** 3 h and 21 h

4a 55 mm
b 52.5 mm and 57.5 mm
c 50 mm and 60 mm
d 47.5 mm and 62.5 mm

5a 101.5 g
b 100.8 g and 102.2 g
c 100.1 g and 102.9 g
d 99.4 g and 103.6 g

6a 114 and 154   **b** 94 and 174
c 74 and 194   **d** 154
e 94   **f** 74
g 134

7a 68%   **b** 95%   **c** 99.7%

8a 95%   **b** 68%
c 99.7%   **d** 50%

9a 50%   **b** 50%   **c** 99.7%

d 68%   **e** 95%   **f** 16%

g 84%   **h** 2.5%

10a 99.7%   **b** 95%   **c** 68%

d 34%   **e** 34%   **f** 47.5%

11a 68%   **b** 99.7%   **c** 95%

d 34%   **e** 16%   **f** 2.5%

g 0.15%   **h** 50%

12a 34%   **b** 49.85%

c 47.5%   **d** 49.85%

e 16%   **f** 0.15%

g 2.5%   **h** 0.15%

13a i 99.7%   **ii** 2.5%

iii 95%

b i 4985   **ii** 125   **iii** 4750

14a i 50%   **ii** 34%   **iii** 95%

b i 1000   **ii** 680   **iii** 1900

15 77.9 mg is three standard deviations above the mean. Although it is possible it is highly unlikely the sample cake mix contains this amount of sodium. This raises the possibility of an error in the analysis.

16a 152   **b** 1.47   **c** 1.45   **d** 0.09

e The data is fairly much normally distributed. Asymmetry appears around the central position. Mean and median are almost equal.

f i 1.38 to 1.56

ii 1.30 (or 1.29) to 1.65

iii 1.21 (or 1.20) to 1.74

g i 24   **ii** 23

17a 1050   **b** 5

c 5   **d** 1.7

e i 3.3 to 6.7

ii 1.5 (or 1.6) to 8.4

iii −0.2 (or −0.1) to 10.1

f i 25   **ii** 25

Exercise 9C

1a −1.7   **b** 1.8   **c** −2.5

d 0.5   **e** 1.3   **f** 2.5

2a 1   **b** 2   **c** 3   **d** 4

e −1   **f** −2   **g** −3   **h** −4

i 0.5   **j** 0.5   **k** 1.5   **l** −1.5

3a 1   **b** 2   **c** −1

d 0   **e** −3   **f** 0.5

4a 0   **b** −2   **c** 2

d −4   **e** 1

5a −2   **b** −1   **c** 0   **d** 1

6 −1.5

7a 2   **b** −2

8a 3   **b** −3

9 Computer investigation

10a 2.5   **b** 1.25   **c** 0.5

d 3   **e** −3

11a $\bar{x} = 60.0$ $\sigma_x \approx 16.5$

b 2.2

c −1.9

d z-score is 2 and expected mark 93

Exercise 9D

1a 70   **b** 50   **c** 38   **d** 26

e 76   **f** 64   **g** 65   **h** 83

2a 33   **b** 49   **c** 17   **d** 41

e 25   **f** 9   **g** 1   **h** 37

i 5   **j** 29   **k** 23   **l** 45

3a 67   **b** 74   **c** 75.5

d 61   **e** 64.5   **f** 70.5

g 57   **h** 53.5   **i** 46.5

j 47.5   **k** 56   **l** 51

4a 59   **b** 71   **c** 83

d 56.6   **e** 63.8   **f** 78.2

g 35   **h** 23   **i** 11

j 43.4   **k** 25.4   **l** 17

5a 16.5   **b** 18.6   **c** 14.7

d 7.2   **e** 5.1

Student	z-score	Hours
a Alexis	1.5	16.5
b Ben	2.2	18.6
c Chris	0.9	14.7
d Debbie	−1.6	7.2
e Evan	−2.3	5.1

6 60.76 mm

7a Holly's fitness test was 3 standard deviations below the mean.

b 54

8a $\bar{x} \approx 14.3$ $\sigma_x \approx 3.3$

b −1.9

c 19

9a $\bar{x} \approx 76.1$ $\sigma_x \approx 7.6$

b 1.6

c 62

10a 198.5 g   **b** 210.5 g

11a Max's result is 1.8 times the standard deviation above the mean.

b 74

Exercise 9E

1a 0

b Maths

c Science

d Maths, English, History and Science

2a 1.5

b 2

c Vietnamese has the better result as it has the highest z-score.

3a 0.24

b 0.33

c No. Ava has a higher z-score in test 2.

4 Task 1 $z = 1.67$

Task 2 $z = 1.33$

∴Michael performed better in task 1 as it has a higher z-score

5 Semester 1 $z = −0.5$ Semester 2 $z = −0.7$

∴Joel performed better in semester 1 as it has the highest z-score.

6 Mathematics $z = 1.57$ Chemistry $z = 1.98$

∴Lachlan performed better in chemistry as it has the highest z-score.

7a 1.45

b 0.85

c Grace performed better in sports coaching as it has the highest z-score.

d No. Her z-score for economics is 0.92, which is below the score for sports coaching.

8a English $z = 0$, Mathematics $z = −2.25$, Biology $z = 2.25$,

Business studies $z = 3$ and Legal studies $z = 1.1$

  b Business studies, biology, legal studies, English and mathematics

  c 2.75

  d Mathematics moves from 5th position to 2nd position.

9a 1.23   **b** 58.6

  c 85   **d** 84

10a Task 1 $z = 1.50$, Task 2 $z = 1.17$, Task 3 $z = 1.13$, Task 4 $z = 1.30$

  b Task 1, Task 4, Task 2 and Task 3

  c Amelia achieved a score of one standard deviation above the mean in all her assessment tasks.

  d Task 1 : 78 Task 2 : 74, Task 3 : 74 Task 4 : 76

11a Technology

  b Technology

  c Multimedia

  d Anthony a merit award for technology ($z = 1.5$), Irene receives a merit award for technology ($z = 1.1$) and Katherine receives a merit award for multimedia ($z = 1.7$)

Exercise 9F

1a 68%   **b** 95%

  c 99.7%   **d** 34%

  e 34%   **f** 47.5%

  g 47.5%   **h** 49.85%

  i 49.85%

2a 68%   **b** 95%   **c** 99.7%

3a 68%   **b** 95%   **c** 99.7%

4a -2 **b** 68%   **c** 95%

5a 95%   **b** 68%

  c 99.7%   **d** 34%

  e 47.5%   **f** 49.85%

  g 34%   **h** 47.5%

  i 49.85%

6a 99.7%   **b** 68%

  c 95%   **d** 49.85%

  e 49.85%   **f** 34%

7a 16%   **b** 2.5%   **c** 0.15%

  d 16%   **e** 2.5%   **f** 0.15%

8a 13.5%   **b** 13.5%

  c 2.35%   **d** 15.85%

  e 81.5%   **f** 83.85%

9a 50%   **b** 16%   **c** 2.5%

  d 50%   **e** 84%   **f** 97.5%

10a 190 g to 210 g

  b 180 g to 220 g

11a 1 and -1

  b 3 and -3

  c 2 and -2

12a -3 **b** 0.15%   **c** 3

13a 95%   **b** 83.85%

  c 2.5%   **d** 16%

  e 50%   **f** 2.5%

  g 5 days   **h** 9 days

14a 47.5% and 72.5%

  b 35% and 85%

  c 22.5% and 97.5%

  d 2.5%

  e 97.5%

  f 84%

  g 78 000

  h 50 400

15a 80.5 cm to 83.5 cm

  b 79 cm to 85 cm

  c 80.5 cm

  d 85 cm

  e 0.15%

  f 16%

  g 1   **h** 80

16a 68%   **b** 136   **c** 13.5%

  d 27   **e** 27   **f** 163

  g 195

17a i 68%   **ii** 2.35%

   iii 97.35%   **iv** 13.5%

  b 96   **c** 15   **d** 300   **e** 15

Review 9

Multiple-choice

1 A

2 C

3 D

4 C

5 A

6 B

7 C

8 D

9 C

10 D

Short-answer

1a 117.6 to 155.4

  b 98.7 to 174.3

  c 79.8 to 193.2

2a 68%   **b** 99.7%

  c 95%   **d** 2.35%

  e 13.5%   **f** 49.85%

3a 2.5%   **b** 2.5%

  c 83.85%

4a 2   **b** -1.5

  c 2.25   **d** -1

5 0.5

6 6

7 68

8a $\bar{x} = 13.31$ $\sigma_x \approx 3.29$

  b -1.9

  c 21.

9a 0.8   **b** 1   **c** 1.5

  d Science   **e** 84.

10 Literacy $z = 1.25$ Numeracy $z = 0.73$

  $\therefore$ Riley performed better in literacy

11a 190   **b** 163   **c** 5   **d** 32

12a 0.2   **b** 46.5 kg

  c 2.5%   **d** 34%

Extended-response

13a 69.994 mm to 70.006 mm

  b 16%

  c 0.15%

  d 15

Chapter 10

Exercise 10A

1a activities

  b duration

  c immediate predecessor

  d scheduling

2a

Activity	Task	Dura-tion (in min)	Imme-diate prede-cessors
A	Turn on water	1	–
B	Wet hands	1	A
C	Clean hands with soap	3	B
D	Rinse off soap	2	C
E	Dry hands	3	D

b Five activities (A to E)

c Clean hands with soap, dry hands (both 3 minutes)

d Total time = 1 + 1 + 3 + 2 + 3 = 10 minutes

e Activity B or wet hands.

f Activity A or turn on water

3a

Activity	Task	Dura-tion (in min)	Imme-diate prede-cessors
A	Find recipe	2	–
B	Prepare ingredients	10	A
C	Cook meal	25	B
D	Serve meal	3	C
E	Clean up	10	D

b Five activities (A to E)

c Find recipe (2 minutes)

d Total time = 2 + 10 + 25 + 3 + 10 = 50 minutes

4a Project: To watch your favorite television show

Activity	Task	Dura-tion (in min)	Imme-diate prede-cessors
A	Find remote control	2	–
B	Turn television on	1	A
C	Select television show	1	B
D	Watch television show	30	C
E	Turn television off	1	D

b Project: To listen to a music playlist

Activity	Task	Dura-tion(in min)	Imme-diate prede-cessors
A	Turn on phone	2	–
B	Unlock phone	1	A
C	Select the music app	1	B
D	Select playlist	3	C
E	Select play	1	D
F	Listen to music	50	E
G	Turn off phone	1	F

c Project: To plant a tree in the garden

Activity	Task	Dura-tion (in min)	Imme-diate prede-cessors
A	Decide on the tree required	10	–
B	Purchase the tree	8	A
C	Dig the hole	12	B
D	Plant the tree	5	C
E	Mulch the tree	3	D
F	Water the tree	5	E

d Project: To bake a cake

Activity	Task	Dura-tion (in min)	Imme-diate prede-cessors
A	Heat oven	10	–
B	Mix ingredients	6	–
C	Put cake mixture in cake tin	3	B
D	Bake the cake	35	A, C
E	Cool the cake	30	D
F	Mix the icing	4	E
G	Ice the cake	8	E, F

e Project: To install a smoke alarm

Activity	Task	Duration (in min)	Immediate predecessors
A	Choose a room	2	–
B	Select a section of the ceiling	2	A
C	Remove the mounting plate from the alarm	2	B
D	Screw the mounting plate into the ceiling	5	C
E	Install the batteries into the alarm	3	D
F	Connect the alarm body to the mounting plate	4	E

5

Activity	Task	Duration (in hours)	Immediate predecessors
A	Buying the food	2	–
B	Preparing the food	3	A
C	Serving the meal	1	B
D	Cleaning up	2	C

6

Activity	Task	Duration (in hours)	Immediate predecessors
A	Buying the laptop	1	–
B	Unpacking the laptop	0.5	A
C	Installing the software	4	B
D	Copying the data	3	C
E	Testing the software with the data	1	D

7 There is more than one correct answer to these questions.

a

Activity	Task	Duration (in min)	Immediate predecessors
A	Get bread and butter	1	–
B	Put bread in toaster	1	A
C	Remove toast from toaster	5	B
D	Butter toast	2	C

b

Activity	Task	Duration (in min)	Immediate predecessors
A	Get pump	1	–
B	Connect pump to valve	1	A
C	Pump tyre to required pressure	5	B
D	Remove pump from valve	1	C

c

Activity	Task	Duration (in min)	Immediate predecessors
A	Get two slices of bread, cheese and butter	1	–
B	Spread butter on bread	3	A

Activity	Task	Dura-tion (in min)	Imme-diate prede-cessors
C	Place cheese between bread	2	B

8a First task is to remove furniture and curtains. It is impossible to prepare and paint walls with furniture and curtains against the wall.

b i Remove furniture and curtains

  ii Prepare walls

  iii Paint walls

  iv Lay new carpet

c Hang new curtains and lay new carpet

d

Activity	Task	Dura-tion (in days)	Imme-diate prede-cessors
A	Remove furniture and curtains	1	–
B	Prepare walls	2	A
C	Paint walls	4	B
D	Lay new carpet	1	C
E	Hang new curtains	1	D
F	Arrange new furniture	1	D, E

9a Defrost the pizza base, prepare the toppings and heat oven

b All of the other tasks

c

Activity	Task	Dura-tion (in min)	Imme-diate prede-cessors
A	Defrost the pizza base	5	–
B	Prepare the toppings	10	–
C	Place the sauce and topping on pizza	2	A, B
D	Heat oven	10	–
E	Cook pizza	25	C, D

Exercise 10B

1a i 4　　**ii** A　**iii** D　**iv** C　**v** A
  b i 6　　**ii** A　**iii** F　**iv** C　**v** A
  c i 6　　**ii** A　**iii** G　**iv** B　**v** A
  d i 6　　　　　　　**ii** A and B
  iii E and F　　**iv** B
  v A and B

2a

Activity	Immediate predecessors
A	–
B	–
C	–
D	C
E	A
F	B, D, E
G	F

b

Activity	Immediate predecessors
R	–
S	R
T	R
U	T
V	S, U

c

Activity	Immediate predecessors
F	–
G	F
H	F
I	G
J	G
K	H, I
L	J
M	K
N	L, M

d

Activity	Immediate predecessors
A	–
B	A
C	A
D	C
E	B
F	D, E
G	F
H	G

e

Activity	Immediate predecessors
A	–
B	–
C	–
D	B
E	A
F	C
G	D, E
H	F, G

f

Activity	Immediate predecessors
A	–
B	–
C	A
D	A
E	B, C
F	D
G	E

3a

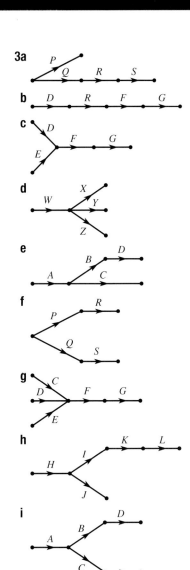

b

c

d

e

f

g

h

i

j

4a

Activity	Immediate predecessors
A	–
B	–
C	A
D	B
E	D
F	C
G	E, F
H	E, F
I	G
J	H
K	I, J

b

Activity	Immediate predecessors
P	–
Q	P
R	P
S	Q
T	Q
U	S, V
V	R
W	R
X	U, T

c

Activity	Immediate predecessors
A	–
B	–
C	–
D	B
E	A
F	C
G	D, E
H	F, G
I	F, G
K	H
L	I
M	K, L

d

Activity	Immediate predecessors
J	–
K	–
L	J
M	N
N	K
O	K
P	N
Q	L, M
R	P
S	O, R
T	Q

5a

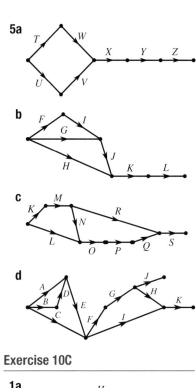

b

c

d

Exercise 10C

1a

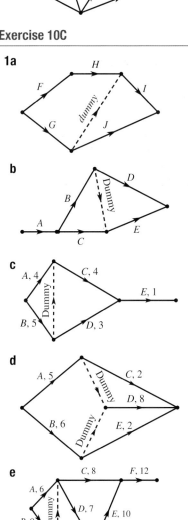

b

c

d

e

2a

Activity	Immediate predecessors
A	–
B	–
C	A
D	A
E	D, B
F	C, E
G	D, B
H	B

b

Activity	Immediate predecessors
P	–
Q	–
R	P
S	P
T	Q
U	R
V	S
W	S, T
X	U
Y	W
Z	V, X, Y

c

Activity	Duration (in mins)	Immediate predecessors
A	3	–
B	9	–
C	5	A
D	8	A
E	2	B
F	3	D
G	7	B, C

d

Activity	Duration (in hours)	Immediate predecessors
A	2	–
B	4	A
C	11	A

Activity	Duration (in hours)	Immediate predecessors
D	5	B
E	8	C
F	6	C
G	1	D, E, F
H	7	G

3a

Activity	Immediate predecessors
A	–
B	–
C	A
D	A
E	B, D
F	C, E
G	C
H	F, G

b

Activity	Immediate predecessors
A	–
B	A
C	A
D	A
E	B
F	C, D
G	D
H	E, F, G
I	G
J	I
K	H

4a Remove panel

b 'Order component' and 'Pound out dent'

5a

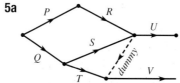

b

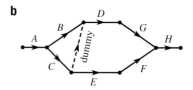

Exercise 10D

1a i 6 **ii** 6 **iii** 9 **iv** 8
b i 6 **ii** 11 **iii** 9 **iv** 13
c A,3 B,2 C,6 D,2
2a i 0 **ii** 2 **iii** 2 **iv** 27
   v 8 **vi** 37
b i 0 **ii** 2 **iii** 31 **iv** 27
   v 37 **vi** 37
3a 12
b 10
c $m = 8$ $n = 8$
d $a = 10$ $b = 11$
e $p = 5$ $q = 10$ $r = 5$ $n = 9$
f $p = 6$ $q = 6$ $r = 4$ $s = 8$
4 $f = 9$ $g = 12$
5a B, 12 **b** 10 **c** 9

6a

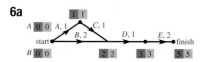

b

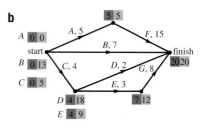

c

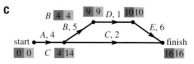

7a

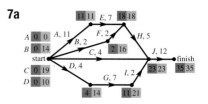

b

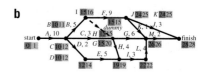

8 a, b, c

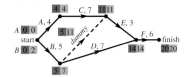

9 a, b, c

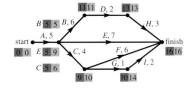

Exercise 10E

1a A: 0 min B: 0 min C: 10 min
   D: 0 min E: 0 min

b A: 0 min B: 2 min C: 1 min
   D: 1 min E: 0 min F: 0 min
   G: 1 min H: 0 min

2a A→F

b A→B→D→G

3a A: 1 day B: 1 day C: 15 days
   D: 0 days E: 0 days F: 0 days

b D→E→F

c 42 days

4a A: 1h B: 0h C: 14h D: 1h E: 0h
   F: 0h G: 1h H: 0h I: 1h J: 0h

b B→E→F→H→J

c 18h

5a

Activity	Duration (weeks)	Immediate predecessors
A	3	–
B	6	–
C	6	A, B
D	5	B
E	7	C, D
F	1	D
G	3	E
H	3	F
I	2	B

b A: 3 wks B: 0 wks C: 0 wks
   D: 7 wks E: 0 wks F: 7 wks
   G: 0 wks H: 7 wks I: 14 wks

c B→C→E→G

d 22 weeks

6 a, b

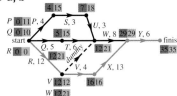

c R→V→X→Y   **d** 35 weeks

7 a, b

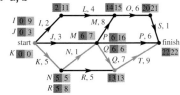

c K→N→Q→T

d 22 weeks

Exercise 10F

1a 14 days   **b** C

c 12 days

2a 17 weeks   **b** A, B or C

c 13 weeks

3a 18 hours   **b** A or F

c 18 hours

4a 14 minutes   **b** A, C, E or G

c 11 minutes

5a B → E → H → J

b 22 hours

c 2 hours

d 6 hours   **e** 20 hours

6a

b A → C → E → H → J

c None.

d 4 hours

7a

b 15 hours

c B→C→E→F

d A is not on the critical path.
   It already has slack time and
   reducing it further has no effect.

e $200

Exercise 10G

1a 10   **b** 13   **c** 14
   d 19   **e** 15   **f** 18

2a C1: 13, C2: 15, C3: 20, C4: 11

b C1: 6, C2: 12, C3: 8,
   C4: 11, C5: 10

c C1: 14, C2: 12, C3: 21

d C1: 12, C2: 16, C3: 16

3a 7   **b** 8   **c** 18
   d 21   **e** 9   **f** 11
   g 8   **h** 18   **i** 57
   j 17   **k** 10   **l** 18

4a

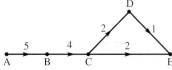

b 3

c

5a

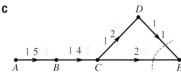

b 18

c

6a

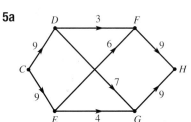

b 13

c

7a

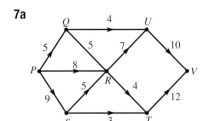

b 17

c

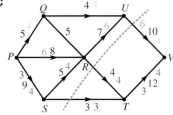

8a Cut 1: 14, Cut 2: 15, Cut 3: 20, Cut 4: 16, Cut 5 is not valid

b Cut 5 does not prevent flow from the source (city A) to sink (city B).

c 13

d One possible solution is shown below.

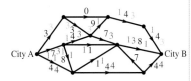

9 Sink 1: 8 kilolitres per minute, Sink 2: 16 kilolitres per minute

10 Outlet 1: 700 kilolitres per minute Outlet 2: 700 kilolitres per minute

Review 10

Multiple-choice

1 D	**2** C	**3** D
4 B	**5** C	**6** A

Short-answer

1a Buying hardware has no immediate predecessor. It is impossible to complete the other five tasks without the hardware.

b i No immediate predecessor
ii Buy hardware
iii Prepare walls

iv Buy hardware
v Sand timber floor
vi Paint walls and seal floor

c

Activity	Task	Dura-tion (in days)	Imme-diate prede-cessors
A	Buy hardware	1	–
B	Prepare walls	1	A
C	Paint walls	4	B
D	Sand timber floor	3	A
E	Seal floor	2	D
F	Put furniture in the room	1	C, E

d

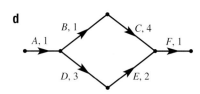

2

Activity	Duration	Immediate predecessors
A	9	–
B	7	–
C	5	A, B
D	7	A, B
E	8	B
F	5	D, E
G	6	C, F

3a

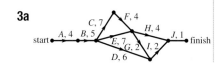

b, c

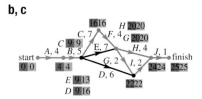

d A→B→C→F→H→J or
A→B→C→F→G→I→J

4a I: 13 h, J: 0 h, K: 13 h, L: 0 h,
M: 2 h, N: 2 h, O: 4 h,
P: 0 h, Q: 0 h

b J→L→P→Q

c 21 hours

5a 26   **b** 15

6 205

Extended-response

7 a, b and c

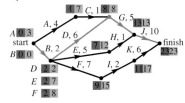

d B→D→G→J

e 23 days

f 6 days

Practice paper 3

1 B	**2** A	**3** C	**4** C
5 B	**6** B	**7** C	**8** B
9 D	**10** D	**11** C	**12** A
13 D	**14** A	**15** A	

16a 2.5%

b i $V_{n+1} = V_n \times 1.008 - 760$
ii $13\,352
iii $112   **iv** $648
v $10\,707.74   **vi** $507.74

c i 400   **ii** 192 cm^2

d i P and Q

ii

Activity	Immediate predecessors
P	–
Q	–
R	P
S	Q
T	R
U	S

17a i

x	−3	−2	−1	0	1	2	3
y	5	0	−3	−4	−3	0	5

ii

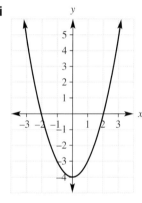

iii

x	−2	−1	0	1	2	3	4
y	0	5	8	9	8	5	0

iv

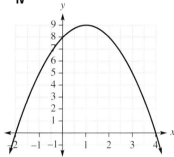

b i $36 724.80

ii $37 234.04

c i Noah's score was 2 standard deviations below the mean.

ii 53

d i A: Float time = 0 − 0 = 0 days

B: Float time = 3 − 3 = 0 days

C: Float time = 12 − 3 = 9 days

D: Float time = 9 − 9 = 0 days

E: Float time = 11 − 11 = 0 days

ii A→B→D→E

e i −2

ii 768 g

iii 68%

18a i $41 698.80

ii $31 216

iii $18 600 per year

b i 50%

ii 84%

iii 99.85%

c i 30

ii

t	0	5	10	15
b	30	75	186	462

iii

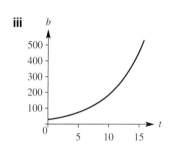

iv 8 hours

d 17